LISP

THIRD EDITION

LISP

THIRD EDITION

Patrick Henry Winston
Massachusetts Institute of Technology

Berthold Klaus Paul Horn
Massachusetts Institute of Technology

▲▼

ADDISON-WESLEY PUBLISHING COMPANY

Reading, Massachusetts • Menlo Park, California • New York
Don Mills, Ontario • Wokingham, England • Amsterdam • Bonn
Sydney • Singapore • Tokyo • Madrid • San Juan • Milan • Paris

Library of Congress Cataloging in Publication Data

Winston, Patrick Henry.
    LISP.

    Includes bibliographical references and index.
    1. LISP (Computer programming language). I. Horn, Berthold Klaus
Paul. II. Title.
QA76.73.L23W56   1989   005.13'3   88-3392
ISBN 0-201-08319-1

Reproduced by Addison-Wesley from camera-ready copy supplied
by the authors.

Reprinted with corrections February, 1993

    14 15 16 17 18 19 20 DO 95

Acknowledgments

The cover painting is by Karen A. Prendergast. The cover design is by Daniel J. Dawson. The fonts are Computer Modern. The text was set using TEX, Donald E. Knuth's typesetting system, with help from Daniel C. Brotsky. Boris Katz prepared the index.

The following people all read large parts of an early draft with incredible care, making suggestions that have led to many improvements.

Daniel G. Bobrow	Xerox Palo Alto Research Center
Terrance Boult	Columbia University
Boris Katz	Massachusetts Institute of Technology
James Devlin	Boston University
Maria Gini	University of Minnesota
W. Eric L. Grimson	Massachusetts Institute of Technology
Masayuki Ida	Aoyama Gakuin University
Jintae Lee	Massachusetts Institute of Technology
Gregor Kiczales	Xerox Palo Alto Research Center
Bil Lewis	Stanford University
David A. Moon	Symbolics
Gordon Novak	University of Texas at Austin
Michael Harrison	University of California at Berkeley

Among these, we must single out Boris Katz, who has read many drafts, contributing enormously to the final result, as he has with previous editions.

Several chapters are based on ideas introduced by Harold Abelson and Gerald Jay Sussman in *Structure and Interpretation of Computer Programs*, their seminal book on the art of programming.

The development of LISP and the COMMON LISP standard was made possible, in large part, by the active encouragement and support of the Defense Advanced Research Projects Agency. In addition, most of the examples in the second part of this book are based on research work sponsored, in large part, by the Defense Advanced Research Projects Agency.

Contents

Multiple-Valued Procedures Embody Transition Trees • Our Interpreter
Uses Explicit Transition-Tree Descriptions • We Use a Macro To Simplify
Tree Definition • A Read, Analyze, and Report Loop Adds a Finishing
Touch • Problems • Summary • References •

Preface

This book is about LISP, a programming language that takes its name from List Processing.

The Book Explains Powerful LISP Programs

The purpose of Part One is to introduce you to the basics of LISP and to important programming concepts. Once you have finished Part One, you will understand the basic ideas of symbol manipulation and will know how to use LISP in contexts that are interesting, albeit simple.

The purpose of Part Two is to introduce some slightly more advanced topics. You need not be familiar with all of them to write big, valuable programs, but you will want to learn about all of them if you want to be counted among LISP's afficionados.

The purpose of Part Three is to demonstrate how LISP is used in practice through complete program examples. We have selected programs with a view toward illustrating not only LISP's features, but also ideas that are important in Artificial Intelligence and related fields. Once you have finished Part Three, you will be ready to begin working with the big programs that are now common in Artificial Intelligence applications.

The chapters of Part One, with selected chapters in Part Two, are appropriate for an introductory subject on LISP. The chapters of Part Three, with selected chapters in Part Two, are appropriate for an intermediate-to-advanced subject on how to put LISP to work.

The Book Uses COMMON LISP

Until about 1984, the LISP programming language appeared to be breaking up into many dialects, with no single dialect dominating the others. Fortunately, however, a powerful group of world-class programming-language experts, representing many key institutions, designed COMMON LISP, a happy amalgam of the features in previous LISPs. COMMON LISP is now solidly established as the commercial standard, widely supported by the major computer manufacturers. Consequently, COMMON LISP is the LISP we use.

The Book Introduces the COMMON LISP Object System

Lately, COMMON LISP has been enriched by the addition of *generic functions*, which give COMMON LISP an *object-oriented* capability. The introduction of generic functions, via CLOS, the COMMON LISP Object System, is the primary reason we wrote this third edition of *LISP*.

The Book Has New Features

In addition to an introduction to CLOS, this third edition incorporates other new features:

- We present improved procedure definitions. For example, we have incorporated optional arguments into many of our procedures, and we have employed a bigger repertoire of LISP conditional and iteration primitives.
- We explain certain topics that were either absent in the previous edition or just touched upon. For example, we explain programming clichés, transforming and filtering procedures, lexical scoping, generators, multiple values, streams, and delayed evaluation.
- We introduce certain other topics of occasional interest. For example, we explain the rudiments of relational databases while discussing natural-language interfaces, and we exhibit an interpreter for a miniature version of PROLOG while discussing backward chaining.

The Chapters of Part One Introduce the Basics of LISP

This section presents a synopsis of the chapters in Part One, the ones that introduce the basic concepts. You should read all of these chapters to acquire a basic understanding of LISP.

- **Chapter 1, Understanding Symbol Manipulation**. This chapter explains why you need to understand the ideas of symbol manipulation, why LISP is the right symbol-manipulation language to learn, and why COMMON LISP is the best LISP to work with.

- **Chapter 2, Basic LISP Primitives**. This chapter introduces many of LISP's basic data types and symbol-manipulation primitives. It also explains many terms that are part of every LISP programmer's vocabulary.

- **Chapter 3, Procedure Definition and Binding**. This chapter explains how you can define your own LISP procedures. It also explains progressive envelopment and comment translation, two techniques for defining procedures.

- **Chapter 4, Predicates and Conditionals**. This chapter introduces testing primitives called predicates and branching primitives called conditionals. Together they make it possible for you to define much more interesting procedures. It also explains problem reduction, a technique for solving problems in general and for defining procedures in particular.

- **Chapter 5, Procedure Abstraction and Recursion**. This chapter introduces the notion of procedure abstraction. It then explains how a procedure may appear in its own definition, thereby describing how recursion works. Recursion is useful whenever the best way for a procedure to solve a problem is to break it into simpler subproblems, each of which the procedure can solve by using itself as a subprocedure.

- **Chapter 6, Data Abstraction and Mapping**. This chapter introduces the notion of data abstraction. It then explains how to define recursive procedures that transform, filter, count, and find. It also introduces the notion of programing cliché and shows that many useful clichés have become LISP primitives.

- **Chapter 7, Iteration on Numbers and Lists**. This chapter explains how to cause something to be done a given number of times or to each element in a list, thereby describing how iteration works.

- **Chapter 8, File Editing, Compiling, and Loading**. Once you know how to define elementary procedures, you need to know how to preserve them for future use. Accordingly, this chapter shows you how to store LISP procedures and data in files for later use.

- **Chapter 9, Printing and Reading**. This chapter explains how a procedure can be made to print and read. It also introduces a LISP printing primitive for fancy printing that is so rich in options, it is like an embedded programming language.

- **Chapter 10, Rules for Good Programming and Tools for Debugging**. This chapter introduces certain rules of good programming that you need to honor if you are to write large, robust, readable, maintainable programs. It particularly recommends abstraction and modularity. In addition, it introduces certain basic debugging primitives that you need to use when you write programs.

The Chapters of Part Two Explain Certain Flourishes

This section presents a synopsis of the chapters in Part Two, the ones that expose some of LISP's more powerful features. You should read at least chapters 11, 12, and 13 to acquire an intermediate understanding of LISP. Chapter 14 is necessary background for chapters 17, 22, and 23. Chapters 15 and 16 are necessary background for part of chapter 25. Chapters 17 and 18 constitute an introduction to how LISP stores and evaluates expressions.

- **Chapter 11, Properties and Arrays**. This chapter describes two popular ways to store and retrieve data. In particular, it introduces properties, which index data by symbols, and arrays, which index data by numbers. It also explains constructor, reader, and writer procedures.

- **Chapter 12, Macros and Backquote**. This chapter explains how to define procedures that differ from ordinary procedures in two ways. First their arguments are not evaluated; and second, wherever they appear, they produce an intermediate result, which acts as if that intermediate result had appeared instead of a call to the procedure.

- **Chapter 13, Structures**. This chapter explains how you can isolate yourself from low-level details of data representation by creating new data types using structures.

- **Chapter 14, Classes and Generic Functions**. This chapter introduces the notion of object-oriented programming, explaining that you may think either in terms of procedures and what they do to objects, or in terms of objects and what gets done to them. It also shows how a generic function is defined in terms of methods, and it explains how the types of the arguments in a call to a generic function determine which method is used.

- **Chapter 15, Lexical Variables, Generators, and Encapsulation**. This chapter first describes how LISP finds values for lexical variables. Next it explains how one procedure can be defined inside another, making it possible to find values for the variables in the inner procedure among the variable values maintained by the outer procedure. Finally, it shows how to create lexical closures, enabling you to encapsulate variables with procedures, restricting access to them.

- **Chapter 16, Special Variables**. This chapter explains special variables and describes how LISP finds values for them.

- **Chapter 17, List Storage, Surgery, and Reclamation**. Part Two concludes with two chapters that explain certain aspects of how

LISP is implemented. In this chapter, LISP is viewed from the memory perspective. The chapter describes how the basic LISP data types are actually represented in terms of bits and bytes. It also explains box-and-pointer notation and certain dangerous, pointer-altering primitives.

- **Chapter 18, LISP in LISP**. In this chapter, LISP is viewed from the interpreter perspective. The chapter describes how LISP actually interprets your LISP procedures. The ideas are explained using an interpreter for a LISPlike language. Curiously, this interpreter itself is written in LISP.

The Chapters of Part Three Concentrate on Applications

This section presents a synopsis of the later chapters, the chapters that explain programs that demonstrate LISP's power. The chapters form groups that can be read selectively.

- **Chapter 19, Examples Involving Search**. This chapter introduces the search problem-solving paradigm, showing how to implement the most popular techniques.
- **Chapter 20, Examples Involving Simulation**. This chapter introduces a program that simulates progress through a project consisting of various tasks, most of which can start only when certain prerequisite tasks are finished.
- **Chapter 21, The Blocks World with Classes and Methods**. This chapter is the first of four that concentrate on the object-oriented point of view, adding to your understanding of object-oriented primitives, introduced in chapter 14. The main illustration in this chapter is a program that moves toy blocks from place to place, moving obstacles as necessary. The chapter also introduces the problem-reduction problem-solving paradigm.
- **Chapter 22, Answering Questions about Goals**. This chapter further develops the program introduced in the previous chapter, showing how to deploy object-oriented auxiliary procedures whose work is done before, after, and around the work of a primary procedure. The chapter also shows how a program can account for its past behavior, answering questions like "How did you ...," "Why did you ...," and "When did you ...."
- **Chapter 23, Constraint Propagation**. In a constraint propagation system, a constraint can be viewed as a box, with terminals, such that the values on some terminals determine the values on others. Often there is no fixed direction to the way the values flow, allowing for flow through constraint boxes in any direction, as circumstances dictate. This chapter shows how to implement a constraint propagation system using CLOS primitives.

- **Chapter 24, Symbolic Pattern Matching**. This chapter is the first of four that explain the ideas involved in simple expert systems. This chapter deals with matching issues, introducing matching programs that compare symbolic expressions to determine if one can be said to be an instance of another.

- **Chapter 25, Streams and Delayed Evaluation**. Some phenomena involve sequences of things flowing through filters. This chapter explains how to think about such computations using the notion of stream. It also shows how the notion of stream can be combined with the notion of delayed evaluation, leading to streams in which the elements are created only when and if needed.

- **Chapter 26, Rule-Based Expert Systems and Forward Chaining**. Expert systems have reached the point where they do all sorts of expert work ranging from financial analysis to engineering design. Many of these problem solvers are based on the use of if-then rules, also known as situation-action rules or productions. This chapter shows how to implement a simple forward-chaining expert system. The main illustration involves animal identification.

- **Chapter 27, Backward Chaining and PROLOG**. This chapter shows how to implement a simple backward-chaining expert system, which apart from syntactic differences, amounts to a simple language, similar to PROLOG. Again the main illustration involves animal identification.

- **Chapter 28, Interpreting Transition Trees**. This chapter is the first of three that explain the ideas involved in simple natural language database interfaces. This chapter, in particular, introduces procedures that interpret language-recognition procedures cast in a form called transition trees.

- **Chapter 29, Compiling Transition Trees**. When a procedure is described in a language other than LISP, an alternative to interpreting the procedure is to translate it into LISP once and for all. This is an instance of the process called compilation. This chapter illuminates the difference between interpreting a procedure and compiling a procedure by introducing a compiler for transition trees to compare with the interpreter of the previous chapter.

- **Chapter 30, Procedure-Writing Programs and Database Interfaces**. Translating English into formal database queries is an exciting application for LISP's procedure-writing ability. It is at the heart of many commercial natural language interfaces. This chapter illustrates how such systems work, using a toy relational database containing information about the tools in a workshop.

- **Chapter 31, Finding Patterns in Images**. Many issues must be faced when designing a program, including tradeoffs between conciseness, efficiency, transparency, and ease of modification. These tradeoffs are illustrated by a program that finds the position and orientation of known star constellations.

- **Chapter 32, Converting Notations, Manipulating Matrices, and Finding Roots**. There are some mathematical calculations for which LISP is well suited. This chapter presents examples in which sparse arrays are manipulated and roots of algebraic equations are found.

A Complementary Book Presents Another Perspective

As in previous editions, this third edition complements *Artificial Intelligence*, Second Edition. In particular, the following topics are discussed in both books, but in this book the emphasis is on the implementation of ideas, rather than on the ideas themselves:

- Search, introduced here in chapter 19.
- Problem reduction and the block-movement system, introduced here in chapter 21.
- Question answering using goal trees, introduced in chapter 22.
- Rule-based expert systems, introduced in chapters 26 and 27.
- Transition trees for natural language analysis, introduced here in chapters 28, 29, and 30.

You May Ignore the Footnotes

The footnotes sprinkled here and there in this book are for the benefit of readers who are well beyond the beginner stage and either discuss esoteric details or point to postponed explanations. Consequently, they may confuse you more than help you.

P.H.W.
B.K.P.H.

1

Understanding Symbol Manipulation

This book is about LISP, a programming language that takes its name from List Processing. The book has three parts, each written to accomplish a particular purpose:

- The purpose of Part One is to help you learn about symbol manipulation and basic LISP programming.
- The purpose of Part Two is to introduce you to some more advanced LISP programming ideas.
- The purpose of Part Three is to excite you about what you can do with LISP.

This brief chapter describes what symbol manipulation is all about, indicates why symbol manipulation is important, and explains why LISP is the right symbol-manipulation language to learn.

Symbol Manipulation Is Like Working with Words and Sentences

Everything in a computer is a string of binary digits, ones and zeros, that everyone calls bits. From one perspective, sequences of bits can be interpreted as a code for ordinary decimal digits. But from another perspective, sequences of bits can be interpreted as a code for wordlike objects and sentencelike objects.

- In LISP, the fundamental things formed from bits are wordlike objects called *atoms*.
- Groups of atoms form sentencelike objects called *lists*. Lists themselves can be grouped together to form higher-level lists.
- Atoms and lists collectively are called *symbolic expressions*, or more succinctly, *expressions*. Working with symbolic expressions is what symbol manipulation using LISP is about.

A symbol-manipulation program uses symbolic expressions to remember and work with data and procedures, just as people use pencil, paper, and human language to remember and work with data and procedures. A symbol-manipulation program typically has procedures that recognize particular symbolic expressions, tear existing ones apart, and assemble new ones.

Two examples of symbolic expressions follow. The parentheses mark where lists begin and end. The first is a description of a structure built out of children's blocks. The second is a description of a certain university.

```
(arch (parts lintel post1 post2)
      (lintel must-be-supported-by post1)
      (lintel must-be-supported-by post2)
      (lintel a-kind-of wedge)
      (post1 a-kind-of brick)
      (post2 a-kind-of brick)
      (post1 must-not-touch post2)
      (post2 must-not-touch post1))

(mit (a-kind-of university)
     (location (cambridge massachusetts))
     (phone 253-1000)
     (schools (architecture
               business
               engineering
               humanities
               science))
     (founder (william barton rogers)))
```

Certainly these are not scary. Both just describe something according to some conventions about how to arrange symbols. Here is another example, this time expressing a rule for determining whether some animal is a carnivore:

```
(identify6
  ((? animal) has pointed teeth)
  ((? animal) has claws)
  ((? animal) has forward eyes)
  ((? animal) is a carnivore))
```

What we see is just another way of expressing the idea that an animal with pointed teeth, claws, and forward-pointing eyes is probably a carnivore. To use such a rule, a program must take it apart, determine if the patterns involving teeth, claws, and eyes are compatible with what is known about a particular animal in a database, and if they are compatible, add the conclusion that the animal is a carnivore to the database. All this is done by manipulating symbols.

LISP Helps Make Computers Intelligent

These days, there is a growing armamentarium of programs that exhibit what most people consider intelligent behavior. Nearly all of these intelligent programs, or seemingly intelligent programs, are written in LISP. Many have great practical importance. Here are some examples:

- Expert problem solvers. One of the first LISP programs did calculus problems at the level of university freshmen. Another early program did geometric analogy problems of the sort found in intelligence tests. Since then, newer programs have configured computers, diagnosed infections of the blood, understood electronic circuits, evaluated geological formations, planned investments, scheduled factories, designed fasteners, invented interesting mathematics, and much more. All are written in LISP.

- Commonsense reasoning. Much of human thinking seems to involve a small amount of reasoning using a large amount of knowledge. Representing knowledge means choosing a vocabulary of symbols and fixing some conventions for arranging them. Good representations make just the right things explicit. LISP is the language in which most research on representation is done.

- Learning. Much work has been done on the learning of concepts by computer, and certainly most of what has been done also rests on progress in representation. LISP again dominates.

- Natural-language interfaces. There is a growing need for programs that interact with people in English and other natural languages. Practical systems have been built for recovering information from databases that are difficult to use otherwise.

- Education and intelligent support systems. To interact comfortably with computers, people must have computers that know what people know and how to tell them more. No one wants a long-winded explanation once they know a lot. Nor does anyone want a telegramlike explanation when just beginning. LISP-based programs are beginning to make user models by analyzing what the user does. These programs use the models to trim or elaborate explanations.

- Speech and vision. Understanding how people hear and see has proved fantastically difficult. It seems that we do not know enough about how the physical world constrains what ends up on our ear drums and retinas. Nevertheless, progress is being made and much of it is made in LISP, even though a great deal of straight arithmetic-oriented programming is necessary. To be sure, LISP has no special advantages for arithmetic-oriented programming. But at the same time, LISP has no disadvantages for arithmetic either.

Consequently, people who want to know about computer intelligence need to understand LISP.

LISP Promotes Productivity and Facilitates Education

LISP is an important language even when computer intelligence is not involved. Here are some examples:

- Applications programming. Talented programmers find that LISP can increase their productivity enormously, enabling them to write big programs much faster and far less expensively. This can have dramatic effects on the way big programs are developed. The old way was to start with multiyear periods of specification, followed by multiyear periods of implementation, leading to systems that produce disappointed, cranky users. The new way is to have prototypes up in a few months, with specification and implementation evolving together, with users constantly helping to shape the final result.

- Systems programming. LISP machines are high-powered workstations programmed from top to bottom in LISP. The operating system, the user utility programs, the editors, the compilers, and the interpreters are all written in LISP, demonstrating LISP's power and versatility.

- Computer science education. LISP facilitates procedure abstraction and data abstraction, thereby emphasizing two supremely important programming ideas. And because LISP is a superb implementation language, LISP is a good language with which to build interpreters and compilers for a variety of languages, including LISP itself.

Given all these examples, it is no surprise that the following is accepted by nearly everyone:

- All computer scientists and computer engineers must understand the power of symbol manipulation in general. Most computer scientists and engineers should understand LISP in particular.

LISP Is the Right Symbol-Manipulation Language To Learn

There are too many programming languages. Fortunately, however, only a few are for symbol manipulation, and of these LISP is the most used. After LISP is understood, most of the other symbol-manipulation languages are easy to learn.

Why has LISP become the most used language for symbol manipulation, and lately, much more? All of the following arguments have adherents:

- The interaction argument. LISP is oriented toward programming at a terminal with rapid response. All procedures and all data can be displayed or altered at will.

- The environment argument. LISP has been used by a community that needed and got the best in editing and debugging tools. For more than two decades, people at the world's largest artificial intelligence centers have created sophisticated computing environments around LISP, making a combination that is unbeatable for writing big, complicated programs.

- The evolution argument. COMMON LISP is built on more than twenty years of continuous experiment and refinement. Consequently, LISP has just the right features.

- The uniformity argument. LISP procedures and LISP data have the same form. One LISP program can use another as data. One LISP program even can create another and use it.

Happily, LISP is an easy language to learn. A few hours of study is enough to understand amazing programs. Previous exposure to some other programming language is not necessary. Indeed, such experience can be something of a handicap, for there can be a serious danger of developing a bad accent: other languages do things differently, and procedure-by-procedure translation leads to awkward constructions and poor programming practice.

One reason LISP is easy to learn is that its syntax is extremely simple. Curiously, LISP's present syntax has strange roots. John McCarthy, LISP's inventor, originally used a sort of old LISP, which is about as hard to read as old English. At one point, however, he wished to use LISP to do a piece of mathematics that required both procedures and data to have the same syntactic form. The resulting form of LISP quickly caught on.

COMMON LISP Is the Right LISP To Learn

The LISP used throughout this book is COMMON LISP. We use COMMON LISP because it is modern, powerful, and widely available. COMMON LISP also is the accepted standard for commercial use. Do not be confused by references to other, strangely-named LISPs. Most are either obsolete dialects or COMMON LISP with company-specific extensions.

Lately, COMMON LISP has been extended to include features for object-oriented programming via CLOS, the COMMON LISP Object System. Several chapters in this book explain how CLOS makes COMMON LISP more powerful.

Beware of False Myths

There is no perfect computer language, and to be sure, LISP has defects. Many of the original defects have been fixed, even though some people mistakenly cite them even today. Among the most pervasive and unfortunate myths are the following:

• Myth: LISP is slow at crunching numbers.

In fact this was true at one time. This historical problem has been corrected by the development of good programs for translating the stuff programmers produce into the instructions that a computer can execute directly, without further decomposition. Said another way, the problem has been corrected by the development of good LISP compilers.

• Myth: LISP is slow.

In fact this also was true at one time. In the old days, LISP was used strictly in research, where interaction is at a premium and high speed for fully debugged application-oriented programs is less important. Today, however, excellent LISP compilers have been developed to support the growing commercial demand for LISP programs.

• Myth: LISP programs are big.

Actually, this is not a myth. Some are. But that is only because LISP makes it possible to create programs that are big enough to know a lot.

• Myth: LISP programs require expensive computers.

A few years ago, getting started with LISP required a million-dollar commitment. Today, on the low end, excellent LISP systems for personal computers start at only a few hundred dollars, and on the high end, even the fanciest LISP systems running on LISP-oriented workstations cost well under a hundred thousand dollars.

• Myth: LISP is hard to read and debug because of all the parentheses.

In fact the parentheses problem goes away as soon as you learn how to use a LISP editing program that helps you put things down on an editing screen properly. No one finds the following to be particularly clear:

```
(defun fibonacci (n) (if (or (= n
0) (= n 1)) 1 (+ (fibonacci (-
n 1)) (fibonacci (- n 2)))))
```

But the equivalent, formatted version is fine after a little experience:

```
(defun fibonacci (n)
  (if (or (= n 0) (= n 1))
      1
      (+ (fibonacci (- n 1))
         (fibonacci (- n 2)))))
```

LISP-oriented editors make it easy to produce the formatted version as it is written.

- Myth: LISP is hard to learn.

LISP earned its bad reputation by being in the company of some hard-to-read books in its youth. Now there are many good ones, each with its own distinguishing features.

Summary

- Symbol manipulation is like working with words and sentences.
- LISP helps make computers intelligent.
- LISP promotes productivity and facilitates education.
- LISP is the right symbol-manipulation language to learn.
- COMMON LISP is the right LISP to learn.
- Beware of false myths. LISP is an easy-to-learn, fast-running, productivity-multiplying language, well-suited to many applications both in and outside of Artificial Intelligence.

References

COMMON LISP was developed by a large group of highly talented people. The result was the remarkable reference manual, the *COMMON LISP Reference Manual*, by Guy L. Steele, Jr., with contributions by Scott E. Fahlman, Richard P. Gabriel, David A. Moon, and Daniel L. Weinreb. Every professional LISP user should own a copy.

For a general introduction to Artificial Intelligence, see *Artificial Intelligence (Second Edition)* by Patrick H. Winston. For a general introduction to the commercial applications of Artificial Intelligence, see *The AI Business: The Commercial Uses of Artificial Intelligence*, edited by Patrick H. Winston and Karen A. Prendergast. See also *The Rise of the Expert Company*, by Edward A. Feigenbaum, Pamela McCorduck, and H. Penny Nii.

For historical perspective on LISP, see McCarthy [1960, 1978]. For historical perspective on the idea of lambda conversion, a key supporting concept, see Church [1941].

For arguments in favor of LISP as a programming language, see the paper by Cornish [1987].

Among the many other textbooks on LISP, we recommend *Programming in COMMON LISP* by Rodney A. Brooks, which is particularly strong on debugging and good programming practice, and we recommend *Structure and Interpretation of Computer Programs*, by Harold Abelson and Gerald Jay Sussman, which is conspicuous for using SCHEME, a dialect of LISP, to teach programming fundamentals.

Other LISP books with good points include *Anatomy of LISP*, by John Allen, *Artificial Intelligence Programming*, by Eugene Charniak *et al.*, *COMMON LISPcraft*, by Robert Wilensky, *Let's Talk LISP*, by Laurent

Siklóssy, and *LISP—A Gentle Introduction to Symbolic Computation*, by David S. Touretzky.

For a complete treatment of the COMMON LISP Object System, see *Object-Oriented Programming in COMMON LISP*, by Sonya E. Keene.

2

Basic LISP
Primitives

The primary purpose of this chapter is to introduce LISP's basic symbol-manipulation primitives. To do this, some primitives are introduced that work on numbers and others are introduced that work on lists. The list-oriented primitives extract parts of lists and build new lists.

A secondary purpose of this chapter is to introduce many terms that make it easier to talk about what LISP does. These terms include prompt, comment, procedure, argument, primitive, program, algorithm, atom, number, symbol, list, element, expression, data type, object, form, evaluation, application, call, value, nesting, top-level, binding, assignment, side effect, function, template, integer, ratio, and floating point.

Some of the terms may be familiar to you already, but in any case, do not recoil in horror. There is no need to memorize definitions. Most of the terms become second nature just through reading, and should you stumble occasionally, a detour through the glossary or index will get you going again.

LISP Means Symbol Manipulation

As with other computer languages, the best way to learn LISP is aggressively, working as quickly as possible toward interesting programs. We therefore move quickly over the basics, occasionally having you look at

things that you may not yet understand completely, with a view toward
motivating as well as explaining.

To get started, imagine sitting in front of a computer terminal. When
LISP is resting, doing nothing, it displays a *prompt* to tell you that it is
waiting for you to type something. In most implementations of COMMON
LISP, the prompt is an asterisk:

```
*
```

The words beyond the semicolon are *comments* inserted for explanation—a
semicolon makes the remainder of the words on a line invisible to LISP.

You begin, as if engaging in a dialog, typing inputs and observing
outputs. Suppose, for example, that you want some help adding numbers.
The proper incantation, once LISP has displayed the prompt, is as follows:

```
* (+ 3.14 2.71)
```

LISP agreeably responds:

```
5.85
```

This is a simple example of LISP's ability to handle arithmetic. Elementary
examples of symbol manipulation are equally straightforward. Suppose, for
example, that we are interested in keeping track of some facts needed in
connection with understanding a children's story about, say, a robot. It
might be important to remember that certain children are friends of the
robot. Typically a name is required to identify such a group, and the name
FRIENDS will do as well as any other. If Dick and Jane and Sally are friends
of the robot, this fact can be remembered by using SETF, whose name is
drawn from set field:

```
* (setf friends '(dick jane sally))
```

Do not worry about the quote mark that appears. Because it would be
awkward to explain the quote mark now, we defer our explanation to later
in this chapter.

At this point, typing FRIENDS causes the list of friends to be typed in
response:

```
* friends
(DICK JANE SALLY)
```

Note that you may use either upper or lower case when you type; LISP
does not care. LISP's response is always in upper case, however. In our
examples, we show the prompt in front of your input whenever we are
showing fragments of dialog between you and LISP. This is to help you
determine whether an expression is an input or an output, particularly
in those situations where we chose to omit some of LISP's more boring
responses

A list similar to the list of friends can be established for enemies:

```
* (setf enemies '(troll grinch ghost))
```

Because friends and enemies tend to be dynamic categories in children's worlds, it is often necessary to change the category that a particular individual belongs to. The ghost ceases to be an enemy and becomes a friend after typing two lines like this:

```
* (setf enemies (remove 'ghost enemies))
* (setf friends (cons 'ghost friends))
```

The first line, with REMOVE, changes the remembered list of enemies to what it was minus the entry GHOST. The second line, with CONS for <u>cons</u>truct, changes the remembered list of friends to what it was plus the entry GHOST. FRIENDS and ENEMIES have been changed such that we now get properly altered responses:

```
* enemies
(TROLL GRINCH)

* friends
(GHOST DICK JANE SALLY)
```

Later we will see how to write a procedure that does the same job. In particular we will understand how the following creates a procedure, named NEWFRIEND, for changing a person from an enemy into a friend:

```
(defun newfriend (name)
  (setf enemies (remove name enemies))
  (setf friends (cons name friends)))
```

With NEWFRIEND, the previous elevation of the status of GHOST can be done more simply by typing only this:

```
* (newfriend 'ghost)
```

LISP Procedures and Data Are Symbolic Expressions

Now is a good time to get some terms straight. First, when left and right parentheses surround something, we call the result a *list* and speak of its *elements*. In our first example, the list (+ 3.14 2.71) has three elements, +, 3.14, and 2.71, separated by spaces.

Note the peculiar location of the +, standing strangely before the two things to be added, rather than between them, as in ordinary arithmetic notation. In LISP the name of the thing to do, the *procedure*, is always specified first, followed then by the things that the procedure is to work with, the *arguments*. Thus 3.14 and 2.71 are the arguments given to the procedure named +.

This so-called *prefix notation* facilitates uniformity, because the procedure name is always in the same place, no matter how many arguments are involved.

We are now prepared to gather together some definitions for important terms, some of which we have used informally already:

- A *procedure* is a step by step specification, expressed in a programming language, of how to do something.
- A procedure, like +, supplied by LISP itself, is called a *primitive*. Although there must be step by step specifications, in some language, for how each primitive is to do its job, you will have no occasion to look at those detailed specifications.
- A procedure supplied by you in terms of LISP primitives is called a *user-defined procedure*.
- A collection of procedures that work together is called a *program*.

There is another term, which we use rarely, but which it is also good to know about:

- An *algorithm* is specification for how to do something. In common usage, an algorithm is an abstract specification, not one in couched in procedure. However, to be an algorithm, a specification must be concrete enough for it to be recast as a procedure.[1]

Now let us look at more examples. For simplicity, we stick to arithmetic for the moment.

```
* (* 9 3)
27
* (/ 27 3)
9
```

Note that the names of the primitives can be single characters like +, - *, and /. This is just a convenience reserved for often-used primitives. Note also that +, *, -, and / can work with any number of arguments, not just two. Just as + keeps on adding, so - will keep on subtracting and / will keep on dividing, when given more than two arguments. There is never any confusion, because the end of the argument sequence is signaled clearly by a right parenthesis.

Now consider the following expression, in which + is followed by something other than raw numbers:

---

[1]Knuth's rigorous definition requires all algorithms to terminate in a finite number of steps. Most theoreticians take a more relaxed view, particularly now that probabilistic algorithms have blurred the notion of what it means to finish in a finite number of steps.

```
* (+ (* 2 2) (/ 2 2))
5
```

If we think of this expression as directions for something to do, it is easy to see that (* 2 2) produces 4, (/ 2 2) produces 1, and these results, fed in turn to +, give 5 as the result. But if, instead, we think of this expression as data, then we see that we have a three-element list: + is the first element, the entire expression (* 2 2) is the second element, and (/ 2 2) is the third. Thus lists themselves can be elements of other lists. Said another way, we permit lists in which individual elements are lists themselves. In part, the representational power of LISP derives from this ability to build nested structures.

Now it is time to be a bit more precise about lists and a few other things, some of which we have introduced informally already:

- Indivisible things like 27, 3.14, and +, which have obvious meaning, as well as things like FOO, B27, and HYPHENATED-SYMBOL are called *atoms*.

- Atoms like 27 and 3.14 are called *numeric atoms*, or more succinctly, *numbers*.

- Atoms like FOO, B27, HYPHENATED-SYMBOL, FIRST, and + are called *symbolic atoms*, or more succinctly, *symbols*.

- A *list* consists of a left parenthesis, followed by zero or more atoms or lists, followed by a right parenthesis.

- Both atoms and lists are called *symbolic expressions*, or more succinctly, *expressions*.[2]

The diagram in figure 2-1 summarizes. All the things shown in the figure— expressions, atoms, numbers, symbols, and lists—are referred to as *data types*. Specific instances of the various data types are called *objects*. Thus 27 is an object that belongs to the number data type; FOO is an object that belongs to the symbol data type.

Later on, in other chapters, you learn that LISP has many other data types, including characters, arrays, strings, and structures.

Note that when you are interested in the value of an expression, it is conventional to refer to that expression as a *form*. If a form is a list, the first element generally is the name of the procedure to be used to produce the value. The process of computing the value of a form is called *evaluation*.

The procedure specified in a form is said to be *applied* or *called* and the result is referred to as the *value* of the form or the *value returned* by the procedure.

---

[2]Symbolic expressions used to be called s-expressions, *s* being short for *symbolic*, to distinguish them from m-expressions, *m* being short for *meta*. M-expressions were used to represent s-expressions only by John McCarthy, as far as we know.

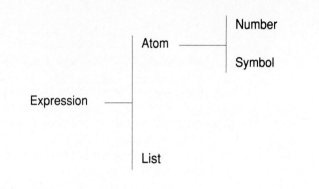

Figure 2-1. LISP's basic data types.

Problems

Problem 2-1: Each of the following things may be an atom, a list, or neither. Identify each accordingly.

```
ATOM
(THIS IS AN ATOM)
(THIS IS AN EXPRESSION)
((A B) (C D)) 3 (3)
(LIST 3)
(/ (+ 3 1) (- 3 1))
)(
((()))
(() ())
((())
())(
((ABC
```

Lists Are Like Bowls

We are trained, practically from birth, to think that parentheses signal unimportance. Consequently, you may want to solidify your understanding of lists by thinking about an analogy with bowls, like those used to store things in your refrigerator. Here, for example, are three such refrigerator bowls:[3]

---

[3]The bowl metaphor was suggested to us by Daniel C. Brotsky.

Because refrigerator bowls are made to fit inside one another, you can put the small bowl inside the medium one, and then you can put the combination of the small and medium bowls inside the big bowl:

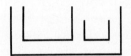

The result is three nested bowls. The small bowl is empty, the medium bowl contains the small bowl, and the big bowl contains the medium bowl.

Alternatively, you can put both the small bowl and the medium bowl inside the big bowl this way:

Here you say that both the small bowl and the medium bowl are empty and that the big bowl contains both the small bowl and the medium bowl.

Of course, we can also put some fruit in the bowls, represented here by As for apples and Ps for pears:

The small bowl is still empty; the medium bowl now contains two apples and one pear; and the big bowl still contains the small and medium bowls.

You could say that the big bowl also contains two apples and a pear, but let us agree to say that the big bowl contains a bowl that contains the two apples and one pear. Thus *contains* means *directly contains*, with no other container intervening.

By analogy, lists are like bowls. Like bowls, lists can be empty. Like bowls, lists can contain other lists. Like bowls, lists can contain things that are not containers.

To make the analogy clearer between lists and bowls, the bowls are drawn using parentheses for sides from now on. Here we have two parentheses bowls:

```
(                    )
(              ) (        )
(              ) (        )
(_____) (_____)
```

Erasing the bottoms and dropping the sides down, we have two lists:

```
(                ) (        )
```

Here is one bowl nested inside another:

```
(    (        )    )
(    (        )    )
(    (_____)    )
(_____)
```

And here is one list inside another:

```
(    (        )    )
```

We say that the lists are *nested* because one list contains another. The inside, empty list is inside another list. Here is another bowl example in which a small and a medium bowl are nested inside a large one:

```
( (          )      )
( (        ) (  ) )
( (_____) (__) )
(_____)
```

And here is the analogous list situation in which two lists are nested inside another:

```
( (        ) (    ) )
```

Now the big list contains two empty lists, just as the big bowl contains two empty bowls. Here is a bowl set involving two apples and a pear:

```
( (          )      )
( ( A A P ) (    ) )
( (_____) (__) )
(_____)
```

And here are three lists along with three symbols:

```
( ( A A P ) (    ) )
```

The big list contains two elements. The first element is a list that contains three elements:

```
( ( A A P ) (    ) )

          |
          |
          v

   ( A A P )
```

The second element of the big list is an empty list:

```
( ( A A P ) (    ) )

              |
              |
              v

          (    )
```

As with bowls, let us agree that *contains* means *directly contains*, with no other list intervening. Let us further agree that the *top-level elements* of a list are contained, in the sense of *directly contained*, by that list. In the following example, the big list contains two top-level elements, both lists, (A A P) and ().

```
( ( A A P ) (    ) )
```

Thinking of lists as bowls makes it clear that the first element of the big list is another list, not the symbol A.

• In LISP, parentheses signal the left and right boundaries of a container, just like the sides of the bowls in the bowl diagrams.

Some procedures only look at the top-level elements of a list, ignoring the elements of elements. Thus it is important to understand the distinction.

FIRST and REST Take Lists Apart

Examples from arithmetic are simple, but arithmetic does not expose LISP's talent for manipulating expressions. Suppose we have an expression like (FAST COMPUTERS ARE NICE). We might like to chip off the first element leaving (COMPUTERS ARE NICE), or we might like to glue on a new first element producing something like (SMALL FAST COMPUTERS ARE NICE). It is time to look at such manipulations starting with basic techniques for dissecting and constructing lists. In particular we must understand the primitives FIRST, REST, APPEND, LIST, and CONS.

The value returned by FIRST is the first element of the list given as its argument. In the following examples, do not worry about the quote marks; we will explain them soon:

```
* (first '(fast computers are nice))
FAST
```

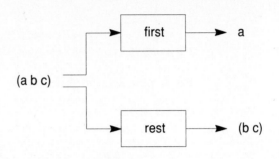

Figure 2-2. FIRST and REST take lists apart.

```
* (first '(a b c))
A
```

REST does the complementary thing. It returns a list containing all but the first element:

```
* (rest '(fast computers are nice))
(COMPUTERS ARE NICE)
* (rest '(a b c))
(B C)
```

Note that REST, unlike FIRST, always returns a list. Remembering the diagram shown in figure 2-2 may help keep the asymmetry of FIRST and REST straight.

Also, when REST is applied to a list with only one element, it returns the *empty list*, which you can denote by either ( ) or NIL; LISP itself prefers NIL:

```
* (rest '(c))
NIL
```

Also, while on the subject of the empty list, it is important to know that when given NIL, FIRST and REST both return NIL, by convention:

```
* (first ())
NIL
* (rest ())
NIL
```

Finally, consider the following example, in which the argument given to FIRST is the two-element list ((A B) (C D)):

```
* (first '((a b) (c d)))
(A B)
```

You might think that the result should be A because A is the first thing you encounter as your eyes scan from left to right. But keep in mind that the elements of ((A B) (C D)) are (A B) and (C D), the first of which is (A B).

Quoting Stops Evaluation

Now it is time to understand those quote marks that have been appearing. To start, suppose that you want the second element of (A B C). One way to get the second element is to use SECOND; another is to use a combination of FIRST and REST:

```
* (first (rest (a b c)))
```

Using FIRST and REST exposes a problem, however. We want REST to take the list (A B C) and give back (B C). Then FIRST would certainly return B, the second element in the original list. But how is LISP to know where the specification of what to do leaves off and the data to be manipulated begins? Look at the embedded list:

```
(a b c)
```

LISP might legitimately think that A is some sort of procedure, perhaps one defined by you. Similarly, the following expression is certainly a list:

```
(rest (a b c))
```

And its first element is surely REST! Thus the following expression could well result in an answer of REST:

```
* (first (rest (a b c)))
```

How far should the evaluation process go into an expression? LISP needs help in making this decision. You specify where to stop evaluation by introducing a single-quote character, '. Thus the following expression returns B:

```
* (first (rest '(a b c)))
B
```

B is returned because the quote mark prevents LISP from wading in and thinking of (A B C) as a form in which A is the name of a procedure to be applied to B and C. Instead, (A B C) is given to REST, which then hands (B C) to FIRST, resulting finally in just plain B. Moving the quote mark changes the result:

```
* (first '(rest (a b c)))
REST
```

Here LISP does not try to take the REST of anything but simply gives the expression (REST (A B C)) to FIRST as a list to work on, resulting in REST because REST is the first element.

Leaving out the quote mark altogether would result in an attempt to use A as a procedure. Because there is no such procedure supplied by LISP, LISP would report that there has been an undefined procedure error.

Incidentally, prefacing an expression with ' is equivalent to nesting that expression inside a QUOTE form, and in old programs, you are likely to see expressions like (QUOTE (A B C)) in place of '(A B C). Providing the ' mark as a shorthand for the longer version is considered a form of *syntactic sugaring.* Nothing new is added to the power of the language, but programs become more readable.[4]

Problems

Problem 2-2: Evaluate the following forms:

```
(first '(p h w))
(rest '(b k p h))
(first '((a b) (c d)))
(rest '((a b) (c d)))
(first (rest '((a b) (c d))))
(rest (first '((a b) (c d))))
(rest (first (rest '((a b) (c d)))))
(first (rest (first '((a b) (c d)))))
```

Problem 2-3: Evaluate the following forms:

```
(first (rest (first (rest '((a b) (c d) (e f))))))
(first (first (rest (rest '((a b) (c d) (e f))))))
(first (first (rest '(rest ((a b) (c d) (e f))))))
(first (first '(rest (rest ((a b) (c d) (e f))))))
(first '(first (rest (rest ((a b) (c d) (e f))))))
'(first (first (rest (rest ((a b) (c d) (e f))))))
```

Problem 2-4: Write sequences of FIRSTs and RESTs that will pick the symbol PEAR out of the following expressions:

```
(apple orange pear grapefruit)
((apple orange) (pear grapefruit))
(((apple) (orange) (pear) (grapefruit)))
(apple (orange) ((pear)) (((grapefruit))))
((((apple))) ((orange)) (pear) grapefruit)
((((apple) orange) pear) grapefruit)
```

---

[4]Actually, the ' character is recognized as a macro character by LISP's reader, which converts '<expression> into (quote <expression>).

Some Old Timers Use CARs and CDRs

Until recently, most LISP programmers used CAR and CDR in place of FIRST and REST.[5] In COMMON LISP, CAR and CDR are still allowed because they can be run together to form composite primitives of the form CxxR, CxxxR, or CxxxxR. Each x denotes either an A, signifying CAR, or a D, signifying CDR. Thus the following are equivalent:

```
* (cadr '(a b c))
≡ (car (cdr '(a b c)))
≡ (first (rest '(a b c)))
```

Note that the left-to-right order of the *a*s and *d*s follows that of the equivalent CARs and CDRs:

```
(cadr <expression>)
```

```
(car (cdr <expression>))
```

In old programs, the most common compositions of CARs and CDRs were CADR and CADDR, which pick out the second and third elements from lists. COMMON LISP offers SECOND and THIRD, FOURTH and on up to TENTH, however. Consequently, in new programs, compositions of CAR and CDR are less commonly used than they were. We do not use them at all in the rest of this book.

SETF Assigns Values to Symbols

So far we have seen how symbolic expressions can be taken apart by evaluating forms that begin with FIRST or REST. We have also seen how arithmetic can be done by evaluating forms that begin with +, -, and other related primitives. It seems as if LISP's goal is always to evaluate something and return a value. This is true for symbols as well as lists. Suppose we type a symbol, followed by a space, and wait for LISP to respond:

---

[5]FIRST and REST were originally called CAR and CDR because of the way they were implemented on the ancient IBM 704 computer. CAR was so called because it was implemented by a 704 instruction that computed the contents of the address portion of a register. Similarly, CDR was so called because it was implemented by a 704 instruction that computed the contents of the decrement portion of a register.

```
* L
```

On seeing L, LISP tries to return a value for it, just as if (+ 3 4) were typed.
But for a symbol, the *value* is something to be looked up, rather than the
result of a computation, as when dealing with lists.

The process of reserving a place in computer memory to store a value
for a symbol is called *binding*. The process of storing a value in that place
is called *assignment*. The process of recovering a value from that place is
one kind of *evaluation*.

LISP binds symbols as they are encountered. One way to assign values
to symbols is to use SETF.[6] This primitive causes the value of its second
argument to be assigned to its first argument. Consider this:

```
* (setf ab-list '(a b))
```

SETF is unusual in that it does *not* evaluate its first argument. SETF is also
unusual in that it does more than just return a value. The value returned by
(SETF AB-LIST '(A B)) is (A B). But, more importantly, when evaluating
(SETF AB-LIST '(A B)), LISP assigns (A B) to the symbol AB-LIST. If we
now type AB-LIST, followed by a space, we see that (A B) comes back:

```
* ab-list
(A B)
```

Anything a procedure has done that persists after it returns its value is
called a *side effect*. Thus the expression (SETF AB-LIST '(A B)) is evaluated
mainly for the side effect of assigning (A B) to AB-LIST.

• A procedure that only computes a value is called a *function*. Strictly
  speaking, according to mathematical convention, procedures that have
  side effects are not functions. Nevertheless, people commonly refer to
  all LISP procedures, somewhat loosely, as functions. Thus SETF is not
  really a function, although it certainly is a procedure.

Once (A B) is assigned to AB-LIST, we can use AB-LIST to work through some
examples using the basic list manipulating primitives. These illustrate that
LISP seeks out the value of symbols not only when they are typed in by
themselves, but also when the symbols appear as arguments to procedures:

```
* ab-list
(A B)
* 'ab-list
ab-list
```

---

[6]The primitive SETQ, an acronym for <u>set</u> <u>q</u>uote, can be used instead of SETF to
attach values to symbols. Most programmers prefer SETF, however, because
SETF can be used not only with symbols, but also with other data types that
you will learn about later.

```
* (first ab-list)
A

* (first 'ab-list)
ERROR

* (rest ab-list)
(B)

* (rest 'ab-list)
ERROR
```

Note that both FIRST and REST print an error message if asked to work on something that is not a list. In general, the content of COMMON LISP's error messages is implementation dependent. In this book, we indicate where some sort of error message is printed by writing ERROR.

**SETF Accepts
Multiple
Symbol-Value Pairs**

Note that you can run several SETFs together in a single SETF. The odd-numbered arguments are not evaluated but the even ones are, as you would expect. Thus one SETF can do the work that would otherwise require many. Only the value of the final argument is returned:

```
* (setf ab-list '(a b)
        xy-list '(x y))
(X Y)
```

Now ab-list and xy-list both have values:

```
* ab-list
(A B)

* xy-list
(X Y)
```

**Certain Atoms
Evaluate to
Themselves**

Before leaving the subject of assignment, we must explain that certain atoms evaluate to themselves, by convention. Among symbols, T and NIL always evaluate to themselves, and you cannot assign anything else to either:

```
* t
T

* nil
NIL
```

```
* (setf t nil)
ERROR
```

All numbers also evaluate to themselves:

```
* 2
2
* 2.71
2.71
```

**CONS, APPEND,
and LIST Construct
Lists**

While FIRST and REST take things apart, CONS, APPEND, and LIST put them together.

CONS takes an expression and a list and returns a new list whose first element is the expression and whose remaining elements are those of the old list:

```
* (cons 'a '(b c))
```

```
(a    b c)
```

Consider these examples:

```
* (setf new-front 'a old-list '(b c))
* (cons new-front old-list)
(A B C)
* (first (cons new-front old-list))
A
* (rest (cons new-front old-list))
(B C)
```

Sometimes it is useful to think in terms of a general pattern that shows how the various parts of an expression fit together. Such general patterns are called *templates*, and by convention, the words in a template between angle brackets are taken as descriptions of what should appear in the position occupied. Then the arguments of the CONS primitive can be described by the following template:

```
(cons <new first element> <a list>)
```

Note then that the following are equivalent, provided that the value of SAMPLE-LIST is a list other than the empty list:

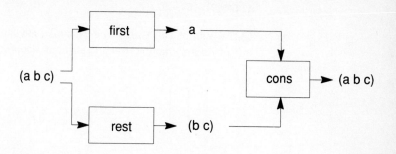

Figure 2-3. CONS can reassemble the pieces returned by FIRST and REST into a new list that looks just like the original.

```
sample-list ≡ (cons (first sample-list) (rest sample-list))
```

The diagram in figure 2-3 shows this inverse relationship between CONS and the FIRST-REST combination.

APPEND combines the elements of all lists supplied as arguments as shown here:

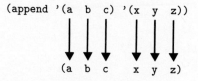

Here are more examples:

```
* (setf ab-list '(a b)
       xy-list '(x y))
* (append ab-list xy-list)
(A B X Y)
* (append ab-list xy-list ab-list)
(A B X Y A B)
* (append ab-list '() xy-list '())
(A B X Y)
* (append 'ab-list xy-list)
ERROR                              ; 'AB-LIST is an atom,
                                   ; not a list.
```

Be sure to understand that APPEND runs the elements of its arguments together, but does nothing to those elements themselves. Note that the value returned in the following example is ((A) (B) (C) (D)), not (A B C D):

```
* (append '((a) (b)) '((c) (d)))
((A) (B) (C) (D))
```

LIST does not run things together like APPEND does. Instead, it makes a list out of its arguments. Each argument becomes an element of the new list:

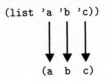

Here are more examples:

```
* (setf front 'a middle 'b back 'c)
```

```
* (list front middle back)
(A B C)
```

```
* (front middle back)
ERROR
```

```
* (setf ab-list '(a b))
```

```
* (list ab-list ab-list)
((A B) (A B))
```

```
* (list ab-list ab-list ab-list)
((A B) (A B) (A B))
```

```
* (list 'ab-list ab-list)
(AB-LIST (A B))
```

Now study how CONS, APPEND, and LIST differ:

```
* (setf ab-list '(a b) cd-list '(c d))
```

```
* (append ab-list cd-list)
(A B C D)
```

```
* (list ab-list cd-list)
((A B) (C D))
```

```
* (cons ab-list cd-list)
((A B) C D)
```

```
* (append ab-list ab-list)
(A B A B)
```

```
* (list ab-list ab-list)
((A B) (A B))
```

```
* (cons ab-list ab-list)
((A B) A B)
```

```
* (append 'ab-list ab-list)
ERROR
```

```
* (list 'ab-list ab-list)
(AB-LIST (A B))
* (cons 'ab-list ab-list)
(AB-LIST A B)
```

Problems

Problem 2-5: Evaluate the following slightly tricky forms:

```
(append '(a b c) '( ))
(list '(a b c) '( ))
(cons '(a b c) '( ))
```

Problem 2-6: Evaluate the following forms in the order given:

```
(setf tools (list 'hammer 'screwdriver))
(cons 'pliers tools)
tools
(setf tools (cons 'pliers tools))
tools
(append '(saw wrench) tools)
tools
(setf tools (append '(saw wrench) tools))
tools
```

Problem 2-7: Evaluate the following form:

```
(cons (first nil) (rest nil))
```

CONS, APPEND, and LIST Do Not Alter Symbol Values

Note carefully that CONS, APPEND, and LIST do not alter the values of their arguments. In the following, for example, neither NEW-FRONT nor OLD-LIST changes when the CONS form is evaluated:

```
* (setf new-front 'a old-list '(b c))
* (cons new-front old-list)
(A B C)
* new-front
A
* old-list
(B C)
```

If your intention is to add a new element to a list assigned to a symbol, thus changing the value of the symbol, you must embed the CONS form in a SETF form. Here is the template:

```
(setf <name of a list> (cons <new element> <name of the list>))
```

And here is an example of the template in use:

```
* (setf new-front 'a list-to-be-changed '(b c))
* (setf list-to-be-changed (cons new-front list-to-be-changed))
(A B C)
* new-front
A
* list-to-be-changed
(A B C)
```

Alternatively, you could use PUSH, a wonderful LISP primitive that takes
two arguments, a new element and a symbol whose value is a list. PUSH
returns a new list, as if CONS appeared in place of PUSH, and assigns the new
list to the symbol:

```
* (setf new-front 'a list-to-be-changed '(b c))
* (push new-front list-to-be-changed)
(A B C)
* list-to-be-changed
(A B C)
```

POP is the equally wonderful complement to PUSH. POP takes one argument,
a symbol whose value is a list. POP returns the first element in the list and
assigns the rest of the list to the symbol:

```
* list-to-be-changed
(A B C)
* (pop list-to-be-changed)
A
* list-to-be-changed
(B C)
```

We rarely use either PUSH or POP in this book. We think PUSH and POP should
be in your vocabulary, but strictly speaking, they are not essential.

**NTHCDR,
BUTLAST, and
LAST Shorten Lists**

Unlike REST, NTHCDR trims off n elements, not just one, with the first argument determining the exact number:

```
* (setf abc-list '(a b c))
* (rest abc-list)
(B C)
```

```
* (nthcdr 2 abc-list)
(C)
```

If the first argument is equal to or greater than the number of elements in the list, NTHCDR returns NIL:

```
* (setf abc-list '(a b c))
* (nthcdr 50 abc-list)
NIL
```

BUTLAST is similar to NTHCDR, but trims off the last n elements, rather than the first. BUTLAST is different from NTHCDR in that the second argument, not the first, determines the number of elements trimmed off:

```
* (setf abc-list '(a b c))
* (butlast abc-list 2)
(A)
* (butlast abc-list 50)
NIL
```

The second argument in BUTLAST forms is optional; if there is no second argument, only one element is trimmed off:

```
* (setf abc-list '(a b c))
* (butlast abc-list)
(A B)
```

It is computationally expensive to trim elements from the back of a list for reasons you learn about much later, in chapter 17. Accordingly, using BUTLAST is more expensive than using NTHCDR.

If you want to add an element to the back of a list, you must use a combination of APPEND and LIST, as there is no complement to CONS:

```
(setf f 'front
      b 'back
      abc-list '(a b c))
* (cons f abc-list)
(FRONT A B C)
* (append abc-list (list b))
(A B C BACK)
```

Note, however, that adding elements to the back of a list is computationally expensive, again for reasons you learn about in chapter 17.

Moving on, LAST returns a list with all but the last element of a list trimmed off:

```
* (setf abc-list '(a b c) ab-cd-list '((a b) (c d)))
```

```
* (last abc-list)
(C)
* (last ab-cd-list)
((C D))
* (last 'abc-list)
ERROR
```

Pause here to note that LAST returns a list containing the last element of a list, not the last element itself. Just as there is nothing that complements CONS, there is nothing that complements FIRST. To extract the last element itself, you must combine FIRST with LAST:

```
* (setf abc-list '(a b c))
* (last abc-list)
(C)
* (first (last abc-list))
C
```

Extracting the last element is computationally expensive, however, so if the lack of primitives analogous to FIRST discourages you from extracting a list's final element, so much the better.

LENGTH and REVERSE Work on Top-Level Elements

The LENGTH primitive counts the number of top-level elements in a list. REVERSE reverses the order of the top-level elements of a list. Both consider the argument they get to be a list of elements, not caring whether the elements themselves are lists or just atoms. Often they are used on lists that have lists as elements, but they do nothing with the insides of those sublists:

```
* (setf ab-list '(a b) ab-cd-list '((a b) (c d)))
* (length ab-list)
2
* (length ab-cd-list)
2
* (length (append ab-list ab-list))
4
* (reverse ab-list)
(B A)
* (reverse ab-cd-list)
((C D) (A B))
* (reverse (append ab-list ab-list))
(B A B A)
```

Problems

Problem 2-8: Evaluate the following forms:

```
(length '(plato socrates aristotle))
(length '((plato) (socrates) (aristotle)))
(length '((plato socrates aristotle)))
(reverse '(plato socrates aristotle))
(reverse '((plato) (socrates) (aristotle)))
(reverse '((plato socrates aristotle)))
```

Problem 2-9: Evaluate the following forms:

```
(length '((car chevrolet) (drink coke) (cereal wheaties)))
(reverse '((car chevrolet) (drink coke) (cereal wheaties)))
(append '((car chevrolet) (drink coke))
        (reverse '((car chevrolet) (drink coke))))
```

ASSOC Looks for Indexed Sublists

The ASSOC primitive is especially tailored to work with a particular kind of association-recording expression called an *association list*, sometimes referred to as an *a-list*.

An association list consists of a list of sublists.[7] The first element of each sublist is used as a *key* for recovering the entire sublist. For example, you could represent some information about a particular person as follows:

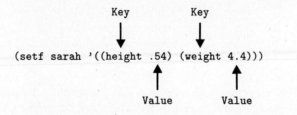

Evidently, *height* and *weight* are keys in the list assigned to SARAH; .54 and 4.4 are values expressed in meters and kilograms.

You retrieve elements from an association list using ASSOC, a key, and the association list:

```
(ASSOC <key> <association list>)
```

Here is an example:

---

[7]Association lists can be lists of *dotted pairs*. To avoid discussing dotted pairs, we limit ourselves to association lists that are lists of lists. Most LISP programmers use dotted pairs rarely or never, except in association lists, and even there, they are not really necessary.

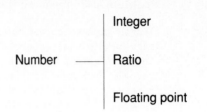

Figure 2-4. LISP's basic numeric data types. A number can be an integer, a ratio, or a floating-point number.

```
* (assoc 'weight sarah)
(WEIGHT 4.4)
```

Note that ASSOC always returns the entire first sublist with a matching key. In the event that more than one sublist has a matching key, only the first is returned and all the rest are said to be *shadowed*.[8]

LISP Offers Integers, Ratios, and Floating-Point Numbers, among Others

The purpose of this section is to discuss three data types, shown in figure 2-4, that are numeric atoms, along with primitives that operate on those data types. The discussion is too long for a footnote, but you need not study it in detail, especially on first reading, unless you want to work with numbers right away.

Three of the most popular types of numbers in LISP are integers, ratios, and floating-point numbers. *Integers*, like 47, represent whole numbers; *ratios*, like 4/7 represent rational numbers; and *floating-point numbers*, like 4.7, represent reals, which, roughly speaking, are numbers with decimal fractions.

Integers usually are written without a decimal point, but if you do include one, be sure that there are no digits following the decimal point because a number with a digit after the decimal point is interpreted as a floating-point number.

The result of division depends on the numbers involved. First of all, with two floating-point arguments, a floating-point number is returned by /, as expected. Consider this example:

```
* (/ 1.234321 1.111)
1.111
```

Next, note that / returns an integer when given two integer arguments that happen to divide evenly:

[8]In later chapters, you see examples in which association lists are used to tie variables and variable values together.

```
* (/ 27 9)
3
```

However, with two integer arguments that do *not* divide evenly, the result is a *ratio*:

```
* (/ 22 7)
22/7
```

When you want a floating-point result, you can use `FLOAT`, a primitive that converts its argument into a floating-point number:

```
* (float (/ 22 7))
3.14286
```

If, instead, you want the answer to be an integer, you use `ROUND`. Note, however, that `ROUND` is one of many LISP primitives that return more than one useful value, each of which is printed on a separate line:

```
* (round (/ 22 7))
3                              ;The nearest integer.
1/7                            ;The remainder.
```

Later on, in chapter 28, you learn how to capture all of the values returned by multiple-valued forms. For now, just imagine that all of the excess values are thrown away when a multiple-valued form is embedded in another computation:

```
* (+ (round (/ 22 7)) (round (/ 7 3)))
5
```

`ROUND` rounds toward the even integer when its argument is midway between two integers:

```
* (round 5 2)
2
```

Something else worth knowing about is the notion of *floating contagion*. If an arithmetic primitive is given one argument that is an integer or a ratio and another that is a floating-point number, then the integer or ratio is converted into a floating-point number before the primitive is applied. Consequently, the following are completely equivalent:[9]

---

[9]If an arithmetic form has many arguments, some of which are integers or ratios and some of which are floating-point numbers, implementations of COMMON LISP are free to combine all of the integers and ratios first, converting only the result to a floating-point number, which is more efficient than argument by argument conversion.

```
* (+ 2 1.5)
3.5
* (+ (float 2) (float 1.5))
3.5
```

Finally, note that some primitives that are usually employed with multiple
arguments also do useful things when given a single argument:

```
* (- 8)
-8
* (- -8)
8
```

Thus - computes the negative of its argument if there is only one, and
(- 8) is equivalent to (- 0 8) Similarly, / computes the reciprocal of its
argument if there is only one, and (/ 2) is equivalent to (/ 1 2):

```
* (/ 1 2)
1/2
* (/ 2)
1/2
```

**A Few Primitives for
Numbers Round Out
a Basic Repertoire**

You cannot get along with just +, -, *, /, FLOAT, and ROUND for long. Consequently, we conclude this chapter with a description of a few more number-
oriented primitives. MAX and MIN, for example, find maxima and minima:

```
* (MAX 2 4 3)
4
* (MIN 2 4 3)
2
```

EXPT calculates powers; it raises its first argument to its second:

```
* (expt 2 3)
8
* (expt 3 2)
9
```

EXPT works with floating-point numbers too:

```
* (expt 3.3 2.2)
13.827085
* (expt 2.2 3.3)
13.48947
```

SQRT, of course, takes the square root, undoing what (EXPT ⟨expression⟩ 2) does:

```
* (sqrt 9)
3
* (expt 3 2)
9
```

If you give SQRT a negative argument, it returns a complex number, a numeric data type that we introduce much later, in chapter 32.

Finally, ABS computes the absolute value:

```
* (abs 5)
5
* (abs -5)
5
```

Problems

Problem 2-10: Evaluate the following forms:

```
* (/ (+ 3 1) (- 3 1))
* (* (MAX 3 4 5) (MIN 3 4 5))
* (MIN (MAX 3 1 4) (MAX 2 7 1))
```

Summary

- LISP means symbol manipulation.
- LISP procedures and data are symbolic expressions.
- Lists are like bowls.
- FIRST and REST take lists apart.
- Quoting stops evaluation.
- Some old timers use CARs and CDRs.
- SETF assigns values to symbols.
- SETF accepts multiple symbol-value pairs.
- Certain atoms evaluate to themselves.
- CONS, APPEND, and LIST construct lists.
- CONS, APPEND, and LIST do not alter symbol values.
- NTHCDR, BUTLAST, and LAST shorten lists.
- LENGTH and REVERSE work on top-level elements.
- ASSOC looks for indexed sublists.
- LISP offers integers, ratios, and floating-point numbers, among others.
- A few primitives for numbers round out a basic repertoire.

3

Procedure
Definition
and Binding

The primary purpose of the chapter is to explain how you can define your own LISP procedures by building them out of LISP primitives and other, previously defined procedures.

A secondary purpose of this chapter is to expand your vocabulary a bit more, introducing the terms *variable*, *parameter*, *body*, *lexical variable*, and *special variable*.

Another secondary purpose of this chapter is to introduce two simple procedure-writing techniques: *progressive envelopment* and *comment translation*.

DEFUN is LISP's Procedure-Definition Primitive

Suppose you want to make a new list out of the first and last elements of a list whose value is MEALS:

```
* (setf meals '(breakfast lunch tea dinner))
(BREAKFAST LUNCH TEA DINNER)
```

Recalling that LAST is a primitive that removes all but the last element from a list, you know that you can make the desired list as follows:

```
* (cons (first meals) (last meals))
(BREAKFAST DINNER)
```

This works because (FIRST MEALS) returns BREAKFAST, (LAST MEALS) returns (DINNER), and putting them together with CONS yields (BREAKFAST DINNER).

Of course CONS, FIRST, and LAST will work on any list:

```
* (setf route2 '(boston cambridge lincoln concord))
(BOSTON CAMBRIDGE LINCOLN CONCORD)
* (cons (first route2) (last route2))
(BOSTON CONCORD)
```

Now suppose you often want to pick the first and last element out of a list. You wish there were a procedure, BOTH-ENDS, such that you could use BOTH-ENDS as a sort of shorthand for the CONS-FIRST-LAST combination:

```
* (both-ends meals)
(BREAKFAST DINNER)
* (both-ends route2)
(BOSTON CONCORD)
```

Happily, you can define BOTH-ENDS to be a procedure, telling LISP what to do when a BOTH-ENDS form is encountered. But before looking at how to define BOTH-ENDS in detail, consider the intended effect: whenever a form involving BOTH-ENDS is encountered, LISP must do four things:

- Reserve a new place in memory to hold a value for WHOLE-LIST. Said another way, LISP must bind WHOLE-LIST.
- Evaluate BOTH-ENDS's argument and store the result in the place reserved for WHOLE-LIST's value. Said another way, LISP must assign a value to WHOLE-LIST.
- Evaluate the form (CONS (FIRST WHOLE-LIST) (LAST WHOLE-LIST)) and return the result.
- Forget about the new place in memory reserved for WHOLE-LIST's value.

It is easier to talk about all this once we have these definitions:

- A *variable* is a symbol thought of as a name for a place to store a value.
- The *parameters* of a procedure are variables that are bound and that have values assigned to them when that procedure is entered.

It is precise, albeit awkward, to say that a variable is bound and that a certain value is assigned to it on entry to a procedure. Consequently, it is standard practice to say, as a sort of shorthand, that the variable is bound to the value. Similarly, it is standard practice to speak of a variable's binding as a synonym for the variable's value.

Thus WHOLE-LIST is to be a parameter in BOTH-ENDS that is bound to (BREAKFAST LUNCH TEA DINNER) when (BOTH-ENDS '(BREAKFAST LUNCH TEA DINNER)) is evaluated.

- The *body* of a procedure consists of the forms that are evaluated when a procedure is used.

Thus (CONS (FIRST WHOLE-LIST) (LAST WHOLE-LIST)) is to be the body of BOTH-ENDS.

Now we are ready to exhibit a definition of BOTH-ENDS, illustrating the use of LISP's procedure-defining primitive, DEFUN, an acronym for <u>de</u>fine <u>fun</u>ction. Note that there is no prompt because we are not showing the give and take of a dialog here:

```
(defun both-ends              ;Procedure's name is BOTH-ENDS.
  (whole-list)                ;Parameter list (just one parameter here).
  (cons (first whole-list)    ;The body (just one form here).
        (last whole-list)))
```

As indicated in the comments, the DEFUN form tells LISP the name of the procedure, the parameter variables to be bound, and the forms to be evaluated. Here is the DEFUN template, in its simplest form, along with our sample procedure.

```
(defun <procedure name>      (defun both-ends
        (<parameter>)          (whole-list)
        <form>)                (cons (first whole-list)
                                     (rest whole-list)))
```

Once BOTH-ENDS is defined using DEFUN, BOTH-ENDS can be used like any other procedure. Here it is in action on the previously bound variables MEALS and ROUTE2:

```
* (both-ends meals)
(BREAKFAST DINNER)
* (both-ends route2)
(BOSTON CONCORD)
```

In both examples, (CONS (FIRST WHOLE-LIST) (LAST WHOLE-LIST)), the procedure's body, was evaluated. In the first example, WHOLE-LIST was bound to the list (BREAKFAST LUNCH TEA DINNER); in the second, WHOLE-LIST was bound to the list (BOSTON CAMBRIDGE LINCOLN CONCORD).

Note that it is conventional, albeit not necessary, to put all parameter variables together with the procedure name on the first line of procedure definitions:

```
(defun both-ends (whole-list)      ;Parameter list on the first line.
  (cons (first whole-list)         ;The body (just one form here).
        (last whole-list)))
```

And if the procedure is short enough, you can even save space by putting the whole thing on one line. For our example, if we shorten WHOLE-LIST to W, we can write:

```
(defun both-ends (w) (cons (first w) (last w)))
```

In general, it is much better to use mnemonic parameter names like WHOLE-LIST, which aid understanding, rather than W, which does not.

Note also that DEFUN does not evaluate its arguments. It just looks at them and establishes a procedure definition. The value that DEFUN gives back is the procedure name, but this is of little consequence, because the main purpose of DEFUN is to establish a definition, not to return some useful value:

```
* (defun both-ends (whole-list)
    (cons (first whole-list)
          (last whole-list)))
BOTH-ENDS
```

Recall that anything a procedure has done that persists after it returns its value is called *a side effect*. The side effect of DEFUN is to set up a procedure definition.

Parameter Variable Values Are Isolated by Virtual Fences

Suppose that WHOLE-LIST has a value apart from WHOLE-LIST's role in BOTH-ENDS:

```
* (setf whole-list '(monday tuesday wednesday thursday friday))
```

You might worry that BOTH-ENDS's action would affect WHOLE-LIST's value. For example, suppose we use BOTH-ENDS with an argument that causes WHOLE-LIST's value to be (BOSTON CAMBRIDGE LINCOLN CONCORD) while BOTH-ENDS is doing its job:

```
* (both-ends '(boston cambridge lincoln concord))
(BOSTON CONCORD)
```

Once BOTH-ENDS is finished, however, the value of WHOLE-LIST appears unchanged:

```
* whole-list
(MONDAY TUESDAY WEDNESDAY THURSDAY FRIDAY)
```

Evidently, the parameter variable bindings established when a procedure is entered are isolated from other variable bindings. It is as if LISP builds a fence to avoid confusion. For example, whenever BOTH-ENDS is called, LISP throws up a fence around the body of BOTH-ENDS that protects any existing value for WHOLE-LIST.

Thus the value of WHOLE-LIST, if any, before BOTH-ENDS is used is the value of WHOLE-LIST once again after LISP finishes evaluating the body of BOTH-ENDS. It does not matter that WHOLE-LIST was bound to a different value inside BOTH-ENDS's fence. Even assigning a new value to WHOLE-LIST inside BOTH-ENDS using SETF has no affect on the value of WHOLE-LIST outside the fence.

Special Variable Values Are Not Isolated by Virtual Fences

Although a virtual fence isolates all of a procedure's parameter bindings, there is no such isolation for variables that are not parameters. Consider this version of BOTH-ENDS, for example:

```
(defun both-ends-with-special-variable ()
  (setf whole-list
        (cons (first whole-list) (last whole-list))))
```

There is no parameter at all in BOTH-ENDS-WITH-SPECIAL-VARIABLE. Thus WHOLE-LIST is *not* a parameter variable, and its value is *not* isolated from the value of WHOLE-LIST outside of the fence erected when a form involving BOTH-ENDS-WITH-SPECIAL-VARIABLE is evaluated:

```
* (setf whole-list '(monday tuesday wednesday thursday friday))
(MONDAY TUESDAY WEDNESDAY THURSDAY FRIDAY)
* (both-ends-with-special-variable)
(MONDAY FRIDAY)
* whole-list
(MONDAY FRIDAY)
```

Thus there are two kinds of variables: those that are isolated by virtual fences and those that are not. Each kind has a name:

- A variable is a *lexical variable* if it is isolated by a virtual fence. For the moment, you may assume that a variable is a lexical variable if it appears inside a procedure in which it is a parameter.
- A variable is a *special variable* if it is *not* isolated by a virtual fence. For the moment, you may assume that a variable is a special variable if it appears inside a procedure in which it is *not* a parameter.

Later on, in chapter 16, you see that there are other factors that determine whether a variable is lexical or special. For now, however, you do not know how to do anything that can get you into trouble.

Procedures Match Parameters to Arguments

The next example introduces BOTH-ENDS-WITH-TWO-PARAMETERS, a procedure with two parameters, rather than just one:

```
(defun both-ends-with-two-parameters (l m)
  (cons (first l) (last m)))
```

The purpose of BOTH-ENDS-WITH-TWO-PARAMETERS is to combine the first element of one list with the last element of another:

```
* (both-ends-with-two-parameters '(breakfast lunch)
                                 '(tea dinner))
(BREAKFAST DINNER)
```

In this example, the temporary value of L becomes (BREAKFAST LUNCH) on entry, and the temporary value of M becomes (TEA DINNER). Note that there is never any confusion about how to match L and M with (BREAKFAST LUNCH) and (TEA DINNER)—LISP knows the correct way to match them up because DEFUN's parameter list specifies the order in which parameters are to be paired with incoming arguments.

Finally, note that a procedure can have not only multiple parameters, but also multiple forms in its body. When there is more than one form in the body, the value returned by the procedure is the value of the last form. Any others are evaluated for side effects only. Here is an example:

```
(defun both-ends-with-side-effect (whole-list)
  (setf last-list-processed whole-list) ;First form in the body.
  (cons (first whole-list)
        (last whole-list)))                ;Second form in the body.
```

The first of the two forms is evaluated only for the side effect of assigning a value to a special variable, LAST-LIST-PROCESSED; the second form is evaluated to produce a result for the BOTH-ENDS-WITH-SIDE-EFFECT procedure.

Thus the general template for DEFUN shows that DEFUN forms can have more than one form in the body as well as more than one parameter in the parameter list:

```
(defun <procedure name>
  (<parameter 1> ... <parameter m>)        ;Many parameters.
  <form 1>                                  ;Many forms
  ...
  <form n>)
```

Problems

Problem 3-1: Define EXCHANGE, a procedure that returns the elements of a two-element list in reverse order:

```
* (setf sinners '(adam eve))
* (exchange sinners)
(EVE ADAM)
```

Problem 3-2: Some people are annoyed by abbreviations like CONS, which is really a shortened form of <u>cons</u>truct. Define a new procedure, CONSTRUCT, that does the same thing.

Problem 3-3: Define ROTATE-LEFT, a procedure that takes a list as its argument and returns a new list in which the former first element becomes the last.

```
* (rotate-left '(a b c))
(B C A)
* (rotate-left (rotate-left '(a b c)))
(C A B)
```

Problem 3-4: Define ROTATE-RIGHT. It is to be like ROTATE-LEFT except that it is to rotate in the other direction. You will want to use BUTLAST.

Problem 3-5: A palindrome is a list that has the same sequence of elements when read from right to left that it does when read from left to right. Define PALINDROMIZE such that it takes a list as its argument and returns a palindrome that is twice as long.

Problem 3-6: When converting between degrees Fahrenheit and degrees Celsius, it is useful to note that $-40°$ Fahrenheit equals $-40°$ Celsius. This observation makes for the following symmetric conversion formulas:

$$C = (F + 40) \times 5/9 - 40,$$
$$F = (C + 40) \times 9/5 - 40.$$

Define conversion procedures, F-TO-C and C-TO-F, using these formulas. Here are some examples of your results in use:

```
* (f-to-c 32)
0
* (f-to-c 98.6)
37.0
* (f-to-c 212)
100
```

LET Forms Bind Parameters to Initial Values

Now it is time to learn about LET, a popular primitive that binds parameters. Along the way we consider several alternative versions of the BOTH-ENDS procedure previously defined this way:

```
(defun both-ends (whole-list)
  (cons (first whole-list) (last whole-list)))
```

Here is an example of a LET form in action:

```
* (setf whole-list '(breakfast lunch tea dinner))
* (let ((element (first whole-list))    ;Bind ELEMENT to initial value.
        (trailer (last whole-list)))    ;Bind TRAILER to initial value.
    (cons element trailer))             ;Combine ELEMENT and TRAILER.
(BREAKFAST DINNER)
```

Evidently, LET arranges for parameters to be bound, just as parameters are bound on entering a procedure. Here is the general template:

```
(let ((<parameter 1> <initial value 1>)
      ...
      (<parameter m> <initial value m>))
  <form 1>
  ...
  <form n>)
```

And here is how the general template matches the example:

```
(let ((<parameter 1>           (let ((element
       <initial value 1>)              (first whole-list))
      (<parameter 2>                  (trailer
       <initial value 2>))            (last whole-list)))
  <form 1>)                     (cons element trailer))
```

Thus LET generally begins with a parameter list consisting of two-element lists, each of which has a parameter variable and an initial value form.

Now we can use a LET form, with initial values, to define a variant of BOTH-ENDS:

```
(defun both-ends-with-let (whole-list)
  (let ((element (first whole-list))    ;Bind ELEMENT to initial value.
        (trailer (last whole-list)))    ;Bind TRAILER to initial value.
    (cons element trailer)))            ;Combine ELEMENT and TRAILER.
```

LET Forms Produce Nested Fences

Whenever a LET form is evaluated, the parameter bindings involved are isolated by a virtual fence, just as they are when a procedure is entered. But now we come to a convention that we will explain in much more detail in chapter 15: whenever a LET form appears inside a procedure definition, the fence for that LET form appears inside the fence for the procedure definition:

```
BOTH-ENDS-WITH-LET's fence ─────────────────────┐
                                                 │
        LET's fence ──────────────────────┐     │
                                     │     │     │
                                     └─────┘     │
                                                 │
 └───────────────────────────────────────────────┘
```

LET Forms Evaluate Initial-Value Forms in Parallel

Note that LET is said to evaluate its initial-value forms in *parallel* because all initial-value forms are evaluated before the fence for the LET is built and before any of the LET's parameters are bound. Accordingly, in the following example, the second initial-value form finds the value of X outside of the fence for the LET; it is not influenced by the binding of X established by the LET itself:

```
* (setf x 'outside)
* (let ((x 'inside)         ;X's parameter value will be INSIDE.
        (y x))              ;Y's parameter value will be OUTSIDE.
    (list x y))
(INSIDE OUTSIDE)
```

If X had not had a value assigned to it by the SETF form, there would have been an error message reporting an unbound variable error.

LET* Forms Evaluate Initial-Value Forms Sequentially

Sometimes, however, you need a version of LET that does parameter binding such that the value of a parameter bound early can be used to compute the value of a parameter bound late. The required alternative to LET is LET*. In the following example, the second initial-value form finds the value of X already established by the LET itself:

```
* (setf x 'outside)
* (let* ((x 'inside)        ;X's parameter value will be INSIDE.
         (y x))             ;Y's parameter value will be INSIDE too.
    (list x y))
(INSIDE INSIDE)
```

LET* is really a shorthand notation for nested LETs. Thus the LET* form above is equivalent to the following multiple LET expression:

```
* (setf x 'outside)
* (let ((x 'inside))
    (let ((y x))
      (list x y)))
(INSIDE INSIDE)
```

The consequent effect is that the evaluation of initial-value forms and the binding of parameters appears to be interdigitated. Accordingly, LET* is said to evaluate its initial-value forms *sequentially*.

Progressive Envelopment and Comment Translation Help Define New Procedures

We now explain two techniques that will help you to work out definitions for your own procedures. For each, we use BOTH-ENDS as an illustration, producing slightly different definitions with each technique. Although these techniques are not really necessary for implementing such a simple procedure, it is instructive to see them all at work on the same procedure, one that is so simple that understanding the procedure cannot get in the way of understanding the techniques.

The first technique for defining procedures is *progressive envelopment*. The basic idea is to work out what combinations of LISP primitives are needed through a sequence of terminal experiments.

To see how progressive envelopment works, imagine that you have yet to see a definition for BOTH-ENDS. To start our implementation by progressive envelopment, we devise a sample expression that BOTH-ENDS could be asked to work on:

```
(setf whole-list '(breakfast lunch tea dinner))
```

With this, we know that the result to be produced is (BREAKFAST DINNER), so we begin to think about how to dig BREAKFAST and DINNER out of the list assigned to WHOLE-LIST, using LISP itself to verify our thoughts. In particular, we note the results returned by FIRST and LAST when applied to the sample expression:

```
* (first whole-list)
BREAKFAST
```

```
* (last whole-list)
(DINNER)
```

With these results in front of us on our terminal's screen, we speculate that we can get what we want by enveloping (FIRST WHOLE-LIST) and (LAST WHOLE-LIST) in a CONS form. Again, we use LISP to verify:

```
* (cons (first whole-list)
        (last whole-list))
(BREAKFAST DINNER)
```

Now that we have what we want, we envelope it further in a DEFUN form, using WHOLE-LIST as a parameter:

```
(defun both-ends (whole-list)     ;Progressive envelopment version.
  (cons (first whole-list)
        (last whole-list)))
```

Finally, we test:

```
* (both-ends '(breakfast lunch tea dinner))
(BREAKFAST DINNER)
```

Progressive envelopment helps you write procedures because it allows you to build complicated things incrementally, one step at a time, with frequent testing to expose bugs as they creep in, reducing the need for localizing them later on.

The next technique for defining procedures is *comment translation*. The basic idea is to think through what to do in English first before trying to translate what needs to be done into LISP forms.

To see how comment translation works, imagine again that we have yet to see a definition for BOTH-ENDS. We start by devising a skeletal definition for BOTH-ENDS with comments appearing instead of forms. Following custom, we use two semicolons in front of comments that have lines to themselves:

```
(defun both-ends (whole-list)
  ;;Extract first element.
  ;;Extract last element.
  ;;Combine the first and last elements.
  )
```

Once the skeleton is in place, we start translating comments to LISP forms:

```
(defun both-ends (whole-list)
  ;;Extract first element.
  (first whole-list)
  ;;Extract last element.
  (first (last whole-list))
  ;;Combine the first and last elements.
  )
```

One more step yields the desired result:

```
(defun both-ends (whole-list)    ;Comment translation version.
  ;;Combine the first and last elements.
  (list
    ;;Extract first element.
    (first whole-list)
    ;;Extract last element.
    (first (last whole-list))))
```

Comment translation has led us to a slightly different definition from the one we produced by progressive envelopment. Both return the desired result.

Comment translation helps you write procedures because it forces you to think about what your procedures are supposed to do before you get bogged down throwing parentheses around. Comment translation also helps you to maintain procedures because good comments are essential later on when you try to reconstruct what you were thinking about at the time you were writing the procedures originally.

Two other useful techniques for defining procedures are *problem reduction*, introduced in chapter 4, and the most powerful technique of all, *procedure abstraction*, introduced in chapter 5.

Summary

- DEFUN is LISP's procedure-definition primitive.
- Parameter variable values are isolated by virtual fences.
- Special variable values are *not* isolated by virtual fences.
- Procedures match parameters to arguments.
- LET forms bind parameter variables to initial values.
- LET forms produce nested fences.
- LET forms evaluate initial-value forms in parallel.
- LET* forms evaluate initial-value forms sequentially.
- Progressive envelopment and comment translation help define new procedures.

4

Predicates
and Conditionals

The principal purpose of this chapter is to explain various tests, which we call *predicates* when we want to be formal. These tests, combined with *conditionals*, enable you to tell LISP how to vary what happens as circumstances dictate, making it possible to define more interesting procedures. Some predicates accept a behavior-altering *keyword argument*.

A secondary purpose of this chapter is to introduce another simple procedure-writing technique, *problem reduction*.

A Predicate Is a Procedure That Returns True or False

A *predicate* is a procedure that returns a value that signals *true* or *false*. False is always signaled by NIL. True is often signaled by the special symbol T, but actually, anything other than NIL is considered to signal true.

Note that T and NIL are special symbols in that their values are preset to T and NIL. That is, the value of T is T and the value of NIL is NIL. Consider these examples:

```
* t
T                                          ;Value of T is T.
* nil
NIL                                        ;Value of NIL is NIL.
```

EQUAL, EQ, EQL, and = Are Equality Predicates

The EQUAL primitive tests two arguments to see if their values are the same expression. EQUAL works for both atoms and lists. If EQUAL's two argument values are the same, then the value returned by EQUAL is T; otherwise the value returned is NIL.

```
* (equal (+ 2 2) 4)
T
* (equal (+ 2 3) 3)
NIL
* (equal '(this is a list) (setf l '(this is a list)))
T
* (equal '(this is a list) l)
T
* (equal '(this is a list) (setf reverse-of-l '(list a is this)))
NIL
* (equal l (reverse reverse-of-l))
T
```

Several predicates determine if their arguments are equal. They range from EQUAL, which is a general purpose predicate, but computationally expensive, to EQ and =, which are special purpose, but efficient:

Name	Purpose
equal	Are two argument values the same expression?
eql	Are two argument values the same symbol or number?
eq	Are two argument values the same symbol?
=	Are two argument values the same number?

Roughly, here is how EQUAL, EQL, EQ, and = are related:[1]

- EQUAL first tests to see if its arguments satisfy EQL. If not, it tries to see if they are *lists* whose elements satisfy EQUAL.
- EQL first tests to see if its arguments satisfy EQ. If not, it tries to see if they are *numbers* of the same type and value.
- EQ tests to see if its arguments are represented by the same chunk of computer memory. They will be if they are identical *symbols*.
- = tests to see if its arguments represent the same number, even if they do not happen to be the same type of number.

It is important to remember that numbers must be numbers of the same type to satisfy EQL.

---

[1]Chapter 17 describes the relationship among the various equality predicates in more detail.

```
* (eql 4 4.0)                        ;Numbers have the different type.
NIL
* (eql 4 4)                          ;Numbers have the same type.
T
```

Numbers that are of different type satisfy =, however:

```
* (= 4 4.0)
T
```

Also, note that the arguments to = must be numbers. Anything else produces an error.

MEMBER Tests for List Membership

The MEMBER predicate tests to see if its first argument is an element of its second argument. Note that MEMBER returns what is left of the list when the matching symbol is encountered:

```
* (setf sentence '(tell me more about your mother please))
* (member 'mother sentence)
(MOTHER PLEASE)
```

The implementers of LISP decided long ago that NIL is NIL, but anything other than NIL is as good as T. Sometimes a predicate returns something other than T on the ground that a more descriptive result can be useful in further computation.

Note also that MEMBER ordinarily returns NIL unless the first argument is a top-level element of the second argument; just being there, buried inside the list, is not enough. For example, MEMBER returns NIL in the following, in which MOTHER is present, but not as a top-level element:

```
* (setf pairs '((father son) (mother daughter)))
* (member 'mother pairs)
NIL
```

Keyword Arguments Modify Behavior

Note that MEMBER normally tests things with EQL, the predicate that works only with symbols and numbers of the same type. When you want MEMBER to look for an element that happens to be a list, you must indicate that you want to test for membership using the EQUAL predicate.

Old versions of LISP had several membership predicates, one for each equality predicate. In COMMON LISP, however, there is just one membership predicate because COMMON LISP has a general mechanism for altering basic behavior by way of *keyword arguments*. To explain keyword arguments, we explain how :TEST and #'EQUAL alter the behavior of MEMBER in the following:

```
* (setf pairs '((maple shade) (apple fruit)))
* (member '(maple shade) pairs)
NIL
* (member '(maple shade) pairs :test #'equal)
((MAPLE SHADE) (APPLE FRUIT))
```

First, any symbol beginning with a colon is said to be a *keyword*. Like T and NIL, keywords always evaluate to themselves:

```
* :test
:TEST
```

Any argument that follows a keyword is a keyword argument. The purpose of a keyword argument is to modify a procedure's basic behavior along the lines suggested by the keyword. Thus the :TEST keyword indicates a change to the basic behavior of the MEMBER predicate. In particular, :TEST indicates that the next argument specifies the test that MEMBER is to use.

Next, to understand the purpose of the #' characters, you must understand the distinction between procedure names and procedure objects. The five characters in the symbol EQUAL constitute a *procedure name*. The computer instructions that actually perform the required test constitute a *procedure object*.

The purpose of the #' characters is to produce a procedure object from a procedure name. Thus DEFUN and #' do complementary things: DEFUN stores procedure descriptions away as procedure objects; #' produces procedure objects from procedure names. The procedure object associated with EQUAL is just what is needed to alter the behavior of MEMBER.

Incidentally, prefacing an expression with #' is equivalent to nesting that expression inside a FUNCTION form, and in old programs, you are likely to see expressions like (FUNCTION EQUAL) in place of #'EQUAL. Providing #', like providing ', is a sort of syntactic sugaring.[2]

Note, however, that #' and ' have quite different purposes, in spite of their visual similarity. One produces a procedure object; the other stops evaluation.

Of course, you may wonder why things have to be so fancy. Why not have LISP expect a procedure name following the :TEST keyword, so that the #' would be unnecessary? After all, LISP expects the first element in forms to be procedure names and must produce procedure objects from those names. The reason is that we want to allow a keyword argument to be a variable whose value is a procedure object, rather than a procedure name. Suppose, for example, that we bind PREDICATE to a procedure object:

---

[2]Actually, the #' character combination is recognized by LISP's reader, which converts #'<expression> into (FUNCTION <expression>).

```
* (setf predicate #'equal)
```

Now we can use PREDICATE's value, a procedure object, in a member form:

```
* (member '(maple shade) '((maple shade) (apple fruit))
        :test predicate)
((MAPLE SHADE) (APPLE FRUIT))
```

Similarly, you may wonder why the :TEST keyword is necessary. Why not have LISP assume that any extra argument is a test-specifying procedure object? The reason is that keywords make more than one kind of behavior alteration possible. For example, MEMBER can be used with another keyword, the :TEST-NOT keyword. If :TEST-NOT appears, MEMBER returns the remainder of the list after the first element, if any, that is *not* the same as the first argument, where the keyword argument determines what *same* means:

```
* (setf pairs '((maple shade) (apple fruit)))

* (member '(maple shade) pairs
        :test-not #'equal)
((APPLE FRUIT))

* (member '(maple shade)
        '((maple shade) (maple shade))
        :test-not #'equal)
NIL
```

LISTP, ATOM, NUMBERP, and SYMBOLP Are Data-Type Predicates

LISP has many predicates that test objects to see whether they belong to a particular data type. Recall that you know about the data types shown in figure 4-1. Accordingly, here are representative data-type predicates:

Name	Purpose
atom	Is it an atom?
numberp	Is it a number?
symbolp	Is it a symbol?
listp	Is it a list?

ATOM is a predicate that tests its argument to see if it is an atom, while NUMBERP tests to see if its argument is a numeric atom and SYMBOLP tests its argument to see if it is a symbol, that is, a nonnumeric atom. LISTP tests its argument to see if it is a list. In the following examples, note that the value of PI is the floating-point approximation to the mathematical constant π.

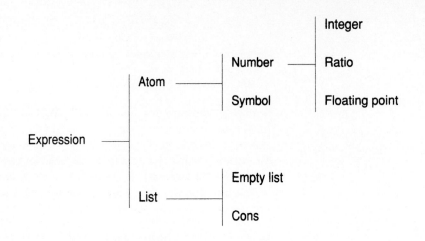

Figure 4-1. The basic data types.

```
* (atom 'pi)
T

* (atom pi)
T

* (numberp 'pi)
NIL

* (numberp pi)
T

* (symbolp 'pi)
T

* (symbolp pi)
NIL

* (listp 'pi)
NIL

* (listp pi)
NIL

* (listp '(this is a list with pi in it))
T
```

Note that predicates often end in *p*, an acronym for p̲redicate. The predicate ATOM is an unfortunate exception that tends to suggest, wrongly, that LIST should be a predicate too.

NIL Is Equivalent to the Empty List

Now it is time to consider an important peculiarity: NIL and the empty list, ( ), are completely equivalent as far as LISP is concerned. NIL and ( ) satisfy the EQ, EQL, and EQUAL predicates, for example:[3]

```
* (eq nil '())
T

* (eql nil '())
T

* (equal nil '())
T
```

By convention, both NIL and the empty list is printed out as NIL:

```
* nil
NIL

* ()
NIL
```

The equivalence of NIL and ( ) is confusing, at first, because it means that NIL and ( ) are both symbols and lists. Thus, both (SYMBOLP '( )) and (LISTP NIL) return T.

```
* (atom nil)
T

* (atom ())
T

* (symbolp nil)
T

* (symbolp ())
T

* (listp nil)
T

* (listp ())
T
```

---

[3]Some say the reason that the equivalence of NIL and ( ) was originally arranged has to do with the instruction set of the ancient 704 computer. Others believe the identity was introduced as a programming convenience, albeit a questionable one. No one seems to know for sure.

**NULL and ENDP
Are Empty-List
Predicates**

The most important predicates for lists, other than `LISTP`, are these:

Name	Purpose
null	Is the argument an empty list?
endp	Is the argument, which must be a list, an empty list?

`NULL` is the predicate that tests to see if its argument is an empty list. `ENDP` is the predicate that tests to see if a list is empty:

```
* (null '(this is not empty))
NIL
* (endp '(this is not empty))
NIL

* (null ())
T

* (endp ())
T
* (null 'this-is-a-symbol)
NIL

* (endp 'this-is-a-symbol)
ERROR
```

These days, `ENDP` is recommended for testing for empty lists, but `NULL` will work too. Note that it is an error to use `ENDP` on anything other than a list.

Curiously, you can think of `NULL` as a data-type test, rather than a list-testing predicate, because the empty list is considered to be a data type. Also, if a list is not an empty list, it must be the result of an explicit `CONS` operation or an implicit `CONS` operation hiding in a `LIST` or other list-building primitive. Thus the *empty list* and the so-called *cons* are the two subtypes of the list data type, as shown in figure 4-2.

There is even a data-type test for conses, named `CONSP`. We do not use it in this book, however.

**There Are Many
Number Predicates**

There are many predicates that work on numbers. For the most part, their meaning is obvious:

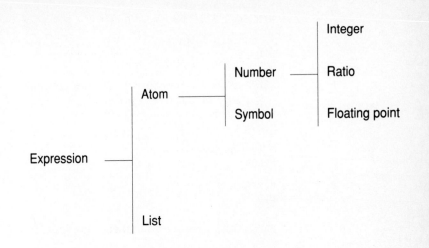

Figure 4-2. The list data type has two basic subtypes.

Name	Purpose
numberp	Is it a number?
zerop	Is it zero?
plusp	Is it positive?
minusp	Is it negative?
evenp	Is it even?
oddp	Is it odd?
>	Are they in descending order?
<	Are they in ascending order?

For some examples, let us establish some variable values:

```
* (setf zero 0 one 1 two 2 three 3 four 4)
* (setf digits (list zero one two three four))
```

Using these values, we can look at the numerical predicates. **NUMBERP** tests its argument to see if it is a number:

```
* (numberp 4)
T

* (numberp four)
T

* (numberp 'four)
NIL
```

```
* (numberp digits)
NIL

* (numberp 'digits)
NIL
```

ZEROP expects a number. It tests its argument to see if it is zero:

```
* (zerop zero)
T

* (zerop 'zero)
ERROR

* (zerop four)
NIL
```

PLUSP tests whether a number is positive:

```
* (plusp one)
T

* (plusp (- one))
NIL

* (plusp zero)
NIL
```

EVENP checks whether a number is even:

```
* (evenp (* 9 7 5 3 1))
NIL

* (evenp (* 10 8 6 4 2))
T
```

The > and < predicates expect their arguments to be numbers. The predicate > tests them to see that they are in strictly descending order, while < checks to see that they are in strictly ascending order. Both may be given one, two, or more arguments.

```
* (> four two)
T

* (> two four)
NIL

* (> three two one)
T

* (> three one two)
NIL
```

Problem 4-1: Define `DIVISIBLE-BY-THREE`, a predicate that determines whether an integer is divisible by 3. Use `REM`, a primitive that takes two integer arguments and returns the remainder left over when the first argument is divided by the second.

```
* (divisible-by-three 6)
T

* (divisible-by-three 7)
NIL

* (divisible-by-three 8)
NIL
```

Problem 4-2: Define `PALINDROMEP`, a predicate that tests its argument to see if it is a list that has the same sequence of symbols when read from right to left as when it is read from left to right:

```
* (palindromep '(a b c b a))
T

* (palindromep '(a b c c b a))
T

* (palindromep '(a b c c c a))
NIL
```

Problem 4-3: Define `RIGHTP`, a predicate that takes three arguments. The arguments are the lengths of the sides of a triangle that may or may not be a right-angle triangle. Because the floating-point representation of real numbers has limited precision, it would be unreasonable to test for exact equality here. Consequently, `RIGHTP` is to return `T` if the sum of the squares of the two shorter sides is within 2% of the square of the longest side. Otherwise `RIGHTP` is to return `NIL`. You may assume that the longest side is given as the first argument:

```
* (rightp 5 4 3)
T

* (rightp 5 3 3)
NIL
```

**AND, OR, and NOT
Enable Elaborate
Testing**

In many situations, it is natural to combine the results of two or more predicates into a combined test. This is done by using AND and OR.

Roughly, AND and OR do what they sound like they should. AND returns NIL if *any* of its arguments evaluates to NIL. OR returns NIL if *all·* of its arguments evaluate to NIL. Note the following details, however:

- The arguments of an AND form are evaluated from left to right: if any of an AND's arguments evaluates to NIL, none of the remaining arguments is evaluated, and the value returned by the AND expression is NIL.
- If all the arguments of an AND form evaluate to something other than NIL, the value returned by the AND form is the value of the last argument.

OR behaves symmetrically:

- The arguments of an OR form are also evaluated from left to right: if any of an OR's arguments evaluates to something other than NIL, none of the remaining arguments is evaluated, and the value returned by the OR expression is that nonNIL value.
- If none of the arguments of an OR form evaluate to something other than NIL, the value returned by the OR form is NIL.

Thus AND and OR make composite tests possible. AND returns nonNIL only if all arguments are nonNIL, whereas OR returns nonNIL if any argument is nonNIL. Both take any number of arguments. Here are some examples:

```
* (setf pets '(dog cat))

* (and (member 'dog pets) (member 'tiger pets))
NIL

* (or (member 'dingo pets) (member 'tiger pets))
NIL

* (and (member 'dog pets) (member 'cat pets))
(CAT)

* (or (member 'dog pets) (member 'tiger pets))
(DOG CAT)
```

Note carefully that AND and OR return the last value computed, when successful, rather than just plain T. In the examples, the last values computed were the values of MEMBER forms, and MEMBER returns the remainder of its second argument whenever it finds its first argument in that second argument.

Finally, NOT just turns nonNIL values into NIL and NIL into T:

```
* (not nil)
T

* (not t)
NIL
```

```
* (not 'dog)
NIL
* (setf pets '(dog cat))
* (member 'dog pets)
(DOG CAT)
* (not (member 'dog pets))
NIL
* (member 'dingo pets)
NIL
* (not (member 'dingo pets))
T
* (and (member 'dog pets) (member 'tiger pets))
NIL
* (and (member 'dog pets) (not (member 'tiger pets)))
T
```

Because NIL and the empty list, ( ), are completely equivalent, NOT actually does the same thing NULL does: both return T if their argument is NIL, and both return NIL if their argument is nonNIL. LISP has both NOT and NULL so that you can clearly indicate whether you are thinking about logical values or about lists.

Problems

Problem 4-4: Evaluate the following forms:

```
(and (listp pi) (setf result 'set-in-first-and))
result
(and (numberp pi) (setf result 'set-in-second-and))
result
```

**Predicates Help
IF, WHEN, and
UNLESS Choose
among Alternatives**

Predicates are most often used to determine which of one or more forms should be evaluated. The choice is often determined by predicates in conjunction with IF. In an IF form, the symbol IF is followed by a test form, as well as something to evaluate and return if the value of the test form is nonNIL and something else to evaluate and return if the value returned by the test form is NIL. Thus the template for IF is as follows:

```
(if <test> <then form> <else form>)
```

The following is a simple example. The result is the symbol DAY if the value of DAY-OR-DATE is a symbol, and DATE, otherwise:

```
* (setf day-or-date 'monday)

* (if (symbolp day-or-date) 'day 'date)
DAY

* (setf day-or-date 9)

* (if (symbolp day-or-date) 'day 'date)
DATE
```

Note that IF forms are unusual in that either the second or third argument is evaluated, but not both. In most forms, all arguments are evaluated.[4]

Note also that IF is called a *conditional* because the result of an IF form depends on the value of its test form. There are several other conditionals that are popular when the full generality of IF is not necessary. In particular, a WHEN can be used instead of an IF whenever the false consequent in an equivalent IF form would be NIL:

```
(if <test> <then form> nil)
≡
(when <test> <then form>)
```

Similarly, an UNLESS can be used instead of an IF whenever the then form in an equivalent IF form would be NIL:

```
(if <test> nil <else form>)
≡
(unless <test> <else form>)
```

Actually, both WHEN and UNLESS can have an unlimited number of arguments. The first argument is always the test form; the last argument always supplies the value if the test's value indicates action; and all of the arguments in between are evaluated for their side effects. In the following example, the value of the WHEN form is NEW-RECORD whenever TEMPERATURE is bigger than HIGH. But note that there is also a side effect: the second argument in the WHEN form is a SETF form that assigns TEMPERATURE to HIGH:

```
* (setf high 98 temperature 102)

* (when (> temperature high)        ;Compare TEMPERATURE with HIGH.
    (setf high temperature)         ;When bigger, change HIGH's value.
    'new-record)                    ;When bigger, return NEW-RECORD.
NEW-RECORD
```

---

[4] IF forms belong to a small group whose members are all treated as special cases by LISP interpreters and compilers. Such forms, and the primitives that identify them, are called, appropriately enough, *special forms*. Other primitives that call for special-case argument handling are generally implemented as macros in which special forms appear.

```
* high
102
```

Note carefully that WHEN and UNLESS are unusual in that their arguments, after the first, are evaluated only when the value of the test indicates that they should be.

Problems

Problem 4-5: Write IF forms that are equivalent to (ABS X), (MIN A B), and (MAX A B).

Predicates Help COND Choose among Alternatives

Although IF, WHEN, and UNLESS are extremely versatile, sometimes you need COND, an even more versatile conditional. Regrettably, COND has a template that calls for particularly peculiar argument evaluation. As shown, the symbol COND is followed by lists called *clauses*:

```
(COND (<test 1> <consequent 1-1> ...)
      (<test 2> <consequent 2-1> ...)
            .
            .
            .
      (<test m> <consequent m-1> ...))
```

As indicated, each clause contains a *test*, as well as zero or more additional forms called *consequents*. The idea is to move through the clauses, evaluating only the test form in each, until a test form is found whose value is nonNIL. The corresponding clause is said to be *triggered*, and its consequent forms are evaluated. The value of the entire COND form is the value of the *last* consequent form in the triggered clause. All consequent forms standing between the test and the last consequent form in the triggered clause are there only for their side effects.

Suppose, for example, that the formula used to compute area depends on whether THING's value is CIRCLE or SPHERE:

```
* (setf thing 'sphere r 1)
1
* (cond ((eq thing 'circle) (* pi r r))
        ((eq thing 'sphere) (* 4 pi r r)))
12.56637
```

If all the test-form values are NIL, the value of the COND form is NIL. If THING's value were LINE, for example, the value of the preceding COND would be NIL.

In the following variation, there is no way to drop through the second clause; THING's value is assumed to be SPHERE if it is not CIRCLE:

```
* (setf thing 'sphere r 1)
1
* (cond ((eq thing 'circle) (* pi r r))
        (t (* 4 pi r r)))        ;THING's value must be SPHERE.
12.56637
```

Many programmers make a habit of including a final clause whose test form is T. That way they clearly signal that the final clause is to be used when none of the others triggers. With a T-triggered clause, there is no way to fall through the conditional, producing the default value, NIL.

If a clause with a nonNIL test form is found that has only a test form and no consequent forms, then the value of the COND form is the value of the test form itself. Consequently, the following variation works just as well as the preceding variation:

```
* (setf thing 'sphere r 1)
1
* (cond ((eq thing 'circle) (* pi r r))
        ((* 4 pi r r)))
12.56637
```

Because (* 4 PI R R) cannot be NIL, the second clause triggers if the first one does not. Because the second clause has only one form, that form is both first and last and therefore is both the test form and the value form. As a matter of style, however, it is better to include the intension-signaling T.

COND is particularly useful when there are more than two cases to consider. In the following example, a probability number between 0 and 1 is converted into one of four symbols:

```
* (setf p .6)
* (cond ((> p .75) 'very-likely)
        ((> p .5) 'likely)
        ((> p .25) 'unlikely)
        (t 'very-unlikely))
LIKELY
```

In the following example, the result is either GLUTTON or NORMAL if BREAKFAST is not empty, and ANOREXIC otherwise:

```
* (setf breakfast '(eggs bacon toast tea))
* (cond ((> (length breakfast) 10) 'glutton) ;Are there more than 10?
        ((not (endp breakfast)) 'normal)      ;Is the list not empty?
        (t 'anorexic))
NORMAL
```

Actually, you need not use ENDP to test BREAKFAST because BREAKFAST is nonNIL whenever there is something in BREAKFAST:

```
* (cond ((> (length breakfast) 10) 'glutton) ;Are there more than 10?
        (breakfast 'normal)                   ;Is BREAKFAST nonNIL?
        (t 'anorexic))
NORMAL
```

As shown, the test form in a COND clause may be a symbol whose value is a list that may or may not be empty. If the list *is not* empty, it triggers the COND clause, because it is not NIL; if the list *is* empty, it does not trigger the clause, because it is the same as NIL. Note, however, that many programmers are offended by the use of naked lists as COND tests.

Problems

Problem 4-6: Compose COND forms that produce the same results as (NOT U), (OR X Y Z), and (AND A B C).

CASE Is Still Another Conditional

Note that IF, WHEN, and UNLESS forms can be viewed as special cases of COND forms because all of those forms could be written as COND forms, albeit usually with some loss of clarity. One more such special case, CASE, belongs in your vocabulary. Like the others, and like COND itself, CASE is unusual because forms containing CASE are evaluated in a special way. The symbol CASE is followed a *key form*, which is followed by *clauses*:

```
(case <key form>
  (<key 1> <consequent 1-1> ...)
  (<key 2> <consequent 2-1> ...)
  .
  .
  .
  (<key m> <consequent m-1> ...))
```

CASE checks the *evaluated* key form against the *unevaluated* keys using EQL. If the key is found, the corresponding clause is triggered and all of the clause's consequents are evaluated.

You use CASE when you would otherwise have a COND in which all of the tests just look for a value among several possibilities. Recall, for example, the following COND form:

```
(cond ((eq thing 'circle) (* pi r r))
      ((eq thing 'sphere) (* 4 pi r r)))
```

Rewritten as a CASE form, it becomes this:

```
(case thing                          ;THING symbol to be evaluated.
  (circle (* pi r r))                ;CIRCLE symbol not to be evaluated.
  (sphere (* 4 pi r r)))             ;SPHERE symbol not to be evaluated.
```

Note, however, that case uses EQL, not EQ.

There are several special cases worth noting. First, if none of the clauses is triggered, CASE returns NIL:

```
* (setf thing 'point r 1)
* (case thing
    (circle (* pi r r))
    (sphere (* 4 pi r r)))
NIL
```

Second, if none of the other clauses is triggered, and if the key in the last clause is either T or OTHERWISE, then the last clause is triggered:

```
* (setf thing 'point r 1)
* (case thing
    (circle (* pi r r))
    (sphere (* 4 pi r r))
    (otherwise 0))
0
```

Finally, if a key is a list, rather than an atom, CASE checks the *evaluated* key form against the *unevaluated* key list using MEMBER. If the key is found in the unevaluated key list, the corresponding clause is triggered and all of the clause's consequents are evaluated:

```
* (setf thing 'ball r 1)
* (case thing
    ((circle wheel) (* pi r r))
    ((sphere ball) (* 4 pi r r))
    (otherwise 0))
12.56637
```

Conditionals Enable DEFUN To Do Much More

Now we are ready to use conditional forms when defining new procedures using DEFUN. Suppose you want EXPRESS-PROBABILITY to be a procedure that takes a probability between 0 and 1 and returns an English interpretation:

```
* (express-probability .8)
VERY-LIKELY

* (express-probability .6)
LIKELY
```

```
ress-probability .4)
LY
ress-probability .2)
NLIKELY
```

y the desired procedure must do a test and act according to the result.
procedure definition will do the job:

```
n express-probability (p)
nd ((> p .75) 'very-likely)
    ((> p .5) 'likely)
    ((> p .25) 'unlikely)
    (t 'very-unlikely)))
```

ll that the `T` in the conditional expression ensures that the last clause
be triggered if the others are not. The `T` is not really necessary, however,
use the same values would result were it left out.[5]

oblem 4-7: Define `CHECK-TEMPERATURE`, a procedure that is to take one
ument, such that it returns `RIDICULOUSLY-HOT` if the argument is greater
n `100`, it returns `RIDICULOUSLY-COLD` if the argument is less than `0`, and
eturns `OK` otherwise.

w that we have explained conditionals, we can explain *problem reduction*,
other procedure-definition technique to add to progressive envelopment
d comment translation, both of which were introduced in chapter 3.

The basic idea is to divide the original problem into several subprob-
ms, each of which is handled separately, possibly by a separate procedure.

To see how problem reduction works, we return to the problem faced
y `BOTH-ENDS` and think of it, somewhat artificially, in terms of what to do
n four cases: what to do if the argument is an empty list, a list of one
element, a list of two elements, and a list of more than two elements:

```
(defun both-ends (whole-list)
  (case (length whole-list)
    (0 ...)                          ;Deal with empty list.
    (1 ...)                          ;Deal with one-element list.
    (2 ...)                          ;Deal with two-element list.
    (t ...)))                        ;Deal with general case.
```

Given this division into subproblems, each can be solved independently:

---

[5]Curiously, using `T` to trigger the final clause does matter if the value form
returns multiple values.

```
(defun both-ends (whole-list)          ;Comment translation version.
  (case (length whole-list)
    (0 NIL)                            ;Deal with empty list.
    (1 (cons (first whole-list)        ;Deal with one-element list.
          whole-list))
    (2 whole-list)                     ;Deal with two-element list.
    (t (cons (first whole-list)        ;Deal with general case.
          (last whole-list)))))
```

Summary

- A predicate is a procedure that returns true or false.
- EQUAL, EQ, EQL, and = are equality predicates.
- MEMBER tests for list membership.
- Keyword arguments modify behavior.
- LISTP, ATOM, NUMBERP, and SYMBOLP are data type predicates.
- NIL is equivalent to the empty list.
- NULL and ENDP are empty-list predicates.
- There are many number-oriented predicates.
- AND, OR, and NOT enable elaborate testing.
- Predicates help IF, WHEN, and UNLESS choose among alternatives.
- Predicates help COND choose among alternatives.
- CASE is still another conditional.
- Conditionals enable DEFUN to do much more.
- Problem reduction helps define new procedures.

5

Procedure
Abstraction
and Recursion

The principal purpose of this chapter is to introduce the powerful idea of *procedure abstraction*, a process that helps you to build large, complicated programs.

A secondary purpose of this chapter is to explain how a procedure can use itself in its own definition, either directly or through an intermediary. This is called *recursion*, and leads to several important concepts, including *singly recursive procedures*, *doubly recursive procedures*, and *tail recursive procedures*.

Recursion is one of several general strategies for controlling how a computation evolves. Accordingly, recursion is said to be one kind of *control strategy*.

Procedure Abstraction Hides Details Behind Abstraction Boundaries

In chapter 3, we introduced BOTH-ENDS, a procedure that produces a list consisting of the first and last element in a given list:

```
* (setf l '(breakfast lunch tea dinner))
* (both-ends l)
(BREAKFAST DINNER)
```

To do its job, BOTH-ENDS must do three things:

- **BOTH-ENDS** must extract the first element.
- It must extract the last element.
- It must combine the two extracted elements.

In chapter 3, **BOTH-ENDS** and several variations did the three things by calling upon LISP primitives directly, and for a simple procedure, calling upon LISP primitives directly is not a bad thing. Consider, however, the following alternative definition, which uses three auxiliary procedures yet to be defined:

```
(defun both-ends (whole-list)              ;Procedure abstraction version.
  (combine-elements                        ;Combine first and last.
    (extract-first-element whole-list)     ;Extract first element.
    (extract-last-element whole-list)))    ;Extract last element.
```

By defining **BOTH-ENDS** this way, you isolate yourself from the details of how combination and extraction are done. After all, while you are thinking about **BOTH-ENDS**, you do not care how the auxiliary procedures do their jobs as long as they produce the proper results. As far as you are concerned, the auxiliary procedures are just abstractions that have a prescribed behavior. You could define them like this:

```
(defun combine-elements (e1 e2)
  (list e1 e2))
(defun extract-first-element (l)
  (first l))
(defun extract-last-element (l)
  (first (last l)))
```

Or, alternatively, you could define the auxiliary procedures like this:

```
(defun combine-elements (e1 e2)
  (cons e1 (cons e2 nil)))
(defun extract-first-element (l)
  (car l))
(defun extract-last-element (l)
  (first (reverse l)))
```

And many other definitions would do as well. You can choose definitions for the auxiliary procedures so that they are easily understood, elegant, or efficient. Or you can have an assistant make the definition choices, isolating yourself completely from the details of how the auxiliary procedures are implemented.

Thinking visually, **BOTH-ENDS** forms a one-procedure layer, with its auxiliary procedures forming a lower layer, and any procedures that use **BOTH-ENDS** forming a higher layer. The way you define **BOTH-ENDS** is unaffected by the choices you make in other layers.

Note, incidentally, that BOTH-ENDS auxiliary procedures have such long names that the names become like comments helping to make the definition of BOTH-ENDS clearer. Many programmers use long procedure names, rather than elaborate comments, on the ground that a procedure with a long name explains itself everywhere it is used, whether commented or not. Thus the use of long procedure names constitutes a sort of *automatic commenting*.

Whenever you deliberately arrange procedures into layers, you are said to be doing *procedure abstraction*, and the layers are called *abstraction layers*. Abstraction layers are separated from one another by *abstraction boundaries*. The abstraction boundaries isolate the implementation details of the procedures in each abstraction layer from the procedures in the next higher layer.

Procedure abstraction is an extremely powerful idea, one that makes big programs possible by virtue of the following crucial benefits:

- Procedure abstraction helps you to think at a high level by helping you to suppress the details of how things are done at a low level. If you wish, you are free to program top down, working on your high-level procedures first, deferring work on your low-level procedures until later.

- Procedure abstraction helps you to keep procedure definitions small and easy to understand.

Now we turn to an important special case of procedure abstraction where the abstraction that a procedure is built on is the procedure itself.

Recursion Allows Procedures To Use Themselves

To calculate the nth power of some number, m, it is sufficient to do the job for the $(n-1)$th power, because this result, multiplied by m, is the desired result for the nth power:

$$m^n = \begin{cases} m \times m^{n-1}, & \text{for } n > 0; \\ 1, & \text{for } n = 0. \end{cases}$$

Ignoring the existence of EXPT, the primitive supplied by LISP itself, assume, temporarily, that we have LOWER-LEVEL-EXPT, a procedure that does, in fact, compute powers. We could then define a new procedure, HIGHER-LEVEL-EXPT, that uses LOWER-LEVEL-EXPT in its definition:

```
(defun higher-level-expt (m n)
  (if (zerop n)
      1                                        ;If N = 0, return 1.
      (* m                                     ;Otherwise, use a lower-
        (lower-level-expt m (- n 1)))))        ; level abstraction.
```

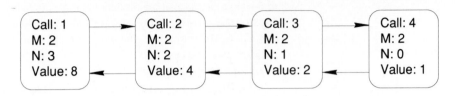

Figure 5-1. A simulation often helps illuminate the strategy of a recursive procedure. Here each call to the RECURSIVE-EXPT procedure reduces the value of N by one and calls itself on the reduced value until N is reduced to zero.

From the perspective of procedure abstraction, two abstraction layers are formed by HIGHER-LEVEL-EXPT and LOWER-LEVEL-EXPT. As far as HIGHER-LEVEL-EXPT is concerned, LOWER-LEVEL-EXPT can go about its job any way it likes. In particular, LOWER-LEVEL-EXPT can do its job by calling any procedure that knows how to compute powers, HIGHER-LEVEL-EXPT for example:

```
(defun lower-level-expt (m n)
  (higher-level-expt m n))
```

But because LOWER-LEVEL-EXPT does nothing other than call HIGHER-LEVEL-EXPT, we might as well substitute HIGHER-LEVEL-EXPT everywhere LOWER-LEVEL-EXPT appears, producing the following definition:

```
(defun higher-level-expt (m n)
  (if (zerop n)
      1
      (* m
         (higher-level-expt m (- n 1)))))         ;Substitution.
```

When a procedure calls itself, the call is said to be a *recursive call*. Definitions that describe a procedure partly in terms of recursive calls are said to be *recursive definitions*. To emphasize that HIGHER-LEVEL-EXPT is recursive, we rename it RECURSIVE-EXPT:[1]

```
(defun recursive-expt (m n)
  (if (zerop n)
      1                                        ;If N = 0, return 1.
      (* m                                     ;Otherwise, multiply M times the
         (recursive-expt m (- n 1)))))         ; result using a smaller exponent.
```

Using figure 5-1, we can easily follow the history of M and N as LISP evaluates (RECURSIVE-EXPT 2 3). The boxes represent the procedure calls involved in the computation. Each call is shown with its order in the sequence of calls, its arguments, and its returned value.

---

[1]Note that our RECURSIVE-EXPT is weaker than EXPT because RECURSIVE-EXPT expects only nonnegative integer exponents.

In the RECURSIVE-EXPT example, each box sprouts only one new branch because each call to RECURSIVE-EXPT can lead to only one new call. A procedure that does this is said to be *singly recursive*. Such procedures are particularly easy to convert into procedures that do *not* call themselves, and therefore are not recursive.

The Fibonacci function provides an example of a procedure that is not singly recursive. Leonardo of Pisa, also known as Fibonacci, was curious about the rate of reproduction of rabbits. To be able to apply formal mathematical methods to the problem, he made some simplifying assumptions:

- There is one immature female rabbit at the beginning of the first month.
- Only mature female rabbits reproduce. It takes one month to become mature.
- Each mature female rabbit produces exactly one female offspring during each month.
- Rabbits live forever.
- The male rabbits can be ignored.

Thus the number of female rabbits added during a particular month equals the number of mature female rabbits. This in turn is the total number of rabbits, mature or immature, a month earlier. Accordingly, the Fibonacci function, $f(n)$, is defined as follows:

$$f(n) = \begin{cases} f(n-1) + f(n-2), & \text{for } n > 1; \\ 1, & \text{for } n = 1; \\ 1, & \text{for } n = 0. \end{cases}$$

Putting this function into LISP, we have the following:

```
(defun fibonacci (n)
  (if (or (= n 0) (= n 1))        ;If N = 0 or 1,
      1                            ; return 1.
      (+ (fibonacci (- n 1))       ;Otherwise recurse using N-1
         (fibonacci (- n 2)))))    ; and N-2.
```

Figure 5-2 shows FIBONACCI computing a result when given 4 as its argument.

Computing Fibonacci numbers this way is more interesting than computing powers of numbers because FIBONACCI can call itself twice, not just once. Hence FIBONACCI is said to be *doubly recursive*. The definition of Fibonacci's function directly suggests such a doubly recursive procedure. But as you can see in figure 5-2, the doubly recursive procedure is inefficient because it solves identical subproblems over and over. We will look at other ways to compute Fibonacci numbers later.

Having seen recursion at work on two simple numerical problems, let us now look at two other examples that show recursion at work on symbolic

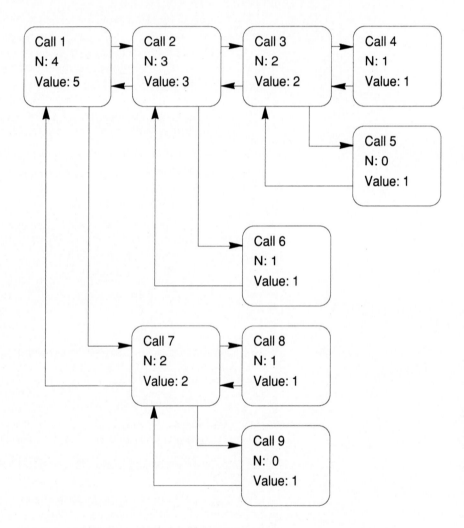

Figure 5-2. A simulation of FIBONACCI. Note that each call to FIBONACCI calls itself twice whenever an argument proves to be too hard to handle directly.

problems. For the first example, consider the following recursive definition for computing the number of elements in a list, ignoring the existence of LENGTH, the primitive supplied by LISP itself:

```
(defun count-elements (l)
  (if (endp l)                    ;Empty list?
      0                           ;Empty list has zero elements.
      (+ 1                        ;Add one to the number in the rest of L.
         (count-elements (rest l)))))
```

Evidently, COUNT-ELEMENTS returns zero immediately when it encounters an empty list. Otherwise, COUNT-ELEMENTS gives up and calls itself on the slightly simplified problem in which the list is one element shorter. Figure 5-3 shows COUNT-ELEMENTS at work on the following problem:

```
* (count-elements '(fast computers are nice))
4
```

Incidentally, note that presenting the LISP definition of COUNT-ELEMENTS is a way of describing what COUNT-ELEMENTS does. Such a description is a useful alternative to a description in English. But because COUNT-ELEMENTS does the same thing as LENGTH, the official LISP primitive, we see that it is possible to describe part of LISP using LISP itself, an idea developed much further in chapter 18.

Recursion Can Be Efficient

Note that whenever COUNT-ELEMENTS works on anything other than an empty list, it calls itself on a simpler problem and then adds one to the result handed back. Now let us look at another way of counting in which nothing is done to the result handed back:

```
(defun count-elements-cleverly (l)
  (count-elements-cleverly-aux l 0))
(defun count-elements-cleverly-aux (l result)
  (if (endp l)
      result
      (count-elements-cleverly-aux (rest l) (+ 1 result))))
```

Note that COUNT-ELEMENTS-CLEVERLY's purpose is only to set up the problem for the auxiliary procedure, COUNT-ELEMENTS-CLEVERLY-AUX, which has two arguments, not just one. The second argument is incremented by one whenever COUNT-ELEMENTS-CLEVERLY-AUX calls itself, thus keeping track of the number of elements that have been skipped over so far.

As shown in figure 5-4, the value returned by each call, except the last one, is just the value returned to it by another call. Conceptually, the final

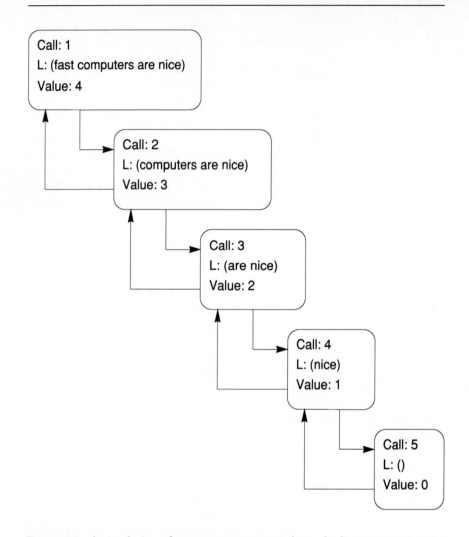

Figure 5-3. A simulation of COUNT-ELEMENTS at work on the list (FAST COMPUTERS ARE NICE).

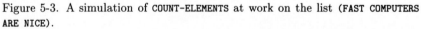

call to COUNT-ELEMENTS-CLEVERLY-AUX can return the value of the final form computed, RESULT, to the procedure that called COUNT-ELEMENTS-CLEVERLY, ignoring all intermediate calls.

Whenever a problem is converted into a new problem such that no further computation is necessary once the new problem is solved, the new problem is said to be a *reduction* of the original problem. Whenever a recursive procedure is defined such that all recursive calls to itself are re-

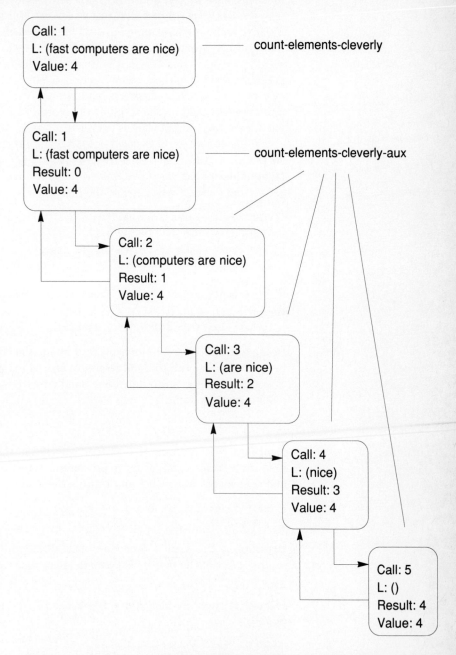

Figure 5-4. A simulation of COUNT-ELEMENTS-CLEVERLY and COUNT-ELEMENTS-CLEVER-LY-AUX at work on the list (FAST COMPUTERS ARE NICE).

ductions, that procedure is said to be *tail recursive.*

Evidently, COUNT-ELEMENTS-CLEVERLY-AUX is a tail recursive procedure because each problem handed to COUNT-ELEMENTS-CLEVERLY-AUX is converted into another problem for COUNT-ELEMENTS-CLEVERLY-AUX such that the answer to the new problem *is* the answer to the original problem. COUNT-ELEMENTS, defined in the previous section, is *not* tail recursive because whenever one call to COUNT-ELEMENTS leads to another, the second call is *not* a reduction of the first: the result of the second call must be incremented by one before the computation is complete.

In the following, both COUNT-ELEMENTS-INDIRECTLY and COUNT-ELEMENTS-BUFFER are tail recursive even though they do not call themselves directly. It is sufficient that whenever there are two successive calls to a procedure, the second call is a reduction of the first.

```
(defun count-elements-mutually (l)
  (count-elements-indirectly l 0))
(defun count-elements-indirectly (l result)
  (if (endp l)
      result
      (count-elements-buffer (rest l) (+ 1 result))))
(defun count-elements-buffer (l result)
  (count-elements-indirectly l result))
```

Because nothing need be remembered about the computations that occur between the first call to a tail recursive procedure and the recursive reduction, tail recursive procedures are handled extremely efficiently by most modern LISP systems.[2]

Problems

Problem 5-1: Ignoring the existence of NTHCDR, the primitive supplied by LISP itself, write a tail recursive procedure, SKIP-FIRST-N that trims off the first n elements from a list and returns the rest:

```
* (skip-first-n 3 '(a b c d e f g h i))
(D E F G H I)
```

Problem 5-2: Write a procedure, KEEP-FIRST-N, not tail recursive, that returns a list of the first n elements in a list. You may assume there are at least n elements.

```
* (keep-first-n 3 '(a b c d e f g h i))
(A B C)
```

---

[2]In particular, modern LISP systems recognize that every procedure eventually leads to a reduction. By returning the value produced by that reduction to the procedure's caller, many stack operations are eliminated.

Problem 5-3: Now write a pair of procedures KEEP-FIRST-N-CLEVERLY and KEEP-FIRST-N-CLEVERLY-AUX, that together make a list of the first n elements in a list. Be sure that KEEP-FIRST-N-CLEVERLY-AUX is tail recursive.

Recursion Can Be Used To Analyze Nested Expressions

Now consider COUNT-ATOMS, a procedure that counts the atoms in a given expression. In the following example, there are seven atoms occurring in the three top-level elements of the list (SQRT (EXPT X 2) (EXPT Y 2)):

```
* (count-atoms '(sqrt (expt x 2) (expt y 2)))
7
```

Here is one way to define COUNT-ATOMS:

```
(defun count-atoms (l)
  (cond ((null l) 0)                    ;L is an empty list?
        ((atom l) 1)                    ;L is an atom?
        (t (+ (count-atoms (first l))   ;L must be a list; recurse.
              (count-atoms (rest l))))))
```

The first two clauses of the COND form deal with the very simplest cases, returning 0 for empty lists and 1 for nonlists. The third clause handles other situations by converting big problems into smaller ones. Lists are broken up using FIRST and REST, and COUNT-ATOMS is called once for each of the two resulting fragments. Because every atom in the list is in one or the other of the two fragments, every atom gets counted, with + combining the results. Eventually, after perhaps many calls to itself, COUNT-ATOMS reduces the hard cases to something that either the first or the second clause of the conditional can handle.

At this point, it is helpful to see how COUNT-ATOMS can take an expression apart and reduce it successively to the simple cases. As shown in figure 5-6, the particular expression whose atoms are to be counted is (SQRT (EXPT X 2) (EXPT Y 2)). Note that the data expression in this case is itself a form, something that you might think of evaluating if you were interested in finding the length of the hypotenuse of a right triangle. Here is an example of a procedure, COUNT-ATOMS, examining a piece of another procedure and performing a computation on it.

At each stage, COUNT-ATOMS's argument gets broken into two smaller pieces. Once the answers for both pieces are in hand, + adds the results together and returns the value.

Computing the number of atoms in an expression this way is more interesting than counting the number of top-level elements in a list because each call to COUNT-ATOMS can create *two* new calls, not just one. Thus COUNT-ATOMS is doubly recursive.

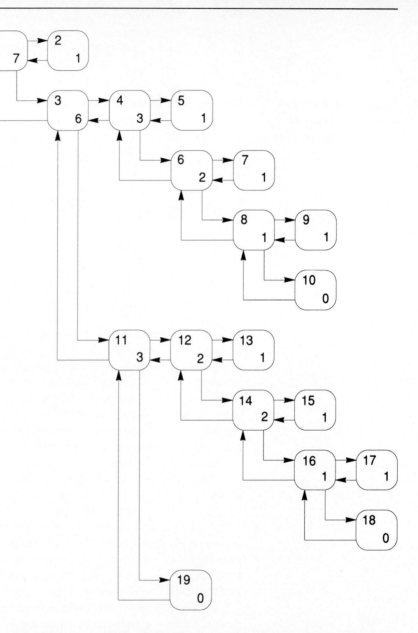

Figure 5-5. Again a simulation helps illuminate the strategy of a recursive procedure. Here the expression (SQRT (EXPT X 2) (EXPT Y 2)) is broken up into its constituent pieces by the procedure COUNT-ATOMS. The numbers in the upper left corners of the boxes are call numbers; those in the lower right corners are values.

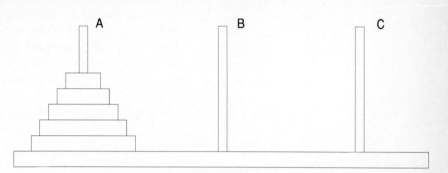

Figure 5-6. The Tower of Hanoi problem, simplified. Transferring the disks from pin A to pin B, without placing a larger disk on a smaller one, requires 31 moves for five disks.

Now you have seen both singly recursive procedures, like `RECURSIVE-EXPT` and `COUNT-ELEMENTS` as well as doubly recursive procedures, like `FIBONACCI` and `COUNT-ATOMS`. Generally, singly recursive procedures are natural for working with various types of sequences, such as the top-level element of a list. Doubly recursive procedures are natural when it comes to exploring trees, such as *all* parts of an expression, even those parts that are deeply embedded.

Note, however, that it is a particular procedure that is said to be singly or doubly recursive. The same result often can be produced by one procedure that is singly recursive, another that is doubly recursive, and a third that is not recursive at all.

Problems

Problem 5-4: The LISP primitives `1+` and `1-` increment and decrement a number by one. Using `1+` and `1-`, write a recursive procedure, `ADD`, for adding two numbers without `+`. Assume that both numbers are positive.

Problem 5-5: An ancient myth has it that in some temple in Hanoi, time is marked off by monks engaged in the transfer of 64 disks from one of three pins to another, as shown in figure 5-6. The universe as we know it will end when they are done. The reason we do not have to concern ourselves about the cosmological implications of this is that their progress is kept in check by some clever rules:

- Only one disk can be moved at a time.
- The disks all have different diameters, and no disk can ever be placed on top of a smaller one.
- Initially all disks are on one pin and each disk rests on a larger one.

The insight leading to the correct sequence of moves comes from the realization that a set of n disks can be transferred from pin A to pin B in these stages: first move the top $(n-1)$ disks from A to the spare pin C; then move the large bottom disk from A to B; and finally, move the $(n-1)$ disks from the spare pin, C, onto pin B. Naturally, moving the $(n-1)$ disks from C to B can be done by the same trick, using pin A as workspace.

Suppose TOWER-OF-HANOI is to count the number of moves required to move a list of pins from one pin to another, given a list of disks:

```
* (tower-of-hanoi '(1))
1
* (tower-of-hanoi '(2 1))
3
* (tower-of-hanoi '(3 2 1))
7
* (tower-of-hanoi '(4 3 2 1))
15
* (tower-of-hanoi '(5 4 3 2 1))
31
* (tower-of-hanoi '(10 9 8 7 6 5 4 3 2 1))
1023
```

Define TOWER-OF-HANOI.

Problem 5-6: Describe the evident purpose of the following procedure:

```
(defun mystery (s)
  (cond ((null s) 1)
        ((atom s) 0)
        (t (max (+ (mystery (first s)) 1)
                (mystery (rest s))))))
```

Problem 5-7: Describe the evident purpose of the following procedure:

```
(defun strange (l)
  (cond ((null l) nil)
        ((atom l) 1)
        (t (cons (strange (first l))
                 (strange (rest l))))))
```

Problem 5-8: Define PRESENTP, a predicate that determines whether a given atom occurs *anywhere* in an expression. PRESENTP differs from MEMBER, in that MEMBER looks only for top-level instances. Symbolic-mathematics systems make use of a procedure like PRESENTP to determine if an expression contains a particular variable. Here are two examples:

```
* (setf formula '(sqrt (/ (+ (expt x 2) (expt y 2)) 2)))
```

```
* (presentp 'x formula)
T
```

```
* (presentp 'z formula)
NIL
```

Problem 5-9: Define `SQUASH`, a procedure that takes an expression as its argument and returns a nonnested list of all atoms found in the expression. Here is an example:

```
* (squash '(a (a (a (a b))) (((a b) b) b) b))
(A A A A B A B B B B)
```

Essentially, this procedure explores the *fringe* of the tree represented by the list given as its argument, and returns a list of all the leaves.

Problem 5-10: A particular definition of a mathematical function, like the Fibonacci function, may directly suggest a LISP procedure for computing it. This is of course not the only, and quite often not the best, procedure. For the Fibonacci function, we can solve a linear recurrence relation for $f(n)$. We obtain Binet's formula in terms of the golden ratio, $(1 + \sqrt{5})/2$, and its inverse, $(\sqrt{5} - 1)/2$:

$$f(n) = \frac{1}{\sqrt{5}} \left[\left(\frac{1 + \sqrt{5}}{2} \right)^{n+1} - \left(\frac{1 - \sqrt{5}}{2} \right)^{n+1} \right].$$

Write a version of `FIBONACCI` that does the computation directly, without recursion.

Optional Parameters Eliminate the Need for Many Auxiliaries

So far, each defined procedure requires an argument for each parameter. Elegantly, you may also define procedures that involve *optional parameters* for which there may not be corresponding arguments.

We start our explanation with `ROOT`, a procedure that finds roots. `ROOT` is to find the square root if given one argument, or the prescribed root if given two:

```
* (root 9)
3.0
```

```
* (root 9 2)
3.0
```

```
* (root 27 3)
3.0
```

To improve `ROOT`, we introduce an optional parameter. There is only one, `N`, in the following example:

```
(defun root (x &optional n)
  (if n
      (expt x (/ 1 n))
      (sqrt x)))
```

Note that all parameters listed after &OPTIONAL are optional parameters. When ROOT is used with just one argument, N is bound to NIL, the default value. Consequently, ROOT uses SQRT:

```
* (root 9)
3.0                              ; Uses SQRT; N bound to NIL.
```

When ROOT is used with two arguments, the optional parameter, N, is bound to the value of the second argument, and ROOT uses EXPT:

```
* (root 27 3)
3.0                              ; Uses EXPT; N bound to 3.
```

You often want to specify default values for the optional parameters, rather than just having those parameters bound to NIL when there is no corresponding argument. You specify your own default values by surrounding the optional parameter and a default-value form with parentheses. In the following version of ROOT, the default value of N is 2:

```
(defun root (x &optional (n 2))
  (expt x (/ 1 n)))
```

If there is no second argument, the default value, 2, is bound to N:

```
* (root 9)
3.0                              ; Uses EXPT; N bound to 2.
```

If there is a second argument, it is bound to N, as before:

```
* (root 27 3)
3.0                              ; Uses EXPT; N bound to 3.
```

Optional parameters often simplify programs by reducing the need for auxiliary procedures. Recall the procedures COUNT-ELEMENTS-CLEVERLY and its auxiliary, COUNT-ELEMENTS-CLEVERLY-AUX. Look back at those programs and note that the only job done by COUNT-ELEMENTS-CLEVERLY is to start COUNT-ELEMENTS-CLEVERLY-AUX off with an appropriate second argument, namely 0. You eliminate the need for COUNT-ELEMENTS-CLEVERLY by making COUNT-ELEMENTS-CLEVERLY-AUX's second parameter an optional parameter, with a default value of 0, and changing its name to something more appropriate:

```
(defun count-with-optional-parameter (l &optional (result 0))
  (if (endp l)
      result
      (count-with-optional-parameter (rest l)
                                     (+ 1 result))))
```

Given this definition, when COUNT-WITH-OPTIONAL-PARAMETER is used with just one argument, the initial value of RESULT is 0. But note that COUNT-WITH-OPTIONAL-PARAMETER is used with two arguments in all recursive calls, and the default value of RESULT is ignored in favor of the value of the supplied argument. This leads to the action shown in figure 5-7.

Problems

Problem 5-11: Suppose that we have a procedure that attaches the symbol PERIOD to the end of a list:

```
(defun punctuate (l) (append l '(period)))
```

Here is an example of PERIOD in use:

```
* (punctuate '(this is an example))
(THIS IS AN EXAMPLE PERIOD)
```

Naturally, it is easy to add other procedures that add QUESTION-MARK or EXCLAMATION-MARK instead. Alternatively, we can rewrite PUNCTUATE so that it takes a second argument:

```
(defun punctuate (l mark) (append l (list mark)))
```

Most sentences end with a period, however, so supplying the second argument every time is annoying. Happily, the optional arguments feature enables you to supply the second argument only when needed. Define a version of PUNCTUATE that takes an optional argument such that it works as follows:

```
* (punctuate '(this is an example))
(THIS IS AN EXAMPLE PERIOD)
* (punctuate '(is this an example) 'question-mark)
(IS THIS AN EXAMPLE QUESTION-MARK)
```

Problem 5-12: The version of FIBONACCI we have already exhibited is inefficient beyond description. Many computations are repeated. Write a version with optional parameters that does not have this flaw. Think of working forward from the first month rather than backward from the nth month.

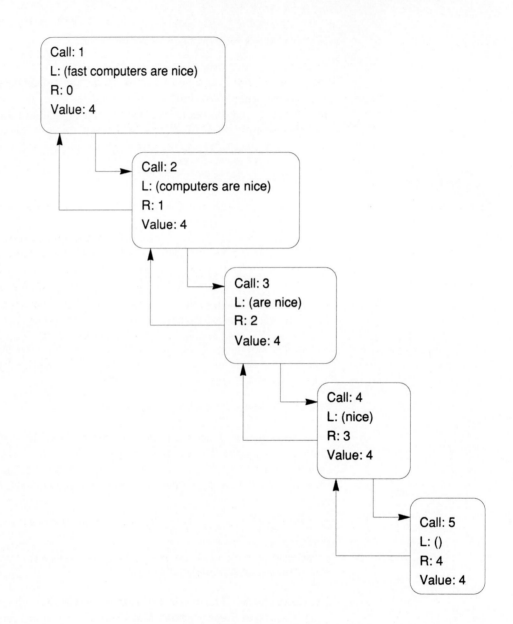

Figure 5-7. A simulation of COUNT-WITH-OPTIONAL-PARAMETER at work on the list (FAST COMPUTERS ARE NICE).

Problem 5-13: Define `TAIL-RECURSIVE-EXPT`, a version of `RECURSIVE-EXPT` that is tail recursive. Use an optional parameter to accumulate partial results. This approach represents a common way of turning a singly recursive procedure into a tail recursive procedure.

Problem 5-14: Define `TAIL-RECURSIVE-REVERSE`, ignoring the existence of `REVERSE`, a primitive supplied by LISP itself. Use the same approach as in the previous problem.

Problem 5-15: Define `CLEVER-COUNT-ATOMS` a version of `COUNT-ATOMS` that uses an optional parameter to hang onto the count accumulated so far in exploring one part of the tree.

Advanced Programmers Use Rest, Key, and Aux Parameters

The optional parameter is just one of several special-purpose parameter types that LISP offers. Because we use these other parameter types sparingly, we give you only a taste of how they work.

First, a rest parameter, marked by `&REST`, is bound to a list of all otherwise unaccounted for argument values. Consider `RAISE`, a procedure that is to raise its first argument to its second, if there is a second argument, and if there are more arguments, to continue raising the result to successive arguments until all are exhausted:

```
* (raise 2)
2                         ;2.

* (raise 2 3)
8                         ;2^3.

* (raise 2 3 5)
32768                     ;(2^3)^5.
```

All the work is done by `RAISE-AUX`, a procedure that takes two arguments:

```
(defun raise-aux (result number-list)
  (if (endp number-list)
      result
      (raise-aux (expt result (first number-list))
                 (rest number-list))))
```

`RAISE` gathers up arguments and starts `RAISE-AUX`. To gather up arguments, it uses a rest parameter:

```
(defun raise (x &rest numbers)
  (raise-aux x numbers))
```

When evaluating (RAISE 2 3 5), X is bound to 2 and NUMBERS is bound to (3 5).

Next, a key parameter, an acronym for <u>key</u>word, is used in situations where there are multiple parameters, but many of them are to be bound to default values most of the time. Were you limited to optional parameters in such situations, you would have to remember the parameter order and supply values for all the parameters that happen to be in front of the ones that you want to bind to nondefault values.

Consider ROTATE-LIST, a procedure that normally is to rotate a list one element to the right:

```
* (rotate-list '(a b c d e))
(E A B C D)
```

But given a :DIRECTION keyword, with LEFT, the rotation is to be the other way:

```
* (rotate-list '(a b c d e) :direction 'left)
(B C D E A)
```

And given a :DISTANCE keyword, the rotation can be any distance to the right:

```
* (rotate-list '(a b c d e) :distance 2)
(D E A B C)
```

And given both keywords, the rotation can be any distance to the left:

```
* (rotate-list '(a b c d e) :direction 'left :distance 2)
(C D E A B)
```

When defining a procedure with key parameters, the keys are marked with &KEY. In the following, for example, DIRECTION and DISTANCE, appearing in ROTATE-LIST, are the key parameters:

```
(defun rotate-list (l &key direction distance)     ;First version.
  (if (eq direction 'left)
      (rotate-list-left l (if distance distance 1))
      (rotate-list-right l (if distance distance 1))))
(defun rotate-list-right (l n)
  (if (zerop n)
      l
      (rotate-list-right (append (last l) (butlast l))
                         (- n 1))))
```

```
(defun rotate-list-left (l n)
  (if (zerop n)
      l
      (rotate-list-left (append (rest l) (list (first l)))
                        (- n 1))))
```

Now when ROTATE-LIST appears in a form, the colon-bearing keywords :DI-RECTION and :DISTANCE may appear as well, marking arguments to be assigned to the DIRECTION and DISTANCE parameters. Note that the bindings are determined by the keywords, not by order. Both of the following do the same thing:

```
* (rotate-list '(a b c d e) :direction 'left :distance 2)
* (rotate-list '(a b c d e) :distance 2 :direction 'left)
```

If there is no argument marked by a matching keyword, the corresponding keyword parameter is bound to NIL. However, you are free to specify default values, if you wish, by combining the keyword with a default-value form. Thus we can write a simpler, more transparent definition for ROTATE-LIST by specifying a default value other than NIL for the distance parameter:

```
(defun rotate-list (l &key direction (distance 1)) ;Better version.
  (if (eq direction 'left)
      (rotate-list-left l distance)
      (rotate-list-right l distance)))
```

There are even fancier things to do with key parameters, but you have seen enough to get a feel for them.

Finally, an aux parameter, an acronym for auxiliary, marked by &AUX is not matched to any arguments at all. Aux parameters are really just LET* parameters in disguise. Here is a definition of BOTH-ENDS-WITH-LET that is similar to one given in chapter 3:

```
(defun both-ends-with-let (whole-list)
  (let* ((element (first whole-list))
         (trailer (last whole-list)))
    (cons element trailer)))
```

Here is an alternate version with two aux parameters, both of which have initial values:

```
(defun both-ends-with-aux
       (whole-list &aux
                      (element (first whole-list))
                      (trailer (last whole-list)))
  (cons element trailer))
```

An aux parameter can also appear without an initial-value form, in which case there are no surrounding parentheses and the initial value is NIL.

Of course, you can combine the various parameter types. Just be sure to keep the optional parameters first, just after the regular parameters. Then comes the sole rest parameter, followed by key parameters, followed by aux parameters.

Only a Few LISP Primitives Are Really Necessary

One marvelous thing about LISP is that so much can be built on so little. Although COMMON LISP is an extremely rich language, with primitives for just about everything, a surprising number of those primitives can be implemented in terms of a small subset of primitives consisting of FIRST, REST, CONS, IF, a few predicates, and a few arithmetic primitives.

Consider LENGTH, for example. If LENGTH were not part of LISP, you could define it yourself in terms of IF, ENDP, +, and REST:[3]

```
(defun user-defined-length (l)
  (if (endp l)
      0
      (+ 1 (user-defined-length (rest l)))))
```

Similarly, you could define APPEND in terms of IF, ENDP, CONS, FIRST, and REST. Here is a version that works on exactly two arguments:

```
(defun user-defined-append2 (l1 l2)
  (if (endp l1)
      l2
      (cons (first l1)
            (user-defined-append2 (rest l1)
                                  l2))))
```

And given a two-argument version, you can build on it to produce a version that works on any number of arguments. In the following, USER-DEFINED-APPEND just gathers up arguments; APPEND-AUX feeds those gathered-up arguments to the previously defined, two-argument procedure USER-DEFINED-APPEND2:

---

[3] Actually, the given definition of USER-DEFINED-LENGTH is not as general as the LENGTH primitive supplied by LISP because it works only on lists, whereas LENGTH works on both lists and one-dimensional arrays.

```
(defun user-defined-append (&rest lists)
  (append-aux lists))
(defun append-aux (lists)
  (if (endp lists)
      nil
      (user-defined-append2 (first lists)
                            (append-aux (rest lists)))))
```

Problems

Problem 5-16: Define USER-DEFINED-LIST to do what the primitive LIST does. Use a rest parameter.

Problem 5-17: Define USER-DEFINED-NTHCDR in terms of IF, ZEROP, -, and REST.

Problem 5-18: Define USER-DEFINED-LAST in terms of IF, ENDP, and REST.

Summary

- Procedure abstraction hides details behind abstraction boundaries.
- Recursion allows procedures to use themselves.
- Recursion can be efficient.
- Recursion can be used to analyze nested expressions.
- Optional parameters eliminate the need for many auxiliaries.
- Advanced programmers use rest, key, and aux parameters.
- Only a few LISP primitives are really necessary.

References

For an excellent treatment of procedure abstraction, see *Structure and Interpretation of Computer Programs*, by Harold Abelson and Gerald Jay Sussman. For other examples of recursive procedures, see Knuth [1968].

6

Data
Abstraction
and Mapping

The principal purpose of this chapter is to introduce the powerful idea of *data abstraction*, a process that helps you to build large, complicated programs.

A secondary purpose of this chapter is to explain how to use recursive procedures to perform a computation on each element in a list. This is useful because it enables you to transform one list into a new list, to filter undesired elements out of a list, to count particular elements, and to find particular elements.

Another secondary purpose of this chapter is to show that your knowledge of programming is embedded partly in broadly applicable templates called *programming clichés*, as well as in your knowledge of primitive procedures. Some clichés ultimately prove so useful that they are incorporated into the language itself. In particular, the utility of transforming, filtering, counting and finding leads to a family of extremely useful primitives that do transforming, filtering, counting, and finding directly. These primitives, which include MAPCAR, REMOVE-IF, REMOVE-IF-NOT, COUNT-IF, and FIND-IF, are commonly called *mapping primitives* because a mapping, in mathematical parlance, connects entities in one domain with entities in another.

Mapping, like recursion, is a general strategy for controlling how a computation evolves. Accordingly, mapping is said to be one kind of *control strategy*.

Still another secondary purpose of this chapter is to explain how you can define procedures using *lambda expressions*. Frequently, transforming, filtering, counting, and finding involves a procedure that is used once and never again. Defining such procedures using lambda expressions can improve a program by bringing procedure descriptions to the places where the procedures are used.

Data Details Stifle Progress

In this section, you see why you should isolate yourself from details of data representation. Suppose, for example, that you want to keep a bibliographic index of the books in your library. You might decide to organize your index so that it includes information about the title, author, and classification for each book. All these things could be represented in a list:

```
(setf book-example-1
      '((Artificial Intelligence) ;Title.
        (Patrick Henry Winston)   ;Author.
        (Technical AI)))          ;Classification.
```

The first element in the representation for a book is a list of the words in the book's title. The second element is a list of the author's names. The third is a list of classification terms. Given this representation for an individual book, it is a simple matter to recover a book's author:

```
* (second book-example-1)
(PATRICK HENRY WINSTON)
```

However, with your data represented this way, there are two immediate problems:

- You have to remember exactly how each kind of data is stored. In big programs, it is impossible to remember your conventions for how each data list is arranged.
- You cannot change the details of data arrangement easily. If you decide to add something to the front of the list, the name of the publisher for example, all your references to other items will have to be changed, creating a bookkeeping nightmare.

Moreover, you cannot even find references to the data in your programs easily because you may have referenced a book's author in any of the following methods:

```
(first (rest <book description>))        ;One method.

(second <book description>)              ;Another method.
```

```
(first (nthcdr 1 <book description>))  ;Still another method.
```

Suppose, nevertheless, that you decide to start implementing your big program with your data couched in ordinary lists. Later on, you might decide you just have to have something better. In particular, you might decide to improve your program by using the association-list approach. In chapter 2, we explained that an association list is a list that consists of sublists, each of which contains a symbol, used as a key, as its first element and an association list value as its second element:

```
(setf book-example-2
      '((title (Artificial Intelligence))
        (author (Patrick Henry Winston))
        (classification (Technical AI))))
```

Recall that you get at association-list elements using ASSOC:

```
* (assoc 'author book-example-2)
(AUTHOR (PATRICK HENRY WINSTON))
* (second (assoc 'author book-example-2))
(PATRICK HENRY WINSTON)
```

There is some hope that you could switch from ordinary lists to association lists, given that you are the only person working on a program. But now suppose that you loan out your books a lot, and you want to keep a record of who has each. Just to push our points to a caricaturized extreme, suppose that you decide to represent information about book loans on a separate association list, combining both association lists into a book-describing list of two elements:

```
(setf book-example-3
      '(((title (Artificial Intelligence))
         (author (Patrick Henry Winston))
         (classification (Technical AI)))
        ((loaned-to (Karen Prendergast))
         (loaned-on (26 May 88)))))
```

Now you have gone from a simple list to a baroque combination of ordinary lists and association lists, bringing up another plague:

- You have to remember complicated combinations of low-level primitives to get at each kind of data.

By this time, if you are working on a program alone, you are ready for a straightjacket. If you are working on a program with other people, you need protection.

You can see that there is a problem even if you are able to make reasonable decisions about data representation from the beginning. Even without the spectre of change, it is just too much trouble to remember how each kind of data is represented so as to know how to get at it properly.

Data Abstraction
Facilitates Progress

The alternative is to hide the details of how your data is represented by isolating that data behind a set of *constructor procedures* that create data, *reader procedures* that retrieve data, and *writer procedures* that change data. Collectively, *constructors*, *readers*, and *writers* are called *access procedures*. In general, the process of detail hiding through access procedures is called *data abstraction*.

Suppose, for example, you decide that BOOK-AUTHOR is the reader procedure for retrieving a book's author. When you start out, BOOK-AUTHOR is defined as follows:

```
(defun book-author (book)    ;Data is in a simple list.
  (second book))
```

And here is an example of BOOK-AUTHOR in use:

```
(setf book-example-1
      '((Artificial Intelligence) ;Title.
        (Patrick Henry Winston)    ;Author.
        (Technical AI)))           ;Index terms.
* (book-author book-example-1)
(PATRICK HENRY WINSTON)
```

Later on, the definition of BOOK-AUTHOR changes each time you decide there just has to be a change in the way data is represented. For example, moving up to association lists requires this:

```
(defun book-author (book)    ;Data is in an association list.
  (second (assoc 'author book)))
```

And here is an example of this new version of BOOK-AUTHOR in use:

```
(setf book-example-2
      '((title (Artificial Intelligence))
        (author (Patrick Henry Winston))
        (classification (Technical AI))))
* (book-author book-example-2)
(PATRICK HENRY WINSTON)
```

Next, the change to a list of two association lists requires still another change:

```
(defun book-author (book)    ;Data is in a list of association lists.
  (second (assoc 'author (first book))))
```

And here is an example of the final version of BOOK-AUTHOR in use:

```
(setf book-example-3
     '(((title (Artificial Intelligence))
        (author (Patrick Henry Winston))
        (classification (Technical AI)))
       ((loaned-to (Karen Prendergast))
        (loaned-on (26 May 88)))))

* (book-author book-example-3)
(PATRICK HENRY WINSTON)
```

Importantly, only the definition of BOOK-AUTHOR has changed as our representation evolved. There is no need whatsoever to change anything at the places where BOOK-AUTHOR is used or even to look at those places. Henceforth, neither you nor your associates have to remember the details of how data is stored. You simply deploy the BOOK-AUTHOR procedure. And if you want to look at the places where the author of a book is referenced, you can find those places easily by looking for BOOK-AUTHOR. In summary, the defects of the original approach are corrected:

- You *do not* have to remember exactly how each kind of data is stored.
- You *can* change the details of data arrangement easily.
- You *can* find references to the data easily.
- You *do not* have to remember complicated combinations of low-level primitives to get at each kind of data. Access procedures are much easier to remember and think about.

Consequently, you should adhere to the following rule: whenever you find yourself using a tangled combination of LISP primitives to access data, you should move that tangled combination into a reader procedure where the details of data arrangement become hidden behind an abstraction barrier.

**You Should
Use Readers,
Constructors, and
Writers Liberally**

So far we have limited our discussion to reader procedures. Obviously, when constructing and changing data, the same problems come up and the same solution applies.

Assume, for the sake of illustration, that books are represented as association lists. Then the following is a constructor:

```
(defun make-book (title author classification)
  (list (list 'title title)
        (list 'author author)
        (list 'classification classification)))
```

The constructor creates a new book, given appropriate arguments:

```
* (setf book-example-4
        (make-book '(Common Lisp)
                   '(Guy Steele)
                   '(Technical Lisp)))
((TITLE (COMMON LISP))
 (AUTHOR (GUY STEELE))
 (CLASSIFICATION (TECHNICAL LISP)))
```

To go along with the constructor, we define a set of readers:

```
(defun book-title (book)
  (second (assoc 'title book)))
(defun book-author (book)
  (second (assoc 'author book)))
(defun book-classification (book)
  (second (assoc 'classification book)))
```

To change an entry, the author for example, we define a writer, BOOK-AUTHOR-WRITER, which just adds a new element to the association list. Because ASSOC always returns the first element with a matching key, there is no harm in leaving the existing author element alone, other than wasting memory:

```
(defun book-author-writer (book author)
  (cons (list 'author author) book))
```

Here is an example in which we add Steele's middle initial to the author entry in BOOK-EXAMPLE-4:

```
* (setf book-example-4
        (book-author-writer book-example-4
                            '(Guy L Steele)))
((AUTHOR (GUY L STEELE))
 (TITLE (COMMON LISP))
 (AUTHOR (GUY STEELE))
 (CLASSIFICATION (TECHNICAL LISP)))
* (book-author book-example-4)
(GUY L STEELE)
```

Alternatively, we can define BOOK-AUTHOR-WRITER as a recursive procedure that replaces the existing author element:

```
(defun book-author-writer (book author)
  (if (eql 'author (first (first book)))
      (cons (list 'author author) (rest book))
      (cons (first book)
            (book-author-writer (rest book) author))))
```

Here is the recursive version in action using the original value of BOOK-EXAMPLE-4:

```
* (setf book-example-4
        (book-author-writer book-example-4
                                 '(Guy L Steele)))
((TITLE (COMMON LISP))
 (AUTHOR (GUY L STEELE))
 (CLASSIFICATION (TECHNICAL LISP)))
* (book-author book-example-4)
(GUY L STEELE)
```

Writers for the other parts of the book description are equally easy to define.

It Is Useful To Transform and To Filter

Once you have created a constructor for books, we can use that constructor to build a list of books, forming a little data base:

```
(setf books
  (list
    (make-book '(artificial intelligence)
               '(patrick henry winston)
               '(technical ai))
    (make-book '(common lisp)
               '(guy l steele)
               '(technical lisp))
    (make-book '(moby dick)
               '(herman melville)
               '(fiction))
    (make-book '(tom sawyer)
               '(mark twain)
               '(fiction))
    (make-book '(the black orchid)
               '(rex stout)
               '(fiction mystery))))
```

Now we can use this data base to illustrate how you can transform one list into a new list, filter undesired elements out of a list, count particular elements, and find particular elements.

For example, you might want to make a *transformation*, producing a list consisting of only the author's names:

```
((PATRICK HENRY WINSTON)
 (GUY L STEELE)
 (HERMAN MELVILLE)
 (MARK TWAIN)
 (REX STOUT))
```

Alternatively, you might want to *filter* all of the entries, extracting only those that satisfy some predicate. For example, you might want a list of all the fiction:

```
(((MOBY DICK) (HERMAN MELVILLE) (FICTION))
 ((TOM SAWYER) (MARK TWAIN) (FICTION))
 ((THE BLACK ORCHID) (REX STOUT) (FICTION MYSTERY))))
```

When transforming a list, the length of the returned list is the same as the
length of the input list. When filtering a list, the length of the output list
is shorter, unless all of the elements in the input list pass the filtering test.

Both of these symbolic computations are easy to do using recursive
LISP procedures.

**Recursive
Procedures Can
Transform and Filter**

Let us begin with a program that makes an author summary. Given the
reader BOOK-AUTHOR, it is easy to write LIST-AUTHORS, a transformation that
makes a list of all the authors in BOOKS:

```
(defun list-authors (books)
  (if (endp books)                          ;Is list empty?
      nil                                   ;If so, return empty list.
      (cons (book-author (first books))     ;Add author of first book.
            (list-authors (rest books)))))  ; to authors of the rest.
* (list-authors books)
((PATRICK HENRY WINSTON)
 (GUY L STEELE)
 (HERMAN MELVILLE)
 (MARK TWAIN)
 (REX STOUT))
```

Filtering the list of books is equally easy. To filter out all but the fiction, for
example, we need FICTIONP, a procedure that uses the book-classification
reader:

```
(defun fictionp (book)
  (member 'fiction (book-classification book)))
```

Here is what happens when FICTIONP is used:

```
* (fictionp '((title (tom sawyer))
             (author (mark twain))
             (classification (fiction))))
(FICTION)
* (fictionp '((title (common lisp))
             (author (guy l steele))
             (classification (technical lisp))))
NIL
```

Thus FICTIONP is the predicate LIST-FICTION-BOOKS needs to separate out
the fiction:

```
(defun list-fiction-books (books)
  (cond ((endp books) nil)                    ;Empty list?
        ((fictionp (first books))             ;It's fiction; keep it.
         (cons (first books)
               (list-fiction-books (rest books))))
        (t (list-fiction-books (rest books))))) ;It's not; omit it.
```

And here is what happens when LIST-FICTION-BOOKS works on BOOKS:

```
* (list-fiction-books books)
(((TITLE (MOBY DICK))
  (AUTHOR (HERMAN MELVILLE))
  (CLASSIFICATION (FICTION)))
 ((TITLE (TOM SAWYER))
  (AUTHOR (MARK TWAIN))
  (CLASSIFICATION (FICTION)))
 ((TITLE (THE BLACK ORCHID))
  (AUTHOR (REX STOUT))
  (CLASSIFICATION (FICTION MYSTERY))))
```

**Recursive
Procedures Can
Count and Find**

Once we can filter a list, it is easy to count the entries that satisfy a predicate or to find a particular entry, albeit inefficiently. To count the fictional entries in BOOKS, for example, we need only use LENGTH on the result returned by LIST-FICTION-BOOKS:

```
* (length (list-fiction-books books))
3
```

Filtering also makes it easy to identify the first entry encountered that satisfies a given predicate. To find the first fictional entry in BOOKS, we need only use FIRST on the result returned by LIST-FICTION-BOOKS:

```
* (first (list-fiction-books books))
((TITLE (MOBY DICK))
 (AUTHOR (HERMAN MELVILLE))
 (CLASSIFICATION (FICTION)))
```

Both solutions are hopelessly inefficient, however, because LISP has to go to the trouble of constructing a new list only to count the elements in it or to extract the first element. Here are more efficient solutions that do not construct a new list:

```
(defun count-fiction-books (books)
  (cond ((endp books) 0)                          ;Empty list?
        ((fictionp (first books))                 ;It's fiction; count it.
         (+ 1 (count-fiction-books (rest books))))
        (t (count-fiction-books (rest books)))))
(defun find-first-fiction-book (books)
  (cond ((endp books) nil)                         ;Empty list?
        ((fictionp (first books))                 ;It's fiction; report it.
         (first books))
        (t (find-first-fiction-book (rest books)))))
```

Problems

Problem 6-1: Suppose that the arguments to FIND-BOOK-BY-TITLE-WORDS are words that may appear in book titles. FIND-BOOK-BY-TITLE-WORDS is to return the first book it finds that has all of those words in its title:

```
* (find-book-by-title-words '(orchid) books)
((TITLE (THE BLACK ORCHID))
 (AUTHOR (REX STOUT))
 (CLASSIFICATION (FICTION MYSTERY)))
* (find-book-by-title-words '(black orchid) books)
((TITLE (THE BLACK ORCHID))
 (AUTHOR (REX STOUT))
 (CLASSIFICATION (FICTION MYSTERY)))
* (find-book-by-title-words '(orchid black) books)
((TITLE (THE BLACK ORCHID))
 (AUTHOR (REX STOUT))
 (CLASSIFICATION (FICTION MYSTERY)))
* (find-book-by-title-words '(blue orchid) books)
NIL
```

To define FIND-BOOK-BY-TITLE-WORDS, we need a procedure that matches words to titles. The primitive LISP procedure SUBSETP is just right:

```
* (subsetp '(black orchid) '(the black orchid))
T
* (subsetp '(orchid) '(common lisp))
NIL
```

Note, incidentally, that SUBSETP is indifferent to element order:

```
* (subsetp '(orchid black) '(the black orchid))
T
```

Using SUBSETP, define FIND-BOOK-BY-TITLE-WORDS.

Clichés Embody Important Programming Knowledge

We have introduced several procedures that attack lists in order to transform, filter, count, and find. The general shape of all these procedures can be captured by templates. Here is the template for LIST-AUTHORS, for example:

```
(defun <transforming procedure> (input-list)
  (if (endp input-list)                        ;Is list empty?
      nil                                      ;If so, return empty list.
      (cons (<element transformer> (first input-list))    ;Transform.
            (<transforming procedure> (rest input-list))))) ;Recurse.
```

Using this template, LIST-AUTHORS is easy to write with the following substitutions:

```
<transforming procedure>    ⟶    list-authors
<element transformer>       ⟶    book-author
```

Importantly, there are many other procedures that are equally easy to write using the transforming-procedure template. When a template is broadly useful, it is said to be a *programming cliché*. Building your own armamentarium of programming clichés is an important part of learning a programming language, just as learning sentence patterns is an important part of learning a natural human language.

Here are some other templates that merit cliché status:

```
(defun <filtering procedure> (input-list)
  (cond ((endp input-list) nil)
        ((<element tester> (first input-list))
         (cons (first input-list)
               (<filtering procedure> (rest input-list))))
        (t (<filtering procedure> (rest input-list)))))
(defun <counting procedure> (input-list)
  (cond ((endp input-list) 0)
        ((<element tester> (first input-list))
         (+ 1 (<counting procedure> (rest input-list))))
        (t (<counting procedure> (rest input-list)))))
(defun <finding procedure> (input-list)
  (cond ((endp input-list) nil)
        ((<element tester> (first input-list))
         (first input-list))
        (t (<finding procedure> (rest input-list)))))
```

Because transforming, filtering, counting, and finding are so useful, LISP has primitives that enable you to do transforming, filtering, counting, and finding directly, without resorting to clichés. These primitives are explained in the following sections.

MAPCAR Simplifies Transforming Operations

The MAPCAR primitive makes it particularly easy to transform lists.[1] To use MAPCAR, you supply the name of a transforming procedure together with a list of elements to be transformed.

The following is a simple example in which a MAPCAR is used to record which numbers in a list are odd using the LISP primitive ODDP. Note the #' preceding ODDP. As you learned in chapter 4, the #' produces a procedure object from a procedure name:

```
* (mapcar #'oddp            ;Procedure object to work with.
          '(1 2 3))         ;Elements to be fed to the procedure.
(T NIL T)
```

When evaluating a MAPCAR form, LISP feeds each element in its second argument to the transforming procedure specified by its first argument. The value returned is a list of the results:

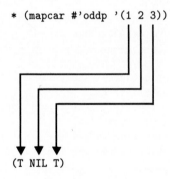

The procedure MAPCAR uses is not restricted to be a procedure of one parameter, but if the procedure has more than one parameter, there must be a corresponding number of lists from which to extract arguments. As shown in the following illustration, MAPCAR can act like an assembly machine, taking one element from each list of arguments and assembling them for a transforming procedure:

---

[1]MAPCAR is perhaps the most unfortunately-named primitive in LISP. The *map* part is all right—it comes from the use of the term *map* in mathematics. The *car* part, however, comes from the now-obsolete CAR primitive mentioned in chapter 2. MAP-ELEMENTS would have been a better name.

```
* (mapcar #'= '(1 2 3) '(3 2 1))
```

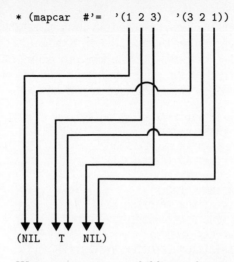

```
(NIL  T  NIL)
```

We now return to our bibliography example. Earlier, we defined a recursive procedure, LIST-AUTHORS, which used BOOK-AUTHOR to extract the names of all the authors:

```
* (list-authors books)
((PATRICK HENRY WINSTON)
 (GUY L STEELE)
 (HERMAN MELVILLE)
 (MARK TWAIN)
 (REX STOUT))
```

Now we have an alternative; we can use MAPCAR:

```
* (mapcar #'book-author books)
((PATRICK HENRY WINSTON)
 (GUY L STEELE)
 (HERMAN MELVILLE)
 (MARK TWAIN)
 (REX STOUT))
```

Consequently, MAPCAR forms offer an alternative to the recursive transformation cliché.

As a programming language evolves, its authors take note of the common clichés that emerge and embody those clichés in language primitives. From this perspective, MAPCAR is an embodiment of the transformation cliché.

As you work with a programming language, you should take note of the common things that you do and view them as your own private clichés. And if your private clichés occur often enough, you should embody them into a private collection of procedures.

REMOVE-IF and REMOVE-IF-NOT Simplify Filtering Operations

Just as MAPCAR offers a way to transform lists, REMOVE-IF and REMOVE-IF-NOT offer a way to filter them.

Earlier, we defined a recursive procedure, LIST-FICTION-BOOKS, which used FICTIONP to filter out all of the books except those that are books of fiction. Now we can use REMOVE-IF-NOT instead:

```
* (remove-if-not #'fictionp books)
(((TITLE (MOBY DICK))
  (AUTHOR (HERMAN MELVILLE))
  (CLASSIFICATION (FICTION)))
 ((TITLE (TOM SAWYER))
  (AUTHOR (MARK TWAIN))
  (CLASSIFICATION (FICTION)))
 ((TITLE (THE BLACK ORCHID))
  (AUTHOR (REX STOUT))
  (CLASSIFICATION (FICTION MYSTERY))))
```

Thus REMOVE-IF-NOT eliminates all elements that do not satisfy a given predicate.

Symmetrically, REMOVE-IF eliminates all elements that do satisfy a given predicate:

```
* (remove-if #'fictionp books)
(((TITLE (ARTIFICIAL INTELLIGENCE))
  (AUTHOR (PATRICK HENRY WINSTON))
  (CLASSIFICATION (TECHNICAL AI)))
 ((TITLE (COMMON LISP))
  (AUTHOR (GUY L STEELE))
  (CLASSIFICATION (TECHNICAL LISP))))
```

COUNT-IF and FIND-IF Simplify Counting and Finding Operations

Just as REMOVE-IF and REMOVE-IF-NOT enable you to filter lists, COUNT-IF and FIND-IF enable you to count the elements that satisfy a test and to find the first element that satisfies a test. In the following, for example, COUNT-IF determines the number of fiction books:

```
* (count-if #'fictionp books)
3
```

And here, FIND-IF finds the first fiction book:

```
* (find-if #'fictionp books)
((TITLE (MOBY DICK))
 (AUTHOR (HERMAN MELVILLE))
 (CLASSIFICATION (FICTION)))
```

**FUNCALL and
APPLY Also Take a
Procedure Argument**

In previous sections, you have learned that MAPCAR, REMOVE-IF, REMOVE-IF-NOT, COUNT-IF, and FIND-IF all require an argument that is a procedure object, or to use the common term, they all have a *procedure argument*.

Sometimes procedure arguments are called *funargs*, an acronym for <u>fun</u>ction <u>arg</u>ument, because the word *function* is used often as a synonym for the word *procedure*.

Two other common primitives use procedure arguments, namely FUN-CALL and APPLY. Because both are important, we explain them here, diverting ourselves momentarily from our explanation of mapping primitives.

FUNCALL applies its first argument's value to its other arguments' values. Here is the template:

```
(funcall #'<procedure specification>
       <argument 1>
       ...
       <argument N>)
```

Thus, the following forms are completely equivalent:

```
(funcall #'first '(e1 e2 e3))
(first '(e1 e2 e3))
```

These forms are equivalent, too:

```
(funcall #'append '(a b) '(x y))
(append '(a b) '(x y))
```

FUNCALL enables you to define procedures that have procedure arguments. Consider TOSS:[2]

```
* (toss '(victim of attack) #'first)
VICTIM
* (toss '(victim of attack) #'rest)
(OF ATTACK)
```

TOSS can be defined this way:

```
(defun toss (argument procedure)
  (funcall procedure argument))
```

TOSS illustrates a key use of FUNCALL: you use FUNCALL when you have assigned a procedure object to a variable and you want to call that procedure object.

Now suppose TOSS were defined this way:

---

[2] TOSS's name suggests an image in which an argument is sent a message in the form of a procedure object. This is not exactly what is meant by the *message passing* language paradigm, however, because the knowledge of what to do is in the procedure object, rather than attached to the argument's data type.

```
(defun toss (argument procedure)          ;Bugged!
  (procedure argument))                   ;Bugged!
```

LISP does not evaluate the first element in a form. Consequently, when LISP looks for a procedure named PROCEDURE, it complains because PROCEDURE is not a defined procedure.

APPLY uses its first argument's value on the elements of its second argument's value, which must be a list. Here is the template:

```
(apply #'<procedure name>
       <list of arguments>)
```

Thus, the following are completely equivalent:

```
(apply #'first '((e1 e2 e3)))
(first '(e1 e2 e3))
```

These are equivalent, too:

```
(apply #'append '((a b) (x y)))
(append '(a b) '(x y))
```

Note the difference between FUNCALL and APPLY carefully:

```
(funcall #'<procedure name> <argument 1> ... <argument N>)

(apply #'<procedure name> <list of arguments>)
```

FUNCALL uses as many arguments as the named procedure requires, plus one for the procedure name. APPLY usually takes two arguments, the procedure name and a list of arguments for the procedure. The list has as many elements as the named procedure requires.

Actually, there are situations in which APPLY appears with more than two arguments. If there are more than two arguments, all but the first and last are combined into a list, to which the last argument is appended. Consequently, the following are equivalent:

```
(apply #'+ '(1 2 3 4 5 6))     ;Argument list fed to + is
                               ; (1 2 3 4 5 6)
(apply #'+ 1 2 3 '(4 5 6))     ;Argument list fed to + is
                               ; (append (list 1 2 3) '(4 5 6))
```

Here is another way to define TOSS, this time using APPLY:

```
(defun toss (argument procedure)
  (apply procedure (list argument)))
```

This version of TOSS demonstrates that APPLY, like FUNCALL, is useful when you want to use a procedure whose name is the value of a parameter.

LAMBDA Defines Anonymous Procedures

Suppose you have defined the procedure `BOOK-LAST-NAME` solely to use it in a single `MAPCAR` transformation:

```
(defun book-last-name (book)
  (first (last (book-author book)))) 
```

```
* (mapcar #'book-last-name books)
(WINSTON STEELE MELVILLE TWAIN STOUT)
```

In this situation, many LISP programmers prefer to replace the name of the transformation procedure, `BOOK-LAST-NAME`, with a description of what to do.

To describe what to do, without defining a named procedure, you use a *lambda expression*. A lambda expression looks very much like a `DEFUN` form. It is just a matter of replacing `DEFUN` by `LAMBDA` and dropping the procedure name:

```
(defun book-last-name (book)
  (first (last (book-author book))))
```

↓

```
(lambda (book)
  (first (last (book-author book))))
```

Because a lambda expression does not attach a name to the procedure it defines, you need some other way to deploy it. One way is to put the lambda expression at the place where a name would go. In our transformation example, the lambda expression replaces `BOOK-LAST-NAME`:

```
* (mapcar #'book-last-name books)
```

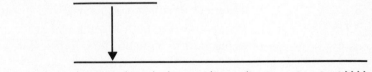

```
* (mapcar #'(lambda (book) (first (last (book-author book))))
          books)
```

The result is the same either way:

```
* (mapcar #'book-last-name
          books)
(WINSTON STEELE MELVILLE TWAIN STOUT)
```

```
* (mapcar #'(lambda (book) (first (last (book-author book))))
          books)
(WINSTON STEELE MELVILLE TWAIN STOUT)
```

You also can substitute lambda expressions for procedure names in REMOVE-IF-NOT and REMOVE-IF forms. Recall that the FICTIONP procedure determines if an individual book is fiction. Given FICTIONP, it is easy to pick out all the works of fiction in BOOKS either by using FICTIONP directly or by converting FICTIONP into a lambda expression:

```
* (remove-if-not
    #'(lambda (book) (member 'fiction (book-classification book)))
    books)
(((TITLE (MOBY DICK))
  (AUTHOR (HERMAN MELVILLE))
  (CLASSIFICATION (FICTION)))
 ((TITLE (TOM SAWYER))
  (AUTHOR (MARK TWAIN))
  (CLASSIFICATION (FICTION)))
 ((TITLE (THE BLACK ORCHID))
  (AUTHOR (REX STOUT))
  (CLASSIFICATION (FICTION MYSTERY))))
```

Using a lambda expression, rather than the name of a procedure defined elsewhere, has the virtue of showing exactly what is to be done at the place where it is done.

Note, however, that using a lambda expression is a bad idea if exactly the same lambda expression appears in many places. When a procedure is to be used in many places, it is better to define it using DEFUN, rather than to describe it repeatedly using LAMBDA. One reason is that defining the procedure in one place saves storage space. Another reason is that there is only one place to be modified in the event you want to change the procedure or fix a bug, not many places spread out all over.

Note also that both FUNCALL and APPLY are happy to use lambda expressions instead of named procedures. Here are two simple illustrations:

```
* (funcall #'(lambda (parameter) (first parameter))
           '(e1 e2 e3))
E1
* (apply #'(lambda (parameter1 parameter2)
             (append parameter1 parameter2))
         '((a b) (x y)))
(A B X Y)
```

Summary

- Data details stifle progress.
- Data abstraction facilitates progress.
- You should use readers, constructors, and writers liberally.
- It is useful to transform and to filter.
- Recursive procedures can transform and filter.
- Recursive procedures can count and find.
- Clichés embody important programming knowledge.
- `MAPCAR` simplifies transforming operations.
- `REMOVE-IF` and `REMOVE-IF-NOT` simplify filtering operations.
- `COUNT-IF` and `FIND-IF` simplify counting and finding operations.
- `FUNCALL` and `APPLY` also take a procedure argument.
- `LAMBDA` defines anonymous procedures.

References

For an excellent treatment of data abstraction, see *Structure and Interpretation of Computer Programs*, by Harold Abelson and Gerald Jay Sussman.

For an introduction to the notion of programming clichés, see Rich and Schrobe [1976] and Waters [1985].

7

Iteration On Numbers and Lists

The principal purpose of this chapter is to explain how to cause something to be done a given number of times or to be done to each element in a list of elements. In these situations, you think in terms of *iterating* a given number of times, using the DOTIMES primitive, or iterating over the elements in a list, using the DOLIST primitive.

A secondary purpose of this chapter is to introduce DO, another iteration primitive, one that is more general, albeit somewhat awkward to use.

Iteration, like recursion and mapping, is a general strategy for controlling how a computation evolves. Accordingly, iteration is said to be one kind of *control strategy*.

DOTIMES Supports Iteration on Numbers

The DOTIMES primitive is popular because it provides a way to write simple counting-oriented iteration procedures. Here is the general template:

```
(dotimes (<count parameter> <upper-bound form> <result form>)
  <body>)
```

When DOTIMES is entered, the *upper-bound form* is evaluated, producing a number, n. Then numbers from 0 to $n-1$ are assigned, one after another, to the count parameter. Thus the count parameter is assigned n times.

For each value, the body is executed. Then, on exit, the count parameter's binding is eliminated and the result form is evaluated, producing the value of the DOTIMES form. If a DOTIMES form has *no* result form, the DOTIMES form returns NIL, and its purpose must be to arrange for side effects.

For an illustration, let us work out a procedure that computes powers of numbers again, this time specified in a way that suggests iteration rather than recursion:

$$m^n = m \times m \times \ldots \times m$$

DOTIMES is just what we need for implementing an iterative power procedure because DOTIMES makes it easy to do something a given number of times.

```
(defun dotimes-expt (m n)
  (let ((result 1))                    ;Initialize result parameter.
    (dotimes (count n result)          ;Evaluate body N times.
      (setf result (* m result)))))    ;Multiply by M again.
```

When DOTIMES is through, the body has been evaluated n times, and the value of RESULT, the result form, is the required power. Note that the count parameter does not appear in the DOTIMES's body in this particular example.

Problems

Problem 7-1: Define DOTIMES-FACTORIAL, using a DOTIMES form. Factorial of n is 1, if n is 0, and n times the factorial of $(n-1)$ otherwise. That is:

$$n! = \begin{cases} n * (n-1)!, & \text{for } n > 0; \\ 1, & \text{for } n = 0. \end{cases}$$

DOLIST Supports Iteration on Lists

The DOLIST primitive is similar to DOTIMES except that the elements of a list are assigned, one after another, to the parameter. Here is the general template:

```
(dolist (<element parameter> <list form> <result form>)
  <body>)
```

When DOLIST is entered, the *list form* is evaluated, producing a list of elements. Then the elements produced by the list form are assigned, one after another, to the element parameter. For each value, the *body* is evaluated. Finally, the element parameter's binding is eliminated and the result form is evaluated, producing the value of the DOLIST form. If a DOLIST form has *no* result form, the DOLIST form returns NIL, and its purpose must be to arrange for side effects.

For illustration, we develop a procedure that counts the number of elements in a list that are below the freezing point of water or above its boiling point, measured in degrees Fahrenheit:

```
* (count-outlyers '(18 75 31 180 270 52))
3
```

The simplest way to implement COUNT-OUTLYERS would be to use COUNT-IF. Another way, one that illustrates DOLIST, is as follows:

```
(setf freezing 32 boiling 212)

(defun count-outlyers (list-of-elements)
  (let ((result 0))                         ;Initialize result parameter.
    (dolist (element list-of-elements       ;Establish DOLIST parameter.
                     result)                ;Result form.
      (when (or (> element boiling)         ;Test element against high.
                (< element freezing))       ;Test element against low.
        (setf result (+ result 1))))))      ;Increment result.
```

In our example, COUNT-OUTLYERS's argument is (18 75 31 180 270 52). Consequently, the value of ELEMENT was 18 during the first evaluation of the body of the DOLIST. Because 18 is less than 32, 1 was added to the result. During the final evaluation, the value of ELEMENT was 52 and the result remained unchanged.

Conveniently, there is a feature that enables immediate termination of a DOLIST or DOTIMES computation. Whenever a (RETURN ⟨expression⟩) form is encountered, the expression is evaluated and becomes the value of the DOLIST. This makes it possible to return the first n outlyers, as soon as n have been found, using the following procedure:

```
(defun first-n-outlyers (n list-of-elements)
  (let ((result 0)                        ;Initialize result.
        (outlyers nil))                   ;Initialize result.
    (dolist (element list-of-elements     ;Establish DOLIST parameter.
                     outlyers)            ;Result form
      (cond ((or (> element boiling)      ;Test element against high.
                 (< element freezing))    ;Test element against low.
             (setf result (+ result 1))   ;Increment result.
             (push element outlyers))     ;Add element to the result.
            ((= n result) (return outlyers))))))  ;Stop when N found.
```

Both COUNT-OUTLYERS and FIRST-N-OUTLYERS perform mapping functions inasmuch as one counts and the other filters. In general, however, DOLIST forms are more often used when the point is to perform some essential side effects, rather than to perform some mapping function. Later on, in chapter 21, for example, you learn about a procedure that clears off all of the things a given object supports:

```
(defun clear-top (object)
  (dolist (obstacle <list of things the object supports> t)
    (get-rid-of obstacle)))
```

In CLEAR-TOP, the only purpose is to set GET-RID-OF to work on each of OBSTACLE's values, not to transform, filter, count, or find something in the list of obstacles.

Problems

Problem 7-2: Write COUNT-OUTLYERS-WITH-COUNT-IF using COUNT-IF instead of DOLIST.

Problem 7-3: Write LIST-OUTLYERS, a procedure that lists the elements in a list that are below the freezing point of water, FREEZING, or above the boiling point, BOILING. While you could do this using REMOVE-IF-NOT, do it instead using DOLIST.

Problem 7-4: Write LIST-OUTLYER-COUNTS, a procedure that counts the temperatures below freezing and above boiling separately, returning a list of the two counts. While you could do this with two separate calls involving COUNT-IF, do it instead using DOLIST.

Problem 7-5: Ignoring the existence of MEMBER, write DOLIST-MEMBER, an iterative version of RECURSIVE-MEMBER:

```
(defun recursive-member (item l)
  (cond ((endp l) nil)
        ((eql item (first l)) t)
        (t (recursive-member item (rest l)))))
```

Note that both RECURSIVE-MEMBER and your solution, unlike MEMBER, are to return T when an item is found.

Problem 7-6: Ignoring the existence of REVERSE, write DOLIST-REVERSE using DOLIST.

DO Is More General than DOLIST and DOTIMES

The DO primitive can be used for iteration when DOLIST and DOTIMES are just not flexible enough. Otherwise, you should avoid DO because it is harder to use.

DO is easier to explain through an immediate example, rather than through an explanation of DO's template. For illustration, we use still another procedure that computes the power of a number:

```
(defun do-expt (m n)
  (do ((result 1)                        ;Bind parameters.
       (exponent n))                     ;Bind parameters.
      ((zerop exponent) result)          ;Test and return.
    (setf result (* m result))           ;Body.
    (setf exponent (- exponent 1))))     ;Body.
```

Note that we have already done this in a simpler way using DOTIMES. Several things must be explained in this more complicated version. Keep in mind that the objective is to multiply n m's together. This will be accomplished by passing n times through the *body*, which in this example consists of the two SETF forms following the DO's test-and-return section.

- The first part of a DO is always occupied by a list of parameters that are all bound to initial values on entering the DO.

Each parameter that has a value before evaluation of the DO is restored to its old value on exit. If there are no parameters, and empty list must be in the first position.

- The second part of a DO determines when the iteration will be terminated and what is returned. This part consists of a list whose initial form is a termination test. The forms that follow in this list are evaluated in turn when the test form's value is nonNIL. The value returned by DO is the value of the last form in this list.

The test is attempted before each pass through the body, including the first pass. The forms after the test form are evaluated only when the test succeeds. All forms between the first and the last are evaluated for side effects only. If there is only one form, it is the test, and DO returns NIL. Consequently, the iteration-terminating part of a DO is not exactly like a clause in a COND, although there are strong similarities.

- The third part of a DO, the body, consists of forms that are evaluated sequentially. All values are ignored, so the evaluations are done only for possible side effects.

In addition to the details illustrated by the DO-EXPT example, several other details that appear in DO forms are important. One concerns the use of RETURN:

- Whenever an expression starting with RETURN is encountered in the body of a DO, the DO is terminated immediately. The value of the terminated DO is the value of the form inside the RETURN expression that stopped the DO.

Thus the following is another way of defining DO-EXPT, albeit an awkward way:

```
(defun do-expt (m n)
  (do ((result 1)                      ;Bind parameters.
       (exponent n))                   ;Bind parameters.
      ()                               ;Test always fails.
    (when (zerop exponent)             ;Test.
      (return result))                 ;Return.
    (setf result (* m result))         ;Body.
    (setf exponent (- exponent 1))))   ;Body.
```

- The parameter specifications can include update forms in addition to variable names and initial-value forms.

Using (RESULT 1 (* M RESULT)), instead of (RESULT 1), in DO's parameter list not only makes 1 the value of RESULT on the first pass, but also makes (* M RESULT) the value of RESULT on subsequent passes. Accordingly, another way to define DO-EXPT is as follows:

```
(defun do-expt (m n)
  (do ((result 1 (* m result))         ;Bind and update parameters.
       (exponent n (- exponent 1)))    ;Bind and update parameters.
      ((zerop exponent) result)))      ;Test and return.
```

Note that the DO in this version of DO-EXPT has no body. All the necessary computation is specified in the parameter update descriptions.

Now you are ready for DO's template in its full-blown glory:

```
(DO ((<parameter 1> <initial value 1> <update form 1>)
     (<parameter 2> <initial value 2> <update form 2>)
     ...
     (<parameter n> <initial value n> <update form n>))
    (<termination test> <intermediate forms, if any> <result form>)
  <body>)
```

Only one important point remains to be explained:

- All initialization forms are evaluated before initial binding. Similarly, all update forms are evaluated before new assignments are done.

Consequently, DO is said to handle its parameters in *parallel*. In this respect, DO is similar to LET. This becomes critical when a DO parameter appears in an initialization or update form. Consider this somewhat silly and definitely defective definition for DO-EXPT:

```
(defun do-expt (m n)                    ;Bugged!
  (do ((result m (* m result))          ;RESULT starts as m not 1.
       (exponent n (- exponent 1))
       (counter (- exponent 1)
                (- exponent 1)))        ;Value of COUNTER is one less
                                        ; than value of EXPONENT.
      ((zerop counter) result)))
```

As written, DO-EXPT will report an error, because there is no value assigned to EXPONENT at the time of the first attempt to get a value for COUNTER by evaluating (- EXPONENT 1).

There are two ways to rescue the situation. The first simply decouples the computation of the EXPONENT and COUNTER update values:

```
(defun do-expt (m n)
  (do ((result m (* m result))          ;RESULT starts as m not 1.
       (exponent n (- exponent 1))       ;Not used in this version!
       (counter (- n 1)                 ;Value of COUNTER is one less
                (- counter 1)))         ; than value of EXPONENT.
      ((zerop counter) result)))
```

Note that this version collapses when the second argument is 0.

Another way to fix the problem is to employ DO*, which is similar to DO, but does a serial, rather than parallel, binding of values. Because DO* is to DO as LET* is to LET, the following works:

```
(defun do-expt (m n)
  (do* ((result m (* m result))         ;RESULT starts as m not 1.
        (exponent n (- exponent 1))
        (counter (- exponent 1)         ;Value of COUNTER is actually
                 (- exponent 1)))       ; one less than value of EXPONENT.
       ((zerop counter) result)))
```

Note that this version also collapses when the second argument is 0.

Problems

Problem 7-7: Define DO-FACTORIAL, using a DO form with an empty body.

Problem 7-8: Ignoring the existence of MEMBER, write DO-MEMBER, an iterative version of RECURSIVE-MEMBER using DO. Like MEMBER, DO-MEMBER is to return the remainder of the list when the item is encountered:

```
(defun recursive-member (item l)
  (cond ((endp l) nil)
        ((eql item (first l)) l)
        (t (recursive-member item (rest l)))))
```

Problem 7-9: Ignoring the existence of REVERSE, a primitive supplied by LISP, write DO-REVERSE using DO.

LOOP Never Stops, Almost

Occasionally, LOOP, still another iteration primitive, is useful. Unlike the other iteration primitives, LOOP forms have a body only:

```
(LOOP <body>)
```

The forms in the body are evaluated over and over. Whenever a (RETURN ⟨expression⟩) form is encountered, as with other iteration primitives, the expression is evaluated and becomes the value of the LOOP as in the following example:

```
* (setf cheers '(cheer cheer cheer))
* (setf loop-count 0)

* (loop
    (when (endp cheers) (return loop-count))
    (setf cheers (rest cheers))
    (setf loop-count (+ loop-count 1)))
3
```

If no return form is ever encountered, LISP continues to evaluate the body of the LOOP.[1]

---

[1] Experimental versions of LISP often include looping primitives with exotic features. Eventually, COMMON LISP's LOOP primitive is likely to incorporate some of those features.

**PROG1 and
PROGN Handle
Sequences Explicitly**

Sometimes the simplest way to get something done may be to evaluate a series of forms sequentially, returning the value of one of them. This is arranged *implicitly* when we use DEFUN, because the body of a defined procedure can consist of any number of forms, with the last form determining the procedure's value. Similarly, LET, LET*, WHEN, and UNLESS expressions can consist of any number of forms, with the last form again determining the expression's value.

Occasionally, however, it is desirable to combine forms *explicitly* into sequences. PROG1 and PROGN do this, as shown by the following examples:

```
* (prog1 (setf a 'x) (setf b 'y) (setf c 'z))
X
* (progn (setf a 'x) (setf b 'y) (setf c 'z))
Z
```

As with DEFUN-defined procedures and LET forms, all but one of the forms are evaluated for side-effects only. Evidently, the one that establishes the value for the entire form is the first for PROG1 and the last for PROGN.

Because the bodies of DEFUNs and LETs can contain any number of forms, PROG1 and PROGN are not much used. Nevertheless, they can be handy, particularly when it is desirable to combine side effects with either or both of the results of an IF form:

```
(if <test>
    (progn <nonNIL side effect> ... <nonNIL consequent>)
    (progn <NIL side effect> ... <NIL consequent>))
```

**Problems and Their
Representation
Determine Proper
Control Strategy**

We can now state some rough guidelines for determining how to select from among the recursion, mapping, and iteration control strategies introduced in this chapter and in chapters 5 and 6.

- If the definition of a mathematical function suggests which control strategy is most appropriate, then use it. Take care, however; there may be other, more efficiently implementable definitions.
- If solving a problem involves diving into an expression, not just looking at the elements in a list, then recursion probably makes sense.
- If solving a problem involves transforming one list into a new list, filtering undesired elements out of a list, counting certain elements, or finding a particular element, then the right thing is probably one of the mapping primitives, MAPCAR, REMOVE-IF, REMOVE-IF-NOT, COUNT-IF, or FIND-IF.
- If a problem calls for doing something over and over again, then try iteration using DOLIST, DOTIMES, or DO.

These rules are only rough guidelines to be augmented as experience increases. Keep in mind that control strategy selection is partly a matter of personal style. You may prefer to use recursion where another person would prefer to use mapping or iteration.

Also keep in mind that implementation details may force a control selection. Many programmers lean toward iteration, rather than recursion, because of efficiency considerations or because of limits on the depth of recursion permitted by particular implementations. In this book, however, we lean toward recursion rather than iteration. We do this, in part, to counterbalance the natural tendency of many people to write strictly iteratively.

Summary

- `DOTIMES` supports iteration on numbers.
- `DOLIST` supports iteration on lists.
- `DO` is more general than `DOLIST` and `DOTIMES`.
- `LOOP` never stops, almost.
- `PROG1` and `PROGN` handle sequences explicitly.
- Problems and their representation determine proper control strategy.

8

File Editing, Compiling, and Loading

Now that you know how to define your own procedures, you will want to start saving them. Accordingly, the principal purpose of this chapter is to explain how to store definitions in files so that you can use them another day without retyping everything.

In addition, there are several secondary purposes: first, we describe how to use *strings* to specify a particular file; second, we show how to use ED to get into an editor so that you can work on a specified file; and third, we explain LOAD, showing you how to tell LISP to evaluate the forms in a file.

Finally, we explain how to use COMPILE-FILE to translate your procedures into equivalent computer instructions. The translated procedures work much faster.

Programs and Data Reside in Files

To create or modify a specified file, you use the ED primitive:

```
(ed <file specification>)
```

ED takes you from LISP and puts you in an editor, as shown in the upper part of figure 8-1. Note that once you have finished working with a file, to get back to LISP you must do something that is prescribed by the particular editor that you use. We provide an example later in this chapter.

To evaluate all the forms in a specified file, once you have returned to LISP, you use the **LOAD** primitive.

```
(load <file specification>)
```

As shown in the lower part of figure 8-1, **LOAD** temporarily redirects LISP's attention from the keyboard to a file until all of the expressions in the file have been evaluated.

File Specifications Tend to Have Baroque Forms

Files are specified by *strings*, which constitute one of LISP's data types. Strings are sequences of characters bounded by double quote characters at the beginning and end. Here is an example showing what happens when you type a string:

```
* "This is a string."
"This is a string."
```

Note that almost any character can appear in a string, even spaces and periods. Note also that lowercase characters remain lowercase characters, even though LISP normally converts lowercase characters into uppercase characters.

We explain strings in more detail in chapter 9. For now, it is enough to know that file names are always specified by strings. Unfortunately, the details are implementation specific because they depend on the operating system that LISP is embedded in. Here are some typical examples:

Operating System	File Specifying String
MS-DOS	/phw/lisp3/searching.lsp
UNIX	/phw/lisp3/searching.lisp
VAX/VMS	[phw.lisp3]searching.lisp.88
Genera	>phw>lisp3>searching.lisp.88

In each instance, there is a file whose *name* is *searching*, whose *type* is *lsp* or *lisp* and whose *version*, if any, is *88*. The rest of the string constitutes a *path*, which specifies the file's position in a file directory hierarchy.

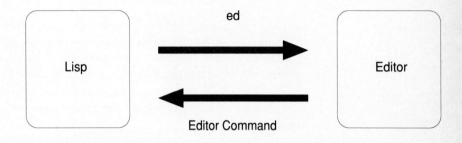

Switching the program in use.

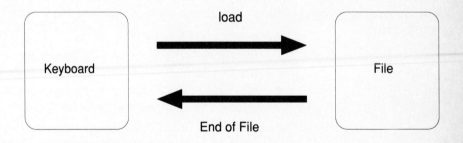

Switching the expression source.

Figure 8-1. ED moves you from LISP to an editor so that you can create or modify a file. LOAD tells LISP to read from a file, rather than from your keyboard, until LISP reaches the end of the file, whereupon LISP reads from your keyboard again.

ED Takes You to an Editor

Now we return to ED, whose argument is always a file-specifying string, like the following one, which conforms to the conventions of MS-DOS:

```
(ed "/phw/lisp3/searching.lsp")
```

Note that among the listed operating systems, only UNIX cares whether the characters in the file specification are in uppercase or lowercase. In the others, you get the same result with (ED "/phw/lisp3/searching.lsp") as with the alternate specification (ED "/PHW/LISP3/SEARCHING.LSP").

You should choose your file names to be as mnemonic as possible. For example, *searching* is a good mnemonic name for a file containing search procedures.

Similarly, your type names should indicate the sort of stuff in the file. Use types like *lisp* or *lsp* for LISP, *data* or *dta* for data, and *text* or *txt* for text.

Of course, you typically edit a file, work with the result, and then edit the same file further. Consequently, whenever you type only (ED), with no file-specifying string, most implementations of LISP assume that you want to edit the same file that you last edited.

EMACS Is a Particularly Powerful LISP Editor

Virtuosity with any editor requires practice and time because there are many basic maneuvers that you must learn about:

- Reading and writing files.
- Adding text.
- Deleting text.
- Moving a blinking character, usually called a *cursor*, that marks the place where additions and deletions are done

Each editor has its own conventions for doing these basic maneuvers. For editing LISP, most programmers prefer the EMACS editor, or one of its descendants, all of which have special commands for working with LISP. Accordingly, we divert ourselves from our discussion of LISP for a few paragraphs to give you a feel for what EMACS is like.

Most of EMACS's special commands involve a *keychord*. To type a keychord, you hold down a modifier key, usually either the key marked *Ctrl* or the one marked *Meta*, and then press the normal alphabetic character. For example, *Ctrl-Meta-F* is the keychord you type by holding down the *Ctrl* and *Meta* keys while pressing the *F* key.

Many keychords move the cursor. *Ctrl-Meta-F*, for example, moves the cursor forward over one LISP expression. The following table lists other representative examples of EMACS's keychords:

Hold ⟶	Ctrl	Meta	Ctrl-Meta	Press ↓
Move to beginning of	line	sentence	definition	A
Move to end of	line	sentence	definition	E
Delete to end of	line	sentence	expression	K
Move back one	character	word	expression	B
Move forward one	character	word	expression	F
Delete next	character	word	expression	D

Other EMACS keychords and keychord sequences handle miscellaneous editing chores such as searching, moving, and substituting. Perhaps the most important of these is *Ctrl-X Ctrl-Z*, the keychord sequence that returns you to LISP from EMACS.

COMPILE-FILE Compiles Files

Once you have prepared a file full of LISP definitions, you either can use those definitions immediately or you can translate those definitions into equivalent computer instructions first. When you use definitions immediately, without translation, a program called the *LISP interpreter* constantly refers to your typed-in definitions and follows those definitions form by form, computing an explicit result for each form.[1]

When you first translate your definitions into sequences of computer instructions, using a program called the *LISP compiler*, your typed-in definitions become available in a completely different, vastly more efficient form. To use those definitions, LISP just executes the computer instructions. There is no reference to your typed-in definitions once the translation process is over.

One way to use the LISP compiler is to evaluate a COMPILE-FILE form, as in the following example:

```
* (compile-file <source file specification>)
```

Given a *source file*, also called a *text file*, COMPILE-FILE produces a *binary file* full of unintelligible computer instructions expressed as bit sequences. The binary file's name and type are implementation dependent, but typically, the binary file's name is the same as the name of the source file, and the type is something that indicates that the file has been produced by the compiler, *bin* for example.

In LISP systems with slow compilers, the tradition is to debug programs using the interpreter first, running the compiler only after development is over. In LISP systems with fast compilers, typically those that ride

---

[1]Actually, the LISP interpreter follows internalized, partially-digested text, in the form of pointers, not the text itself.

on top of LISP-oriented hardware, the tradition is to work with compiled code exclusively.

Note, however, that the choice between interpreting and compiling is not a black and white choice: LISP allows you to combine uncompiled procedure definitions with compiled procedure definitions as you like. You can work with a multiple-file system for a while, change something in one of the files, and reload that file or a compiled version, without any reloading or recompilation of any other file. You can even compile individual procedures, once they have been defined, using the `COMPILE` primitive:

```
(compile <name of a procedure to be compiled>)
```

Because part of a system can be compiled without compiling or recompiling the rest, LISP compilers are said to be *incremental*.[2]

LOAD Causes LISP To Read from Files

Normally, LISP listens to you as you type characters at the keyboard. `LOAD` switches LISP to reading from a file. If the file is a source file, LISP reads from the file, evaluating all the forms, as if it were watching you type characters on your keyboard, until there are no more characters to be absorbed from the file. If the file is a binary file, LISP reads from the file until there are no more compiled definitions to be read.

Like `ED`, `LOAD`'s argument is a file-specifying character string. Suppose, for example, you or someone else has created a file using `ED` this way:

```
* (ed "/phw/lisp3/searching.lsp")
```

To ask LISP to read from that file, you use `LOAD` with the same file specification:

```
* (load "/phw/lisp3/searching.lsp")
```

If you have compiled the file, you use `LOAD` with the file specification appropriate to your LISP system's conventions for naming binary files. The following is representative:

```
* (load "/phw/lisp3/searching.bin")
```

---

[2]Most modern LISP-oriented editors allow you to evaluate forms one at a time, while still in the editor, so that you can alter procedure definitions one at a time without reloading an entire file. Many editors even allow you to compile procedure definitions while editing, whereupon the compiled definition is pressed into immediate service.

Summary

- Programs and data reside in files.
- File specifications tend to have baroque Forms.
- ED takes you to an editor.
- EMACS is a particularly powerful LISP editor.
- COMPILE-FILE compiles files.
- LOAD causes LISP to read from files.

References

EMACS was developed by Richard M. Stallman. For an early discussion, see Stallman [1979].

9

Printing
and Reading

The principal purpose of this chapter is to introduce PRINT, READ, and FOR-MAT, which are primitives that help procedures communicate with you, the LISP user. Primitives like PRINT and FORMAT help procedures to supply information; primitives like READ help procedures to get information.

A secondary purpose of this chapter is to introduce WITH-OPEN-FILE, a primitive that enables you to read from files and to write into files. With WITH-OPEN-FILE, you can read expressions from data files one at a time, as they are needed for processing, and you can write expressions into files as they become ready for storage.

**PRINT and READ
Facilitate Simple
Printing and
Reading**

The PRINT primitive evaluates its single argument, prints it on a new line, and prints a trailing space character. Here, for example, PRINT prints the value of the symbol TEMPERATURE:

```
* (setf temperature 100)
* (print temperature)
100                          ;PRINT's printing action does this.
100                          ;This is the value of the PRINT form.
```

Note that the value returned by `PRINT` is the unaltered value of its argument. In the next example, the value of the `PRINT` form is used as an argument in another form:

```
* (if (< -1 (print (- temperature 98.6)) +1)      ;Print a value.
      'normal
      'abnormal)
1.4                                 ;Value printed by PRINT form.
ABNORMAL                            ;Value returned by IF form.
```

Of course, the argument in a `PRINT` form can be any expression, not just a symbol:

```
* (setf name 'kirsh symptoms '(fever rash nausea))
* (print (list 'patient name
               'presented (length symptoms)
               'symptoms symptoms))
(PATIENT KIRSH PRESENTED 3 SYMPTOMS (FEVER RASH NAUSEA)) ;Side effect.
(PATIENT KIRSH PRESENTED 3 SYMPTOMS (FEVER RASH NAUSEA)) ;Value.
```

When the primitive `READ` is encountered, LISP stops and waits for you to type an expression. Consequently, using `READ` by itself causes total inactivity until you type some expression. In the following example, you have typed `KIRSH`, followed by a space:

```
* (read)kirsh
KIRSH
```

Because `READ` prints nothing to indicate that it is waiting, not even a carriage return, it is usually a good idea to use a `PRINT` form to prompt the user, indicating what kind of response is expected, as in the following example:

```
* (let ((p nil))                  ;P's initial value is NIL.
    (print                        ;Prompt.
      '(please type a patient name))
    (setf p (read))               ;Get name from user.
    (print (append '(ok the name is) ;Compose and print message.
                   (list p)))
    p)                            ;Final form inside LET is P.
(PLEASE TYPE A PATIENT NAME) kirsh ;Prompt plus user's response.
(OK THE NAME IS KIRSH)            ;Acknowledgement message.
KIRSH                             ;The value returned by the LET.
```

**FORMAT Enables
Exotic Printing**

Sooner or later, you will want your LISP programs to print more elegant, neater-looking, sentencelike messages which contain both uppercase and lowercase characters, along with a period or other punctuation. LISP's `FORMAT` primitive makes such messages possible.

In chapter 8, we introduced strings, pointing out that strings are a data type. Particular strings are character sequences bounded by double quote characters at the beginning and end. The simplest `FORMAT` form just prints a string on your terminal with no double quote marks and no movement to a fresh line:

```
* (format t "Hello!")Hello!          ;Format prints Hello!
NIL                                  ;Format's value is NIL.
```

The `T` tells `FORMAT` to print on your terminal. Instead of `T`, there can be a symbol that connects `FORMAT` to an output file, as described in the next section.

To print a character string on a fresh line, you simply add a tilde, followed by a percent sign, at the places where you want to start a fresh line:

```
* (format t "~%Hello!")
Hello!                               ;FORMAT prints Hello!
NIL                                  ;FORMAT's value is NIL.
* (format t "~%Hello!~%I'm ready to start now.")
Hello!                               ;Printed by FORMAT.
I'm ready to start now.              ;Printed by FORMAT.
NIL                                  ;FORMAT's value.
```

A tilde is said to introduce a *directive*. The `%` directive tells `FORMAT` to start a fresh line. The `&` directive normally tells `FORMAT` to start a fresh line too, but not if already at a fresh line. In the following example, back to back `%` directives produce two fresh lines, whereas a `%` directive followed by a `&` produces only one fresh line:

```
* (progn (format t "~%Line followed by % sign directive.~%")
         (format t "~%Line preceded by % sign directive.~%")
         (format t "~&Line preceded by & sign directive."))
Line followed by % sign directive.      ;Concluding % sign directive.
                                        ;Preceding % sign directive.
Line preceded by % sign directive.      ;Concluding % sign directive.
Line preceded by & sign directive.      ;Preceding & sign directive.
NIL
```

You use `&` when you want to be sure you start off on a fresh line, but you do not know if some other `FORMAT` form has finished with a fresh-line directive.

There are many other directives in addition to % and &. In fact, FORMAT offers so many options, each with its own particular directive, that learning about all of them is like learning a separate language. Fortunately, you can do quite a lot with %, &, and just one more, the A directive, which tells FORMAT to insert the value of an additional argument, one that appears after FORMAT's character string:

```
* (format t                                      ;Print on your terminal.
        "~%The next patient is ~a."              ;An A directive appears.
        name)                                    ;The A's matching argument.
The next patient is KIRSH.                       ;Side effect.
NIL                                              ;Value.
```

Of course, if there is more than one A directive, there must be more than one additional argument.

```
* (format t
        "~%Patient ~a presented ~a symptoms ~a."
        name                              ;Argument for first A.
        (length symptoms)                 ;For the second A.
        symptoms)                         ;For the third A.
Patient KIRSH presented 3 symptoms (FEVER RASH NAUSEA). ;Side effect.
NIL                                                     ;Value.
```

FORMAT also makes it possible to print in tabulated columns. The way to do it is to insert a column-width number into the A-directive. Thus the 10A directive tells FORMAT to print the next argument, as before, and then to print enough space characters to fill up a space ten characters wide:

```
* (format t "~%Patient: ~10aSymptoms: ~a" name (length symptoms))
Patient: KIRSH      Symptoms: 3   ;Ten characters in KIRSH plus spaces.
NIL                               ;The value returned.
```

Problems

Problem 9-1: In a previous problem in chapter 5, you defined TOWER-OF-HANOI, a procedure which counts the number of moves required to move a stack of disks from one pin to another under the following conditions:

• Only one disk can be moved at a time.
• The disks all have different diameters, and no disk can ever be placed on top of a smaller one.
• Initially all disks are on one pin and each disk rests on a larger one.

The official solution, expanded a bit so as to pass along the names of the pins involved in the moves, looks like this:

```
(defun tower-of-hanoi (disks from to spare)
  (if (endp disks)
      0
      (+ (tower-of-hanoi (rest disks) from spare to)
         1
         (tower-of-hanoi (rest disks) spare to from)))))
```

Now for the problem. Modify TOWER-OF-HANOI so that it prints a series of instructions for moving disks, rather than counting the number of moves, as in the following example:

```
* (tower-of-hanoi '(3 2 1) 'a 'b 'c)
Move 1 from A to B.
Move 2 from A to C.
Move 1 from B to C.
Move 3 from A to B.
Move 1 from C to A.
Move 2 from C to B.
Move 1 from A to B.
NIL
```

WITH-OPEN-FILE Enables Reading from Files

From time to time, you will want to read expressions from a file, processing them one by one. To see why, suppose that you have a file containing a data base of patient records, like the following, only much bigger:

```
((David Kirsh) (fever rash))
((Georg Hegel) (fever headache))
((Immanuel Kant) (nausea))
((Rene Descartes) (nausea))
((Jean-Paul Sartre) (nausea stomachache))
```

Now you need a way to read these individual patient descriptions into LISP one at a time, as needed. That is, you need to tie READ forms to files such that expressions are extracted from a file, rather than taken from you as you type.

To tie READ forms to files, you need to know about *streams*. Conceptually, streams are LISP objects that serve as sources or sinks for data. Many streams are connected on one end to files. Streams connected to files that supply data are called *input streams*; streams connected to files that receive data are called *output streams*.

On the other end, opposite the file end, input streams are involved in READ forms; output streams are involved in PRINT and FORMAT forms.

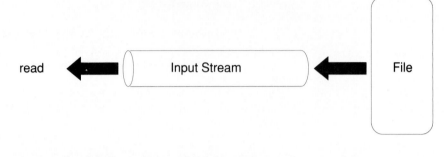

Figure 9-1. WITH-OPEN-FILE connects READs to files via input streams

Streams are created, variables are bound to them, and they are connected to files using the primitive WITH-OPEN-FILE. The template for WITH-OPEN-FILE therefore must enable three things to be specified: the name of a variable to be bound to the stream, the name of the file the stream is to be connected to, and whether the stream is for input or output:

```
(with-open-file (<stream name>
                 <file specification>
                 :direction <:input or :output>)
  ...)
```

Within a WITH-OPEN-FILE form for an input stream, READ forms can specify that reading is to be done from the file, via an input stream, by including the stream name in the READ form:

```
(with-open-file (<stream name>
                 <file specification>
                 :direction :input)
  ...
  (read <stream name>)
  ...)
```

Conceptually, input streams act as connectors between files and READs. As shown in figure 9-1, expressions come out of a file, flow through an input stream, and emerge from a READ.

In the following example, an input stream is created and the symbol PATIENT-STREAM is bound to it. The input stream is connected to the file specified by the character string, which happens to specify a file according to the conventions of the MS-DOS operating system. Finally, the direction is specified as a keyword argument, with :DIRECTION announcing the presence of the keyword argument, and another keyword, :INPUT, serving as the keyword argument:

```
(with-open-file (patient-stream "/phw/lisp3/patients.lsp"
                                :direction :input)
 ...)
```

Inside the WITH-OPEN-FILE form, PATIENT-STREAM can appear in READ forms, indicating that READ is to read from the file via the input stream, not from you via the keyboard. In the following example, the two expressions are read and immediately printed:

```
* (with-open-file (patient-stream "/phw/lisp3/patients.lsp"
                                  :direction :input)
    (dotimes (n 2) (print (read patient-stream)))))
((DAVID KIRSH) (FEVER RASH))              ;First expression read.
((GEORG HEGEL) (FEVER HEADACHE))          ;Second expression read.
NIL
```

Like LET forms, WITH-OPEN-FILE forms return the value of the last form contained. In this example, there is only one form, a DOTIMES form, whose value is NIL.

Optional Arguments in READ Forms Specify End-of-File Treatment

Now the next natural thing is to examine each expression in a file, not just the first two. But this introduces a problem because READ will panic and signal an error if it hits the end of a file unless you tell it not to. One approach would be to mark the end of the file by inserting some special expression. A better approach is to tell READ not to panic by supplying NIL as a second optional argument:

```
(read patient-stream nil)
```

When NIL is supplied as a second argument, READ returns NIL when the end of a file is encountered, rather than halting and announcing an error.

In the following example, the READ forms return patient descriptions until there are no more, whereupon READ returns NIL, leading to the termination of the DO loop:

```
* (with-open-file (patient-stream "/phw/lisp3/patients.lsp"
                                  :direction :input)
    (do ((patient (read patient-stream nil)
                  (read patient-stream nil)))
        ((not patient))
      (print patient)))
((DAVID KIRSH) (FEVER RASH))
((GEORG HEGEL) (FEVER HEADACHE))
((IMMANUEL KANT) (NAUSEA))
((RENE DESCARTES) (NAUSEA))
((JEAN-PAUL SARTRE) (NAUSEA STOMACHACHE))
NIL
```

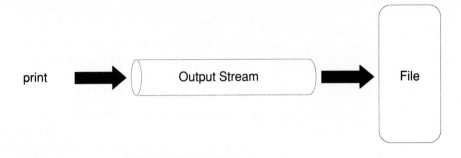

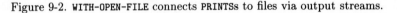

Figure 9-2. WITH-OPEN-FILE connects PRINTSs to files via output streams.

WITH-OPEN-FILE Enables Printing to Files

Output streams are used in the other direction, connecting PRINT to output files, as shown in figure 9-2. WITH-OPEN-FILE sets things up, as in input case, only this time with :OUTPUT appearing in place of :INPUT:

```
(with-open-file (<stream name>
                 <file specification>
                 :direction :output)
  ...
  (print <expression whose value is to be printed> <stream name>)
  ...)
```

In the following example, both input and output streams are at work, with all nauseous patients ending up in a new file, as determined by the NAUSEATED-P predicate:

```
(defun nauseated-p (description)
  (member 'nausea (second description)))
* (with-open-file (patient-stream "/phw/lisp3/patients.lsp"
                                   :direction :input)
    (with-open-file (nausea-stream "/phw/lisp3/nausea.lsp"
                                    :direction :output)
      (do ((patient-description (read patient-stream nil)
                                (read patient-stream nil)))
          ((not patient-description))
        (when (nauseated-p patient-description)
          (print patient-description nausea-stream)))))
NIL
```

Note that nothing appears on your terminal, but the new file has the following contents:

```
((IMMANUEL KANT) (NAUSEA))
((RENE DESCARTES) (NAUSEA))
((JEAN-PAUL SARTRE) (NAUSEA STOMACHACHE))
```

Finally, note the following:

- Each time you open an input file with a particular name, using WITH-OPEN-FILE, LISP starts reading all over again, from the beginning.

- Each time you open an output file with a particular name, using WITH-OPEN-FILE, you create a new, empty file.

- There are other ways to connect input-output streams to files, other than WITH-OPEN-FILE. Using WITH-OPEN-FILE is usually the best way, however, because WITH-OPEN-FILE always ensures that files will be left in a tidy state, even if an error occurs inside WITH-OPEN-FILE causing premature termination.

Problems

Problem 9-2: Sometimes NIL can appear in a file. In such situations, (READ ⟨input stream⟩ NIL) could return NIL before encountering the end of a file, promoting confusion and error. To avoid this confusion and error, you can supply still another optional argument that is returned on encountering the end of a file. Many programmers use EOF for end-of-file:

```
(read patient-stream nil 'eof)
```

Show how to print out all the patient records in the patient description file using a READ form with an EOF argument.

Problem 9-3: In chapter 6, five book descriptions were combined into one list assigned to BOOKS:

```
(setf books
      (list
        (make-book '(artificial intelligence)
                   '(patrick henry winston)
                   '(technical ai))
        (make-book '(common lisp)
                   '(guy l steele)
                   '(technical lisp))
        (make-book '(moby dick)
                   '(herman melville)
                   '(fiction))
        (make-book '(tom sawyer)
                   '(mark twain)
                   '(fiction))
        (make-book '(the black orchid)
                   '(rex stout)
                   '(fiction mystery))))
```

You would never type such an expression directly into LISP for two reasons: first, you could not expect to type so much without mistakes; and second, you want a permanent bibliography, not one that will vanish when you terminate your session with LISP.

Consequently, it is much more natural to create a file in which the SETF form is the sole contents. Reading from the file, using LOAD, would assign the list of book descriptions to BOOKS.

Usually it is better to put just the book descriptions in the file without the SETF, just as in the patient-descriptions example. Explain why.

Problem 9-4: FORMAT also can print to output streams. You need only replace the T with an output stream name. Show how you would create a file containing the following, given the usual patients in the patients file:

```
Patient 1 is not nauseous.
Patient 2 is not nauseous.
Patient 3 is nauseous.
Patient 4 is nauseous.
Patient 5 is nauseous.
```

READ Does Not Evaluate Expressions, but EVAL Evaluates Twice

The READ primitive returns an expression that you type or that appears in a file, *not* an expression's value. If you want to compute the value of an expression returned by READ, you must use EVAL, a primitive that first evaluates its argument and then evaluates the result. Consider this example first:

```
* (setf form-to-evaluate '(+ 2 2))   ;Variable's value is assigned.
(+ 2 2)

* form-to-evaluate                    ;Variable's value is a form.
(+ 2 2)

* (eval form-to-evaluate)             ;Value of that form is a number.
4
```

Now consider an example with READ. When (READ) is embedded in an EVAL form, (READ) is evaluated because it is an argument in a form. Then there is a second evaluation because the form is an EVAL form:

```
* (read)(+ 2 2)        ;You type (+ 2 2) for READ.
(+ 2 2)                ;READ returns (+ 2 2).

* (eval (read))(+ 2 2) ;You type (+ 2 2) for READ.
4                      ;EVAL evaluates READ's result.
```

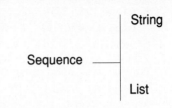

Figure 9-3. Both lists and strings belong to the sequence data type.

Problems

Problem 9-5: Define ECHO1, a procedure that reads expressions and returns them without evaluation, and define ECHO2, a procedure that returns with evaluation:

Special Primitives Manipulate Strings and Characters

Eventually, you may want your LISP procedures to know what a user types or what a file holds on a character by character basis, rather than on the expression by expression basis provided by READ.

Accordingly, we must discuss strings in more detail, and we must introduce *characters*, still another data type. Like other LISP data types, strings and characters are each associated with their own family of primitives, including primitives that read them. At this point, there is no need for you to memorize what these primitives do, as our purpose is only to give you a feel for what strings and characters are all about. String and character primitives are used rarely in the rest of this book.

We begin with strings. Because both lists and strings involve ordered sets of elements, both belong to the *sequence data type*, as indicated in figure 9-3.

Because both lists and strings are sequences, many primitives work equally well on both. Consider LENGTH and REVERSE, for example:

```
* (length '(a b c))
3
* (length "abc")
3
* (reverse '(a b c))
(C B A)
* (reverse "abc")
"cba"
```

ELT, an acronym for <u>el</u>emen<u>t</u>, also works equally well on both lists and strings. If the first argument in an ELT form is a list, then ELT returns the element specified by the second argument, where 0 specifies the first element.

```
* (elt '(a b c) 0)
A
* (elt '(a b c) 2)
C
```

On the other hand, if the first argument in an ELT form is a string, then ELT returns the character specified by the second argument. Character objects are printed with a # symbol, followed by a backslash: prefix:

```
* (elt "abc" 0)
#\a
* (elt "abc" 2)
#\c
```

While many primitives work on both lists and strings, others are specific to one or the other. To determine if two strings are the same, for example, you use STRING= or STRING-EQUAL, primitives that work only on strings. STRING= is case sensitive; STRING-EQUAL is not:

```
* (string= "abc" "xyz")
NIL
* (string= "abc" "abc")
T
* (string= "abc" "ABC")
NIL
* (string-equal "abc" "xyz")
NIL
* (string-equal "abc" "abc")
T
* (string-equal "abc" "ABC")
T
```

To determine if two characters are the same, you use CHAR= or CHAR-EQUAL, primitives that work only on characters. CHAR= is case sensitive; CHAR-EQUAL is not:

```
* (char= #\a #\b)
NIL
* (char= #\a #\a)
T
* (char= #\a #\A)
NIL
* (char-equal #\a #\b)
NIL
```

```
* (char-equal #\a #\a)
T
* (char-equal #\a #\A)
T
```

To determine if one string is contained in another, use SEARCH. If SEARCH's first argument is contained in its second, the result is the position where the match starts. Otherwise, SEARCH returns NIL:

```
* (search "Katz" "Katz, Boris")
0
* (search "Boris" "Katz, Boris")
6
* (search "Pushkin" "Katz, Boris")
NIL
```

To make the SEARCH insensitive to case, you must add CHAR-EQUAL as a keyword argument; otherwise SEARCH compares characters using CHAR=:[1]

```
* (search "BORIS" "Katz, Boris")
NIL
* (search "BORIS" "Katz, Boris" :test #'char-equal)
6
```

Like LENGTH, REVERSE, and ELT, SEARCH is actually a sequence primitive, working on both lists and strings. Here are examples involving strings:

```
* (search '(katz) '(katz boris))
0
* (search '(boris) '(katz boris))
1
* (search '(pushkin) '(katz boris))
NIL
```

READ-LINE and READ-CHAR Read Strings and Characters

The READ-LINE and READ-CHAR primitives are useful for reading strings and characters from a terminal or file. READ-LINE absorbs characters up to the point where either a carriage return or end of file occurs and then produces two values. The first value is a string consisting of the characters preceding the carriage return or end of file. The second value is usually NIL, but if READ-LINE encounters the end of file while reading a line, the second value is T. Once you type (READ-LINE) in the following example, nothing else happens until you type some characters followed by a carriage return:

---

[1] Actually, SEARCH defaults to EQL, like other primitives that do equality tests, but EQL calls CHAR= when faced by characters, a detail that was too early to discuss in chapter 4, where EQL was introduced.

```
* (read-line)This is a READ-LINE test.
"This is a READ-LINE test."
NIL
```

READ-CHAR reads just one character from a terminal or file:

```
* (read-char)x
#\x

* (read-char)X
#\X
```

Both READ-LINE and READ-CHAR accept optional arguments following the pattern set by READ. If there is a first argument, it names a stream to read from. If there is a second, and if it is NIL, READ-LINE and READ-CHAR return NIL when the very next thing is the end of a file, rather than signaling an error.

To illustrate, suppose that you keep names, telephone numbers, and login identifiers in a file identified by the string "PEOPLE.AIL" with the following contents:

```
Horn, Berthold          5863            BKPH
Katz, Boris             6032            BORIS
Winston, Patrick        6754            PHW
Woven Hose Cafe         577-8444
```

Now suppose you want to write FETCH, a procedure that looks through such files for a line containing a particular substring, whereupon the whole line is to be printed. WITH-OPEN-FILE sets up the appropriate stream, and READ-LINE reads lines from the file, one at a time. SEARCH tests each line until one matches the given fragment, whereupon FORMAT prints the line:

```
(defun fetch (fragment file)
  (with-open-file (line-stream file :direction :input)
    (do ((line (read-line line-stream nil)
               (read-line line-stream nil)))
        ((not line) (format t "~%No such entry!"))
      (when (search fragment line :test #'char-equal)
        (format t "~%~a" line)
        (return t)))))
```

Here are examples of FETCH in action:

```
* (fetch "Katz" "people.ail")
Katz, Boris             6032            BORIS
T
```

```
* (fetch "Pushkin" "people.ail")
No such entry!
NIL
```

Summary   • PRINT and READ facilitate simple printing and reading.
                     • FORMAT enables exotic printing.
                     • WITH-OPEN-FILE enables reading from files.
                     • Optional arguments in READ forms specify end-of-file treatment.
                     • WITH-OPEN-FILE enables printing to files.
                     • READ does not evaluate expressions, but EVAL evaluates twice.
                     • Special primitives manipulate strings and characters.
                     • READ-LINE and READ-CHAR read strings and characters.

10

Rules for Good Programming and Tools for Debugging

The principal purposes of this chapter are to introduce certain *rules of good programming practice* and to explain certain key *debugging primitives*, especially TRACE, STEP, and BREAK.

Following Rules of Good Programming Practice Helps You To Avoid Bugs

Books on productivity emphasize the principle that rework is a costly alternative to doing things right the first time. Specializing to programming, the principle is that debugging is a costly alternative to writing bug-free procedures the first time.

Although it is impossible to avoid bugs altogether, there are *rules of good programming practice* that help you avoid many. To help you appreciate the rules, we borrow one of the procedures you will learn about later in chapter 21, rewriting it so that it becomes an exaggerated example of bad programming practice:

```
(defun put-on (arg1 arg2)
  (and (action1 arg1)
       (action2 arg1 arg2)
       (action3 arg1))))
```

PUT-ON's purpose, as you learn in chapter 21, is to arrange for one block to be placed on another by a simulated, one-handed robot. As it stands, however, PUT-ON is incomprehensible. To make it better, we start with the following rule:

- Procedures should be commented liberally. Put descriptive paragraphs before definitions and staccato notes inside them.

Using this rule, the overall approach of PUT-ON emerges.

```
;;; PUT-ON arranges for one object to be placed on another.
;;; PUT-ON succeeds only if all its subprocedures succeed.

(defun put-on (arg1 arg2)
  (and (action1 arg1)              ;Grasp the object,
       (action2 arg1 arg2)         ;Move it to the support
       (action3 arg1))))           ;Ungrasp it.
```

Alternatively, we could achieve much the same effect by using another rule:

- Procedure and variable names should be descriptive.

Descriptive names make programs largely self commenting, as you can see from the following, improved version of PUT-ON:

```
(defun put-on (object support)
  (and (grasp object)
       (move object support)
       (ungrasp object))))
```

Again, the overall approach emerges. Even though you do not see the definitions of the subprocedures, their purpose is evident.

The advantage of descriptive names, relative to comments, is that procedures carry their names wherever they go, whereas instances of a procedure may be unevenly commented. Of course for maximum clarity, you should use both descriptive names and comments:

```
;;; PUT-ON arranges for one object to be place on another.
;;; PUT-ON succeeds only if all its subprocedures succeed.

(defun put-on (object support)
  (and (grasp object)              ;Grasp the object,
       (move object support)       ;Move it to the support
       (ungrasp object))))         ;Ungrasp it.
```

At this point, you can see that three other rules are obeyed already:

- Procedures should be short.
- Procedures should have only a few arguments.
- Procedures should be built around goals.

Our example procedure is certainly short and certainly has only a few arguments. The goal it is built around is to put one object on another; the goals of the procedures it calls are to grasp an object, to move it, and to let go.

The next rule makes it less risky to deploy procedures in situations that are different from those for which they were originally conceived:

- Procedures should presume as little as possible about the situation in effect when they are called.

To illustrate, note that as it stands, there is no reason to suppose that there is space on the support for the object to be placed on it. Assuming that GET-SPACE gets space, if there is any, the following eliminates a presumption:

```
;;; PUT-ON arranges for one object to be place on another
;;; if there is sufficient room.  PUT-ON succeeds only if
;;; all its subprocedures succeed.

(defun put-on (object support)
  (when (get-space object support)    ;See if there is space.
    (and (grasp object)               ;If there is, grasp the object,
         (move object support)        ; move it to the support
         (ungrasp object))))          ; and ungrasp it.
```

The next rule also makes it less risky to deploy procedures in situations that are different from those for which they were originally conceived:

- Procedures should report on what is going on when they encounter unexpected situations.

To follow this rule, we modify PUT-ON again. Now PUT-ON not only returns NIL if it fails, but also says why:

```
;;; PUT-ON arranges for one object to be place on another
;;; if there is sufficient room.  PUT-ON succeeds only if
;;; all its subprocedures succeed.

(defun put-on (object support)
  (if (get-space object support)        ;See if there is space.
      (and (grasp object)               ;If there is, grasp the object,
           (move object support)        ; move it to the support
           (ungrasp object))            ; and ungrasp it.
      (format t "~&Sorry, there is no room for ~a on ~a."
              object                    ;Otherwise complain, and
              support)))                ; return NIL.
```

**Big Programs
Require Abstraction
and Modularity**

So far, we have concentrated on individual procedures, only occasionally
looking at situations in which several procedures work together. Later on,
when we describe big programs several other rules of good programing practice become important. Two of them focus on abstraction. In chapter 5,
you learned that procedure abstraction has to do with hiding the details
of how procedures are implemented. In chapter 6, you learned that data
abstraction has to do with hiding the details of how data is represented:

- Use procedure abstraction. It is a powerful idea.
- Use data abstraction. It is a powerful idea.

By using procedure and data abstraction, you can concentrate more on the
work at hand and less on distracting details.

Procedure and data abstraction divide procedures into layered groups.
You can, of course, divide the parts of a big program another way, by
dividing your procedures into functional groups. To use the standard term,
each functional group is called a *module*. Programs containing recognizable
modules are said to be *modular*.

If only a few of a module's procedures interact with procedures outside
the module, and if those procedures are well commented and written in
accordance with the rules of good programing practice, then the module is
said to have a *clean interface*, which leads to the following:

- Make your programs modular. Give each module a clean interface.

Generally, each module in a big program resides in a separate file, making
the modularity quite explicit.

**Most Programmers
use TRACE, STEP,
and BREAK with
Varying Frequency**

But no matter how carefully you attend to the rules of good programming
practice, there will be bugs. To root them out, you use *debugging primitives*
such as the three described in the following sections. Most programmers
use the first, TRACE, extensively; the second, STEP, never; and the third,
BREAK, occasionally.

**TRACE Causes
Procedures To Print
Their Arguments
and Values**

There are occasions when things just do not work out, no matter how
carefully you honor the rules of good programming practice. Strange results
appear, or worse yet, your machine seems to drop dead, perhaps printing
an error message that is too opaque to help.

Often TRACE is the right way to start tracking down the problem, for
TRACE is the champion of debugging tools. TRACE's effect is to cause entry
and exit information to be printed for the procedures supplied as arguments.

To see how TRACE works, suppose we have defined a procedure, COUNT-
ATOMS, that we think will count all of the atoms in an expression:

```
(defun count-atoms (expression)          ;Bugged!
  (if (atom expression)
      1
      (+ (count-atoms (first expression))
         (count-atoms (rest expression)))))
```

Unfortunately, when we try COUNT-ATOMS, we are disappointed. In a test case, COUNT-ATOMS returns 7 when we expect 4:

```
* (count-atoms '((this is) (a test)))
7
```

At this point, it is time to try TRACE. First we say that we want to trace COUNT-ATOMS. Note that the argument is *not* quoted:

```
* (trace count-atoms)
T
```

Next, we try COUNT-ATOMS again on our test case. Now arguments and values are printed, with the indentation indicating the level of recursion. Note that the exact form of the printed information is implementation dependent.[1]

```
* (count-atoms '((this is) (a test)))
ENTERING: COUNT-ATOMS, ARGUMENT LIST: (((THIS IS) (A TEST)))
 ENTERING: COUNT-ATOMS, ARGUMENT LIST: ((THIS IS))
  ENTERING: COUNT-ATOMS, ARGUMENT LIST: (THIS)
  EXITING: COUNT-ATOMS, VALUE: 1
  ENTERING: COUNT-ATOMS, ARGUMENT LIST: ((IS))
   ENTERING: COUNT-ATOMS, ARGUMENT LIST: (IS)
   EXITING: COUNT-ATOMS, VALUE: 1
   ENTERING: COUNT-ATOMS, ARGUMENT LIST: (NIL)
   EXITING: COUNT-ATOMS, VALUE: 1
  ...
```

Things go well up to the point where COUNT-ATOMS attacked NIL. Mysteriously, the result was 1.

We attempt a repair in the next section. But first, we want to introduce a trace example that involves tracing several procedures simultaneously.

In chapter 5, we saw that the number of rabbits descendant from a single female, after n months, is the sum of the number of rabbits after $n - 1$ months and after $n - 2$ months. Consequently we can break the computation up into three parts:

---

[1] The implementation-dependent examples in this book approximate the conventions of GOLDEN COMMON LISP^{TM}, which is a product of Gold Hill Computers, of Cambridge, Massachusetts.

```
(defun current (n)                              ;Bugged!
  (+ (minus-one n) (minus-two n)))
(defun minus-one (n)
  (current (- n 1)))
(defun minus-two (n)
  (current (- n 2)))
```

Now we try a test case for which we expect the answer to be **13**. We get a mysterious error message instead:

```
* (current 6)
ERROR
```

At this point, we may have no idea what is going on, so we trace everything:

```
* (trace current minus-one minus-two)
T
```

Next we try our test case again:

```
* (current 6)
ENTERING: CURRENT, ARGUMENT LIST: (6)
 ENTERING: MINUS-ONE, ARGUMENT LIST: (6)
  ENTERING: CURRENT, ARGUMENT LIST: (5)
   ENTERING: MINUS-ONE, ARGUMENT LIST: (5)
    ENTERING: CURRENT, ARGUMENT LIST: (4)
     ENTERING: MINUS-ONE, ARGUMENT LIST: (4)
      ENTERING: CURRENT, ARGUMENT LIST: (3)
       ENTERING: MINUS-ONE, ARGUMENT LIST: (3)
        ENTERING: CURRENT, ARGUMENT LIST: (2)
         ENTERING: MINUS-ONE, ARGUMENT LIST: (2)
          ENTERING: CURRENT, ARGUMENT LIST: (1)
           ENTERING: MINUS-ONE, ARGUMENT LIST: (1)
            ENTERING: CURRENT, ARGUMENT LIST: (0)
             ENTERING: MINUS-ONE, ARGUMENT LIST: (0)
              ENTERING: CURRENT, ARGUMENT LIST: (-1)
                 . . .
```

By this time we note that we are trying to compute the number of rabbits before we started, at time zero and earlier. As in the COUNT-ATOMS example, we have a good idea about where things are going wrong. We suspect that the insidious *drop-through* bug has struck: evidently there is nothing that terminates recursion.

We attempt a repair in the section after next. But first, to conclude this section, note that UNTRACE stops the tracing of the procedures supplied as arguments, turning off the effect of TRACE. Suppose we are tracing CUR-RENT, MINUS-ONE, and MINUS-TWO, and we want to trace only CURRENT. Again, note that the arguments are *not* quoted:

```
* (untrace minus-one minus-two)

* (current 6)
ENTERING: CURRENT, ARGUMENT LIST: (6)
 ENTERING: CURRENT, ARGUMENT LIST: (5)
  ENTERING: CURRENT, ARGUMENT LIST: (4)
   ENTERING: CURRENT, ARGUMENT LIST: (3)
    ENTERING: CURRENT, ARGUMENT LIST: (2)
     ENTERING: CURRENT, ARGUMENT LIST: (1)
      ENTERING: CURRENT, ARGUMENT LIST: (0)
       ENTERING: CURRENT, ARGUMENT LIST: (-1)
          ...
```

Alternatively, we could evaluate UNTRACE with no arguments to stop the tracing of all procedures currently traced.

**STEP Causes
Procedures To
Proceed One Step
at a Time**

Once we have a good idea where things are going wrong, perhaps by tracing, we can watch LISP's performance in detail, following its action one step at a time. This can be done using STEP.

For example, consider the COUNT-ATOMS procedure introduced in the previous section. Having concluded that we must test for the empty list, we write this more complicated, but also incorrect version:

```
(defun count-atoms (expression)          ;Bugged!
  (cond ((atom expression) 1)
        ((null expression) 0)
        (t (+ (count-atoms (first expression))
              (count-atoms (rest expression))))))
```

When we try COUNT-ATOMS, we see that it mysteriously produces the same result as before, returning seven instead of four as it should:

```
* (count-atoms '((this is) (a test)))
7
```

When we try tracing the new version, we again see the same thing we saw before. Evidently, COUNT-ATOMS produces a weird result when its argument's value is NIL:

```
* (count-atoms '((this is) (a test)))
ENTERING: COUNT-ATOMS, ARGUMENT LIST: (((THIS IS) (A TEST)))
 ENTERING: COUNT-ATOMS, ARGUMENT LIST: ((THIS IS))
  ENTERING: COUNT-ATOMS, ARGUMENT LIST: (THIS)
  EXITING: COUNT-ATOMS, VALUE: 1
  ENTERING: COUNT-ATOMS, ARGUMENT LIST: ((IS))
   ENTERING: COUNT-ATOMS, ARGUMENT LIST: (IS)
   EXITING: COUNT-ATOMS, VALUE: 1
   ENTERING: COUNT-ATOMS, ARGUMENT LIST: (NIL)
   EXITING: COUNT-ATOMS, VALUE: 1

 ...
```

Consequently, we decide to use STEP on the form (COUNT-ATOMS NIL), hoping that as we move through the body of COUNT-ATOMS, one step at a time, the scales will fall from our eyes.

Unfortunately, the way we work with STEP is highly implementation dependent. In the implementation we work with, each expression is printed out before evaluation, whereupon LISP pauses. After we press the ↓ key, LISP proceeds into the expression to work on the expression's arguments. In the following example, we just press the ↓ key until we hit something interesting, whereupon we press the END key to terminate stepping:

```
* (step (count-atoms nil))
  (COUNT-ATOMS NIL)                      ;STEP prints form to be evaluated.
   NIL                                   ;STEP prints form's argument.
    NIL = NIL                            ;Value of argument is NIL.
   (COND ((ATOM EXPRESSION) 1) ...)      ;Now STEP works on the body.
    (ATOM EXPRESSION)                    ;First form in COND to compute.
     EXPRESSION                          ;Argument is EXPRESSION.
      EXPRESSION = NIL                   ;EXPRESSION's value is NIL.
     (ATOM EXPRESSION) = T               ;What?
1
```

Aha! We forgot that NIL not only is the empty list, but also is an atom. Naturally ATOM returns T when its argument is NIL. Our unfortunate ordering of the COND clauses in COUNT-ATOMS is such that the clause that is supposed to handle the empty list is never triggered. One fix is to reverse the first and second clauses:

```
(defun count-atoms (expression)
  (cond ((null expression) 0)
        ((atom expression) 1)
        (t (+ (count-atoms (first expression))
              (count-atoms (rest expression))))))
```

Now the test case works out fine:

```
* (count-atoms '((this is) (a test)))
4
```

BREAK Stops Evaluation so that You Can Evaluate Forms

We can insert a BREAK form anywhere where we think we can learn something useful by looking at variable bindings, evaluating a form, or even assigning a new value to a variable.

For example, suppose we attempt to fix the problem with our rabbit procedures by adding a terminating test to CURRENT:

```
(defun current (n)                            ;Bugged!
  (if (= n 1)
      1
      (+ (minus-one n) (minus-two n)))))

(defun minus-one (n)
  (current (- n 1)))

(defun minus-two (n)
  (current (- n 2)))
```

When we try this modified version of CURRENT, it still fails in the same way as before:

```
* (current 6)
ERROR
```

We decide to trace CURRENT, but the result does not help much:

```
* (trace current)
ENTERING: CURRENT, ARGUMENT LIST: (6)
 ENTERING: CURRENT, ARGUMENT LIST: (5)
  ENTERING: CURRENT, ARGUMENT LIST: (4)
   ENTERING: CURRENT, ARGUMENT LIST: (3)
    ENTERING: CURRENT, ARGUMENT LIST: (2)
     ENTERING: CURRENT, ARGUMENT LIST: (1)
     EXITING: CURRENT, VALUE: 1
     ENTERING: CURRENT, ARGUMENT LIST: (0)
      ENTERING: CURRENT, ARGUMENT LIST: (-1)
      ...
```

Evidently, we still have a drop-through bug of some sort. Becoming frustrated, we insert two BREAK forms in order to pinpoint the problem. Note that BREAK forms have an argument, a string, which is printed when the break form is evaluated:

```
(defun current (n)                              ;Contains another bug!
  (if (= n 1)
      1
      (+ (minus-one n) (minus-two n)))))
(defun minus-one (n)
  (when (< (- n 1) 1) (break "N is too small in MINUS-ONE"))
  (current (- n 1)))
(defun minus-two (n)
  (when (< (- n 2) 1) (break "N is too small in MINUS-TWO"))
  (current (- n 2)))
```

We try again:

```
* (current 6)                       ;We try CURRENT.
N is too small in MINUS-TWO  ;A BREAK form prints its argument.
1> n                                ;We ask for the value of N.
2                                   ;The value is two.
1> (- n 2)                          ;We ask for the value handed to CURRENT.
0                                   ;It is 0, of course.
...
```

At this point, we have several options. We could reset the value of N using
SETF; we could attempt to evaluate other forms; we could discontinue the
current computation completely; or we could continue on from the BREAK
form.

To discontinue, we press a prescribed keychord to escape from BREAK. In
some implementations, the keychord is *Ctrl-C*, but note that *Ctrl-C* is not
part of COMMON LISP. To continue from where a BREAK stops evaluation, we
press another prescribed keychord. In some implementations, the keychord
is *Ctrl-P*, but again note that *Ctrl-P* is not part of COMMON LISP. If we
do elect to continue, the value returned by a BREAK form is NIL.

Returning to the example, the problem evidently arose because MINUS-
TWO asked CURRENT to compute how many rabbits there were at time 0.
Among the various ways to fix the situation, the easiest is to ensure that
MINUS-TWO never gets 2 as its argument by generalizing the test in CURRENT:

```
(defun current (n)
  (if (< n 2)
      1
      (+ (minus-one n) (minus-two n)))))
```

Now our test case works out:

```
* (current 6)
13
```

TIME, DESCRIBE, and DRIBBLE Are Helpful Too

The TRACE, STEP, and BREAK primitives only scratch the surface of what can be done with debugging in LISP systems. There are many other helpful primitives.

TIME, for example, calculates how long it takes to compute a form:

```
* (time (current 6))
Evaluating: (CURRENT 6)            ;Printed information.
Elapsed time: 0:00.06              ;Printed information.
13                                 ;Value returned.
* (time (current 12))
Evaluating: (CURRENT 12)           ;Printed information.
Elapsed time: 0:00.50              ;Printed information
233                                ;Value returned.
```

From this, we learn, interestingly, that our implementation of CURRENT takes time far worse than proportional to the size of its argument.

DESCRIBE is another helpful debugging primitive. As its name suggests, DESCRIBE prints helpful information about any LISP object:

```
* (setf symbol-example '(a b c))
* (describe 'symbol-example)
It is a symbol.
   Its global value is: (A B C).
   Its function definition is unbound.
   Its property list is empty.
* (defun procedure-example (x) (another-procedure x))
PROCEDURE-EXAMPLE
* (describe 'procedure-example)
It is a symbol.
   Its global value is unbound.
   Its function definition is: (LAMBDA (X) (ANOTHER-PROCEDURE X)).
   Its property list is empty.
```

DRIBBLE makes it possible for you to create a transcript of your interaction with LISP. As the following illustrates, you begin by handing DRIBBLE a file specification as described in chapter 8:

```
* (dribble <file specification>)    ;Start dribbling to the file.
...                                  ;Everything here is recorded
* (dribble)                          ;Stop dribbling.
```

Once you have stopped dribbling, you can then examine what happened, at your leisure, by printing the dribbled file or by examining it with your editor:

```
* (ed <file specification>)
```

Debugging Is Implementation Specific

Unfortunately, the exact behavior of the debugging primitives is inappropriate for detailed discussion here because the behavior of these primitives is implementation specific.

You should, however, experiment with TRACE, STEP, BREAK, TIME, DESCRIBE, and DRIBBLE to see what they do in the implementation you work with. You should also learn how to do the following in the implementation you work with:

- Interrupt an ongoing evaluation, enter a debugging mode, fix something, and continue. In the implementation we work with, this is done by typing the keychord *Ctrl-Break* to interrupt, followed by *Ctrl-P* to continue.
- Interrupt an ongoing computation in preparation for starting over from scratch. This is useful when a program appears to be running for an excessive amount of time. In our implementation, this is done by typing the keychord *Ctrl-Break* to interrupt, followed by *Ctrl-C* to start over from scratch.

Summary

- Following rules of good programming practice helps you to avoid bugs.
- Big programs require abstraction and modularity.
- Most programmers use TRACE, STEP, and BREAK with varying frequency.
- TRACE causes procedures to print their arguments and values.
- STEP causes procedures to proceed one step at a time.
- BREAK stops evaluation so that you can evaluate forms.
- TIME, DESCRIBE, and DRIBBLE are helpful too.
- Debugging is implementation specific.

References

For an excellent treatment of debugging and good programming practice, see *Programming in COMMON LISP*, by Rodney Brooks.

11

Properties
and Arrays

So far, you know how to assign values to symbols using SETF, and you know how to retrieve those values using LISP's ordinary evaluation process. The purpose of this chapter is to introduce *property lists* and *arrays*, which provide other ways to store and retrieve data. First you learn about properties, for which retrieval and storage is done using symbols as object-specifying indexes.

Next you learn about arrays, for which the retrieval and storage is done using one or more integers as object-specifying indexes.

For both properties and arrays, you learn about the appropriate constructor procedures for creating information, reader procedures for retrieving information, and writer procedures for changing information.

**Each Way of
Storing Data Has
Constructors,
Readers, and Writers**

In chapter 6, we explained that it is important to know how to create new data, to retrieve old data, and to change old data. Consequently, for any way of storing data, there are three kinds of access procedures:

- A procedure that creates data is a constructor.
- A procedure that extracts data is a reader.
- A procedure that changes data is a writer.

**Properties
Enable Storage in
Symbolically Indexed
Places**

Symbols may have *property values* as well as ordinary values. Because property values are stored in places named by symbols, the values can be said to be *symbolically indexed*. The collection of property names and values associated with a symbol is said to constitute its *property list*.

Suppose, for example, that you have decided to use symbols to represent people. You then could use properties to store the names of each person's parents and children.

Symbol	Parents Property	Children Property
patrick	(robert dorothy)	(sarah)
karen	(james eve)	(sarah)

Thus, we use the word *value* in two ways: first, we talk of the *value* of a form, either list or atom; and second, we talk of the value of some particular property of a symbol.

**GET and SETF are
the Custodians of
Properties**

It seems natural to learn how to store a property value before learning how to retrieve it. But curiously, the template for retrieving values is part of the template for storing values, so let us look at retrieval first.

The primitive GET retrieves a property value from a symbol:

```
(get <symbol> <property name>)
```

For example, once we have made (ROBERT DOROTHY) the PARENTS property of PATRICK, the following works:

```
* (get 'patrick 'parents)
(ROBERT DOROTHY)
```

Thus GET is the reader primitive for properties.

To attach a property value to a symbol, we use SETF:

```
(setf (get <symbol> <property name>) <property value>)
```

Note carefully that the first argument to SETF is the same form used to retrieve the property value once it is there. The second argument is the thing you want the property value to be. Thus the first argument is the *reader form*, the form that produces the current property value. The second argument supplies the replacement value. The value returned by SETF is the replacement value:

```
* (setf (get 'patrick 'parents) '(robert dorothy))
(ROBERT DOROTHY)
```

Thus SETF, used together with GET, is the writer for properties. The first time SETF is used on a particular symbol with a particular property, it creates a property. Thus SETF serves a dual role when used with properties: because SETF creates a property, it is a constructor; and because it places data in the property, it is a writer.

It is important to note that (GET ⟨SYMBOL⟩ ⟨PROPERTY NAME⟩) returns NIL if there is no such property for the symbol. This means that you cannot use GET to distinguish a property with value NIL from the absence of a property. Accordingly, the use of NIL as a property value is in questionable taste.

Also, as far as GET is concerned, properties can be removed using (SETF (GET <symbol> <property name>) NIL), although it is better programming practice to use REMPROP:

```
(remprop <symbol> <property name>)
```

Here is an example:

```
* (setf (get 'bag 'contents) '(bread butter))
(BREAD BUTTER)
* (get 'bag 'contents)
(BREAD BUTTER)
* (remprop 'bag 'contents)
T
* (get 'bag 'contents)
NIL
```

One way to think about a symbol's value is to think of it as a privileged property—one that you get at by evaluating the symbol, rather than by using GET together with a property name.

Problems

Problem 11-1: Assume that if a person's father is known, the father's name is given as the value of the FATHER property. Define GRANDFATHER, a procedure that returns the name of a person's paternal grandfather, if known, or NIL otherwise.

Problem 11-2: Define ADAM, a procedure that returns the most distant male ancestor of a person through the paternal line, working through the FATHER property. If no male ancestor is known, the procedure is to return the name given as its argument. For simplicity, assume that no name is ever used twice.

Problem 11-3: Define ANCESTORS, a procedure that returns a list consisting of the person given as its argument together with all known ancestors of the person. It is to work through both the FATHER and MOTHER properties. You may assume that related people do not have children together; that is, there is never a way to get to any ancestor by two distinct paths.

Problem 11-4: Suppose each city in a network of cities and highways is represented by a symbol. Further suppose that each city has a property named NEIGHBORS. The value of the NEIGHBORS property is a list of all the other cities for which there is a direct highway connection.

Define CONNECT, a procedure that takes two cities as arguments and puts each into a list which is the value of the NEIGHBORS property of the other. Write CONNECT such if a connection is already in place, CONNECT changes nothing and returns NIL; otherwise CONNECT returns T.

Problem 11-5: Suppose that the value of the POSITION property is a list of two coordinates. Assuming a flat earth, write DISTANCE, a procedure that calculates the distance between two cities based on the values of their POSITION properties. Remember that SQRT calculates square roots.

Arrays Enable Storage in Numerically Indexed Places

An *array* is a data type in which expressions are stored in places identified by integer indexes. Consequently, the values associated with an array can be said to be *numerically indexed*.

Here, for example, is a one-dimensional array, which represents four parts bins, each of which hold either nails, nuts, bolts, or washers:

0	1	2	3
nails	nuts	bolts	washers

The NAILS symbol indicates that the first bin, the one with an index of 0, holds nails. The NAILS symbol is said to be an *element* of the array.

Now for an example of a two-dimensional array, consider an array that represents a checkerboard, with 64 places for data, at the beginning of a game. Each element corresponding to a white square holds an X. Each element corresponding to a black square holds a symbol indicating whether the square is empty or filled with a black or white piece. In this example, we use E to abbreviate e̲mpty, B to abbreviate b̲lack, and W to abbreviate w̲hite. The first index for the leftmost black piece is 0 and the second is 1. The first index for the rightmost white piece is 7 and the second is 6:

	0	1	2	3	4	5	6	7
0	X	B	X	B	X	B	X	B
1	B	X	B	X	B	X	B	X
2	X	B	X	B	X	B	X	B
3	E	X	E	X	E	X	E	X
4	X	E	X	E	X	E	X	E
5	W	X	W	X	W	X	W	X
6	X	W	X	W	X	W	X	W
7	W	X	W	X	W	X	W	X

To use arrays, as with all other techniques for storing data, you need to know how to construct them and you need to know how to get data into and out of them. That is, you need to know about the appropriate constructors, readers, and writers.

MAKE-ARRAY, AREF, and SETF are the Custodians of Arrays

To construct an array in the first place, you need to tell LISP how many dimensions it has *and* how large each dimension is. This is done using MAKE-ARRAY; the argument is a list whose length is the number of dimensions and whose elements specify the size of the corresponding dimension:

```
                      The only dimension ranges from 0 to 3.
                                        ↓
* (setf part-bins (make-array '(4)))

                                     First dimension ranges from 0 to 7.
                                                      ↓
* (setf checker-board (make-array '(8 8)))
                                          ↑
                      Second dimension ranges from 0 to 7.
```

When an array has but one dimension, you can abbreviate MAKE-ARRAY's argument, supplying only a number that specifies the size of that dimension, rather than a list of numbers. Here, for example, is an alternate way to set up an array for the parts bins:

The only dimension ranges from 0 to 3.

```
* (setf part-bins (make-array 4))
```

Normally, you want to set up your arrays with initial elements in each of
the array's positions. There are two common ways to do this. One way
is to include an :INITIAL-ELEMENT keyword along with the desired initial
element. In the following examples, each array element in the PART-BINS
form is initialized to E:

```
* (setf part-bins (make-array 4 :initial-element 'e))
#(E E E E)
```

Note that MAKE-ARRAY returns a strange-looking thing. Do not be alarmed.
The strange-looking thing is strange only because it is LISP's way of representing arrays on a screen or on paper.

   Another way of initializing an array is to include an :INITIAL-CONTENTS
keyword along with the desired initial elements wrapped up in an initial-
contents expression. As shown in the following example, the top-level elements of the initial-contents expression are lists of elements. The first list
of elements corresponds to the array elements that have 0 as the first index,
the second corresponds to those that have 1, and so on.

```
* (setf checker-board
        (make-array '(8 8)
                        :initial-contents
                        '((X B X B X B X B)
                          (B X B X B X B X)
                          (X B X B X B X B)
                          (E X E X E X E X)
                          (X E X E X E X E)
                          (W X W X W X W X)
                          (X W X W X W X W)
                          (W X W X W X W X))))
#2A((X B X B ...)
    (B X B X ...)
    (X B X B ...)
    (E X E X ...)
    ...)
```

Again, MAKE-ARRAY returns a strange-looking thing; this time it is LISP's
way of representing multidimensional arrays on a screen or on paper.

   To make use of an array, once it is created, you need to know how to
use reader and writer primitives to get data out of and into the various
array positions, each of which is identified by its numerical indexes.

Let us concentrate on the array assigned to `PART-BINS`, which is a one-dimensional array, with positions from 0 to 3, as established when the array was created.

Like with properties, the form used to retrieve values from an array is part of the form used to store values. Consequently, let us again look at retrieval first. To get at the data in the array assigned to `PART-BINS`, once the data has been inserted, you simply use `AREF`, for <u>a</u>rray <u>ref</u>erence, together with the array and an integer indicating which place you are interested in:

```
* (aref part-bins 0)          ;Expression stored in place 0.
EMPTY

* (aref part-bins 3)          ;Expression stored in place 3.
EMPTY

* (aref checker-board 0 3)    ;Expression stored in place (0 3).
B

* (aref checker-board 3 0)    ;Expression stored in place (3 0).
E
```

Thus `AREF` is the reader procedure for arrays. Now to get fresh data into the array, you deploy `SETF`, along with `AREF`:

```
(setf (aref part-bins 0) 'nails)      ;Store expression in place 0.
(setf (aref part-bins 1) 'nuts)       ;Store expression in place 1.
(setf (aref part-bins 2) 'bolts)      ;Store expression in place 2.
(setf (aref part-bins 3) 'washers)    ;Store expression in place 3.
```

Thus `SETF`, when used with `AREF`, is the writer procedure for arrays. Note that the first argument to `SETF` is the reader form we use to retrieve the array value once it is there.

User-defined array-handling procedures typically count up the elements in an array that satisfy some predicate. For example, the following procedure counts up all the elements of `PART-BINS` that are the same as a given argument:

```
(defun count-bins-with-specified-part (part)
  (let ((result 0))
    (dotimes (n 4 result)
      (when (eq part (aref part-bins n))
        (setf result (+ result 1))))))
```

Hence:

```
* (count-bins-with-specified-part 'washers)
1
```

The next procedure, COUNT-ELEMENTS-WITH-SPECIFIED-PART is more general because it works on any one-dimensional array, not specifically on the array assigned to PART-BINS. Because the given array may be of any length, COUNT-ELEMENTS-WITH-SPECIFIED-PART uses the primitive ARRAY-DIMENSION, which returns a dimension's size, given an array and a dimension, thereby determining the correct upper bound for the counting parameter, N:

```
(defun count-elements-with-specified-part (part array)
  (let ((result 0))
    (dotimes (n (array-dimension array 0) result)
      (when (eq part (aref array n))
        (setf result (+ result 1))))))
```

Note that DOTIMES is extremely popular in procedures that involve looking at the elements in an array.

Problems

Problem 11-6: Write STATIC-VALUE, a procedure that counts the number of white pieces minus the number of black pieces in the CHECKER-BOARD array. Assume ordinary pieces are represented by W and B and kings are represented by W-KING and B-KING. Also assume one king is worth two ordinary pieces.

Summary

- Each way of storing data has constructors, readers, and writers.
- Properties enable storage in symbolically indexed places.
- GET and SETF are the custodians of properties.
- Arrays enable storage in numerically indexed places.
- MAKE-ARRAY, AREF, and SETF are the custodians of arrays.

12

Macros
and Backquote

So far you know how to define ordinary procedures whose arguments are always evaluated. Their purpose has been either to produce a value or to produce useful side effects.

The primary purpose of this chapter is to show how to define *macro procedures*, which do their work in two steps: first, macros use their arguments to build intermediate forms; and second, macros evaluate the intermediate form to produce a value. You can define macro procedures that are easy to work with even though the evaluation of those procedures may involve complicated LISP forms.[1]

A secondary purpose of this chapter is to introduce the *backquote mechanism*, which simplifies programming tasks that can be viewed as filling in templates. In particular, building the intermediate forms of macros often can be viewed as filling in templates, accounting for the popularity of backquoted forms in macro procedures.

---

[1]When a macro is compiled, the intermediate form is *not* evaluated. Instead, the intermediate form is spliced into the place where the macro appears, eliminating the macro call. Thus the intermediate form is computed only once, at the time of compilation, and the macro call disappears. Many programmers take advantage of the compile-time splicing to produce fast-running programs.

Macros Translate and Then Evaluate

So far, you have used DEFUN to define ordinary procedures, which accept arguments and produce a value. Now you will use DEFMACRO to define procedures called *macro procedures*, which have the following characteristics:

- Macros do not evaluate their arguments.
- Evaluating the body of a macro produces a form.
- The form is evaluated to produce a value.

Macros are popular, in part, because they make it possible to have a transparent syntax on the surface and a legal LISP form in the background. The job of the macro is to translate from one to another before starting evaluation:

$$\text{Transparent form} \longrightarrow \text{LISP form} \longrightarrow \text{Value of LISP form}$$

Let us start with a simple example, even though it is a bit contrived. Imagine that you want to print the symbol ALARM whenever a certain variable, PRESSURE, become greater than zero. To do this, suppose you decide to create a new procedure, WHEN-PLUSP, that evaluates its second argument only when its first argument's value is positive:

```
* (setf pressure -3)

* (when-plusp pressure (print 'alarm))    ;Second argument not evaluated.
NIL                                        ;Value returned.

* (setf pressure 3)

* (when-plusp pressure (print 'alarm))    ;Second argument evaluated.
ALARM                                      ;Value printed.
ALARM                                      ;Value returned.
```

Because the second argument to WHEN-PLUSP is to be evaluated when the value of the first argument is positive, WHEN-PLUSP can be viewed as a replacement for a WHEN form:

```
* (setf pressure -3)

* (when (plusp pressure) (print 'alarm))
NIL

* (setf pressure 3)

* (when (plusp pressure) (print 'alarm))
ALARM
ALARM
```

But suppose you try to define WHEN-PLUSP this way:

```
(defun when-plusp-with-bug (number result)        ;Bugged!
  (when (plusp number) result))                   ;Bugged!
```

Because this version of WHEN-PLUSP-WITH-BUG is an ordinary procedure, both of its arguments are always evaluated before the body is evaluated. Therefore the second argument is evaluated no matter what the first argument's value is, whereas the intent is that the second argument is to be evaluated only if the first argument's value is positive.

The difference is not just a matter of efficiency. Because the second argument is a form with a side effect, the use of WHEN-PLUSP-WITH-BUG, as defined, produces a different computation from the WHEN conditional that WHEN-PLUSP-WITH-BUG is intended to replace. The form (WHEN-PLUSP-WITH-BUG PRESSURE (PRINT 'ALARM)) always prints ALARM, even when the value returned is NIL:

```
* (setf pressure -3)
* (when-plusp-with-bug pressure (print 'alarm))
ALARM                                             ;Incorrect value printed!
NIL                                               ;Correct value returned.
* (setf pressure 3)
* (when-plusp-with-bug pressure (print 'alarm))
ALARM                                             ;Correct value printed.
ALARM                                             ;Correct value returned.
```

To avoid the undesired evaluation, you must define WHEN-PLUSP as a macro procedure, rather than as an ordinary procedure. The only difference between the appearance of a macro definition and an ordinary definition is that one uses DEFMACRO and the other uses DEFUN.

```
(defmacro <macro name>
  (<parameter 1> <parameter 2> ... <parameter m>)
  <form 1> <form 2> ... <form n>)
```

Here is how to define WHEN-PLUSP as a macro:

```
(defmacro when-plusp-macro (number result)        ;Name and parameters.
  (list 'when                                     ;Body.
        (list 'plusp number)
        result))
```

When evaluated, the listing and quoting produce an intermediate WHEN form, which then is evaluated. Assuming that PRESSURE's value is positive, the intermediate form leads to the eventual evaluation of the second argument:

```
* (when-plusp-macro pressure (print 'alarm))
```

(when (plusp pressure) (print 'alarm))   ;Given form is translated.

ALARM   ;New form is evaluated.
ALARM

Assuming that PRESSURE's value is negative, the intermediate WHEN form does not lead to the eventual evaluation of the second argument:

```
* (when-plusp-macro pressure (print 'alarm))
```

(when (plusp pressure) (print 'alarm))   ;Old form is translated.

NIL   ;New form is evaluated.

Thus macros exploit the fact that LISP forms are just expressions meant to be evaluated, and consequently, LISP forms can be constructed with the same primitives that generally manipulate LISP expressions.

The Backquote Mechanism Simplifies Template Filling

LISP's backquote mechanism makes it easy to create and to complete templatelike expressions in which only a few, variable, details need to be filled in. The normal quote, ', isolates an entire expression from evaluation. Backquote, `, is not so absolute. Whenever a comma appears inside a backquoted expression, the subexpression immediately following the comma is replaced by its value:

```
* (setf variable 'test)
TEST
* `(THIS IS A ,VARIABLE)
(THIS IS A TEST)
```

Backquote also allows a comma conjoined to an at sign, ,@. This combination unquotes the following expression, just as comma does, but the resulting value must be a list. The elements in this list are *spliced* into the list in which the ,@ appears, rather than *inserted* as an element:

```
* (setf variable '(more difficult example))
(MORE DIFFICULT EXAMPLE)
```

```
* `(this is a ,variable)
(THIS IS A (MORE DIFFICULT EXAMPLE))
* `(this is a ,@variable)
(THIS IS A MORE DIFFICULT EXAMPLE)
```

The Backquote Mechanism Simplifies Macro Writing

Of course, the backquote mechanism is perfect for making and filling macro templates. For example, the WHEN-PLUSP macro can be viewed as filling in the following template:

```
(when (plusp <template slot for number>)
  <template slot for result when number is positive>)
```

Rewriting this template in backquote form produces this:

```
`(when (plusp ,number) ,result)
```

Using a backquote template is usually much better than flailing around a lot with CONS, LIST, APPEND, and the like. Here then is a better way to define WHEN-PLUSP using backquote:

```
(defmacro when-plusp-with-backquote (number result)
  `(when (plusp ,number) ,result))
```

This is better because the backquote template makes it clearer what the form to be evaluated is to look like. Even so, it can still be difficult to understand a macro definition someone else has written or even your own after a while. Consequently, it is good programming practice to include a comment with every macro definition to illustrate what the macro does:

```
(defmacro when-plusp-with-backquote (number result)
  ;; Sample translation:
  ;; (when-plusp-with-backquote p (print 'alarm))
  ;; → (when (plusp p) (print 'alarm))
  `(when (plusp ,number) ,result))
```

Optional, Rest, and Key Parameters Enable More Powerful Macros

You frequently want to define macro procedures that have a variable number of arguments. For example, you might want a version of WHEN-PLUSP that is more like WHEN in that the first argument's value determines if the other arguments are evaluated, the last argument supplies the WHEN-PLUSP form's value, and all other arguments are evaluated for their side effects. To write such macro procedures, you need a way of slurping up an indefinite number of arguments.

Fortunately, macros, like ordinary procedures, can have optional, rest, and even key parameters. For our WHEN-PLUSP problem, an &REST parameter does the job nicely:

```
(defmacro when-plusp-with-rest (number &rest rest)
  `(when (plusp ,number) ,@rest))     ;Splice in extra arguments.
```

Problems

Problem 12-1: Suppose you are an enthusiastic user of GET, but for obscure historical reasons, you do not like to use SETF when working with properties. Create PUT, a macro procedure that takes three arguments, a symbol, a value, and a property name, such that PUT translates

```
(PUT <symbol> <value> <property name>)
```

into

```
(SETF (GET <symbol> <property name>) <value>)
```

Problem 12-2: You decide to create GETQ and PUTQ. Your GETQ is to translate

```
(getq <symbol> <property>)
```

into

```
(get '<symbol> <property>)
```

and PUTQ is to translate

```
(putq <symbol> <property> <value>)
```

into

```
(setf (get '<symbol> property) value)
```

Problem 12-3: Imagine that the designers of LISP had forgotten to include the UNLESS primitive. Irritated, you decide to define your own UNLESS primitive, which you call WHEN-NIL. Define WHEN-NIL such that it translates

```
(when-nil <trigger> <result>)
```

into

```
(when (not <trigger>) <result>)
```

Problem 12-4: Suppose, for some immensely peculiar reason, you want a form of LET that does not evaluate initial value forms. Define LETQ such that LETQ arranges the following translation:

```
(letq ((<variable1> <value1>)
       (<variable2> <value2>)
       ...)
   <body>)
```

↓

```
(let ((<variable1> '<value1>)
      (<variable2> '<value2>)
      ...)
  <body>)
```

Problem 12-5: The DEFUN template is somewhat unfortunate. Some language designers think it is prettier to combine the procedure name with the parameters so that the first argument is a list that resembles a form. Define DEFINE, a macro that uses DEFUN, but has the following template:

```
(define (<procedure name> <parameter 1> . . . <parameter n>)
  <body>)
```

Problem 12-6: Define PUNCTUATE, a procedure that takes any number of arguments. The first argument must be a list. All other arguments are to be gathered up and appended to the end of the first:

```
* (punctuate '(this is an example) 'so 'to 'speak)
(THIS IS AN EXAMPLE SO TO SPEAK)
```

Problem 12-7: Define PUNCTUATE-MACRO, a macro procedure that takes any number of arguments. The first argument must be a list. All other arguments are to be gathered up and appended to the end of the first. The first argument is to be evaluated, but the rest are not:

```
* (punctuate-macro '(this is an example) so to speak)
(THIS IS AN EXAMPLE SO TO SPEAK)
```

Macros Deserve Their Own File

Big programs are usually separated into many files, one of which is devoted to macros. This makes it easier to be sure that the macros are processed first if the LISP program is compiled. You want the macros to be processed first because many compilers assume that all yet-to-be-defined procedures are ordinary procedures, blundering badly whenever one turns out to be a macro.

Summary

- Macros translate and then evaluate.
- The backquote mechanism simplifies template filling.
- The backquote mechanism simplifies macro writing.
- Optional, rest, and key parameters enable more powerful macros.
- Macros deserve their own file.

13

Structures

Beginning programmers often use complicated nested lists to represent data items. Experienced programmers often think in different terms, however. They isolate themselves from low-level details, so as to concentrate on high-level concepts.

The principal purpose of this chapter is to explain how you can isolate yourself from low-level details of data representation by using user-defined data types called *structure types*, which come with automatically created *access procedures*.[1]

Structure Types Facilitate Data Abstraction

The utility of data abstraction through access procedures is so considerable that LISP has elaborate apparatus for automatically creating new data types that are collectively called *structure types*.

You define new structure types, specifying particular *field names* and *default values*. Once you have defined a new structure type, you construct and use instances of that structure type. However, in keeping with the spirit of data abstraction, you are not allowed to look at the way instances

---

[1] Many LISP experts feel that the introduction of classes into COMMON LISP has made structure types obsolescent. They argue that classes, which we describe in chapter 14, provide the same capabilities in a better way.

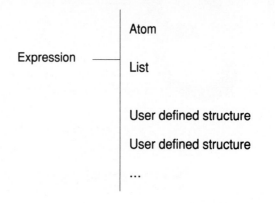

Expression — Atom / List / User defined structure / User defined structure / ...

Figure 13-1. Structure types are part of LISP's data type hierarchy.

of structure types are represented internally, for you are supposed to be isolated from that internal representation. Figure 13-1 shows that your structure types form their own corner of our evolving type hierarchy.

DEFSTRUCT is the primitive that creates new structure types. The following is an example showing what a DEFSTRUCT form looks like. It happens to create the data type named PERSON, with fields for a person's sex and personality:

```
(defstruct person
  (sex nil)                    ;Default value is NIL.
  (personality 'nice))         ;Default value is NICE.
```

Here is the general template for DEFSTRUCT:

```
(defstruct <structure name>
  (<field name 1> <default value 1>)
  (<field name 2> <default value 2>)
  ...
  (<field name n> <default value n>))
```

And here is what is done by DEFSTRUCT forms:

• DEFSTRUCT creates a constructor procedure.
• DEFSTRUCT creates reader procedures for getting things out of an instance's fields.
• DEFSTRUCT generalizes SETF, to serve as writer when used in combination with the readers.
• DEFSTRUCT creates a predicate for testing objects to see if they are instances of the DEFSTRUCT-defined data type.

Again, note that DEFSTRUCT defines new structure types. It *does not* create instances. Instead, DEFSTRUCT automates the creation of a data-constructor procedure, many data-reader procedures, and a data-type predicate, as well as generalizing SETF to handle the new data type.

The name of the constructor procedure created when the DEFSTRUCT form is evaluated is a combination of MAKE- with the structure type's name. In the example, the result is MAKE-PERSON. Here is an example of how the MAKE-PERSON procedure is used:

```
(setf person-instance-1 (make-person))
```

When MAKE-PERSON is evaluated, it constructs a completely new instance whose fields are filled by evaluating the default expressions given when DEFSTRUCT created the PERSON structure type. This leaves PERSON-INSTANCE-1 with one nonNIL field value:

Field	Value	How it Got There
Personality	Nice	Supplied in DEFSTRUCT form.

Note these different purposes of DEFSTRUCT and MAKE-PERSON carefully:

- DEFSTRUCT creates MAKE-PERSON, a instance constructor.
- MAKE-PERSON constructs a particular instance, which happens to be assigned to PERSON-INSTANCE-1.

You can override any default field value by using a field-identifying keyword together with the desired value. As you have seen in other chapters, keywords are prefixed by a colon, as in the following example:

```
(setf person-instance-2 (make-person :sex 'female))
```

This leaves PERSON-INSTANCE-2 with two nonNIL field values:

Field	Value	How it Got There
Sex	Female	Supplied in MAKE-PERSON form.
Personality	Nice	Supplied in DEFSTRUCT form.

Structure Types Enable Storage in Procedurally Indexed Places

You do not need to know how the data in the various fields of an instance are stored because you get your data back using the reader procedures that DEFSTRUCT also creates automatically, along with the constructor. The names of the reader procedures created when the DEFSTRUCT form is evaluated are a combination of the structure type's name and the field name:

```
* (person-sex person-instance-2)
FEMALE
* (person-personality person-instance-2)
NICE
```

Because you get at your data using specially produced reader procedures, the data can be said to be *procedurally indexed*.

Of course you need a way of altering existing field values. DEFSTRUCT takes care of this too. However, it creates no new procedures. Instead, DEFSTRUCT generalizes SETF, so that it works with instance fields. Suppose, for example, that you want to put FEMALE in the SEX field of the PERSON-INSTANCE-1 instance. Here is how:

```
* (setf (person-sex person-instance-1) 'female)
* (person-sex person-instance-1)
FEMALE
```

This leaves PERSON-INSTANCE-1 with these nonNIL field values:

Field	Value	How it Got There
Sex	Female	Supplied in SETF form.
Personality	Nice	Supplied in DEFSTRUCT form.

Again, as with properties and arrays, the first argument to SETF is always an access form that produces the field value, and the second argument supplies the field's replacement value.

Hence there is no new writer procedure; DEFSTRUCT just arranges for the existing SETF writer to be generalized. Thus SETF works with instances of structure types as well as with symbols, properties, and arrays. In fact, SETF's name comes from its use with instances of structure types, as SETF is an acronym for <u>set</u> <u>f</u>ield.

Individual Structure Types Are New Data Types

Each time DEFSTRUCT is used, it creates a new data type. Along with a constructor and many readers for the new data type, DEFSTRUCT creates a data-type predicate. For example, when DEFSTRUCT creates the PERSON data type, it also create PERSON-P, the predicate that tests objects to see if they are instances of the PERSON data type:

```
* (person-p person-instance-1)
T
* (person-p '(this is a list -- not a person instance))
NIL
```

Finally, note that you must anticipate all the fields you want when you use DEFSTRUCT. You cannot use SETF to create a field that was not mentioned when DEFSTRUCT was used. Thus the following is an error for our example:

```
* (setf (person-surname person-instance-1) 'winston)
ERROR
```

Problems

Problem 13-1: Define a structure type for rocks that contains fields for a rock's color, size, and worth. Arrange for the default color to be gray, the default size to be pebble, and the default worth to be nothing.

Problem 13-2: Use MAKE-ROCK, automatically defined in the previous problem, to create a gold nugget, with gold color, default size, and high worth. Assign the instance representing the gold nugget to the symbol HIGH-HOPES.

Problem 13-3: Too bad, your rock turned out to be fool's gold. Modify the instance assigned to HIGH-HOPES such that the worth is nothing. Then make a table showing the values and how the values got there for all the fields in the instance.

One Structure Type Can Include the Fields of Another

We often think of hierarchical relationships in which one thing is a specialization of another. For example, a salesperson is a person who likes to sell products and a hacker is a person who likes to write programs. But in spite of some differences, salespeople and hackers are all employees, which means that salespeople and hackers both have values for the attributes that are common to all employees, like length of service, for example.

Importantly, it is possible to reflect specialization relationships in structure types. Here is how:

```
(defstruct employee
  (length-of-service 0)
  (payment 'salary))

(defstruct (hacker (:include employee))
  (preferred-language 'lisp))
```

In the hacker DEFSTRUCT form, the name of the structure type has been replaced by a list that gives not only the name but also an indication that the structure type is to include fields and default values from the EMPLOYEE structure type. Thus a hacker has a length of service field, with a default value of 0, as all employees do.

```
* (setf employee-example (make-employee))
* (setf hacker-example (make-hacker))

* (employee-length-of-service employee-example)
0
```

```
* (hacker-length-of-service hacker-example)
0
```

Note that the reader procedure prefixed by `EMPLOYEE-` will work on objects that are instances of the specialized structure type.

```
* (employee-length-of-service hacker-example)
0
```

In addition to a `LENGTH-OF-SERVICE` field, hackers have a `PAYMENT` field, with a default value of `SALARY`, as well as a `PREFERRED-LANGUAGE` field, with a default value of `LISP`, which exists in `HACKER` instances only:

```
* (employee-payment hacker-example)
SALARY
```

```
* (hacker-preferred-language hacker-example)
LISP
```

You can arrange for one structure type to include another with one or more of the fields repeated in both. In such cases, the default in the more specialized structure type takes precedence and is said to *shadow* the default in the more general, included structure type. In the following `SALESPERSON` structure type, for example, the peculiar extension to the `:INCLUDE` mechanism indicates that salespeople, like all employees, have payment fields, but unlike other employees, the default value is `COMMISSION`, not `SALARY`.

```
(defstruct (salesperson (:include employee (payment 'commission)))
  (preferred-car 'mercedes))

* (setf salesperson-example (make-salesperson))

* (employee-payment hacker-example)
SALARY

* (employee-payment salesperson-example)
COMMISSION
```

Problems

Problem 13-4: Define a structure type for studs of the kind that houses are built of, with default size of `2X4`, a default length of `8`, and a default strength of `MEDIUM`. Then define a structure type for oak studs in terms of ordinary studs. Indicate that the strength of oak studs is high.

Structure Types Are Important Components of Big Systems

At first thought, it might seem that a firm resolve to stick with just association lists or just properties would offer many of the same advantages as a commitment to structure types. Structure types are superior in the following ways, however:

- The access procedures for instances are efficient.

There is no need to walk down a long list, looking for a match to a symbolic index. Instead, LISP implementers go to great lengths to make sure that DEFSTRUCT produces efficient instance constructors, readers, and writers.

- The fields of a structure type are defined, once and for all.

No one can add or subtract fields on whim in obscure corners of a big program, making the program proportionately hard to comprehend as a whole. Many programmer teams arrange for all structure types to be defined in a central file, heavily commented.

DESCRIBE Prints Descriptions

Earlier, we said that you are supposed to access an instance only via its access procedures; you are not supposed to know how an instance is represented internally. Occasionally, however, you want to look at what is in an instance while you are debugging. Accordingly, the DESCRIBE primitive prints descriptive information in an implementation-specific way, as in the following examples:

```
* (describe person-instance-1)
It is a Named Instance of type PERSON.
   Its field names and values are:
   SEX - FEMALE
   PERSONALITY - NICE

* (describe person-instance-2)
It is a Named Instance of type PERSON.
   Its field names and values are:
   SEX - FEMALE
   PERSONALITY - NICE
```

DEFSTRUCTs Deserve Their Own File

Big, multiply-authored programs are usually separated into many files, one of which is usually devoted to heavily commented DEFSTRUCTs. Such a file is like a bulletin board in that the authors use it to post conventions for the data their programs work on and exchange.

Summary
- Structure types facilitate data abstraction.
- Structure types enable storage in procedurally indexed places.
- Individual structure types are new data types.
- One structure type can include the fields of another.
- Structure types are important components of big systems.
- `DESCRIBE` prints descriptions.
- `DEFSTRUCT`s deserve their own file.

14

Classes
and Generic
Functions

The principal purpose of this chapter is to introduce the object-oriented programming paradigm, explaining that you may think either in terms of procedures and what they do to objects or in terms of objects and what gets done to them.

Thinking in terms of objects leads to the introduction of the CLOS primitives, where CLOS is an acronym for COMMON LISP Object System.[1] CLOS primitives make it possible to define *generic functions*, which are families of procedures called *methods*.

What to Do Depends on What You Do it to

No doubt about it, the way you do something strongly depends on what you are doing it to:

● The way you eat a meal depends on whether it is a hamburger or chateaubriand.

● The way you move a stone depends on whether it is a pebble or a boulder.

---

[1] People argue about how CLOS should be pronounced. Some like to pronounce it so that it sounds a bit like the word *Claus* in *Santa Claus*. Others prefer a pronunciation that sounds like *sea loss*.

- The way you read a book depends on whether it is a children's reader or a mathematical treatise on quantum electrodynamics.

- The way you play middle C on an instrument depends on whether it is a piano or a clarinet.

You Can Make Ordinary Procedures Data Driven, Albeit Awkwardly

Suppose, to take a simple example, that you define structure types for certain planar figures:

```
(defstruct triangle
  (base 0)
  (altitude 0))

(defstruct rectangle
  (width 0)
  (height 0))

(defstruct circle
  (radius 0))
```

Now suppose you want a procedure that calculates areas. Here is one way to define it, using the data-type predicates automatically generated by DEFSTRUCT:

```
(defun area (figure)
  (cond ((triangle-p figure)
         (* 1/2
            (triangle-base figure)
            (triangle-altitude figure)))
        ((rectangle-p figure)
         (* (rectangle-width figure)
            (rectangle-height figure)))
        ((circle-p figure)
         (* pi (expt (circle-radius figure) 2)))))
```

Although there is nothing really wrong with AREA, as defined, the approach invites problems later on when you want to cover more and more figures. Definitions will grow to multiple pages, and you will be unable to resist the temptation to start nesting the conditionals in an attempt to pull similar things together, as in the following caricature, in which we treat squares separately:

```
(defun area (figure)
  (cond ((triangle-p figure)
         (* 1/2
            (triangle-base figure)
            (triangle-altitude figure)))
        ((rectangle-p figure)
         (let ((a (rectangle-width figure))
               (b (rectangle-height figure)))
           (if (= a b)
               (expt a 2)
               (* a b ))))
        ((circle-p figure)
         (* pi (expt (circle-radius figure) 2)))))
```

Eventually, your procedure will be difficult to understand and impossible to debug. Looking for a way out, you might define individual procedures for dealing with each kind of figure:

```
(defun triangle-area (figure)
  (* 1/2
     (triangle-base figure)
     (triangle-altitude figure)))
(defun rectangle-area (figure)
  (* (rectangle-width figure)
     (rectangle-height figure)))
(defun circle-area (figure)
  (* pi (expt (circle-radius figure) 2)))
```

But because you will never remember all the procedure names, you are forced to define AREA again, with some improvement through shortening:

```
(defun area (figure)
  (cond ((triangle-p figure)
         (triangle-area figure))
        ((rectangle-p figure)
         (rectangle-area figure))
        ((circle-p figure)
         (circle-area figure))))
```

Now the definition of AREA is broken up into manageable subprocedures and AREA itself just funnels its argument to the appropriate subprocedure.

What you really want, however, is an automatic mechanism that knows how to retrieve the appropriate data-type specific version of AREA. Although you can write retrieval procedures by hand, you would prefer to have all that detail handled for you automatically.

Methods Are Procedures Selected from Generic Functions by Argument Types

Fortunately, you can, in fact, break up definitions into pieces, each of which is applied automatically when arguments of particular types are involved. Each piece is called a *method*; each collection of methods that share the same name is called a *generic function*.[2]

Methods are defined in a manner similar to procedures, with two exceptions: first, DEFMETHOD is used instead of DEFUN; and second, the parameter list is generalized so that you can stipulate which data types the method is to be associated with. Here, for example, are the one-parameter methods for computing area:

```
(defmethod area ((figure triangle))        ;Method for triangles.
  (* 1/2
     (triangle-base figure)
     (triangle-altitude figure)))

(defmethod area ((figure rectangle))       ;Method for rectangles.
  (* (rectangle-width figure)
     (rectangle-height figure)))

(defmethod area ((figure circle))          ;Method for circles.
  (* pi (expt (circle-radius figure) 2)))
```

Note that each of the three AREA methods has the same name. Together, the three methods constitute the AREA generic function.

Note also that the parameter, FIGURE, that appeared in earlier DEFUN forms, has been replaced, for example, by (FIGURE TRIANGLE), an expression that not only names the parameter, but also specifies that the method is used only when the FIGURE parameter is bound to a TRIANGLE instance. In this context, the TRIANGLE data type is called a *parameter specializer*.

Hence the first of the three AREA methods is applied only when AREA forms appear in which the argument is a triangle; in general, each AREA method is applied only when an AREA form is evaluated in which the argument matches the parameter specializer:

```
* (setf triangle (make-triangle :base 2 :altitude 3))
* (setf rectangle (make-rectangle :width 5 :height 7))
* (setf circle (make-circle :radius 11))

* (area triangle)          ;Matches triangle method.
3
```

---

[2]We would, of course, prefer to use the term *generic procedure*, rather than the term *generic function*, because generic functions can have side effects, making the use of *function* a bit at odds with mathematical convention. We march with computer scientists, however, not mathematicians.

```
* (area rectangle)              ;Matches rectangle method.
35

* (area circle)                 ;Matches circle method.
380.13
```

The examples so far are narrow in two ways: first, the example parameter specializers are all structure types, whereas in fact many other data types can be parameter specializers; and second, the example methods have only one parameter, whereas in fact they can have any number, just like ordinary procedures.

Nevertheless, you can begin to understand two perspectives on programming. One, the *data-driven perspective*, is built around the idea that each combination of argument types determines which version of a procedure to use. From the data-driven perspective, AREA is a family of methods and AREA's argument determines which of those methods is used.

Another perspective, the *object-oriented perspective*, is built around the idea that a data type should be thought of as a bundle of procedures in addition to a bundle of data-type objects. From the object-oriented perspective, structure types like TRIANGLE, RECTANGLE, and CIRCLE are hooks on which to hang the various methods that make up AREA and other generic functions.

Note, however, that the object-oriented perspective is a natural perspective for AREA because the methods in AREA have just one parameter. Thinking in terms of the object-oriented perspective is a little less natural with the examples in subsequent sections, however, because the methods have more than one specialized parameter. Nevertheless, it remains traditional to refer to the kind of programming enabled by generic functions and methods as *object-oriented programming*.

Classes Resemble Structure Types but Resonate Better with Generic Functions

Although we have introduced the generic function idea using structure types, they are really meant to go with *classes*, a related, yet importantly different family of data types.

Because both classes and structure types have fields and field values, the definition of a class resembles the definition of a structure type, but when working with classes, you must be much more specific about what you want. DEFSTRUCT does a lot by default; DEFCLASS does little by default, as suggested by the following DEFCLASS template. Note that when working with classes the convention is to use the word *slot* rather than *field*:

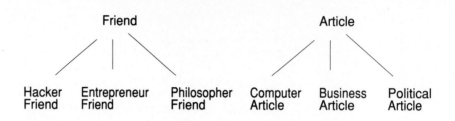

Figure 14-1. The basic ARTICLE and FRIEND class hierarchy. ARTICLE is a superclass of COMPUTER-ARTICLE, BUSINESS-ARTICLE, and POLITICAL-ARTICLE, each of which is a subclass of ARTICLE.

```
(defclass <class name> <list of direct superclasses> ;Basic template.
  (((<slot name 1> :accessor <accessor procedure 1>
                   :initform <initial-value form 1>
                   :initarg <argument marking symbol 1>)
   ...
   (<slot name n> :accessor <accessor procedure n>
                  :initform <initial-value form n>
                  :initarg <argument marking symbol n>)))
```

We must explain several things about the DEFCLASS template, starting with the list of direct superclasses. Classes are usually arranged in hierarchies, like those illustrated in figure 14-1.[3] When you can reach one class by walking up a series of connections, the lower class is called a *subclass* of the upper one, and the upper one is called a *superclass* of the lower one. It is also common to say that a class is more *specialized* than any of its superclasses.

The connections are called *inheritance links* because each class inherits slots from its superclasses. Two classes are said to be *directly connected* when they are connected together via a single inheritance link rather than through a chain of inheritance links. The superclass is a *direct superclass* of the subclass, and the subclass is a *direct subclass* of the superclass. You record hierarchy information in each class definition by including a list of direct superclasses just after the name of the class itself.

Now we turn to the slot specifications. Normally, you want to be able to both read and write slot values. Accordingly, you are expected to supply a name that is used directly as a reader and indirectly as a writer when combined with SETF. In the vocabulary of CLOS, these names are called *accessors*.

---

[3]Of course structure types can be arranged in hierarchies too, but you must use the :INCLUDE syntax, which we consider awkward and ugly compared with the parentheses syntax that is always part of a class definition.

Note that the slot specifications appear in a list, and each slot specification may have an initial-value form. If it does, it must be explicitly marked as an initial-value form by the keyword :INITFORM.

One important difference between classes and structure types is that you make new instances with the primitive MAKE-INSTANCE, along with the class name, rather than with a more specifically named constructor. Here is the template:

```
(make-instance '<class name>)
```

When you use MAKE-INSTANCE, each initial-value form is evaluated, producing initial values for their corresponding slots. Alternatively, you can specify a slot value in a MAKE-INSTANCE form. You must anticipate such occasions, however, by supplying an argument-marking symbol when the class is defined. The argument-marking symbol, usually a keyword, is marked by the keyword :INITARG as in the following example in which the ARTICLE class is defined with :TITLE and :AUTHOR as argument-marking symbols:

```
(defclass article ()
  ((title :accessor article-title :initarg :title)
   (author :accessor article-author :initarg :author)))
```

Note that ARTICLE has no direct superclasses, as the list of direct superclasses is empty. Each slot is to have an initial value supplied when instances are created, and each slot has an accessor procedure.

As we work through an example, you see that the only purpose of the article class is to serve as a slot-defining superclass for other classes. In particular, the accessor procedures are actually methods that are available when working with any subclass of the article class as defined here:

```
(defclass computer-article (article) ())

(defclass business-article (article) ())

(defclass political-article (article) ())
```

Plainly, all three classes are subclasses of the article class. None of the three has any slots other than those inherited from the article class along with accessor methods for those inherited slots.

Any Nonoptional Argument's Class Can Help Select a Method

Many methods have only one parameter specializer, but there is no restriction to just one; the particular method to be applied can be determined by as many nonoptional arguments as you like.

Suppose, for example, that you want to build a program that monitors events, generates messages, and routes those messages to appropriate people. Or, to take a suggestive, albeit whimsical example, suppose you want to notify your friends about journal articles that you think they will be interested in.

Our example involves the ARTICLE class and its three direct subclasses, all already defined. It also involves a FRIEND class, which has three direct subclasses:

```
(defclass friend ()
  ((name :accessor friend-name :initarg :name)))
(defclass hacker-friend (friend) ())
(defclass entrepreneur-friend (friend) ())
(defclass philosopher-friend (friend) ())
```

Now that we have eight classes, arranged in two hierarchies, suppose you have recently read three worthy articles, one of each kind. As with structure types, you override default slot values by using a slot-identifying keyword together with the desired value:

```
(setf articles
      (list (make-instance 'business-article
                           :title "Memory Prices Down")
            (make-instance 'computer-article
                           :title "Memory Speeds Up")
            (make-instance 'political-article
                           :title "Memory Impugned")))
```

Further suppose you have four friends:

```
(setf friends
      (list (make-instance 'hacker-friend :name 'Dan)
            (make-instance 'hacker-friend :name 'Gerry)
            (make-instance 'entrepreneur-friend :name 'Philip)
            (make-instance 'philosopher-friend :name 'David)))
```

Now you could write a procedure to iterate through your friends and your articles, sending computer mail to each about each. But because there is no standardized COMMON LISP mail interface, we limit the example to printing a reminder on your terminal.

First we define an ordinary procedure for printing. Note that the double quote marks, ", in the format string are preceded by backslashes.

The reason is that double quote marks normally terminate strings, so any that are to appear inside the string have to be marked somehow, and the backslash is, by convention, the marking character:

```
(defun print-notification (article friend)
  (format t "~%Tell ~a about \"~a.\""
          (friend-name friend)
          (article-title article))
  t)
```

Next we use PRINT-NOTIFICATION inside nested DOLISTs:

```
* (dolist (friend friends)
    (dolist (article articles)
      (print-notification article friend)))
Tell DAN about "Memory Prices Down."
Tell DAN about "Memory Speeds Up."
Tell DAN about "Memory Impugned."
Tell GERRY about "Memory Prices Down."
Tell GERRY about "Memory Speeds Up."
Tell GERRY about "Memory Impugned."
Tell PHILIP about "Memory Prices Down."
Tell PHILIP about "Memory Speeds Up."
Tell PHILIP about "Memory Impugned."
Tell DAVID about "Memory Prices Down."
Tell DAVID about "Memory Speeds Up."
Tell DAVID about "Memory Impugned."
NIL
```

But of course you do not want to annoy your friends with a lot of electronic mail about articles they are not interested in. Accordingly, you decide to make use of the following table of interests, somehow:

	Business	Politics	Computers
Hackers			√
Entrepreneurs	√		
Philosophers	√	√	√

To use the table, you decide to write methods for PROCESS, a generic function that takes two arguments, one for the friend and the other for the article. Once those methods are written, you can substitute PROCESS for PRINT-NOTIFICATION in the nested DOLISTs:

```
(dolist (friend friends)
  (dolist (article articles)
    (process friend article)))
```

Now hackers like computer articles and entrepreneurs like business articles, so there should be PROCESS methods to reflect those interests, both of which use PRINT-NOTIFICATION to actually do the printing:

```
(defmethod process ((friend hacker-friend)
                     (article computer-article))
  (print-notification article friend))

(defmethod process ((friend entrepreneur-friend)
                     (article business-article))
  (print-notification article friend))
```

Note, incidentally, that all of our PROCESS methods have exactly the same number of parameters. This is not a coincidence: CLOS prescribes that only nonoptional parameters can be specialized and that all of the methods associated with a particular generic function must have the same number of parameters.

Classes Enable Method Inheritance

According to the table relating articles to friends, philosophers read everything. You could, of course, handle them with three distinct methods, one for each of the article types, but there is a better approach that involves a method whose second parameter, ARTICLE, is specialized to the ARTICLE class instead of one of its subclasses:

```
(defmethod process ((friend philosopher-friend)
                     (article article))
  (print-notification article friend))
```

Now a method is said to be an *applicable method*, given a particular call to a generic function, if the arguments involved are the same as the classes of the corresponding parameter specializers or subclasses of those parameter specializers. Thus the preceding PROCESS method is an applicable method with respect to any form in which the first argument belongs to the PHILOSOPHER-FRIEND class and in which the second argument belongs to the ARTICLE class or any of ARTICLE's subclasses.

Finally, to complete the generic function, you need a method that prints nothing when applied in all other friend-and-article situations:

```
(defmethod process ((friend friend)
                      (article article)))
```

This method is an applicable method whenever there is no other more specific method whose first argument belongs to a subclass of the FRIEND class and whose second argument belongs to a subclass of the ARTICLE class. Without this method, uninteresting articles would cause errors because there would be no method that would know what to do with them.

Note, incidentally, that there is a class named T that is an implicit superclass of all other classes. Thus you could cover all friends and articles with an alternative method whose parameters are specialized to T:

```
(defmethod process ((friend t)
                      (article t)))
```

If you wish, you can exploit a convention: when a parameter appears alone, without a parameter specializer, it is as if the parameter specializer were T. Accordingly, the following alternative method is equivalent to the previous method:

```
(defmethod process (friend article))
```

Note, however, that some programmers do not like to make a method more generally applicable than it has to be in normal operation. That way, if an unexpectedly general argument appears, a no-applicable-method error is signaled. Other programmers feel that using specialization for argument type checking is questionable programming practice.

Finally, you can get a better feel for how the parameter specializers of our methods are related to the class hierarchy by examining figure 14-2.

Among the applicable methods, only one is usually applied, and it is said to be the applicable method that *takes precedence* over all the other applicable methods. The procedure for determining which method takes precedence over all the other applicable methods is explained in a subsequent section. For the example developed in this section, the precedence procedure returns the method specialized to ARTICLE and FRIEND only if none of the other methods are applicable.

With these four methods forming the PROCESS generic function, your iteration prints only the appropriate reminders:

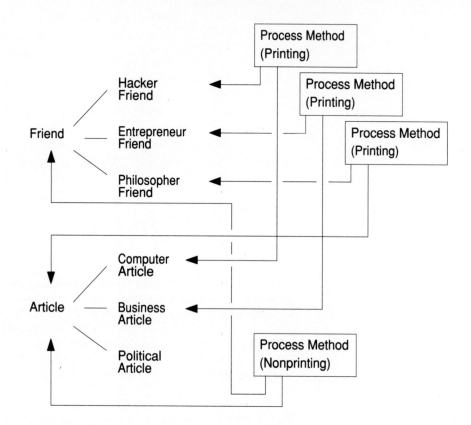

Figure 14-2. The basic FRIEND and ARTICLE class hierarchies, rearranged on the page so as to fit in four methods that form the PROCESS generic function. Arrows connect methods to the classes identified by their parameter specializers.

```
* (dolist (friend friends)
    (dolist (article articles)
      (process friend article)))
Tell DAN about "Memory Speeds Up."
Tell GERRY about "Memory Speeds Up."
Tell PHILIP about "Memory Prices Down."
Tell DAVID about "Memory Prices Down."
Tell DAVID about "Memory Speeds Up."
Tell DAVID about "Memory Impugned."
NIL
```

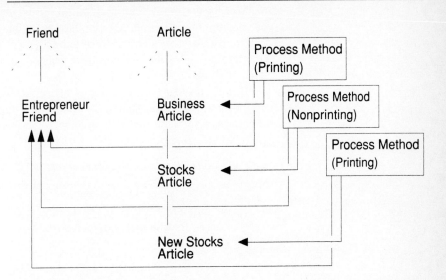

Figure 14-3. STOCKS-ARTICLE and NEW-STOCKS-ARTICLE extend the basic ARTICLE and FRIEND class hierarchy, and two new methods extend the PROCESS generic function. Arrows connect methods to the classes identified by their parameter specializers. If an article is known to be about new stocks, the entrepreneur friends are notified about it, as they would be if an article were just known to be a business article. The entrepreneur friends are not notified, however, about articles on stocks, an intermediate class.

Problems

Problem 14-1: Suppose you learn that philosophers do not like computer articles. Write one new method that prevents you from sending them notices about computer articles without preventing any other notices from getting through.

Problem 14-2: Now suppose all of your friends are interested in music. Create a new class of article for music and write a PROCESS method that tells everyone about them without disturbing anything else.

The Most Specific Method Takes Precedence over the Others

Suppose, as shown in figure 5-1, that one kind of business article is the stocks article and one kind of stocks article is the new-stocks article. We say that new-stocks articles constitute a direct subclass of the stocks articles and a subclass of both the stocks articles and the business articles. Conversely, the business articles are a direct superclass of the stocks articles and a superclass of both the stocks articles and the new stocks articles.

You have already seen an example in which you are reminded to tell your entrepreneur friends about business articles. And because stocks articles and new-stocks articles are subclasses of business articles, you are reminded to tell your entrepreneur friends about any article defined in terms of those classes as well.

But if you like, you can define other methods, with more specialized parameter specializers, that are applied only for the stocks or new-stocks subclasses, displacing methods associated with superclasses. First you define those subclasses:

```
(defclass stocks-article (business-article) ())
(defclass new-stocks-article (stocks-article) ())
```

Next, you indicate that your entrepreneur friends are not interested in stocks articles, for the method specialized to stocks articles does nothing:

```
(defmethod process ((friend entrepreneur-friend)
                     (article stocks-article)))
```

And if you want to be really fancy, you can add still another method, this time indicating that while your entrepreneur friends may not be interested in stocks articles in general, they are interested in new-stocks articles:

```
(defmethod process ((friend entrepreneur-friend)
                     (article new-stocks-article))
  (print-notification article friend))
```

You can test these two new methods as follows:

```
* (process
    (make-instance 'entrepreneur-friend :name 'jack)
    (make-instance 'stocks-article :title "Stock Prices Up"))
NIL
* (process
    (make-instance 'entrepreneur-friend :name 'jill)
    (make-instance 'new-stocks-article
                   :title "New-Stock Prices Up"))
Tell JILL about "New-Stock Prices Up."
T
```

Parameter Order Helps Determine Method Precedence

Now to make method selection a bit more intricate, suppose we define a subclass of HACKER-FRIEND, along with two new methods, one of which uses the new subclass as a parameter specializer and does no notification:

```
(defclass retired-hacker-friend (hacker-friend) ())
```

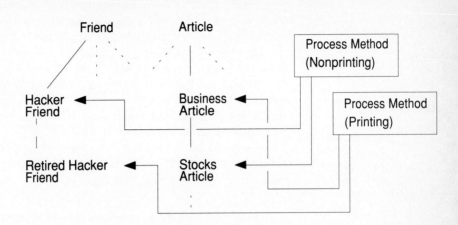

Figure 14-4. `RETIRED-HACKER-FRIEND` extends the growing `FRIEND` and `ARTICLE` class hierarchy, and two new methods extend the `PROCESS` generic function. Arrows connect methods to the classes identified by their parameter specializers. Both new methods have parameter specializers that are either the same as or subclasses of hacker friends and business articles. The one that prints a message takes precedence when `PROCESS` is applied to a retired hacker friend and a stocks article because it has a more specific specializer for the first argument.

```
(defmethod process ((friend retired-hacker-friend)
                    (article business-article))
  (print-notification article friend))

(defmethod process ((friend hacker-friend)
                    (article stocks-article)))
```

The first of the new `PROCESS` methods, which prints a reminder, is specialized by `RETIRED-HACKER-FRIEND` and `BUSINESS-ARTICLE` and the second, which prints nothing, is specialized by `HACKER-FRIEND` and `STOCKS-ARTICLE`. As shown in figure 14-4, the first of the new methods is more specialized, relative to the second method if you consider only the first parameter, and less specialized if you consider only the second parameter.

Which method, then, is the right one for retired hackers and stocks articles, as in the following test case:

```
(process
  (make-instance 'retired-hacker-friend :name 'test-friend)
  (make-instance 'stocks-article :title "Test Article"))
```

When there is more than one applicable method, the one that takes precedence is determined by a left-to-right comparison of the corresponding parameter specializers in the applicable methods. As comparison proceeds, any method whose parameter specializer is less specific than another method's parameter specializer is eliminated. Comparison proceeds until there is only one survivor.

In our example, three methods could be applied, the two new ones plus the one that was defined with FRIEND and ARTICLE as parameter specializers. The one that is applied is the one specialized by RETIRED-HACKER-FRIEND and BUSINESS-ARTICLE, not the one specialized by HACKER-FRIEND and STOCKS-ARTICLE, and not the one specialized by FRIEND and ARTICLE. The reason is that among the first-parameter specializers, RETIRED-HACKER-FRIEND, HACKER-FRIEND, and FRIEND, RETIRED-HACKER-FRIEND is clearly the most specific. Hence, the following is printed:

```
* (process
    (make-instance 'retired-hacker-friend :name 'test-friend)
    (make-instance 'stocks-article :title "Test Article"))
Tell TEST-FRIEND about "Test Article."
T
```

But this is still a simple example because each class has only one superclass. Unlike structure types, classes can have any number of superclasses.

Simple Rules Approximate the Complicated Class Precedence Algorithm

Suppose we create a new kind of article that is about the use of computers in politics:

```
(defclass computer-political-article
  (computer-article political-article)
  ())
```

Recall that a method has been defined already that deals explicitly with hacker friends and computer articles:

```
(defmethod process ((friend hacker-friend)
                    (article computer-article))
  (print-notification article friend))
```

Now suppose you define another method that deals explicitly with hacker friends and political articles:

```
(defmethod process ((friend hacker-friend)
                    (article political-article)))
```

Will you be reminded to tell your hacker friends about such articles? One argument is that you will be, on the ground that you do tell them about computer articles; another argument is that you will *not* be, on the ground that you do *not* tell them about political articles.

Framing the problem in terms of a test case, the question is whether or not anything is printed by the following form:

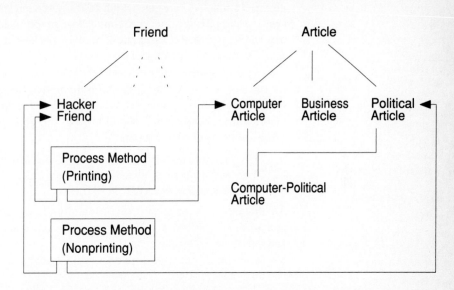

Figure 14-5. COMPUTER-POLITICAL-ARTICLE extends the FRIEND and ARTICLE class hierarchy once again. A hierarchy-walking procedure determines that the PROCESS method that prints a message takes precedence over the one that does not.

```
(process
  (make-instance 'hacker-friend :name 'test-friend)
  (make-instance 'computer-political-article
                 :title "Computer Politics Article Test"))
```

The answer must be determined by the class hierarchy. Looking first at the first argument, we find three applicable methods, two of which are specialized to HACKER-FRIEND and the general method that is specialized to FRIEND. Plainly HACKER-FRIEND is more specific than FRIEND so the general method is eliminated from consideration.

Next, the first parameter of both surviving methods is specialized to FRIEND so the second parameter must be examined to decide between them. The relevant part of the class hierarchy is shown in figure 14-5, in which the inheritance links emerging from the COMPUTER-POLITICAL-ARTICLE class are arranged left-to-right in the same order that they appear in the DEFCLASS form for the COMPUTER-POLITICAL-ARTICLE class.

Evidently, two surviving PROCESS methods have parameter specializers that are superclasses of the argument classes. One has specializers HACKER-FRIEND and COMPUTER-ARTICLE, and the other has specializers HACKER-FRIEND and POLITICAL-ARTICLE.

Because both COMPUTER-ARTICLE and POLITICAL-ARTICLE are in the class hierarchy above COMPUTER-POLITICAL-ARTICLE, their relative positions in the hierarchy must determine which takes precedence over the other. In general, the applicable method that takes precedence over the others is the one whose parameter specializer appears earliest in what is called the *class precedence list*.

The procedure that determines the class precedence list does its job by walking about in the class hierarchy above the argument's class according to a complicated algorithm explained in the appendix. Although that algorithm is complicated, the following, increasingly refined rules give the same result in most situations:

- The depth-first rule: Whenever possible, the hierarchy-walking procedure walks upward, away from the argument's class, adding classes to the class precedence list as it goes.

To illustrate, we digress from friends and articles to deal with the less concrete, but appropriately varied hierarchies shown in figure 14-6. For the particularly simple situation shown on the left in figure 14-6, there are no classes with multiple superclasses. Consequently, the depth-first rule is the only rule needed.

- The left-to-right rule: A class with more than one superclass is called a *split*. Whenever the hierarchy-walking procedure encounters a split, it explores the hierarchies above the split in left-to-right order.

For the situation shown in the middle in figure 14-6, there is one split, but there are no classes that can be reached in more than one way. Consequently, the depth-first rule and the left-to-right rule are the only rules needed. All the classes above the leftmost direct superclass are added to the precedence list first; next come the classes above the middle direct superclass; and finally the classes above the rightmost direct superclass.

- The up-to-join rule: A class that can be reached in more than one way from the argument's class is called a *join*. When a join is encountered for the first time, the hierarchy-walking procedure stops, without adding the join to the precedence list. Similarly, when a join is encountered again, it stops, unless the join is encountered for the last time. When a join is encountered for the last time, the hierarchy-walking procedure adds that join to the precedence list and continues on through.

For the situation shown on the right in figure 14-6, there is a join that can be reached in three ways. Consequently, the depth-first rule, the left-to-right rule, and the up-to-join rule are all needed. The join acts as a dead end until the last time the hierarchy-walking procedure encounters it, whereupon the join is added to the precedence list and the hierarchy-walking procedure continues on through.

In CLOS class hierarchies, the class STANDARD-OBJECT is considered to be an implicit superclass of all DEFCLASS-defined classes. Similarly, T is

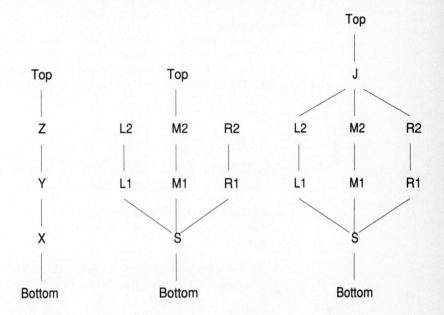

Figure 14-6. Three precedence-ordering situations. On the left, the procedure that determines the class precedence list walks straight up the hierarchy, producing the class precedence list Bottom-X-Y-Z-Top. In the middle, there is a place where there are multiple superclasses, a split, producing the class precedence list Bottom-S-L1-L2-M1-M2-R1-R2. On the right, there is both a split and a join, producing the class precedence list Bottom-S-L1-L2-M1-M2-R1-R2-J-Top.

considered to be an implicit superclass of `STANDARD-OBJECT` and many of LISP's ordinary data types.

Thus in our `COMPUTER-POLITICAL-ARTICLE` example, the class precedence list is as follows:

```
computer-political-article     ; Split
computer-article               ; Leftmost superclass.
political-article              ; Rightmost superclass.
article                        ; Join
standard-object                ; Implicit superclass.
t                              ; Implicit superclass.
```

Consequently, the method whose second parameter specializer comes first in the class precedence list is the one specialized by `COMPUTER-ARTICLE`,

not the one specialized by POLITICAL-ARTICLE. Thus we have the following
result:

```
* (process
    (make-instance 'hacker-friend :name 'test-friend)
    (make-instance 'computer-political-article
                   :title "Computer Politics Article Test"))
Tell TEST-FRIEND about "Computer Politics Article Test."
T
```

Problems

Problem 14-3: Suppose you define a class for articles about the politics
of computers, the POLITICAL-COMPUTER-ARTICLE class:

```
(defclass political-computer-article
  (political-article computer-article)
  ())
```

What does the class precedence list look like for the second argument when
evaluating the following form? Is anything printed?

```
(process
  (make-instance 'hacker-friend :name 'test-friend)
  (make-instance 'computer-political-article
                 :title "Computer Political Article Test"))
```

**Methods Can Be
Specialized to
Individual Instances**

So far, our examples have involved methods that are specialized to classes.
Occasionally, you may want to be even more specific, specializing a method
to a particular instance.

Suppose, for example, that your friend Philip is far too busy to be
notified about any articles. To ensure that Philip is never notified, you substitute the expression (EQL ⟨instance for Philip⟩) into a PROCESS method
in the place where you have used a class name before. The instance for
Philip happens to be the third element in the FRIENDS list:

```
(setf philip (third friends))
(defmethod process ((friend (eql philip))
                    (article article)))
```

This new PROCESS method takes precedence over all other PROCESS methods because an EQL specialized method is more specific than any class-
specialized method. As the method does no notification, Philip will never
hear about anything.

Problems

Problem 14-4: Suppose that there is a particular article that you want to include in your list of articles, but you do not want to tell anyone about it:

```
(setf special-case-article
      (make-instance 'business-article :title "Squashing Friends"))
```

Next you create the following method:

```
(defmethod process ((friend friend)
                     (article (eql special-case-article))))
```

To your surprise, however, notifications about the article are still sent. Why?

Method Selection Involves Three Steps

In this chapter, you have learned about which methods are applicable methods and about how to pick out the applicable method that takes precedence over all the others. The procedures involved actually do more than pick out one method; they produce a complete precedence ordering for all applicable methods. Here is a summary:

- A method is said to be an *applicable method*, given a particular call to a generic function, if the arguments involved are instances of the classes that are the method's parameter specializers or subclasses of those parameter specializers.

- Using the class hierarchy above the first argument, the class precedence algorithm is used to establish the precedence ordering. Three simple rules produce the same result as the class precedence algorithm in most situations.

- If two or more applicable methods have the same specializer for the first parameter, leading to a precedence tie, then their precedence order is determined by using the hierarchy-walking procedure together with the class hierarchies above other arguments. The other arguments are used in left-to-right order until there are no remaining ties.

We explain the utility of a complete precedence ordering later on, in chapters 21 and 22, where we show how many methods, not just one, may be used when a particular generic function is called.

Object-Oriented Programming Offers Advantages, Not Magic

As you have seen, object-oriented programming with classes, methods, and generic functions does the following for you:

- The appropriate data-type specific versions of your procedures are retrieved automatically.

- Procedures are reused automatically. Rather than duplicating a procedure for each class it applies to, you arrange your classes in a class hierarchy such that a single method can handle all the appropriate instances. This is useful for small programs and rapidly becomes essential as programs grow large.

Later on, in chapter 21, you learn that object-oriented programming also enables procedures to be assembled automatically from bits and pieces.

None of this is magic, of course. You could, in principle, do everything by hand without object-oriented programming. But with object-oriented programming, as embodied in CLOS, you avoid a great deal of dull and error-prone work.

Thus you should think of object-oriented programming as a critically important productivity-increasing tool, one that is used constantly by advanced LISP programmers. You should also understand that many object-oriented programming ideas and many CLOS primitives lie beyond what we have introduced in this chapter. Chapters 21 and 22 introduce some of those methods and primitives, yet still provide only an introduction.

Summary

- What to do depends on what you do it to.
- You can make ordinary procedures data driven, albeit awkwardly.
- Methods are procedures selected from generic functions by argument types.
- Classes resemble structure types but resonate better with generic functions.
- Any nonoptional argument's class can help select a method.
- Classes enable method inheritance.
- The most specific method takes precedence over the others.
- Parameter order helps determine method precedence.
- Multiple superclasses require sophisticated precedence computations.
- Methods can be specialized to individual instances.
- Method selection involves three steps.
- Object-oriented programming offers advantages, not magic.

References   For a complete treatment of the COMMON LISP Object System, see *Object-Oriented Programming in COMMON LISP*, by Sonya E. Keene.

Much of the enthusiasm for object-oriented programming in LISP can be traced to an unpublished paper by Howard I. Cannon [1982] and to the subsequent introduction of classlike objects, called flavors, into various versions of LISP.

15

Lexical Variables
Generators
and Encapsulation

The principal purpose of this chapter is to explain how one procedure can be defined inside another, making it possible to find a value for a variable even if it is not a parameter of the procedure that the variable appears in. The effect is a tight coupling between procedures and the subprocedures that are defined inside them.

A secondary purpose of this chapter is to explain another way to arrange for the fences of one procedure to appear inside the fences of another using *lexical closures*. This enables instances of free variables to be *encapsulated*, severely restricting access to their bindings.

Encapsulation, in turn, makes it possible to define sophisticated *generator procedures* that produce new values each time they are called even though they have no arguments.

Note that some programming athletes use the ideas in this chapter extensively; others do not. Some consider the ideas to be fundamental; others think of them as special purpose. In any event, the ideas are subtle, so be prepared to slow down.

LETs Produce
Nested Fences

In chapter 3, we explained that nested fences are produced when a **LET** form appears inside a procedure definition. In this section, we explain how parameter variable values are retrieved when fences are nested. To illustrate, we use the same BOTH-ENDS-WITH-LET procedure introduced in chapter 3:

```
(defun both-ends-with-let (whole-list)
  (let ((leading (first whole-list))           ;Bind LEADING.
        (trailing (first (last whole-list))))  ;Bind TRAILING.
    (list leading trailing)))                  ;Combine.
```

Now imagine that each fence has a gate and a gatekeeper. The gatekeeper maintains a list of the variables on the parameter list of the procedure. BOTH-ENDS-WITH-LET has one parameter, WHOLE-LIST, which its gatekeeper keeps track of. The LET form inside of BOTH-ENDS-WITH-LET has two parameters, LEADING and TRAILING, which its gatekeeper keeps track of:

```
BOTH-ENDS-WITH-LET's fence
    Gatekeeper's list: WHOLE-LIST


        LET's fence
            Gatekeeper's list: LEADING, TRAILING
```

Note that every variable instance that appears inside the LET's fence must also appear inside BOTH-ENDS-WITH-LET's fence, because the LET's fence is inside BOTH-ENDS-WITH-LET's fence.

Now suppose (BOTH-ENDS-WITH-LET '(BREAKFAST LUNCH TEA DINNER)) is to be evaluated. LISP first builds a fence around the body of the BOTH-ENDS-WITH-LET procedure and then sets up a list of parameter variables and variable values for the fence's gatekeeper:

```
BOTH-ENDS-WITH-LET's fence
    Gatekeeper's list:
    WHOLE-LIST's value is (BREAKFAST LUNCH TEA DINNER)
```

While evaluating the body of the BOTH-ENDS-WITH-LET procedure, LISP encounters a LET form, whereupon LISP evaluates the LET's initial-value forms:

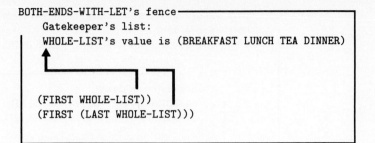

Once the initial-value forms are evaluated, the LET's fence is established, the parameters are bound, and the LET's body form is evaluated:

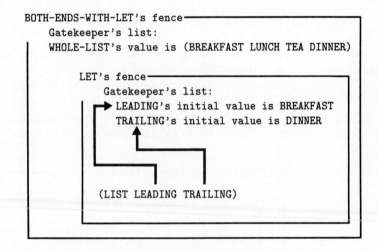

Sometimes parameters appear alone, with no initial value forms. Such parameters have NIL assigned to them as initial values. Thus the following variant of BOTH-ENDS also works:

```
(defun both-ends-with-funny-let (whole-list)
  (let (leading trailing)                    ;Bind both to NIL.
    (setf leading (first whole-list))        ;Assign new value.
    (setf trailing (first (last whole-list))) ;Assign new value.
    (list leading trailing)))                ;Combine.
```

Once the LET form in BOTH-ENDS-WITH-FUNNY-LET has been encountered, we have these fences and parameter bindings:

```
BOTH-ENDS-with-funny-let's fence
    Gatekeeper's list:
    WHOLE-LIST's value is (BREAKFAST LUNCH TEA DINNER)

       LET's fence
           Gatekeeper's list:
               LEADING's initial value is NIL
               TRAILING's initial value is NIL
```

Nested Fences Provide Variable Values

Each time the LISP evaluation machinery seeks a variable's value, the evaluator asks the surrounding fence's gatekeeper about the variable. If the gatekeeper has the variable on his list, he hands over the value. Otherwise, he lets the LISP evaluator move on to the next fence's gatekeeper. Accordingly, when WHOLE-LIST is encountered inside the LET's fence, LISP must move outside the LET's fence to find a value:

```
BOTH-ENDS-with-funny-let's fence
    Gatekeeper's list:
    WHOLE-LIST's value is (BREAKFAST LUNCH TEA DINNER)

       LET's fence
           Gatekeeper's list:
               LEADING's initial value is NIL
               TRAILING's initial value is NIL



           (SETF LEADING (FIRST WHOLE-LIST))
           (SETF TRAILING (FIRST (LAST WHOLE-LIST)))
```

On the other hand, once LEADING and TRAILING get their new values, those new values are found inside the LET's fence:

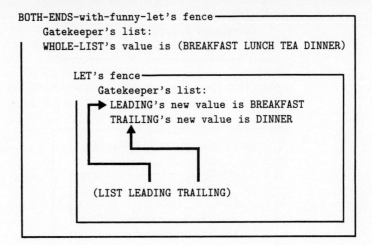

Procedure Calls Usually Do Not Produce Nested Fences

Now let us consider the fences created when one procedure calls another. A procedure's fence surrounds only those variables that appear *explicitly* in the corresponding body of the procedure. Consider these procedures, for example:

```
(defun both-ends-with-helpers (whole-list)
  (list (front-end whole-list) (back-end whole-list)))
```

```
(defun front-end (m)
  (first m))
```

```
(defun back-end (n)
  (first (last n)))
```

The variable WHOLE-LIST appears in BOTH-ENDS-WITH-HELPERS's body; M and N do not. Thus BOTH-ENDS-WITH-HELPERS's fence surrounds WHOLE-LIST, but not M or N:

```
BOTH-ENDS-WITH-HELPERS
    Gatekeeper's list: WHOLE-LIST
```

```
FRONT-END
    Gatekeeper's list: M
```

```
BACK-END
    Gatekeeper's list: N
```

Note that the fences for FRONT-END and BACK-END do not appear inside the fence for BOTH-ENDS-WITH-HELPERS. The following diagram is *incorrect*:

```
BOTH-ENDS-WITH-HELPERS                          Wrong!
    Gatekeeper's list: WHOLE-LIST               Wrong!
                                                Wrong!
        FRONT-END                               Wrong!
            Gatekeeper's list: M                Wrong!
                                                Wrong!
                                                Wrong!
        BACK-END                                Wrong!
            Gatekeeper's list: N                Wrong!
                                                Wrong!
                                                Wrong!
                                                Wrong!
```

Thus one procedure's fence does not include variables from another procedures fence just because one calls the other.

Problems

Problem 15-1: For the following version of BOTH-ENDS, show what the fence diagram looks like at the point where (LIST LEADING TRAILING) is evaluated, given that the argument is (BREAKFAST LUNCH TEA DINNER). Be sure to indicate where the values for LEADING and TRAILING will be found.

```
(defun both-ends-with-nesting (whole-list)
  (let ((leading (first whole-list)))
    (let ((trailing (first (last whole-list))))
      (list leading trailing))))
```

Problem 15-2: Explain what LISP will do, given the following procedures, on the given test case:

```
(defun both-ends (whole-list)
  (list (front-end) (back-end)))
(defun front-end ()
  (first whole-list))
(defun back-end ()
  (first (last whole-list)))
* (both-ends '(breakfast lunch tea dinner))
```

Nested Definitions do Produce Nested Fences

The LABELS primitive enables you to define one procedure inside another. By an odd convention, this determines that the fences built for the two procedures will be nested, just as the fences for nested LET forms are nested. Such nesting allows LISP to find values for free variables, if any, in the inner procedure. Here is a template for one simple use of LABELS:

```
(defun <procedure name> <parameters>
  (labels (<embedded procedure definition>)
    <body of labels>))
```

And here is an example of the template in use:

```
(defun first-of-first-with-labels (l)
  (labels ((aux (m) (first m)))      ;Embedded LABELS definition.
    (first (aux l))))
```

FIRST-OF-FIRST-WITH-LABELS produces the following result:

```
* (first-of-first-with-labels '((a b) (c d)))
A
```

Given the definition of FIRST-OF-FIRST-WITH-LABELS, with the AUX procedure embedded inside LABELS, the fence built for AUX lies inside of the fence built for LABELS, which in turn lies inside the fence for FIRST-OF-FIRST-WITH-LABELS:

```
FIRST-OF-FIRST-WITH-LABELS
     Gatekeeper's list: L

    LABELS
         Gatekeeper's list: AUX

       AUX
           Gatekeeper's list: M
```

Thus LABELS is analogous to LET in that both LABELS and LET arrange for fences to be thrown up.

The key difference between LABELS and LET is that the gatekeepers for LABELS fences keep track of procedure names, not symbol values. Procedures defined in LABELS forms cannot be used outside of the corresponding LABELS fence.

The nesting produced by LABELS matters a great deal when there are free variables to be handled. To see why, consider the following definition, in which AUX does not have M as a parameter:

```
(defun first-of-first-with-funny-labels (l)
  (labels ((aux () (first l)))
    (first (aux))))
```

Happily, because AUX is part of a LABELS form, FIRST-OF-FIRST-WITH-FUNNY-LABELS's gatekeeper provides L's value, even inside AUX, as shown:

```
FIRST-OF-FIRST-WITH-FUNNY-LABELS
    Gatekeeper's list: L

    LABELS
        Gatekeeper's list: AUX

        AUX
            Gatekeeper's list:
```

Now for a more realistic example, suppose the purpose of INSIDE is to determine if a symbol appears anywhere inside a nested expression. The following definition of INSIDE has INSIDE-AUX embedded in it via LABELS:

```
(defun inside (x e)
  (labels
    ((inside-aux (e)                              ;Name and parameters.
       (cond ((atom e) (eq x e))                  ;Body of INSIDE-AUX.
             ((endp e) nil)                        ;Body of INSIDE-AUX.
             (t (or (inside-aux (first e))         ;Body of INSIDE-AUX.
                    (inside-aux (rest e)))))))     ;Body of INSIDE-AUX.
    (inside-aux e)))                               ;Body of LABELS.
```

The fences are as follows. Note that although there are many recursive calls to INSIDE-AUX, each of which requires a new fence, the fences for INSIDE-AUX do *not* nest inside each other:

```
INSIDE's fence
     Gatekeeper's list: X, E

   LABELS
       Gatekeeper's list: INSIDE-AUX

     Fence for first call to INSIDE-AUX
         Gatekeeper's list: E



     Fence for second call to INSIDE-AUX
         Gatekeeper's list: E



     ...
```

Note also that LISP can find values for each instance of X and E:

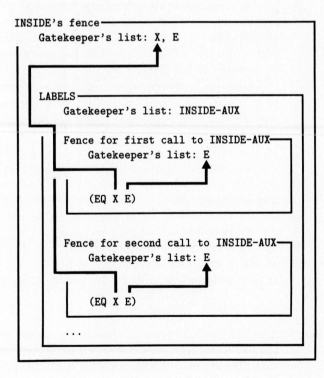

```
INSIDE's fence
     Gatekeeper's list: X, E



   LABELS
       Gatekeeper's list: INSIDE-AUX

     Fence for first call to INSIDE-AUX
         Gatekeeper's list: E


       (EQ X E)


     Fence for second call to INSIDE-AUX
         Gatekeeper's list: E


       (EQ X E)

     ...
```

Here is the general template for `LABELS`:

```
(labels
  (((<first embedded procedure name>
      <first embedded procedure's parameters>
      <body of first embedded procedure>)
   (<second embedded procedure name>
      <second embedded procedure's parameters>
      <body of second embedded procedure>)
   ...)
  <body of labels>)
```

Again, note that the embedded procedures are available only inside the `LABELS`'s body. If used elsewhere, LISP complains.

Thus `LABELS` is a way of defining one procedure inside another. We emphasize that it is useful to define one procedure inside another, with `LABELS`, because of the following convention:

- If the definition of a procedure `OUTER-PROCEDURE` contains a definition for a procedure `INNER-PROCEDURE`, then the fences thrown up for `INNER-PROCEDURE` will appear inside the fences thrown up for `OUTER-PROCEDURE`.

We have explained that the responsibility of a procedure or `LET`'s gatekeeper extends only to the variable symbols that appear *explicitly* in the body of the procedure or `LET` form. Similarly, the responsibility of a `LABELS`'s gatekeeper extends only to the procedure-name symbols that appear *explicitly* in the body of the `LABELS` form.

Such explicitly-appearing variables and procedure names are said to be in the *lexical scope* of the gatekeeper. Because scoping has to do with variables and procedure names that appear explicitly in the written form of each procedure, `LET`, and `LABELS`, the phrase *textual scoping* would be better than the phrase *lexical scoping*, but we are stuck with tradition.

The variables and procedure names that appear on a gatekeeper's list are always lexical variables and lexical procedure names. Lexical variables and procedure names are said to be bound by the corresponding procedure, `LET`, or `LABELS` form. It is more precise to say that those variables and procedure names are *lexically bound*.

Of course, variables can be bound lexically by `LET*`, `DO`, and `DO*` forms as well as by procedures and `LET` forms. We deal only with procedures and `LET` forms in our examples to shorten our explanation.

Generators Produce Sequences

This section introduces *generator procedures*, which are procedures that produce a sequence of related values as they are used. For example, suppose that the purpose of `POWER-OF-TWO` is to deliver powers of two, starting with $2^1 = 2$.

```
* (power-of-two)
2

* (power-of-two)
4

* (power-of-two)
8
```

Evidently, POWER-OF-TWO is a generator that keeps track of which power of two is to be returned next.

Now we define POWER-OF-TWO in a simple way in preparation for defining it in a more sophisticated way. First, we use SETF to assign a value to PREVIOUS-POWER-OF-TWO:

```
(setf previous-power-of-two 1)
```

PREVIOUS-POWER-OF-TWO appears inside the POWER-OF-TWO generator:

```
(defun power-of-two ()
  (setf previous-power-of-two (* previous-power-of-two 2)))
```

Because PREVIOUS-POWER-OF-TWO is *not* on POWER-OF-TWO's parameter list, it is a special variable. We introduced special variables in chapter 3, and we discuss special variables in more detail in chapter 16. For now, you need only remember that special variables are not isolated by virtual fences. Consequently, PREVIOUS-POWER-OF-TWO's value outside POWER-OF-TWO can be referenced and reset inside POWER-OF-TWO, enabling the POWER-OF-TWO generator to do the right thing:

```
* (power-of-two)        ;PREVIOUS-POWER-OF-TWO's value is 1.
2

* (power-of-two)        ;PREVIOUS-POWER-OF-TWO's value is 2.
4

* (power-of-two)        ;PREVIOUS-POWER-OF-TWO's value is 4.
8
```

Because PREVIOUS-POWER-OF-TWO keeps the POWER-OF-TWO generator procedure on track, remembering the previous value produced, PREVIOUS-POWER-OF-TWO is said to be a *state variable*.

There is nothing really wrong with using special variables as state variables. However, some programmers dislike having the state variable exposed. In principle, other procedures could alter it inadvertently. Also, in principle, there could be more than one power-of-two generator, each of which would require its own previous-power-of-two variable. Consequently, it would be nice to encapsulate the state variable so that only one procedure can get at it.

Nameless Procedures Produce Nested Fences

In chapter 6, we explained that nameless procedures, defined by lambda expressions, frequently occur in transforming and filtering forms. For example, the following transformation squares all the numbers in a list using a nameless squaring procedure:

```
(defun square-all-elements (list-of-numbers)
  (mapcar #'(lambda (n) (* n n))
          list-of-numbers))
* (square-all-elements '(1 2 3))
(1 4 9)
```

Now because the nameless procedure is defined inside the definition of SQUARE-ALL-ELEMENTS, the fences thrown up for the nameless procedure appear inside those thrown up for SQUARE-ALL-ELEMENTS:

```
SQUARE-ALL-ELEMENTS's fence ─────────────────────────
    Gatekeeper's list: LIST-OF-NUMBERS

    Nameless procedure's fence───────────────────
        Gatekeeper's list: N
```

Thus one key property of nameless procedures is that the fences thrown up for a nameless procedure lie inside the fences thrown up for any procedure that contains the lambda-defined nameless procedure.

Nameless Procedures Can Be Assigned to Variables

Another key property of nameless procedures is that they can be assigned to variables and the variables can appear wherever the nameless procedure can. For example, the squaring procedure can be assigned to the variable SQUARE-PROCEDURE:

```
* (setf square-procedure #'(lambda (n) (* n n)))
* (mapcar square-procedure '(1 2 3))
(1 4 9)
```

Similarly, a nameless procedure can be assigned to a variable and we can use the variable in a FUNCALL form instead of the nameless procedure itself:

```
* (setf square-procedure #'(lambda (n) (* n n)))
* (funcall square-procedure 2)
4
```

**The Free Variables
in Nameless
Procedures Can Be
Encapsulated**

Now we can define a nameless procedure that computes powers of two, rather than squares, assigning the nameless procedure to the variable POWER-OF-TWO:

```
(setf power-of-two
  #'(lambda ()
      (setf previous-power-of-two (* previous-power-of-two 2))))
```

Because there is no surrounding expression in which PREVIOUS-POWER-OF-TWO is a parameter, LISP takes it to be a special variable. Once we give PREVIOUS-POWER-OF-TWO an initial value, we can produce a sequence of powers of two by using POWER-OF-TWO's value in funcall forms:

```
* (setf previous-power-of-two 1)
1
* (funcall power-of-two)
2
* (funcall power-of-two)
4
* (funcall power-of-two)
8
```

Now suppose we evaluate a LET form in which PREVIOUS-POWER-OF-TWO is a parameter:

```
(let ((previous-power-of-two 1))
  ...)
```

Plainly, PREVIOUS-POWER-OF-TWO becomes the responsibility of the LET's gatekeeper:

```
LET's fence ───────────────────────────────────────────
    Gatekeeper's list: PREVIOUS-POWER-OF-TWO

│
```

If we could just arrange for the fences for our nameless procedure to be built inside such a LET's fence, then the value for PREVIOUS-POWER-OF-TWO would be determined by the LET's gatekeeper.

Now recall that when a lambda-defined, nameless procedure appears inside another expression with parameters, then the fences for the nameless procedure are thrown up inside the fences for the surrounding parameter-containing form. Thus we need to insert our nameless procedure definition inside our LET form. Note that the nameless, lambda-defined procedure is returned when the LET form is evaluated, becoming assigned to the POWER-OF-TWO variable as before:

```
(setf power-of-two
      (let ((previous-power-of-two 1))
        #'(lambda ()
            (setf previous-power-of-two
                  (* previous-power-of-two 2)))))
```

Now the fences for the nameless procedure appear inside the fence for the
LET:

```
LET's fence
     Gatekeeper's list: PREVIOUS-POWER-OF-TWO

     Lambda-defined procedure's fence
        Gatekeeper's list is empty

        (setf previous-power-of-two
              (* previous-power-of-two 2))
```

Each time the nameless procedure is used, the binding for PREVIOUS-POWER-
OF-TWO maintained by the LET gatekeeper's fence is accessed and changed:

```
* (funcall power-of-two)
2

* (funcall power-of-two)
4

* (funcall power-of-two)
8
```

Encapsulation Enables the Creation of Sophisticated Generators

Thus the sophisticated way to create generators is to encapsulate free
variables in lambda definitions by embedding the lambda definition in a
parameter-containing form.

Now that we have explained how this lambda-based encapsulation is
done, you can of course produce multiple POWER-OF-TWO generators:

```
(setf g1
      (let ((previous-power-of-two 1))
        #'(lambda ()
            (setf previous-power-of-two
                  (* previous-power-of-two 2)))))
```

```
(setf g2
    (let ((previous-power-of-two 1))
      #'(lambda ()
          (setf previous-power-of-two
                (* previous-power-of-two 2)))))
```

Note, however, that such generators have no names. Rather, they are assigned to variables, and they must be called using FUNCALL, an arbitrary and somewhat clumsy convention. Thus G1 and G2 cannot be used in procedure position because they are not defined procedures; rather, their values are procedures:

```
* (g1)
ERROR
```

In summary, you can encapsulate the free variables in a lambda definition by placing the lambda definition inside a form in which the free variables appear as parameters. In our example, the LET form encapsulates an instance of the PREVIOUS-POWER-OF-TWO variable. Only the lambda-defined, nameless procedure appearing in the LET can use and change the binding associated with that particular instance of PREVIOUS-POWER-OF-TWO.

But what if you want to reset PREVIOUS-POWER-OF-TWO's encapsulated variable? One way, albeit clumsy, is to return two procedures from the LET expression, not just one. In the following example, the LET returns not only a next-value procedure but also a reset procedure:

```
(setf procedures
    (let ((previous-power-of-two 1))
      (list #'(lambda ()
                (setf previous-power-of-two 1))
            #'(lambda ()
                (setf previous-power-of-two
                      (* previous-power-of-two 2))))))
(setf power-of-two-reset (first procedures)
      power-of-two-value (second procedures))
```

Now both procedures can be deployed:

```
* (funcall power-of-two-value)
2

* (funcall power-of-two-value)
4

* (funcall power-of-two-reset)
1
```

```
* (funcall power-of-two-value)
2
```

The better, more elegant way to give more than one procedure access to an encapsulated variable is to add a so-called *dispatch procedure* whose job is to dig up the procedure that you really want from inside a fence. Here is the general idea:

- Inside a LET form, you create several lambda-defined procedures, each of which you assign to a variable.

- Inside the same LET form, you create another lambda-defined procedure, the dispatch procedure, that takes one procedure-identifying argument. The dispatch procedure is the only thing returned from the LET form.

- The dispatch procedure's value is to be the procedure identified by the procedure-identifying argument.

Examine the following example in preparation for more explanation:

```
(setf generator-with-dispatch-procedure
  (let ((previous-power-of-two 1)
        (reset-procedure
          #'(lambda ()
              (setf previous-power-of-two 1)))
        (value-procedure
          #'(lambda ()
              (setf previous-power-of-two
                    (* previous-power-of-two 2)))))
    ;;The dispatch procedure:
    #'(lambda (accessor)
        (cond ((eq 'reset accessor) reset-procedure)
              ((eq 'value accessor) value-procedure)))))
```

Because the lambda-defined procedures all appear inside the LET form, their fences are all thrown up inside the LET's fence. Hence the dispatch procedure has access to the values of RESET-PROCEDURE and VALUE-PROCEDURE, both of which have procedures assigned to them. Hence the following form's values are procedures whose fences are thrown up inside the LET's fence:

```
(funcall generator-with-dispatch-procedure 'reset)
(funcall generator-with-dispatch-procedure 'value)
```

To use these procedures, you simply embed them in another FUNCALL form:

```
* (funcall (funcall generator-with-dispatch-procedure 'value))
2
* (funcall (funcall generator-with-dispatch-procedure 'value))
4
* (funcall (funcall generator-with-dispatch-procedure 'reset))
1
* (funcall (funcall generator-with-dispatch-procedure 'value))
2
```

Many purists consider it unfortunate that COMMON LISP allows symbols to be attached to both a procedure and a value. In SCHEME, a LISP dialect widely used to teach programming concepts, only one thing can be assigned to a symbol, and that thing can be either a procedure or a value. Consequently, once a procedure is assigned to a symbol, that symbol can appear in a form's procedure position, and there is no need for any analog to FUNCALL. This makes for prettier forms in the dispatch example:

```
* ((generator-with-dispatch-procedure 'value))    ;SCHEME version.
2
* ((generator-with-dispatch-procedure 'value))    ;SCHEME version.
4
* ((generator-with-dispatch-procedure 'reset))    ;SCHEME version.
1
* ((generator-with-dispatch-procedure 'value))    ;SCHEME version.
2
```

Generators Can Be Defined by other Procedures

Rather than make multiple generators by hand, it is better to create a generator-defining procedure:

```
(defun make-power-of-two-generator ()
  (let ((previous-power-of-two 1)
        (reset-procedure
          #'(lambda ()
              (setf previous-power-of-two 1)))
        (value-procedure
          #'(lambda ()
              (setf previous-power-of-two
                    (* previous-power-of-two 2)))))
    ;;The dispatch procedure:
    #'(lambda (accessor)
        (cond ((eq 'reset accessor) reset-procedure)
              ((eq 'value accessor) value-procedure)))))
```

Now POWER-OF-TWO generators are easier to define:

```
(setf g1 (make-power-of-two-generator))
(setf g2 (make-power-of-two-generator))
```

Both G1 and G2 have PREVIOUS-POWER-OF-TWO variables protected by their own LET fences, now embedded inside MAKE-POWER-OF-TWO-GENERATOR fences.

Nameless Procedures Become Lexical Closures

Procedure objects produced by a combination of #' and lambda are called *lexical closures*. The reason the term *lexical closure* is used because the word *closure* suggests that fences are involved and because the word *lexical* suggests that the fences are placed according to the rules of lexical scoping. In our generator examples, the fences built for the lambda-defined procedures appear inside the fences built for the LETs because the lambda expressions appear inside the LETs.

Because there is no convenient printed form for the fence information, the printed form of a lexical closure looks, obscurely enough, something like #<LEXICAL CLOSURE ...>.

Note that a lambda expression, by itself, is not a procedure object. Consequently, a lambda expression cannot be applied until it becomes part of a closure. Until that transformation occurs, there is no information about where to build a fence when the lambda-defined procedure is used.

Summary

- LETs produce nested fences.
- Nested fences provide variable values.
- Procedure calls usually do not produce nested fences.
- Nested definitions do produce nested fences.
- Generators produce sequences.
- Nameless procedures produce nested fences.
- Nameless procedures can be assigned to variables.
- The free variables in nameless procedures can be encapsulated.
- Encapsulation enables the creation of sophisticated generators.
- Generators can be defined by other procedures.
- #' makes nameless procedures into lexical closures.

References

For an excellent treatment of generators and lexical encapsulation, see *Structure and Interpretation of Computer Programs*, by Harold Abelson and Gerald Jay Sussman.

16

Special Variables

The principal purpose of this chapter is to explain how LISP finds values for *special variables* using a *stack*. In chapters 3 and 15, you learned about lexical variables and how LISP finds their values using fences and gatekeepers. Although most variables in LISP are lexical, rather than special, it is important to understand both.

Bindings Could Be Kept on a Record of Calls

You have seen that LISP normally assumes that variables are lexical variables and uses the virtual-fence approach to look for their values. In this section, you learn about another approach that LISP uses to find variable values that does not use fences. Consider these definitions:

```
(defun first-of-first1 (l)
  (first (auxiliary1 l)))
(defun auxiliary1 (l)
  (first l))
```

With these definitions, there is an L on the gatekeeper's list for both FIRST-OF-FIRST1 and AUXILIARY1. LISP has no difficulty finding a value for L inside AUXILIARY1's fence:

```
FIRST-OF-FIRST1's fence              AUXILIARY1's fence
    Gatekeeper's list: L                 Gatekeeper's list: L
```

Now consider the following alternative definitions in which `AUXILIARY2` has no `L` on its parameter list:

```
(defun first-of-first2 (l)
  (first (auxiliary2)))

(defun auxiliary2 ()
  (first l))
```

With these definitions, if LISP were to use virtual fences, LISP would not find `L`'s value when needed. `L`'s value is kept by a gatekeeper inside a different fence:

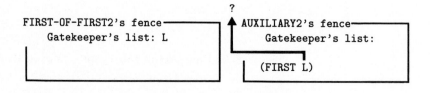

Here is the result produced:

```
* (first-of-first2 '((a b) (c d)))
ERROR
```

Now we use these two versions of `FIRST-OF-FIRST` to learn about another way that LISP finds variable values. First, imagine that LISP keeps a complete record of how procedures and `LET`s and `DO`s call one another. Here is what the record of calls looks like after `FIRST-OF-FIRST1` calls `AUXILIARY1`:

```
FIRST-OF-FIRST1 ──────────────────▶ AUXILIARY1
```

Instead of fences and gatekeepers, LISP can be instructed, in a manner we explain in the next section, to attach bindings for programmer-designated parameters to the record of calls. Here is what happens when both `FIRST-OF-FIRST1` and `AUXILIARY1` have an `L` on their parameter list:

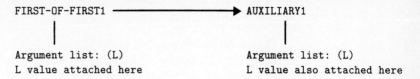

Using a record of calls, LISP finds a value for a variable by walking upward until it locates a place where the variable's binding has been attached. As shown, the value of L required in FIRST-OF-FIRST1 is found immediately in FIRST-OF-FIRST1, and the value of L required in AUXILIARY1 is found immediately in AUXILIARY1.

Now consider the example involving FIRST-OF-FIRST2 and AUXILIARY2, assuming that LISP has been instructed to attach the binding for L to the record of calls:

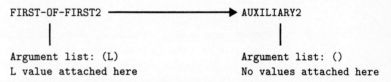

Because AUXILIARY2 does not have an L on its parameter list, L's value, required in AUXILIARY2, is not found associated with AUXILIARY2. Consequently, LISP walks up the record of calls, finding L's value associated with FIRST-OF-FIRST2. Now our test form evaluates properly:

```
* (first-of-first2 '((a b) (c d)))
A
```

If LISP walks all the way up the record of calls without finding an attached binding, then lisp looks for a *global value*, established, for example, by a SETF form. In a subsequent sections, we introduce the DEFVAR primitive and explain that it too can establish global values.

Some Variables Are Declared To Be Special Forevermore

Because LISP assumes, by default, that variables are to be handled by fence gatekeepers, you must tell LISP about any variables that you want to be handled in a different, nonstandard way.

As we explained briefly in chapter 3, one way to tell LISP that a variable instance is to be a *special variable*, handled without the use of gatekeepers, is to use the variable in a place where no gatekeeper can supply a value. Note, however, that this effects only the variable instance involved and does not arrange for variable bindings to be placed on the record of calls.

To force a variable's bindings to be placed on the record of calls, you must be more explicit. You use the primitive DEFVAR, as in the following example:

```
(DEFVAR L)
```

Once a variable is named in a DEFVAR form, it is a *special variable* wherever it subsequently appears. If a declared special variable appears on a parameter list, LISP knows it must attach bindings to the record of calls, not to a gatekeeper's list. Similarly, if a declared special variable appears in a form, LISP knows it must look for its value on the record of calls, not on a gatekeeper's list.

Now note the following terminology: a variable is said to have a *special binding* whenever that variable's binding is attached to the record of calls; a variable is said to have a *lexical binding* whenever that variable's binding is placed on a gatekeeper's list. Variables normally have lexical bindings; variables have special bindings if they have been declared to be special by DEFVARs.

Plainly the purpose of DEFVAR forms is to tell LISP do something in a special way, not to produce a value. Such forms are called *declarations*. Declarations must appear before the procedures that depend on them. Most programmers usually put all declarations at the beginning of their programs, constituting a sort of program preface.

Also, many programmers use asterisks at the beginning and end of variables that are declared to be special. That way, whenever such a variable appears as a parameter, it is clear that its value is to be found on the record of calls, not on a gatekeeper's list. Asterisks are not required, however. We use asterisks only when we want it to be particularly plain that a variable has been declared special.

Special-Variable Bindings Are Actually Kept on a Stack

For a further illustration of how LISP handles special variables, consider the following definitions of INSIDE and INSIDE-AUX, two procedures that determine if a given atom appears inside a given expression at any level. Note that *X* is declared special before either of the two procedures is defined:

```
(defvar *x*)
(defun inside (*x* e)              ;*X* is specially bound,
  (inside-aux e))                  ;E is lexically bound.

(defun inside-aux (e)              ;E is lexically bound.
  (cond ((atom e) (eq *x* e))      ;Instance of *X*.
        (t (or (inside-aux (first e))
               (inside-aux (rest e))))))
```

Here is the record of calls for (INSIDE 'A '(A B)) at the moment when A is found and recursion stops:

```
INSIDE ──────────▶ INSIDE-AUX ──────────▶ INSIDE-AUX
```

In the first call to INSIDE-AUX, LISP must find a value for *X*. To do so, it walks up the record of calls one level, finding a value for *X* in INSIDE. In the second call to INSIDE-AUX, LISP must walk up the record of calls two levels, to INSIDE again.

Now consider the record of calls for (INSIDE 'B '(A B)):

```
INSIDE ──▶ INSIDE-AUX ──┬──▶ INSIDE-AUX
                        └──▶ INSIDE-AUX ──▶ INSIDE-AUX
```

Now INSIDE-AUX is invoked four times before the B is dug out of (A B). In each case, the value of *X* is obtained by following the record of calls up to INSIDE, where *X* is specially bound.

So far, the records of calls that we have seen contain procedure calls only. But instances of LET, LET*, DO, and DO* all appear on the record of calls along with instances of procedures. Thus variables can be specially bound by instances of LET, LET*, DO, and DO* as well as by procedures.

Actually, to find special-variable values, LISP needs only part of the record of calls. Consider the record of calls involved in finding a value for (INSIDE 'B '(A B)):

```
INSIDE ──▶ INSIDE-AUX ──┬──▶ INSIDE-AUX
                        └──▶ INSIDE-AUX ──▶ INSIDE-AUX
```

All LISP needs at this point is the bottom branch, the one that leads to the currently active procedure:

The branch that leads to the currently-active procedure grows and shrinks as LISP enters and exits from procedures:

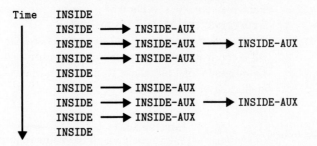

Turning this diagram 90 degrees counterclockwise produces the following diagram:

```
INSIDE          INSIDE-AUX    INSIDE-AUX    INSIDE-AUX   ...
                INSIDE        INSIDE-AUX    INSIDE
                              INSIDE
TIME ──────────────────────────────────────────────────────▶
```

Drawn this way, the required part of the record of calls resembles a stack of cafeteria trays, growing and shrinking as trays are added and taken away. Consequently, LISP is said to maintain a *stack* of procedure calls.

Once a procedure call disappears from the active part of the record of calls, the special-variable values maintained by that call disappear as well. Consequently, special variables are said to have *dynamic extent*. Because special variables have dynamic extent, they are sometimes called *dynamic variables*.

Note that the record of calls is manufactured only when LISP evaluates procedures, LETs, or DOs. Suppose, for example, that CONTAINS is like INSIDE, except that the order of the arguments is reversed:

```
(defun contains (e *x*)            ;*X* is specially bound,
  (inside-aux e))                  ;E is lexically bound.
(defun inside (*x* e)              ;*X* is specially bound,
  (inside-aux e))                  ;E is lexically bound.
(defun inside-aux (e)              ;E is lexically bound.
  (cond ((atom e) (eq *x* e))      ;Instance of *X*.
        (t (or (inside-aux (first e))
               (inside-aux (rest e)))))))
```

Both procedures CONTAINS and INSIDE have *X* as a parameter. Thus *X*'s value in INSIDE-AUX may come from either CONTAINS or INSIDE, depending on the record of calls:

```
CONTAINS   →   INSIDE-AUX        One possibility.
INSIDE     →   INSIDE-AUX        Another possibility.
```

Thus the place to look for the value of a particular instance of *X* must be determined dynamically, as LISP is working. There is no way to tell exactly where *X*'s value will come from by just looking at the definitions of CONTAINS, INSIDE, and INSIDE-AUX.

Recall that you can tell exactly where the values of lexical variables will come from when you look at procedure definitions. This is one reason the designers of LISP chose to use virtual fences as the default mechanism for finding variable values.

DEFVAR Can Assign as Well as Declare

You can use DEFVAR to assign a global value to a variable as well as to declare a variable to be special. For example, the following form not only declares that *INTEREST-RATE* is special, but also assigns .07 to *INTEREST-RATE*.

```
* (defvar *interest-rate* .07)
0.07
```

Note, however, that DEFVAR assigns a value to a variable only when there is none to start with:

```
* (defvar *interest-rate* .07)
.07

* *interest-rate*
.07

* (defvar *interest-rate* .08)
NIL

* *interest-rate*
.07
```

The reason for this odd behavior is that you often want to reload heavily edited files when debugging. When you reload an edited file, you generally do not want to reinitialize special-variable values.

Some Variable Instances Can Be Special while Others Are Lexical

Consider these procedures:

```
(defun time (mpg gallons speed)
  (/ (compute-distance gallons) speed))

(defun compute-distance (gallons)
  (* mpg gallons))
```

The instance of the variable named MPG in the TIME procedure is a lexical variable. The instance of the variable named MPG in the COMPUTE-DISTANCE procedure is taken to be a special variable because according to the way fences are thrown up, no gatekeeper can supply MPG's value inside COMPUTE-DISTANCE.

Consequently, the given procedures will not work unless MPG is made special by a DEFVAR before the definition of TIME is evaluated:

```
* (time 25 10 50)           ;No DEFVAR used.
ERROR

* (time 25 10 50)           ;DEFVAR used.
5
```

Note that you can tell LISP to bind a variable specially in just one procedure by using the DECLARE primitive to make a local declaration. Here is how:

```
(defun time (mpg gallons speed)
  (declare (special mpg))
  (/ (compute-distance gallons) speed))
```

You can do this sort of thing if you wish a variable to be lexically bound in some places and specially bound in others. It is a bad idea, however. It is better to use two variables with different names.

Both Lexical and Special Variables Can Be Free Variables

Finally, we must explain the concept of *free variable*.

- An instance of a *special variable* is *free* with respect to a procedure, LET, or DO if LISP roars past the entry for that procedure, LET, or DO on the record of calls when seeking a value for the variable.

- An instance of a *lexical variable* is *free* with respect to a procedure, LET, or DO if LISP roars past the gatekeeper for that procedure, LET, or DO when seeking a value for the variable.

- An instance of a special variable for which there is no procedure, LET, or DO that supplies a value is a *globally free variable*.

Summary

- Bindings could be kept on a record of calls.
- Some variables are declared to be special forevermore.
- Special-variable bindings are actually kept on a stack.
- DEFVAR can assign as well as declare.
- Some variable instances can be special while others are lexical.
- Both lexical and special variables can be free variables.

17

List Storage,
Surgery,
and Reclamation

The principal purpose of this chapter is to describe how atoms and lists are represented in a computer. You need to understand the ideas in this chapter to use certain primitives, such as NCONC and DELETE, that alter existing expressions surgically, rather than by copying. The ideas in this chapter also clarify the relationships among the various equality predicates.

Lists Can Be Represented by Boxes and Pointers

It is time to learn a little about how lists can be represented inside a computer, distinguishing text from bits.

Viewed as *text*, LISP expressions are sequences of characters like those you see on a screen, in a file, or printed on a piece of paper. Inside a computer, those characters are represented, ultimately, as configurations of two-valued switches called *bits*.

Usually, it is convenient to represent the contents of memory in an abstract way that stands above any particular set of implementation choices. A *box-and-pointer diagram* stands a little above the actual bits and words in a computer, but still records what list objects look like more precisely than text does:

Word	Meaning
Text	The stuff you see on a page
Bits	The stuff inside the computer
Boxes and pointers	A representation level between text and bits

A list, in box-and-pointer notation, is a string of boxes linked by arrowlike *pointers* emerging from their right sides, terminated by a box with a slash in its right side:

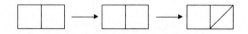

The elements of the list are indicated by the pointers emerging from the left sides of the boxes:

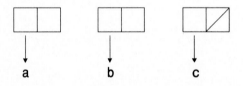

Of course, the elements of a list may be lists themselves. Here is what (A (B (C))) looks like:

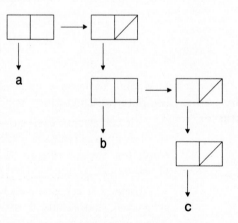

Of course, you can place the boxes on the page any way you like, this way for example:

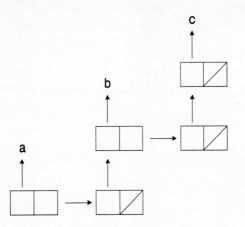

Box-and-pointer diagrams are analogous to the bowl diagrams discussed in chapter 2. Each group of boxes linked by right pointers is like a bowl: to see why, look at the box-and-pointer diagram for (A (B (C))) when surrounded by bowls:

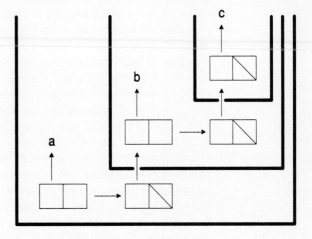

In summary, there are atoms and there are two-pointer entities, which we call boxes that tie things together. The boxes are also known as *cons cells* or *conses*.

Boxes and Pointers Can Be Represented by Bytes

The details of how boxes and pointers are represented in a computer are highly implementation dependent. In this section, we describe one simple approach in general terms.[1]

Conceptually, the memory of most contemporary computers consists of numbered *bytes*, each of which consists of eight bits. The number of a particular byte is called its *address*. In the following diagram, for example, the decimal address of the first byte is 4,194,305 and its binary contents is 0000 0000:

Address	Byte Contents (Binary)
4,194,305	0000 0000
4,194,306	0100 0000
4,194,307	0000 0000
4,194,308	0000 0101
...	...

Of course, a sequence of one or more bytes can represent a number, and that number can be a byte address. Consequently, the contents of a sequence of bytes may be said to contain the starting address of another sequence of bytes. Interpreted this way, the first sequence of bytes is said to contain a pointer to the other. Thus the sequence of four bytes above, beginning at the decimal address 4,194,305, contains a pointer to the sequence of four bytes whose starting address is 10000000000000000000101 in binary, which is 4,194,309 in decimal. Four-byte pointers are adequate for memories of up to 2^{32} bytes, which is considered plenty by today's standards.

Now if four bytes can contain one pointer, then eight bytes can represent two four-byte pointers. Consequently, the pointers required by a box can be represented by a sequence of eight bytes. An extra leading byte, the *data type byte*, containing the *data type bits*, is usually included in order to hold information signifying, for example, that the particular chunk of nine bytes represents part of a list, or from another perspective, a box.

A complete list may be represented by nine-byte boxes threaded together by the second of their two pointers, with the first of their two pointers specifying the elements of the list. A reserved pointer, typically four bytes full of binary zeros, signals the end of the list, thus representing NIL, or from another perspective, a slash in a box.

And finally, a symbol often is represented by suitable data type bits together with four-byte pointers to its value, property list, procedure defi-

---

[1]The details of our implementation-dependent discussion is based roughly on GOLDEN COMMON LISP[TM], which is a product of Gold Hill Computers of Cambridge, Massachusetts.

nition, and the sequence of characters by which the symbol is known when printed.

CONS Builds New Lists by Depositing Pointers in Free Boxes

LISP maintains a list of spare boxes, linked by their right pointers, for use in constructing new lists. This list of spare boxes is called the free storage list. The CONS primitive operates by removing the first box on the free storage list and by depositing new pointers into this first box. Suppose, for example, that the value of EXAMPLE1 is (B C):

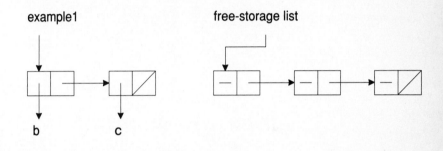

Now if (SETF EXAMPLE1 (CONS 'A EXAMPLE1)) is evaluated, the CONS consumes a spare box from the free storage list, and the SETF redirects the pointer from EXAMPLE1:

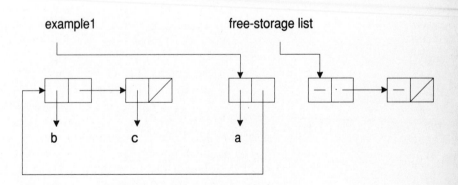

APPEND Builds New Lists by Copying

In a moment we explain how APPEND works. First we set up some values that will help. As a mnemonic aid, let the values of the symbols ABC and XYZ be the lists (A B C) and (X Y Z):

```
* (setf abc '(a b c) 'xyz '(x y z))
```

The box-and-pointer diagrams for ABC and XYZ are as follows:

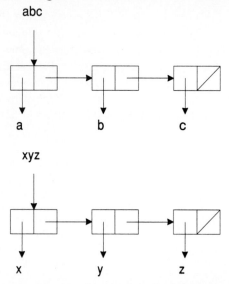

It might seem that evaluating the form (SETF ABCXYZ (APPEND ABC XYZ)) should change the contents of the last box in the representation of the list (A B C):

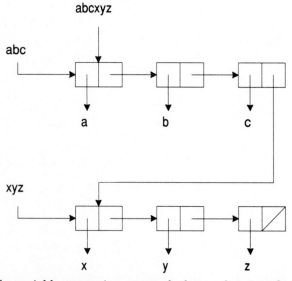

As far as the variable ABCXYZ is concerned, the result is just fine: the newly revised boxes would represent the list (A B C X Y Z), as desired. Also, the value of XYZ is unchanged. Unfortunately, the value of ABC has been

changed. It is now, unexpectedly, (A B C X Y Z), not (A B C)! Given that
APPEND should leave the values of its arguments intact, it must work in some
other way.

The following diagram illustrates what APPEND really does. The first
list is copied, using spare boxes from the free storage list, and then the
second list is attached to the copy:

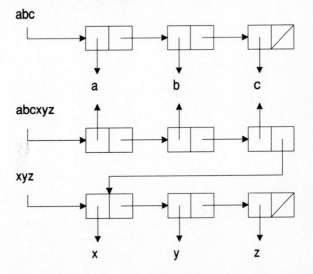

**NCONC and
DELETE Can
Alter Box Contents
Dangerously**

Unlike APPEND, the NCONC primitive smashes two lists together by a surgical
change to the last box in the first list. Consequently, NCONC alters the value
of any variable whose value is represented by a pointer into that first list:

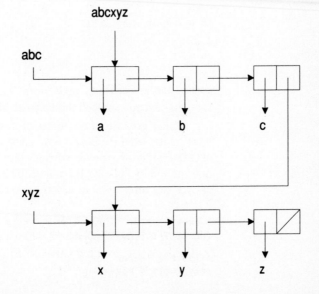

Note the following contrast:

```
* (setf abc '(a b c) xyz '(x y z))

* (setf bc (rest abc))
(B C)

* (setf yz (rest xyz))
(Y Z)

* (setf abcxyz (append abc xyz))
(A B C X Y Z)

* abc
(A B C)

* xyz
(X Y Z)

* bc
(B C)

* yz
(Y Z)

* (setf abcxyz (nconc abc xyz))
(A B C X Y Z)

* abc
(A B C X Y Z)

* xyz
(X Y Z)

* bc
(B C X Y Z)

* yz
(Y Z)
```

NCONC, like APPEND, can take more than two lists. The last box of each of
the lists, except that of the last list, are altered by NCONC.

DELETE gets rid of instances of its first argument that appear at the top
level in its second. If the first element in the list is a matching element,
DELETE simply skips over it when handing back a value. Otherwise, DELETE
does its job by splicing the matching elements out of the list. Consequently,
DELETE can alter symbol assignments peculiarly as a side effect:

```
* (setf tosses '(heads tails tails heads tails))
(HEADS TAILS TAILS HEADS TAILS)

* (delete 'heads tosses)
(TAILS TAILS TAILS)
```

```
* tosses
(HEADS TAILS TAILS TAILS)
```

It is best to combine the DELETE with a SETF, to insure that the value of TOSSES is properly changed, independent of which elements happened to get deleted.

Note that the surgical behavior of DELETE can be avoided. The thing to do is to use REMOVE, a primitive that copies boxes, rather than altering them. REMOVE is similar to, but simpler than REMOVE-IF and REMOVE-IF-NOT, primitives that were introduced earlier.

```
* (setf tosses '(heads tails tails heads tails))
(HEADS TAILS TAILS HEADS TAILS)
* (remove 'heads tosses)
(TAILS TAILS TAILS)
* tosses
(HEADS TAILS TAILS HEADS TAILS)
```

Note, incidentally, that both DELETE and REMOVE, like MEMBER, can take a keyword argument that alters the test used to determine equality. Consequently, if DELETE's or REMOVES's first argument is a list, then the :TEST keyword and the EQUAL predicate should be used to signal that EQUAL is the right test, instead of EQL, which is the default:

```
* (delete '(heads tails)
          '((alpha omega) (heads tails) (zenith nadir)))
((ALPHA OMEGA) (HEADS TAILS) (ZENITH NADIR))
* (delete '(heads tails)
          '((alpha omega) (heads tails) (zenith nadir))
          :test #'equal)
((ALPHA OMEGA) (ZENITH NADIR))
* (remove '(heads tails)
          '((alpha omega) (heads tails) (zenith nadir)))
((ALPHA OMEGA) (HEADS TAILS) (ZENITH NADIR))
* (remove '(heads tails)
          '((alpha omega) (heads tails) (zenith nadir))
          :test #'equal)
((ALPHA OMEGA) (ZENITH NADIR))
```

SETF Also Can Alter Box Contents Dangerously

Importantly, SETF can do box surgery in certain circumstances. Suppose, for example, that the first argument in a SETF form is (FIRST ⟨list⟩). SETF alters the first box representing the list by replacing its left half by a pointer to the second argument. Consider, for example, the following:

```
* (setf fact1 '(big computers are nice))
(BIG COMPUTERS ARE NICE)

* (setf (first fact1) 'fast)
FAST
```

The pointer to `BIG` has been replaced by a pointer to `FAST` in the first of the boxes representing (BIG COMPUTERS ARE NICE):

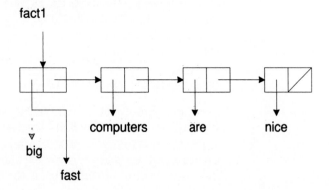

From the box-and-pointer diagram, we see that the value of `FACT1` has been changed:

```
* fact1
(FAST COMPUTERS ARE NICE)
```

Similarly, `SETF` also does surgery when the first argument is (REST ⟨list⟩). `SETF` alters the first box representing the list by replacing its right half by a pointer to the second argument. Consider these:

```
* (setf fact2 '(apples are good for you))
(APPLES ARE GOOD FOR YOU)

* (setf (rest fact2) '(were bad for adam))
(WERE BAD FOR ADAM)
```

Now only `APPLES` is retained from `FACT2`, as the following diagram shows:

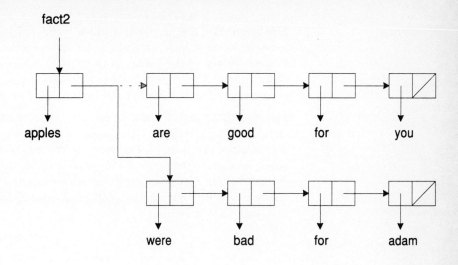

The value of FACT2 has changed:

```
* fact2
(APPLES WERE BAD FOR ADAM)
```

Note that you can create a circular list if you use SETF carelessly:

```
* (setf fact3 '(circle))
(CIRCLE)

* (setf (rest fact3) fact3)
(CIRCLE CIRCLE CIRCLE ....
```

We have altered (CIRCLE), producing a *circular list* that has a pointer back to itself, as shown in the following diagram:

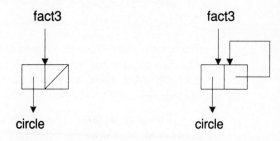

Whenever you attempt to print out such a circular list, LISP's printing procedure gets stuck until you interrupt it.

Problems

Problem 17-1: A *queue* is a linearly ordered set of things that can be accessed using enqueuing and dequeuing operations. ENQUEUE adds a new item to the tail of the queue, while DEQUEUE removes an item from the head of the queue. A list can be used to represent a queue, with the first element corresponding to the item at the head of the queue.

Define ENQUEUE and DEQUEUE as macros. ENQUEUE takes two arguments, the item to be enqueued and the name of a variable whose value is the list representing the queue. The value is the enlarged list. DEQUEUE takes a single argument, the name of the variable whose value is the list. The value returned is the item dequeued. In both cases the value of the variable is changed to reflect the new contents of the queue. Do not copy the list when enqueuing a new item.

EQ Checks Pointers Only

You learned in chapter 4 that EQ returns T if both its arguments' values are the same symbol. In these respects, EQ is similar to EQUAL. If the two arguments are lists, however, things are a bit more complicated. Consider the following:

```
* (setf l1 (list 'a 'b 'c))
(A B C)


* (setf l2 (list 'a 'b 'c))
(A B C)


* (setf l3 l2)
(A B C)
```

Each time LIST is used, it assembles a list using new boxes drawn from the free storage list repository. Consequently, while the values of L1 and L2 both print as (A B C), the two values are represented by distinct box sequences.

The SETF in (SETF L3 L2), on the other hand, attaches a pointer from its first argument to the box structure that its second argument points to. Hence the values of L2 and L3 both print as (A B C), and moreover, the two values are represented by the same box sequences. All of this is illustrated in this diagram:

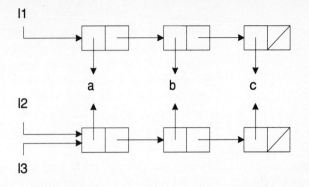

Now certainly, both (EQUAL L1 L2) and (EQUAL L2 L3) return T because the values of L1 and L2 are exact copies of one another and because the values of L2 and L3 are represented by exactly the same boxes. L1 is equal to L2 in a way that is slightly different from the way that L2 is equal to L3, but EQUAL could not care less.

The primitive EQ does care. For EQ, two lists are equal only if they are represented by the same boxes. Copies are not considered equal in the EQ sense. Thus (EQ L1 L2) returns NIL whereas (EQ L2 L3) returns T.

•   Two lists that are EQUAL may not be EQ.

•   Any two lists that are EQ are also always EQUAL.

Why use EQ instead of EQUAL? Again the answer usually is a matter of efficiency. It is usually slightly faster to check whether two symbols are the same using EQ. Of course, if you are comparing two things that may be lists, rather than symbols, you should use EQUAL.

Garbage Collection Reclaims Abandoned Memory

Consider this sequence:

```
* (setf example2 (list 'a 'b 'c))
(A B C)
* (setf example2 (list 'x 'y 'z))
(X Y Z)
```

Like CONS, the primitive LIST builds a new list by taking material from the free storage list. The structure is accessible via the value of EXAMPLE2. But we changed the value of EXAMPLE2 immediately. The previous structure is no longer accessible from any symbol. To be sure, the value of EXAMPLE2 can be made to be (A B C) again, but only by taking new boxes from the free storage list and rebuilding.

There is no point in wasting the boxes in the now inaccessible list. Somehow they should be returned to the free storage list so that they can

be used again. Note, however, that we cannot just return the boxes when
they are snipped off: other structures may be pointing to them. Instead,
we just continue using up new boxes, allowing the no-longer used ones to
languish. When we finally do run out of space, we must do something to
determine which boxes can be reused. *Garbage collection* is the technical
term for what needs to be done.

**LISP Allows You
To Write Inefficient
Procedures**

In general, programming languages should handle low-level details while
you think about what you want to do. One example in LISP is automatic
recovery of unused memory via garbage collection. Another is floating
contagion in arithmetic forms.

Like most good things, however, you can come to rely too much on
LISP's detail-handling capability. In particular, LISP allows you to write
procedures that are hopelessly inefficient because they spend too much time
depositing pointers in boxes and generating garbage to be collected.

To illustrate, suppose LISP had no **REVERSE** primitive. You could write
the following, but should not:

```
(defun user-reverse (l)                    ;Hopelessly inefficient.
  (if (endp l)
      nil
      (append (user-reverse (rest l))
              (list (first l)))))
```

Here is why this version of **REVERSE** is so bad:

* If there are n elements in the list to be reversed, **USER-REVERSE** recurses
  n times.
* For each recursive call, **USER-REVERSE** calls **APPEND** and **LIST**.
* In the first call to **USER-REVERSE**, n boxes are consumed by **APPEND** and
  LIST. In the second call, $n-1$ are consumed. In the final call, none
  are consumed.

Hence the number of boxes consumed in reversing a list of length n is as
follows:

$$n + (n-1) + \cdots + 0 = \frac{n^2 + n}{2}.$$

The theorists say that such a computation is order n^2.

Now consider the following alternative. For each element in the list,
there is just one explicit call to **CONS** consuming one box. The computation
is order n, which is much better than order n^2:

```
(defun user-reverse (l &optional result)        ;Reasonably efficient.
  (if (endp l)
      result
      (user-reverse (rest l)
                    (cons (first l) result)))))
```

For short lists, either version of USER-REVERSE is fine. For long lists, using
an order n^2 procedure rather than an order n procedure can waste a lot of
time and memory, leading to the following maxim:

- Avoid frivolous box consumption. Be especially careful with APPEND.

Another way to improve efficiency is to use surgery-oriented primitives,
thereby consuming no new boxes at all. Suppose, for example, that you
want a procedure that substitutes the symbol PERSON for every instance of
the symbol MAN in any expression given as an argument. Call this procedure
LIBERATE1. It can be defined as follows using CONS:

```
(defun liberate1 (s)                      ;First version.
  (cond ((eq s 'man) 'person)             ;Replace MAN.
        ((atom s) s)                      ;Keep other atoms.
        (t (cons (liberate1 (first s))    ;Recurse on first
                 (liberate1 (rest s))))))) ; and rest.
```

The FIRST and REST rip the given argument apart again and again until the
atoms are reached, and then reassemble a near copy using CONS to build
it. If the list is deeply nested, this can take a lot of time even if there are
few instances of MAN to replace. The CONS operation itself takes time, and
in addition, CONS depletes free storage. The more free storage is used, the
more reclamation is needed later.

In the following version, the original list is not copied. Instead, local
surgery is performed whenever an instance of MAN is encountered. If a lot
of liberation is to be done, time can be saved.

```
(defun liberate2 (s)                      ;Second version.
  (cond ((eq s 'man) 'person)             ;Useful when MAN is at the top level.
        ((atom s) s)                      ;Keep atoms.
        ((eq (first s) 'man)              ;If MAN spotted in front of a list,
         (setf (first s) 'person)         ; replace with PERSON surgically,
         (liberate2 (rest s)))            ; and look again.
        (t (liberate2 (first s))          ;Recurse on first
           (liberate2 (rest s))           ; and rest.
           s)))                           ;Return result.
```

However, using this version of LIBERATE can be dangerous, because it alters the list that is supplied by an argument. Examples using LIBERATE1 and LIBERATE2 show how:

```
* (setf test '(chair man))
(CHAIR MAN)
* (liberate1 test)
(CHAIR PERSON)
* test
(CHAIR MAN)
```

Evidently, doing (LIBERATE1 TEST) does not change the value of TEST. Now consider this:

```
* (liberate2 test)
(CHAIR PERSON)
* test
(CHAIR PERSON)
```

Now the value of TEST has changed because LIBERATE2 alters boxes. Such changes can be confusing and lead to bugs:

- LISP does not completely prevent the abuse of arguments. Generality provides hanging rope.
- You must be extremely careful with NCONC, DELETE, and box-altering SETF forms. Unless you are desperately eager to improve efficiency, avoid them.

Accordingly, we use neither NCONC nor DELETE in any other chapter, and we rarely use box-altering forms of SETF.

Problems

Problem 17-2: You might expect the following version of USER-REVERSE to be quite fast because it uses NCONC in place of APPEND. Curiously, the NCONC version becomes progressively slower than the version that uses CONS as the length of the list increases, even though it consumes no new boxes. Explain.

```
(defun user-reverse (1)              ;Moderately inefficient.
  (if (endp 1)
      nil
      (nconc (user-reverse (rest 1))
             (list (first 1)))))
```

Problem 17-3: Ignoring the existence of NREVERSE, a primitive supplied by LISP itself, write USER-DEFINED-NREVERSE, a procedure that reverses a list by manipulating pointers in the list's existing boxes.

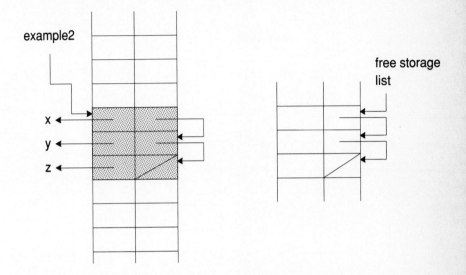

Figure 17-1. Results of a garbage collector's marking phase. Marked cells are shown shaded.

Simple Garbage Collectors Use the Mark and Sweep Approach

Simple garbage collectors have two phases. In the first phase, the garbage collector runs through memory, starting from the values, properties, and procedure definitions of all symbols, together with all the forms involved in the current computation, marking all of the boxes representing the expressions encountered. Once the marking phase is finished, a sweep phase passes through memory sequentially, taking note of unmarked boxes and returning them to the free storage list.

The marking may be done by altering one of the bits in the memory boxes, if any are otherwise unused, or by maintaining a table containing one bit per box. The choice is influenced strongly by the architecture of the computer. Figure 17-1 illustrates what the garbage collector's marker does in an area that contains the boxes representing the current value of EXAMPLE2 and nothing else. Figure 17-2 illustrates how the sweep phase handles a previously marked area.

Typically, a garbage collector is invoked automatically when the free storage list is near exhaustion, and some small icon flashes on the screen indicating that garbage collection is in progress.

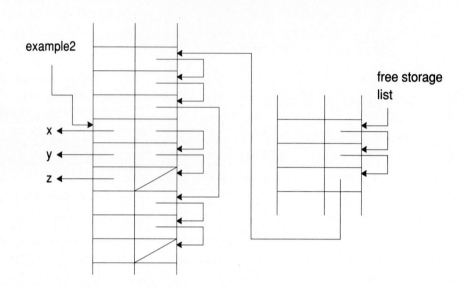

Figure 17-2. Results of a garbage collector's sweeping phase. The free storage list is enlarged.

Simulation Procedures Expose Garbage Collection Details

For most LISP programmers, it is enough to know that garbage collection reclaims abandoned memory. If you want to know more about how garbage collection is done, you can read about a simple, albeit imaginary, garbage collector described in this section. In our imaginary garbage collector, specified as a LISP procedure, you see a bit of LISP described in terms of LISP itself, a theme we concentrate on in chapter 18.

To keep our explanation simple, we confine our imaginary garbage collector to working with boxes and symbol values, ignoring properties, procedure definitions, and memory involved in ongoing computation.

Now suppose memory is simulated by a one-dimensional array. Each element in the array is analogous to some bits in memory, and array indexes are analogous to memory addresses.

To store information about boxes, symbols, and free memory, we partition the array into four-element chunks. Each four-element chunk represents either a box, a symbol, or free memory according to the following list of conventions:

- The first element in each four-element chunk indicates what data type the chunk represents. In our simulated memory, the first element of a chunk contains BOX, SYMBOL, or FREE, with FREE indicating unused or abandoned memory. In a typical real implementation, a few bits in a data type byte would indicate the type.

- The second element in each four-element chunk indicates whether the chunk has been marked. In our simulated memory, the value of the second element of a chunk is either MARKED or UNMARKED. In a typical real implementation, a single mark bit in the data type byte would indicate whether the chunk is marked or not.

- For boxes, the third and fourth elements represent pointers. In our simulated memory, the value of the third and fourth elements of a chunk are either the indexes of the first elements of other chunks or NIL, with NIL representing a pointer to the empty list. In a real implementation, the pointers would be represented by some number of bytes, with the exact number depending on the available memory in the computer.

- For symbols, the third element contains the name of the symbol, and the fourth element contains either the index of the first element of another chunk or NIL or UNBOUND, with UNBOUND indicating that the symbol has no value. In a real implementation, the fact that a symbol has no value would be indicated by another bit reserved in the data type byte.

- For free memory, the third element is not used and always contains NIL. The fourth element contains the index of the first element of the next chunk or NIL if the chunk is the last of the chunks that are associated with free memory.

Thus the initial state of a tiny ten element memory, with no symbols or lists represented, could be simulated by the following array assigned to MEMORY, in which we have inserted extra spaces to make the contents easier to comprehend:

```
(setf memory (make-array 40 :initial-contents
  '(free      unmarked  nil      4        ;Elements 0–3.
    free      unmarked  nil      8        ;Elements 4–7.
    free      unmarked  nil      12       ;Elements 8–11.
    free      unmarked  nil      16       ;Elements 12–15.
    free      unmarked  nil      20       ;Elements 16–19.
    free      unmarked  nil      24       ;Elements 20–23.
    free      unmarked  nil      28       ;Elements 24–27.
    free      unmarked  nil      32       ;Elements 28–31.
    free      unmarked  nil      36       ;Elements 32–35.
    free      unmarked  nil      nil      ;Elements 36–39.
  )))
```

Now suppose the value of NEXT-FREE-CHUNK is the address of the first element of the first free chunk and the value of LAST-FREE-CHUNK is the address of the first element of the last free chunk:

```
(setf next-free-chunk 0 last-free-chunk 36)
```

Primitives like SETF, CONS, and LIST consume boxes from the free storage list. Suppose, for example, that you evaluate (SETF X (LIST 'A 'B)). Then our simulated memory might look as follows, where we have again inserted extra spaces to make MEMORY's value easier to comprehend:

```
* memory
#(SYMBOL      UNMARKED   X        4          ;Elements 0–3.
  BOX         UNMARKED   8        12         ;Elements 4–7.
  SYMBOL      UNMARKED   A        UNBOUND    ;Elements 8–11.
  BOX         UNMARKED   16       NIL        ;Elements 12–15.
  SYMBOL      UNMARKED   B        UNBOUND    ;Elements 16–19.
  FREE        UNMARKED   NIL      24         ;Elements 20–23.
  FREE        UNMARKED   NIL      28         ;Elements 24–27.
  FREE        UNMARKED   NIL      32         ;Elements 28–31.
  FREE        UNMARKED   NIL      36         ;Elements 32–35.
  FREE        UNMARKED   NIL      NIL        ;Elements 36–39.
  )
```

Now the free-memory indexes are as follows:

```
* next-free-chunk
20
* last-free-chunk
36
```

Next, suppose we evaluate (SETF X (LIST 'L 'M)). Now MEMORY's value is changed, with more of the free boxes consumed:

```
* memory
#(SYMBOL      UNMARKED   X        20         ;Elements 0–3.
  BOX         UNMARKED   8        12         ;Elements 4–7.
  SYMBOL      UNMARKED   A        UNBOUND    ;Elements 8–11.
  BOX         UNMARKED   16       NIL        ;Elements 12–15.
  SYMBOL      UNMARKED   B        UNBOUND    ;Elements 16–19.
  BOX         UNMARKED   24       28         ;Elements 20–23.
  SYMBOL      UNMARKED   L        UNBOUND    ;Elements 24–27.
  BOX         UNMARKED   32       NIL        ;Elements 28–31.
  SYMBOL      UNMARKED   M        UNBOUND    ;Elements 32–35.
  FREE        UNMARKED   NIL      NIL        ;Elements 36–39.
  )
```

And, of course, the value of NEXT-FREE-CHUNK changes:

```
* next-free-chunk
36
```

```
* last-free-chunk
36
```

MARK Places Marks on Useful Chunks

Now we introduce PLACE-MARKS, a procedure that follows pointers through boxes and marks all boxes and symbols encountered. Note that a non-numeric index indicates that PLACE-MARKS has hit either NIL or UNBOUND, whereupon PLACE-MARKS does nothing. Note that PLACE-MARKS also ignores already-marked boxes:

```
(defun place-marks (index)
  (when (numberp index)
    (unless (eq 'marked (aref memory (+ 1 index)))
      (setf (aref memory (+ 1 index)) 'marked)
      (when (eq 'box (aref memory index))
        (place-marks (aref memory (+ 2 index)))
        (place-marks (aref memory (+ 3 index)))))))
```

Then the first phase in garbage collection is to start PLACE-MARKS off at each memory position corresponding a symbol with a value. Conveniently, (ARRAY-DIMENSION MEMORY 0) determines the size of the array's 0th dimension:

```
(defun mark ()
  (do ((index 0 (+ 4 index)))
      ((= index (array-dimension memory 0)))
    (when (and (eq 'symbol (aref memory index))
               (not (eq 'unbound (aref memory (+ 3 index)))))
      (setf (aref memory (+ 1 index)) 'marked)
      (place-marks (aref memory (+ 3 index))))))
```

Once (MARK) is evaluated, MEMORY's value is as follows, with only five of the ten chunks marked:

```
* memory
#(SYMBOL     MARKED      X      20         ;Elements 0-3.
  BOX        UNMARKED    8      12         ;Elements 4-7.
  SYMBOL     UNMARKED    A      UNBOUND    ;Elements 8-11.
  BOX        UNMARKED    16     NIL        ;Elements 12-15.
  SYMBOL     UNMARKED    B      UNBOUND    ;Elements 16-19.
  BOX        MARKED      24     28         ;Elements 20-23.
  SYMBOL     MARKED      L      UNBOUND    ;Elements 24-27.
  BOX        MARKED      32     NIL        ;Elements 28-31.
  SYMBOL     MARKED      M      UNBOUND    ;Elements 32-35.
  FREE       UNMARKED    NIL    NIL        ;Elements 36-39.
  )
```

SWEEP Collects Unmarked Chunks

With everything useful protected by marking, SWEEP converts each unprotected chunk into a free chunk and inserts the newly freed chunk at the end of the trail of free chunks that starts at the place pointed to by NEXT-FREE-CHUNK and ends at the place pointed to by LAST-FREE-CHUNK. The value of LAST-FREE-CHUNK is altered accordingly.

```
(defun sweep ()
  (do ((index 0 (+ 4 index)))
      ((= index (array-dimension memory 0)))
    (unless (or (eq 'free (aref memory index))
                (eq 'marked (aref memory (+ 1 index))))
      (setf (aref memory index) 'free)
      (setf (aref memory (+ 2 index)) nil)
      (setf (aref memory (+ 3 index)) nil)
      (setf (aref memory (+ 3 last-free-chunk)) index)
      (setf last-free-chunk index))
    (setf (aref memory (+ 1 index)) 'unmarked)))
```

Now when (SWEEP) is evaluated, all of the marks are removed and all abandoned symbols and boxes are recovered:

```
* memory
#(SYMBOL     UNMARKED    X         20          ;Elements 0–3.
   FREE      UNMARKED    NIL       8           ;Elements 4–7.
   FREE      UNMARKED    NIL       12          ;Elements 8–11.
   FREE      UNMARKED    NIL       16          ;Elements 12–15.
   FREE      UNMARKED    NIL       NIL         ;Elements 16–19.
   BOX       UNMARKED    24        28          ;Elements 20–23.
   SYMBOL    UNMARKED    L         UNBOUND     ;Elements 24–27.
   BOX       UNMARKED    32        NIL         ;Elements 28–31.
   SYMBOL    UNMARKED    M         UNBOUND     ;Elements 32–35.
   FREE      UNMARKED    NIL       4           ;Elements 36–39.
   )
```

Combining MARK and SWEEP, we have COLLECT-GARBAGE:

```
(defun collect-garbage () (mark) (sweep))
```

Marking Can Be Done without Recursion

The marking procedure introduced in the previous section has one major flaw. As it runs through memory, the PLACE-MARKS procedure calls itself recursively, requiring considerable memory to keep track of the state of the computation. In fact, running through complicated expressions could require more memory than the total available to keep track of the state of computation.

Fortunately, it is possible to build a nonrecursive garbage collector that does no recursion. The one presented in the next section is based on Floyd's modification of an algorithm independently discovered by Deutsch and by Schorr and Waite.

Our Nonrecursive Marking Procedure Leaves a Trail of Pointers

The general approach is to leave a trail behind the marking procedure as it runs through memory so that it can find its way back out of the box arrangement. The trick is to leave the trail without consuming extra memory by cleverly reversing pointers.

Figure 17-3 illustrates. As the nonrecursive marking procedure moves down, it reverses the pointers behind it so that it can find its way back up. As the marking procedure moves up, it reverses the pointers again so that the box arrangement ends up the way it began.

The only really complicated part has to do with marking boxes. The following nonrecursive marking procedure, NR-PLACE-MARKS, is complicated only because it must deal separately with so many situations. First, a chunk may represent a box or symbol. For either a chunk or box, NR-PLACE-MARKS may encounter it moving down or moving up. If the chunk is a box, it may be either marked or unmarked.

On the way down through a box, the NR-PLACE-MARKS procedure first deposits a back pointer in the place normally occupied by the box's left pointer. Then NR-PLACE-MARKS proceeds to examine the memory that previosly hung below the box's left pointer.

When NR-PLACE-MARKS hits a box on the way up for the first time, NR-PLACE-MARKS moves the back pointer from the left-pointer place to the right-pointer place, marks the box, and proceeds to examine the arrangement below the box's right pointer.

Finally, when NR-PLACE-MARKS hits a box on the way up the second time, the box will have been marked, signaling the marking procedure to keep on going up:

```
(defun nr-place-marks
       (last-chunk this-chunk &aux next-chunk (direction 'down))
  (loop
    (case (aref memory this-chunk)
      (box
        (case direction
          (down (setf next-chunk (aref memory (+ 2 this-chunk)))
                (setf (aref memory (+ 2 this-chunk)) last-chunk))
          (up
            (case (aref memory (+ 1 this-chunk))
              (unmarked
                (setf (aref memory (+ 1 this-chunk)) 'marked)
                (setf next-chunk (aref memory (+ 3 this-chunk)))
                (setf (aref memory (+ 3 this-chunk))
                      (aref memory (+ 2 this-chunk)))
                (setf (aref memory (+ 2 this-chunk)) last-chunk)
                (setf direction 'down))
              (marked
                (setf next-chunk (aref memory (+ 3 this-chunk)))
                (setf (aref memory (+ 3 this-chunk)) last-chunk)
                (setf direction 'up))))))
      (symbol
        (case direction
          (down (setf (aref memory (+ 1 this-chunk)) 'marked)
                (setf next-chunk last-chunk)
                (setf direction 'up))
          (up (return)))))
    (when next-chunk
      (setf last-chunk this-chunk
            this-chunk next-chunk))))
```

Note that this version of NR-PLACE-MARKS requires two arguments, not just
one. Accordingly, a new version of MARK, NR-MARK, calls NR-PLACE-MARKS with
both the location of the current symbol and the location of the symbol's
value:

```
(defun nr-mark ()
  (do ((index 0 (+ 4 index)))
      ((= index (array-dimension memory 0)))
    (when (and (eq 'symbol (aref memory index))
               (not (eq 'unbound (aref memory (+ 3 index)))))
      (setf (aref memory (+ 1 index)) 'marked)
      (place-marks index (aref memory (+ 3 index))))))
```

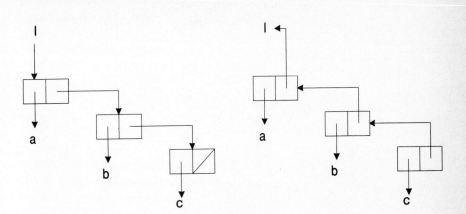

Figure 17-3. A pointer-reversing marking procedure at work. The original box structure is shown first, followed by the box structure at the deepest point in the marking process. The next step is to return to the original box structure using the reversed pointers. Thus clever pointer manipulation enables the entire structure to be marked without requiring extra memory.

Some Garbage Collectors Are Incremental

Some newer garbage collectors do not use the mark-and-sweep idea. Instead they do a little garbage collection with each CONS, either explicit or implicit. They never stop for a complete purge. Consequently, they are better suited to situations for which it would be disastrous to stop processing for seconds or minutes to collect garbage.

Summary

- Lists can be represented by boxes and pointers.
- Boxes and pointers can be represented by bytes.
- CONS builds new lists by depositing pointers in free boxes.
- APPEND builds new lists by copying.
- NCONC and DELETE can alter box contents dangerously.
- SETF also can alter box contents dangerously.
- EQ checks pointers only.
- Garbage collection reclaims abandoned memory.
- LISP allows you to write inefficient procedures.
- Simple garbage collectors use the mark and sweep approach.
- Simulation procedures expose garbage collection details.
- MARK places marks on useful chunks.
- SWEEP collects unmarked chunks.
- Marking can be done without recursion.

- Our nonrecursive marking procedure leaves a trail of pointers.
- Some garbage collectors are incremental.

18

LISP
In
LISP

The purpose of this chapter is to show how LISP's evaluation procedure can be described in terms of LISP itself. In particular, we present an interpreter for MICRO LISP, a simple LISPlike language with just a few primitives for working with symbols and lists.

It Is Easy To Build a Simple Interpreter for a LISPlike Language

In chapter 8, we explained that an interpreter is a program that constantly refers to procedure definitions, following those definitions form by form, and computing an explicit result for each form. To keep things straight as we introduce an interpreter for MICRO LISP, let us begin with some naming conventions:

- The names of MICRO LISP's built-in, primitive procedures begin with M-. Thus M-FIRST, M-REST, and M-CONS are the MICRO LISP analogs to FIRST, REST, and CONS in LISP.

- The names of the LISP procedures needed to implement MICRO LISP begin with MICRO-. Thus MICRO-EVAL and MICRO-APPLY are procedures defined in LISP in order to interpret MICRO LISP expressions.

The key procedures of the MICRO LISP interpreter are MICRO-EVAL and MICRO-APPLY. MICRO-EVAL works on two arguments, a *form* and an association list of variable bindings called the *environment*. MICRO-EVAL's job is to

evaluate atoms and special-case forms directly and to convert other forms
into a procedure name or procedure description and a list of evaluated arguments for MICRO-APPLY. The specially recognized, special-case forms are
called *special forms*.

The MICRO-APPLY procedure works on two arguments, a *procedure name*
or *procedure description* and a list of *evaluated arguments*. MICRO-APPLY's
job is to compute results for primitive procedures and to convert other
procedures into forms and environments for MICRO-EVAL.

Now let us consider MICRO-EVAL in detail. MICRO-EVAL's first argument
is a form to be evaluated, and its second argument is the environment. If
the form given to MICRO-EVAL is a numeric atom, it is returned as is. If the
form is T or NIL, it is returned as is. If the form is any symbol other than T
or NIL, its value is found in the environment association list and returned:

```
(defun micro-eval (form &optional environment)
  (if (atom form)
      (cond ((numberp form) form)
            ((eq t form) t)
            ((eq nil form) nil)
            (t (second (assoc form environment))))
      ...))
```

If the form given to MICRO-EVAL is not an atom, then MICRO-EVAL checks to see
if the form is a special form. If the procedure is M-QUOTE, for example, then
MICRO-EVAL just returns the argument without evaluation. If the procedure
is M-IF, the first argument is evaluated, with the result determining which
of the other two arguments is evaluated to produce the result:

```
(defun micro-eval (form &optional environment)
  (if (atom form)
      ...
      (case (first form)
        (m-quote (second form))
        (m-if (if (micro-eval (second form) environment)
                  (micro-eval (third form) environment)
                  (micro-eval (fourth form) environment)))
        ...)))
```

If the form is not a special form, then MICRO-EVAL evaluates all the arguments and hands the procedure and the evaluated arguments off to MICRO-
APPLY:

```
(defun micro-eval (form &optional environment)
  (if (atom form)
      ...
      (case (first form)
        ...
        (t (micro-apply
             (first form)
             (mapcar #'(lambda (x) (micro-eval x environment))
                     (rest form)))))))
```

When `MICRO-EVAL` hands `MICRO-APPLY` a primitive like `M-FIRST`, `M-REST`, or `M-CONS`, `MICRO-APPLY` does the appropriate thing directly using a LISP primitive:

```
(defun micro-apply (procedure argument-values)
  (if (symbolp procedure)
      (case procedure
        (m-first (first (first argument-values)))
        (m-rest (rest (first argument-values)))
        (m-cons (cons (first argument-values)
                      (second argument-values)))
        (m-endp (endp (first argument-values)))
        (m-not (not (first argument-values)))
        (m-eq (eq (first argument-values)
                  (second argument-values)))
        ...)
      ...))
```

If the procedure handed to `MICRO-APPLY` is a name, but not a recognized name, then `MICRO-APPLY` gets a procedure description from the property list of the name and calls itself recursively, substituting the procedure description for the name.

```
(defun micro-apply (procedure argument-values)
  (if (symbolp procedure)
      (case procedure
        ...
        (t (micro-apply (get procedure 'm-lambda)
                        argument-values)))
      ...))
```

If the procedure handed to `MICRO-APPLY` is not a name, `MICRO-APPLY` assumes it is a procedure description in the form of an m-lambda expression, which is analogous to a lambda expression in LISP:

```
(m-lambda <parameters> <body>)
```

When handed an m-lambda description `MICRO-APPLY` simply evaluates the
body after preparing an environment in which the m-lambda parameters
are paired with argument values using `BIND-VARIABLES`:

```
(defun micro-apply (procedure argument-values)
  (if (symbolp procedure)
      ...
      (micro-eval (third procedure)
                  (bind-variables (second procedure)
                                  argument-values))))

(defun bind-variables (variables values &optional a-list)
  (append (mapcar #'list variables values) a-list))
```

MICRO-EVAL and MICRO-APPLY Work Together To Evaluate Forms

Here then are `MICRO-EVAL` and `MICRO-APPLY` as developed so far, with some
error-catching flourishes to look for unbound variables and undefined procedures:

```
(defun micro-eval (form &optional environment)
  (if (atom form)
      (cond ((numberp form) form)
            ((eq t form) t)
            ((eq nil form) nil)
            (t (let ((binding (assoc form environment)))
                 (if binding
                     (second binding)
                     (error
                       "I could find no variable binding for ~a."
                       form)))))
      (case (first form)
        (m-quote (second form))
        (m-if (if (micro-eval (second form) environment)
                  (micro-eval (third form) environment)
                  (micro-eval (fourth form) environment)))
        (t (micro-apply
             (first form)
             (mapcar #'(lambda (x) (micro-eval x environment))
                     (rest form)))))))
```

```
(defun micro-apply (procedure argument-values)
  (if (symbolp procedure)
      (case procedure
        (m-first (first (first argument-values)))
        (m-rest (rest (first argument-values)))
        (m-cons (cons (first argument-values)
                      (second argument-values)))
        (m-endp (endp (first argument-values)))
        (m-not (not (first argument-values)))
        (m-eq (eq (first argument-values)
                  (second argument-values)))
        (t (let ((procedure-description (get procedure 'm-lambda)))
             (if procedure-description
                 (micro-apply procedure-description
                              argument-values)
                 (error
                   "I could find no procedure description for ~a."
                   procedure)))))
      (micro-eval (third procedure)
                  (bind-variables (second procedure)
                                  argument-values))))
```

Both MICRO-EVAL and MICRO-APPLY use ERROR, a LISP primitive that is similar to BREAK, introduced in chapter 10, except that you cannot continue the current computation beyond the evaluation of an ERROR form. To go on, you must reset LISP by typing some implementation-dependent keychord. You use ERROR forms in places where their evaluation signals that there has been a fatal error. Like BREAK, ERROR prints a format string, with optional arguments, and then enters a debugging mode.

```
* (error "There has been a fatal error.")
ERROR
There has been a fatal error.
>
```

Now, in summary, here is what MICRO-EVAL and MICRO-APPLY do:

- MICRO-EVAL handles atoms directly, usually by looking up a binding on the environment association list.

- If the form handed to MICRO-EVAL is a special form that requires non-standard argument evaluation, like a form involving M-QUOTE or M-IF, MICRO-EVAL evaluates only the appropriate arguments and performs the necessary computation itself.

- Otherwise MICRO-EVAL evaluates all of the form's arguments and then hands the procedure name or procedure description and the evaluated arguments over to MICRO-APPLY.

- MICRO-APPLY handles simple primitives, like M-FIRST and M-REST, directly.
- If the procedure handed to MICRO-APPLY is a name, MICRO-APPLY fetches a procedure description from the name's property list.
- Otherwise MICRO-APPLY handles procedure descriptions, usually in the form of m-lambda expressions, by preparing an appropriate form and environment for MICRO-EVAL.

Traces Show How MICRO-EVAL and MICRO-APPLY Work Together

To see how all this fits together, let us walk through an example. To keep things as simple as possible, we start by using just the primitive M-FIRST, watching how MICRO-EVAL and MICRO-APPLY cooperate:

```
* (micro-eval '(m-first (m-quote (a b c))))
A
```

This looks simple, and in fact the interaction of MICRO-EVAL and MICRO-APPLY is simple, as the following trace demonstrates:

```
* (trace micro-eval micro-apply)
* (micro-eval '(m-first (m-quote (a b c))))
ENTERING: MICRO-EVAL: ((M-FIRST (M-QUOTE (A B C))))
 ENTERING: MICRO-EVAL: ((M-QUOTE (A B C)) NIL)
 EXITING: MICRO-EVAL: (A B C)
 ENTERING: MICRO-APPLY: (M-FIRST ((A B C)))
 EXITING: MICRO-APPLY: A
EXITING: MICRO-EVAL: A
A
```

Now to take a slightly more difficult example, we put a lambda-style description of a procedure named M-SECOND onto the property list of the symbol M-SECOND under the property M-LAMBDA:

```
(setf (get 'm-second 'm-lambda)
      '(m-lambda (l) (m-first (m-rest l))))
```

Now MICRO-EVAL can evaluate forms containing M-SECOND:

```
* (micro-eval '(m-second (m-quote (a b c))))
B
```

Seeing that M-SECOND is a name for a procedure, rather than a lambda expression, a procedure-describing m-lambda expression is retrieved from the property list of M-SECOND. Thus the form (M-SECOND (M-QUOTE (A B C))) is equivalent to another form containing an m-lambda expression:

```
* (micro-eval '((M-LAMBDA (L) (M-FIRST (M-REST L)))
                (M-QUOTE (A B C))))
B
```

This time the trace shows action on the environment association list:

```
* (micro-eval '(m-second (m-quote (a b c))))
ENTERING: MICRO-EVAL: ((M-SECOND (M-QUOTE (A B C))) NIL)
 ENTERING: MICRO-EVAL: ((M-QUOTE (A B C)) NIL)
 EXITING: MICRO-EVAL: (A B C)
 ENTERING: MICRO-APPLY: (M-SECOND ((A B C)))
  ENTERING: MICRO-APPLY: ((M-LAMBDA (L) (M-FIRST (M-REST L)))
                          ((A B C)))
   ENTERING: MICRO-EVAL: ((M-FIRST (M-REST L)) ((L (A B C))))
    ENTERING: MICRO-EVAL: ((M-REST L) ((L (A B C))))
     ENTERING: MICRO-EVAL: (L ((L (A B C))))
     EXITING: MICRO-EVAL: (A B C)
     ENTERING: MICRO-APPLY: (M-REST ((A B C)))
     EXITING: MICRO-APPLY: (B C)
    EXITING: MICRO-EVAL: (B C)
    ENTERING: MICRO-APPLY: (M-FIRST ((B C)))
    EXITING: MICRO-APPLY: B
   EXITING: MICRO-EVAL: B
  EXITING: MICRO-APPLY: B
 EXITING: MICRO-APPLY: B
EXITING: MICRO-EVAL: B
B
```

This concludes the basic development of MICRO LISP. From here, more and more power can be developed by bootstrapping, using MICRO LISP's own procedure-defining mechanism, just as we did when we defined M-SECOND. Here is another example, one using M-IF:

```
(setf (get 'm-append 'm-lambda)
      '(m-lambda (l1 l2)
         (m-if (m-endp l1)
               l2
               (m-cons (m-first l1)
                       (m-append (m-rest l1) l2)))))
* (micro-eval '(m-append (m-quote (a b c)) (m-quote (x y z))))
(A B C X Y Z)
```

Quite a lot of recursion is required to handle this example: MICRO-EVAL is called 38 times and MICRO-APPLY is called 21 times.

Problems

Problem 18-1: Define MICRO-READ-EVAL-PRINT, a procedure that prints a prompt, reads a form, evaluates the form using MICRO-EVAL, prints the result, and repeats, as in the following example:

```
* (micro-read-eval-print)
Micro > (m-quote a)
A
Micro > (m-first (m-quote (a b c)))
A
Micro > (m-rest (m-quote (a b c)))
(B C)
Micro > ...
```

Problem 18-2: Add the necessary machinery to MICRO-EVAL such that expressions of the following form define new procedures by placing m-lambda expressions on the property list of procedure names as shown in the following example:

```
* (micro-eval '(m-defun m-append (l1 l2)
                  (m-if (m-endp l1)
                        l2
                        (m-cons (m-first l1)
                                (m-append (m-rest l1) l2)))))
M-APPEND
* (get 'm-append 'm-lambda)
(M-LAMBDA (L1 L2)
  (M-IF (M-ENDP L1)
        L2
        (M-CONS (M-FIRST L1)
                (M-APPEND (M-REST L1) L2))))
```

Closures Encapsulate Environments

Suppose you want to add an analog of APPLY to MICRO LISP. All you need to do is add another piece to MICRO-EVAL:

```
(defun micro-eval (form &optional environment)
  (if (atom form)
      ...
      (case (first form)
        ...
        (m-apply
          (micro-apply
            (micro-eval (second form) environment)
            (micro-eval (third form) environment)))
        ...)))
```

Once MICRO-EVAL recognizes M-APPLY, forms like the following are evaluated easily:

```
* (micro-eval '(m-apply
                 (m-quote (m-lambda (x y)
                                     (m-cons x (m-cons y nil))))
                 (m-quote (a b))))
(A B)
```

In the following example, we bury one m-lambda expression inside another:

```
* (micro-eval '(m-apply
                 (m-quote
                   (m-lambda (x y)
                     (m-apply
                       (m-quote
                         (m-lambda (l m)
                           (m-cons l (m-cons m nil))))
                       (m-cons x (m-cons y nil)))))
                 (m-quote (a b))))
(A B)
```

Importantly, a new environment is created each time an m-lambda expression is applied in accordance with the rules of lexical scoping. When **MICRO-APPLY** converts the outer m-lambda expression and its arguments into a form and an environment, the environment produced is `((X A) (Y B))`. When **MICRO-APPLY** converts the inner m-lambda expression, the environment produced is `((L A) (M B))`.

Now consider the following, similar example, in which `X` and `Y` are free variables with respect to the inner m-lambda expression:

```
* (micro-eval '(m-apply
                 (m-quote
                   (m-lambda (x y)
                     (m-apply
                       (m-quote
                         (m-lambda ()
                           (m-cons x (m-cons y nil))))
                       (m-quote ()))))
                 (m-quote (a b))))
ERROR
I could find no variable binding for X.
>
```

The problem is that MICRO LISP has created new environments for both m-lambda expressions. The bindings for `X` and `Y` are not available for the evaluation of the inner m-lambda's body.

The way to fix the problem is to add closure-handling mechanisms to **MICRO-APPLY** and **MICRO-EVAL**. An m-closure expression is like an m-lambda expression with **M-CLOSURE** substituted for **M-LAMBDA** and an extra element, an environment:

```
(m-lambda <parameters> <body>)

(m-closure <parameters> <body> <environment>)
```

When a generalized MICRO-APPLY encounters an m-closure expression, rather than an m-lambda expression, it adds new variable bindings to the environment carried by the m-closure expression, rather than creating a completely new environment:

```
(defun micro-apply (procedure argument-values)  ;Version with closures.
  (if (symbolp procedure)
      (case procedure
        (m-first (first (first argument-values)))
        (m-rest (rest (first argument-values)))
        (m-cons (cons (first argument-values)
                      (second argument-values)))
        (m-endp (endp (first argument-values)))
        (m-not (not (first argument-values)))
        (m-eq (eq (first argument-values)
                  (second argument-values)))
        (t (let ((procedure-description (get procedure 'm-lambda)))
             (if procedure-description
                 (micro-apply procedure-description argument-values)
                 (error
                   "I could find no procedure description for ~a."
                   procedure)))))
      (case (first procedure)
        (m-lambda                                              ;New.
          (micro-eval (third procedure)
                      (bind-variables (second procedure)
                                      argument-values)))
        (m-closure                                             ;New.
          (micro-eval (third procedure)
                      (bind-variables (second procedure)
                                      argument-values
                                      (fourth procedure)))))))
```

Now on to closure creation. Once appropriately generalized, MICRO-EVAL converts m-lambda expressions into m-closure expressions whenever those m-lambda expressions are contained in an M-FUNCTION form. Thus (M-FUNCTION (M-LAMBDA <parameters> <body>)), when evaluated by MICRO-EVAL, becomes (M-CLOSURE <parameters> <body> <environment>). The required change to MICRO-EVAL is straightforward:

```
(defun micro-eval (form &optional environment) ;Version with closures.
  (if (atom form)
      (cond ((numberp form) form)
            ((eq t form) t)
            ((eq nil form) nil)
            (t (let ((binding (assoc form environment)))
                 (if binding
                     (second binding)
                     (error
                       "I could find no variable binding for ~a."
                       form)))))
      (case (first form)
        (m-quote (second form))
        (m-if (if (micro-eval (second form) environment)
                  (micro-eval (third form) environment)
                  (micro-eval (fourth form) environment)))
        (m-apply
          (micro-apply (micro-eval (second form) environment)
                       (micro-eval (third form) environment)))
        (m-function                        ;New.
          `(m-closure ,(second (second form))
                      ,(third (second form))
                      ,environment))
        (t (micro-apply
             (first form)
             (mapcar #'(lambda (x) (micro-eval x environment))
                     (rest form)))))))
```

With these additions to MICRO-APPLY and MICRO-EVAL, we can repeat the
trouble-causing example using M-FUNCTION instead of M-QUOTE:

```
* (micro-eval '(m-apply
                 (m-function
                   (m-lambda (x y)
                     (m-apply
                       (m-function
                         (m-lambda ()
                           (m-cons x (m-cons y nil))))
                       (m-quote ()))))
                 (m-quote (a b))))
  (A B)
```

Now there is no problem. From the inner m-lambda expression, MICRO-EVAL
produces the following m-closure expression:

```
(m-closure () (m-cons x (m-cons y nil)) ((x a) (y b)))
```

From this m-closure expression and an empty argument list, MICRO-APPLY concludes that ((X A) (Y B)) is the proper environment for evaluating the m-closure expression's body, (M-CONS X (M-CONS Y NIL)).

Problems

Problem 18-3: Modify MICRO-EVAL such that forms involving M-SETQ are handled. M-SETQ is to assign its evaluated second argument to its unevaluated first argument.

Problem 18-4: Using M-FUNCTION and M-SETQ, create a generator procedure, M-TOGGLE, such that successive evaluations of a form containing M-TOGGLE alternately return Ts and NILs, as in the following example:

```
* (micro-eval '(m-toggle))
NIL

* (micro-eval '(m-toggle))
T

* (micro-eval '(m-toggle))
NIL

* (micro-eval '(m-toggle))
T
...
```

Special Variable Binding Can Be Arranged

In MICRO LISP, the values of all variables are determined by the environment. We implemented MICRO-EVAL and MICRO-APPLY such that variables obey the laws of lexical scoping. Each time a procedure is applied, a new environment is created, unless that procedure is described in terms of an m-closure expression.

We could have elected to implement MICRO LISP such that all variables are special variables. Using the rules that apply to special variables, each time a procedure is applied, variable bindings are added to the existing environment. The required changes to MICRO-EVAL and MICRO-APPLY are slight. In MICRO-EVAL, we amend only the call to MICRO-APPLY to include a third argument, the environment:

```
(defun micro-eval (form &optional environment)
  (if (atom form)
      (cond ...)
      (case (first form)
        ...
        (m-apply
          (micro-apply (micro-eval (second form) environment)
                       (micro-eval (third form) environment)
                       environment))              ;New.
        ...
        (t (micro-apply
             (first form)
             (mapcar #'(lambda (x) (micro-eval x environment))
                     (rest form))
             environment)))))                     ;New
```

In MICRO-APPLY, we add the environment variable to the parameter list and include the current environment in the environment-producing form:

```
(defun micro-apply (procedure argument-values environment)
  (if (symbolp procedure)
      (case ...)
      (case (first procedure)
        (m-lambda
          (micro-eval (third procedure)
                      (bind-variables (second procedure)
                                      argument-values
                                      environment)))    ;New.
        ...)))
```

Because these versions of MICRO-EVAL and MICRO-APPLY treat all variables as special variables, the following form, which produced an error before, yields an answer here:

```
* (micro-eval '(m-apply
                 (m-quote
                   (m-lambda (x y)
                     (m-apply
                       (m-quote
                         (m-lambda ()
                           (m-cons x (m-cons y nil))))
                       (m-quote ()))))
                 (m-quote (a b))))
(A B)
```

**LISP Does
Call-by-Value
Rather Than
Call-by-Reference**

In the world of programming languages, there are two commonly employed options for handling procedure arguments. They are referred to as *call by reference* and *call by value*. To understand the difference, consider the following version of BOTH-ENDS:

```
(defun both-ends-with-setf (whole-list)
  (setf whole-list (cons (first whole-list) (last whole-list))))
```

There is really no reason to have a SETF in BOTH-ENDS-WITH-SETF, other than to illustrate one subtle point: using SETF to change the value of a procedure's parameter variable does not change the value of the corresponding argument variable when a procedure is used. For example, suppose we evaluate the following forms:

```
* (setf route '(boston cambridge lincoln concord))
```

```
* (both-ends-with-setf route)          ;ROUTE appears as an argument.
(BOSTON CONCORD)                       ;WHOLE-LIST's value changed
                                       ; inside BOTH-ENDS-WITH-SETF.
```

```
* route                                ;ROUTE's value was not effected.
(BOSTON CAMBRIDGE LINCOLN CONCORD)
```

On entering BOTH-ENDS-WITH-SETF, the parameter variable WHOLE-LIST is bound to the value of ROUTE. While evaluating the body of BOTH-ENDS-WITH-SETF, the value of WHOLE-LIST is reset to (BOSTON CONCORD), but resetting WHOLE-LIST has no effect on ROUTE; ROUTE's value remained unchanged.

In some languages, WHOLE-LIST and ROUTE are tied together in analogous circumstances, such that a change to a parameter variable on the inside of a procedure would be reflected in a change to the corresponding argument variable on the outside.

- Because using SETF to change the value of a procedure's parameter variable does not change the value of a corresponding argument variable, LISP is said to obey the conventions of *call by value*. When parameter variables and matching argument variables are tied together, the language is said to be *call by reference*.[1]

---

[1] Although LISP is a call-by-value language, the value of an argument can be changed by a change to a parameter if that change is done by certain surgical primitives that alter lists like those described in chapter 17. Only pointers to lists are copied, not lists themselves.

**LISP Can Be
Defined in LISP**

It may seem weird, but MICRO LISP could be modified and extended to become a language that is more and more like LISP itself. Because we already have described MICRO LISP using LISP, we must conclude that LISP can be described using LISP. Describing how LISP works using LISP as a tool is similar to the way a dictionary defines words in terms of other, presumably simpler words. LISP can be defined in terms of a small number of primitive procedures.

To avoid confusion, keep in mind that LISP interpretation requires a procedure, and LISP itself is a clear, transparent language for expressing procedures; therefore, the LISP interpretation procedure might just as well be implemented as a program in LISP.

That this can be done using only EVAL, APPLY, and a few other simple procedures suggests that a primitive LISP can be created by writing a few procedures in some other implementation language, followed by translating those procedures into machine language using the implementation language's compiler. Do not be misled, however. Although a primitive LISP is easy to write, a good implementation of COMMON LISP, with all its features, is a major undertaking.

**Fancy Control
Structures Usually
Start Out as Basic
LISP Interpreters**

Inserting a layer of interpretation is the first step toward implementing fancy control structures. An interpreter interposed between LISP and user programs provides the programming-language potter with plenty of clay. This is the way many very-high-level languages are first implemented and tested.

Summary

- It is easy to build a simple interpreter for a LISPlike language.
- MICRO-EVAL and MICRO-APPLY work together to evaluate forms.
- Traces show how MICRO-EVAL and MICRO-APPLY work together.
- Closures encapsulate environments.
- Special variable binding can be arranged.
- LISP does call-by-value rather than call-by-reference.
- LISP can be defined in LISP.
- Fancy control structures usually start out as basic LISP interpreters.

19

Examples
Involving
Search

The principal purpose of this chapter is to start your transition from the study of LISP as a programming language to your use of LISP as a problem-solving tool.

A secondary purpose of this chapter is to explore the well-known problem of *search* because search is ubiquitous in one form or another. The search procedures developed in this chapter find paths through maplike nets. Similar procedures do jobs ranging from robot motion planning to factory scheduling.

Breadth-First and Depth-First Searches Are Basic Strategies

The search problem is illustrated in figure 19-1. As shown, there is a starting place, S, at position (0 3); many intermediate places; and a finishing place, F, at position (11 3). The problem is to find a path from S through some of the intermediate places to F.

Formally, places are called *nodes*. The connections between nodes are called *arcs*. If it is possible to go from a node A to node B in one step, and vice versa, then A and B are called neighbors.

Our general strategy for search is to manipulate a list of partial paths, from the start node to intermediate nodes, until one of the partial paths is extended far enough to become an acceptable complete path. We call the

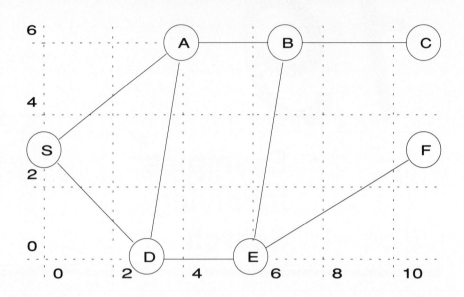

Figure 19-1. A typical search problem. The circles are nodes and the lines between them are arcs. The general problem is to find a path between one specified node, S, and another, F.

list of partial paths the *partial-path queue* because the first partial path on the list is always the one that is to be extended first. Here are the details:

- We create an initial partial-path queue consisting of just one partial path. The initial partial path is to contain the start node only.

- We extend the first partial path on the queue to all the neighbors of that path's terminal node. Then we replace the first partial path with the newly extended partial paths, adding the new partial paths to the appropriate places in the partial-path queue.

- We continue until one of the partial paths becomes an acceptable complete path from the start node to the finish node.

Thinking in terms of implementation, let us represent nodes as symbols, paths as lists of symbols, and the queue as a list of paths. Thus the first partial path in the example is (S) and the first queue of partial paths is ((S)).

The initial partial-path queue is then augmented by extending (S), the one partial path that is on the queue. This initial partial path is replaced by two new partial paths, one extending from S to A and another from S to D. Repeated replacement of the first partial path eventually produces a complete path from S all the way to F.

The general strategy leads to a variety of particular strategies depending on how the partial paths are added to the partial-path queue.

The general strategy is expressed in a procedure named NET-SEARCH. When you first call NET-SEARCH, you hand it a start and a finish node. In this situation, with no optional argument supplied, the first thing that NET-SEARCH does is to convert its starting-place argument into a one-element queue consisting of a single partial path. The form (LIST START) creates the partial path, and that partial path becomes the only element of the queue through another application of LIST:

```
(defun net-search (start finish &optional
                                (queue (list (list start))))
  ...)
```

In general, however, NET-SEARCH is to call itself recursively, with a current queue as the third argument. Consequently, NET-SEARCH needs to check the queue to see if it is empty. If the queue is empty, there are no further partial paths to consider and NET-SEARCH must fail:

```
(defun net-search (start finish &optional
                                (queue (list (list start))))
  (cond ((endp queue) nil)                ;Queue empty?
        ...))
```

If the queue is not empty, NET-SEARCH needs to see if the first partial path on the queue is a complete path. To make it easy to test paths for completion, let us represent each path in reverse order, such that the partial path from S to A is represented as (A S). To determine if such a reverse-order path is complete, we need only look at the first list element using FIRST:

```
(defun net-search (start finish &optional
                                (queue (list (list start))))
  (cond ((endp queue) nil)                      ;Queue empty?
        ((eq finish (first (first queue)))      ;Finish found?
         (reverse (first queue)))               ;Return path.
        ...))
```

And if the first partial path is not a complete path, NET-SEARCH needs to try again by calling itself recursively. This time, however, there are three arguments, not just two, as there is now an established queue:

```
(defun net-search (start finish &optional
                             (queue (list (list start))))
   (cond ((endp queue) nil)                      ;Queue empty?
         ((eq finish (first (first queue)))      ;Finish found?
          (reverse (first queue)))               ;Return path.
         (t (net-search start finish <new queue>)))) ;Try again.
```

Thus the only remaining problem has to do with forming a new queue. The first step is to write EXTEND, a procedure that extends a path.

But before we can write EXTEND, we must find a way to represent the arcs. Because we have already decided to represent the nodes with symbols, we attach properties to those symbols to represent the arcs. Thus the following SETF form captures the structure of the net shown in figure 25–1:

```
(setf (get 's 'neighbors) '(a d)
      (get 'a 'neighbors) '(s b d)
      (get 'b 'neighbors) '(a c e)
      (get 'c 'neighbors) '(b)
      (get 'd 'neighbors) '(s a e)
      (get 'e 'neighbors) '(b d f)
      (get 'f 'neighbors) '(e))
```

Having recorded the arcs as node properties, it is easy to find the neighbors of any node:

```
* (get 'd 'neighbors)
(S A E)
```

Consequently, you might think that the following appropriately transform the list of neighbors into new paths:

```
(defun extend (path)                                   ;Bugged!
  (mapcar #'(lambda (new-node) (cons new-node path))   ;Bugged!
          (et (first path) 'neighbors)))               ;Bugged!
```

The problem with this version of EXTEND is that it happily builds circular paths:

```
* (extend '(d a s))
((S D A S)                      ;Circular! Goes back to S.
 (A D A S)                      ;Circular! Goes back to A.
 (E D A S))                     ;Ok.
```

So let us add some apparatus to eliminate circular paths. We need only filter out any path for which the terminal node appears anywhere else:

```
(defun extend (path)
  (print (reverse path))                              ;Print path.
  (mapcar #'(lambda (new-node) (cons new-node path))  ;Form new paths.
          (remove-if #'(lambda (neighbor) (member neighbor path))
                     (get (first path) 'neighbors))))
```

Note that we added a form that prints the path that is about to be extended, in the normal start-to-termination order, so as to make it easy to see what is going on later. Now the circular paths are eliminated before they can cause trouble:

```
* (extend '(d a s))
(S A D)                                               ;Path to be extended.
((E D A S))                                           ;Just one noncircular path.
```

Now that we have written EXTEND, we can write DEPTH-FIRST, a version of NET-SEARCH that forms a new queue by adding all new partial paths to the front of the queue:

```
(defun depth-first (start finish &optional
                                 (queue (list (list start))))
  (cond ((endp queue) nil)                    ;Queue empty?
        ((eq finish (first (first queue)))     ;Finish found?
         (reverse (first queue)))              ;Return path.
        (t (depth-first                        ;Try again.
             start
             finish
             (append (extend (first queue))    ;New paths in front.
                     (rest queue))))))          ;Skip extended path.
```

Now that we have DEPTH-FIRST, we can try it on our example:

```
* (depth-first 's 'f)
(S)                                                   ;Initial path.
(S A)
(S A B)
(S A B C)                                             ;Dead end.
(S A B E)
(S A B E D)                                           ;Extensions all circular.
(S A B E F)                                           ;Complete path.
```

DEPTH-FIRST is said to do *depth-first search* because depth-first search moves deeply into the net as quickly as possible, extending one partial path as far as possible, ignoring other partial paths until needed.

In BREADTH-FIRST, new partial paths are added to the end of the queue:

```
(defun breadth-first (start finish &optional
                                   (queue (list (list start))))
  (cond ((endp queue) nil)                      ;Queue empty?
        ((eq finish (first (first queue)))      ;Finish found?
         (reverse (first queue)))               ;Return path.
        (t (breadth-first                       ;Try again.
            start
            finish
            (append (rest queue)                ;Skip extended path.
                    (extend (first queue)))))))) ;New paths in back.
```

Here is the result of using BREADTH-FIRST on the problem previously solved with DEPTH-FIRST:

```
* (breadth-first 's 'f)
(S)                                   ;Initial path.
(S A)                                 ;Two-node paths generated.
(S D)
(S A B)                               ;Three-node paths generated.
(S A D)
(S D A)
(S D E)
(S A B C)                             ;Four-node paths generated.
(S A B E)
(S A D E)
(S D A B)
(S D E B)
(S D E F)                             ;Complete path.
```

BREADTH-FIRST is said to do *breadth-first search* because breadth-first search extends all partial paths out to a uniform length before extending any to a greater length.

Problems

Problem 19-1: Rewrite DEPTH-FIRST such that it uses a DO form to work on the queue, rather than recursion.

Problem 19-2: In depth-first search, all of the partial paths in the queue at a given point in the search are related to one another in a simple way: each is the extension by one node of the partial path after it in the queue. The queue might, for example, look like this:

```
((D C B A) (C B A) (B A) (A))
```

Consequently you actually need to keep track of only the longest path in the queue, that is, the first partial path, because the queue could always be reconstructed from this path. Write a version of the procedure DEPTH-FIRST that does not explicitly construct a queue, merely a path that is passed along in the recursive calls, along with the start and finish nodes.

**Best-First Search
and Hill-Climbing
Require Sorting**

Sometimes it is possible to make a good guess about how far a given node is from the finish. If so, it may make sense to extend the path that leads to a place closest to the finish. This strategy is called *best-first search*.

Identifying the path that leads to the best place so far can be done, albeit somewhat wastefully, by ordering the paths completely. This is done using SORT, a primitive that takes a list and a two-parameter predicate. SORT rearranges the list such that if you feed any two of the rearranged list's elements to the predicate in the same order that they appear in the rearranged list, the predicate returns nonNIL:

```
* (sort '(3 1 4 1 5 9) #'<)
(1 1 3 4 5 9)
```

Note that SORT, like NCONC and DELETE, alters box contents:

```
* (setf pi-front '(3 1 4 1 5 9))
* (sort pi-front #'<)
(1 1 3 4 5 9)
* pi-front
(3 4 5 9)
```

Accordingly, if you want to retain the original list, copy it using the COPY-LIST before sorting:

```
* (setf pi-front '(3 1 4 1 5 9))
* (sort (copy-list pi-front) #'<)
(1 1 3 4 5 9)
* pi-front
(3 1 4 1 5 9)
```

Using SORT to sort the queue, BEST-FIRST is easy to implement:

```
(defun best-first (start finish &optional
                                (queue (list (list start))))
  (cond ((endp queue) nil)                     ;Queue empty?
        ((eq finish (first (first queue)))     ;Finish found?
         (reverse (first queue)))              ;Return path.
        (t (best-first                         ;Try again.
             start
             finish
             (sort (append (extend (first queue))
                           (rest queue))
                   #'(lambda (p1 p2) (closerp p1 p2 finish)))))))
```

Soon we will work on the predicate, CLOSERP. First, however, we need a way of estimating the distance remaining. For a map traversal problem, the straight-line distance is usually a good heuristic measure of distance remaining, although not always reliable. This requires coordinate knowledge, which we can add to the nodes via a COORDINATES property:

```
(setf (get 's 'coordinates) '(0 3)
      (get 'a 'coordinates) '(4 6)
      (get 'b 'coordinates) '(7 6)
      (get 'c 'coordinates) '(11 6)
      (get 'd 'coordinates) '(3 0)
      (get 'e 'coordinates) '(6 0)
      (get 'f 'coordinates) '(11 3))
```

With the COORDINATES properties in place, STRAIGHT-LINE-DISTANCE does the required computation:

```
(defun straight-line-distance (node-1 node-2)
  (let ((coordinates-1 (get node-1 'coordinates))
        (coordinates-2 (get node-2 'coordinates)))
    (sqrt (+ (expt (- (first coordinates-1)
                      (first coordinates-2))
                   2)
             (expt (- (second coordinates-1)
                      (second coordinates-2))
                   2)))))
```

Given STRAIGHT-LINE-DISTANCE, it is easy to decide if one partial path terminates closer to the finish than another:

```
(defun closerp (path-1 path-2 target-node)
  (< (straight-line-distance (first path-1) target-node)
     (straight-line-distance (first path-2) target-node)))
```

And with CLOSERP, we can test BEST-FIRST:

```
* (best-first 's 'f)
(S)                              ;Initial path.
(S A)                            ;A is closer to F than D is.
(S A B)
(S A B C)                        ;Dead end.
(S A B E)
(S A B E F)                      ;Complete path.
```

Note that BEST-FIRST was fooled in this instance because A is closer to F than D is. Ultimately, this led the search to the partial path from A to C. Although C is close to F by straight-line distance, C is a dead end.

For *hill-climbing search*, the strategy differs from the one for best-first search in that the new queue is made by sorting the new neighbors and placing them at the head of the queue, rather than by sorting the whole queue.

Problems

Problem 19-3: Our implementation of BEST-FIRST is inefficient because the entire queue is sorted even though most of it is in the right order already:

```
(sort (append (extend (first queue))      ;Needs sorting.
              (rest queue))               ;Already sorted.
      #'(lambda (p1 p2) (closerp p1 p2 finish)))
```

Define a new version of BEST-FIRST using MERGE, a primitive that efficiently combines two previously-sorted lists into a new list sorted the same way:

```
* (merge 'list
         '(1 3 5 7 9)
         '(0 2 4 6 8)
         #'<)
(0 1 2 3 4 5 6 7 8 9)
```

Note that the first argument in MERGE forms always indicates the desired type of the result. This is needed because MERGE accepts two strings, as well as two lists, and even one list and one string as long as both the list and the string contain data objects accepted by the merge predicate. Given that the argument types can be either lists, or strings, or both, the value can be either a list or a string, and LISP wants you to decide which it should be. The following two examples involve a string of characters, a list of characters, and CHAR<, a primitive that returns T if its two arguments are ordered in the usual numeric or alphabetic way:

```
* (merge 'list "13579" '(#\0 #\2 #\4 #\6 #\8) #'char<)
(#\0 #\1 #\2 #\3 #\4 #\5 #\6 #\7 #\8 #\9)
* (merge 'string "13579" '(#\0 #\2 #\4 #\6 #\8) #'char<)
"0123456789"
```

Problem 19-4: Define HILL-CLIMB, a search procedure that does hill climbing. Note that HILL-CLIMB is to produce the following results, which in our example are the same as the results produced by BEST-FIRST:

```
* (hill-climb 's 'f)
(S)                                   ;Initial path.
(S A)                                 ;A is closer to F than D is.
(S A B)
(S A B C)                             ;Dead end.
(S A B E)
(S A B E F)                           ;Complete path.
```

Problem 19-5: Define PATH-LENGTH, a procedure that returns the length of a path through a list of nodes, assuming that the distance between adjacent nodes on the list is the straight line distance, as computed by STRAIGHT-LINE-DISTANCE.

Next define SHORTERP, a predicate that takes two paths as arguments and returns T when the first path is shorter than the second.

Finally, define BRANCH-AND-BOUND, a search procedure that extends the shortest path on the queue. It is guaranteed to produce the shortest path from start to finish, even though all paths may not be fully extended to the finish.

Note that BRANCH-AND-BOUND is to produce the following results:

```
* (branch-and-bound 's 'f)
(S)                                ;Initial path.
(S D)                              ;Shortest path extended.
(S A)
(S D E)
(S A B)
(S D A)
(S A D)
(S A B C)
(S D E F)                          ;Shortest path complete.
```

Problem 19-6: Define BEAM, a search procedure similar to BREADTH-FIRST, but that extends only a specified number of the best paths of each length, where *best* means terminates closest to the goal. The name BEAM is used because *beam search* looks at a small number of ways to continue, just as a person with a flashlight looks at a small part of the world.

The following illustrate. Note that the specified number of paths to extend is given as BEAM's third argument. Note also that BEAM may fail to find any path even though there is one:

```
* (beam 's 'f 1)
(S)                                ;Initial path.
(S A)                              ;Just one two-node path extended.
(S A B)                            ;Just one three-node path extended.
(S A B C)                          ;Dead end.
NIL                                ;Failure.

* (beam 's 'f 2)
(S)                                ;Initial path.
(S A)                              ;Two two-node paths extended.
(S D)
(S A B)                            ;Two three-node paths extended.
(S D E)
(S D E F)                          ;Complete path.
```

```
* (beam 's 'f 3)
(S)                                          ; Initial path.
(S A)                                        ; Only two two-node paths to extend.
(S D)
(S A B)                                      ; Three three-node paths extended.
(S D E)
(S D A)
(S D E F)                                    ; Complete path.
```

Problem 19-7: In a *PERT chart*, for program evaluation and review technique, nodes represent tasks, each of which takes a known amount of time. Directed branches represent precedence relations, such that if there is an branch from task *A* to task *B*, then task *A* must be done before work can begin on task *B*. In chapter 20, we explain a program that simulates the flow of work through PERT charts. Here we treat PERT charts as nets to be searched.

Suppose we alter the net we have been working with, introducing directed arcs, as shown in figure 19-2 and as captured in this SETF form:

```
(setf (get 's 'successors) '(a d)
      (get 'a 'successors) '(b d)
      (get 'b 'successors) '(c e)
      (get 'c 'successors) '()
      (get 'd 'successors) '(e)
      (get 'e 'successors) '(f)
      (get 'f 'successors) '())
```

Further suppose that we attach a property to each task node indicating how much time each takes:

```
(setf (get 's 'time-consumed) 3
      (get 'a 'time-consumed) 2
      (get 'b 'time-consumed) 4
      (get 'c 'time-consumed) 3
      (get 'd 'time-consumed) 3
      (get 'e 'time-consumed) 2
      (get 'f 'time-consumed) 1)
```

Now write ALL-PATHS, a procedure that returns a list of all noncircular paths starting from a given node. Note that ALL-PATHS is to produce the following final result:

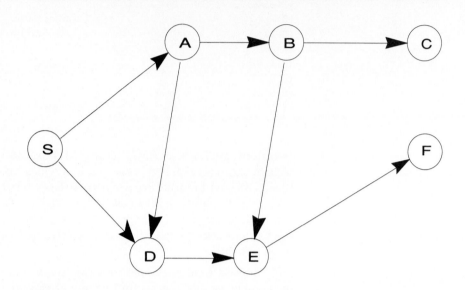

Figure 19-2. A PERT chart. Circles represent tasks and the lines between them represent precedence relations.

```
* (all-paths 's)
((S A D E F)
 (S A B E F)
 (S A B C)
 (S D E F))
```

You must change extend so that it uses the SUCCESSOR property rather than the NEIGHBORS property and you should delete the form in EXTEND that prints the path, to avoid an avalanche of detail. To get all incomplete paths to the front of the queue, use SORT together with FIRST-PATH-INCOMPLETE-P, a predicate that returns T if the first of two arguments is an incomplete path:

```
(defun first-path-incomplete-p (p1 p2)
  (not (endp (extend p1))))      ;Second argument ignored.
```

Problem 19-8: Write TIME-CONSUMED, a procedure that determines how much time is consumed by the tasks in a path.

Next, write LONGERP, a procedure that takes two paths as arguments and returns T if the first path is more time consuming than the second.

Finally, modify ALL-PATHS, the procedure you developed in the previous problem, so that it returns the *critical path*, the one taking the longest time. Delays along the critical path delay the entire project.

Note that CRITICAL-PATH is to produce the following result:

```
* (critical-path 's)
(S A B E F)
```

Problem 19-9: It is inefficient to sort a queue completely when all that you really want is for the right path to be in front. Write `MOVE-BEST-TO-FRONT`, a procedure that takes a queue and a predicate and returns a revised queue with the best element in front.

Note that `MOVE-BEST-TO-FRONT` is to produce the following results:

```
* (move-best-to-front '((b a s) (d a s) (a d s) (e d s)) #'shorterp)
((E D S) (B A S) (D A S) (A D S))
```

In your solution, you will probably want to use a `DOLIST` form, and you will probably want to use a `REMOVE` form with an `EQUAL` test.

Problems about Measuring Out a Volume of Water

Imagine being given two crocks of different volumes, a and b. The crocks may be filled from a source or emptied into a sink. In addition, water can be poured from one into the other until it is filled or until the crock from which water is being poured is emptied. The problem is to measure out a given volume, c.

First of all, we insist that this volume fit into one or the other of the two crocks. Thinking about it carefully, it is clear that only certain volumes can be measured out this way. For example, if b is twice a, it is not possible to measure out amounts other than a and twice a. In fact, if both a and b are multiples of n, only multiples of n can be measured out. We can now deduce the general rule that only multiples of the greatest common divisor of a and b can be achieved.

Assuming that the volumes of the two crocks are such that c is achievable, let us proceed to consider sequences of possible moves. A little thought makes it clear that it never makes sense to back up, undoing what has been achieved so far. As a result, water always moves in one direction: from the source it goes into one crock; from there, into the other; and from there, it is finally poured out. We do not have to search a huge tree of possible moves, because most moves do not make sense. It is sufficient to repeat a series of transfers in one direction, checking at each step whether one of the two crocks happens to contain the correct amount of water.

Problem 19-10: Recalling that *a* and *b* are the capacities of the two crocks, write TRANSFER such that the following occurs:

• If the right amount is in crock A, stop.

• If the right amount is in crock B, stop.

• If crock A is full, empty it.

• If crock B is empty, fill it.

• If the water in crock B will fit into crock A, empty crock B into crock A.

• Otherwise, fill crock A from crock B.

Note that TRANSFER is always to be called with arguments reflecting the current contents of the two crocks, the capacities of the two crocks, and the desired amount of water. Here is an example of TRANSFER in action:

```
* (transfer 0 0 3 5 2)
I can produce 2 units in B.
((FILL B) (FILL A FROM B))
```

Problem 19-11: Using TRANSFER, write WATER-CROCK, a procedure that is to return the results of calling TRANSFER if a water crock solution is possible. Here are examples of water crock in action:

```
* (water-crock 3 5 2)
I can produce 2 units in B.
((FILL B) (FILL A FROM B))

* (water-crock 3 6 2)
Sorry, I cannot produce 2 units.
NIL
```

You will probably want to use REM, the primitive that returns the remainder of its first argument when divided by its second, and GCD, a primitive that returns the greatest common devisors of two integers:

```
* (rem 28 22)
6

* (rem 22 14)
8

* (gcd 28 22)
2

* (gcd 22 14)
2
```

**Problems about
Placing Queens on
a Chess Board**

How is it possible to place n queens on an n by n chess board so that
they do not threaten each other? A queen in chess can move along the
column, the row, and the two diagonals through her present position. We
can encode the positions on the board by numbering the rows and columns.
Thus solutions to the 4×4 problem can be represented as four-element lists
of two-element lists of row and column numbers, with ((0 1) (1 3) (2 0)
(3 2)) corresponding to the following nonthreatening arrangement:

```
* (print-board '((0 1) (1 3) (2 0) (3 2)))
*---------*
| . Q . . |
| . . . Q |
| Q . . . |
| . . Q . |
*---------*
NIL
```

Note that the row and column indexes start at zero.

Problem 19-12: Write PRINT-BOARD, an auxiliary procedure to print out a
board configuration as shown in the example, given the list of coordinates.

Problem 19-13: Now the task is to write QUEEN, a procedure that finds all
solutions for a given board size. First, however, you need a predicate that
determines whether two queens threaten each other. The following will do:

```
(defun threat (i j a b)          ;One queen at (i, j); other at (a, b).
  (or (= i a)                    ;Same row.
      (= j b)                    ;Same column.
      (= (- i j) (- a b))        ;SW-NE diagonal.
      (= (+ i j) (+ a b))))      ;NW-SE diagonal.
```

Now remember that you are to represent configurations of queens using
lists of two-element sublists, each sublist containing the row and column
number of one queen on the board. Suppose now that we plan to add a
queen to a partially developed board. The following predicate will tell us
whether the position (n, m) for the new queen is safe:

```
(defun conflict (n m board)
  (cond ((endp board) nil)
        ((threat n
                 m
                 (first (first board))
                 (second (first board)))
         t)
        (t (conflict n m (rest board)))))
```

With these preliminaries out of the way we can tackle the problem. Write
`QUEEN` such that it tries all possible placements.

Let the single argument, `SIZE`, specify the size of the board. This will
be eight for a full chess board, but it is interesting to watch the program
at work on smaller boards too. There are no solutions for 2×2 and 3×3
boards, for example, but there are two for a 4×4 board:

```
* (queen 2)
NIL

* (queen 3)
NIL

* (queen 4)
*---------*
| . Q . . |
| . . . Q |
| Q . . . |
| . . Q . |
*---------*
*---------*
| . . Q . |
| Q . . . |
| . . . Q |
| . Q . . |
*---------*
NIL
```

Summary
- Breadth-first and depth-first searches are basic strategies.
- Best-first search and hill-climbing require sorting.

References

For a general introduction to search, see chapter 4 of *Artificial Intelligence
(Second Edition)* by Patrick H. Winston. Knuth [1973] and Aho, Hopcroft,
and Ullman [1974] cover search more deeply.

Euclid's algorithm for finding the greatest common divisor is discussed
in Brown [1971].

20

Examples
Involving
Simulation

The principal purpose of this chapter is to continue your transition from the study of LISP as a programming language to your use of LISP as a problem-solving tool.

A secondary purpose of this chapter is to explain how programs can *simulate* real-world activities, because simulation, like search, is frequently part of problem solving. The program developed in this chapter does project simulation, which is broadly useful in itself. Similar programs simulate such wildly differing things as signals flowing through circuits and parts flowing through factories.

**Projects Involve
Events and Tasks**

Suppose you are in charge of getting your company into new quarters. Having carefully thought about what needs to be done, you know that you need to select a space, negotiate a lease, produce an office plan, prepare the space, obtain furniture, and move.

In the vernacular of project planning and analysis, the things to do are called *tasks*, and the instants when a task is either started or finished are called *events*.

No task can start until all of its prerequisite tasks, if any, are finished. Customarily, the prerequisite dependencies are shown in a diagram called

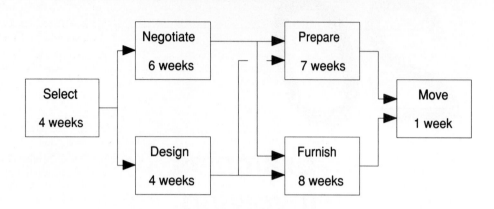

Figure 20-1. A PERT chart. Each arrow between tasks indicates a prerequisite dependency: the task at the tail must be finished before the task at the head can begin.

a *PERT chart*, where PERT is an acronym for <u>P</u>rogram <u>E</u>valuation and <u>R</u>eview <u>T</u>echnique. Figure 20-1 is a PERT chart for our example.

Assuming each task begins as soon as all prerequisite tasks are finished, the way tasks constrain events is expressed in a simple formula in which $t(i)$ represents the time when prerequisite i is complete, d represents the task duration, and $t(o)$ represents the time when the task is finished:

$$t(o) = \max_i t(i) + d$$

Structures Can Represent Events and Tasks

We now develop a program that simulates project progress. It is to be a *simulator* because it is to examine the events in the same order in which those events occur in the actual project. This makes it easy for the simulator to produce a schedule of events, with times increasing, like the following:

```
Time 0:  starting  SELECT.
Time 4:  finishing SELECT.
Time 4:  starting  NEGOTIATE.
Time 4:  starting  DESIGN.
Time 8:  finishing DESIGN.
Time 10: finishing NEGOTIATE.
Time 10: starting  PREPARE.
Time 10: starting  FURNISH.
Time 17: finishing PREPARE.
Time 18: finishing FURNISH.
Time 18: starting  MOVE.
Time 19: finishing MOVE.
```

Our approach is to develop structures for events and tasks first, and then to develop procedures that simulate plan progress. For events, we need a structure with fields for the time, the task whose completion corresponds to the event, and all the tasks that cannot start until the event occurs.

```
(defstruct event              ;Temporary version.
  (time 'unknown)
  (input-task nil)
  (output-tasks nil))
```

For tasks, we need a structure with fields for a name, for all the events that must occur before the task begins, the event that corresponds to the task's completion, and the task duration.

```
(defstruct task               ;Temporary version.
  (name 'unknown)
  (input-events nil)
  (output-event nil)
  (duration 'unknown))
```

Next consider CONNECT, a utility procedure for connecting events and tasks together:

```
(defun connect (task output inputs)
  (setf (task-input-events task) inputs)       ;Inputs
  (dolist (event inputs)
    (push task (event-output-tasks event)))
  (setf (task-output-event task) output)       ;Output
  (setf (event-input-task output) task))
```

Using CONNECT we can connect up our sample PERT chart as follows:

```
(let ((s (make-task :duration 4 :name 'select))
      (n (make-task :duration 6 :name 'negotiate))
      (d (make-task :duration 4 :name 'design))
      (p (make-task :duration 7 :name 'prepare))
      (f (make-task :duration 8 :name 'furnish))
      (m (make-task :duration 1 :name 'move))
      (e1 (make-event :time 0))
      (e2 (make-event)) (e3 (make-event))
      (e4 (make-event)) (e5 (make-event))
      (e6 (make-event)) (e7 (make-event)))
  (setf *start* e1)
  (connect s e2 (list e1))    (connect n e3 (list e2))
  (connect d e4 (list e2))    (connect p e5 (list e3 e4))
  (connect f e6 (list e3 e4)) (connect m e7 (list e5 e6))
  'done)
```

Note that the special variable *START* is bound to the first event. Without *START*, none of the events or tasks would be accessible after the LET form is evaluated.

Our general approach to PERT chart analysis is to create `SIMULATE-EVENT`
and `SIMULATE-TASK`, which work their way from one end of the PERT chart
to the other, simulating project progress.

First consider `SIMULATE-EVENT`. When called, it puts a time in an event's
`TIME` field and calls `SIMULATE-TASK` on each of the tasks in the event's `OUTPUT-
TASKS` field:

```
(defun simulate-event (time event)
  (setf (event-time event) time)
  (dolist (output-task (event-output-tasks event))
    (simulate-task output-task)))
```

Now consider `SIMULATE-TASK`. When times are available for all of the events
in a task's `INPUT-EVENTS` field, as determined by `EVENT-TIMES-KNOWN-P`, it
is easy to compute the start time, using `LATEST-TIME`, and it is easy to
compute the finish time for the task:

```
(defun simulate-task (task)
  (when (event-times-known-p (task-input-events task))
    (let* ((start-time (latest-time (task-input-events task)))
           (finish-time (+ (task-duration task) start-time)))
      ...)))

(defun event-times-known-p (list-of-events)
  (not (find-if-not
         #'(lambda (event) (numberp (event-time event)))
         list-of-events)))

(defun latest-time (events)
  (apply #'max (mapcar #'event-time events)))
```

Now suppose `SIMULATE-TASK` simply prints its start and finish time, using
two auxiliary procedures, `ANNOUNCE-START-TIME` and `ANNOUNCE-FINISH-TIME`,
and calls `SIMULATE-EVENT`. Note the 9T and 19T directives in the `FORMAT`
forms. They mean skip to the ninth and nineteenth columns:

```
(defun simulate-task (task)                      ;Bugged!
  (when (event-times-known-p (task-input-events task))
    (let* ((start-time (latest-time (task-input-events task)))
           (finish-time (+ (task-duration task) start-time)))
      (announce-start-time start-time (task-name task))
      (announce-finish-time finish-time (task-name task))
      (simulate-event finish-time (task-output-event task)))))

(defun announce-start-time (time name)
  (format t "~%Time ~a:~9tstarting~19t~a." time name))
```

```
(defun announce-finish-time (time name)
  (format t "~%Time ~a:~9tfinishing~19t~a." time name))
```

The problem with this definition of SIMULATE-TASK is that tasks are simulated in the order that they are encountered as LISP recurses through SIMULATE-TASK and SIMULATE-EVENT, not in the order that they occur in time.

Plainly, if SIMULATE-TASK is to simulate tasks, the evaluation of the printing and propagation forms must be deferred until the appropriate moment. This illustrates:

```
* (simulate-event 0 *start*)
Time 0:  starting  SELECT.
Time 4:  finishing SELECT.
Time 4:  starting  DESIGN.
Time 8:  finishing DESIGN.
Time 4:  starting  NEGOTIATE.
Time 10: finishing NEGOTIATE.
Time 10: starting  FURNISH.
Time 18: finishing FURNISH.
Time 10: starting  PREPARE.
Time 17: finishing PREPARE.
Time 18: starting  MOVE.
Time 19: finishing MOVE.
DONE
```

But before we explain what needs to be done, you must endure a diversion.

Event and Task Structures Require Special Printing Procedures

When you print a structure or an expression containing a structure, LISP normally prints the structure according to the following template:

```
#s(<structure type> <field name> <field value> ...)
```

For example, suppose you print the event structure assigned to *START* *before* you connect it to task structures:

```
* *start*
#s(EVENT :TIME 0 :INPUT-TASK NIL :OUTPUT-TASKS NIL)
```

Unfortunately, if you try to print the same structure *after* it is connected to task structures, you encounter a problem:

```
* *start*
#s(EVENT :TIME 0
         :INPUT-TASK NIL
         :OUTPUT-TASKS
         (#s(TASK :NAME SELECT
                  :INPUT-EVENTS
                  (#s(EVENT :TIME 0
                            :INPUT-TASK NIL
                            :OUTPUT-TASKS

                            ...
```

Printing an event structure requires printing the contents of two fields with task structures in them, both of which have event fields. Printing the contents of those event fields requires printing the original event structure again, starting a endless circle.

Fortunately, there is a way to change the way structures are printed. You simply replace the structure name in the structure definition with an expression that includes the name of a printing procedure:

```
<structure name>
```

↓

```
(<structure name> (:PRINT-FUNCTION <name of printing procedure>))
```

Here is the revised definition of the event structure:

```
(defstruct (event (:print-function print-event))
  (time 'unknown)
  (input-task nil)
  (output-tasks nil))
```

With this altered structure definition in place, whenever LISP wants to print an event structure, LISP applies PRINT-EVENT to the structure. PRINT-EVENT, like all structure-printing procedures, must accept three arguments, even though you are not compelled to use them. LISP arranges for the first argument to be the structure to be printed. LISP further arranges for the second argument to be the stream that LISP is currently printing to and for the third to be how far printing has progressed down into a nesting of data objects.

For PRINT-EVENT, we do not use the second and third arguments, so we just bind them, appropriately enough, to a rest parameter named IGNORE:

```
(defun print-event (structure &rest ignore)
  (format t "<event structure>"))
```

As defined, PRINT-EVENT also ignores the structure argument. All events are printed as identical strings specified in the FORMAT form appearing in PRINT-EVENT:

```
* (make-event)
<event structure>
```

MAKE-EVENT still produces a structure, as before, with field values that can be accessed and changed. All that has changed is the way the structure is printed.

Similarly, we redefine the task structure, adding **PRINT-TASK**, a printing procedure for tasks. **PRINT-TASK** is similar to **PRINT-EVENT**, except that when a task structure is printed, **PRINT-TASK** includes the task's name in the printed string:

```
(defstruct (task (:print-function print-task))
  (name 'unknown)
  (input-events nil)
  (output-event nil)
  (duration 'unknown))

(defun print-task (structure &rest ignore)
  (format t "<task structure for ~a>" (task-name structure)))

* (make-task)
<task structure for UNKNOWN>
```

An Event List Keeps Simulation in Step with the Simulated Project

Returning to simulation, we solve our evaluation-order problem by maintaining ***EVENT-SEQUENCE***, a special variable whose value is a list of forms to be evaluated, keeping those forms ordered by their time-indicating arguments. Before showing the necessary modifications to our simulation procedures, we first illustrate how the value of ***EVENT-SEQUENCE*** is to change in working our example problem.

The following shows the result of the first call to **SIMULATE-EVENT**, which of course calls **SIMULATE-TASK**.

```
* (defvar *event-sequence* nil)
* (simulate-event 0 *start*)
* *event-sequence*
((ANNOUNCE-START-TIME 0 'SELECT)
 (ANNOUNCE-FINISH-TIME 4 'SELECT)
 (SIMULATE-EVENT 4 <event structure>))
```

Now suppose we start popping elements off of ***EVENT-SEQUENCE***, evaluating each using **EVAL**, explained in chapter 9. The first two times, the list assigned to ***EVENT-SEQUENCE*** becomes shorter and a message is printed:

```
* (eval (pop *event-sequence*))
Time 0:  starting    SELECT.
NIL
* *event-sequence*
((ANNOUNCE-FINISH-TIME 4 'SELECT)
 (SIMULATE-EVENT 4 <event structure>))

* (eval (pop *event-sequence*))
Time 4:  finishing   SELECT.
NIL
* *event-sequence*
((SIMULATE-EVENT 4 <event structure>))
```

Next time, however, the first element is a `SIMULATE-EVENT` form. Evaluating it produces two calls to `SIMULATE-TASK`, one to work on the `NEGOTIATE` task and the other, on `DESIGN`. Each of the two calls leads to three new forms in the ordered list assigned to `*EVENT-SEQUENCE*`:

```
* (eval (pop *event-sequence*))
NIL
* *event-sequence*
((ANNOUNCE-START-TIME 4 'NEGOTIATE)
 (ANNOUNCE-START-TIME 4 'DESIGN)
 (ANNOUNCE-FINISH-TIME 8 'DESIGN)
 (SIMULATE-EVENT 8 <event structure>)
 (ANNOUNCE-FINISH-TIME 10 'NEGOTIATE)
 (SIMULATE-EVENT 10 <event structure>))
```

By now, you see the general picture. We add new print and simulate forms to an event sequence. Because the event sequence is ordered by time, we ensure that `SIMULATE-TASK` works on the tasks in the same sequence followed in the actual project.

To actually get forms on the ordered list assigned to `*EVENT-SEQUENCE*` we use `ADD-TO-EVENT-SEQUENCE`, which sorts elements according to `EARLIER-FIRST-P`. Forms with identical times are arranged with finish announcements first, followed by event simulations:

```
(defun add-to-event-sequence (form)
  (setf *event-sequence*
        (sort (cons form *event-sequence*)
              #'earlier-first-p)))
(defun earlier-first-p (x y)
  (cond ((< (second x) (second y)) t)
        ((= (second x) (second y))
         (cond ((eq 'announce-finish-time (first x)) t)
               ((eq 'announce-finish-time (first y)) nil)
               ((eq 'simulate-event (first x)) t)
               ((eq 'simulate-event (first y)) nil)))))
```

Returning to SIMULATE-TASK, we must construct the appropriate forms using backquote and add them to the event list using ADD-TO-EVENT-SEQUENCE:[1]

```
(defun simulate-task (task)
  (when (event-times-known-p (task-input-events task))
    (let* ((start-time (latest-time (task-input-events task)))
           (finish-time (+ (task-duration task) start-time)))
      (add-to-event-sequence
        `(announce-start-time ,start-time ',(task-name task)))
      (add-to-event-sequence
        `(announce-finish-time ,finish-time ',(task-name task)))
      (add-to-event-sequence
        `(simulate-event ,finish-time ,(task-output-event task))))))
```

To complete our program, we add a SIMULATE procedure that does what we have done by hand so far. After setting *EVENT-SEQUENCE* to NIL and calling SIMULATE-EVENT to start the simulation, SIMULATE simply iterates, with the list assigned to *EVENT-SEQUENCE* shrinking and growing, until the list is empty:

```
(defun simulate (starting-event time)
  (setf *event-sequence* nil)
  (simulate-event time starting-event)
  (loop
    (if (endp *event-sequence*)
        (return 'done)
        (eval (pop *event-sequence*)))))
```

Here then is SIMULATE, in action, producing the desired result:

```
* (simulate *start* 0)
Time 0:  starting  SELECT.
Time 4:  finishing SELECT.
Time 4:  starting  NEGOTIATE.
Time 4:  starting  DESIGN.
Time 8:  finishing DESIGN.
Time 10: finishing NEGOTIATE.
Time 10: starting  PREPARE.
Time 10: starting  FURNISH.
Time 17: finishing PREPARE.
Time 18: finishing FURNISH.
Time 18: starting  MOVE.
Time 19: finishing MOVE.
DONE
```

---

[1] There is a better way, albeit more sophisticated, using lexical closures. We explore it in a problem.

Problems

Problem 20-1: Suppose you change your mind, realizing that you cannot start working on the office-move project until day ten. You rerun the simulation with a surprising, disturbing result:

```
* (simulate *start* 10)
Time 10: starting  SELECT.
Time 14: finishing SELECT.
Time 14: starting  NEGOTIATE.
Time 14: starting  DESIGN.
Time 18: finishing DESIGN.
Time 18: starting  PREPARE.
Time 18: starting  FURNISH.
Time 20: finishing NEGOTIATE.
Time 20: starting  PREPARE.
Time 20: starting  FURNISH.
...
DONE
```

The problem is that the results of the first simulation are still lying about in the events. You could, of course, recreate the entire net from scratch, with fresh structures, but it is more elegant to create time-forgetting procedures instead. Noting that time forgetting need not happen in any particular order, define FORGET-EVENT and FORGET-TASK such that (FORGET-EVENT ⟨event⟩) causes the time of the event and all dependent events to be reset to UNKNOWN. Then redefine simulate so that it works properly, even when rerunning a simulation.

Problem 20-2: Occasionally, you learn that the time required by a task has been incorrectly estimated. Write REVISE-TASK-DURATION, a procedure that resets the time in a task's DURATION field and prints a revised schedule of all dependent events:

```
* (simulate *start* 0)

* (revise-task-duration *design* 7)
Time 4:  starting   DESIGN.
Time 11: finishing  DESIGN.
Time 11: starting   PREPARE.
Time 11: starting   FURNISH.
Time 18: finishing  PREPARE.
Time 19: finishing  FURNISH.
Time 19: starting   MOVE.
Time 20: finishing  MOVE.
DONE
```

Be sure to use one of the forgetting procedures that you developed in the preceding problem. Also, you may find it convenient to use SIMULATE-TASK and a piece of SIMULATE.

Problem 20-3: Our approach to adding forms to the *EVENT-SEQUENCE* list has the virtue of producing a readable list which helps you understand what is going on. On the other hand, our approach has the defect of requiring ugly, hard to write backquote forms. It would be nicer if SIMULATE-TASK could be defined this way:

```
(defun simulate-task (task)
  (when (event-times-known-p (task-input-events task))
    (let* ((start-time (latest-time (task-input-events task)))
           (finish-time (+ (task-duration task) start-time)))
      (add-to-event-sequence
        (announce-start-time start-time (task-name task)))
      (add-to-event-sequence
        (announce-finish-time finish-time (task-name task)))
      (add-to-event-sequence
        (simulate-event finish-time (task-output-event task))))))
```

To do this, redefine ADD-TO-EVENT-SEQUENCE to be a macro so that its argument is not evaluated. Note that ADD-TO-EVENT-SEQUENCE cannot just sort the new form into the *EVENT-SEQUENCE* list, however, for there would be no way to recover variable values when the new form is evaluated later.

Summary

- Projects involve events and tasks.
- Structures can represent events and tasks.
- Simulation procedures can propagate event times.
- Event and task structures require special printing procedures.
- An event list keeps simulation in step with the simulated project.

21

The Blocks World
With Classes
and Methods

The principal purpose of this chapter is to reinforce your understanding of the object-oriented programming paradigm introduced in chapter 14.

One secondary purpose of this chapter is to exhibit a program that is larger than those in earlier chapters with a view toward illustrating procedure abstraction and data abstraction. In particular, we describe a blocks-manipulation program to be used by a one-handed robot operating in a world that consists of a few blocks lying on a table.

Another secondary purpose is to illustrate the *problem reduction* paradigm, a problem-solving paradigm that goes hand in hand with the idea of procedure abstraction. Most of the problems in the blocks world are transformed into one or more subproblems, hiding the details of just how those subproblems are solved.

The Blocks-World Program Handles Put-On Commands

Figure 21-1 shows the blocks world. Here are the rules according to which the blocks are to be manipulated:

- There are three kinds of movable objects: bricks, wedges, and balls.
- The robot has one hand. It can grasp any movable block that has nothing on top of it.

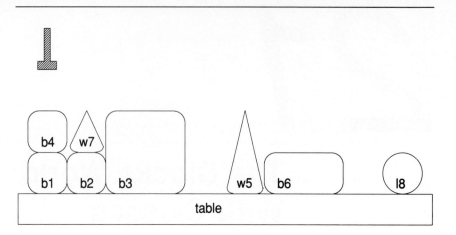

Figure 21-1. A particular situation in the blocks world. Several moves are required to put block B1 on block B2.

- Every block is either held by the hand or supported by exactly one brick or the table. No block can overhang from its support.
- Although a movable block can be moved to the top of a wedge or a ball, neither wedges nor balls can support anything.
- Supporting bricks can support more than one block, as long as there is room.
- The table is wide enough for all of the blocks to fit on it at once.

In the course of moving the blocks, the robot often has to move obstructions out of the way. Given the arrangement shown in figure 21-1, for example, the robot's blocks manipulation program suggests the following action when you want to put block B1 on top of block B2:

```
* (put-on b1 b2)
Move hand to pick up W7 at location (3 4).
Grasp W7.
Move W7 to top of TABLE at location (8 0).
Ungrasp W7.
Move hand to pick up B4 at location (1 4).
Grasp B4.
Move B4 to top of TABLE at location (16 0).
Ungrasp B4.
Move hand to pick up B1 at location (1 2).
Grasp B1.
Move B1 to top of B2 at location (2 2).
Ungrasp B1.
T
```

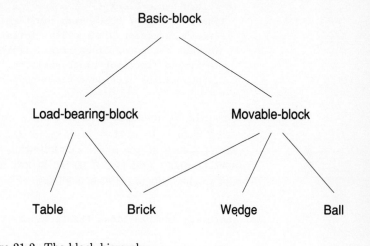

Figure 21-2. The block hierarchy.

Object-Oriented Programming Shifts Attention from Procedures to Objects

Now we could develop a blocks manipulation program from a procedure-oriented perspective. We could think about the various sorts of things that need to be done, perhaps concentrating on bricks, ignoring the possibility that we might want to generalize to other sorts of objects like wedges or balls. Later on, if we were to decide to generalize, we would have to alter existing programs to test for special cases. Procedures would become bloated and hard to debug. Worse yet, new bugs would inevitably cause collapse even on previously handled cases.

Consequently, we elect to develop a blocks manipulation program from an object-oriented perspective. In developing the blocks program from an object-oriented perspective, we think early on about the things we want to deal with, we arrange them into a class hierarchy, and then we write methods to cover some of those things. Later on, if we decide to extend the program by adding new classes, we need only add new methods to handle those classes. Old methods remain untouched, reducing the probability that our program will collapse on previously handled cases.

Object-Oriented Programming Begins with Class Specification

Our blocks world contains several block classes, as shown in the classification tree of figure 21-2.

First, we define a class for blocks, the BASIC-BLOCK class. Each accessor procedure has a BLOCK- prefix. The position slot is to be occupied by a list of the x and y coordinates.

```
(defclass basic-block ()
  ((name :accessor block-name :initarg :name)
   (width :accessor block-width :initarg :width)
   (height :accessor block-height :initarg :height)
   (position :accessor block-position :initarg :position)
   (supported-by :accessor block-supported-by :initform nil)))
```

Once the BASIC-BLOCK class is defined, defining other classes is easy. Because each is a subclass of BASIC-BLOCK, there is no need to repeat the
slot specifiers at any level. The following expressions define the classes for
MOVABLE-BLOCK and LOAD-BEARING-BLOCK; note that we add a SUPPORT-FOR
slot to the LOAD-BEARING-BLOCK class:

```
(defclass movable-block (basic-block) ())
```

```
(defclass load-bearing-block (basic-block)
  ((support-for :accessor block-support-for :initform nil)))
```

Next we arrange for the BRICK, WEDGE, and BALL classes:

```
(defclass brick (movable-block load-bearing-block) ())
```

```
(defclass wedge (movable-block) ())
```

```
(defclass ball (movable-block) ())
```

Next we have a class for the table, which we define as a load-bearing block,
but not as a movable block:

```
(defclass table (load-bearing-block) ())
```

And finally, we need a class for the hand:

```
(defclass hand ()
  ((name :accessor hand-name :initarg :name)
   (position :accessor hand-position :initarg :position)
   (grasping :accessor hand-grasping :initform nil)))
```

With all these classes defined, we proceed to create all the individual bricks,
wedges and balls, along with the table, placing all the blocks at initial
positions shown in figure 21-3.

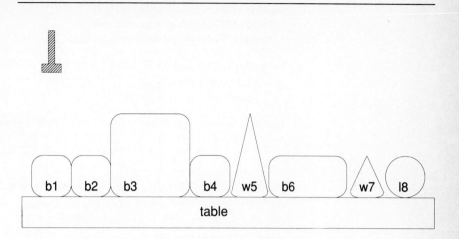

Figure 21-3. The initial position of the blocks in the blocks world.

```
(defvar *blocks*
 (list
  (make-instance 'table :name 'table :width 20 :height 0 :position '(0 0))
  (make-instance 'brick :name 'b1 :width 2 :height 2 :position '(0 0))
  (make-instance 'brick :name 'b2 :width 2 :height 2 :position '(2 0))
  (make-instance 'brick :name 'b3 :width 4 :height 4 :position '(4 0))
  (make-instance 'brick :name 'b4 :width 2 :height 2 :position '(8 0))
  (make-instance 'wedge :name 'w5 :width 2 :height 4 :position '(10 0))
  (make-instance 'brick :name 'b6 :width 4 :height 2 :position '(12 0))
  (make-instance 'wedge :name 'w7 :width 2 :height 2 :position '(16 0))
  (make-instance 'ball  :name 'l8 :width 2 :height 2 :position '(18 0))
))
```

At this point, the only way to get at the instances of the classes is through the list assigned to *BLOCKS*. For increased convenience, we assign each instance to the symbol found in its name slot. We do this using SET, which is like SETF, except that SET evaluates both its arguments, the first of which must evaluate to the name of a special variable:

```
(dolist (l *blocks*) (set (block-name l) l))
```

There is a symbol for each block, and the value of that symbol is the appropriate block-describing instance.

Now it is time to fill in the SUPPORTED-BY and SUPPORT-FOR slots. All the bricks rest on the table initially:

```
(dolist (l (remove table *blocks*))
  (push l (block-support-for table))
  (setf (block-supported-by l) table))
```

Note that PUSH, like SETF, works just fine with slot accessor forms as well as with variable names.

Finally, we need a hand:

```
(defvar *hand* (make-instance 'hand :name '*hand* :position '(0 6)))
```

Problems

Problem 21-1: Define a constructor, MAKE-BLOCK, that creates blocks with ordinary arguments rather than key arguments. With your new constructor, the following will do the same thing:

```
* (make-instance 'ball :name '18
                       :width 2
                       :height 2
                       :position '(18 0))
* (make-block 'ball '18 2 2 18 0)
```

Problem 21-2: Our initialization of the blocks world is awkward because we have not yet introduced the procedures for moving blocks around. Consequently, we must pick places on the table for each block by hand. Anticipating the PUT-ON procedure, which arranges for all BLOCK-SUPPORT-FOR and BLOCK-SUPPORTED-BY slots to be properly maintained, initialize the blocks world in another way.

Slot Readers Are Generic Functions

The slot accessor procedures are actually generic function methods. Accordingly, you can define additional methods that complement those that are created automatically when you define your classes.

Consider BLOCK-SUPPORT-FOR, for example. When we created the LOAD-BEARING-BLOCK class, we indicated that there is to be an accessor method, BLOCK-SUPPORT-FOR, for the SUPPORT-FOR slot. The CLOS inheritance rules ensure that this automatically created method works on bricks and on the table because BRICK and TABLE are subclasses of LOAD-BEARING-BLOCK. It will not work on wedges and balls, however, because WEDGE and BALL are not subclasses of LOAD-BEARING-BLOCK.

The problem is that we want to be able to apply BLOCK-SUPPORT-FOR to any object instance without explicitly testing its class to be sure that the automatically-created method is applicable. Consequently, we need to augment the automatically-created method with one that acts like a slot reader for everything that is *not* a load-bearing block:

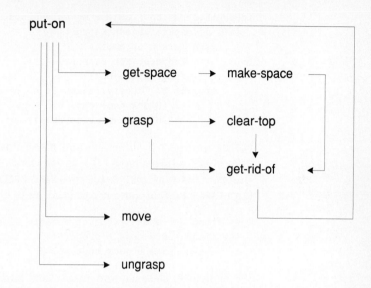

Figure 21-4. The blocks manipulation program uses many short goal-oriented methods. PUT-ON means put one brick on another. PUT-ON is used both to accomplish the main goal and to help clear away obstacles.

```
(defmethod block-support-for ((object basic-block))
  nil)
```

This new method returns NIL because only load-bearing blocks can support things. Note that it acts as if it were reading a value from a SUPPORT-FOR slot although it is applied only to object instances without a SUPPORT-FOR slot.

The Blocks-World Program's Methods Are Transparent

Our robot's blocks manipulation program consists of the generic functions shown in figure 21-4. The arrows represent generic function calls that always occur.

The goal of PUT-ON is to place one object on another. The work is done by finding a place using GET-SPACE and then grasping the object, moving it, and ungrasping, using the primitives GRASP, MOVE, and UNGRASP. Thus the problem-solving technique used in PUT-ON is an example of *problem reduction* because the problem of placing an object on another is broken up into simpler problems. Because the same general approach puts any type of block on any type of block, we can define a general PUT-ON method as follows:

```
(defmethod put-on ((object movable-block) (support basic-block))
  (if (get-space object support)
      (and (grasp object)
           (move object support)
           (ungrasp object))
      (format t "~&Sorry, there is no room for ~a on ~a."
              (block-name object)
              (block-name support)))))
```

PUT-ON returns T if successful and NIL if not. GET-SPACE, MAKE-SPACE, and
FIND-SPACE return places. To do its work, GET-SPACE tries FIND-SPACE. If
that does not work, GET-SPACE tries MAKE-SPACE. MAKE-SPACE is more powerful
than FIND-SPACE because it can clear away obstructions to make room:

```
(defmethod get-space ((object movable-block) (support basic-block))
  (or (find-space object support)
      (make-space object support)))
```

We explain FIND-SPACE and MAKE-SPACE later. Now, however, we turn to
GRASP. You might be surprised at GRASP's complexity, but GRASP has many
things to check. First, the hand may be grasping the correct object, in
which case there is nothing to do. If the hand is not grasping the correct object, GRASP must be sure that the top of the object is cleared off
or else clear it off using CLEAR-TOP. Next, GRASP must get rid of anything
that it happens to be holding using GET-RID-OF. After that, GRASP prints
appropriate messages and puts appropriate values in the hand's slots:

```
(defmethod grasp ((object movable-block))
  (unless (eq (hand-grasping *hand*) object)
    (when (block-support-for object) (clear-top object))
    (when (hand-grasping *hand*)
      (get-rid-of (hand-grasping *hand*)))
    (format t "~&Move hand to pick up ~a at location ~a."
            (block-name object)
            (top-location object))
    (setf (hand-position *hand*) (top-location object))
    (format t "~&Grasp ~a." (block-name object))
    (setf (hand-grasping *hand*) object))
  t)
```

GRASP, like PUT-ON and most of the other methods yet to be defined, returns
T if successful and NIL if not.

UNGRASP lets go by modifying the GRASPING slot of the hand. Note,
however, that the modification happens only if UNGRASP is sure there is a
support. If the SUPPORTED-BY slot contains NIL, then UNGRASP does nothing
and returns NIL:

```
(defmethod ungrasp ((object movable-block))
  (when (block-supported-by object)
    (format t "~&Ungrasp ~a." (block-name object))
    (setf (hand-grasping *hand*) nil)
    t))
```

GET-RID-OF is really simple. It puts an object on the table:

```
(defmethod get-rid-of ((object movable-block))
  (put-on object table))
```

MAKE-SPACE is nothing more than a repeated appeal to GET-RID-OF to clear away space for a new object. The loop containing GET-RID-OF returns as soon as enough clutter has been cleared away to make enough room for FIND-SPACE to succeed:

```
(defmethod make-space ((object movable-block) (support basic-block))
  (dolist (obstruction (block-support-for support))
    (get-rid-of obstruction)
    (let ((space (find-space object support)))
      (when space (return space)))))
```

Now let us turn to CLEAR-TOP. Its purpose is to remove all the objects directly supported by something the hand is supposed to grasp. This is done by looping until each object found in the SUPPORT-FOR slot is disposed of by GET-RID-OF:

```
(defmethod clear-top ((support load-bearing-block))
  (dolist (obstacle (block-support-for support) t)
    (get-rid-of obstacle)))
```

Finally, in between grasping and ungrasping, objects are moved. MOVE prints appropriate messages and revises location slots. MOVE also calls upon REMOVE-SUPPORT and ADD-SUPPORT, which take care of keeping the SUPPORT-FOR and SUPPORTED-BY properties up-to-date:

```
(defmethod move ((object movable-block) (support basic-block))
  (remove-support object)
  (let ((newplace (get-space object support)))
    (format t "~&Move ~a to top of ~a at location ~a."
            (block-name object)
            (block-name support)
            newplace)
    (setf (block-position object) newplace)
    (setf (hand-position *hand*) (top-location object)))
  (add-support object support)
  t)
```

REMOVE-SUPPORT and ADD-SUPPORT are auxiliary methods that do bookkeeping. Because MOVE can move only movable objects, REMOVE-SUPPORT is always called with a movable-object argument; hence the parameter specializer is, in a sense, redundant:

```
(defmethod remove-support ((object movable-block))
  (let ((support (block-supported-by object)))
    (when support
      (setf (block-support-for support)
            (remove object (block-support-for support)))
      (setf (block-supported-by object) nil)
      t)))
```

Suppose we assume MOVE can move a movable object to any other object, load bearing or not. If the target object is not a load bearing object, the hand must hold the moved object in position. If the target object is a load bearing object, we want to add a support relation so that the hand can let go.

Thus, in the general case, ADD-SUPPORT does nothing, but if the supporting object is a load-bearing block, ADD-SUPPORT acts:

```
(defmethod add-support ((object movable-block)
                        (support basic-block))
  t)
(defmethod add-support ((object movable-block)
                        (support load-bearing-block))
  (push object (block-support-for support))
  (setf (block-supported-by object) support)
  t)
```

The blocks-manipulation methods, with the assistance of a few number-crunching methods introduced in a later section, handle the problem posed as the chapter opened. However, we can improve it and increase your understanding of CLOS by working a bit more on MOVE.

Before and After Methods Simplify Bookkeeping

So far, you have learned about what are called primary methods, of which only one is used whenever a generic function appears in a form. Conveniently, there are two other kinds of methods, the :BEFORE methods and the :AFTER methods.

Like primary methods, :BEFORE or :AFTER methods have parameter specializers. Whenever :BEFORE or :AFTER methods are applicable methods with respect to a form, all applicable :BEFORE methods are applied, from the most specific to the least specific, then the most specific primary method is applied, and finally, all applicable :AFTER methods are applied, from the least specific to the most specific. The primary method is still the one that determines the form's value.

The `:BEFORE` and `:AFTER` methods are frequently used in supporting roles, enabling primary methods to remain unencumbered by bookkeeping detail.

Consider `REMOVE-SUPPORT` and `ADD-SUPPORT`, for example. Both have a supporting role with respect to the `MOVE` method. Moreover, the `REMOVE-SUPPORT` form is evaluated before the other forms in `MOVE` and the `ADD-SUPPORT` form is evaluated after other forms in `MOVE`:

```
(defmethod move ((object movable-block)
                 (support basic-block))
  (remove-support object)
  (let ((newplace (get-space object support)))
    ...
    )
  (add-support object support)
  t)
```

Accordingly, `REMOVE-SUPPORT` and `ADD-SUPPORT` are natural candidates for redoing as `:BEFORE` and `:AFTER` methods. Both can be removed from `MOVE`, with the intention of converting them into `:BEFORE` and `:AFTER` methods in the `MOVE` generic function:

```
(defmethod move ((object movable-block)      ;New version.
                 (support basic-block))
  (let ((newplace (get-space object support)))
    ...)
  t)
```

And the following is the result of converting the old `REMOVE-SUPPORT` methods into a single new `MOVE` method marked by `:BEFORE`. We include a second, ignored parameter in our new `MOVE` method. This is necessary because other `MOVE` methods have two parameters and because all of the methods belonging to the same generic function must have the same number of parameters:

```
(defmethod move :before ((object movable-block) ignored-parameter)
  (let ((support (block-supported-by object)))
    (when support
      (format t "~%Removing support relations between ~a and ~a."
        (block-name object) (block-name support))
      (setf (block-support-for support)
            (remove object (block-support-for support)))
      (setf (block-supported-by object) nil)
      t)))
```

Similarly, the old `ADD-SUPPORT` methods have become a single `MOVE` method marked by `:AFTER`. Again we have added a `FORMAT` form:

```
(defmethod move :after ((object movable-block)
                        (support load-bearing-block))
  (format t "~%Adding support relations between ~a and ~a."
          (block-name object) (block-name support))
  (setf (block-support-for support)
        (cons object (block-support-for support)))
  (setf (block-supported-by object) support)
  t)
```

Now we can test our changes, starting with all the blocks on the table:

```
* (progn (put-on b2 w7)
         (put-on b1 b2))
Move hand to pick up B2 at location (3 2).
Grasp B2.
Removing support relations between B2 and TABLE.
Move B2 to top of W7 at location (16 2).
Move B2 to top of TABLE at location (2 0).
Adding support relations between B2 and TABLE.
Ungrasp B2.
Move hand to pick up B1 at location (1 2).
Grasp B1.
Removing support relations between B1 and TABLE.
Move B1 to top of B2 at location (2 2).
Adding support relations between B1 and B2.
Ungrasp B1.
T
```

Note that the :AFTER method is not activated when the brick, B2, is placed on the wedge, W7. Consequently, no support relation is placed, and B2 must be returned to the table before B1 can be grasped.

Problems

Problem 21-3: Define a new class, NON-LOAD-BEARING-BLOCK, a superclass of WEDGE and BALL and a subclass of BASIC-BLOCK. Next, arrange for an appropriate message to be printed whenever you put any object on top of a wedge or ball.

Problem 21-4: You can simplify the initialization of the blocks, eliminating the DO forms, by adding an :AFTER method to INITIALIZE-INSTANCE, a generic function that is called by MAKE-INSTANCE. Here is a template for the new method:

```
(defmethod initialize-instance
           :after
           ((block basic-block) &key name)
  <body>)
```

Finish the definition by filling in the template. You may assume that the table is the first object to be defined.

Problem 21-5: In the previous problem, you simplified the initialization of the blocks world by creating an :AFTER method for INITIALIZE-INSTANCE. In another problem, you simplified the initialization by putting each block on the table using PUT-ON. Combine the two solutions by using PUT-ON inside an :AFTER method for INITIALIZE-INSTANCE.

Problem 21-6: Define another PUT-ON method such that you get the following result:

```
* (put-on table b1)
Sorry, you cannot move a table.
NIL
```

Slot Writers Are Generic Functions

The primary MOVE method now looks as follows, once bookkeeping details have been pushed off into :BEFORE and :AFTER methods:

```
(defmethod move ((object movable-block) (support basic-block))
  (let ((newplace (get-space object support)))
    (format t "~&Move ~a to top of ~a at location ~a."
            (block-name object)
            (block-name support)
            newplace)
    (setf (block-position object) newplace)
    (setf (hand-position *hand*) (top-location object)))
  t)
```

Noting that accessor procedures are actually generic functions, you can push still other bookkeeping details off into other :BEFORE and :AFTER methods, eliminating the form dealing with the hand from the primary MOVE method:

```
(defmethod move ((object movable-block) (support basic-block))
  (let ((newplace (get-space object support)))
    (format t "~&Move ~a to top of ~a at location ~a."
            (block-name object)
            (block-name support)
            newplace)
    (setf (block-position object) newplace))
  t)
```

To do this, you must define a new :AFTER method for the writer that goes
along with BLOCK-POSITION, the generic function for reading the POSITION
slot in MOVABLE-BLOCK object instances. Such writer methods are defined
using a slight modification of the usual DEFMETHOD template. The place
usually occupied by a single-symbol generic function name holds (SETF
⟨reader name⟩), which is considered a two-symbol generic function name:

```
(defmethod (setf block-position)
           :after
           (new-position (object movable-block))
  (setf (hand-position *hand*) (top-location object)))
```

This DEFMETHOD form creates a method that is applied after the evaluation
of anything of the following form in which OBJECT's value belongs to the
MOVABLE-BLOCK class or one of its subclasses:

```
(setf (block-position object) <new position>)
```

Problem 21-7: Suppose you want to add a graphic module to the blocks
manipulation program. One way would be to add forms wherever a block's
position slot is changed. Describe a better way.

**Object-Oriented
Programming
Enables Automatic
Procedure Assembly**

In chapter 14, we noted that object-oriented programming offers automatic
retrieval for data-type specific procedure versions and automatic procedure
reuse. Now that you have learned about :BEFORE and :AFTER methods, you
can see that there is another related advantage: procedures are assembled
from bits and pieces automatically.

You Can Control How Instances Are Printed

If you try to print an instance, or an expression containing an instance, LISP may print something unpredictably ugly because CLOS does *not* prescribe a printed form for instances. Fortunately, however, CLOS has a generic function, PRINT-OBJECT, which is used by LISP whenever LISP wants to print an instance. By adding your own PRINT-OBJECT methods, you can control how your instances are printed.

The first parameter in all PRINT-OBJECT methods specializes the method to a particular class. The second parameter is bound on entry to a stream to print to. For our example, the first argument is to be an instance of the BASIC-BLOCK class. The name of the block involved is printed inside some descriptive text:

```
(defmethod print-object ((x basic-block) stream)
  (format stream "#<block ~a>" (block-name x)))
```

Now you can print the value of B1 or the value of *BLOCKS*:

```
* b1
#<block b1>

* *blocks*
(#<block b1>
 #<block b2>
 #<block b3>
 #<block b4>
 #<block w5>
 #<block b6>
 #<block w7>
 #<block 18>
 #<block table>)
```

The Number-Crunching Methods Can Be Ignored

Neither FIND-SPACE nor TOP-LOCATION is easy to implement, particularly if the implementation is to be general. Fortunately, however, you can ignore them as they do not introduce any important ideas. Alternatively, you can look at the limited implementation given in this section.

To begin, we assume that we can treat all objects as if they were bricks with integer dimensions in a two-dimensional world. We further assume that all supported objects must rest on only one support with no overhang.

Our assumptions enable us to follow the strategy illustrated in figure 21-5. We imagine that the left edge of the object to be placed is lined up with the left edge of the proposed support. Next, we see if the object to be placed overlaps any other supported objects in that position. If there

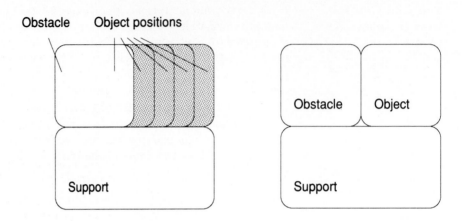

Figure 21-5. To find a place for a new object, we imagine the object in all possible positions, checking for intersection until one of the possible positions proves acceptable.

is overlap, we move the object to be placed one unit to the right and try again. We repeat until we find an acceptable place or there are no places left to try.

FIND-SPACE embodies our strategy. We implement it as an ordinary procedure, not as a method. There is little point in creating a method if there is only one way to do something, a way that is independent of argument class.

```
(defun find-space (object support)
  (dotimes (offset (+ 1 (- (block-width support)
                           (block-width object))))
    (unless (intersections-p object offset
                             (first (block-position support))
                             (block-support-for support))
      (return (list (+ offset (first (block-position support)))
                    (+ (second (block-position support))
                       (block-height support)))))))
```

FIND-SPACE needs a way to determine if two objects intersect. Our assumptions make this a simple job; INTERSECTIONS-P, another ordinary procedure, just compares the left and right sides of the object to be placed against the left and right sides of each possible obstacle. There is no intersection if the left side of the object is to the right of the right side of the obstacle, or if the right side of the object is to the left of the left side of the obstacle:

```
(defun intersections-p (object offset base obstacles)
  (dolist (obstacle obstacles)
    (let* ((ls-proposed (+ offset base))
           (rs-proposed (+ ls-proposed (block-width object)))
           (ls-obstacle (first (block-position obstacle)))
           (rs-obstacle (+ ls-obstacle (block-width obstacle))))
      (unless (or (>= ls-proposed rs-obstacle)
                  (<= rs-proposed ls-obstacle))
        (return t)))))
```

TOP-LOCATION, still another ordinary procedure, finds the top center of an object by simple calculations using the width and height of the object:

```
(defun top-location (object)
  (list (+ (first (block-position object))
           (/ (block-width object) 2))
        (+ (second (block-position object))
           (block-height object))))
```

Problems

Problem 21-8: Suppose we generalize the definition of BASIC-BLOCK to include a home position so that whenever a block is to be placed on the table, it can be placed at the home position:

```
(defclass basic-block ()
  ((name :accessor block-name :initarg :name)
   (width :accessor block-width :initarg :width)
   (height :accessor block-height :initarg :height)
   (position :accessor block-position :initarg :position)
   (home-position :accessor block-home-position :initform nil)
   (supported-by :accessor block-supported-by :initform nil)))
```

Then, after we have created the blocks, we can arrange for their initial positions to be their home positions:

```
(dolist (l (remove table *blocks*))
  (setf (block-home-position l) (block-position l)))
```

Define a GET-SPACE method, specialized situations in which the table is the support, that always returns the home position. When so defined, GET-SPACE ensures that no block's home position ever can be occupied by some other block.

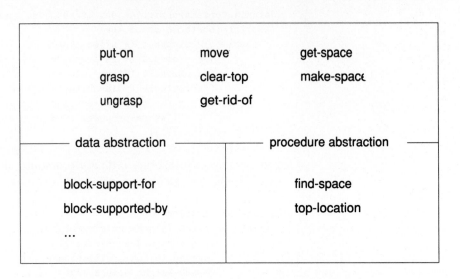

Figure 21-6. The blocks world illustrates both a data-abstraction boundary and a procedure-abstraction boundary. The data-abstraction boundary is a byproduct of class specification. The procedure-abstraction boundary is a deliberate consequence of isolating place-oriented computations.

The Blocks-World Program Illustrates Abstraction

The blocks world program is a good example of several kinds of abstraction. One kind is illustrated by nearly every procedure because procedure abstraction is a natural byproduct of organizing procedures around goals: each goal-oriented procedure does little more than call other goal-oriented procedures without caring how those other procedures do their job.

Other abstraction examples are suggested in figure 21-6. Because the program uses instances of classes to represent objects, the details of how data are represented are hidden behind a data-abstraction boundary automatically produced when the various classes were defined. Similarly, because the details of place manipulation are hidden behind FIND-SPACE and TOP-LOCATION, there is a procedure-abstraction boundary as well.

Summary

- The blocks-world program handles put-on commands.
- Object-oriented programming shifts attention from procedures to objects.
- Object-oriented programming begins with class specification.
- The blocks-world program's methods are transparent.
- Before and after methods simplify bookkeeping.

- Accessors are generic functions.
- Object-oriented programming enables automatic procedure assembly.
- You can control how object are printed.
- The number-crunching methods can be ignored.
- The blocks-world program illustrates abstraction.

References

The blocks world appear as the domain of discourse in Winograd's early work on natural language [1972]. For a general introduction to the blocks world and problem reduction, see chapter 2 of *Artificial Intelligence (Second Edition)* by Patrick H. Winston.

For a complete treatment of the COMMON LISP Object System, see *Object-Oriented Programming in COMMON LISP*, by Sonya E. Keene.

22

Answering Questions about Goals

The principal purpose of this chapter is to further reinforce your understanding of the object-oriented programming paradigm introduced in chapter 14 and developed further in chapter 21.

A secondary purpose of this chapter is to explain how a program can answer questions about *how* and *why* it has done things the way it has. Because our robot's blocks manipulation program is organized around methods that work toward identifiable goals, it is easy to add a little extra machinery to it that records how the robot's blocks manipulation methods have called upon one another in the form of a history-remembering *goal tree*. Once a goal tree has been built, simple question-answering procedures can answer *how* and *why* questions by searching the goal tree and commenting on what they find.

The Blocks-World Program Can Introspect into its Own Operation

Consider the problem illustrated in figure 21-1. While solving the problem the robot's blocks manipulation program, once suitably modified, can build a goal tree, captured in a set of classes as shown in figure 22-1. In the goal tree, each node represents a situation in which a method was invoked. Most nodes branch out into other nodes that represent methods called to help out.

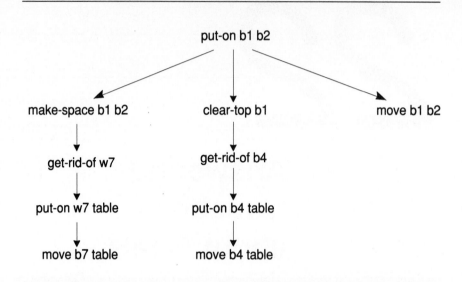

Figure 22-1. A goal tree built by a modified blocks manipulation program. Goal trees make it easy to answer certain questions about *how*, *why*, and *when*. In general, moving one level down handles questions about how; one level up, why; and all the way to the top, when.

Why questions are the first to think about. "Why did you put W7 on the table?" is correctly answered by finding a suitable occurrence of PUT-ON in the goal tree, looking up to the next higher node, and answering that the action was performed in order to get rid of W7. The question, "Why did you do that?" then requires another step up the tree, producing a remark about making space for B1 on B2. Repeating the question produces an answer involving the desire to put B1 on B2, and repeating again leads to the universal, top-level response, "Because you told me to."

Questions about *how* go the other way. "How did you put B1 on B2?" causes a response stating that a place was made for B1 on B2, B1 was cleared off, and B1 was moved to B2. Asking about the first action, making a place, results in a remark about getting rid of W7. Asking about getting rid of W7 causes a remark about putting W7 on the table. Asking about that leads to a statement that W7 was moved to the table.

Questions about *when* can be handled too. The trick is to trace up from the node asked about, all the way to the top of the tree to the node that represents the originating command. Thus "When did you move W7 to the table?" can be answered by noting that it was done while B1 was being put on B2.

Here then is a summary of how to answer *how*, *why*, and *when* questions:

- *Why* questions are answered either by moving one step up the goal tree and describing the goal found there or by saying "Because you told me to!"

- *How* questions are answered by either enumerating the goals found one step down in the goal tree or by saying "I just did it!"

- *When* questions are answered by a reference to a top-level goal.

Thus a tree of generic function calls makes it possible to answer *how, why,* and *when* questions related to accomplished actions. How can the blocks-world program construct such a tree? One way is to build some extra machinery into the existing blocks-world program by adding new methods.

Remembering Generic Function Calls Creates a Goal Tree

Each time a method is used, we want to record several associated things such as who called it, whom it calls, and the values of the arguments. One natural place to put such information is in a node class:

```
(defclass node ()
  ((parent :accessor node-parent :initform nil)
   (children :accessor node-children :initform nil)
   (action :accessor node-action :initform nil)))
```

Now we must arrange to create a node each time a method is called. In our example, MAKE-SPACE calls GET-RID-OF and GET-RID-OF calls PUT-ON. A node representing the call to GET-RID-OF therefore must have a node representing an occurrence of MAKE-SPACE in its parent slot and another node representing an occurrence of PUT-ON in its children slot.

Next we must explain how the blocks-world program can be modified to generate such nodes as it does its work. For illustration, we start with GET-RID-OF:

```
(defmethod get-rid-of ((object movable-block))
  (put-on object table))
```

When GET-RID-OF is called, we want the following to happen:

- A node for the particular occurrence of GET-RID-OF is constructed.

- The nodes for the occurrence of GET-RID-OF and for the corresponding occurrence of the calling method are tied together via their parent and children slots.

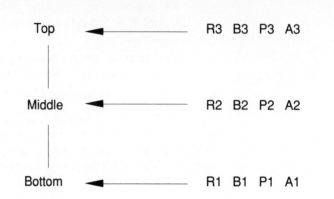

Figure 22-2. Three classes, each of which is associated with one :`AROUND` method (R), one :`BEFORE` method (B), one primary method (P), and one :`AFTER` method (A), all belonging to the same generic function. The rules of method combination specify that the calling order is R1–R2–R3–B1–B2–B3–P1–P2–P3–A3–A2–A1, assuming that the :`AROUND` and primary methods contain appropriate (`CALL-NEXT-METHOD`) forms.

To get these things done, take note that there are :`AROUND` methods, as well as :`BEFORE`, :`AFTER`, and primary methods. Like :`BEFORE` and :`AFTER` methods, :`AROUND` methods are used frequently in supporting roles, enabling primary methods to be wrapped up inside methods that perform necessary, but distracting chores, especially when those chores require knowledge of the primary method's result.

To deal with :`AROUND` methods, we have to generalize the handling of :`BEFORE`, primary, and :`AFTER` methods as introduced in chapter 21. First, the most specific :`AROUND` method is applied. If an applied :`AROUND` method evaluates a (`CALL-NEXT-METHOD`) form, then the next most specific :`AROUND` method is applied, and its value becomes the value of the (`CALL-NEXT-METHOD`) form.

Figure 22-2 illustrates using a one-parameter generic function with :`AROUND`, :`BEFORE`, primary, and :`AFTER` methods specialized by each of three classes, `BOTTOM`, `MIDDLE`, and `TOP`. Now suppose the generic function is called with an argument that belongs to the `BOTTOM` class. Assuming that all the :`AROUND` methods involve the evaluation of a (`CALL-NEXT-METHOD`) form, the list of applied methods begins as R1–R2–R3–....

If there are no more :`AROUND` methods, and a (`CALL-NEXT-METHOD`) form has been evaluated in each of them, then the :`BEFORE`, primary, and :`AFTER` methods are applied. But if any of the :`AROUND` methods fails to evaluate a (`CALL-NEXT-METHOD`) form, all the other methods are ignored.

If all the :`AROUND` methods evaluate a (`CALL-NEXT-METHOD`) form, the

:BEFORE methods are applied next, from the most specific to the least specific. For the example in figure 22-3, the list of applied methods continues as R1–R2–R3–B1–B2–B3–....

Next the most specific primary method is applied. In previous chapters, only one primary method could be applied because we had not yet introduced the (CALL-NEXT-METHOD) primitive. Now, however, note that if an applied primary method evaluates a (CALL-NEXT-METHOD) form, then the next most specific primary method is applied, and its value becomes the value of the (CALL-NEXT-METHOD) form. The value of the first primary method applied is the value returned by the (CALL-NEXT-METHOD) form in the last :AROUND method. For the example, the list of applied methods continues as R1–R2–R3–B1–B2–B3–P1–P2–P3–....

Finally, the :AFTER methods are applied, from the least specific to the most specific. For the example, the list of applied methods concludes as R1–R2–R3–B1–B2–B3–P1–P2–P3–A3–A2–A1.

The value of the first :AROUND method is the value returned overall.

We can use :AROUND methods to build a history tree of nodes. First, however, we create a top-level node and assign it to *CURRENT-NODE*, which is declared to be special. It will end up as the only node with NIL in its parent slot:

```
(defvar *current-node* (make-instance 'node))
```

Next we have a partial definition of an :AROUND method for GET-RID-OF:

```
(defmethod get-rid-of :around ((object movable-block))
  (let* ((parent *current-node*)
         (*current-node* (make-instance 'node))
         (primary-method-value (call-next-method)))
    ...
    primary-method-value))
```

The first thing to note is that the value returned is the value of PRIMARY-METHOD-VALUE and PRIMARY-METHOD-VALUE is bound to the value of (CALL-NEXT-METHOD). And because there is to be just one :AROUND method for GET-RID-OF, the value of (CALL-NEXT-METHOD) will be the value of the primary method. Hence the value of the :AROUND method is the value of the primary method. The :AROUND method serves only as a sort of wrapper, a wrapper that builds the history tree.

The next thing to note is that the LET* form introduces PARENT-NODE, which happens to be a lexical variable by default, and *CURRENT-NODE*, which is a special variable by virtue of its appearance in a preceding DEFVAR form.

Now think carefully about how LET* forms are evaluated. First the LET*'s first initial-value form is evaluated, offering up the current value

for *CURRENT-NODE*. Because *CURRENT-NODE* is a special variable, PARENT-
NODE is bound to the value of *CURRENT-NODE* at the time GET-RID-OF is
called. Thus the history of generic function calls determines the value of
PARENT-NODE. Then, once PARENT-NODE is bound to the value of *CURRENT-
NODE*, a node is created by (MAKE-INSTANCE 'NODE) and the result becomes
CURRENT-NODE's new value.

Now to manipulate PARENT and *CURRENT-NODE*, we define two auxiliary
methods, ATTACH-PARENT, which ties parent and child nodes together, and
ATTACH-ACTION, which attaches an action description to a node:

```
(defmethod attach-parent ((child node) (parent node))
  (setf (node-parent child) parent)        ;Attach parent to child.
  (setf (node-children parent)             ;Attach child to parent.
        (append (node-children parent)
                (list child))))
(defmethod attach-action ((node node) action)
  (setf (node-action node) action))
```

As it stands, we expect ACTION's value to be a list, and we could specialize
it to LIST, forcing LISP to signal a no-applicable-method error if our expec-
tation is violated. As we noted in chapter 14, however, some programmers
feel that using specialization for argument type checking is questionable
programming practice.

Blending ATTACH-PARENT and ATTACH-ACTION into GET-RID-OF we have
the following new, tree-building version:

```
(defmethod get-rid-of :around ((object movable-block))
  (let* ((parent *current-node*)
         (*current-node* (make-instance 'node))
         (primary-method-value (call-next-method)))
    (when primary-method-value
      (attach-parent *current-node* parent)
      (attach-action *current-node*
                     (list 'get-rid-of object)))
    primary-method-value))
```

Evidently, unless PRIMARY-METHOD-VALUE's value is NIL, the newly created
node is attached to its parent.

**Macros Enable
Method-Defining
Procedures To Be
Defined**

Naturally, it would be tedious to construct such history-remembering methods by hand. It is easier to do it with a method-defining macro, DEFINE-
HISTORY-METHOD. Note that it calls REMOVE-SPECIALIZERS, an auxiliary procedure that transforms a list of specialized parameters into a list of parameters:

```
(defmacro define-history-method (name parameters &rest body)
  `(defmethod ,name :around ,parameters
       (let* ((parent *current-node*)
              (*current-node* (make-instance 'node))
              (primary-method-value (call-next-method)))
     (when primary-method-value
       (attach-parent *current-node* parent)
       (attach-action *current-node*
                      (list ',name
                            ,@(remove-specializers parameters))))
     primary-method-value)))
```

REMOVE-SPECIALIZERS could be defined as a method specialized to lists,
but there is no particularly good reason to because REMOVE-SPECIALIZERS
is never called on anything other than lists. Also, note that REMOVE-
SPECIALIZERS never expects to see any optional, rest, key, or aux parameters:

```
(defun remove-specializers (parameter-list)
  (mapcar #'(lambda (element)
              (if (listp element)
                  (first element)
                  element))
          parameter-list))
```

Using DEFINE-HISTORY-METHOD, we can identify those methods that we want
to contribute to the history tree.

Problems

Problem 22-1: Define a version of REMOVE-SPECIALIZERS that works even
if optional, rest, key, or aux parameters are present. It is to return a list
of the ordinary parameters only, as in the following example:

```
* (remove-specializers '((object movable-block)
                         (support basic-block)
                         &rest ignore))
(OBJECT SUPPORT)
```

You will probably want to make use of LAMBDA-LIST-KEYWORDS, which is a
variable whose value is a list of all parameter-marking keywords.

**The Goal Tree Is
Easy to Display**

Using DEFINE-HISTORY-METHOD, we can add :AROUND methods to keep track of
whichever methods we want. Our choice is to redefine PUT-ON, GET-RID-OF,
MAKE-SPACE, CLEAR-TOP, and MOVE:

```
(define-history-method put-on ((object movable-block)
                               (support basic-block)))
(define-history-method get-rid-of ((object movable-block)))
(define-history-method make-space ((object movable-block)
                                   (support basic-block))
(define-history-method clear-top ((support load-bearing-block)))
(define-history-method move ((object movable-block)
                             (support basic-block)))
```

Once we have these new tree-building methods, we need a technique for displaying the results. In a problem, you will develop a program that displays diagrams like the one shown below in which arrows show the relationships among generic function calls:

```
* (show-tree *current-node*)
TOP-OF-TREE
  *--> (PUT-ON B1 B2)
        |--> (MAKE-SPACE B1 B2)
        |     *--> (GET-RID-OF W7)
        |           *--> (PUT-ON W7 TABLE)
        |                 *--> (MOVE W7 TABLE)
        |--> (CLEAR-TOP B1)
        |     *--> (GET-RID-OF B4)
        |           *--> (PUT-ON B4 TABLE)
        |                 *--> (MOVE B4 TABLE)
        *--> (MOVE B1 B2)
NIL
```

Note, however, that the arrows are redundant because indentation alone is enough to show the relationships among generic function calls:

```
* (show-simple-tree *current-node*)
TOP-OF-TREE
  (PUT-ON B1 B2)
    (MAKE-SPACE B1 B2)
      (GET-RID-OF W7)
        (PUT-ON W7 TABLE)
          (MOVE W7 TABLE)
    (CLEAR-TOP B1)
      (GET-RID-OF B4)
        (PUT-ON B4 TABLE)
          (MOVE B4 TABLE)
    (MOVE B1 B2)
NIL
```

SHOW-SIMPLE-TREE is easy to implement as an ordinary procedure. We do need a new format directive, however. When a T directive appears, it means skip to the column identified by the number that stands between the tilde and the T:

```
* (format t "~%~2tSkip to second column.")
  Skip to second column.
NIL
```

Whenever a V appears in place of the number, it means use the next argument as the number:

```
* (format t "~%~vtSkip to second column." 2)
  Skip to second column.
NIL
```

We also need to specialize the PRINT-OBJECT procedure so that object instances are printed as names only, particularly when the contents of an ACTION slot is printed. In chapter 21, we arranged for object instances to be printed as follows:

```
* b1
#<block b1>
```

Now we want object instances to be printed as names only:

```
* b1
B1
```

Hence we redefine the PRINT-OBJECT method:

```
(defmethod print-object ((x basic-block) stream)
  (format stream "~a" (block-name x)))
```

Now we can define SHOW-SIMPLE-TREE:

```
(defun show-simple-tree (node &optional (indentation 0))
  (format t "~&~vt~a"
          indentation
          (or (node-action node) 'top-of-tree))
  (dolist (node (node-children node))
    (show-simple-tree node (+ 2 indentation))))
```

The Goal Tree Answers Questions

Now it is time to do more sophisticated things with the goal tree. FIND-ACTION, defined as an ordinary procedure, searches through the goal tree looking for a node whose ACTION slot contains an expression that matches the given action.

```
(defun find-action (given-form &optional (node *current-node*))
  (let ((node-form (node-action node)))
    (if (equal given-form node-form)
        node
        (dolist (child (node-children node))
          (let ((result (find-action given-form child)))
            (when result (return result)))))))
```

Given FIND-ACTION, it is easy to create TELL-WHY, which announces why something was done:

```
* (tell-why GET-RID-OF W7)
I did (GET-RID-OF W7) because I wanted to (MAKE-SPACE B1 B2).
DONE

* (tell-why MAKE-SPACE B1 B2)
I did (MAKE-SPACE B1 B2) because I wanted to (PUT-ON B1 B2).
DONE

* (tell-why put-on b1 b2)
I did (PUT-ON B1 B2) because you told me to.
DONE
```

As shown below, TELL-WHY calls TELL-WHY-AUX, which is mostly machinery to deal with special cases.

```
(defmacro tell-why (name &rest parameters)
  `(tell-why-aux (list ',name ,@parameters)))

(defun tell-why-aux (given-action)
  (let ((node (find-action given-action)))
    (if (not (null node))
        (cond ((node-action (node-parent node))
               (format t "~&I did ~a because I wanted to ~a."
                       given-action
                       (node-action (node-parent node))))
              (t (format t "~&I did ~a because you told me to."
                         given-action)))
        (format t "~&I did not ~a." given-action))
    'done))
```

Note that all of the arguments of TELL-WHY will be evaluated, except for the name argument, when the body of the macro is evaluated. That is what you want, after all, because you want TELL-WHY to search for forms involving prescribed nodes, not the symbols those prescribed nodes happen to be assigned to.

Problems

Problem 22-2: Define `TELL-HOW` and `TELL-HOW-AUX`. They arrange a search for a given description in the nodes in the tree hanging from the node `*CURRENT-NODE*`. If the given description is found, the nodes immediately below are printed, as in the following example:

```
* (tell-how get-rid-of w7)
I did (GET-RID-OF W7) by the following operations:
  (PUT-ON W7 TABLE)
DONE

* (tell-how put-on w7 table)
I did (PUT-ON W7 TABLE) by the following operations:
  (MOVE W7 TABLE)
DONE

* (tell-how move w7 table)
I did (MOVE W7 TABLE) by just doing it.
DONE
```

Problem 22-3: Define `TELL-WHEN` and `TELL-WHEN-AUX`. They arrange a search for a given description in the nodes in the tree hanging from the node `*CURRENT-NODE*`. If the given description is found, the highest node above the given node is printed, as in the following examples:

```
* (tell-when get-rid-of w7)
I did it while I (PUT-ON B1 B2).
DONE
```

Problem 22-4: Define `SHOW-TREE` such that it prints history trees with arrows as in this example:

```
* (show-tree *current-node*)
TOP-OF-TREE
  *--> (PUT-ON B1 B2)
        |--> (MAKE-SPACE B1 B2)
        |      *--> (GET-RID-OF W7)
        |             *--> (PUT-ON W7 TABLE)
        |                    *--> (MOVE W7 TABLE)
        |--> (CLEAR-TOP B1)
        |      *--> (GET-RID-OF B4)
        |             *--> (PUT-ON B4 TABLE)
        |                    *--> (MOVE B4 TABLE)
        *--> (MOVE B1 B2)
NIL
```

You will probably need to use `CONCATENATE`, a primitive that we do not discuss elsewhere. When the first argument in a `CONCATENATE` form evaluates to `STRING` and the other arguments are strings, the value returned is a string produced by running the other arguments together:

```
* (concatenate 'string "abc" "xyz")
"abcxyz"
```

Summary

- The blocks-world program can introspect into its own operation.
- Remembering generic function calls creates a goal tree.
- Macros enable method-defining procedures to be defined.
- The goal tree is easy to display.
- The goal tree answers questions.

References

For a general introduction to using goal trees to answer questions, see chapter 6 of *Artificial Intelligence (Second Edition)* by Patrick H. Winston.

23

Constraint
Propagation

The principal purpose of this chapter is to provide another example of the object-oriented programming paradigm introduced in chapter 14 and developed further in chapters 21 and 22.

A secondary purpose of this chapter is to illustrate the *constraint propagation* problem-solving paradigm. In a constraint propagation system, a constraint can be viewed as a box with terminals such that the values on some terminals determine the values on others.

Constraints Propagate Numbers through Arithmetic Boxes

You are already familiar with the idea of constraint propagation because you understand simple algebra. You know, for example, that the following equation, along with values for any two of the variables, allows you to find the value of the third variable:

$$x + y = z.$$

Using the vocabulary of constraint propagation, addition and other basic arithmetic operators can be viewed as constraint boxes that can determine missing terminal values when enough of the other terminal values are known. As shown in figure 23-1, knowing both addends allows the addition box to calculate the sum. Alternatively, if the sum and one of the addends

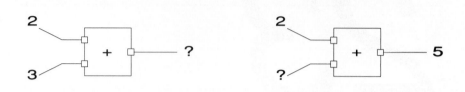

Figure 23-1. Viewed as a constraint box, addition enables one missing terminal value to be calculated given values on the other two terminals.

is known, the addition box calculates the value of the other addend. Accordingly, we say that the addition constraint can propagate values toward any of the terminals as circumstances dictate.

When many arithmetic constraint boxes are connected together to form a net, a few known values can have far-reaching effects as constraint boxes propagate values from connection to connection. It would make sense to call this phenomenon *propagation of values through constraints*, but it is more customary, albeit idiomatic, to call it *constraint propagation*.

But rather than building a program for constraint propagation through arithmetic boxes, we think that it is more instructive to develop a more complicated example involving the propagation of probability bounds.

**Constraints
Propagate
Probability Bounds
through Logic Boxes**

Suppose you like to buy stocks just before splits are announced. To decide if a stock is about to split, you habitually consult four advisors. Two are Wall Street brokers and two are mystics. You consider the brokers, as a group, to believe that a stock will split if either of the brokers believes that it will; and similarly, you consider the mystics, as a group, to believe that a stock will split if either of the mystics believes that it will. Being conservative, you believe that a stock will split only if both the brokers group and the mystics group believe that it will.

There are many approaches to representing such opinions as numbers. Most of those approaches translate opinions into probability numbers that indicate how frequently an assertion is true. Probability numbers range from 0 to 1, with 1 representing the idea that an assertion is certainly true and 0 representing the idea that an assertion is certainly false.

The approach we explain here is more sophisticated because each opinion is translated into a range of probability numbers, not just one. The range is specified by a lower bound on assertion probability and an upper bound, as shown in figure 23-2.

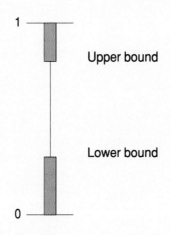

Figure 23-2. Our constraint system deals with upper and lower bounds on probability.

Upper and lower bounds enable us to deal with advisors who refuse to be pinned down precisely. With upper and lower bounds, we can capture statements like, "I do not know enough to give you a probability that the stock will split, but I do know enough to say that the probability is definitely between .25 and .75." Of course, the upper and lower bounds converge to one number if an advisor is willing to express an exact probability.

Individual opinions can be tied together in various ways. Figure 23-3 shows how the various opinions in our stock-split example fit together with constraint boxes in between.

Of course, the constraint boxes are more complicated than those in the arithmetic boxes, being based on probability theory, not simple algebra. Fortunately, to develop a constraint-propagation program, you need neither understand probability theory nor look at the constraint derivations. It is enough to get a feel for how the constraints work.

Consider, for example, the following constraint equations, which govern the action of one kind of constraint box. For any such box, a and b represent inputs, and o represents the output. Also $l(a)$, $l(b)$, and $l(o)$

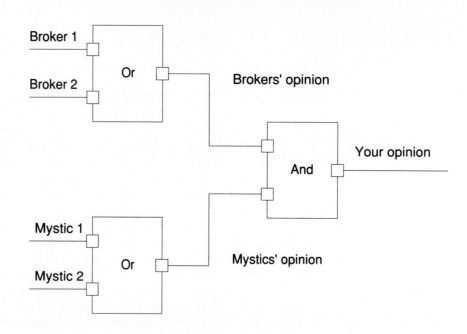

Figure 23-3. The opinion of the broker group is that the stock will split if either thinks so. Similarly, the opinion of the mystic group is that the stock will split if either thinks so. However, your opinion is that the stock will split only if both the broker group and the mystic group think so.

represent lower bounds, and $u(a)$, $u(b)$, and $u(o)$ represent upper bounds:

$$u(a) \leq u(o)$$
$$l(a) \geq l(o) - u(b)$$
$$u(b) \leq u(o)$$
$$l(b) \geq l(o) - u(a)$$
$$u(o) \leq u(a) + u(b)$$
$$l(o) \geq \max[l(a), l(b)]$$

By looking at extreme cases, you can see that this set of constraints is reminiscent of the Or constraint in logic. For example, the first equation indicates that if the lower bound of either of the inputs is 1, then the lower bound of the output is also 1. In English, this means that if either of the input assertions is certainly true, then the output assertion is certainly true as well. Similarly, if the upper bound on the output assertion is 0, then the upper bounds of the input assertions are also 0. In English, this means that if the output assertion is certainly false, then both input assertions must be false as well.

Actually, the special cases are no accident because the sample constraint equations are intended to be a generalization of the notion of Or. Other groups of constraint equations are intended to be generalizations of And and Not.

When a group of assertions and logical constraints are combined, they form what is called an *inference net*. Accordingly, when we combine assertions and constraint boxes, they form a special kind of inference net.

With inference nets, we use the words *input* and *output* loosely because the constraints enable propagation from any terminal to any terminal. You saw this already when considering extreme cases. You see it again in figure 23-4, where upper and lower probability bounds propagate through an Or box from an input to the output, and in figure 23-5, where upper and lower probability bounds propagate through an Or box from the output to the two inputs.

Classes Represent Assertions and Logical Constraints

Now that you know a bit about propagating probability bounds, we can develop an object-oriented program to do the propagation. With our program, each time we specify an assertion's bounds anywhere in an inference net, the constraint boxes can spread a wave of new bounds in all directions, stopping only at those points where the new bounds are not as good as the existing ones.

Our approach is to concentrate on assertions and constraints, developing classes for both. Next we develop subclasses of the constraint-box class for Ands, Ors, and Nots. Then, we develop constraint-propagating methods specialized to the assertion class and to the Or and And subclasses of the constraint class.

For assertions, we need a class with slots for a name, the upper and lower probability bounds, and a list of all the constraints that the assertion is connected to:

```
(defclass assertion ()
  ((name        :accessor assertion-name :initarg :name)
   (lower-bound :accessor assertion-lower-bound :initform 0)
   (upper-bound :accessor assertion-upper-bound :initform 1)
   (constraints :accessor assertion-constraints :initform nil)))
```

For constraints, figure 23-6 shows the classes we are about to create. First, the CONSTRAINT class exhibits slots for a name and for an output assertion. We also need slots for inputs, but the number depends on whether the constraint has two terminals or three, as captured by the BINARY-CONSTRAINT and TERNARY-CONSTRAINT classes:

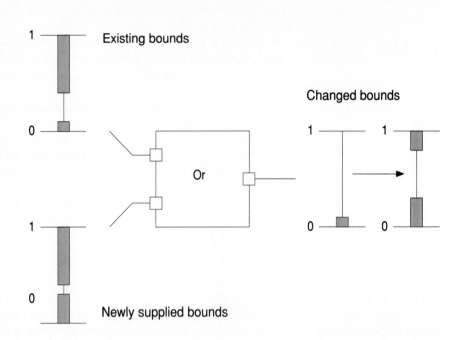

1
0

Existing bounds

Changed bounds

Or

1   1
0   0

1
0

Newly supplied bounds

Figure 23-4. Bounds on assertion probabilities propagate through constraint
boxes. Here the propagation is from left to right. New bounds on the lower of
the two inputs, together with the existing bounds on the other input, constrains
the output probability to lie between .3 and .8.

```
(defclass constraint ()
  ((name    :accessor constraint-name :initarg :name)
   (output :accessor constraint-output)))

(defclass binary-constraint (constraint)
  ((input :accessor constraint-input)))

(defclass ternary-constraint (constraint)
  ((input-a :accessor constraint-input-a)
   (input-b :accessor constraint-input-b)))
```

Note that BINARY-CONSTRAINT and TERNARY-CONSTRAINT are useful because
they, like CONSTRAINT, capture common slots required in the classes we really
need:

```
(defclass not-box (binary-constraint) ())
```

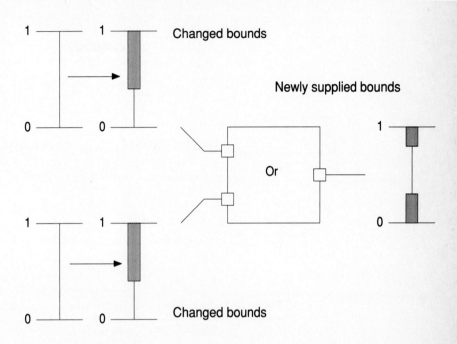

Figure 23-5. Bounds on assertion probabilities propagate through constraint boxes. Here the propagation is from right to left. New bounds on an output probability, indicating that the probability must lie between .3 and .8, constrains both input probabilities to lie between 0 and .4.

```
(defclass or-box (ternary-constraint) ())

(defclass and-box (ternary-constraint) ())
```

Note that the slot specifications of the two ternary constraints, OR-BOX and AND-BOX, are exactly the same, and only a little different from the binary constraint, NOT-BOX. Evidently the reason they are all defined is not that they have different slots, but that they enable us to define propagation methods that are specialized to each individually.

Before defining the propagation methods, we need to wire assertions and constraints together to capture the content of our stocks problem. This utility method is for wiring up Not boxes:

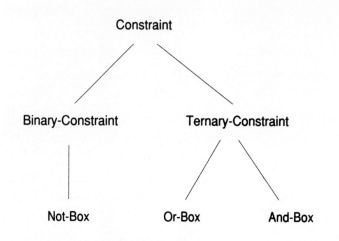

Figure 23-6. The class hierarchy for opinion constraints.

```
(defmethod connect2 ((c constraint)
                     (i assertion)
                     (o assertion))
  (setf (constraint-input  c) i)
  (setf (constraint-output c) o)
  (push c (assertion-constraints i))
  (push c (assertion-constraints o)))
```

And this one is for wiring up Or and And boxes:

```
(defmethod connect3 ((c constraint)
                     (a assertion)
                     (b assertion)
                     (o assertion))
  (setf (constraint-input-a c) a)
  (setf (constraint-input-b c) b)
  (setf (constraint-output  c) o)
  (push c (assertion-constraints a))
  (push c (assertion-constraints b))
  (push c (assertion-constraints o)))
```

The following creates constraint boxes, assigns them to variable names, and produces the connections we need:

```
(let ((assertions
        (list (make-instance 'assertion :name 'broker1)
              (make-instance 'assertion :name 'broker2)
              (make-instance 'assertion :name 'broker-opinion)
              (make-instance 'assertion :name 'mystic1)
              (make-instance 'assertion :name 'mystic2)
              (make-instance 'assertion :name 'mystic-opinion)
              (make-instance 'assertion :name 'your-opinion)))
      (constraints
        (list (make-instance 'or-box :name 'broker-constraint)
              (make-instance 'or-box :name 'mystic-constraint)
              (make-instance 'and-box :name 'your-constraint))))
  (dolist (l constraints) (set (constraint-name l) l))
  (dolist (l assertions) (set (assertion-name l) l))
  (connect3 broker-constraint broker1 broker2 broker-opinion)
  (connect3 mystic-constraint mystic1 mystic2 mystic-opinion)
  (connect3 your-constraint
            broker-opinion
            mystic-opinion
            your-opinion))
```

Generic Functions Enforce Constraints

Now we are ready to introduce the methods required to propagate values. Our general approach is to create various specializations of PROPAGATE-VIA-BOX, a generic function that propagates values through constraint boxes.

The form for all ternary constraint methods is the same. Each has a parameter that is specialized to a particular constraint class. Each has a parameter that identifies where the propagation is coming from. Each has a LET* form that binds inputs, outputs, and various bounds to variables with short names, enabling concise, easier-to-read propagation formulas:

```
(defmethod propagate-via-box ((constraint <constraint class>))
  (let* <variable bindings for a b o la ua lb ub lo and uo>
    (propagate-via-assertion o constraint <propagation formulas>)
    (propagate-via-assertion a constraint <propagation formulas>)
    (propagate-via-assertion b constraint <propagation formulas>)))
```

Consider the OR method, for which we have already exhibited the equations. Its bulk consists mostly of the parameter binding, which is followed by forms that propagate values to the connected assertions:

```
(defmethod propagate-via-box ((constraint or-box))
  (let* ((a (constraint-input-a constraint))
         (b (constraint-input-b constraint))
         (o (constraint-output constraint))
         (la (assertion-lower-bound a))
         (ua (assertion-upper-bound a))
         (lb (assertion-lower-bound b))
         (ub (assertion-upper-bound b))
         (lo (assertion-lower-bound o))
         (uo (assertion-upper-bound o)))
    (propagate-via-assertion o constraint (max la lb) (+ ua ub))
    (propagate-via-assertion a constraint (- lo ub) uo)
    (propagate-via-assertion b constraint (- lo ua) uo)))
```

Turning now to Ands, the governing equations are as follows. Note that unlike Ors, Ands do not constrain either $l(a)$ or $l(b)$:

$$u(a) \leq u(o) - l(b) + 1$$
$$l(a) \geq 0$$
$$u(b) \leq u(o) - l(a) + 1$$
$$l(b) \geq 0$$
$$u(o) \leq \min[u(a), u(b)]$$
$$l(o) \geq l(a) + l(b) - 1$$

Accordingly, the AND-BOX method is defined as follows; only the specialization of the CONSTRAINT parameter and the propagation formulas distinguish it from the OR-BOX method:

```
(defmethod propagate-via-box ((constraint and-box))
  (let* ((a (constraint-input-a constraint))
         (b (constraint-input-b constraint))
         (o (constraint-output constraint))
         (la (assertion-lower-bound a))
         (ua (assertion-upper-bound a))
         (lb (assertion-lower-bound b))
         (ub (assertion-upper-bound b))
         (lo (assertion-lower-bound o))
         (uo (assertion-upper-bound o)))
    (propagate-via-assertion o constraint (+ la lb -1) (min ua ub))
    (propagate-via-assertion a constraint 0 (+ 1 (- uo lb)))
    (propagate-via-assertion b constraint 0 (+ 1 (- uo la)))))
```

Now we need a propagation method for assertions. It has a parameter that is specialized to the assertion class, along with a parameter that identifies where the propagation is coming from. It has a LET* form with parameters bound to old and new upper and lower bounds:

```
(defmethod propagate-via-assertion ((assertion assertion)
                                    (source constraint)
                                    lower
                                    upper)
  (let* ((old-upper (assertion-upper-bound assertion))
         (old-lower (assertion-lower-bound assertion))
         (new-upper (max 0 (min old-upper upper)))
         (new-lower (min 1 (max old-lower lower))))
  ...))
```

Note that the proposed upper and lower bounds are filtered so that they cannot be worse than they were, nor can they move outside the zero-to-one range allowed for probabilities even when the constraint equations produce numbers that are less than zero or greater than one.

Once the LET* parameters are bound, each proposed bound is compared with the existing bound, and if it is different, the new bound is placed in the appropriate slots. Then if either of the bounds has changed, a message is printed and values are propagated to the connected constraints. Note that the FORMAT form contains a 4,2F directive, meaning print a floating-point number with two digits beyond the decimal point, occupying four spaces:

```
(defmethod propagate-via-assertion ((assertion assertion)
                                    (source constraint)
                                    lower
                                    upper)
  (let* ((old-upper (assertion-upper-bound assertion))
         (old-lower (assertion-lower-bound assertion))
         (new-upper (max 0 (min old-upper upper)))
         (new-lower (min 1 (max old-lower lower))))
    (unless (= old-upper new-upper)
      (setf (assertion-upper-bound assertion) new-upper))
    (unless (= old-lower new-lower)
      (setf (assertion-lower-bound assertion) new-lower))
    (when (or (/= old-lower new-lower) (/= old-upper new-upper))
      (format t "~%Constraint ~a has modified ~a's values:")
      (format t "~%[~4,2f, ~4,2f] --> [~4,2f, ~4,2f]"
              (constraint-name source)
              (assertion-name assertion)
              old-lower old-upper
              new-lower new-upper)
      (dolist (constraint (assertion-constraints assertion))
        (propagate-via-box constraint)))))
```

Now all we need is a way of initiating the propagation. An INITIATE-PROPAGATION method does the job. It just fills in slots with the values supplied, prints a message, and propagates the supplied values to all connected constraints:

```
(defmethod initiate-propagation ((assertion assertion)
                                 lower
                                 upper)
   (setf (assertion-upper-bound assertion) upper)
   (setf (assertion-lower-bound assertion) lower)
   (format t "~%You have started propagation from ~a with values:"
           (assertion-name assertion))
   (Format t "~%[~4,2f, ~4,2f]"
           lower upper)
     (dolist (constraint (assertion-constraints assertion))
       (propagate-via-box constraint)))
```

More Information Moves Probability Bounds Closer

Now everything is in place for our example. To begin, assume that none of the four advisors have submitted opinions. Then the probability bounds associated with a stock split are $[0, 1]$, as shown in figure 23-7.

Suppose that you learn that BROKER1's opinion is that the probability bounds associated with a stock split are $[.25, .75]$. You can initiate propagation through the inference net with the following results:

```
* (initiate-propagation broker1 .25 .75)
You have started propagation from BROKER1 with values:
[0.25, 0.75]
Constraint BROKER-CONSTRAINT has modified BROKER-OPINION's values:
[ 0.0, 1.00] --> [0.25, 1.00]
NIL
```

Now the probability bounds are as shown in figure 23-8.

Learning the opinions of BROKER2, MYSTIC1, and MYSTIC2 leads to the following results:

```
* (initiate-propagation broker2 .33 .66)
You have started propagation from BROKER2 with values:
[0.33, 0.66]
Constraint BROKER-CONSTRAINT has modified BROKER-OPINION's values:
[0.25, 1.00] --> [0.33, 1.00]
NIL

* (initiate-propagation mystic1 .15 .15)
You have started propagation from MYSTIC1 with values:
[0.15, 0.15]
Constraint MYSTIC-CONSTRAINT has modified MYSTIC-OPINION's values:
[ 0.0, 1.00] --> [0.15, 1.00]
NIL
```

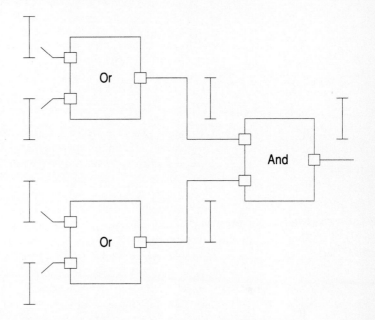

Figure 23-7. An inference net in its initial state, with $[0, 1]$ probability bound on all assertions.

```
* (initiate-propagation mystic2 .85 .85)
You have started propagation from MYSTIC2 with values:
[0.85, 0.85]
Constraint MYSTIC-CONSTRAINT has modified MYSTIC-OPINION's values:
[0.15, 1.00] --> [0.85, 1.00]
Constraint YOUR-CONSTRAINT has modified YOUR-OPINION's values:
[ 0.0, 1.00] --> [0.18, 1.00]
NIL
```

Now the final probability bounds are as shown in figure 23-9.

Of course, the results are different if YOUR-CONSTRAINT is an Or rather than an And. In particular, the bounds associated with the YOUR-OPINION assertion are much tighter, as you can see if you reset all bounds to $[0, 1]$ and experiment again:

```
* (initiate-propagation broker1 .25 .75)
You have started propagation from BROKER1 with values:
[0.25, 0.75]
```

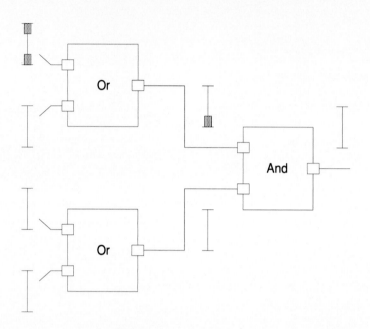

Figure 23-8. The inference net after one broker's probability bounds are known.

```
Constraint BROKER-CONSTRAINT has modified BROKER-OPINION's values:
[ 0.0, 1.00] --> [0.25, 1.00]
Constraint YOUR-CONSTRAINT has modified YOUR-OPINION's values:
[ 0.0, 1.00] --> [0.25, 1.00]
NIL

* (initiate-propagation broker2 .33 .66)
You have started propagation from BROKER2 with values:
[0.33, 0.66]
Constraint BROKER-CONSTRAINT has modified BROKER-OPINION's values:
[0.25, 1.00] --> [0.33, 1.00]
Constraint YOUR-CONSTRAINT has modified YOUR-OPINION's values:
[0.25, 1.00] --> [0.33, 1.00]
NIL

* (initiate-propagation mystic1 .15 .15)
You have started propagation from MYSTIC1 with values:
[0.15, 0.15]
Constraint MYSTIC-CONSTRAINT has modified MYSTIC-OPINION's values:
[ 0.0, 1.00] --> [0.15, 1.00]
NIL
```

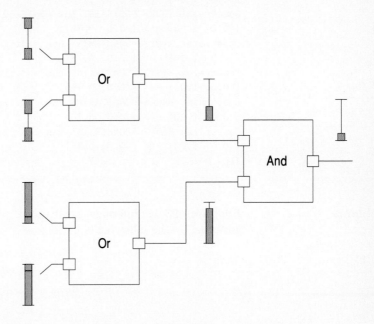

Figure 23-9. The inference net after all probability bounds are known.

```
* (initiate-propagation mystic2 .85 .85)
You have started propagation from MYSTIC2 with values:
[0.85, 0.85]
Constraint MYSTIC-CONSTRAINT has modified MYSTIC-OPINION's values:
[0.15, 1.00] --> [0.85, 1.00]
Constraint YOUR-CONSTRAINT has modified YOUR-OPINION's values:
[0.33, 1.00] --> [0.85, 1.00]
NIL
```

Now suppose you approach the inference net from another direction. You decide on your own that the bounds associated with the YOUR-OPINION assertion are [.50, .75].

After resetting all bounds to [0, 1], retaining the Or interpretation for YOUR-CONSTRAINT, you get the following result with the output constrained. Evidently, no advisor can think that the upper bound on the probability that the stock will split is greater than .75:

```
* (initiate-propagation your-opinion .5 .75)
You have started propagation from YOUR-OPINION with values:
[0.50, 0.75]
```

```
Constraint YOUR-CONSTRAINT has modified BROKER-OPINION's values:
[ 0.0, 1.00] --> [ 0.0, 0.75]
Constraint YOUR-CONSTRAINT has modified MYSTIC-OPINION's values:
[ 0.0, 1.00] --> [ 0.0, 0.75]
Constraint MYSTIC-CONSTRAINT has modified MYSTIC1's values:
[ 0.0, 1.00] --> [ 0.0, 0.75]
Constraint MYSTIC-CONSTRAINT has modified MYSTIC2's values:
[ 0.0, 1.00] --> [ 0.0, 0.75]
Constraint BROKER-CONSTRAINT has modified BROKER1's values:
[ 0.0, 1.00] --> [ 0.0, 0.75]
Constraint BROKER-CONSTRAINT has modified BROKER2's values:
[ 0.0, 1.00] --> [ 0.0, 0.75]
NIL
```

Problems

Problem 23-1: Inference nets also involve Nots, with only one input, governed by the following equations:

$$u(i) \leq 1 - l(o)$$
$$l(i) \geq 1 - u(o)$$
$$u(o) \leq 1 - l(i)$$
$$l(o) \geq 1 - u(i)$$

Devise a corresponding NOT-BOX method.

Problem 23-2: Sometimes you know that two sources of opinion are independent because neither uses information used by the other. Knowing that the two inputs to an Or or And constraint box are independent makes that Or or And constraint box an independent Or or And. The equations for independent Or and And boxes produce much tighter constraints than ordinary Or and ordinary And boxes.

Produce a class and a method for independent Or boxes using the following equations. Be sure there will be no division by zero.

$$u(a) \leq \frac{u(o) - l(b)}{1 - l(b)}$$

$$l(a) \geq \frac{l(o) - u(b)}{1 - u(b)}$$

$$u(b) \leq \frac{u(o) - l(a)}{1 - l(a)}$$

$$l(b) \geq \frac{l(o) - u(a)}{1 - u(a)}$$

$$u(o) \leq u(a) + u(b) - u(a) \times u(b)$$
$$l(o) \geq l(a) + l(b) - l(a) \times l(b)$$

Summary
- Constraints propagate numbers through arithmetic boxes.
- Constraints propagate probability bounds through logic boxes.
- Classes represent assertions and logical constraints.
- Generic functions enforce constraints.
- More information moves probability bounds closer.

References   For a general introduction to constraint propagation, see chapter 3 of *Artificial Intelligence (Second Edition)* by Patrick H. Winston.

Our treatment of probability bounds is based on Quinlan [1983].

24

Symbolic Pattern Matching

The principal purpose of this chapter is to introduce the ideas of pattern matching and to develop two pattern-matching procedures. The basic procedure, MATCH, compares a *pattern expression* with an *ordinary expression* to see if the ordinary expression is an instance of the pattern expression. The more advanced procedure, UNIFY, is an implementation of the *unification* matching algorithm, an algorithm that compares two pattern expressions to see if they can be made identical by a consistent set of substitutions.

The basic pattern-matching procedure is a key element in an animal-identifying, forward-chaining, rule-based expert system developed in chapter 26. The unification matching procedure is a key element in a backward-chaining, PROLOGlike language developed in chapter 27.

A secondary purpose of this chapter is to review several procedure-writing techniques: progressive envelopment, problem reduction, comment translation, and procedure abstraction.

Matching Compares Patterns and Datums Element by Element

Let us begin by thinking in terms of matching a *pattern* and an ordinary expression. Because the ordinary expression is used to represent bits of knowledge about some real or imagined world, we call the ordinary expression a *datum*. For example, the following datums could indicate that apples are red and oranges are orange:

```
(color apple red)                              ;Datum examples.
(color orange orange)
```

Unlike datums, patterns can contain elements called *pattern variables*. To make pattern variables easy to recognize, we encapsulate them in two-element lists whose first element is a ? and whose second element is the pattern variable. For example, the pattern variables x and y appear in the following patterns:

```
(color (? x) red)                              ;Pattern examples.
(color apple (? y))
(color (? x) (? y))
(color (? x) (? x))
```

When a pattern contains no pattern variables, that pattern matches a datum match only if the pattern is exactly the same as the datum, with each corresponding position occupied by the same atom. Thus the pattern, (COLOR APPLE RED) successfully matches the datum (COLOR APPLE RED), but (COLOR APPLE RED) fails to match (COLOR APPLE GREEN).

When a pattern does contains pattern variables, the pattern-variable expressions initially act like wild cards. Whenever there is a single pattern-variable expression in a pattern, anything at all is allowed in the corresponding place in the datum. Thus (COLOR (? X) RED) matches (COLOR APPLE RED).

Note that the correspondence of pattern-variable expressions to datum elements is remembered and pattern variables are somehow bound to datum elements. If the same pattern-variable expression appears more than once in a single pattern, only the initial appearance acts like a wild card; subsequent appearances act like the datum element corresponding to the first appearance.

Thus (COLOR (? X) (? X)) fails to match (COLOR APPLE RED). The pattern variable expression (? X) acts like a wild card the first time it is encountered, binding X somehow to APPLE, but the second time (? X) is encountered, it acts like APPLE, which fails to match the corresponding datum element, RED. On the other hand, (COLOR (? X) (? X)) does match (COLOR ORANGE ORANGE). Again, the pattern variable expression (? X) acts like a wild card the first time it is encountered, associating X with ORANGE, and the second time (? X) is encountered, it acts like ORANGE, which matches the corresponding datum element, ORANGE.

There is one prominent exception to the conventions for remembering pattern-variable bindings. This exception is for pattern-variable expressions in which the variable-name position is occupied by the underscore character. Even though underscore is a perfectly good symbol, pattern-variable expressions containing underscore act as if there were no variable to associate with a datum element. Hence (? _) always acts like a wild card and underscore is said to be the *anonymous variable*. Thus (COLOR (? _) (? _)) matches (COLOR APPLE RED).

MATCH Keeps Variable Bindings on an Association List

Although LISP itself has no pattern matching built in, it is easy to write a pattern-matching program in LISP. Hence, we say that LISP is a good *implementation language* for pattern matchers.

Our first matching procedure, MATCH, works by *first-rest recursion*, taking patterns and datums apart using FIRST and REST until they are both reduced to the point where matching is easy. Thus MATCH reduces the problem of matching (COLOR (? X) RED) with (COLOR APPLE RED) to the problem of matching COLOR with COLOR and ((? X) RED) with (APPLE RED). Then MATCH reduces the problem of matching ((? X) RED) with (APPLE RED) to the problem of matching (? X) with APPLE and (RED) with (RED). Finally, the problem of matching (RED) with (RED) is reduced to matching RED with RED and NIL with NIL.

But before you can understand how MATCH is implemented, you need to understand that MATCH keeps track of associations between pattern variables and datum elements using an association list of bindings. When a pattern and datum match, the association list is returned, as in the following examples:

```
* (match '(color (? x) red)
         '(color apple red))
((X APPLE))

* (match '(color apple (? y))
         '(color apple red))
((Y RED))

* (match '(color (? x) (? y))
         '(color apple red))
((Y RED) (X APPLE))
```

Of course, if there are no pattern variables, or if only the anonymous pattern variable appears, the association list will be empty:

```
* (match '(color apple red)
         '(color apple red))
NIL
```

```
* (match '(color (? _) red)
          '(color apple red))
NIL
* (match '(color (? _) (? _))
          '(color apple red))
NIL
```

Note that NIL indicates that the pattern matches the datum and that there
are no bindings. This contrasts with the usual use of NIL because NIL
usually signals that something has failed.

Because NIL cannot mean that a match has failed, MATCH returns the
symbol FAIL when the pattern and datum do not match:[1]

```
* (match '(color apple orange)
          '(color apple red))
FAIL
* (match '(color (? x) (? x))
          '(color apple red))
FAIL
```

Now in preparation for understanding MATCH, let us construct four auxiliary
procedures for adding bindings to association lists, for finding bindings
in association lists, and for extracting the key and value from particular
bindings.

First, let us construct ADD-BINDING, a procedure that adds a binding to
an association list, given a pattern-variable expression like (? X) and a value
like APPLE. To construct ADD-BINDING, we use the progressive envelopment
technique, introduced in chapter 3, starting with sample values for three
variables, PATTERN-VARIABLE-EXPRESSION, DATUM, and BINDINGS:

```
(setf pattern-variable-expression '(? x))
(setf datum 'apple)
(setf bindings '((y red)))
```

First, we dig the pattern variable out of the pattern-variable expression:

```
* (second pattern-variable-expression)
X
```

Next we combine the pattern variable with the datum:

```
* (list (second pattern-variable-expression)
         datum)
(X APPLE)
```

Next, we add this to the front of the association list:

---

[1]MATCH really needs to return two values: one indicating success or failure and
   one providing the association list on success. You learn about LISP's multiple-
   values feature later, in chapter 28.

```
* (cons (list (second pattern-variable-expression)
              datum)
        bindings)
((X APPLE) (Y RED))
```

Finally, we encapsulate what we have done, creating the `ADD-BINDING`, `EXTRACT-VARIABLE`, and **MAKE-BINDING** procedures, adding just a bit to handle the anonymous variable:

```
(defun add-binding (pattern-variable-expression datum bindings)
 (if (eq '_ (extract-variable pattern-variable-expression))
     bindings
     (cons (make-binding
             (extract-variable pattern-variable-expression)
             datum)
           bindings)))

(defun extract-variable (pattern-variable-expression)
  (second pattern-variable-expression))

(defun make-binding (variable datum)
  (list variable datum))
```

Here are examples of `ADD-BINDING` in action, exhibiting both of the result expressions in the `IF` expression:

```
* (add-binding '(? x) 'apple '((y red)))
((X APPLE) (Y RED))

* (add-binding '(? _) 'apple '((y red)))
((Y RED))
```

The following procedure for finding a binding is equally straightforward, but note that no effort is made to retrieve bindings for pattern-variable expressions in which the anonymous pattern variable appears:

```
(defun find-binding (pattern-variable-expression binding)
  (unless (eq '_ (extract-variable pattern-variable-expression))
    (assoc (extract-variable pattern-variable-expression) binding)))
```

Here are three examples:

```
* (find-binding '(? x) '((x apple) (y red)))
(X APPLE)

* (find-binding '(? y) '((x apple) (y red)))
(Y RED)
```

```
* (find-binding '(? _) '((x apple) (y red)))
NIL
```

Finally, the two procedures for extracting keys and values are truly simple; they are useful because they have a data-abstraction quality. Unlike FIRST and SECOND, EXTRACT-KEY and EXTRACT-VALUE clearly indicated that an element of an association list is under examination.

```
(defun extract-key (binding)
  (first binding))

(defun extract-value (binding)
  (second binding))
```

Matching Is Easily Implemented by a Recursive Procedure

Now let us see how to implement MATCH. We adopt the problem reduction technique, dividing the general problem up into several more specific problems:

```
(defun match (p d &optional bindings)
  (cond
    ((and (atom p) (atom d))        ;Easy: both arguments are atoms.
     ...)
    ((and (listp p) (eq '? (first p)))  ;Hard: pattern is a variable.
     ...)
    ((and (listp p) (listp d))      ;Hard: both arguments are lists.
     ...)
    (t 'fail)))                     ;Default. Fail.
```

As indicated by the first clause in the COND, there is just one easy case: the pattern and the datum are both atoms. As indicated in the following expansion, two atoms match only if they are the same atom, which MATCH determines using EQL. If they are the same, then MATCH returns the current value of BINDINGS, whatever it is; if the atoms are not the same, MATCH returns the symbol FAIL.

```
(defun match (p d &optional bindings)
  (cond
    ((and (atom p) (atom d))              ;Are both arguments atoms?
     (if (eql p d) bindings 'fail))       ;If EQL, ok; if not, fail.
    ...))
```

Next, the following expansion shows what to do when the pattern is a pattern-variable expression. Evidently, the first thing to do is to see if there is already an entry for the pattern variable on the association list of bindings using FIND-BINDING. If an entry for the pattern variable is found, then MATCH tries again with the pattern variable's binding substituted for the pattern variable itself. If the pattern variable is not on the association list of bindings, then ADD-BINDING composes a new entry for that association list, which is then returned:

```
(defun match (p d &optional bindings)
  (cond
    ...
    ((and (listp p) (eq '? (first p)))      ;Is pattern a variable?
     (let ((binding (find-binding p bindings)))  ;Find binding, if any.
       (if binding                          ;Is there a binding?
           (match (extract-value binding)   ;If so, substitute.
                  d
                  bindings)
           (add-binding p d bindings))))    ;If not, add binding.
    ...))
```

The next expansion shows what to do when the pattern is not a variable, but both the pattern and datum are lists. After all, you may want to match patterns and datums in which the elements are not just lists of atoms and pattern-variable expressions:

```
* (match '(((? p) is-a person) with (hair (? h)))
         '((patrick is-a person) with (hair blond)))
((HAIR BLOND) (PERSON PATRICK))
```

Nested pattern and datum expressions are broken up using FIRST and REST. But note in the following that the REST parts are matched only if the FIRST parts match successfully. Moreover, if the REST parts are matched at all, they are matched using the association list produced by matching the FIRST parts:

```
(defun match (p d &optional bindings) ;Final version!
  (cond
    ...
    ((and (listp p) (listp d))           ;Are both pattern and datum lists?
     (let ((result (match (first p)      ;Match pattern's first element
                          (first d)      ; with datum's first element
                          bindings)))    ; using current bindings.
       (if (eq 'fail result)             ;Do first elements fail to match?
           'fail                         ;If so, fail.
           (match (rest p)               ;If not, match the
                  (rest d)               ; rest of the elements
                  result))))             ; using new bindings.
    ...))
```

Problem reduction helps you write procedures because it is often less difficult to solve several subproblems than it is to solve one big problem.

Matching Is Better Implemented Using Procedure Abstraction

Although we have explained a version of MATCH that handles all cases in one
chunk of procedure, it is easier and prettier to implement MATCH using procedure abstraction, with auxiliary procedures handling the various cases.
Let us indicate what auxiliary procedures we need and how those auxiliary
procedures should fit together by combining problem reduction together
with the comment translation technique:

```
(defun match (p d &optional bindings)
  (cond
    ((and (atom p) (atom d))
     ;;See if P and D are the same.
     ;;If so, return the value of BINDINGS.
     ;;Otherwise, return FAIL.
     ...)
    ((and (listp p) (eq '? (first p)))
     ;;See if the pattern variable is known.
     ;;If it is, substitute its value and try again.
     ;;Otherwise, add new binding.
     ...)
    ((and (listp p) (listp d))
     ;;See if the first parts match producing new bindings.
     ;;If they do not match, fail.
     ;;If they do match, try the rest parts using the resulting bindings.
     ...)
    (t 'fail)))
```

Now let us translate the comments into LISP procedures:

```
(defun match-atoms (p d bindings)
  ;;See if P and D are the same:
  (if (eql p d)
      ;;If so, return the value of BINDINGS:
      bindings
      ;;Otherwise, return FAIL.
      'fail))
(defun match-variable (p d bindings)
  (let ((binding (find-binding p bindings)))
    ;;See if the pattern variable is known:
    (if binding
        ;;If it is, substitute its value and try again:
        (match (extract-value binding) d bindings)
        ;;Otherwise, add new binding:
        (add-binding p d bindings))))
(defun match-pieces (p d bindings)
  (let ((result (match (first p) (first d) bindings)))
    ;;See if the first parts match producing new bindings:
    (if (eq 'fail result)
        ;;If they do not match, fail.
        'fail
        ;;If they do match, try the rest parts using the resulting bindings:
        (match (rest p) (rest d) result))))
```

Assembling these procedures, we have the following, simpler version of MATCH, with all of the action hidden behind an abstraction barrier:

```
(defun match (p d &optional bindings)
  (cond ((and (atom p) (atom d))
         (match-atoms p d bindings))
        ((and (listp p) (eq '? (first p)))
         (match-variable p d bindings))
        ((and (listp p) (listp d))
         (match-pieces p d bindings))
        (t 'fail)))
```

Of course, for the complete procedure abstraction treatment, the testing can be put behind an abstraction barrier as well:

```
(defun elements-p (p d)
  (and (atom p) (atom d)))
(defun variable-p (p)
  (and (listp p) (eq '? (first p))))
(defun recursive-p (p d)
  (and (listp p) (listp d)))
```

Now MATCH is extremely compact and transparent:

```
(defun match (p d &optional bindings)
  (cond ((elements-p p d)
         (match-atoms p d bindings))
        ((variable-p p)
         (match-variable p d bindings))
        ((recursive-p p d)
         (match-pieces p d bindings))
        (t 'fail)))
```

Problems

Problem 24-1: Suppose that you wish to specify that a pattern element is to match a datum element only if the datum element satisfies one or more predicates. You can, once we introduce the *restriction feature*.

To use the restriction feature, you write pattern-variable expressions of the following form:

(? <variable name> <predicate 1> ... <predicate n>)

The idea is that the corresponding position in the datum must be occupied by an expression that satisfies all of the predicates listed in the restriction. Thus we can define predicates like PATRIOTIC-COLOR-P or 4LETTER-COLOR-P:

```
(defun patriotic-color-p (x) (member x '(red white blue)))
```

```
(defun 4letter-color-p (x) (member x '(pink blue)))
```

Such predicates can be used in pattern restrictions to limit the class of acceptable symbols in the corresponding datum positions, as in the following examples:

```
* (match '(color (? x) (? y patriotic-color-p))
         '(color apple red))
((Y RED) (X APPLE))
* (match '(color (? x) (? y patriotic-color-p 4letter-color-p))
         '(color apple red))
FAIL
```

First, write PREDICATES-SATISFIED-P, a predicate that returns T if all the predicates supplied as a first argument return T when applied to the second argument, as in these examples:

```
* (predicates-satisfied-p '(patriotic-color-p) 'red)
T
```

```
* (predicates-satisfied-p '(patriotic-color-p 4letter-color-p) 'red)
NIL
```

Next, modify `MATCH-VARIABLE` such that `MATCH` handles restrictions properly.

Unification Is Generalized Matching

The purpose of `UNIFY` is to match two patterns rather than one pattern and one datum. Although `UNIFY` is not required in most matching situations, it is required for the backward-chaining, PROLOGlike language introduced in chapter 27.

Consider the following examples. Each pattern pair matches in the sense that repeated substitutions from the resulting association list make both patterns identical:

```
* (unify '(color (? x) (? y))
         '(color apple red))
((Y RED) (X APPLE))              ;Patterns become (COLOR APPLE RED).
* (unify '(color apple red)
         '(color (? l) (? m)))
((M RED) (L APPLE))              ;Patterns become (COLOR APPLE RED).
* (unify '(color (? x) (? y))
         '(color (? l) (? m)))
((Y (? M)) (X (? L)))           ;Patterns become (COLOR (?~L) (?~M).
* (unify '(color (? x) (? y))
         '(color (? x) (? y)))
((Y (? Y)) (X (? X)))           ;Patterns become (COLOR (?~X) (?~Y).
```

Our implementation of `UNIFY` strongly resembles our implementation of `MATCH`. The top-level procedures are the same except for substituting `UNIFY` for `MATCH` and adding a `COND` clause that looks for pattern variables in the second argument:

```
(defun unify (p1 p2 &optional bindings)
  (cond ((elements-p p1 p2)              ;Are both atoms?
         (unify-atoms p1 p2 bindings))   ;If yes, ok; if no, fail.
        ((variable-p p1)                 ;Is P1 a variable?
         (unify-variable p1 p2 bindings)) ;Unify using bindings.
        ((variable-p p2)                 ;Is P2 a variable?
         (unify-variable p2 p1 bindings)) ;Unify using bindings.
        ((recursive-p p1 p2)             ;Are both lists?
         (unify-pieces p1 p2 bindings))  ;Unify pieces.
        (t 'fail)))
```

Two of the three auxiliary procedures, `UNIFY-ATOMS` and `UNIFY-PIECES`, are identical to the auxiliary procedures `MATCH-ATOMS` and `MATCH-PIECES` except for substituting `UNIFY` for `MATCH`:

```
(defun unify-atoms (p1 p2 bindings)   ;Identical to MATCH-ATOMS.
  (if (eql p1 p2) bindings 'fail))

(defun unify-pieces (p1 p2 bindings)  ;Identical to MATCH-PIECES.
  (let ((result (unify (first p1) (first p2) bindings)))
    (if (eq 'fail result)
        'fail
        (unify (rest p1) (rest p2) result))))
```

Only UNIFY-VARIABLE differs more substantially from its analog, MATCH-VARIABLE, and they differ only in a subtle way that many implementers forget about or choose to ignore for the sake of speed. But for complete generality, UNIFY-VARIABLE, unlike MATCH-VARIABLE, must avoid matching a variable against an expression that contains the same variable.[2] Consider the following, somewhat contrived examples:

```
* (unify '((? x) with (hair blond))
         '((patrick is-a person) with (hair blond)))
((X (PATRICK IS-A PERSON)))           ;X matches a list of symbols.

* (unify '((? x) with (hair blond))
         '((patrick is-a (? y)) with (hair blond)))
((X (PATRICK IS-A (? Y))))            ;X matches thing with Y inside.

* (unify '((? x) with (hair blond))
         '((patrick is-a (? x)) with (hair blond)))
FAIL                                  ;X cannot match thing with X inside.
```

Our subsequent use of UNIFY involves no trouble-causing situations in which a careless matcher would match a variable with an expression containing the same variable. Nevertheless, we implement UNIFY-VARIABLE as if there were such situations by incorporating an auxiliary procedure, INSIDEP:

```
(defun unify-variable (p1 p2 bindings)
  (let ((binding (find-binding p1 bindings)))    ;Find binding, if any.
    (if binding                                  ;Is there a binding?
        (unify (extract-value binding) p2 bindings) ;If yes, use value.
        (if (insidep p1 p2 bindings)             ;Is P1 inside P2?
            'fail                                 ;If yes, fail.
            (add-binding p1 p2 bindings)))))      ;If no, add binding.
```

INSIDEP is happy only if its first argument is strictly inside its second; equal does not count as inside:

---

[2]The matchers in PROLOG implementations usually are not unification matchers because they happily match variables with expressions that contain them.

```
(defun insidep (variable expression bindings)
  (if (equal variable expression)
      nil
      (inside-or-equal-p variable expression bindings)))
```

INSIDE-OR-EQUAL-P does all the real work. It recursively rips into its second
argument, replacing any variable it finds with that variable's value if there
is one:

```
(defun inside-or-equal-p (variable expression bindings)
  (cond ((equal variable expression) t)
        ((atom expression) nil)
        ((eq '? (first expression))
         (let ((binding (find-binding expression bindings)))
           (when binding
             (inside-or-equal-p variable
                                (extract-value binding)
                                bindings))))
        (t (or (inside-or-equal-p variable
                                  (first expression)
                                  bindings)
               (inside-or-equal-p variable
                                  (rest expression)
                                  bindings)))))
```

Summary

- Matching compares patterns and datums element by element.
- MATCH keeps variable bindings on an association list.
- Matching is easily implemented by a recursive procedure.
- Matching is better implemented using procedure abstraction.
- Unification is generalized matching.

References

For a general introduction to unification, see chapter 7 of *Artificial Intelligence (Second Edition)* by Patrick H. Winston.

25

Streams and Delayed Evaluation

One principal purpose of this chapter is to introduce *object streams*, which appear in a key role in the following problem-solving chapters, chapter 26 and chapter 27.

Another principal purpose of this chapter is to introduce *delayed evaluation*, a way of encapsulating directions for doing a computation so that the computation can be done later, at the time when it is absolutely certain that the computation is needed.

Streams Are Sequences of Data Objects

Abstractly, a *stream* is any producer or consumer of a sequence of data objects. Input/output operations, for example, are natural producers and consumers of sequences of data objects, so it is natural to think in terms of reading information from streams connected to input files and writing information to streams connected to output files.

Many procedures are also natural producers and consumers of data objects because sequences of data objects flow through them. In such situations, it is convenient to refer to the flowing data-object sequences as streams.

Note carefully the key distinguishing feature of streams: the data objects in them are meant to be processed in a definite order, from the front of the stream toward the back; similarly, data objects added to them are meant to be added at the back.

**We Can Represent
Streams Using Lists**

We could, in principle, represent a stream as a list of objects. Then we could get at the first stream object using FIRST, and we could trim the first object off of a stream using REST. One problem with this approach is that you could get at the elements of the stream using primitives like SECOND and NTH, thus diverting you from thinking of a stream as a sequence of objects that must be processed in the order that they appear. Another problem is that you could not tell at a glance whether an instance of FIRST or REST is supposed to be working on a stream or an ordinary list. And still another problem is that you would not be prepared to understand the more powerful and sophisticated representation for streams introduced in the next section.

Consequently, we suppress the temptation to represent streams as lists of stream objects. Instead, we represent streams as two-element lists in which the first element is the first object in the stream and the second element is itself a stream. Empty streams are represented by the symbol EMPTY-STREAM. Here are examples:

```
empty-stream                             ;Empty stream.
(object1 empty-stream)                   ;One-object stream.
(object1 (object2 empty-stream))         ;Two-object stream.
(object1 (object2 (object3 empty-stream))) ;Three-object stream
```

With this representation, we can now start to produce a few stream access procedures, the simplest of which are as follows:

```
(defun stream-endp (stream) (eq stream 'empty-stream))
(defun stream-first (stream) (first stream))
(defun stream-rest (stream) (second stream))
(defun stream-cons (object stream) (list object stream))
```

In addition, we need three other, more complicated stream-handling access procedures, one of which is STREAM-APPEND, which we implement in terms of the simpler stream-manipulation procedures:

```
(defun stream-append (stream1 stream2)
  (if (stream-endp stream1)
      stream2
      (stream-cons (stream-first stream1)
                   (stream-append (stream-rest stream1)
                                  stream2)))))
```

Suppose, for example, that we create two streams using STREAM-CONS:

```
* (setf stream1
        (stream-cons 'object-a
                        (stream-cons 'object-b
                                        'empty-stream)))
(OBJECT-A (OBJECT-B EMPTY-STREAM))
* (setf stream2
        (stream-cons 'object-x
                        (stream-cons 'object-y
                                        'empty-stream)))
(OBJECT-X (OBJECT-Y EMPTY-STREAM))
```

We can append the two streams using STREAM-APPEND:

```
* (stream-append stream1 stream2)
(OBJECT-A (OBJECT-B (OBJECT-X (OBJECT-Y EMPTY-STREAM))))
```

STREAM-CONCATENATE makes a single stream of objects from a stream of streams of objects:

```
(defun stream-concatenate (streams)
  (if (stream-endp streams) 'empty-stream
    (if (stream-endp (stream-first streams))
        (stream-concatenate (stream-rest streams))
      (stream-cons (stream-first (stream-first streams))
                        (stream-concatenate
                          (stream-cons (stream-rest (stream-first streams))
                                        (stream-rest streams)))))))
```

Here is an example:

```
* (setf stream-of-streams
        (stream-cons stream1
                        (stream-cons stream2 'empty-stream)))
((OBJECT-A (OBJECT-B EMPTY-STREAM))
 ((OBJECT-X (OBJECT-Y EMPTY-STREAM)) EMPTY-STREAM))
* (stream-concatenate stream-of-streams)
(OBJECT-A (OBJECT-B (OBJECT-X (OBJECT-Y EMPTY-STREAM))))
```

Next, STREAM-TRANSFORM is analogous to MAPCAR in that STREAM-TRANSFORM applies a given procedure to each object in a stream, producing a new stream:

```
(defun stream-transform (procedure stream)
  (if (stream-endp stream)
      'empty-stream
      (stream-cons (funcall procedure (stream-first stream))
                        (stream-transform procedure
                                        (stream-rest stream)))))
```

Here is an example of STREAM-TRANSFORM in action:

```
* (setf number-stream
        (stream-cons 2
                     (stream-cons 3
                                  'empty-stream)))
(2 (3 EMPTY-STREAM))

* (stream-transform #'(lambda (number) (expt 2 number))
                    number-stream)
(4 (8 EMPTY-STREAM))
```

Next, STREAM-MEMBER determines if a given thing is an object in a stream.
Note that STREAM-MEMBER, unlike MEMBER, uses EQUAL:

```
(defun stream-member (object stream)
  (cond ((stream-endp stream) nil)
        ((equal object (stream-first stream)) t)
        (t (stream-member object (stream-rest stream)))))
```

In chapters 26 and 27, we need to add objects to the end of streams that
are assigned to particular variables. STREAM-REMEMBER is a macro that does
the job. Note that it returns the object, if successfully added, or NIL if the
object is already in the stream:

```
(defmacro stream-remember (object variable)
  `(unless (stream-member ,object ,variable)
     (setf ,variable
           (stream-append ,variable
                          (stream-cons ,object
                                       'empty-stream)))
     ,object))
```

Consider this example in which LONG-STREAM's value is a stream of four
objects:

```
* long-stream
(OBJECT-A (OBJECT-B (OBJECT-X (OBJECT-Y EMPTY-STREAM))))

* (stream-remember 'last-object long-stream)
LAST-OBJECT

* long-stream
(OBJECT-A
  (OBJECT-B
    (OBJECT-X
      (OBJECT-Y
        (LAST-OBJECT EMPTY-STREAM)))))
```

```
* (stream-remember 'last-object long-stream)
NIL
```

Now that we have explained what basic streams are, we digress in the next section to explain how the evaluation of a form can be delayed until the form is needed. After that, we bring streams and delayed evaluation together, showing how to evaluate the forms that create stream elements only when those stream elements are needed.

We Can Delay Evaluation by Encapsulation

Suppose that while looking through your mail, you stumble across a scientific paper that looks interesting. Rather than evaluating it yourself, however, you pass it on to a friend along with a scribbled note suggesting that he read it from your perspective.

Analogous situations occur in programming. One procedure prepares a form to be evaluated later by another. Inasmuch as the form is not evaluated when it is prepared, but only later, the evaluation is said to be *delayed evaluation.*

Note carefully that delayed evaluation is to be done using the variable bindings of the procedure that prepared the form, just as the scientific paper is to be read from the perspective of the person who suggested it be read.

Suppose, for example, that one procedure's name is SKIMMER, and another's is THINKER. Your first thought might be that SKIMMER could just pass along the form, with THINKER evaluating it, perhaps using EVAL. Unfortunately, if the form has variables, those variables' values are determined by the fence thrown up for the call to THINKER, not by the fence that was thrown up for SKIMMER. To make this clearer, we define SKIMMER to be a procedure that prepares an EXPT form and we define THINKER to be a procedure that simply evaluates whatever form it is given:

```
(defun skimmer (n)
  '(expt n 2))
(defun thinker (form)
  (eval form))
```

Now suppose you try to evaluate the following forms:

```
* (skimmer 2)
(EXPT N 2)
* (thinker (skimmer 2))
ERROR
```

SKIMMER handed THINKER the form (EXPT N 2) to be evaluated later inside THINKER. Unfortunately, although N is bound to 2 inside the fence thrown up for SKIMMER, N has no binding inside the fence thrown up for THINKER:

```
SKIMMER ──────────────────────────────────────────┐
     Gatekeeper's list: N                          │
  │                                                │
  └────────────                                    │
                                                   │
                                                   │
```

```
THINKER───────────────────────────────────────────┐
     Gatekeeper's list                             │
  │                                                │
  └────────────                                    │
                                                   │
```

Somehow, you need a way to force LISP to evaluate the form inside SKIMMER's fence, even though the evaluation is called for later, inside THINKER.

In chapter 15, where we discussed generator procedures, you learned that you can determine the fence in which a form is evaluated by encapsulating the form inside a nameless procedure. Here, the trick is to encapsulate the form to be evaluated inside a nameless procedure while inside SKIMMER. Then the nameless procedure can be called inside THINKER:

```
(defun skimmer (n)                          ; New version.
  #'(lambda () (expt n 2)))

(defun thinker (procedure)                  ; New version.
  (funcall procedure))
```

Now the fence for the nameless procedure will be thrown up inside the fence thrown up for SKIMMER when the nameless procedure was defined:

```
SKIMMER ──────────────────────────────────────────┐
     Gatekeeper's list: N                          │
  │                                                │
  │   Nameless procedure's fence ───────────┐      │
  │        Gatekeeper's list:                │      │
  │     │                                    │      │
  │     └────────────                        │      │
  │                                          │      │
  └──────────────────────────────────────────      │
                                                   │
```

The form that caused trouble before causes no trouble now. SKIMMER returns a nameless procedure that contains the form to be evaluated. As always, the nameless procedure is something to be applied, not something to look at and not something to type in:

```
* (skimmer 2)
#<LEXICAL-CLOSURE 53C:F708>
```

When the nameless procedure is called inside THINKER, the form is evaluated, with the variable values drawn from the fence thrown up for SKIMMER:

```
* (thinker (skimmer 2))
4
```

Of course, in this illustration, nothing is really gained. There is no reason why the form, (EXPT N 2), should not be evaluated in SKIMMER, with the value handed to THINKER, rather than the form. The power of encapsulation emerges only when it is not clear whether a form will ever need to be evaluated at the time the form is composed.

Now we define two macros for encapsulating forms and for subsequently evaluating encapsulated forms. These macros not only do what we did by hand before, but also signal their intent by their names:

```
(defmacro encapsulate (form)
  `#'(lambda () ,form))
(defmacro expose (procedure)
  `(funcall ,procedure))
```

With these macros, SKIMMER and THINKER can be defined this way:

```
(defun skimmer (n)                       ;Still another version.
  (encapsulate (expt n 2)))
(defun thinker (procedure)               ;Still another version.
  (expose procedure))
* (thinker (skimmer 2))
4
```

We Can Represent Streams Using Delayed Evaluation

Now we combine two ideas, streams and delayed evaluation via encapsulation. To start out, suppose we construct a stream of powers of two using our existing stream procedures:

```
* (setf power-of-two-stream
        (stream-cons (expt 2 2)
                     (stream-cons (expt 2 3)
                                  'empty-stream)))
(4 (8 EMPTY-STREAM))
```

Note that both powers are computed before the stream is available for further processing. If only the first of the two stream objects happens to be used in further processing, then the work of computing the second power is wasted. Although the time wasted in computing one power of two in our illustration is insignificant, the time wasted in complicated computations can be enormous.

Now, however, we introduce a more sophisticated representation for streams, one which enables us to defer the computations that produce

stream objects until they are needed. We still represent the empty stream as
EMPTY-STREAM, and we still represent other streams as lists of two elements.
But in contrast to our first implementation, the second element in the two-
element list representing a stream is not an evaluated argument of STREAM-
CONS. Instead, the second element is a nameless procedure that produces
the remainder of the stream when called. This requires us to change the
definition of STREAM-CONS, making it a macro:

```
(defmacro stream-cons (object stream)
  `(list ,object #'(lambda () ,stream)))
```

And here is the result produced by the same stream-constructing form you
saw at the opening of this section:

```
* (setf power-of-two-stream
        (stream-cons (expt 2 2)
                     (stream-cons (expt 2 3)
                                  'empty-stream)))
(4 #<LEXICAL CLOSURE 1A4:C6C6>)
```

Note that the second element in the two-element list representing the
stream is a nameless procedure. If we call the nameless procedure, we
get the rest of the stream, with only the first object missing:

```
* (funcall (second power-of-two-stream))
(8 #<LEXICAL CLOSURE 1A4:C26A>)
```

And if we call the second nameless procedure, we get the rest of the stream
again, with the first and second objects missing and only the empty stream
remaining:

```
* (funcall (second (funcall (second power-of-two-stream))))
EMPTY-STREAM
```

Now it is clear that we need a new definition of STREAM-REST to complement
our new definition of STREAM-CONS. The newly defined STREAM-REST needs to
treat the second element appearing in its argument as a procedure to be
called:

```
(defun stream-rest (stream)
  (funcall (second stream)))
```

Now STREAM-FIRST, unchanged from our first implementation, and STREAM-
REST produce the following results. As you look at them, note carefully
when the EXPT forms are actually evaluated:

```
* (setf power-of-two-stream                    ;(EXPT 2 2) evaluated.
      (stream-cons (expt 2 2)
                   (stream-cons (expt 2 3)
                                'empty-stream)))
(4 #<LEXICAL CLOSURE 18C:A61D>)
* (stream-first power-of-two-stream)
4
* (setf power-of-two-stream
      (stream-rest power-of-two-stream))  ;(EXPT 2 3) evaluated.
(8 #<LEXICAL CLOSURE 18C:7C5>)
* (stream-first power-of-two-stream)
8
* (setf power-of-two-stream (stream-rest power-of-two-stream))
EMPTY-STREAM
```

Thus the EXPT forms are evaluated only as we march through the stream, not all at once when the stream is constructed.

Although our new definitions of STREAM-CONS and STREAM-REST are certainly adequate, we can inject a little elegance in them by using ENCAPSULATE and EXPOSE, which we defined in the previous section. With that, our basic stream procedures look like this:

```
(defun stream-endp (stream) (eq stream 'empty-stream))
(defun stream-first (stream) (first stream))
(defun stream-rest (stream) (expose (second stream)))   ;New.
(defmacro stream-cons (object stream)                   ;New.
  `(list ,object (encapsulate ,stream)))
```

Once you understand the basic procedures, the rest is easy. Because we built the remaining stream-handling procedures on top of the basic four, their definitions in this implementation are the same as those in the first implementation.

Problems

Problem 25-1: Consider the following procedure, which produces a stream of n squares:

```
(defun make-square-stream (n)
  (if (zerop n)
      'empty-stream
      (stream-cons (expt n 2) (make-square-stream (- n 1)))))
```

With our first implementation of stream-handling procedures, the result for $n = 3$ is as follows:

```
* (make-square-stream 3)
(9 (4 (1 EMPTY-STREAM)))
```

With our second implementation, the result looks a bit different:

```
* (setf square-stream (make-square-stream 3))
(9 #<LEXICAL CLOSURE 1C4:FE64>)
```

While evaluating the preceding form, (EXPT N 2) is evaluated with N bound
to 3. While evaluating the following form, (EXPT N 2) is evaluated twice,
once with N bound to 2 and once with N bound to 1:

```
(stream-rest
  (stream-rest
    (stream-rest square-stream)))
EMPTY-STREAM
```

Show the fences that determine the variable bindings used in the evaluation
of the preceding form.

Problem 25-2: Suppose we create the following stream:

```
* (setf power-of-two-stream
        (stream-cons (expt 2 2)
                     (stream-cons (expt 2 3)
                                  'empty-stream)))
```

The form (EXPT 2 3) is evaluated only when STREAM-REST is applied:

```
* (stream-rest power-of-two-stream)
(8 #<LEXICAL CLOSURE 1BC:B1B7>)
```

Unfortunately, it will be evaluated over and over if STREAM-REST is applied
over and over:

```
* (stream-rest power-of-two-stream)      ;(EXPT 2 3) evaluated.
(8 #<LEXICAL CLOSURE 1BC:7821>)

* (stream-rest power-of-two-stream)      ;(EXPT 2 3) evaluated again.
(8 #<LEXICAL CLOSURE 1BC:72C0>)
```

Define a new version of ENCAPSULATE such that the encapsulated form is
never evaluated more than once. The first time, a switch is to be set and
the value is to be remembered. Subsequently, the remembered value is to
be offered up without another evaluation of the encapsulated form.

Problem 25-3: Approach the issue exposed in the previous problem another way. Rather than modifying ENCAPSULATE, modify STREAM-REST so that
whenever it calls EXPOSE on a closure, it replaces that closure with its value,
as the following sequence illustrates:

References   **377**

```
* (setf power-of-two-stream
        (stream-cons (expt 2 2)
                     (stream-cons (expt 2 3)
                                  'empty-stream)))
(4 #<LEXICAL CLOSURE 164:EBD4>)

* (stream-rest power-of-two-stream)
(8 #<LEXICAL CLOSURE 16C:448E>)

* power-of-two-stream
(4 (8 #<LEXICAL CLOSURE 16C:448E>))

* (stream-rest (stream-rest power-of-two-stream))
EMPTY-STREAM

* power-of-two-stream
(4 (8 EMPTY-STREAM))
```

To handle the problem, you will need the primitive FUNCTIONP which returns
T if its argument is any procedure that can be applied, a closure for example.

Summary

- Streams are sequences of data objects
- We can represent streams using lists.
- We can delay evaluation by encapsulation.
- We can represent streams using delayed evaluation.

References

For an excellent treatment of streams, see *Structure and Interpretation of
Computer Programs*, by Harold Abelson and Gerald Jay Sussman.

26

Rule-Based
Expert Systems and
Forward Chaining

The principal purpose of this chapter and chapter 27 is to explain problem-solving programs that are based on matching simple rules to given problems. These programs are often called *rule-based expert systems*, and sometimes they are called *if-then systems* or *situation-action systems* or *production-rule systems*.

In this chapter, we explain how to implement a *forward-chaining rule-based program* that reasons forward from *assertions* to a *conclusion*. Our main example involves identification in the animal world.

Forward Chaining Means Working from Antecedents to Consequents

The following rules are typical of the things we learn as we accumulate new recognition skills:

- If an animal is a parent of a child, then the child's species is the same as the parent's.
- If an infection is a primary bacteremia, and it has entered by way of the gastrointestinal tract, then there is evidence that the infecting organism is bacteroides.

In these rules, the givens are called *antecedent assertions*. The conclusions are called *consequent assertions*. Because we assume that each rule has exactly one consequent assertion, the rules have the following form:

```
If      <antecedent assertion 1> is true,
        <antecedent assertion 2> is true,
        . . .
then    <consequent assertion> is true.
```

These rules are called *if-then rules*, *antecedent-consequent rules*, *situation-action rules*, *production rules*, or just *rules*. Programs based on rules do many practical recognition jobs.

A rule-based system does *forward chaining* if it starts with a collection of assertions and tries all available rules over and over, adding new assertions as it goes, until no rule can produce a new assertion.

In contrast, a rule-based system uses *backward chaining* if it starts with a hypothesis and tries to verify that hypothesis using things that are known already.

In both types of rule-based system, we need a way to represent assertions and rules. One good way is to create assertion and rule streams, as described in the next section.

We Use Streams To Represent Assertions and Rules

Let us agree that assertions are represented as lists of symbols like the following:

```
(bozo is a dog)
```

Our forward-chaining system, to be described, examines sequences of assertions, looking for those that match patterns. Consequently, it is natural to combine assertions into an assertion stream that our forward-chaining system processes.

The first thing we need is a procedure to get new assertions into the assertion stream. The following procedure, REMEMBER-ASSERTION, does the job, using stream procedures borrowed from chapter 25. Either the plain stream procedures or the stream procedures using delayed evaluation can be used, but to keep our examples simple and informative, assume that we are using the plain ones. Were we to use the set with delay, the values returned would contain obfuscating lexical closures, rather than illuminating expressions.

```
(defun remember-assertion (assertion)
  (stream-remember assertion *assertions*))
```

Note that the assertion stream is assigned to the symbol *ASSERTIONS*. Also recall from chapter 25 that STREAM-REMEMBER inserts new assertions at the end of the stream, so that later on, when the assertion stream is processed, the assertions are processed in the order that they are remembered. Once REMEMBER-ASSERTION is defined, here is how *ASSERTIONS* could be initialized:

```
(setf *assertions* 'empty-stream)
(remember-assertion '(bozo is a dog))
(remember-assertion '(deedee is a horse))
(remember-assertion '(deedee is a parent of sugar))
(remember-assertion '(deedee is a parent of brassy))
```

Now the value of *ASSERTIONS* is as follows:

```
* *assertions*
((BOZO IS A DOG)
 ((DEEDEE IS A HORSE)
  ((DEEDEE IS A PARENT OF SUGAR)
   ((DEEDEE IS A PARENT OF BRASSY) EMPTY-STREAM))))
```

Now let us turn to the representation of rules. We represent a rule as a list containing the rule's name, its antecedents, and its single consequent:

```
(<name>
 <antecedent assertion 1>
 <antecedent assertion 2>
 ...
 <antecedent assertion n>
 <consequent assertion>)
```

Later on, we need to get at the various parts of individual rules. Three simple procedures do the job:

```
(defun rule-name (rule) (first rule))

(defun rule-ifs (rule) (butlast (rest rule)))

(defun rule-then (rule) (first (last rule)))
```

REMEMBER-RULE is analogous to REMEMBER-ASSERTION, but REMEMBER-RULE adds to the stream assigned to *RULES*, rather than to the stream assigned to *ASSERTIONS*:

```
(defun remember-rule (rule)
  (stream-remember rule *rules*))
```

Now we can initialize *RULES* as follows, providing only a single rule for illustration. The rule captures the idea that if a parent belongs to a certain species, then the parent's child belongs to that species as well:

```
(setf *rules* 'empty-stream)
(remember-rule
  '(identify
        ((? animal) is a (? species))
        ((? animal) is a parent of (? child))
        ((? child) is a (? species))))
```

Thus the value of *RULES* is as follows:

```
* *rules*
((IDENTIFY ((? ANIMAL) IS A (? SPECIES))
         ((? ANIMAL) IS A PARENT OF (? CHILD))
         ((? CHILD) IS A (? SPECIES)))
 EMPTY-STREAM)
```

Our First Pass Concentrates on MATCH and the Binding Stream

Pattern variables make it possible for a rule to match a database of assertions in many ways. Keeping track of every possibility is not too difficult because we use a binding stream in which each element is an association list of pattern variable bindings.

Consider the use of a single rule with multiple antecedents. The first thing to do is to match the first antecedent in the rule against each assertion in the database using MATCH, borrowed from chapter 24. For each match, MATCH's initial association list is empty because there are no initial variable bindings. Most matches fail, in general, but some may succeed. Each success produces an association list of bindings. These association lists form an initial binding stream.

Working with our sample assertion and rule streams, two assertions in the database match ((? ANIMAL) IS A (? SPECIES)), the first antecedent in the only rule we have. One matching assertion is (BOZO IS A DOG); the other is (DEEDEE IS A HORSE). Together they determine the following two-element binding stream:

```
(((SPECIES DOG) (ANIMAL BOZO))
 (((SPECIES HORSE) (ANIMAL DEEDEE)) EMPTY-STREAM))
```

Once the first antecedent has been handled, the next thing to do is to match the second antecedent in the rule against each assertion in the database, but this time with an association list from the initial binding stream. Some association lists in the initial binding stream may lead to one or more association lists in the second binding stream. Other association lists from the initial binding stream condemn the matcher to fail on all assertions and lead to nothing in the second binding stream.

In our example, ((? ANIMAL) IS A PARENT OF (? CHILD)) is the second antecedent of the only rule. Using the first association list in the input binding stream, ((SPECIES DOG) (ANIMAL BOZO)), the pattern does not match any assertion in our database, producing an empty output binding stream. However, using the second association list in the input binding stream, ((SPECIES HORSE) (ANIMAL DEEDEE)), the pattern matches two assertions in the database, producing an output binding stream with two elements. Combining the empty output binding stream, from ((SPECIES DOG) (ANIMAL BOZO)), with the two-element one, from ((SPECIES HORSE) (ANIMAL DEEDEE)), we have this:

```
(((CHILD SUGAR) (SPECIES HORSE) (ANIMAL DEEDEE))
 (((CHILD BRASSY) (SPECIES HORSE) (ANIMAL DEEDEE))
  EMPTY-STREAM))
```

The next thing to do is to repeat for each antecedent. For our example, there are only two antecedents, so we are already finished.

Conceptually, it is best to think of filtering a binding stream through a cascaded set of filters. The characteristics of each filter are jointly determined by one antecedent and by the existing assertions in the assertion stream.

The binding stream stretches and shrinks like a rubber band as it moves from filter to filter. For each way of matching the rule to the assertion database, an association list emerges in the binding stream that leaves the final filter. The consequent must be processed for every such association list, replacing all pattern variables in the consequent using an association list from the surviving elements of the binding stream.

The process of replacing variables with variable values is called *instantiation*. Using the two surviving elements in the example, there are two ways to instantiate ((? CHILD) IS A (? SPECIES)), the consequent assertion. These two instantiations yield two new assertions:

```
(sugar is a horse)
(brassy is a horse)
```

Our Second Pass Concentrates on the Procedures that Surround MATCH

Now that we have explained what is to be done, we turn to an explanation of the procedures that do the work. We begin with TRY-ASSERTION, which is the most basic procedure in our forward-chaining program. TRY-ASSERTION matches a pattern against an assertion, given an association list of bindings, using MATCH. If the pattern does match the assertion, TRY-ASSERTION returns a single-element binding stream consisting of the resulting association list; otherwise, TRY-ASSERTION returns the empty stream:

```
(defun try-assertion (pattern assertion bindings)
  (let ((result (match pattern assertion bindings)))
    (if (eq 'fail result)
        'empty-stream
        (stream-cons result 'empty-stream))))
```

Here are a few examples of TRY-ASSERTION in action:

```
* (try-assertion '((? animal) is a (? species))
                 '(bozo is a dog)
                 nil)
(((SPECIES DOG) (ANIMAL BOZO)) EMPTY-STREAM)
```

```
* (try-assertion '((? animal) is a parent of (? child))
                 '(deedee is a parent of sugar)
                 '((species dog) (animal bozo)))
EMPTY-STREAM


* (try-assertion '((? animal) is a (? species))
                 '(deedee is a horse)
                 nil)
(((SPECIES HORSE) (ANIMAL DEEDEE)) EMPTY-STREAM)


* (try-assertion '((? animal) is a parent of (? child))
                 '(deedee is a parent of sugar)
                 '((species horse) (animal deedee)))
(((CHILD SUGAR) (SPECIES HORSE) (ANIMAL DEEDEE))
 EMPTY-STREAM)
```

Given TRY-ASSERTION, which matches a pattern to a single assertion, we
can define MATCH-PATTERN-TO-ASSERTIONS, which matches a pattern to all
of the assertions in the list assigned to *ASSERTIONS*. In MATCH-PATTERN-
TO-ASSERTIONS, the combination of TRY-ASSERTION with STREAM-TRANSFORM
produces a stream of binding streams, which STREAM-CONCATENATE converts
back into a binding stream of association lists:

```
(defun match-pattern-to-assertions (pattern bindings)
  (stream-concatenate
    (stream-transform
      #'(lambda (assertion) (try-assertion pattern
                                           assertion
                                           bindings))
      *assertions*)))
```

Here are some examples of MATCH-PATTERN-TO-ASSERTIONS in action:

```
* (match-pattern-to-assertions '((? animal) is a (? species))
                               nil)
(((SPECIES DOG) (ANIMAL BOZO))
 (((SPECIES HORSE) (ANIMAL DEEDEE)) EMPTY-STREAM))


* (match-pattern-to-assertions
    '((? animal) is a parent of (? child))
    '((species dog) (animal bozo)))
EMPTY-STREAM
```

```
* (match-pattern-to-assertions
    '((? animal) is a parent of (? child))
    '((species horse) (animal deedee)))
(((CHILD SUGAR) (SPECIES HORSE) (ANIMAL DEEDEE))
 (((CHILD BRASSY) (SPECIES HORSE) (ANIMAL DEEDEE))
  EMPTY-STREAM))
```

Thus MATCH-PATTERN-TO-ASSERTIONS produces a binding stream of association lists, given a pattern and an initial association list. Next we can move on to define FILTER-BINDING-STREAM, which uses STREAM-TRANSFORM to apply MATCH-PATTERN-TO-ASSERTIONS once for each association list in the binding stream. Once again, STREAM-CONCATENATE converts the resulting stream of binding streams back into a stream of association lists:

```
(defun filter-binding-stream (pattern stream)
  (stream-concatenate
    (stream-transform
      #'(lambda (bindings)
          (match-pattern-to-assertions pattern bindings))
      stream)))
```

The following are some examples of FILTER-BINDING-STREAM in action. Note that (NIL EMPTY-STREAM) is a single-element binding stream consisting of a single, empty association list:

```
* (filter-binding-stream '((? animal) is a (? species))
                         '(nil empty-stream))
(((SPECIES DOG) (ANIMAL BOZO))
 (((SPECIES HORSE) (ANIMAL DEEDEE)) EMPTY-STREAM))
* (filter-binding-stream '((? animal) is a parent of (? child))
                         '(((species dog) (animal bozo))
                           (((species horse) (animal deedee))
                            empty-stream)))
(((CHILD SUGAR) (SPECIES HORSE) (ANIMAL DEEDEE))
 (((CHILD BRASSY) (SPECIES HORSE) (ANIMAL DEEDEE))
  EMPTY-STREAM))
* (filter-binding-stream
    '((? animal) is a parent of (? child))
    (filter-binding-stream '((? animal) is a (? species))
                           '(nil empty-stream)))
(((CHILD SUGAR) (SPECIES HORSE) (ANIMAL DEEDEE))
 (((CHILD BRASSY) (SPECIES HORSE) (ANIMAL DEEDEE))
  EMPTY-STREAM))
```

The next thing we need is a procedure that uses FILTER-BINDING-STREAM once for each pattern in a list of patterns:

```
(defun apply-filters (patterns initial-input-stream)
  (if (endp patterns)
      initial-input-stream
      (apply-filters (rest patterns)
                     (filter-binding-stream (first patterns)
                                            initial-input-stream))))
```

Note that the call to FILTER-BINDING-STREAM works on the first of the remaining patterns. This ensures that the patterns in multiple-antecedent rules are filtered in the order in which they appear in the rule. Note that the input to the first filter is a binding stream containing just one association list, which is empty:

```
* (apply-filters '(((? animal) is a parent of (? child))
                   ((? animal) is a (? species)))
                 '(nil empty-stream))
(((CHILD SUGAR) (SPECIES HORSE) (ANIMAL DEEDEE))
 (((CHILD BRASSY) (SPECIES HORSE) (ANIMAL DEEDEE))
  EMPTY-STREAM))
```

The consequent part of the rule is instantiated for each element, if any, in the binding stream that emerges from the final filter. The consequent instantiation is done by INSTANTIATE-VARIABLES, which uses EXTRACT-VALUE and FIND-BINDING, both defined in chapter 24. Note that the first COND clause takes care of patterns bound to NIL, among others:

```
(defun instantiate-variables (pattern a-list)
  (cond
    ((atom pattern) pattern)
    ((eq '? (first pattern))
     (extract-value (find-binding pattern a-list)))
    (t (cons (instantiate-variables (first pattern) a-list)
             (instantiate-variables (rest pattern) a-list)))))
```

Here are examples of INSTANTIATE-VARIABLES in action:

```
* (instantiate-variables
    '((? child) is a (? species))
    '((child sugar) (species horse) (animal deedee)))
(SUGAR IS A HORSE)
```

```
* (instantiate-variables
    '((? child) is a (? species))
    '((child brassy) (species horse) (animal deedee)))
(BRASSY IS A HORSE)
```

We are ready for USE-RULE. It uses APPLY-FILTERS to apply FILTER-BINDING-STREAM to each of a rule's antecedents. Then the instantiated consequents are added to the assertion stream using REMEMBER-ASSERTION. Note that USE-RULE uses reader procedures, RULE-NAME, RULE-IFS, and RULE-THEN, to dig the name, the antecedents, and the consequent out of the rule:

```
(defun use-rule (rule)
  (let ((binding-stream
          (apply-filters (rule-ifs rule)
                          (stream-cons nil 'empty-stream))))
     (do ((binding-stream binding-stream
                          (stream-rest binding-stream))
         (success-switch nil))
        ((stream-endp binding-stream) success-switch)
       (let ((result (instantiate-variables
                       (rule-then rule)
                       (stream-first binding-stream))))
         (when (remember-assertion result)
           (format t "~%Rule ~a indicates ~a."
                   (rule-name rule) result)
           (setf success-switch t)))))))
```

Now we can try USE-RULE:

```
* (use-rule '(identify
               ((? animal) is a (? species))
               ((? animal) is a parent of (? child))
               ((? child) is a (? species))))
Rule IDENTIFY indicates (SUGAR IS A HORSE).
Rule IDENTIFY indicates (BRASSY IS A HORSE).
T
```

This produces a modified list of assertions:

```
* *assertions*
((BOZO IS A DOG)
 ((DEEDEE IS A HORSE)
  ((DEEDEE IS A PARENT OF SUGAR)
   ((DEEDEE IS A PARENT OF BRASSY)
    ((SUGAR IS A HORSE)                    ;New.
     ((BRASSY IS A HORSE)                  ;New.
      EMPTY-STREAM))))))
```

Now all that remains is to use USE-RULE on all rules using FORWARD-CHAIN.
But note that whenever a new assertion is added to the assertion stream,
a rule that previously failed may succeed. Consequently, the rule stream
must be reprocessed whenever any rule produces a new assertion. As soon
as there are no new assertions, a message is printed and FORWARD-CHAIN
returns:

```
(defun forward-chain ()
    (do ((rule-stream *rules* (stream-rest rule-stream))
         (repeat-switch nil))
        ((stream-endp rule-stream)
         (if repeat-switch
             (progn
               (format t "~%I am trying the rules again.")
               (forward-chain))
             (progn
               (format t "~%Nothing new noted.")
               'done)))
      (when (use-rule (stream-first rule-stream))
        (setf repeat-switch t))))
```

In our one-rule example, working with the original assertions, FORWARD-
CHAIN just makes a single call to USE-RULE, producing the behavior you saw
above in the USE-RULE example, together with a second pass to see if any
of the first-pass conclusions lead to new results:

```
* (forward-chain)
Rule IDENTIFY indicates (SUGAR IS A HORSE).
Rule IDENTIFY indicates (BRASSY IS A HORSE).
I am trying the rules again.
Nothing new noted.
DONE
```

**Simple Rules Help
Identify Animals**

If an animal has hair or gives milk, it is a mammal. If an animal eats meat,
it is a carnivore. Encoding knowledge like this in if-then rules produces the
following zoo-oriented rules:

```
(setf *rules* 'empty-stream)
(remember-rule '(identify1
                   ((? animal) has hair)
                   ((? animal) is a mammal)))
(remember-rule '(identify2
                   ((? animal) gives milk)
                   ((? animal) is a mammal)))
```

```
(remember-rule '(identify3
                   ((? animal) has feathers)
                   ((? animal) is a bird)))

(remember-rule '(identify4
                   ((? animal) flies)
                   ((? animal) lays eggs)
                   ((? animal) is a bird)))

(remember-rule '(identify5
                   ((? animal) eats meat)
                   ((? animal) is a carnivore)))

(remember-rule '(identify6
                   ((? animal) has pointed teeth)
                   ((? animal) has claws)
                   ((? animal) has forward eyes)
                   ((? animal) is a carnivore)))

(remember-rule '(identify7
                   ((? animal) is a mammal)
                   ((? animal) has hoofs)
                   ((? animal) is an ungulate)))

(remember-rule '(identify8
                   ((? animal) is a mammal)
                   ((? animal) chews cud)
                   ((? animal) is an ungulate)))

(remember-rule '(identify9
                   ((? animal) is a mammal)
                   ((? animal) is a carnivore)
                   ((? animal) has tawny color)
                   ((? animal) has dark spots)
                   ((? animal) is a cheetah)))

(remember-rule '(identify10
                   ((? animal) is a mammal)
                   ((? animal) is a carnivore)
                   ((? animal) has tawny color)
                   ((? animal) has black stripes)
                   ((? animal) is a tiger)))

(remember-rule '(identify11
                   ((? animal) is an ungulate)
                   ((? animal) has long neck)
                   ((? animal) has long legs)
                   ((? animal) has dark spots)
                   ((? animal) is a giraffe)))

(remember-rule '(identify12
                   ((? animal) is an ungulate)
                   ((? animal) has black stripes)
                   ((? animal) is a zebra)))
```

```
(remember-rule '(identify13
                  ((? animal) is a bird)
                  ((? animal) does not fly)
                  ((? animal) has long neck)
                  ((? animal) has long legs)
                  ((? animal) is black and white)
                  ((? animal) is an ostrich)))

(remember-rule '(identify14
                  ((? animal) is a bird)
                  ((? animal) does not fly)
                  ((? animal) swims)
                  ((? animal) is black and white)
                  ((? animal) is a penguin)))

(remember-rule '(identify15
                  ((? animal) is a bird)
                  ((? animal) flies well)
                  ((? animal) is an albatross)))

(remember-rule '(identify16
                  ((? animal) is a (? species))
                  ((? animal) is a parent of (? child))
                  ((? child) is a (? species))))
```

Now suppose we create assertions as follows:

```
(setf *assertions* 'empty-stream)
(remember-assertion '(robbie has dark spots))
(remember-assertion '(robbie has tawny color))
(remember-assertion '(robbie eats meat))
(remember-assertion '(robbie has hair))
(remember-assertion '(suzie has feathers))
(remember-assertion '(suzie flies well))
```

Given these rules and assertions, FORWARD-CHAIN produces the following behavior:

```
* (forward-chain)
Rule IDENTIFY1 indicates (ROBBIE IS A MAMMAL).
Rule IDENTIFY3 indicates (SUZIE IS A BIRD).
Rule IDENTIFY5 indicates (ROBBIE IS A CARNIVORE).
Rule IDENTIFY9 indicates (ROBBIE IS A CHEETAH).
Rule IDENTIFY15 indicates (SUZIE IS AN ALBATROSS).
I am trying the rules again.
Nothing new noted.
DONE
```

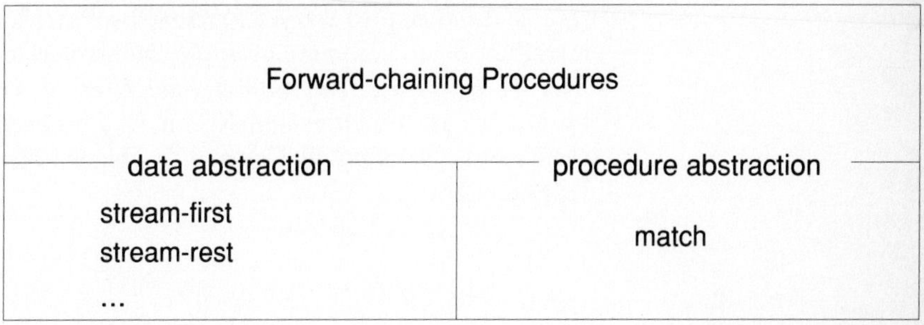

```
┌─────────────────────────────────────────────────────────────┐
│                                                               │
│                  Forward-chaining Procedures                  │
│                                                               │
├──────── data abstraction ────────┬──── procedure abstraction ─┤
│        stream-first              │                            │
│        stream-rest               │         match              │
│        ...                       │                            │
└───────────────────────────────────┴───────────────────────────┘
```

Figure 26-1. The forward-chaining problem solver has both a data-abstraction boundary and procedure-abstraction boundary.

Rules Facilitate Question Answering and Probability Computing

One reason rule-based problem solvers are popular is that they can be extended with programs that explain how conclusions are reached and programs that determine how probable the program's answers are.

As we explained in chapter 22, a remembered goal tree makes it possible to answer *how* and *why* questions. Because a record of rule use can be viewed as a goal tree, building a question-answering system on top of a rule-based problem solver is straightforward.

And as we explain in chapter 23, an inference net makes it possible to propagate probability bounds. Because a record of rule use can be viewed as an inference net, building a probability system on top of a rule-based problem solver is also straightforward.

Our Forward-Chaining Program Illustrates Abstraction

The forward-chaining problem solver illustrates both data abstraction and procedure abstraction, as suggested in figure 26-1. Because the program uses assertion streams, all the detail of how data is represented is hidden behind a data-abstraction boundary. And because all the detail of pattern matching is hidden behind MATCH, there is a procedure-abstraction boundary as well.

Summary

- Forward chaining means working from antecedents to consequents.
- We use streams to represent assertions and rules.
- Our first pass concentrates on MATCH and the binding stream.
- Our second pass concentrates on the procedures that surround MATCH.
- Simple rules help identify animals.
- Rules facilitate question answering and probability computing.
- Our forward-chaining program illustrates abstraction.

References   For a general introduction to rule-based expert systems, see chapter 6 of *Artificial Intelligence (Second Edition)* by Patrick H. Winston. For a general introduction to commercial applications of rule-based expert systems, see *The AI Business: The Commercial Uses of Artificial Intelligence*, edited by Patrick H. Winston and Karen A. Prendergast. See also *The Rise of the Expert Company*, by Edward A. Feigenbaum, Pamela McCorduck, and H. Penny Nii.

27

Backward Chaining and PROLOG

The principal purpose of this chapter and chapter 26 is to explain problem-solving systems that are based on matching simple rules to given problems.

In this chapter, we concentrate on *backward-chaining* systems that reason backward from a hypothesis looking for assertions that support the hypothesis.

Apart from syntax, our implementation of a backward-chaining system is within a hair of being a simple version of PROLOG, a popular backward-chaining language. Like PROLOG, our program looks at all possible ways of chaining backward through rules to verify hypotheses.

As in chapter 26, our main example involves identification in the animal world.

Our Backward Chainer Borrows Access Procedures from our Forward Chainer

In chapter 25, we defined two sets of procedures for operating on streams. Using either set of stream procedures, we can define REMEMBER-ASSERTION and REMEMBER-RULE, both of which were introduced in chapter 25:

```
(defun remember-assertion (assertion)
  (stream-remember assertion *assertions*))
```

```
(defun remember-rule (rule)
  (stream-remember rule *rules*))
```

Using these two procedures we can prepare *ASSERTIONS* and *RULES* for
backward-chaining experiments:

```
(setf *assertions* 'empty-stream)
(remember-assertion '(deedee has hair))
(remember-assertion '(bozo is a mammal))
(setf *rules* 'empty-stream)
(remember-rule '(identify
                    ((? animal) has hair)
                    ((? animal) is a mammal)))
```

Although either set of stream procedures works, for the illustrations in
this chapter, we use the simple set, the one without delayed evaluation.
The reason is that we want to make our explanations clearer by showing
examples of what each procedure returns. Were we to use the set with
delay, the values returned would be unintelligible.

**Backward Chaining
Means Working
from Consequents
to Antecedents**

Recall that a problem solver is doing *backward chaining* if it starts with a
hypothesis and tries to verify that hypothesis using things that are known
already. The strategy followed by our backward-chaining program is as
follows:

- Look for an assertion in the database that matches a hypothesis. Do
  this using MATCH, borrowed from chapter 24.
- If there is no matching assertion, look for a rule whose consequent
  matches the hypothesis. Because both the hypothesis and the consequent may have pattern variables, do this using UNIFY, borrowed from
  chapter 24.
- For any rule whose consequent matches the hypothesis, try to verify
  each of the rule's antecedents recursively, thinking of each as a subhy-
  pothesis. If each antecedent is verified, then the hypothesis is verified.

**Our First Pass
Concentrates on
MATCH, UNIFY,
and the Binding
Stream**

In preparation for explaining the procedures that surround MATCH and UNIFY
in our backward-chaining program, we walk through a few simple examples.
First suppose the hypothesis is that Bozo is a mammal. For this, it is
sufficient to match the hypothesis against the assertions in the database
with no initial bindings. The first try fails; the second succeeds, returning
an empty list of bindings:

```
* (match '(bozo is a mammal) '(deedee has hair) nil)
FAIL

* (match '(bozo is a mammal) '(bozo is a mammal) nil)
NIL
```

Now suppose the hypothesis is that Deedee is a mammal. Neither database assertion matches:

```
* (match '(deedee is a mammal) '(deedee has hair) nil)
FAIL

* (match '(deedee is a mammal) '(bozo is a mammal) nil)
FAIL
```

But the hypothesis does match the consequent of the sample identification rule, **IDENTIFY**, returning a single element list of bindings, where **ANIMAL** is bound to **DEEDEE**:

```
* (unify '(deedee is a mammal)
         '((? animal) is a mammal)
         nil)
((ANIMAL DEEDEE))
```

We can try to verify the rule's antecedent, ((? ANIMAL) HAS HAIR), matching it against the assertions in the database. The first assertion tried works:

```
* (match '((? animal) has hair)
         '(deedee has hair)
         '((animal deedee)))
((ANIMAL DEEDEE))
```

Note carefully that the supplied binding list is no longer empty: it is the list produced by unifying the hypothesis with the rule's consequent. Note also that the result is the same binding list with nothing new added. Hence the rule's antecedent is verified, and we conclude that Deedee is a mammal.

Now we work through a harder example. The hypothesis is that something is a mammal, and we expect a binding list for each such thing found. One of the two database assertions matches:

```
* (match '((? x) is a mammal) '(deedee has hair) nil)
FAIL

* (match '((? x) is a mammal) '(bozo is a mammal) nil)
((X BOZO))
```

But the hypothesis also matches the consequent of the rule, producing a single binding list in which the value of **X** is a variable expression:

```
* (unify '((? x) is a mammal)
         '((? animal) is a mammal)
         nil)
((X (? ANIMAL)))
```

To verify the rule's antecedent, ((? ANIMAL) HAS HAIR), we match it with database assertions using the new binding list:

```
* (match '((? animal) has hair)
         '(deedee has hair)
         '((x (? animal))))
((ANIMAL DEEDEE) (X (? ANIMAL)))
```

Again, the antecedent matches the first database assertion, this time adding a new binding to the resulting binding list. Thus the ((? X) IS A MAMMAL) hypothesis produces two binding lists: one by direct match of the hypothesis with a database item and one by using the rule.

Our Second Pass Concentrates on the Procedures that Surround MATCH and UNIFY

It is time to see how our backward-chaining program arranges for MATCH and UNIFY to be used as just sketched. Ultimately, we define BACKWARD-CHAIN, a procedure that produces the following results:

```
* (backward-chain '(bozo is a mammal))
YES

* (backward-chain '(deedee is a mammal))
YES

* (backward-chain '(bozo is a mammal) '(deedee is a mammal))
YES

* (backward-chain '(bozo is a mammal) '(bozo has spots))
NO

* (backward-chain '((? x) is a mammal))
-->     X = BOZO
-->     X = DEEDEE
NO-MORE
```

Most of BACKWARD-CHAIN is devoted to printing a neat result, translating an association list of bindings into a pretty answer. The part that produces the association lists of bindings is straightforward:

```
(defun backward-chain (&rest patterns)
  (let ((binding-stream
          (apply-filters patterns
                         (stream-cons nil 'empty-stream)))
        ...)
    ...))
```

Later, we expose the rest of BACKWARD-CHAIN. For now, note in passing that BACKWARD-CHAIN can handle any number of patterns. The patterns are the foundation for a sequence of binding-stream filters. The initial input to the sequence of filters is a stream whose only element is an empty binding list. The deployment of the filters is handled by APPLY-FILTERS, a procedure borrowed from our forward-chaining program:

```
(defun apply-filters (patterns initial-input-stream)
  (if (endp patterns)
      initial-input-stream
      (apply-filters (rest patterns)
                     (filter-binding-stream (first patterns)
                                            initial-input-stream))))
```

The two arguments handed to FILTER-BINDING-STREAM are a pattern and a stream processed by filters based on other patterns. In our example, the arguments in the first call to APPLY-FILTERS are the hypothesis pattern, (BOZO IS A MAMMAL), and a binding stream containing a single empty binding list, (NIL EMPTY-STREAM).

When FILTER-BINDING-STREAM calls itself, the arguments are NIL and the same single-element stream as before, (NIL EMPTY-STREAM). This second call, with no pattern, immediately returns (NIL EMPTY-STREAM), the single-element stream. Thus for our example, the result of the call to APPLY-FILTERS is the same as the result that would be obtained by calling FILTER-BINDING-STREAM as follows:

```
(filter-binding-stream '(bozo is a mammal)
                       '(nil empty-stream))
```

The version of FILTER-BINDING-STREAM we need here is more general than the one that we managed with in chapter 26. It must look for the pattern not only in the database but also among the rule consequents:

```
(defun filter-binding-stream (pattern stream)
  (stream-concatenate
    (stream-transform
      #'(lambda (bindings)
          (stream-concatenate
            (stream-cons
              (match-pattern-to-assertions pattern bindings)
              (stream-cons
                (match-pattern-to-rules pattern bindings)
                'empty-stream))))
      stream)))
```

MATCH-PATTERN-TO-ASSERTIONS, which is borrowed without modification from our forward-chaining program, works on all the database assertions using TRY-ASSERTION:

```
(defun match-pattern-to-assertions (pattern bindings)
  (stream-concatenate
    (stream-transform
      #'(lambda (assertion) (try-assertion pattern
                                           assertion
                                           bindings))
      *assertions*)))
```

TRY-ASSERTION, like MATCH-PATTERN-TO-ASSERTIONS, is borrowed from our forward-chaining program:

```
(defun try-assertion (pattern assertion bindings)
  (let ((result (match pattern assertion bindings)))
    (if (eq 'fail result)
        'empty-stream
        (stream-cons result 'empty-stream))))
```

When you ask if Bozo is a mammal, BACKWARD-CHAIN, working through APPLY-FILTERS, applies MATCH-PATTERN-TO-ASSERTIONS to (BOZO IS A MAMMAL) as illustrated in the following form, producing a single-element binding stream:

```
* (match-pattern-to-assertions '(bozo is a mammal) nil)
(NIL EMPTY-STREAM)
```

This result is produced by two calls to TRY-ASSERTION, one of which produces a single-element stream and the other, an empty stream:

```
* (try-assertion '(bozo is a mammal) '(bozo is a mammal) nil)
(NIL EMPTY-STREAM)
```

```
* (try-assertion '(bozo is a mammal) '(deedee has hair) nil)
EMPTY-STREAM
```

STREAM-CONCATENATE, appearing in MATCH-PATTERN-TO-ASSERTIONS, puts them together:

```
* (stream-concatenate
    '((nil empty-stream) empty-stream))
(NIL EMPTY-STREAM)
```

FILTER-BINDING-STREAM also works on the pattern using MATCH-PATTERN-TO-RULES, which uses TRY-RULE:

```
(defun match-pattern-to-rules (pattern bindings)
  (stream-concatenate
    (stream-transform
      #'(lambda (rule) (try-rule pattern rule bindings))
      *rules*)))

(defun try-rule (pattern rule bindings)
  (let* ((rule (make-variables-unique rule))
         (result (unify pattern (rule-then rule) bindings)))
    (if (eq 'fail result)
        'empty-stream
        (apply-filters (rule-ifs rule)
                       (stream-cons result
                                    'empty-stream)))))
```

Note that TRY-RULE does not use a rule itself, but rather a copy produced by MAKE-VARIABLES-UNIQUE. As you will see when MAKE-VARIABLES-UNIQUE is defined, the variable names are changed in the copy. One reason is that this allows the same variables to be used in more than one rule without confusion. Another is that a rule can be called upon in the course of verifying one of its own antecedents, as shown later in a problem. If variables were to have the same names whenever a rule is encountered, the bindings appropriate to one deployment of the rule could shadow those of the other, recursive deployments, leading to disaster.

Thus MAKE-VARIABLES-UNIQUE produces the following transformation of IDENTIFY:

```
* (make-variables-unique '(identify
                            ((? animal) has hair)
                            ((? animal) is a mammal)))
(IDENTIFY
  ((? ANIMAL90) HAS HAIR)
  ((? ANIMAL90) IS A MAMMAL))
```

To keep our explanation uncluttered, however, we pretend that the rule is returned as is, without variable substitutions. In our particular examples, the rule does not lead to its own use; hence there is no possibility of confusion.

When dealing with the hypothesis that Bozo is a mammal, `TRY-RULE` determines that the pattern matches the consequent of `IDENTIFY` using `UNIFY`:

```
* (unify '(bozo is a mammal) '((? animal) is a mammal) nil)
((ANIMAL BOZO))
```

This means that the call to `APPLY-FILTERS` in `TRY-RULE` will work on the pattern `((? ANIMAL) HAS HAIR)` with `((ANIMAL BOZO))` serving as the only binding list in the input binding stream. But because `BOZO` is not known to have hair, the result is an empty binding stream:

```
* (apply-filters '(((? animal) has hair))
                 '(((animal bozo)) empty-stream))
EMPTY-STREAM
```

Because `APPLY-FILTERS` produces an empty binding stream, `TRY-RULE` and `MATCH-PATTERN-TO-RULES` do too:

```
* (match-pattern-to-rules '(bozo is a mammal) nil)
EMPTY-STREAM
```

To review, `MATCH-PATTERN-TO-ASSERTIONS` produces a stream containing one empty association list, `(NIL EMPTY-STREAM)`. `MATCH-PATTERN-TO-RULES` produces `EMPTY-STREAM`, which is an empty stream. Because `FILTER-BINDING-STREAM` combines the two results, the call to `FILTER-BINDING-STREAM` caused by the call to `APPLY-FILTERS` in `BACKWARD-CHAIN` produces a stream containing one empty association list:

```
* (filter-binding-stream '(bozo is a mammal)
                         '(nil empty-stream))
(NIL EMPTY-STREAM)
```

When the hypothesis is that Deedee is a mammal, the result is obtained a bit differently. `BACKWARD-CHAIN` calls `APPLY-FILTERS`, which causes a call to `FILTER-BINDING-STREAM`, which calls both `MATCH-PATTERN-TO-ASSERTIONS` and `MATCH-PATTERN-TO-RULES`. This time `MATCH-PATTERN-TO-ASSERTIONS` comes up empty handed:

```
* (match-pattern-to-assertions '(deedee is a mammal) nil)
EMPTY-STREAM
```

But now `MATCH-PATTERN-TO-RULES` leads to interesting behavior. First `TRY-RULE` determines that the pattern matches the consequent of `IDENTIFY`, as it did before:

```
* (unify '(deedee is a mammal) '((? animal) is a mammal) nil)
((ANIMAL DEEDEE))
```

This means the call to APPLY-FILTERS in TRY-RULE will work on ((? ANIMAL) HAS HAIR) with ((ANIMAL DEEDEE)) serving as the initial binding list. And because DEEDEE is known to have hair, the result is as follows:

```
* (apply-filters '(((? animal) has hair))
                 '(((animal deedee)) empty-stream))
(((ANIMAL DEEDEE)) EMPTY-STREAM)
```

Because APPLY-FILTERS produces a single-element binding stream, TRY-RULE and MATCH-PATTERN-TO-RULES do too:

```
* (match-pattern-to-rules '(deedee is a mammal) nil)
(((ANIMAL DEEDEE)) EMPTY-STREAM)
```

To review again, MATCH-PATTERN-TO-ASSERTIONS produces EMPTY-STREAM and MATCH-PATTERN-TO-RULES produces (((ANIMAL DEEDEE)) EMPTY-STREAM). The call to FILTER-BINDING-STREAM constructed by the call to APPLY-FILTERS in BACKWARD-CHAIN therefore has the following result:

```
* (filter-binding-stream '(deedee is a mammal)
                         '(NIL EMPTY-STREAM))
(((ANIMAL DEEDEE)) EMPTY-STREAM)
```

When the hypothesis is that something is a mammal, the result is produced both by MATCH-PATTERN-TO-ASSERTIONS and MATCH-PATTERN-TO-RULES. Without going into so much detail, here is a synopsis of what happens:

```
* (match-pattern-to-assertions '((? x) is a mammal) nil)
(((X BOZO)) EMPTY-STREAM)
* (unify '((? x) is a mammal) '((? animal) is a mammal) nil)
((X (? ANIMAL)))
* (apply-filters '(((? animal) has hair))
                 '(((x (? animal))) empty-stream))
(((ANIMAL DEEDEE) (X (? ANIMAL))) EMPTY-STREAM)
* (match-pattern-to-rules '((? x) is a mammal) nil)
(((ANIMAL DEEDEE) (X (? ANIMAL))) EMPTY-STREAM)
* (filter-binding-stream '((? x) is a mammal)
                         '(NIL EMPTY-STREAM))
(((X BOZO))
 (((ANIMAL DEEDEE) (X (? ANIMAL))) EMPTY-STREAM))
```

Finally, we return to BACKWARD-CHAIN. In addition to deploying filters, it has to arrange for a pretty output. If there are no pattern variables in the hypothesis, the output is just YES or NO. Otherwise, the output is a display of each unique set of bindings for the hypothesis variables. Note that there are several auxiliary procedures that are explained in the next section:

```
(defun backward-chain (&rest patterns)
  (let ((binding-stream
          (apply-filters patterns
                         (stream-cons nil 'empty-stream)))
        (variables (list-variables patterns))
        (displayed-answers nil))
    (if (endp variables)
        (if (stream-endp binding-stream)
            'no
            'yes)
        (do ((binding-stream binding-stream
                             (stream-rest binding-stream)))
            ((stream-endp binding-stream) 'no-more)
          (let ((answer
                  (make-answer variables
                               (stream-first binding-stream))))
            (unless (member answer displayed-answers
                            :test #'equal)
              (display-answer answer)
              (setf displayed-answers
                    (cons answer displayed-answers)))))))))
```

Completing Our Backward-Chaining Program Involves a Few Auxiliary Procedures

In this section, we expose several auxiliary procedures that do boring but necessary jobs. Many were introduced in BACKWARD-CHAIN. For example, LIST-VARIABLES makes a list of the variables that appear in a pattern:

```
* (list-variables '((? x) is a mammal))
(X)
```

MAKE-ANSWER constructs an association list of variable bindings for the variables produced by LIST-VARIABLES using an element of the binding stream:

```
* (make-answer '(x) '((X BOZO)))
((X BOZO))

* (make-answer '(x) '((ANIMAL DEEDEE) (X (? ANIMAL))))
((X DEEDEE))
```

LIST-VARIABLES is defined as follows:

```
(defun list-variables (tree &optional names)
  (cond ((atom tree) names)
        ((eq '? (first tree))
         (if (member (second tree) names)
             names
             (append names (rest tree))))
        (t (list-variables (rest tree)
                           (list-variables (first tree)
                                           names)))))
```

And here is MAKE-ANSWER:

```
(defun make-answer (variables bindings)
  (instantiate-variables
    (mapcar #'(lambda (variable)
                (list variable (list '? variable)))
            variables)
    bindings))
```

MAKE-ANSWER uses INSTANTIATE-VARIABLES, a procedure that replaces variable expressions using a binding list:

```
* (instantiate-variables '(x (? x))
                         '((animal deedee) (x (? animal))))
(X DEEDEE)
```

Note that INSTANTIATE-VARIABLES must be generalized from the version used in chapter 26 because a variable may be replaced with an expression that itself requires variable replacement. In the example, (? X) is replaced by (? ANIMAL), which is replaced in turn by DEEDEE. Here is the new definition:

```
(defun instantiate-variables (pattern a-list)
  (cond ((atom pattern) pattern)
        ((eq '? (first pattern))
         (let ((binding (find-binding pattern a-list)))
           (if binding
               (instantiate-variables (extract-value binding)
                                      a-list)
               pattern)))
        (t (cons (instantiate-variables (first pattern)
                                        a-list)
                 (instantiate-variables (rest pattern)
                                        a-list)))))
```

The only auxiliary procedure left to explain in BACKWARD-CHAIN is DISPLAY-ANSWER:

```
(defun display-answer (answers)
  (format t "~&-->")
  (dolist (answer answers)
    (format t " ~a = ~a" (first answer) (second answer)))))
```

Finally, to define MAKE-VARIABLES-UNIQUE, an auxiliary used in TRY-RULE, we need GENTEMP, a primitive that generates a new symbol whose name is formed by concatenating the name of its argument with a unique number:

```
* (gentemp 'x)
X26

* (gentemp 'x)
X27

* (gentemp 'y)
Y28
```

Using GENTEMP, MAKE-VARIABLES-UNIQUE is easy to define. Variables are extracted using LIST-VARIABLES and replaced using INSTANTIATE-VARIABLES:

```
(defun make-variables-unique (rule)
  (let ((variables (list-variables rule)))
    (dolist (variable variables rule)
      (setf rule
            (instantiate-variables
              rule
              (list (list variable
                          (list '? (gentemp variable)))))))))
```

Simple Rules Help Identify Animals

Now we can revisit our zoo-oriented database, this time with a view toward experimenting with backward chaining. Here are the assertions we introduced in chapter 26:

```
(setf *assertions* 'empty-stream)
(remember-assertion '(robbie has dark spots))
(remember-assertion '(robbie has tawny color))
(remember-assertion '(robbie eats meat))
(remember-assertion '(robbie has hair))
(remember-assertion '(suzie has feathers))
(remember-assertion '(suzie flies well))
```

And here are a few of the rules, just the ones we need for our experiments here:

```
(setf *rules* 'empty-stream)
(remember-rule '(identify1
                 ((? animal) has hair)
                 ((? animal) is a mammal)))
(remember-rule '(identify3
                 ((? animal) has feathers)
                 ((? animal) is a bird)))
(remember-rule '(identify5
                 ((? animal) eats meat)
                 ((? animal) is a carnivore)))
(remember-rule '(identify9
                 ((? animal) is a mammal)
                 ((? animal) is a carnivore)
                 ((? animal) has tawny color)
                 ((? animal) has dark spots)
                 ((? animal) is a cheetah)))
(remember-rule '(identify15
                 ((? animal) is a bird)
                 ((? animal) flies well)
                 ((? animal) is a albatross)))
```

Suppose we ask if Robbie is a cheetah. Rule IDENTIFY9 says he is if he is a mammal, a carnivore, and has the right color and spots. Rule IDENTIFY1 says he is a mammal because he has hair, and rule IDENTIFY5 says he is a carnivore because he eats meat. The correct color and spots are determined by looking directly at the assertions in the database. Hence Robbie is a cheetah as BACKWARD-CHAIN demonstrates:

```
* (backward-chain '(robbie is a cheetah))
YES
```

Similarly, rule IDENTIFY15, working in concert with rule IDENTIFY3, shows that Suzie is an albatross:

```
* (backward-chain '(suzie is a albatross))
YES
```

Next we ask what Robbie is, introducing a pattern variable. All the rules get tried in this example:

```
* (backward-chain '(robbie is a (? x)))
-->      X = MAMMAL
-->      X = CARNIVORE
-->      X = CHEETAH
NO-MORE
```

Similarly, we can ask what Suzie is. Again, all the rules get tried:

```
* (backward-chain '(suzie is a (? x)))
-->     X = BIRD
-->     X = ALBATROSS
NO-MORE
```

Alternatively, we can ask what everyone is:

```
* (backward-chain '((? animal) is a (? x)))
-->     ANIMAL = ROBBIE X = MAMMAL
-->     ANIMAL = SUZIE  X = BIRD
-->     ANIMAL = ROBBIE X = CARNIVORE
-->     ANIMAL = ROBBIE X = CHEETAH
-->     ANIMAL = SUZIE  X = ALBATROSS
NO-MORE
```

Problems

Problem 27-1: Create a database of assertions in which Laura is a parent of Robert, Robert is a parent of Patrick, and Patrick is a parent of Sarah. Next create a database of rules that capture the following ideas:

- If person x is a parent of person y, then x is an ancestor of y.
- If person x is a parent of person y, and person y is an ancestor of z, then x is an ancestor of z.

Problem 27-2: The assertions and rules in the previous problem enable our backward chainer to verify that Robert is an ancestor of Patrick:

```
* (backward-chain '(ancestor robert patrick))
YES
```

The reasoning step as follows:

- Rule FAMILY1 indicates that Robert is an ancestor of Patrick because Robert is a parent of Patrick.

In the same format, explain the reasoning that shows Laura is an ancestor of Sarah:

```
* (backward-chain '(ancestor laura sarah))
YES
```

Also, indicate whether either of the rules is used more than once in verifying that Laura is an ancestor of Sarah.

Our Backward Chainer Implements a Language like PROLOG

You have seen that our backward-chaining program unleashes matching and backward-chaining procedures. PROLOG is an entire programming language built around matching and backward chaining.

The differences between our program and PROLOG, in simple situations, are just a matter of syntax:

Our Program	PROLOG
`(remember-assertion '(bozo is a mammal))`	`mammal(bozo).`

`(remember-rule`
` '(identify1`
`    ((? animal) has hair)`
`    ((? animal) is a mammal)))`
	`mammal(Animal):-`
	`    hair(Animal).`

`(backward-chain '(deedee is a mammal))`	`?- mammal(deedee).`
`(backward-chain '((? x) is a mammal))`	`?- mammal(X).`

Note that in PROLOG, variables are indicated by initial uppercase characters, and PROLOG uses prefix notation. We have implemented `BACKWARD-CHAIN` such that the answers are reported just as many implementations of PROLOG report them.

Problems

Problem 27-3: PROLOG allows hypotheses with instances of the anonymous variable that match anything but do not accumulate values. Using the syntax of our backward-chaining program, here is an example, using our Bozo-Deedee database of assertions and rules:

```
* (backward-chain '((? _) is a mammal))
YES

* (backward-chain '((? _) is a (? _)))
YES
```

Because `MATCH` and `UNIFY` already handle the anonymous variable, only a small change need be made to our backward-chaining program in the `LIST-VARIABLES` procedure. Make it.

Problem 27-4: PROLOG actually does not list more than one set of variable values unless you ask it to by pressing an implementation-dependent character, usually a semicolon or comma. In the following example, using our animal recognition database of assertions and rules, a new set is printed each time the comma key is pressed:

```
* (backward-chain '((? x) is a (? y)))
-->     X = ROBBIE       Y = MAMMAL,
-->     X = SUZIE        Y = BIRD,
-->     X = ROBBIE       Y = CARNIVORE,
-->     X = ROBBIE       Y = CHEETAH,
-->     X = SUZIE        Y = ALBATROSS,
NO-MORE
```

Typing any other character causes the answer-printing process to abort:

```
* (backward-chain '((? x) is a (? y)))
-->     X = ROBBIE       Y = MAMMAL,
-->     X = SUZIE        Y = BIRD,
-->     X = ROBBIE       Y = CARNIVORE.
NO-MORE
```

Modify BACKWARD-CHAIN such that the comma convention is followed. You need, of course, a way of reading characters, one at a time, and a way of testing characters to see what they are. Use READ-CHAR to read characters, character by character:

```
* (read-char)
```

Use CHAR= to test two characters for equality. Recall that LISP's convention for specifying a particular object of the character data type, as introduced in chapter 9, is to preface the character with a # symbol, followed by a backslash.

Our Backward-Chaining Program Illustrates Abstraction

Like the forward-chaining problem solver introduced in chapter 26, the backward-chaining problem solver illustrates both data abstraction and procedure abstraction. Because the program uses assertion streams, all the detail of how data is represented is hidden behind a data-abstraction boundary. And because all the detail of pattern matching is hidden behind MATCH and UNIFY, there is a procedure-abstraction boundary as well. Thus the same abstraction boundaries that served forward chaining serve again with backward chaining, as shown figure 27-1.

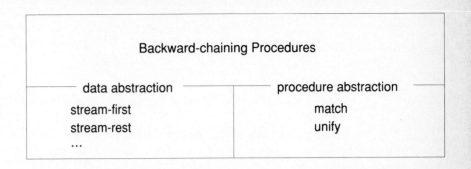

Figure 27-1. The backward-chaining problem solver illustrates both a data-abstraction boundary and a procedure-abstraction boundary. The stream and matching procedures are the same as those used in forward chaining except that MATCH has been joined by UNIFY.

Summary
- Our backward-chaining system borrows database access procedures from our forward-chaining system.
- Backward chaining means working from consequents to antecedents.
- Our first pass concentrates on MATCH, UNIFY, and the binding stream.
- Our second pass concentrates on the procedures that surround MATCH and UNIFY.
- Completing our backward-chaining program involves a few auxiliary procedures.
- Simple rules help identify animals.
- Our backward-chaining program implements a PROLOGlike language.
- Our backward-chaining program illustrates abstraction.

References

For a general introduction to rule-based expert systems, see chapter 6 of *Artificial Intelligence (Second Edition)* by Patrick H. Winston. For a general introduction to commercial applications of rule-based expert systems, see *The AI Business: The Commercial Uses of Artificial Intelligence*, edited by Patrick H. Winston and Karen A. Prendergast. See also *The Rise of the Expert Company*, by Edward A. Feigenbaum, Pamela McCorduck, and H. Penny Nii.

For an excellent treatment of PROLOG, see *PROLOG Programming for Artificial Intelligence*, by Ivan Bratko.

28

Interpreting
Transition Trees

The principal purpose of this chapter is to show how LISP can be used to implement other languages via an *interpreter*, a program that follows procedure descriptions incrementally, doing what the procedure descriptions specify. Specifically, we introduce an interpreter for transition trees, showing how to build a program that accepts questions and commands expressed in an ordinary natural language, such as English, and produces answers by way of appropriate interactions with a database.

A secondary purpose of this chapter is to introduce MULTIPLE-VALUE-BIND and VALUES. With these primitives, you can define and make use of procedures that return any number of values, not just one.

And of course, another secondary purpose of this chapter is to explain transition trees, which is the key idea used in building commercial-grade natural-language database interfaces.

Procedures Can Produce Multiple Values

Before we begin our discussion of natural language, we explain how to handle those occasions when you want a procedure to return more than one value. For example, suppose you are a highly paid consultant. You charge d dollars for each 8-hour day plus h dollars for each additional hour in a fraction of a day. To calculate your fees you divide total hours

worked by 8, producing both a quotient, q, and a remainder, r. Your fee
is $d \times q + h \times r$.

To get both the quotient and the remainder out of a division, you use
the primitive TRUNCATE, which returns two values:

```
* (truncate 20 8)
2                                             ;Quotient
4                                             ;Remainder
```

Because most procedures expect a form to return just one value, excess
values are usually thrown away. Thus TRUNCATE looks like it returns just
the quotient to higher-level forms:

```
* (print (truncate 20 8))                     ;Form containing TRUNCATE.
2                                             ;Printed by PRINT.
2                                             ;PRINT's value.
```

Fortunately, there is a way to capture excess values, however. You simply
bind variables to them using MULTIPLE-VALUE-BIND. Here is the template:

```
(multiple-value-bind
      <list of variables to be bound>
      <form returning multiple values>
  <body>)
```

Using MULTIPLE-VALUE-BIND, the variables are bound, one after the other,
to the values returned by the multiple-value form. Then the forms in the
body are evaluated, with the last of those forms producing the value for
the entire MULTIPLE-VALUE-BIND form. Here, for example, the FEE procedure
uses MULTIPLE-VALUE-BIND to bind two variables to the two values emerging
from TRUNCATE:

```
(defun fee (hours-worked daily-rate hourly-rate)
  (multiple-value-bind
        (quotient remainder)            ;Variables to be bound.
        (truncate hours-worked 8)       ;Values to be assigned.
    (+ (* daily-rate quotient)          ;Body.
       (* hourly-rate remainder)))))

* (fee 20 1000 200)
2800
```

Now that you know how to capture multiple values, you need to know how
to produce them with your own procedures, not just with those supplied
as primitives. You produce multiple values using VALUES, according to the
following template:

```
(values <first value to be returned>
        ...
        <last value to be returned>)
```

When VALUES appears with no arguments, the number of values returned is zero. Accordingly, if you do not want a procedure to print anything when it returns, for aesthetic reasons, you can use (VALUES) as the final form in that procedure.

Now suppose that you offer a discount if your customer pays your bill within 10 days. You can write a procedure, FEE-AND-DISCOUNT, that returns both your fee and the discount, rounded to the nearest dollar, using VALUES:

```
(defun fee-and-discount
       (hours-worked daily-rate hourly-rate discount-percent)
  (let* ((fee (fee hours-worked daily-rate hourly-rate))
         (discount (round (* fee (/ discount-percent 100)))))
    (values fee discount)))                    ;Two values returned.

* (fee-and-discount 20 1000 200 15)
2800                                           ;First value returned.
420                                            ;Second value returned.
```

When VALUES appears in the absence of MULTIPLE-VALUE-BIND, only the first of the multiple values is relayed to the calling procedure. In the following example, the FEE-AND-DISCOUNT form produces two values, but only the first of the two values is used:

```
* (* 1/2 (fee-and-discount 20 1000 200 15))
1400
```

In the presence of MULTIPLE-VALUE-BIND, multiple values are captured for further use within the body of the MULTIPLE-VALUE-BIND form. In the following example, both of the values of FEE-AND-DISCOUNT are used:

```
* (multiple-value-bind (fee discount)
      (fee-and-discount 20 1000 200 15)
    (- fee discount))
2380
```

Thus VALUES and MULTIPLE-VALUE-BIND normally work in tandem. VALUES produces multiple values and MULTIPLE-VALUE-BIND binds variables to those values. There are other ways to capture multiple values, but MULTIPLE-VALUE-BIND is both representative and adequate for our purpose in this chapter.

Natural-Language Interfaces Produce Database Commands

To do its job, a natural-language interface translates questions and commands expressed in a natural language, such as English, into the database commands required by a particular database, generally a database that lies outside LISP in a separate database system. Inasmuch as we discuss database systems later, you must be content, for the moment, with our assurance that certain database access forms somehow call upon a database system that knows about tools. One such form counts them and prints the result:

```
* (db-call '(db-count saws))
1
```

Another database access form prints properties:

```
* (db-call '(db-show saws))
| CLASS | COLOR | SIZE   | WEIGHT | PEG   |
| ----- | ----- | ------ | ------ | ----- |
| SAW   | BLACK | MEDIUM | HEAVY  | (2 6) |
```

DB-CALL, DB-COUNT, and DB-SHOW are described in more detail in chapter 30. Meanwhile, just note that databases are much easier to use if a natural language interface stands in front of them. Then the interaction can look like this:

```
> Count the saws.
1
> Describe the saws.
| CLASS | COLOR | SIZE   | WEIGHT | PEG   |
| ----- | ----- | ------ | ------ | ----- |
| SAW   | BLACK | MEDIUM | HEAVY  | (2 6) |
> ...
```

Now it is easy to specify what a natural language interface does:

- A natural language interface translates questions and commands expressed in a natural language into questions and commands expressed in a database language.

Transition Trees Capture English Syntax

A *grammar* is a set of patterns that describe legal sentences. A *semantic grammar* is a grammar whose patterns involve semantic categories, like *tool*, not just syntactic categories, like *noun*. The grammar we are about to explain is a *transition-tree semantic grammar*. Figure 28-1 exhibits three simple transition trees that express some of the regularities involved in simple questions and commands involving tools.

A *parser* is a program that analyzes sentences, determining how they are put together. To see how a parser can use transition trees, note that a transition tree consists of a tree of nodes linked by labeled arcs. To parse a sentence, a tree-based parser tries to traverse the tree along a path that is compatible with the words in the sentence. If the parser succeeds, the sentence is said to be *parsed*.

Imagine that we have implemented a tree-based parser, and consider the sentence, "Count the saws," together with the INTERFACE tree shown in figure 28-1. The first word in the sentence, *count*, is compatible with the first symbol of the first branch in the INTERFACE tree, allowing our tree-based parser to penetrate the INTERFACE tree along that first branch.

Now note that the next symbol in the INTERFACE tree, >objects, is prefixed by a greater-than symbol, meant to suggest a rightward-pointing arrow. This means that it is time for our tree-based parser to leave the INTERFACE tree temporarily, jumping into the corresponding OBJECTS tree.

In the OBJECTS tree, the first symbol, THE, is compatible with the sentence word *the*, leading to a four-way branch node. The next sentence word, *saws*, is compatible with the first and only symbol of the first branch.

Now our tree-based parser comes to a terminal node in the OBJECTS tree, thus succeeding in finding a path through the OBJECTS tree. On succeeding, the parser notes the RTN symbol inside the terminal node, which indicates that the parser is to return the value of a terminal form. In the OBJECTS tree, the terminal form is 'SAWS.

Because the sentence words enable the parser to traverse the OBJECTS tree, the parser returns to the INTERFACE tree and moves just past the >objects symbol. Usefully, the OBJECTS symbol is bound by the parser to the value of the terminal form encountered in the OBJECTS tree, SAWS.

The parser has now reached a terminal node in the INTERFACE tree. Because the terminal node is marked with an IF-END-RTN symbol, the parser succeeds only if there are no more words in the sentence under analysis. Inasmuch as all of the words in the sentence, "Count the saws," have been used up, the parser succeeds and returns the value of the terminal form, (DB-CALL '(DB-COUNT ,OBJECTS)). Because the symbol OBJECTS has been bound to SAWS, the backquote form evaluates to (DB-COUNT SAWS). Accordingly, it is reasonable to expect the call to the companion database to produce a count.

Now it is time to summarize what our imagined transition tree parser does:

- Legitimate sentences and sentence fragments are compatible with paths through trees. The transition tree parser attempts to traverse such a path.

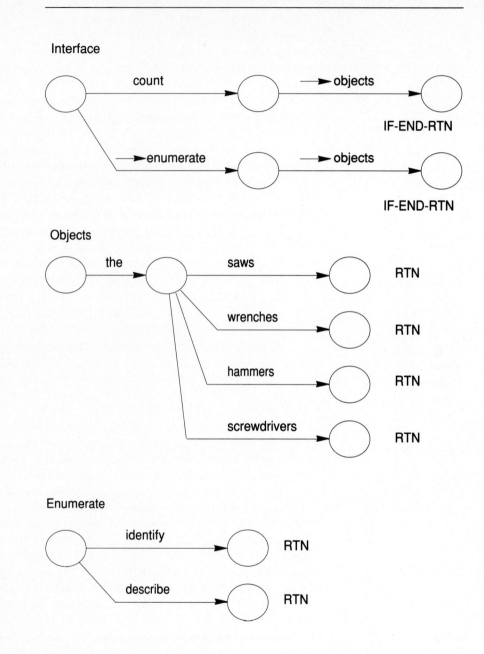

Figure 28-1. Three simple transition trees representing the structure of some simple commands.

- On reaching a branch node, the parser tries to traverse the branches, one at a time, until it traverses one completely or there are no more branches.

- On encountering an ordinary symbol in a tree, the parser moves on only if a sentence or sentence fragment has a word corresponding to that symbol.

- On encountering a symbol specially marked by a > prefix, the parser moves on only if it can traverse the tree corresponding to that specially-marked symbol.

- On reaching either an unmarked terminal node or a terminal node marked with an RTN symbol, the parser succeeds.

- On reaching a terminal node marked by an IF-END-RTN symbol, the parser succeeds only if there are no more words left in the sentence.

- On succeeding at a node marked by a RTN symbol or an IF-END-RTN symbol, the parser evaluates a terminal form, and the tree's name is bound to the terminal form's value. On succeeding at an unmarked node in a tree, the tree's name is bound to NIL.

A Transition Tree Interpreter Follows an Explicit Description

An *interpreter* is a program that follows procedure descriptions incrementally, doing what the procedure descriptions specify.

To implement an interpreter for our transition tree parser, we need a notation for describing transition trees in LISPlike form. Our notational choices are illustrated in the following expressions:

```
;;Description of INTERFACE transition tree:
(brnchs
  (count > objects if-end-rtn
                  (db-call `(db-count ,objects)))
  (> enumerate > objects if-end-rtn
                       (db-call `(db-show ,objects))))
```

```
;;Description of OBJECTS transition tree:
(the brnchs
     (saws          rtn 'saws)
     (wrenches      rtn 'wrenches)
     (hammers       rtn 'hammers)
     (screwdrivers  rtn 'screwdrivers))
```

```
;;Description of ENUMERATE transition tree:
(brnchs (identify)
        (describe))
```

Evidently, our notational choices are as follows:

- Transition trees are denoted by lists. If a transition tree has multiple branches, then the corresponding list will have embedded lists.
- Branch nodes are denoted by the symbol BRNCHS. Each branch is represented by a list.
- Each transition tree name, marked by a > in diagrams, is denoted by a > followed by the tree name.
- Each terminal node marked by an RTN in diagrams is denoted by RTN, followed by a terminal form.
- Each terminal node marked by an IF-END-RTN in diagrams is denoted by IF-END-RTN, followed by a terminal form.

Multiple-Valued Procedures Embody Transition Trees

To implement our transition tree parser, we create a procedure for each tree. Thus there are three procedures for our sample transition-tree system, one each for the INTERFACE, ENUMERATE, and OBJECTS trees. Each of these procedures takes a list of words and returns three values when successful. The first value is T if that procedure has found a path through the corresponding transition tree, or NIL otherwise; the second is the value of the terminal form, if any, or NIL otherwise; and the third is a list of the words that remain to be processed. Here are examples of the INTERFACE procedure in action:

```
* (interface '(count the saws))    ;The INTERFACE procedure in action.
1                                   ;Side effect of terminal form.
T                                   ;It succeeded.
NIL                                 ;Terminal form's value.
NIL                                 ;No more words to process.
* (interface '(this is nonsense))   ;The INTERFACE procedure in action.
NIL                                 ;It failed.
NIL
(THIS IS NONSENSE)
```

And here are two examples involving the OBJECTS and ENUMERATE trees:

```
* (enumerate '(describe the saws))  ;The ENUMERATE procedure in action.
T                                   ;It succeeded.
NIL                                 ;No terminal form.
(THE SAWS)                          ;Remaining words.
* (objects '(the saws))             ;The OBJECTS procedure in action.
T                                   ;It succeeded.
SAWS                                ;Terminal form's value.
NIL                                 ;No more words to process
```

Now to implement these transition tree procedures, we arrange for each to hand its argument to a universal transition tree interpreter named INTERPRET-TREE. Here are the definitions for our three transition tree procedures:

```
(defun interface (word-list)
  (interpret-tree
    '(brnchs
       (count > objects if-end-rtn
         (db-call `(db-count ,objects)))
       (> enumerate > objects if-end-rtn
         (db-call `(db-show ,objects))))
    word-list))

(defun objects (word-list)
  (interpret-tree
    '(the brnchs
         (saws rtn 'saws)
         (wrenches rtn 'wrenches)
         (hammers rtn 'hammers)
         (screwdrivers rtn 'screwdrivers))
    word-list))

(defun enumerate (word-list)
  (interpret-tree
    '(brnchs (identify)
            (describe))
    word-list))
```

Note that each tree definition looks like this:

```
(defun <name of tree> (word-list)
  (interpret-tree '<tree description> word-list))
```

Our Interpreter Uses Explicit Transition-Tree Descriptions

The INTERPRET-TREE procedure has three parameters, two mandatory and one optional. The first, TREE, is bound to a transition tree; the second, WORD-LIST, is bound to a list of words to be processed; and the third, A-LIST, is bound to an association list used for binding tree names to the values of terminal forms:

```
(defun interpret-tree (tree word-list &optional a-list)
  ...)
```

The body of INTERPRET-TREE is a giant COND form. The first clause, the one that handles the simplest case, looks for the end of a tree:

```
(defun interpret-tree (tree word-list &optional a-list)
  (cond ((endp tree) ...)
        ...))
```

Now that you have seen that a procedure can return multiple values, we can arrange for our interpreter, INTERPRET-TREE, to produce the three values required for each transition tree procedure. In the simple end-of-tree case, the three values are T, NIL, and the value of WORD-LIST:

```
(defun interpret-tree (tree word-list &optional a-list)
  (cond ((endp tree) (values t nil word-list))
        ...))
```

Of course, total failure is the other simple case:

```
(defun interpret-tree (tree word-list &optional a-list)
  (cond ...
        (t (values nil nil word-list))))
```

Now as we run through the other possibilities, note that INTERPRET-TREE is a recursive procedure that chews its way down trees and sentences, appropriately handling symbols, branches, trees, and terminal forms as they are encountered. For example, suppose that the first of the remaining words is the same as a symbol in the tree. INTERPRET-TREE skips both and calls itself on the remainder of the tree and the remainder of the word list:

```
(defun interpret-tree (tree word-list &optional a-list)
  (cond ...
        ((eq (first tree) (first word-list))
         (interpret-tree (rest tree) (rest word-list) a-list))
        ...))
```

The most convoluted clause takes care of subtrees, signaled by >s. Because all trees are embedded in procedure definitions, it is easy to get into the appropriate tree by applying the corresponding subprocedure to the list of remaining words. Then the values returned are captured by the MULTIPLE-VALUE-BIND form:

```
(defun interpret-tree (tree word-list &optional a-list)
  (cond ...
        ((eq '> (first tree))
         (multiple-value-bind
             (result binding word-list)
             (funcall (second tree) word-list)
           ...))
        ...))
```

If the work on the subtree succeeds, RESULT's value is T. As shown in the following fragment, INTERPRET-TREE then calls itself with carefully constructed arguments. The first argument, the tree argument, has the > symbol and the tree name trimmed off. The second argument, the word list argument, is bound to the list of words remaining after processing the tree. And the third argument, the association list argument, is augmented by an entry that binds the name of the tree to the value of the terminal expression found in the tree, or to NIL if there was no terminal expression.

```
(defun interpret-tree (tree word-list &optional a-list)
  (cond ...
        ((eq '> (first tree))
         (multiple-value-bind
             (result binding word-list)
             (funcall (second tree) word-list)
           (when result
             (interpret-tree (rest (rest tree))
                             word-list
                             (cons (list (second tree) binding)
                                   a-list)))))
        ...))
```

Note that a single NIL is returned if RESULT's value is NIL. You might think this could be a problem if the calling procedure is expecting INTERPRET-TREE to return multiple values. There is no error, however, because if there are too few values for the parameters in a MULTIPLE-VALUE-BIND form, the excess parameters are bound to NIL.

Of course, there may be a RTN or an IF-END-RTN at the end of the tree, indicating that there are forms to evaluate. The following COND clauses, together with an auxiliary procedure, recognize these cases and arrange for an auxiliary procedure to evaluate the terminal forms:

```
(defun interpret-tree (tree word-list &optional a-list)
  (cond ...
        ((eq 'rtn (first tree))
         (values t
                 (evaluate-forms (rest tree) a-list)
                 word-list))
        ((and (eq 'if-end-rtn (first tree))
              (endp word-list))
         (values t
                 (evaluate-forms (rest tree) a-list)
                 nil))
        ...))
```

The auxiliary procedure, EVALUATE-FORMS, needs to do a bit of work before it
can evaluate terminal forms because terminal forms may contain tree names
bound to values on the association list. The first branch in the INTERFACE
tree, for example, has the following single-element list of terminal forms,
which is handed to EVALUATE-FORMS:

```
((db-call `(db-count ,objects)))
```

Note that the comma indicates that the OBJECTS symbol is to be replaced
by the value of the OBJECTS symbol. Consequently, for the terminal form to
produce the right answer, the association list bindings must become symbol
values.

If the sentence is "Count the saws," then the association list, just
before terminal-form evaluation, is as follows:

```
((objects saws))
```

To evaluate the terminal forms properly, we can use a LET form based on
the association list and the terminal forms:

```
(let ((objects 'saws))                  ;From the association list.
  (db-call `(db-count ,objects)))  ;From the terminal forms.
```

We can produce the desired LET form and get it evaluated by using a backquote template together with EVAL:

```
(defun evaluate-forms (forms a-list)
  (eval `(let ,(make-let-variables a-list)
             ,@forms)))
```

Inside EVALUATE-FORMS, the auxiliary procedure, MAKE-LET-VARIABLES, constructs the list of variable-value pairs using another backquote template:

```
(defun make-let-variables (a-list)
  (mapcar #'(lambda (pair)
              `(,(first pair) ',(second pair))) a-list))
```

Here is an example of MAKE-LET-VARIABLES in action:

```
* (make-let-variables '((objects saws)))
((OBJECTS 'SAWS))
```

And here is an example of EVALUATE-FORMS in action:

```
* (evaluate-forms '((db-call `(db-count ,objects)))
                  '((objects saws)))
1              ;Printed as a side effect of DB-COUNT.
NIL            ;The value of EVALUATE-FORMS.
```

Note that the definition of EVALUATE-FORMS allows for multiple terminal
forms although only the value of the last one is returned. Thus EVALUATE-
FORMS resonates with LISP's general inclination to allow for additional side-
effect forms in such places as procedure bodies, COND clauses, and LET and
DO forms.

Another auxiliary procedure, INTERPRET-BRANCHES, introduced below,
handles branches, once the branch-signaling symbol, BRNCHS, is noted. Basi-
cally, INTERPRET-BRANCHES tries INTERPRET-TREE on the first branch, captures
the values returned using MULTIPLE-VALUE-BIND, and tests the first value to
see if INTERPRET-TREE succeeded on the first branch. If INTERPRET-TREE did
succeed, all the values are passed along; otherwise, INTERPRET-BRANCHES tries
the next branch:

```
(defun interpret-tree (tree word-list &optional a-list)
  (cond ...
        ((eq 'brnchs (first tree))
         (interpret-branches (rest tree) word-list a-list))
        ...))
(defun interpret-branches (branches word-list a-list)
  (if (endp branches)
      (values nil nil word-list)
      (multiple-value-bind (result binding words-left-over)
          (interpret-tree (first branches) word-list a-list)
        (if result
            (values result binding words-left-over)
            (interpret-branches (rest branches)
                                word-list
                                a-list)))))
```

You may wonder why INTERPRET-BRANCHES cannot be simpler, perhaps looking like the following:

```
(defun interpret-branches (branches word-list a-list)    ;Bugged!
  (if (endp branches)                                    ;Bugged!
      (values nil nil word-list)                         ;Bugged!
      (or (interpret-tree (first branches) ...)          ;Bugged!
          (interpret-branches (rest branches) ...))))    ;Bugged!
```

The reason is that AND and OR ignore multiple values, except for the last form.[1]   Similarly, COND ignores all but the first value returned by each clause's trigger. The only way to avoid recomputing the results produced by INTERPRET-TREE on a successful branch is to capture those results explicitly.

Now you have seen all the pieces of INTERPRET-TREE. Here they are assembled together:

```
(defun interpret-tree (tree word-list &optional a-list)
  (cond ((endp tree) (values t nil word-list))
        ((eq (first tree) (first word-list))
         (interpret-tree (rest tree) (rest word-list) a-list))
        ((eq '> (first tree))
         (multiple-value-bind
             (result binding word-list)
             (funcall (second tree) word-list)
           (when result
             (interpret-tree (rest (rest tree))
                             word-list
                             (cons (list (second tree) binding)
                                   a-list)))))
        ((eq 'rtn (first tree))
         (values t
                 (evaluate-forms (rest tree) a-list)
                 word-list))
        ((and (eq 'if-end-rtn (first tree))
              (endp word-list))
         (values t (evaluate-forms (rest tree) a-list) nil))
        ((eq 'brnchs (first tree))
         (interpret-branches (rest tree) word-list a-list))
        (t (values nil nil word-list))))
```

We Use a Macro To Simplify Tree Definition

So that it will be easier to define transition tree procedures, we now define DEFINE-TREE, a procedure that defines pattern-described procedures. With the backquote mechanism, defining DEFINE-TREE is mainly a matter of converting the general description of the desired DEFUN form into backquote form inside a macro procedure:

---

[1]Obscure reasons, having to do with the efficiency of compiled programs, force this peculiarity.

```
(defmacro define-tree (name-of-tree tree-description)
  `(defun ,name-of-tree (word-list)
     (interpret-tree ',tree-description word-list)))
```

Given DEFINE-TREE, we define our transition tree procedures this way:

```
(define-tree interface
  (brnchs
    (count > objects if-end-rtn
                    (db-call `(db-count ,objects)))
    (> enumerate > objects if-end-rtn
                      (db-call `(db-show ,objects)))))

(define-tree objects
  (the brnchs
      (saws        rtn 'saws)
      (wrenches    rtn 'wrenches)
      (hammers     rtn 'hammers)
      (screwdrivers rtn 'screwdrivers)))

(define-tree enumerate
  (brnchs (identify)
          (describe)))
```

A Read, Analyze, and Report Loop Adds a Finishing Touch

And finally, we define RUN-INTERFACE, a procedure that embeds the IN-TERFACE procedure in a read-analyze-report loop that prompts users for questions and commands with a > character:

```
* (run-interface)
> Count the saws.
1
> Describe the saws.
| CLASS | COLOR | SIZE   | WEIGHT | PEG   |
| ----- | ----- | ------ | ------ | ----- |
| SAW   | BLACK | MEDIUM | HEAVY  | (2 6) |
> ...
```

Before we define RUN-INTERFACE, however, we need to introduce STRING-TRIM, a primitive that trims away all the characters that appear in one string from both the front and back ends of another string:

```
* (string-trim ".!?" "Count the saws.")
"Count the saws"
```

```
* (string-trim ".!?" "Count the saws!")
"Count the saws"
```

With STRING-TRIM, we can define READ-SENTENCE, a procedure that reads a
line of characters and turns it into a list of words. READ-SENTENCE does its job
using WITH-INPUT-FROM-STRING, a LISP primitive that is like WITH-OPEN-FILE,
but uses a string as a text source instead of a file. WITH-INPUT-FROM-STRING
sets up a stream variable between the string and READ:

```
(defun read-sentence ()
  (with-input-from-string
      (input (string-trim ".?!" (read-line)))
    (do ((word (read input nil)
               (read input nil))
         (sentence nil))
        ((not word) (return (reverse sentence)))
      (push word sentence)))))
```

Here is an example of READ-SENTENCE in action:

```
* (read-sentence)Count the saws.
(COUNT THE SAWS)
```

Now we are ready for RUN-INTERFACE:

```
(defun run-interface ()
  (print '>)
  (do ((input (read-sentence) (read-sentence)))
      ((endp input)
       (format t "~&Ok, goodbye.")
       (values))
    (unless (interface input)
      (format t "~&Sorry, I can't understand that.~
              ~&Press the return key if you want to stop."))
    (print '>)))
```

Problems   **Problem 28-1:** Modify DEFINE-TREE so that if the variable *DEBUG* is
nonNIL, the name of each transition tree procedure is printed on entry and
return, along with the words, as suggested by the following examples:

```
* (interface '(count the saws))
INTERFACE entered with (COUNT THE SAWS).
OBJECTS entered with (THE SAWS).
OBJECTS succeeded consuming (THE SAWS).
1
INTERFACE succeeded consuming (COUNT THE SAWS).
T
NIL
NIL
* (interface '(this is nonsense))
INTERFACE entered with (THIS IS NONSENSE).
ENUMERATE entered with (THIS IS NONSENSE).
ENUMERATE failed leaving (THIS IS NONSENSE).
INTERFACE failed leaving (THIS IS NONSENSE).
NIL
```

Problem 28-2: Modify `INTERPRET-BRANCHES` so that if the variable `*DEBUG*` is nonNIL, each branch is printed on entry and on exit, along with a success or failure indication:

```
* (interface '(count the wrenches))
Starting on   (COUNT > OBJECTS ...).
Starting on   (SAWS RTN 'SAWS).
Failed on     (SAWS RTN 'SAWS).
Starting on   (WRENCHES RTN 'WRENCHES).
Succeeded on  (WRENCHES RTN 'WRENCHES).
2
Succeeded on  (COUNT > OBJECTS ...).
T
NIL
NIL
```

Problem 28-3: Suppose that you want to have transition trees that handle sentences of the form "...mother..." no matter how many words precede and follow the word *mother*. Add a feature to `INTERPRET-TREE` such that the asterisk in the following pattern means accept any number of words, including zero, such that the sentence fits, and assigns the two lists of accepted words to `WORDS` and `MORE-WORDS`:

```
(* words mother * more-words if-end-rtn ...)
```

You may want to try using a `DO` form that trims off words one at a time until `INTERPRET-TREE` succeeds on the remainder.

Problem 28-4: It is easy to write a simple version of a program that seems to interact with people at a terminal much like the way one type of psychiatrist interacts with people on the couch:

```
* (doctor)
(SPEAK UP)

> (I AM WORRIED ABOUT THE LISP QUIZ)
(HOW LONG HAVE YOU BEEN WORRIED ABOUT THE LISP QUIZ)

> (SINCE MY MOTHER CALLED LAST NIGHT)
(TELL ME MORE ABOUT YOUR FAMILY)

> (THEY ALL HATE COMPUTERS EXCEPT FOR ME)
(DO MACHINES FRIGHTEN YOU)

> (YES)
(PLEASE DO NOT BE SO SHORT WITH ME)

> (YOU ARE FRUSTRATING ME)
(EARLIER YOU SPOKE OF YOUR MOTHER)

> (DARN)
(PLEASE DO NOT USE LANGUAGE LIKE THAT)

> (STOP IT)
(I DID NOT UNDERSTAND THAT)
(TYPE NIL IF YOU WANT TO STOP)

> NIL
(OK -- OUR TIME IS UP ANYWAY)
```

To implement the doctor-imitating program, we begin with DOCTOR, the procedure that couples you to the Doctor transition tree:

```
(defun doctor ()
  (defvar mother nil)                 ;MOTHER used in the transition tree.
  (let ((mother nil))
    (print '(speak up))
    (print '>)
    (do ((input (read) (read)))
        ((endp input)
         (print '(ok -- our time is up anyway))
         (values))
      (multiple-value-bind (result value)
                           (doctor-tree input)
        (if value
            (print value)
            (progn
              (print '(i did not understand that))
              (print '(type nil if you want to stop)))))
      (print '>))))
```

Your job is to implement DOCTOR-TREE, a transition tree procedure, based on the sample dialog, that recognizes sentences and returns appropriate responses. Here is a fragment you can start with:

```
(define-tree doctor-tree
  (brnchs (i am worried about * words if-end-rtn
           `(how long have you been worried about ,@words))
          ...))
```

Your procedure will be similar in spirit to the key procedure in DOCTOR, also known as ELIZA, a classic program that seemed to understand sentences.

Note that your DOCTOR procedure will have no real understanding of the user. It builds no model of the problems it seems to discuss, but depends instead on superficial keyword observations.

Problem 28-5: It is easy to write a simple version of STUDENT, a program that converts algebra word problems into LISP expressions. Here is an example of what the STUDENT program is to do:

```
* (student '(the revenue is 3 times the square of the costs))
(= (THE REVENUE) (* 3 (EXPT (THE COSTS) 2)))
```

To implement the student-imitating program, we begin with STUDENT, the procedure that couples you to STUDENT-TREE:

```
(defun student (words)
  (multiple-value-bind
      (result value)
      (student-tree words)
    value))
```

Your job is to implement STUDENT-TREE, a transition tree procedure, based on the example, that recognizes algebra constructions expressed in English and returns equations. Here is a fragment you can start with:

```
(define-tree student-tree
  (brnchs (* words is * more-words if-end-rtn
           `(= ,(student words) ,(student more-words)))
          (the sum of * words and * more-words if-end-rtn
           `(+ ,(student words) ,(student more-words)))
          ...
          (* words if-end-rtn
           (if (numberp (first words))
               (first words)
               words)))))
```

Your procedure will be similar in spirit to the key procedure in STUDENT, a classic program that solved high-school algebra problems.

Note that your STUDENT procedure will have no real understanding of mathematics. Like the DOCTOR program, it is limited to superficial manipulations based on keywords.

Summary
- Procedures can produce multiple values.
- Natural-language interfaces produce database commands.
- Transition trees capture English syntax.
- A transition tree interpreter follows an explicit description.
- Multiple-valued procedures embody transition trees.
- Our interpreter uses explicit transition-tree descriptions.
- We use a macro to simplify tree definition.
- A read-analyze-report loop adds a finishing touch

References

For a general introduction to natural language understanding, see chapter 9 of *Artificial Intelligence (Second Edition)* by Patrick H. Winston. For a general introduction to commercial natural language systems, see *The AI Business: The Commercial Uses of Artificial Intelligence*, edited by Patrick H. Winston and Karen A. Prendergast.

For early work on transition trees, see Bobrow and Fraser [1969], Winograd [1972], Woods [1972], and Kaplan [1972]. Our treatment is based partly on the work of Hendrix *et al.* and partly on the work of Harris [1977].

29

Compiling
Transition Trees

The principal purpose of this chapter is to take a second look at language interfaces by implementing a *compiler* for transition trees. Take note that we will be talking about compiling in a general sense meaning translating from one language into another, directly useful one. This is different from the more restricted sense that implies that the translation is into some computer's basic instruction set.

Transition Trees Can Be Compiled from Transparent Specifications

In principle, you can translate perspicuous transition tree descriptions into LISP procedures that LISP can use directly, without an interpreter standing in between. For example, the following definition would serve, in principle, for the ENUMERATE procedure:

```
(defun enumerate (word-list)
  (when (member (first word-list) '(identify describe))
    (values t nil (rest word-list))))
```

Unfortunately, the translation can be much more difficult for more complicated transition trees. However, a program can do the job for us. In general, a *compiler* is a program that translates procedure descriptions from one language into another. A transition tree compiler translates transition tree procedure descriptions into LISP.

Once we develop a compiler, definitions for our simple transition tree grammar can be written as follows:

```
(compile-tree interface
  (brnchs
    (count > objects if-end-rtn
                  (db-call `(db-count ,objects)))
    (> enumerate > objects if-end-rtn
                    (db-call `(db-show ,objects)))))

(compile-tree objects
  (the brnchs
      (saws        rtn 'saws)
      (wrenches    rtn 'wrenches)
      (hammers     rtn 'hammers)
      (screwdrivers rtn 'screwdrivers)))

(compile-tree enumerate
  (brnchs (identify)
        (describe)))
```

Compilers Treat Programs as Data

Now the problem is to create a tree-to-LISP compiler. Fortunately, the job involves nothing more than the symbol-manipulating flair so characteristic of LISP.

Much of the work of COMPILE-TREE is to be done by COMPILE-ELEMENTS, a procedure that walks down the defining tree, converting each element of the tree into a suitable form. Here, for example, is the form that COMPILE-ELEMENTS is to produce when it gets to the leaf of a tree:

```
* (compile-elements '())
(VALUES T NIL WORD-LIST)
```

It is easy to get compile-elements to do the right thing in this simple case:

```
(defun compile-elements (tree)
  (cond ((endp tree) '(values t nil word-list))
        ...))
```

In the rest of COMPILE-ELEMENTS, we make heavy use of the backquote mechanism to fill in templates with the proper expressions. For example, if there is a symbol at the beginning of a transition tree, the following result is what we want:

```
* (compile-elements '(<word> ...))
(LET ((CURRENT-WORD (FIRST WORD-LIST))
      (WORD-LIST (REST WORD-LIST)))
  (WHEN (EQ CURRENT-WORD '<WORD>)
    <result of using COMPILE-ELEMENTS on ...>))
```

The following is the appropriate backquote template, which happens to be
in the final clause of the COND in COMPILE-ELEMENTS:

```
(defun compile-elements (tree)
  (cond ...
        (t `(let ((current-word (first word-list))
                  (word-list (rest word-list)))
              (when (eq current-word ',(first tree))
                ,(compile-elements (rest tree)))))))
```

Here is what we want for terminal forms:

```
* (compile-elements '(rtn <terminal expressions>))
(VALUES T (PROGN <terminal expressions>) WORD-LIST)
* (compile-elements '(if-end-rtn <terminal expressions>))
(WHEN (ENDP WORD-LIST)
      (VALUES T (PROGN <terminal expressions>) NIL))
```

And here are the backquote forms:

```
(defun compile-elements (tree)
  (cond ...
        ((eq 'rtn (first tree))
         `(values t (progn ,@(rest tree)) word-list))
        ((eq 'if-end-rtn (first tree))
         `(when (endp word-list)
            (values t (progn ,@(rest tree)) nil)))
        ...))
```

Now look at the way we handle calls to subtree transition trees. First, the
subtree procedure is applied to WORD-LIST's value, producing three values
captured by MULTIPLE-VALUE-BIND. If the value bound to RESULT is T, then
work proceeds on the rest of the tree.

```
* (compile-elements '(> <subtree name> ...))
(MULTIPLE-VALUE-BIND
  (RESULT <subtree name> WORD-LIST)
  (<subtree name> WORD-LIST)
  (WHEN RESULT
    <result of using COMPILE-ELEMENTS on ...>))
```

Again, we obtain the desired result with the following backquote form:

```
(defun compile-elements (tree)
  (cond ...
        ((eq '> (first tree))
         `(multiple-value-bind (result ,(second tree) word-list)
              (,(second tree) word-list)
            (when result
              ,(compile-elements (rest (rest tree))))))
        ...))
```

Branches are considerably more complicated. Here is what we want if there
are two:

```
* (compile-elements '(brnchs <branch1> <branch2>))
(MULTIPLE-VALUE-BIND
    (RESULT BINDING WORDS-LEFT-OVER)
    <result of using COMPILE-ELEMENTS on branch1>
  (IF RESULT
      (VALUES RESULT BINDING WORDS-LEFT-OVER)
      (MULTIPLE-VALUE-BIND
          (RESULT BINDING WORDS-LEFT-OVER)
          <result of using COMPILE-ELEMENTS on branch2>
        (IF RESULT
            (VALUES RESULT BINDING WORDS-LEFT-OVER)
            NIL))))
```

To handle branches, COMPILE-ELEMENTS uses an auxiliary procedure:

```
(defun compile-elements (tree)
  (cond ...
        ((eq 'brnchs (first tree))
         (compile-branches (rest tree)))
        ...))

(defun compile-branches (forms)
  (unless (endp forms)
    `(multiple-value-bind (result binding words-left-over)
         ,(compile-elements (first forms))
       (if result
           (values result binding words-left-over)
           ,(compile-branches (rest forms))))))
```

Putting together all the parts of COMPILE-ELEMENTS, we have the following:

```
(defun compile-elements (tree)
  (cond ((endp tree) '(values t nil word-list))
        ((eq '> (first tree))
         `(multiple-value-bind (result ,(second tree) word-list)
              (,(second tree) word-list)
            (when result
                ,(compile-elements (rest (rest tree))))))
        ((eq 'brnchs (first tree))
         (compile-branches (rest tree)))
        ((eq 'rtn (first tree))
         `(values t (progn ,@(rest tree)) word-list))
        ((eq 'if-end-rtn (first tree))
         `(when (null word-list)
            (values t (progn ,@(rest tree)) nil)))
        (t `(let ((current-word (first word-list))
                  (word-list (rest word-list)))
              (when (eq current-word ',(first tree))
                ,(compile-elements (rest tree)))))))
```

Now to actually create tree procedures, we want definitions of the following form:

```
(defun <name of tree> (word-list)
  (compile-elements '<tree description>))
```

To produce such procedures, we bottle up the appropriate DEFUN form in a backquote template inside a macro procedure:

```
(defmacro compile-tree (name tree)
  `(defun ,name (word-list)
     ,(compile-elements tree)))
```

The simplest transition tree in our grammar is ENUMERATE. To compile it, we use COMPILE-TREE:

```
(compile-tree enumerate
  (brnchs (identify)
          (describe)))
```

COMPILE-TREE then produces the following definition for the ENUMERATE tree. Note that this definition is much more complicated than the one we produced by hand earlier in this chapter:

```
(defun enumerate (word-list)
  (multiple-value-bind
    (result binding words-left-over)
    (let ((current-word (first word-list))          ;First branch starts.
          (word-list (rest word-list)))
      (when (eq current-word 'identify)
        (values t nil word-list)))
    (if result                                      ;First branch succeed?
        (values result binding words-left-over)     ;If so succeed.
        (multiple-value-bind                         ;If not, try harder.
          (result binding words-left-over)
          (let ((current-word (first word-list))    ;Second branch starts.
                (word-list (rest word-list)))
            (when (eq current-word 'describe)
              (values t nil word-list)))
          (if result                                ;Second succeed?
              (values result binding words-left-over) ;Succeed.
              nil)))))                                ;Give up.
```

In general, compilers tend to produce longer procedures than people do because compiler authors often sacrifice brevity in the simple cases for uniformity in all cases.

For more difficult situations, the difference is not one of simplicity, however, but rather one of correctness. When things get complicated, human programmers make mistakes, whereas the compiler plods ahead with its unlimited capacity to tolerate tedium.

Compiled Programs Run Faster

Compilers translate programs from a *source language* to a *target language*. When the compiled program runs, neither the source-language version nor the compiler is around to help figure things out. Once compiled, a program is on its own. For example, in the compiled transition trees, the tree specifications are present only implicitly in the LISP procedures.

Interpreters follow source-language procedures one step at a time. The source-language procedures are always there to refer to. For example, in working with interpreted transition trees, tree specifications are always explicit, retaining their original form.

Generally, interpreters are easier to write. Generally, compiled programs run faster. On sample problems, our compiled transition tree procedures run three times faster than our interpreted transition tree procedures.

Compilers Are Usually Major Undertakings

In the transition tree example, LISP is both the compiler's implementation language and the compilation's target language. Creating the compiler was straightforward because compiling is a symbol-manipulating task for which LISP is eminently suited. Often compilers translate from source languages into languages lying close to the basic instruction set of some computer to achieve high running speed. Developing such compilers is much harder, especially if the compiler itself must be written in a low-level, computer-specific assembler language, because maximum efficiency is an absolute requirement.

LISP Itself Is Either Compiled or Interpreted

First we used a LISP program to interpret transition tree descriptions. Then we used another LISP program to compile transition tree descriptions into LISP programs.

Of course LISP programs themselves are descriptions of procedures, and as such, they can be interpreted by a program written using the basic machine instructions of a computer or they can be compiled into programs written in those basic instructions.

This makes for the curious set of possibilities shown in figure 29-1. The translation of LISP into basic instructions is a symbol-manipulation job. Hence it is nicely accomplished by a program written in LISP. Said another way, LISP is a good language for writing a LISP compiler. But then the LISP compiler itself is a LISP program that can be compiled. Once compiled, the compiler can compile itself. Indeed the first program a new LISP compiler usually compiles is itself, relying on an interpreter or a previous compiler to get the self-compilation done.

As you would expect, compiled LISP programs run much faster than interpreted LISP programs. Increases in speed by factors of ten to twenty are typical.

Problems

Problem 29-1: Add a feature to COMPILE-ELEMENTS such that the asterisk in the following pattern means accept any number of words, including zero, such that the sentence fits, and assigns the two lists of accepted words to the symbols WORDS and MORE-WORDS:

```
(* words mother * more-words if-end-rtn ...)
```

You may want to have COMPILE-ELEMENTS create a DO form in which words are trimmed off one at a time until the remaining words successfully match the remainder of the pattern.

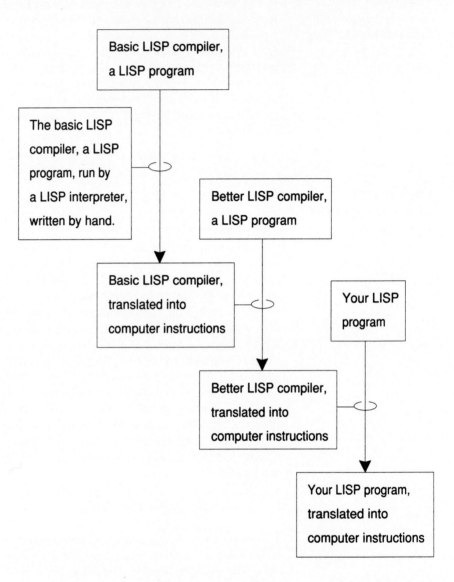

Figure 29-1. Each new version of the LISP compiler is compiled by the previous version. At the very beginning, the original compiler is compiled using an interpreter. User programs are either run by the current version of the interpreter or compiled by the last compiler in the chain. One compiler is better than another if it runs faster or if it produces faster or smaller programs or if it handles more of the language it is compiling.

Summary

- Transition trees can be compiled from transparent specifications.
- Compilers treat programs as data.
- Compiled programs run faster.
- Compilers are usually major undertakings.
- LISP itself is either compiled or interpreted.

30

Procedure-Writing Programs and Database Interfaces

The principal purpose of this chapter is to show that a problem-solving program also may write its own programs and evaluate them in the normal course of problem solving. The particular program developed here deals again with the tool world, now answering more sophisticated questions.

The answers are produced by creating programs for a simulated *relational database* that we pretend exists already. Consequently, our development illustrates some of the ideas involved when building an English interface for database access.

Grammars Can Be Sophisticated

The transition tree grammar introduced in chapter 28, covering just a few lines, is too simple to illustrate more than the rudiments of the transition tree approach to building language interfaces. In this chapter, we introduce a slightly more sophisticated transition tree grammar, covering just a few pages, to make our examples more lifelike. Note that this grammar is still minute when compared with commercial-grade grammars.

Here are some sample sentences of the sort our more sophisticated transition tree grammar handles for some tools hanging on a pegboard:

```
> Count the long screwdrivers.
(interface '(Count the long screwdrivers))
3
> Show me the length of the blue screwdriver.
(interface '(Show me the size of the blue screwdriver))
| SIZE |
| ---- |
| LONG |
> Print the size and weight of the red screwdrivers.
(interface '(Print the size and weight of the red screwdrivers))
| SIZE  | WEIGHT |
| ----- | ------ |
| LONG  | HEAVY  |
| SHORT | LIGHT  |
> Describe the red screwdrivers.
(interface '(describe the red screwdrivers))
| CLASS       | COLOR | SIZE  | WEIGHT | PEG   |
| ----------- | ----- | ----- | ------ | ----- |
| SCREWDRIVER | RED   | LONG  | HEAVY  | (6 2) |
| SCREWDRIVER | RED   | SHORT | LIGHT  | (7 2) |
```

To deal with these questions, our more sophisticated transition tree grammar has transition trees that you have not yet seen and more complicated versions of the ones you have.

Answering Requests Is Done in Three Steps

The shape of the request-answering system is illustrated by figure 30-1. Note the following:

- The first step in answering a request is to analyze the question, expressed in a natural language, using a transition tree.
- Next a construction procedure manufactures a procedure for an external database.
- Then the procedure is evaluated, producing the desired result.

Most Database Commands Transform Relations into Relations

A *relation* is a named set of *records*. Each record, in turn, is like a LISP structure in that it contains *fields*, which are analogous to structure slots.

A *relational database* is a database built around the relation concept. A typical relational database provides a small number of commands for displaying and manipulating databases. We now explain a few of those commands, all of which we preface with a DB- prefix to make it clear that they are database commands, not LISP procedures. DB-SHOW, for example, produces a printed report in which each line corresponds to a record and

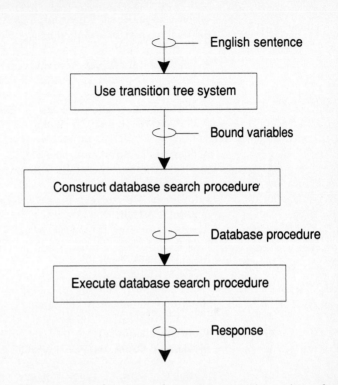

Figure 30-1. The structure of a system that answers questions using a database. Note that a program writes a procedure and then executes that procedure.

each column corresponds to a field. Assuming we have somehow created a database of screwdrivers, here is what DB-SHOW might do when asked to display it:

```
* (db-show screwdrivers)
| CLASS       | COLOR | SIZE  | WEIGHT | PEG   |
| ----------- | ----- | ----- | ------ | ----- |
| SCREWDRIVER | BLUE  | LONG  | LIGHT  | (4 2) |
| SCREWDRIVER | BLACK | LONG  | LIGHT  | (5 2) |
| SCREWDRIVER | RED   | LONG  | HEAVY  | (6 2) |
| SCREWDRIVER | RED   | SHORT | LIGHT  | (7 2) |
```

Sometimes, you only care about the number of items in a database, not their descriptions, making DB-COUNT a useful command:

```
* (db-count screwdrivers)
4
```

Unlike DB-SHOW and DB-COUNT, most database commands transform one relation into another. For example, DB-SELECT picks out those records whose field values satisfy specified constraints:

```
* (db-show (db-select screwdrivers with color eql red))
| CLASS       | COLOR | SIZE  | WEIGHT | PEG   |
| ----------- | ----- | ----- | ------ | ----- |
| SCREWDRIVER | RED   | LONG  | HEAVY  | (6 2) |
| SCREWDRIVER | RED   | SHORT | LIGHT  | (7 2) |
```

A companion command, DB-PROJECT, picks out particular fields, dropping the rest, and by convention, eliminating any duplicates:

```
* (db-show (db-project screwdrivers over size weight))
| SIZE  | WEIGHT |
| ----- | ------ |
| LONG  | LIGHT  |
| LONG  | HEAVY  |
| SHORT | LIGHT  |
```

DB-UNION combines two relations:

```
* (db-show hammers)
| CLASS  | COLOR | SIZE  | WEIGHT | PEG   |
| ------ | ----- | ----- | ------ | ----- |
| HAMMER | BLUE  | LARGE | HEAVY  | (4 6) |

* (db-show wrenches)
| CLASS  | COLOR | SIZE  | WEIGHT | PEG   |
| ------ | ----- | ----- | ------ | ----- |
| WRENCH | GRAY  | SMALL | LIGHT  | (6 6) |
| WRENCH | GRAY  | LARGE | HEAVY  | (8 6) |

* (db-show (db-union hammers wrenches))
| CLASS  | COLOR | SIZE  | WEIGHT | PEG   |
| ------ | ----- | ----- | ------ | ----- |
| HAMMER | BLUE  | LARGE | HEAVY  | (4 6) |
| WRENCH | GRAY  | SMALL | LIGHT  | (6 6) |
| WRENCH | GRAY  | LARGE | HEAVY  | (8 6) |
```

English Questions Correspond to Database Commands

To answer questions using a relational database, you simply compose the basic commands appropriately. For example, to answer the question "Print the size and weight of the red screwdrivers," you start by selecting the red screwdrivers from the screwdriver database:

```
(db-select screwdrivers with color eql red)
```

Next, you eliminate all of the fields except for size and weight:

```
(db-project (db-select screwdrivers with color eql red)
            over size weight)
```

And finally, to get a nice report, you hand the result to the report-printing command:

```
(db-show (db-project (db-select screwdrivers
                                with color eql red)
                     over size weight))
```

Unfortunately, composing commands can be tedious, particularly when the questions are convoluted. Fortunately, composing commands can be done by a LISP procedure in response to requests expressed in natural language.

**Our Simulated
Database Supports
an Improved
Grammar**

Now that you know more about how database commands work, we can build a much stronger interface grammar than the one that was introduced in chapter 28. In this stronger interface grammar, all the interaction between LISP and the database takes place in the generalized INTERFACE tree:

```
(compile-tree interface
  (brnchs
    (count > objects if-end-rtn
       (db-call `(db-count ,objects)))
    (how many > objects are there if-end-rtn
       (db-call `(db-count ,objects)))
    (> enumerate > objects if-end-rtn
       (db-call `(db-show ,objects)))
    (> present the > attributes of > objects if-end-rtn
       (db-call
         `(db-show
            (db-project ,objects over ,@attributes)))))))
```

Evidently, database commands are composed using a backquote template inside INTERFACE. We pretend that those database commands are sent to an external database by handing them to DB-CALL, a procedure that directs the database commands to our database simulating LISP procedures.

For example, with the appropriate values for OBJECTS and ATTRIBUTES, the backquote template produces the correct database commands for answering the question "Print the size and weight of the red screwdrivers," as shown:

```
* (setf objects '(db-select screwdrivers with color eql red)
        attributes '(size weight))

* `(db-show (db-project ,objects over ,@attributes))
(DB-SHOW
  (DB-PROJECT (DB-SELECT SCREWDRIVERS WITH COLOR EQL RED)
              OVER SIZE WEIGHT))
```

Now it is time to see how appropriate values for OBJECTS and ATTRIBUTES can be produced by appropriate transition tree procedures. We begin with the transition tree for ATTRIBUTES, along with a transition tree for ATTRIBUTE:

```
(compile-tree attributes
  (brnchs (> attribute > attributes rtn (cons attribute
                                              attributes))
          (and > attribute       rtn (list attribute))
          (> attribute           rtn (list attribute))))

(compile-tree attribute
  (brnchs (class      rtn 'class)
          (color      rtn 'color)
          (size       rtn 'size)
          (weight     rtn 'weight)
          (position   rtn 'peg)
          (location   rtn 'peg)))
```

The ATTRIBUTE tree is straightforward; it simply looks for attributes and returns a field name, which is usually the same as the attribute name. The ATTRIBUTES tree, on the other hand, is a bit more complicated, because it has to be able to handle one or more attributes, possibly with an *and* stuck between the final two if there are two or more. In our sample, all three branches are required to handle the list (SIZE AND WEIGHT). The first call to ATTRIBUTES hands (AND WEIGHT) to the second call, which in turn hands (WEIGHT) to the third call.

A similar pair of transition trees handles attribute values, which we need in preparation for understanding OBJECTS. These two transition trees produce triples for the DB-SELECT command, rather than single symbols, but otherwise they are quite like the ATTRIBUTES-ATTRIBUTE combination:

```
(compile-tree attribute-values
  (brnchs (> attribute-value > attribute-values
           rtn (append attribute-value attribute-values))
          (and > attribute-value rtn attribute-value)
          (> attribute-value rtn attribute-value)))
```

```
(compile-tree attribute-value
  (brnchs (large      rtn '(size eql large))
          (medium     rtn '(size eql medium))
          (small      rtn '(size eql small))
          (long       rtn '(size eql long))
          (short      rtn '(size eql short))
          (black      rtn '(color eql black))
          (blue       rtn '(color eql blue))
          (red        rtn '(color eql red))
          (yellow     rtn '(color eql yellow))
          (gray       rtn '(color eql gray))
          (heavy      rtn '(weight eql heavy))
          (light      rtn '(weight eql light))))
```

On to objects. Unlike the simple OBJECTS tree introduced in chapter 28,
the OBJECTS tree in this chapter can deal with attributes, such as *red*, as in
"the red screwdrivers," with help from the DETERMINER and OBJECT trees:

```
(compile-tree objects
  (brnchs (> determiner > objects rtn objects)
          (> attribute-values > object
             rtn `(db-select ,object with ,@attribute-values))
          (> object rtn object)))

(compile-tree determiner
  (brnchs (a) (the)))

(compile-tree object
  (brnchs (saw        rtn 'saws)
          (saws       rtn 'saws)
          (hammer     rtn 'hammers)
          (hammers    rtn 'hammers)
          (wrench     rtn 'wrenches)
          (wrenches   rtn 'wrenches)
          (screwdriver rtn 'screwdrivers)
          (screwdrivers rtn 'screwdrivers)))
```

Note that a backquote template in OBJECTS composes the DB-SELECT command from the values of OBJECT and ATTRIBUTE-VALUES:

```
* (setf object 'screwdrivers
        attribute-values '(color eql red))
* `(db-select ,object with ,@attribute-values)
(DB-SELECT SCREWDRIVERS WITH COLOR EQL RED)
```

Finally, a few other small transition trees are involved:

```
(compile-tree enumerate
  (brnchs (identify)
          (describe)))
```

```
(compile-tree present
  (brnchs (show me)
          (what is)
          (what are)
          (give)
          (display)
          (print)
          (present)))
(compile-tree object1 (> objects rtn objects))
(compile-tree object2 (> objects rtn objects))
```

Problems

Problem 30-1: Define MULTIPLE-OBJECTS, a transition tree procedure that can handle object descriptions as in "the red screwdrivers and the gray wrenches." Note that the database command DB-UNION must appear in your solution.

The Relational Database Can Be Faked

While we have pretended that DB-SHOW, DB-COUNT, DB-SELECT, and DB-PROJECT are commands for a relational database separate from LISP, it is easy enough to create a simple relational database inside LISP that provides a simulated underpinning for our natural language interface.

But first, some decisions have to be made about representation. Our approach is to represent each relation as a list of field names followed by lists of field values. Here, for example, is a relation assigned to SCREWDRIVERS:

```
* screwdrivers
((CLASS          COLOR   SIZE    WEIGHT  PEG)
 (SCREWDRIVER    BLUE    LONG    LIGHT   (4 2))
 (SCREWDRIVER    BLACK   LONG    LIGHT   (5 2))
 (SCREWDRIVER    RED     LONG    HEAVY   (6 2))
 (SCREWDRIVER    RED     SHORT   LIGHT   (7 2)))
```

With this representation, we can implement procedures to simulate all the basic database commands used in our illustrations. Of these commands, DB-COUNT and DB-UNION are the simplest. DB-COUNT simply prints the result produced by LENGTH, returning no values:

```
(defun db-count (relation)
  (format t "~&~a" (length (rest relation)))
  (values))
```

And DB-UNION appends records, removing any duplicates found with REMOVE-DUPLICATES, a primitive that eliminates redundant list elements:

```
(defun db-union (&rest records)
  (cons (first (first records))
        (remove-duplicates (apply #'append
                                  (mapcar #'rest records))
                  :test #'equal)))
```

Some of the other commands are more difficult to implement. Consider DB-PROJECT, for example. In real database systems, command arguments are not quoted. Accordingly, DB-PROJECT is defined as a macro so that its arguments need not be quoted:

```
(defmacro db-project (relation &optional over &rest projections)
  `(cons ',projections
         (db-project-aux (first ,relation) (rest ,relation)
                         ',projections)))
```

Evidently, DB-PROJECT arranges for DB-PROJECT-AUX to receive symbols whose values are a list of field names, a list of records, and a quoted list of field names to project the relation over. DB-PROJECT-AUX creates new records by extracting all the specified field-value pairs from each of the old records. Note that it uses POSITION, a LISP primitive that returns the position of an element in a list, counting the first element as the 0th:

```
(defun db-project-aux (fields records projections)
  (remove-duplicates
    (mapcar
      #'(lambda (record)
          (mapcar
            #'(lambda (projection)
                (nth (position projection fields) record))
            projections))
      records)
    :test #'equal))
```

Note that we implement DB-PROJECT-AUX with a MAPCAR that works its way down the list of fields supplied, rather than with a REMOVE-IF-NOT that works its way down the record chucking out everything that does not belong. Our choice is dictated by our desire to arrange the fields in the new records in the order specified in DB-PROJECT.

DB-SELECT works like DB-PROJECT inasmuch as both hand off the real work to auxiliaries:

```
(defmacro db-select (relation &optional over &rest triples)
  `(cons (first ,relation)
         (db-select-aux (first ,relation)
                        (rest ,relation)
                        ',triples)))
```

The auxiliary procedure, DB-SELECT-AUX, filters the records by checking the specified fields to be sure that their values satisfy the specified constraints:

```
(defun db-select-aux (fields records triples)
  (if (endp triples)
      records
      (remove-if-not
        #'(lambda (record)
            (funcall (second triples)
                     (nth (position (first triples) fields)
                          record)
                     (third triples)))
        (db-select-aux fields records (nthcdr 3 triples)))))
```

Of course, with all of these database commands simulated in LISP, the definition of DB-CALL becomes completely simple:

```
(defun db-call (arg) (eval arg))
```

Problems

Problem 30-2: To make it easier to create relations, define a macro, MAKE-RELATION, such that MAKE-RELATION has the following behavior:

```
* (make-relation screwdrivers
    (class            color    size      weight    peg)
    (screwdriver      blue     long      light     (4 2))
    (screwdriver      black    long      light     (5 2))
    (screwdriver      red      long      heavy     (6 2))
    (screwdriver      red      short     light     (7 2)))

* screwdrivers
((class color size weight peg)
 (screwdriver blue long light (4 2))
 (screwdriver black long light (5 2))
 (screwdriver red long heavy (6 2))
 (screwdriver red short light (7 2)))
```

Problem 30-3: Define `DB-SHOW`. Because you want to size the columns to fit the widest symbols in them, your answer probably will not be pretty. Also, you probably will want to use several features of LISP that we have not yet introduced. One feature you need is a version of the `A` directive, used in `FORMAT` forms, in which the letter *v* stands between the tilde and the letter *a*. This directive is useful when one argument determines the number of columns to another argument, as in the following example:

```
* (format t "~%| ~va |"
         10                         ;Number of columns to be used.
         'saw)                      ;Thing to be printed.
| SAW        |                      ;Result.
NIL
```

Another feature you need is the `MAKE-STRING` primitive. It makes a string of a given length filled with a character announced by an `:INITIAL-ELEMENT` keyword:

```
* (make-string 5 :initial-element #\-)
"-----"
```

Finally, you need to know that `FORMAT` forms used with `NIL` rather than `T` do not print. Instead, they return the character string that would have been printed if `T` had been used. Such `FORMAT` forms are particularly useful for converting symbol names into character strings:

```
* (format nil "~a" 'screwdrivers)
"SCREWDRIVERS"
```

Problem 30-4: Suppose we add a branch to the `INTERFACE` tree such that it can recognize questions of the form "How far is the red screwdriver from the saw:"
(interface '(how far is the red screwdriver from the saw))

```
(compile-tree interface
  (brnchs
    ...
    (how far is > object1 from > object2 if-end-rtn ...)))
```

To answer such questions, we need a procedure that can compute distances:

```
(defun report-distance (a b)
  (format t "~&~a"
          (sqrt (+ (expt (- (first a) (first b)) 2)
                   (expt (- (second a) (second b)) 2)))))
```

Given `REPORT-DISTANCE`, the required distance is reported given the following terminal form together with an appropriate definition for `DB-EXTRACT-VALUE`:

```
(report-distance (db-call `(db-extract-value ,object1 over peg))
                 (db-call `(db-extract-value ,object2 over peg)))
```

Define DB-EXTRACT-VALUE. Use DB-PROJECT-AUX as an auxiliary procedure. Make DB-EXTRACT-VALUE complain if the projected relation produces more than one record or more than one field.

Problem 30-5: Relational databases always have a join command, which is useful when you must stitch multiple databases together to answer a question. Write DB-JOIN such that it combines the records in two relations by appending the fields of one to the fields of another, but only when a specified predicate holds between specified field values, as illustrated by the following:

```
* (db-show suppliers)
| SUPPLIER   | TOOL-SOLD   |
| ---------- | ----------- |
| BRAXTON    | SAW         |
| BRAXTON    | HAMMER      |
| HICKS      | HAMMER      |
| HICKS      | WRENCH      |
| SCREWLOOSE | SCREWDRIVER |
* (db-show customers)
| CUSTOMER | TOOL-NEEDED |
| -------- | ----------- |
| SMITH    | HAMMER      |
| WESSON   | HAMMER      |
| WESSON   | SCREWDRIVER |
* (db-show (db-join suppliers customers
                with tool-sold eql tool-needed))
| SUPPLIER   | TOOL-SOLD   | CUSTOMER | TOOL-NEEDED |
| ---------- | ----------- | -------- | ----------- |
| BRAXTON    | HAMMER      | SMITH    | HAMMER      |
| BRAXTON    | HAMMER      | WESSON   | HAMMER      |
| HICKS      | HAMMER      | SMITH    | HAMMER      |
| HICKS      | HAMMER      | WESSON   | HAMMER      |
| SCREWLOOSE | SCREWDRIVER | WESSON   | SCREWDRIVER |
```

Problem 30-6: What question is answered by the following database expression:

```
* (db-show
   (db-project
    (db-join suppliers customers
            with tool-sold eql tool-needed)
    over supplier))
```

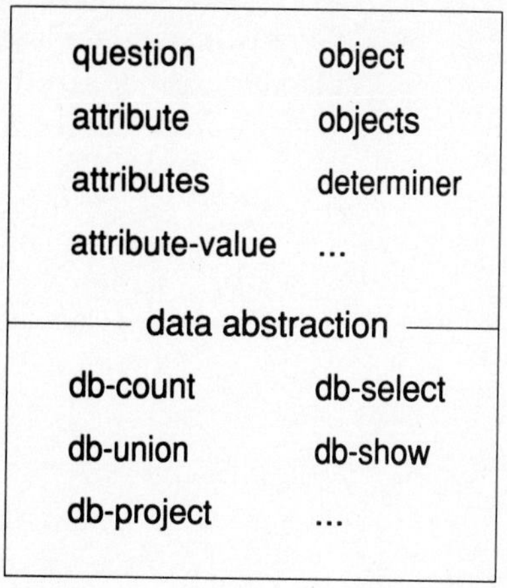

question	object
attribute	objects
attributes	determiner
attribute-value	...
── data abstraction ──	
db-count	db-select
db-union	db-show
db-project	...

Figure 30-2. The transition tree interpreter and the database simulator meet at a data-abstraction boundary.

Problem 30-7: What question is answered by the following database expression:

```
* (db-show
    (db-project
      (db-join
        suppliers
        (db-select
          (db-union saws hammers wrenches screwdrivers)
          with class member (hammer wrench))
        over tool-sold eql class)
      over supplier))
```

The Database Illustrates Data Abstraction

The interaction between the transition tree interpreter and the simulated database is a good example of data abstraction because all the detail of how data is represented is hidden behind a clearly marked data-abstraction boundary as suggested in figure 30-2.

Summary

- Grammars can be sophisticated.
- Answering requests is done in three steps.
- Most database commands transform relations into relations.

- English questions correspond to database commands.
- Our simulated database supports an improved grammar.
- The relational database can be faked.
- The database illustrates data abstraction.

31

Finding Patterns
in Images

The primary purpose of this chapter is to illustrate some methods for matching spatial patterns using a variety of features of LISP that we have introduced. A secondary purpose is to explore some of the issues faced when designing a program. These include tradeoffs between conciseness, efficiency, readability, and ease of program modification. We will also have an opportunity to see how some simple numerical procedures can be implemented.

The examples are drawn from pattern matching in two dimensions. Specifically, the procedures find the position and orientation of a known pattern, as well as recognizing such patterns from a library of model patterns. Initially, we deal with patterns of isolated points, such as stars in a constellation. We then extend these methods to lines, as in an image of an industrial part in front of a robot camera.[1]

Generating All Possible Matches Helps Isolate the Correct Match

Suppose that we are looking at a portion of the night sky and we would like to determine which part of the sky we are looking at. This can be accomplished by recognizing some familiar pattern of stars, such as one

[1] We do not treat *pattern classification* here, a subject that, strictly speaking, involves mapping multidimensional feature vectors into integers.

Figure 31-1. To find out which portion of the sky we are looking at, we match bright spots in the image with stars in stored models of constellations.

of the constellations. Figure 31-1, for example, shows the pattern of the brightest stars in the constellation Orion and also an image of a portion of the sky containing various bright spots. There are two tasks:

- Matching some of the bright spots in the image of the sky with stars in the model of one of the constellation.
- Determining the transformation between the coordinates of the image and the coordinates of the model.

These two tasks are closely interrelated: it is hard to do one without the other—or, said another way, if we have solved either one of the two problems, the other is easier to deal with.

To simplify the algebra, we will pretend that the sky is flat, so that the positions of stars can be described using two Cartesian coordinates. Similarly, we will use Cartesian coordinates to describe the positions of bright spots in a planar image.

The methods developed here also have less prosaic applications: We can think of the "spots" as feature points in an image of something other than the sky. These feature points are places in the image that are especially easy to identify, such as the corners of polygonal regions of constant brightness. The images might be of a flat industrial part on a conveyor belt, for example, taken with a camera that is oriented with its optical axis perpendicular to the belt.

We represent each model constellation by a list of stars and the image by a list of bright spots. could equally well have used one-dimensional arrays, because it is just as easy to step through the elements of a simple array using `DOTIMES` as it is to step through the elements of a simple list using `DOLIST`. Arrays are convenient when we have to be able to get at items in random order, because it takes the same amount of time to get to each of the elements. Array access, however, is typically a little more costly than going through a list if it is just a matter of stepping through sequentially. Other tradeoffs between these two alternate representations are explored a little later in this chapter.

To make a clear distinction between the two things to be matched, different names are used for corresponding entities, namely stars and spots. We also use different variable names for coordinates, and define two different structures to represent stars in the model and bright spots in the image. In addition, we arrange for stars to have names while spots are numbered. Each star and each spot could have been represented using a list containing the name or number, as well as the coordinates, but it is better to use a structure, because we may need to alter the representation later to include more information:

```
(defstruct star (name) (x) (y))          ;Structure for star.


(defstruct spot (number) (u) (v))        ;Structure for spot.
```

Here u and v are coordinates in an image, while x and y are coordinates in some global coordinate system in which all of the constellation models are described. In our flat sky model, the transformation from one to the other involves a rotation and a translation:

$$x = c\,u - s\,v + x_0,$$
$$y = s\,u + c\,v + y_0,$$

where $c = \cos\theta$ and $s = \sin\theta$, while θ is the angle between corresponding axes in the two coordinate systems. Further, x_0 and y_0 are the offsets of the origin of the image coordinate system in the model coordinate system. This transformation is illustrated in figure 31-2. Part of our matching task is the recovery of the transformation parameters c, s, x_0 and y_0.

We start by developing a matching procedure that does not pay attention to any constraints on possible matches between stars and spots:

```
(defun find-match (stars spots)          ;Find spots to match stars.
  (find-match-sub nil stars spots))      ;Start—no matched pairs.
```

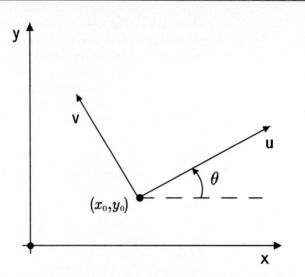

Figure 31-2. The transformation from image coordinates, u and v, to global coordinates, x and y, used in the stored model, consists of a rotation through an angle θ and a translation x_0 in the x direction and a translation y_0 in the y direction.

```
(defun find-match-sub (pairs stars spots)          ;First version.
  (if (endp stars)                                 ;More stars to match?
      (print-pairs (reverse pairs))                ;Just print the result.
      (let ((star (first stars)))                  ;First star in list.
        (dolist (spot spots)                       ;Try each spot in turn.
          (find-match-sub (cons (list star spot)   ;Add new pair,
                                pairs)             ; to exiting pairs.
                          (rest stars)             ;Remaining stars.
                          (remove spot spots))))))) ;Remaining spots.
```

Here PAIRS is a list of two-element lists, each of which contains a star and the corresponding bright spot. At a particular point in the matching process, PAIRS contains the state of the match so far, while STARS contains the stars not yet matched and SPOTS contains the spots not yet used in the match. Note that there is an asymmetry between the way we treat stars and spots: we must find a match for every star, while some spots may remain unmatched. This is reasonable, because the image of a portion of the sky is likely to contain bright spots corresponding to stars other than those belonging to a particular constellation. Also, some spots sensed might correspond to stars that were too dim to be included in the model constellation. We deal later with the more general situation were we also allow some stars to remain unmatched.

Each time we incorporate a star in the match, it is removed from the front of the list of remaining stars. Similarly, each time a spot is incorporated in a match, it is removed from the list of remaining spots. We have to use the primitive REMOVE, in this case, however, because the spot to be removed need not be at the front of the list of spots. This takes considerable computational effort, because part of the list has to be copied, namely the part up to where the element occurs that is to be removed. Note that we cannot use the surgical primitive DELETE here, because the list without the deletion has to be available for use after the recursive call to FIND-MATCH-SUB.

We could have avoided the use of REMOVE by passing along the original, complete list of bright spots and checking each time whether a spot has already been used in a partial match, that is, whether it occurs in one of the pairs in the list PAIRS. This, of course, is expensive too, because we now have to search through the elements of PAIRS before we can use a particular spot in the match.

In this situation, using an array instead of a list to represent the set of spots would have certain advantages. The reason is that we can easily mark the spots that have already been used in a partial match by a flag in a second, parallel array. We would have to be careful, however, to reset the flag when we return from the recursive call to FIND-MATCH-SUB!

We could achieve the same effect by adding a flag to the structure representing a spot. The flag is set before the recursive call and reset after. It is a little odd though to include something in the data structure that has nothing to do with the entity represented, instead being merely a convenient way of keeping track of the state of a computation. As you have seen before, there are typically a large number of different ways of implementing a particular algorithm. Sometimes improvements in computational efficiency have to be weighed against reduced readability and flexibility in future modifications. Here we stick with the simple representation for both stars and spots as lists, because the procedure is easier to read that way, and also easier to modify.

When a complete match has been found, the result is to be printed out:

```
(defun print-pairs (pairs)                    ;First version.
  (format t "~%")
  (dolist (pair pairs)                         ;Step through elements of list.
    (let ((star (first pair)) (spot (second pair)))
      (format t "(star ~a = spot ~a) "         ;Print out one pair.
              (star-name star) (spot-number spot)))))
```

Note that FIND-MATCH-SUB, as it stands, will print out all possible ways of matching stars with spots, without any constraint on the matches. So if there are n stars and m spots (with $m \geq n$), we will generate

$$\frac{m!}{(m-n)!}$$

matches. These are all the ways of picking spots to pair up with stars. When $m = n$, the above procedure provides us with a convenient way of generating all permutations of n elements. Here is a test case that illustrates this:

```
* (find-match
    (list (make-star :name "alpha" :x 0.0 :y 1.0)
          (make-star :name "beta" :x 0.0 :y 0.0)
          (make-star :name "gamma" :x 1.5 :y 1.0))
    (list (make-spot :number 1 :u 0.03 :v 1.50)
          (make-spot :number 2 :u 1.00 :v 1.52)
          (make-spot :number 3 :u 0.51 :v 0.02)))
(star alpha = spot 1) (star beta = spot 2) (star gamma = spot 3)
(star alpha = spot 1) (star beta = spot 3) (star gamma = spot 2)
(star alpha = spot 2) (star beta = spot 1) (star gamma = spot 3)
(star alpha = spot 2) (star beta = spot 3) (star gamma = spot 1)
(star alpha = spot 3) (star beta = spot 1) (star gamma = spot 2)
(star alpha = spot 3) (star beta = spot 2) (star gamma = spot 1)
```

Constraints Are Needed To Isolate the Correct Match

We clearly need some mechanism for discriminating between different ways of matching stars with spots. Now stars have different *magnitudes*.[2] Correspondingly, spots in the image will have different brightnesses. Once again we use different names for related quantities in order to minimize the opportunity for confusion when thinking about what is matched with what. We can modify the structures for stars and spots to include this additional information:

```
(defstruct star (name) (x) (y) (magnitude))
(defstruct spot (number) (u) (v) (brightness))
```

Note that we do not have to rewrite any of the code for accessing the coordinates when we add this new information. This is one of the advantages gained by using structures.

Measurements of brightness cannot be made with perfect accuracy, so we have to allow for the possibility of a small difference when we test whether a spot could match a star:

---

[2]The magnitude of a star is measured on a logarithmic scale, where a difference of five magnitudes corresponds to a ratio of 100 in brightness.

```
(defun similar-magnitude (star spot)        ;Similar magnitude?
  (let ((star-m (star-magnitude star))      ;Get star's magnitude.
        (spot-m (spot-brightness spot)))    ;Get spot's brightness.
    (< (abs (- star-m spot-m)) 1.0)))       ;Within tolerance?
```

Here we have assumed that estimates of the stars magnitude based on the measured brightness are never more than one magnitude in error. In practice it would probably be more convenient to use a global special variable for the tolerance rather than burying it in this procedure.

Now we can incorporate a check in FIND-MATCH-SUB so that we pursue only partial matches composed of pairs of spots and stars whose brightnesses match within the specified tolerance:

```
(defun find-match-sub (pairs stars spots)     ;Second version
  (if (endp stars)                            ;More stars to match?
      (print-pairs (reverse pairs))           ;Just print the result.
      (let ((star (first stars)))             ;First star in list.
        (dolist (spot spots)                  ;Try each spot in turn.
          (when (similar-magnitude star spot) ;Similar in brightness?
            (find-match-sub (cons (list star spot)  ;Add new pair,
                                  pairs)            ; to existing pairs.
                            (rest stars)            ;Remaining stars,
                            (remove spot spots)))))))    ; & spots.
```

We can also modify PRINT-PAIRS to print more information:

```
(defun print-pairs (pairs)                    ;Second version.
  (format t "~%")
  (dolist (pair pairs)                         ;Step through elements of list.
    (let ((star (first pair)) (spot (second pair)))
      (format t "~%(star ~a (~5,2F) = spot ~a (~5,2F))"
              (star-name star) (star-magnitude star)
              (spot-number spot) (spot-brightness spot)))))
```

Note that the test we added to FIND-MATCH-SUB can dramatically decrease the number of matches explored, provided that the error in brightness measurements is small enough. Whole branches of the search tree are pruned away when a spot proposed as a possible match to a particular star has a significantly different brightness from the star. In fact, if we could measure brightness with unlimited accuracy, our job would be done, because a star's magnitude would then be a unique identifying characteristic. We could then ignore the geometric information, as we have done so far. In practice, however, measurements of brightness have limited accuracy and the procedure may find several potential matches that each pass the brightness comparison tests.

The Search Tree Can Be Pruned Using Geometric Information

Let us look at ways of pruning the search tree further using information about the spatial relationship between the stars in a constellation. So far we have used only a unary test, one that applies to a single star and a single spot—now let us consider a binary test. The distance between stars is not changed by rotation or translation in the image plane. So distance is independent of the coordinate transformation we are searching for, and thus comparison of distances between stars and corresponding spots gives us a convenient additional filtering test for proposed partial matches. Note that this binary test is more expensive than the unary brightness test, because we have to compare the distances between the proposed new star and all of the stars already included in the partial match with the corresponding distances between the proposed new spot and all of the spots already included in the partial match. If these distances can be measured with high accuracy, however, then this test will remove almost all erroneous partial matches.

We start by defining procedures for computing distances between stars and distances between spots:

```
(defun distance-stars (a b)                    ;Distance between stars.
  (distance (star-x a) (star-y a) (star-x b) (star-y b)))

(defun distance-spots (a b)                    ;Distance between spots.
  (distance (spot-u a) (spot-v a) (spot-u b) (spot-v b)))

(defun distance (xs ys xf yf)                  ;Euclidean distance.
  (let ((dx (- xf xs)) (dy (- yf ys)))
    (sqrt (+ (* dx dx) (* dy dy)))))
```

Next we compare the distances between a pair of stars to the distance between the corresponding pair of bright spots in the image:

```
(defun similar-distances (pair-a pair-b)          ;Distances similar?
  (let* ((star-a (first pair-a)) (spot-a (second pair-a))
         (star-b (first pair-b)) (spot-b (second pair-b))
         (dstars (distance-stars star-a star-b))  ;Between stars.
         (dspots (distance-spots spot-a spot-b))) ;Between spots.
    (< (abs (- dstars dspots)) 0.1)))             ;Within tolerance?
```

Here we have arbitrarily assumed that the accuracy with which we can measure positions in the image allows us to determine distances between spots to an accuracy of 0.1 units. Again, in practice it would be more convenient to use a global special variable for this tolerance rather than burying it in the procedure.

Next we need a procedure that performs the distance check on all of the distances between the new pair and pairs in the existing partial match:

```
(defun distances-check (new pairs)                ;Check out new pair,
  (dolist (pair pairs t)                          ; against other pairs.
    (unless (similar-distances new pair) (return nil))))
```

The DOLIST here returns T when it terminates normally after testing every pair in the list PAIRS. If a particular pair does not pass the SIMILAR-DISTANCES test, however, the loop is terminated prematurely by the (RETURN NIL) form.

We should note at this stage that in the search for the correct match, the distance between a particular pair of spots is likely to be recomputed many times. It thus makes sense to compute all of the pairwise distances once, ahead of time, and to save them, perhaps in a two-dimensional array. The same goes for the pairwise distances between stars in the model. We do not do this here in order to simplify the exposition.

Now we are ready to incorporate DISTANCES-CHECK in FIND-MATCH-SUB:

```
(defun find-match-sub (pairs stars spots)         ;Third version.
  (if (endp stars)                                ;More stars to match?
      (print-pairs (reverse pairs))               ;Just print the result.
      (let ((star (first stars)))                 ;First star in list.
        (dolist (spot spots)                      ;Try each spot in turn.
          (when (similar-magnitude star spot)     ;Similar in brightness?
            (let ((new (list star spot)))         ;New pair to check out.
              (when (distances-check new pairs)    ;Compatible?
                (find-match-sub (cons new pairs)   ;New pair.
                                (rest stars)
                                (remove spot spots)))))))))
```

Here is a test case for FIND-MATCH with an extra spot that remains unmatched:

```
* (find-match
    (list (make-star :name "alpha" :x 0.0 :y 1.0 :magnitude 0.0)
          (make-star :name "beta" :x 0.0 :y 0.0 :magnitude 0.5)
          (make-star :name "gamma" :x 1.5 :y 1.0 :magnitude 1.0))
    (list (make-spot :number 1 :u 0.03 :v 1.50 :brightness 0.7)
          (make-spot :number 2 :u 1.00 :v 1.52 :brightness 0.2)
          (make-spot :number 3 :u 0.51 :v 0.02 :brightness 1.9)
          (make-spot :number 4 :u 1.00 :v 0.01 :brightness 1.3)))
(star alpha ( 0.00) = spot 2 ( 0.20))
(star beta ( 0.50) = spot 1 ( 0.70))
(star gamma ( 1.00) = spot 4 ( 1.30))
NIL
```

Only one match is found that satisfies the constraints on the brightnesses of the spots and on the distances between spots.

Matches Have to be Checked for Global Consistency

If the accuracy of image position measurement is high, this procedure will typically find the correct match, and only the correct match, unless the constellation has an unusual symmetric spatial pattern. If on the other hand, the accuracy is limited, there may be several different matches between stars and spots that pass the pairwise distance test. Also, some of the matches that pass the pairwise distance test may not make sense globally. Consider, for example, a match between a constellation and some spots arranged in a pattern that is the mirror-image of the constellation. There is in general no rotation and translation that will bring the constellation and the set of spots into alignment, yet all of the pairwise distances will match. This means that we should perform a check on the whole pattern when we reach a leaf of the search tree. The check involves estimating a transformation from the image to the model and then verifying that this transformation maps all of the spots to positions near to the stars that they have been matched with.

At this point we need to decide how to represent the transformation. We could just use a list of the rotation angle and the two offsets, but for ease of future modification we instead define a simple structure:

```
(defstruct transform (c) (s) (xo) (yo))
```

Note that we chose here to represent the rotation by the cosine and the sine of the rotation angle rather than by the angle itself. There are a number of advantages to this redundant scheme, one of which is that we do not have to evaluate any trigonometric or inverse trigonometric functions. Next, we may want a simple procedure for printing out a transformation:

```
(defun print-transform (trans)
  (let ((c (transform-c trans)) (s (transform-s trans))
        (xo (transform-xo trans)) (yo (transform-yo trans)))
    (format t "~%c = ~a s = ~a xo = ~a yo = ~a" c s xo yo)))
```

We will also need a procedure for transforming from image coordinates to the model coordinates:

```
(defun map-uv-to-xy (u v trans)                ;From image to model.
  (let ((c (transform-c trans)) (s (transform-s trans))
        (xo (transform-xo trans)) (yo (transform-yo trans)))
    (values (+ (- (* c u) (* s v)) xo)
            (+ (+ (* s u) (* c v)) yo))))
```

Note the use of VALUES to return the two coordinates.

We next discuss the algebra for recovering the coordinate transformation. Readers less interested in the mathematical details may wish to skip the next page or so, where the procedure FIND-TRANSFORM is developed.

Our task is to find the parameters of the transformation, namely c, s, x_0, and y_0. The transformation is fully determined by two corresponding pairs. The translation is just the difference between the centroid of the two stars and the rotated centroid of the two corresponding bright spots in the image. The rotation itself can be found by considering the vector connecting the two stars and the vector connecting the two spots. The dot-product of these two vectors is proportional to the cosine of the angle between them, while the magnitude of the cross-product is proportional to the sine of the angle between them. To be precise, if $(x_a, y_a)^T$ and $(x_b, y_b)^T$ are the coordinates of the two stars, while $(u_a, v_a)^T$ and $(u_b, v_b)^T$ are the coordinates of the corresponding spots, then

$$k\,c = (\delta u, \delta v, 0)^T \cdot (\delta x, \delta y, 0)^T,$$

while

$$k\,s = (\delta u, \delta v, 0)^T \times (\delta x, \delta y, 0)^T \cdot (0, 0, 1)^T$$

for some constant k, where $\delta x = (x_b - x_a)$, $\delta y = (y_b - y_a)$, $\delta u = (u_b - u_a)$, and $\delta v = (v_b - v_a)$.

We are now ready to write a simple version of the procedure FIND-TRANSFORM:

```
(defun find-transform (pairs)               ;Get transformation.
  (if (< (length pairs) 2)                   ;Need two pairs.
      (error "Too few pairs for transformation")
      (find-transform-sub (first pairs) (second pairs))))


(defun find-transform-sub (pair-a pair-b)              ;Minimal version.
  (let* ((star-a (first pair-a)) (spot-a (second pair-a))
         (star-b (first pair-b)) (spot-b (second pair-b))
         (xa (star-x star-a)) (ya (star-y star-a))
         (xb (star-x star-b)) (yb (star-y star-b))
         (ua (spot-u spot-a)) (va (spot-v spot-a))
         (ub (spot-u spot-b)) (vb (spot-v spot-b)))
    (find-transform-aux xa ya xb yb ua va ub vb)))


(defun find-transform-aux (xa ya xb yb ua va ub vb)
  (let ((dx (- xb xa)) (dy (- yb ya))              ;Vector (dx, dy).
        (du (- ub ua)) (dv (- vb va))              ;Vector (du, dv).
        (xm (/ (+ xb xa) 2)) (ym (/ (+ yb ya) 2))  ;Centroid x & y.
        (um (/ (+ ub ua) 2)) (vm (/ (+ vb va) 2))) ;Centroid u & v.
    (multiple-value-bind (c s) (dot-and-cross dx dy du dv)
      (let ((xo (- xm (- (* c um) (* s vm))))
            (yo (- ym (+ (* s um) (* c vm)))))
        (make-transform :c c :s s :xo xo :yo yo)))))
```

```
(defun dot-and-cross (dx dy du dv)
  (let ((kc (+ (* dx du) (* dy dv)))            ;Dot-product.
        (ks (- (* dy du) (* dx dv))))           ;Cross-product.
    (normalize-c-s kc ks)))

(defun normalize-c-s (kc ks)                    ;Normalize two values
  (if (and (zerop kc) (zerop ks))               ; that are proportional
      (error "K C = 0 and K S = 0")
      (let ((k (sqrt (+ (* kc kc) (* ks ks)))))
        (values (/ kc k) (/ ks k)))))           ; to cosine and sine.
```

In writing NORMALIZE-C-S we made use of the fact that the sum of squares
of the sine and cosine of an angle should be equal to one.

Once we have an estimate of the transformation, we can use it to check
the proposed match:

```
(defun check-matched-pairs (pairs trans)        ;Do pairs really match?
  (dolist (pair pairs t)
    (let* ((star (first pair)) (spot (second pair))
           (x (star-x star)) (y (star-y star))
           (u (spot-u spot)) (v (spot-v spot)))
      (multiple-value-bind (xs ys) (map-uv-to-xy u v trans)
        (unless (point-match x y xs ys) (return nil))))))

(defun point-match (x y xs ys)                  ;Similar coordinates?
  (and (< (abs (- xs x)) 0.1) (< (abs (- ys y)) 0.1)))
```

The DOLIST here returns T if all of the pairs pass the test. The loop is
terminated prematurely by (RETURN NIL) if any one of them fails. Note that
we have, once again, arbitrarily assumed that the accuracy of measurement
allows us to determine positions to within 0.1 units.

Using just the first two pairs in the list of matched pairs, by the way,
is not the best approach when the data are known to be corrupted by
measurement noise.

Now it is time to integrate FIND-TRANSFORM and CHECK-MATCHED-PAIRS
into FIND-MATCH-SUB. While we are at it, let us also change the procedure
so that it returns the list of pairs and the transformation, rather than just
printing it. At this stage, a potential match has to satisfy constraints on
brightness and pairwise distances, as well as passing the final verification
of the transformation, so it is very unlikely that anything but the correct
match will be found. This means that we can just return the first match
that passes all of the tests, rather than considering all possible matches,
thus saving some computational effort.

The following version of FIND-MATCH-SUB returns the matched pairs and
the transform if a satisfactory match is found. If for some reason a match
is not satisfactory, NIL is returned and the search continues.

```
(defun find-match-sub (pairs stars spots)        ;Fourth version.
  (if (endp stars)                               ;More stars to match?
      (find-match-check (reverse pairs))         ;No, check the match.
      (let ((star (first stars)))                ;First star in list.
        (dolist (spot spots)                     ;Try each spot in turn.
          (when (similar-magnitude star spot)    ;Similar brightness?
            (let ((new (list star spot)))        ;New pair to check out.
              (when (distances-check new pairs)     ;Compatible?
                (let ((ans (find-match-sub (cons new pairs)
                                           (rest stars)
                                           (remove spot spots))))
                  (when ans (return ans)))))))))) ;Drop out.
(defun find-match-check (pairs)                  ;Obtain transformation,
  (let ((trans (find-transform pairs)))          ; and check it.
    (when (check-matched-pairs pairs trans) ;Return NIL if no go,
      (list pairs trans))))                   ; else pairs & transform.
```

To make the results easier to understand, it is convenient to print the pairs in an abbreviated form. Accordingly, we write PRINT-PAIRS and combine it with PRINT-TRANSFORM in PRINT-FIND-MATCH:

```
(defun print-pairs (pairs)                       ;Third version.
  (format t "~%")
  (dolist (pair pairs)
    (let ((star (first pair)) (spot (second pair)))
      (format t "(~a = ~a) " (star-name star) (spot-number spot)))))
(defun print-find-match (stars spots)            ;Find match
  (let ((result (find-match stars spots)))        ; and print it.
    (when result
      (let ((pairs (first result)) (trans (second result)))
        (print-pairs pairs)
        (print-transform trans)))))
```

Here is a test case:

```
* (print-find-match
    (list (make-star :name "alpha" :x 0.0 :y 1.0 :magnitude 0.0)
          (make-star :name "beta" :x 0.0 :y 0.0 :magnitude 0.5)
          (make-star :name "gamma" :x 1.5 :y 1.0 :magnitude 1.0))
    (list (make-spot :number 1 :u 0.03 :v 1.50 :brightness 0.7)
          (make-spot :number 2 :u 1.00 :v 1.52 :brightness 0.2)
          (make-spot :number 3 :u 0.51 :v 0.02 :brightness 1.9)
          (make-spot :number 4 :u 1.00 :v 0.01 :brightness 1.3)))
(alpha = 2) (beta = 1) (gamma = 4)
c = 0.0206141 s = 0.999788 xo = 1.499063 yo = -0.046018
NIL
```

We have permitted bright spots to go unmatched, because the image may
contain bright spots corresponding to stars belonging to more than one
constellation. Also, some stars may not have been included in the description of the constellation because they are too dim, or because they are close
to earth and thus appear to move a significant amount as time passes. We
have insisted so far, however, that all stars in the given constellation must
find a match. We should relax this condition also, because some of the
stars in the constellation may lie outside the field of view of the imaging
device, may be obscured by clouds, or may be too dim for the particular
sensor we are using.

One way to allow for such mismatches is to introduce "wild-card"
spots, that is, spots that will match any star, no matter what its magnitude
or its geometric position. We could append a list of such special spots to
the list of bright spots passed to FIND-MATCH. We then have to be careful to
modify SIMILAR-MAGNITUDE and SIMILAR-DISTANCES so that they ignore these
wild-card spots. An alternative is to ignore a particular star in FIND-MATCH
if the DOLIST terminates without finding a matching spot for it in any of
the recursive calls. Note that we can now no longer simply terminate the
search when we find the first match, because it might be a match consisting
mostly of wild-cards. Instead, we have to look through all possibilities and
choose the one with the largest number of matched pairs:

```
(defun find-match-sub (pairs stars spots)       ;Fifth version.
  (if (endp stars)                              ;More stars to match?
      (find-match-check (reverse pairs))        ;No, check the match.
      (let ((star (first stars))                ;First star in list.
            (best nil)                          ;Best match so far.
            (m-b 0))                            ;Pairs in best match.
        (dolist (spot spots)                    ;Try each spot in turn.
          (when (similar-magnitude star spot)   ;Same brightness?
            (let ((new (list star spot)))       ;New pair to check out.
              (when (distances-check new pairs) ;Distances compatible?
                (let* ((ans (find-match-sub
                              (cons new pairs)
                              (rest stars)
                              (remove spot spots)))
                       (m (length (first ans))))   ;How many pairs?
                  (when (> m m-b) (setf m-b m best ans)))))))
        (let* ((ans (find-match-sub pairs       ;Ignore one star.
                                    (rest stars)
                                    spots))
               (m (length (first ans))))        ;How many pairs?
          (when (> m m-b) (setf m-b m best ans)))
        best)))                                 ;Return the best.
```

```
(defun find-match-check (pairs)              ;Obtain transformation,
  (unless (< (length pairs) 2)               ; and check it.
    (let ((trans (find-transform pairs)))
      (when (check-matched-pairs pairs trans)  ;NIL if no go,
        (list pairs trans)))))                 ; pairs & transform.
```

Note that we had to add a test to FIND-MATCH-CHECK to ensure that FIND-TRANSFORM has at least two pairs to work with. This is necessary, because we allow wild-card matches and so there will be times when we call FIND-MATCH-CHECK with most stars matched with wild-card spots, that is, when these stars are not included in pairs found in the list PAIRS.

Here is a test case where one star remains unmatched:

```
* (print-find-match
    (list (make-star :name "alpha" :x 0.0 :y 1.0 :magnitude 0.0)
          (make-star :name "beta" :x 0.0 :y 0.0 :magnitude 0.5)
          (make-star :name "gamma" :x 1.5 :y 1.0 :magnitude 1.0)
          (make-star :name "delta" :x 1.0 :y 0.5 :magnitude 1.5))
    (list (make-spot :number 1 :u 0.03 :v 1.50 :brightness 0.7)
          (make-spot :number 2 :u 1.00 :v 1.52 :brightness 0.2)
          (make-spot :number 3 :u 0.51 :v 0.02 :brightness 1.9)
          (make-spot :number 4 :u 1.00 :v 0.01 :brightness 1.3)))
(alpha = 2) (beta = 1) (gamma = 4)
c = 0.020614 s = 0.999788 xo = 1.49906 yo = -0.046018
```

An important factor to be aware of is that the new version of FIND-MATCH-SUB typically will have to look at many more potential matches than the earlier versions where we insisted that each star find a matching bright spot in the image. The search tree has to be explored to its full depth even when all of the comparisons of brightnesses and pairwise distances fail. This is because we allow each star to be matched with a wild-card bright spot.

To see how much more work might be involved, we note that the unconstrained problem is equivalent to one where we have added n wild-card spots to the existing m spots, where n is the number of stars. The number of possible matches now equals

$$\frac{(m+n)!}{m!}$$

which is typically a larger number than what we had to contend with before.

**Keeping Track
of Mismatches
Improves Efficiency**

How can we limit the computational effort expended in searching? First of all, we should rewrite FIND-MATCH-CHECK to limit the number of unmatched stars, in addition to checking that there are enough matches to find the transformation.

Rejecting a partial match right at the end, however, is not a such a clever idea because we may have already put a lot of effort into partial matches that are doomed to fail. We should really reject such partial matches as soon as they contain too many wild-card matches.

This means that we have to keep track of how many wild-card matches there are in FIND-MATCH-SUB, rather than just testing right at the end in FIND-MATCH-CHECK:

```
(defun find-match (stars spots)              ;Find spots to match stars.
  (find-match-sub nil stars spots 0))        ;Start—no wild-cards.

(defun find-match-sub (pairs stars spots k)  ;Sixth version.
  (if (endp stars)                           ;More stars to match?
      (find-match-check (reverse pairs))     ;No, check the match.
      (unless (> k 3)                        ;Too many wild-cards?
        (let ((star (first stars))           ;First star in list.
              (best nil)                      ;Best match so far.
              (m-b 0))                        ;Pairs in best match.
          (dolist (spot spots)               ;Try each spot in turn.
            (when (similar-magnitude star spot) ;Same brightness?
              (let ((new (list star spot)))    ;New pair to check.
                (when (distances-check new pairs)  ;Compatible?
                  (let* ((ans (find-match-sub (cons new pairs)
                                              (rest stars)
                                              (remove spot spots)
                                              k))
                         (m (length (first ans)))) ;How many pairs?
                    (when (> m m-b) (setf m-b m best ans)))))))
          (let* ((ans (find-match-sub pairs    ;Ignore one star.
                                      (rest stars)
                                      spots
                                      (+ k 1)))
                 (m (length (first ans))))      ;How many pairs?
            (when (> m m-b) (setf m-b m best ans)))
          best))))                             ;Return the best.
```

After we try to match a particular star with all of the spots in the list of spots, we drop out of the DOLIST, and the star is matched against a wild-card bright spot. This means that it is dropped from the list STARS, but not included in a pair in PAIRS, and we increment the count of wild-card matches. We arbitrarily limit the number of wild-card matches to three in the above version of FIND-MATCH-SUB. A more sophisticated test could be inserted here that takes into account the number of pairs in the list PAIRS as well as the number of stars remaining in STARS and the number of spots remaining in SPOTS in addition to the number of wild-card matches so far.

The Cost of Filtering Has To Be Weighed against the Cost of Searching

The comparison of star magnitudes and spot brightnesses greatly reduces the number of partial matches to be explored further. The comparison of distances between pairs of stars and corresponding pairs of spots helps to prune the search tree even more. Continuing in this vein, we may wish to consider filtering tests involving not one or two, but three stars and three spots. An example would be a test comparing the angles of the triangle formed by three spots with the angles in the triangle formed by the corresponding stars. Such ternary tests are likely to help prune the search tree even further, but are also very costly.

We need to apply a unary test only to the bright spot in the image to be matched to a particular star. The computational cost of such a test is independent of the size of the partial match. A binary test, on the other hand, must be applied to the new spot and all of the spots already included in the partial match. Thus the computational cost grows linearly with the size of the partial match. A ternary test must be applied to all pairs of spots in the partial match. If a partial match contains k stars and k spots, then the test must be applied $k(k-1)/2$ times. The computational cost grows quadratically in this case.

An important consideration in the design of filtering tests is that it should not be necessary to recover the coordinate transformation in order to apply the test, because this typically involves a large amount of computation. Thus quantities that are invariant with respect to the transformation are of particular interest. Obviously, brightnesses are unaffected by the coordinate transformation. More interestingly, the distances between points are preserved by rotation and translation, as are the angles between lines connecting the points.

There is a tradeoff between the effort expended on checking that partial matches satisfy the constraints and the effort involved in verifying that a complete match is acceptable. The more careful we are in checking that partial matches satisfy constraints, the fewer complete matches have to be checked for global consistency. Normally this implies that we should attempt to discover as many constraints as possible. If, however, the verification of the consistency of a complete match is simple, then it does not make sense to be very stringent in the testing of the constraint on partial matches.

In designing matching procedures, we also have to be careful how we pick the tolerances in the constraint checks. If we make the tolerances too tight, the correct match may at times be rejected if it happens to include particularly noisy measurements (false negatives). We may, on the other hand, accept incorrect matches that happen to be similar to the correct match, if we make the tolerances too loose (false positives). So in this case we can not afford to just accept the first match found. We have to collect

them all and pick the best one. This means that we must develop some
measure of the quality of a match.

**Multiple Matching
Attempts Lead to
Recognition**

Suppose now that we have a list of constellations, each consisting of a name
and a list of stars:

```
(defstruct constellation (name) (stars))
```

We wish to find the constellation that matches the pattern of bright spots
in the image:

```
(defun recognize-constellation (spots constellations)
  (dolist (constellation constellations)
    (let* ((stars (constellation-stars constellation))
           (ans (find-match stars spots)))
      (when ans
        (let ((trans (second ans)))
          (return (list constellation trans)))))))
```

This procedure returns both the constellation and the transformation that
maps the bright spots onto the stars in the constellation. Recognition is
simple once we have the matching procedures that determine the coordinate
transformation.

Problems

Problem 31-1: The brightness of some stars varies with time, in some
cases periodically and in some not. In any case, the variation is almost
always within a limited range (if we exclude super novas!). We can represent
such a range by a list of the minimum and the maximum brightness. Modify
SIMILAR-MAGNITUDE to allow for variable stars.

Problem 31-2: Write the procedure MAP-XY-TO-UV for converting from
model coordinates to image coordinates. Test it to make sure it is an
inverse to MAP-UV-TO-XY.

Problem 31-3: In the procedure POINT-MATCH, the error in x and y is
tested separately. It makes more sense to compute the length of the error
vector. Modify the procedure accordingly.

Problem 31-4: The version of FIND-TRANSFORM introduced in the text arbitrarily uses the first two matched pairs to estimate the coordinate transformation. If the corresponding stars are close together, the estimate of
the rotation will tend to be less accurate than if one had chosen stars that
are far apart. Write MOST-DISTANT-PAIRS, a procedure that returns a list of
the two pairs that contain the stars that are the furthest from each other.
Then incorporate this procedure in FIND-TRANSFORM.

Problem 31-5: In the version of FIND-TRANSFORM above, only two pairs were used. In the presence of measurement error we should really apply a least-squares approach to all of the available data. That is, we wish to minimize:

$$E = \sum_{i=1}^{n}\big(x_i - (c\,u_i - s\,v_i + x_0)\big)^2 + \big(y_i - (s\,u_i + c\,v_i + y_0)\big)^2.$$

It is convenient here to shift the origin to the centroids, that is, to subtract the average values from each of the coordinates. So we will use $x_i' = (x_i - \bar{x})$, $y_i' = (y_i - \bar{y})$, $u_i' = (u_i - \bar{u})$, and $v_i' = (v_i - \bar{v})$, where $\bar{x}$, $\bar{y}$, $\bar{u}$, and $\bar{v}$ are the averages of $\{x_i\}$, $\{y_i\}$, $\{u_i\}$, and $\{v_i\}$, respectively. Note that the average values of the new, shifted coordinates are all zero.

The sum of squares of the errors can be rewritten in the form

$$E = \sum_{i=1}^{n}\big(x_i' - (c\,u_i' - s\,v_i' + x_0')\big)^2 + \big(y_i' - (s\,u_i' + c\,v_i' + y_0')\big)^2,$$

where

$$x_0' = x_0 - \big(\bar{x} - (c\,\bar{u} - s\,\bar{v})\big),$$
$$y_0' = y_0 - \big(\bar{y} - (s\,\bar{u} + c\,\bar{v})\big).$$

It is easy to see that the sum of squares of the errors is minimized when $x_0' = 0$ and $y_0' = 0$, given that the sum of the shifted coordinates is zero. So we want

$$x_0 = \bar{x} - (c\,\bar{u} - s\,\bar{v}),$$
$$y_0 = \bar{y} - (s\,\bar{u} + c\,\bar{v}).$$

Knowing this, we can rewrite the sum of squares of errors in the form

$$E = \sum_{i=1}^{n}\big(x_i' - (c\,u_i' - s\,v_i')\big)^2 + \big(y_i' - (s\,u_i' + c\,v_i')\big)^2,$$

or

$$E = A - 2(c\,C + s\,S) + B,$$

where

$$A = \sum_{i=1}^{n}\big(x_i'^2 + y_i'^2\big), \quad \text{and} \quad B = \sum_{i=1}^{n}\big(u_i'^2 + v_i'^2\big),$$

while

$$C = \sum_{i=1}^{n}\big(x_i'u_i' + y_i'v_i'\big) \quad \text{and} \quad S = \sum_{i=1}^{n}\big(y_i'u_i' - x_i'v_i'\big).$$

The extrema of this expression occur where $s\,C = c\,S$. At the minimum,

$$c = \frac{C}{\sqrt{C^2 + S^2}} \quad \text{and} \quad s = \frac{S}{\sqrt{C^2 + S^2}},$$

because $c^2 + s^2 = 1$. Write a new version of `FIND-TRANSFORM` that uses these results to compute the best-fit transformation.

Problem 31-6: When we use the least-squares method to recover the best-fit transformation, we can also obtain a measure of goodness of fit. The sum of squares of errors equals

$$E = A - 2(c\,C + s\,S) + B$$

which, at the minimum, where $sC = cS$, equals

$$E = A - 2\sqrt{C^2 + S^2} + B.$$

Modify `FIND-TRANSFORM` to return a list containing both the best-fit transformation and the root-mean-square error ($\sqrt{E/n}$). Use the root-mean-square error in `FIND-MATCH-CHECK` to check the quality of the match, rather than using `CHECK-MATCHED-PAIRS`.

Problem 31-7: In the fourth version of `FIND-MATCH-SUB`, we stopped searching as soon as we found a match that satisfied the constraints and passed the test on the transformation. If we make the tests very lenient, there may be more than one way to match stars with spots that satisfies all of the tests. In this case, we may want to search for all such matches and return them in a list for further analysis rather than just returning the first match. Modify the fourth version of `FIND-MATCH-SUB` accordingly.

Problem 31-8: What is wrong with the following attempt at the fifth version of `FIND-MATCH-SUB`, a procedure that permits stars to go unmatched?

```
(defun find-match-sub (pairs stars spots)          ; Buggy fifth version.
  (if (endp stars)                                 ; More stars to match?
      (find-match-check (reverse pairs))           ; No, check the match.
      (let ((star (first stars)))                  ; First star in list.
        (or (dolist (spot spots)                   ; Try each spot in turn.
              (when (similar-magnitude star spot)  ; Brightness?
                (let ((new (list star spot)))      ; New pair.
                  (when (distances-check new pairs) ; Compatible?
                    (let ((ans (find-match-sub
                                (cons new pairs)
                                (rest stars)
                                (remove spot spots))))
                      (when ans (return ans)))))))  ; Drop out.
            (find-match-sub pairs (rest stars) spots))))) ; Ignore.
```

Note how the primitive `OR` is used here: if no viable matches are found for a particular star, the `DOLIST` returns `NIL`. In this case a recursive call to `FIND-MATCH-SUB` is made with one star dropped from the list `STARS`.

Problem 31-9: If the image covers a large portion of the sky it may contain bright spots corresponding to stars from more than one constellation. Write a procedure, called `RECOGNIZE-CONSTELLATION`, that returns all of the constellations that match, rather than just the first one.

Problem 31-10: In the procedure for recognizing multiple constellations that you developed in the previous problem, each constellation is matched against the full set of bright spots, even though matches with other constellations may already have occurred. Rewrite `RECOGNIZE-CONSTELLATION` so that it avoids wasting time matching stars with bright spots that have already been accounted for.

Problem 31-11: Suppose that we did not know the focal length of the camera used to take the images of the sky, and consequently did not know the scale of the image. Then the transformation to be recovered would have to include scaling, in addition to rotation and translation. This makes the problem considerably more difficult, because distances are no longer preserved and we cannot use the convenient binary test that compares distances between stars to distances between spots.

Angles between lines are preserved, however, and so the ternary test discussed earlier can be used. We could compare the actual angles. Alternatively, we can compare the shapes of the triangles by comparing ratios of the lengths of the sides. Define `SIMILAR-TRIANGLES`, a procedure that checks whether the two triangles formed by the stars and the spots have similar shapes. As usual, allow for some small error in measurement.

Problem 31-12: If we allow scaling of the image, we have to augment our procedures for recovering the transformation to determine the scale. If the transformation is obtained from just two pairs of stars and spots, the scale factor can be obtained from the ratio of the distance between the stars to the distance between the corresponding spots. If, on the other hand, we want more accurate results we may wish to use a least squares approach. The best-fit scale factor turns out to be the ratio of the root-mean-square deviation of the stars from their centroid to the root-mean-square deviation of the corresponding spots from their centroid. Write the procedure `FIND-SCALE` that determines the best-fit scale given the list `PAIRS`.

Project 31-1: The sky is not planar. The position of a real star is given in terms of right ascension and declination, not Cartesian coordinates. Right ascension, α, and declination, δ, are like longitude and latitude on the celestial sphere. We can define the "distance" between stars in terms of their angular separation. The angular separation can be found using spherical trigonometry. Alternatively, we can use the fact that the dot-product of vectors pointing at the two stars is proportional to the cosine of the angle between them, while the magnitude of the cross-product is proportional to the sine of this angle. The unit vector

$$(\cos \delta \cos \alpha, \, \cos \delta \sin \alpha, \, \sin \delta)^T$$

points at the star with right ascension α and declination δ. Assume now that a new structure is used to represent stars:

```
(defstruct real-star (name) (ascension) (declination) (magnitude))
```

Write a version of the procedure DISTANCE-STARS that uses the magnitude of the sine of the angle between the directions of the two stars as a measure of the distance between them.

Project 31-2: In the previous project we discovered the changes we have to make to DISTANCE-STARS in order to accommodate a spherical sky. We have to make a corresponding change to DISTANCE-SPOTS, because we now use the angle between the directions of stars, rather than Euclidean distance in the image plane. If we assume for convenience that the focal length of the camera is one, then a vector in the direction of the bright spot in the image at (x, y) is given by

$$(x, y, 1)^T.$$

Note that this is <u>not a unit</u> vector, but that we can obtain a unit vector by dividing by $\sqrt{x^2 + y^2 + 1}$. Use the method developed in the previous project to find the magnitude of the sine of the angle between the directions toward two spots. Rewrite DISTANCE-SPOTS accordingly. Observe that now DISTANCE-SPOTS no longer has the same structure as DISTANCE-STARS.

Project 31-3: With a spherical sky, the transformation from directions in the camera coordinate system to the celestial coordinate system consists of a three-dimensional rotation (rather than a two-dimensional rotation and translation, as we have assumed so far). This rotation can be found if we know the directions of two stars in the celestial coordinate system and of two corresponding spots in the camera coordinate system.

Any rotation can be described in terms of an axis and an angle. Let ω be a unit vector in the direction of the axis of the rotation, while θ is the angle of rotation. Suppose that the vector c_1 in the camera coordinate system is taken into the vector s_1 in the celestial coordinate system. Because rotation preserves the lengths of vectors and the angles between them, we must have

$$c_1 \cdot \omega = s_1 \cdot \omega$$

or $(s_1 - c_1) \cdot \omega = 0$. That is, ω is perpendicular to $(s_1 - c_1)$. Suppose next that the vector c_2 is taken into the vector s_2 by the rotation. Then we may conclude by similar reasoning that ω is perpendicular to $(s_2 - c_2)$. Now a vector perpendicular to two given vectors is parallel to their cross-product. So

$$\omega \parallel (s_1 - c_1) \times (s_2 - c_2).$$

We can easily construct a unit vector from this cross-product.

We still have to find the angle of rotation, θ. Now $c_3 = c_1 \times \omega$ and $s_3 = s_1 \times \omega$ are two vectors in a plane perpendicular to ω, and it should be clear that c_3 is mapped into s_3 by the rotation. Thus the angle between c_3

Figure 31-3. We can match the edges found in an image with lines in models of polygonal objects. This allows us to recognize which object we are looking at, as well as finding the translation and rotation that will bring the image into alignment with the stored model.

and s_3 is equal to θ. We can find this angle by noting that the dot-product of these two vectors is proportional to the cosine of the angle, while the cross-product is parallel to ω and has magnitude proportional to the sine of the angle (a method that should by now be familiar!).

Write a new version of FIND-TRANSFORM that applies when the sky is spherical. The least-squares solution of this problem, by the way, is quite a bit harder, although elegant.

Edges Provide More Constraint than Points

The methods we have developed for matching stars in a constellation with bright spots in an image could be applied to images of two-dimensional polygonal objects if we first located isolated features, such as the corners of corresponding polygonal image regions of more or less constant brightness. A line drawing, on the other hand, provides a more complete description of a planar polygonal object. An edge map, to be matched to such a model line drawing, may be obtained from a real gray-level image using one of the many edge-finding algorithms that have been developed in the past twenty years. Figure 31-3 illustrates the relationship between edges in the image and lines in the stored model.

An edge in an image typically separates two regions of different gray level. This difference in gray levels makes it possible to assign a direction to the edge: If you go from the start of an edge to its end, the bright region will be on your right. The same ordering of end points applies to lines in the model. Without this ordering information we would have to deal with many two-way ambiguities in matching.

Edges provide more constraint than points, but require a bit more effort on our part. We look once more for unary and binary tests on proposed partial matches that depend on quantities that are independent of the sought-after coordinate transformation.

If the transformation consists only of rotation and translation, then the length of a line should be equal to the length of the corresponding edge. We can use a simple unary test that compares the length of an edge in the image with the length of a line on the model. Several binary tests are possible. Perhaps the simplest binary test compares the angle between two edges to the angle between the corresponding lines in the model.

Once again, in order to keep the two things to be matched clearly separated in our mind, we use different terms, namely edges in the image and lines in the model. Furthermore, we use different variable names for coordinates in the image and coordinates in the stored geometric models. Correspondingly, we define two different structures:

```
(defstruct line (xs) (ys) (xf) (yf))

(defstruct edge (us) (vs) (uf) (vf))
```

The line starts at (x_s, y_s) and ends at (x_f, y_f). Similarly, the edge starts at (u_s, v_s) and ends at (u_f, v_f).

We can now write procedures for computing the lengths of lines and edges, and for comparing the length of an edge with the length of the corresponding line:

```
(defun line-length (l)                        ;Length of line.
  (distance (line-xs l) (line-ys l) (line-xf l) (line-yf l)))

(defun edge-length (e)                         ;Length of edge.
  (distance (edge-us e) (edge-vs e) (edge-uf e) (edge-vf e)))

(defun similar-length (line edge)              ;Similar length?
  (let ((dl (line-length line)) (el (edge-length edge)))
    (< (abs (- dl el)) 0.1)))
```

Note that we once again have chosen a small tolerance to allow for errors in the measurement of the edge in the image. Again, in practice it would be more convenient to use a global special variable for this tolerance rather than burying it in the procedure.

For the simple binary test we have to compare the angles between lines to the angle between edges. The following procedures return the cosine and the sine of the angle between two lines and two edges respectively:

```
(defun angle-between-lines (line-a line-b)
  (let ((xs-a (line-xs line-a)) (ys-a (line-ys line-a))
        (xf-a (line-xf line-a)) (yf-a (line-yf line-a))
        (xs-b (line-xs line-b)) (ys-b (line-ys line-b))
        (xf-b (line-xf line-b)) (yf-b (line-yf line-b)))
    (angle-between-sub xs-a ys-a xf-a yf-a xs-b ys-b xf-b yf-b)))
(defun angle-between-edges (edge-a edge-b)
  (let ((us-a (edge-us edge-a)) (vs-a (edge-vs edge-a))
        (uf-a (edge-uf edge-a)) (vf-a (edge-vf edge-a))
        (us-b (edge-us edge-b)) (vs-b (edge-vs edge-b))
        (uf-b (edge-uf edge-b)) (vf-b (edge-vf edge-b)))
    (angle-between-sub us-a vs-a uf-a vf-a us-b vs-b uf-b vf-b)))
(defun angle-between-sub (xs-a ys-a xf-a yf-a xs-b ys-b xf-b yf-b)
  (let ((dx-a (- xf-a xs-a)) (dy-a (- yf-a ys-a))
        (dx-b (- xf-b xs-b)) (dy-b (- yf-b ys-b)))
    (dot-and-cross dx-a dy-a dx-b dy-b)))
```

We are now ready to check whether the angle between two edges is similar
to the angle between two lines:

```
(defun similar-angles (pair-a pair-b)
  (let ((line-a (first pair-a)) (edge-a (second pair-a))
        (line-b (first pair-b)) (edge-b (second pair-b)))
    (multiple-value-bind (c-l s-l)
        (angle-between-lines line-a line-b)
      (multiple-value-bind (c-e s-e)
          (angle-between-edges edge-a edge-b)
        (< (abs (- (* c-l s-e) (* c-e s-l))) 0.1)))))
```

Here we have computed the sine of the difference of the angles, rather than
the difference of angles itself. One reason for doing this is that we then
do not have to use trigonometric functions or their inverses. Note that
we have arbitrarily set a limit of 0.1 on the magnitude of the sine of the
difference of the two angles, which corresponds to about $5.74°$.

We will need to check the angles between a new edge and all edges in
a partial match against the angles between a new line and all lines in the
partial match. A procedure for doing this is easily written using DISTANCES-
CHECK as a template:

```
(defun angles-check (new pairs)                    ;Check out new pair,
  (dolist (pair pairs t)                           ; against other pairs.
    (unless (similar-angles new pair) (return nil))))
```

It is also easy now to write a simple procedure for recovering the transformation using the procedure FIND-TRANSFORM developed earlier as a model.
We can obtain the transformation directly from one matched pair:

```
(defun find-edge-transform (pairs)              ;Get edge transformation,
  (if (null pairs)                              ; using single pair.
      (error "Not enough pairs for transformation")
      (find-edge-transform-sub (first pairs))))

(defun find-edge-transform-sub (pair)           ;Minimal version.
  (let* ((line (first pair)) (edge (second pair))
         (xs (line-xs line)) (ys (line-ys line))
         (xf (line-xf line)) (yf (line-yf line))
         (us (edge-us edge)) (vs (edge-vs edge))
         (uf (edge-uf edge)) (vf (edge-vf edge)))
    (find-transform-aux xs ys xf yf us vs uf vf)))
```

Here we have used `FIND-TRANSFORM-AUX` defined earlier for use in the star matching task. Note that in practice, it would be unwise to base the estimate of the transformation on so little information. It is better to apply a least-squares method to all of the information in the match.

Next, we write `FIND-EDGE-CHECK`, the procedure that finds a transformation and checks the matched pairs using this transformation. This is based on `FIND-MATCH-CHECK`:

```
(defun find-edge-check (pairs)                      ;Obtain transformation,
  (unless (endp pairs)                              ; and check it.
    (let ((trans (find-edge-transform pairs)))      ;Transformation.
      (when (check-edge-pairs pairs trans)          ;NIL if no go,
        (list pairs trans)))))                      ; pairs & transform.

(defun check-edge-pairs (pairs trans)                   ;Do pairs really match?
  (dolist (pair pairs t)
    (let* ((line (first pair)) (edge (second pair))
           (xs (line-xs line)) (ys (line-ys line))
           (xf (line-xf line)) (yf (line-yf line))
           (us (edge-us edge)) (vs (edge-vs edge))
           (uf (edge-uf edge)) (vf (edge-vf edge)))
      (multiple-value-bind (xsd ysd) (map-uv-to-xy us vs trans)
        (multiple-value-bind (xfd yfd) (map-uv-to-xy uf vf trans)
          (unless (and (point-match xs ys xsd ysd)
                       (point-match xf yf xfd yfd))
            (return nil)))))))
```

This procedure uses `POINT-MATCH`, a procedure defined earlier for use in the star matching task. Now we are ready to write the procedure `FIND-EDGE-MATCH`, based on our last version of `FIND-MATCH`, merely replacing stars with lines, and spots with edges:

```
(defun find-edge-match (lines edges)            ;Find edges to match lines.
  (find-edge-match-sub nil lines edges 0))      ;Start—no wild-cards.
```

```
(defun find-edge-match-sub (pairs lines edges k)      ;Edge version.
  (if (endp lines)                                    ;More lines to match?
      (find-match-check (reverse pairs))              ;No, check the match.
      (unless (> k 3)                                 ;Too many wild-cards?
        (let ((line (first lines))                    ;First line in list.
              (best nil)                              ;Best match so far.
              (m-b 0))                                ;Pairs in best match.
          (dolist (edge edges)                        ;Try each edge in turn.
            (when (similar-length line edge)          ;Similar length?
              (let ((new (list line edge)))           ;New pair to check.
                (when (angles-check new pairs)        ;Angles compatible?
                  (let* ((ans (find-edge-match-sub
                               (cons new pairs)
                               (rest lines)
                               (remove edge edges)
                               k))
                         (m (length (first ans))))    ;How many pairs?
                    (when (> m m-b) (setf m-b m best ans))))))))
          (let* ((ans (find-match-sub pairs           ;Ignore one edge.
                                      (rest lines)
                                      edges
                                      (+ k 1)))
                 (m (length (first ans))))            ;How many pairs?
            (when (> m m-b) (setf m-b m best ans)))
          best))))                                    ;Return the best.
```

Finally, suppose that we have a list of polygonal objects, each consisting of a name and a list of lines as defined by the structure:

```
(defstruct object (name) (lines))
```

We wish to find the polygonal object that matches the pattern of edges found in the image:

```
(defun recognize-object (edges objects)
  (dolist (object objects)
    (let* ((lines (object-lines object))
           (ans (find-match lines edges)))
      (when ans
        (let ((trans (second ans)))
          (return (list object trans)))))))
```

This procedure returns both the object and the transformation that maps the edges in the image onto the lines in the model object. So recognition is simple once we have the matching procedures that determine the coordinate transformation.

Problems

Problem 31-13: In most cases, the two sides of an edge can be distinguished, because the image is brighter on one side of the edge than it is on the other. This does not always happen, however. Let us assume, for purposes of this problem, that there is no direct way of distinguishing the two ends of an edge. So there is no way of telling which end of an edge should match which end of a line. We will have to be prepared for a situation where an edge is matched to the correct line, but the ends happen to be interchanged.

Modify SIMILAR-ANGLES and ANGLE-BETWEEN-EDGES to take care of the fact that the computed angle may be off by 180°.

Problem 31-14: If the end points of edges and lines are not ordered, as in the previous problem, we can no longer use just a single edge-to-line match to estimate the transformation, because there is now a two-way ambiguity. Modify FIND-EDGE-TRANSFORM to use two matched pairs instead.

Problem 31-15: If the end points are not ordered, as in the previous problems, we also have to be careful when we test a transformation. Rewrite CHECK-EDGE-PAIRS accordingly.

Problem 31-16: If the end points of lines are given, there is more to their pairwise relationships than just the angle between them. We can, for example, find the intersection of the two lines, when extended, and measure the distance of the beginning and end of each line from that common reference point. The two lines give rise to four distances that can be compared to the corresponding four distances obtained from the edges. Note that these four distances can be calculated without recovering the coordinate transformation, and thus are suitable for a filtering test. Write the procedure LINE-SIGNATURE that will return the four distances of the end points of two lines from their mutual point of intersection. Also write the procedure EDGE-SIGNATURE that does the corresponding thing for edges.

Problem 31-17: If we allow multiple objects in the field of view, then they may overlap. In this case an edge may be partially obscured by another polygonal object. Thus the length of an edge in the image may be less than the length of the corresponding line in the model. Modify SIMILAR-LENGTH accordingly. Would you expect the matching problem to become harder with this change?

Summary

- Generating all possible matches helps find the correct match.
- Constraints are needed to isolate the correct match.
- The search tree can be pruned using geometric information.
- Matches have to be checked for global consistency.

- Matching is harder if mismatches are allowed.
- Keeping track of mismatches improves efficiency.
- The cost of filtering has to be weighed against the cost of searching.
- Multiple matching attempts lead to recognition.
- Edges provide more constraint than points.

References

Methods for recognition and determination of an object's position and attitude have been explored by Grimson and Lozano-Pérez [1984]. These methods have been extended to deal with three-dimensional objects, curved objects, as well as articulated and parameterized objects by Grimson and Lozano-Pérez [1987]. A different approach to recognition and attitude determination exploits something called the extended Gaussian image, introduced by Horn [1984]. This method was used in a robot system that picks an object out of a pile of objects, as described by Horn and Ikeuchi [1984].

If we consider a spherical sky and note that bright spots in the image actually define directions, then the transformation from image coordinates to model coordinates involves a three-dimensional rotation. The closed-form solution of the least-squares problem of recovering the three-dimensional translation, rotation, and scaling relating two coordinate systems was discovered by Horn [1987]. In our case we are dealing with a somewhat simpler case, because there is no translation and the scale is assumed known, but the same method can be used.

More information about machine vision can be found in the book *Robot Vision* by Horn [1986].

32

Converting Notations Manipulating Matrices and Finding Roots

The purpose of this chapter is to explore procedures for numerical computations. For many, the first exposure to programming is through examples of this kind.

It Is Easy to Translate Infix Notation to Prefix

Many find it inconvenient and error-prone to translate mathematical formulas into prefix notation. Therefore let us develop a simple LISP procedure that performs this translation automatically.

An arithmetic expression will be represented as a list of operands and operators, as in this example:

(A + B * C)

The usual precedence among arithmetic operators will be enforced. In the above expression, for example, * has higher precedence than +, so that the expression indicates a computation where B and C are multiplied first and then the result is added to A. Ordering can be enforced by enclosing a subexpression in parentheses, making a sublist. Consequently we have the following equivalence:

```
(A + (B * C))   ≡   (A + B * C)
```

Thus in this case, the extra parentheses around `B * C` are not really needed. The parentheses are required, however, in the following example:

```
((A + B) * (C + D))
```

We start by exhibiting `WEIGHT`, a procedure that returns the precedence weighting of an operator. Here we could have used `COND` and `EQL` to advantage, but the procedure is more perspicuous if we use `CASE` introduced in chapter 4:

```
(defun weight (operator)              ;Determine weight of operator.
  (case operator
    (= 0)
    (+ 1)
    (- 1)
    (* 2)
    (/ 2)
    (\\ 2)
    (^ 3)
    (t 9)))                           ;Unrecognized operator.
```

Note that in the above we allowed for an operator, \, intended to represent a remainder operation. Recall that in LISP, the backslash, \, signals unusual treatment for the following character. As a result, it is necessary in the above procedure to use \\ to get the equivalent of a single \.

Also note that the actual values of the weights are of no significance, only the ordering of the weights matters. In the given procedure, operators that are not recognized are arbitrarily given a large weight, namely 9. This convention is exploited later in one of the problems.

Next we must look up the appropriate symbol for the LISP primitive that implements a given operator:

```
(defun opcode (operator)              ;Get appropriate primitive
  (case operator
    (= 'setf)
    (+ '+)
    (- '-)
    (* '*)
    (/ '/ )
    (\\ 'rem)
    (^ 'expt)
    (t operator)))                    ;Unrecognized operator.
```

The symbols of unrecognized operators are just copied—we could instead have generated an error when an unrecognized operator is found.

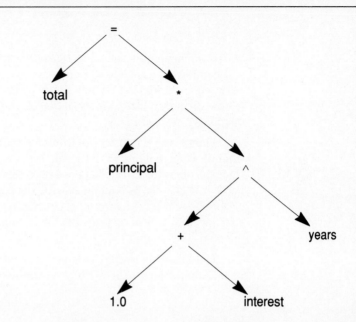

Figure 32-1. An arithmetic expression in prefix form can be represented as a tree. The operators lie at the internal nodes, and the leaves are the operands. The equivalent infix form can be found by a simple depth-first exploration of this tree.

The symbols denoting the primitives that perform simple arithmetic operations happen to be the symbols normally used to represent those operations in ordinary mathematical formulas. This correspondence is convenient, but perhaps slightly confusing here. In OPCODE, + is used in two different ways: in the first instance we are checking whether the given formula contains this symbol; in the second instance we are referring to the primitive that performs addition.

Now then, the *prefix* form of an arithmetic expression can be represented as a tree. Figure 32-1, for example, shows a tree corresponding to the following:

```
(setf total (* principal (expt (+ 1.0 interest) years)))
```

The *infix* form is essentially a linear string obtained by depth-first exploration of the tree representing the arithmetic expression.

By tracing along the outer boundary of the tree, we obtain the following:

```
(total = principal * (1.0 + interest) ^ years)
```

There are many methods for translating from one form to the other. We will employ a linear left-to-right scan, where operands and operators not yet used in producing output are kept in a list. For clarity, we actually use two separate lists, one for OPERANDS and one for OPERATORS, to stack up operands and operators.

Things are added to the fronts of the lists when the operator at the head of what remains of the arithmetic expression, AE, has a larger weight than the operator at the head of OPERATORS. Otherwise, the operator at the head of OPERATORS is combined with the top two operands at the head of OPERANDS. Whenever a piece of the result has been assembled in this fashion, that piece is added to the front of the operand list as a new composite operand.

The following simple example illustrates by showing successive stages in the translation of the arithmetic expression A + B * C:

OPERATORS	OPERANDS	AE
()	()	(A + B * C)
()	(A)	(+ B * C)
(+)	(A)	(B * C)
(+)	(B A)	(* C)
(* +)	(B A)	(C)
(* +)	(C B A)	()
(+)	((* B C) A)	()
()	((+ A (* B C)))	()

When precedence is forced using sublists, the procedure simply calls itself recursively on the sublist. The value returned is the translated result. Here is the procedure INF-TO-PRE that does the translation:

```
(defun inf-to-pre (ae)
  (if (atom ae) ae                       ;Check for easy case.
      (inf-aux ae nil nil)))             ;Start with empty stacks.

(defun inf-aux (ae operators operands)
  (inf-iter (rest ae)                    ;Work on rest after
            operators
            (cons (inf-to-pre (first ae))  ; recursing on first.
                  operands)))
```

```
(defun inf-iter (ae operators operands)
  (cond ((and (endp ae) (endp operators))        ;Termination?
         (first operands))                        ;Result.
        ((and (not (endp ae))                     ;Not end of AE?
              (or (endp operators)                ;Empty stack?
                  (> (weight (first ae))          ;Compare weights.
                     (weight (first operators)))))
         (inf-aux (rest ae)
                  (cons (first ae) operators)     ;Push operator
                  operands))                       ; and continue.
        (t (inf-iter ae
                     (rest operators)             ;Pop operator,
                     (cons (list (opcode (first operators))
                                 (second operands)  ; construct
                                 (first operands))  ; result,
                           (rest (rest operands))))))))  ; pop operands.
```

Here is an example of INF-TO-PRE in action:

```
* (inf-to-pre '(total = principal * (1.0 + interest) ^ years))
(setf total (* principal (expt (+ 1.0 interest) years)))
```

Problems

Problem 32-1: It is simple to translate prefix to infix. Write PRE-TO-INF without worrying about removing redundant parentheses. The following is a test case:

```
* (pre-to-inf
   '(setf total (* principal (expt (+ 1.0 interest) years))))
(total = (principal * ((1.0 + interest) ^ years)))
```

Problem 32-2: Improve PRE-TO-INF so that it will not put in redundant levels of parentheses. It should do the following, for example:

```
* (pre-to-inf
   '(setf total (* principal (expt (+ 1.0 interest) years))))
(total = principal * (1.0 + interest) ^ years)
```

Problem 32-3: Add a tracing mechanism to INF-TO-PRE that prints the values of AE, OPERANDS, and OPERATORS whenever they change. Let the tracing operation be under control of *TRACE-FLAG*, a global free variable.

Problem 32-4: Operators of the same weight now lead to code that nests left to right. While this is the usual convention for most programming languages, it is at times desirable to have operations nested right to left. Change one line in INF-TO-PRE, as developed in a previous problem, so as to change its behavior as follows:

```
* (inf-to-pre '(a + b + c + d))        ;Existing definition.
(+ (+ (+ a b) c) d)

* (inf-to-pre '(a + b + c + d))        ;Desired definition.
(+ a (+ b (+ c d)))
```

Problem 32-5: Sometimes it is convenient to indicate a multiplication simply by juxtaposing two operands without an intervening *. Modify INF-TO-PRE to permit implicit multiplication by checking for the presence of an operand where an operator is expected. Note that the operand may be an atom or a list. Here is a test case

```
* (inf-to-pre '(a b c + e f g))
(+ (* (* a b) c) (* (* e f) g))
```

Problem 32-6: To make it possible to add new operators easily, it is better to store information on their property lists instead of encasing them in procedures like WEIGHT and OPCODE. Make INF-TO-PRE extensible by looking up the precedence weight and the appropriate primitive on the property lists of the operators.

Problem 32-7: Add comparison operators, like < and >, and logical operators, like & (for AND) and | (for OR), noting the convention that logical operators have less weight than the usual arithmetic operators. Also, & has more weight than |. Here is an example of the modified procedure at work:

```
* (inf-to-pre '(a + b < c + d & a + c > b + d))
(and (< (+ a b) (+ c d)) (> (+ a c) (+ b d)))
```

Project 32-1: We have not allowed unary operators like -, SQRT, and SIN. Add a check for the presence of an operator where INF-TO-PRE is looking for an operand, to implement this extension. Unary operators have highest precedence weight.

Project 32-2: In PRE-TO-INF there is an implicit assumption that operators have two operands. Rewrite the procedure so it will deal correctly with situations such as

```
* (pre-to-inf '(+ (* a b c) (* d e f) (/ a b)))
(a * b * c + d * e * f + a / b)
```

Sparse Matrices Can Be Represented as Lists of Lists

Matrices are conveniently represented using arrays. When they get large this can become unwieldy. In the case of sparse matrices, storage is wasted on the large number of 0 entries, which also lead to useless arithmetic operations. Adding 0 and multiplying by 0 can be avoided if just the nonzero elements are stored.

A sparse vector can be represented conveniently as a list of two-element sublists. Each sublist contains an index and the corresponding component. So the vector expressed as $[1.2, 0.0, 3.4, 0.0, 0.0, -6.7, 0.0]^T$ can be represented by the list ((1 1.2) (3 3.4) (6 -6.7)). Locating a particular component requires additional work, but storage and computation is conserved when large sparse vectors are manipulated.

First, let us develop a procedure that multiplies a sparse vector by a scalar. This can be done easily by multiplying one component and recursively applying the same procedure to the rest of the vector.

```
(defun sparse-scale-v (scale v)
  (if (zerop scale) nil                              ;Special case.
      (if (endp v) nil                               ;Termination?
          (let ((fv (first v)))                      ;Grab first entry.
            (cons (list (first fv)                   ;Copy index.
                        (* scale (second fv)))        ;Scale component.
                  (sparse-scale-v scale (rest v))))))) ;Recurse.
```

Hence:

```
* (sparse-scale-v 2 '((1 1.2) (3 3.4) (6 -6.7)))
((1 2.4) (3 6.8) (6 -13.4))
```

Note the special treatment of the case when the scale factor is zero.

Next we apply a similar program structure to the problem of calculating the dot product of two sparse vectors. At each step we check whether the components at the head of the lists have matching indexes. If they do, the product of the corresponding components is calculated. Otherwise the component with the lower index is discarded, and the procedure is applied recursively to what remains.

```
(defun sparse-dot-product (a b)
  (if (or (endp a) (endp b)) 0                       ;Termination?
      (let ((fa (first a)) (fb (first b)))           ;Grab components.
        (cond ((< (first fa) (first fb))
               (sparse-dot-product (rest a) b))       ;Shorten A.
              ((< (first fb) (first fa))
               (sparse-dot-product a (rest b)))       ;Shorten B.
              (t (+ (* (second fa) (second fb))       ;Multiply.
                    (sparse-dot-product (rest a)
                                        (rest b)))))))) ;Recurse.
```

Here is an example:

```
* (sparse-dot-product '((1 2) (3 3) (6 4))
                      '((1 1) (6 3)))
14
```

We do not need much more than this to add two sparse vectors, as long as we are careful to construct the representation of the result correctly:

```
(defun sparse-v-plus (a b)
  (cond ((endp a) b)                            ;Termination?
        ((endp b) a)                            ;Termination?
        (t (let ((fa (first a)) (fb (first b)))) ;Grab components.
           (cond ((< (first fa) (first fb))
                  (cons fa                        ;Copy component.
                        (sparse-v-plus (rest a) b)))
                 ((< (first fb) (first fa))
                  (cons fb                        ;Copy component.
                        (sparse-v-plus a (rest b))))
                 (t (cons (list (first fa)        ;Copy index.
                                (+ (second fa)
                                   (second fb)))   ;Add.
                          (sparse-v-plus (rest a)
                                         (rest b)))))))))  ;Recurse.
```

Here is an example

```
* (sparse-v-plus '((1 2) (3 3) (6 4))
                 '((1 1) (6 3)))
((1 3) (3 3) (6 7))
```

Sparse matrices can be represented as lists of sublists. Here we chose to think of the matrix as composed of column vectors. Each sublist contains a column index and a sparse vector representing the corresponding column. The following is a representation of the 3×3 identity matrix:

```
((1 ((1 1)))
 (2 ((2 1)))
 (3 ((3 1))))
```

The product of a matrix with a vector is the vector obtained by listing the dot products of each of the rows of the matrix with the vector. Our representation is organized around columns, so to make use of the definition, we would have to transpose the matrix. This may be inefficient or inconvenient, however. Fortunately, we can also obtain the product of the matrix and the vector by scaling each column of the matrix by the corresponding component of the vector and then adding up the scaled columns, treating each as a vector. The following procedure clarifies:

```
(defun sparse-m-times-v (m v)
  (if (or (endp v) (endp m)) nil                ;Termination?
      (let ((fv (first v)) (fm (first m)))      ;Grab components.
        (cond ((< (first fv) (first fm))
               (sparse-m-times-v m (rest v)))   ;Shorten V.
              ((< (first fm) (first fv))
               (sparse-m-times-v (rest m) v))   ;Shorten M.
              (t (sparse-v-plus
                   (sparse-scale-v (second fv) (second fm))
                   (sparse-m-times-v (rest m) (rest v)))))))))
```

Now we are ready for matrix multiplication. There are many ways of looking at the product, C, of two matrices A and B. The (i,j)th element of C is the dot product of the ith row of A and the jth column of B, for example. Thus the jth column of C is the product of the matrix A and the jth column of B. We can use this relationship to obtain the product of two matrices as follows:

```
(defun sparse-m-times (ma mb)
  (if (endp mb) nil                             ;Termination?
      (let ((fb (first mb)))                    ;Grab first component.
        (cons (list (first fb)                  ;Copy index.
                    (sparse-m-times-v ma (second fb)))
              (sparse-m-times ma (rest mb)))))) ;Recurse.
```

Thus multiplication of sparse matrices is simple, given all the auxiliary procedures. Here is a simple example:

```
* (sparse-m-times '((1 ((2 2))) (2 ((1 1))) (3 ((3 1))))
                  '((1 ((2 3))) (2 ((3 3))) (3 ((1 4)))))
((1 ((1 3))) (2 ((3 3))) (3 ((2 8))))
```

Problems

Problem 32-8: Write a procedure to extract the nth component of a sparse vector.

Problem 32-9: There is no special provision in SPARSE-V-PLUS for the situation when the sum of two components happens to be zero. Change the procedure SPARSE-V-PLUS so that this component is not inserted in the result.

Problem 32-10: Does it matter whether we let the indexes of the components of a sparse vector run from 0 to $(n-1)$ or from 1 to n?

Problem 32-11: Write `SPARSE-V-PRINT`, a procedure that prints a sparse vector as a row of numbers (even though we are thinking of them here as column vectors). The procedure should fill in 0s for components that do not appear and simply stop after the last nonzero component. Assume that the index of the first component is 1.

Problem 32-12: Using `SPARSE-V-PLUS` as a model, write `SPARSE-M-PLUS` for adding two sparse matrices.

Problem 32-13: The product of a vector and a matrix is a vector obtained by listing the dot products of the vector with each of the columns of the matrix. Employ this definition to write the procedure `SPARSE-V-TIMES-M`.

Problem 32-14: Write `SPARSE-M-TRANSPOSE`, a procedure for transposing a sparse matrix. Here is an example of this procedure in use:

```
* (sparse-m-transpose '((1 ((2 3))) (2 ((3 3))) (3 ((2 8) (3 7)))))
((2 ((1 3) (3 8))) (3 ((2 3) (3 7))))
```

Problem 32-15: The ith row of C, the product of two matrices A and B, is the product of the ith row of A and the matrix B. Write another version of `SPARSE-M-TIMES` based on this observation. Use `SPARSE-M-TRANSPOSE` and `SPARSE-V-TIMES-M` defined in earlier problems.

Project 32-3: Write `SPARSE-M-PRINT`, a procedure that prints each row of a sparse matrix on a separate line. It may help to use `SPARSE-M-TRANSPOSE` and a procedure similar to `SPARSE-V-PRINT`. To get a neat looking result it is necessary to determine the largest column and row indexes that occur in the sparse matrix.

Complex Numbers Constitute Another Numeric Data Type

In the following sections we often deal with complex numbers. Fortunately, LISP has built-in primitives for working with complex numbers. A complex number is represented as a combination of its real and imaginary parts, each part being an integer, a ratio, or a floating-point number. The real and imaginary parts of a given complex number have to be of the same type. When printed, the real and imaginary parts are shown between parenthesis, preceded by the prefix `#C`:

```
* (sqrt -1.0)
#C(0.0 1.0)
```

We can construct complex numbers from their real and imaginary parts using `COMPLEX`, together with `COS` and `SIN`, which produce the cosine and sine, given an angle measured in radians:

```
* (complex (cos (/ pi 2)) (sin (/ pi 2)))
#C(0.0 1.0)
```

The real and imaginary parts of a complex number can be extracted using
REALPART and IMAGPART, hence:

```
(complex (realpart z) (imagpart z))   ≡    z
```

The conjugate of a complex number can be obtained using CONJUGATE, so:

```
(conjugate z)   ≡    (complex (realpart z) (- (imagpart z)))
```

The primitive COMPLEXP tests whether a number is complex:

```
* (complexp (sqrt -1.0))
T
```

We can obtain the modulus (magnitude) and argument (phase angle) of a
complex number using ABS and PHASE:

```
* (abs (sqrt -1.0))
1.0
* (phase (sqrt -1.0))
1.5707963
```

The result of PHASE is in radians, in the range $-\pi$ to π, so that for nonzero
complex numbers, the phase is equivalent to the angle whose tangent is the
ratio of the real and imaginary parts of the complex number. That angle
also can be determined by ATAN, a primitive that can take two numbers,
calculate their ratio, and produce the angle whose tangent is equal to that
ratio:

```
(phase z)   ≡    (atan (imagpart z) (realpart z))
```

The phase angle of zero is arbitrarily defined to be zero.

The arithmetic primitives +, -, *, and / can be used to manipulate
complex numbers. If the arguments given are not all of the same type, then
the rules of *complex contagion* are followed. When a non-complex number
is to be combined with a complex number, the non-complex number is first
converted to a complex number with imaginary part equal to zero[1].

Some of the irrational and transcendental primitives, for example,
EXPT, LOG, and SQRT, may produce a complex result when given real arguments:

---

[1]When the real and imaginary parts of the result of a computation are ratios,
and the imaginary part happens to be zero, then the result is converted to a
ratio. This is the rule of *rational canonicalization*. Such conversion to a non-
complex number does not occur if the real and imaginary parts are floating-
point numbers.

```
* (expt -1 1/3)
#C(0.25 0.86625)
```

In this case, we note that EXPT does not return -1, even though -1 certainly
is a cube root of -1. The reason is that it returns the *principal value*, rather
than just any one of the roots.

**Roots of Quadratic
Equations Are Easy
To Calculate**

Now let us construct a collection of procedures for finding the roots of
algebraic equations with real coefficients. These equations may have several
roots, and these roots may be complex, so the procedures should return a
list, each element of which may be a complex number.

Finding the roots of an equation from its coefficients by means of a
finite number of rational operations and extraction of roots is called solution
by radicals. The solutions by radicals of algebraic equations of the third
and fourth degree were discovered in the sixteenth century. Early in the
nineteenth century, P. Ruffini and N. H. Abel showed that the general
algebraic equation whose degree is greater than four cannot be solved by
radicals. We will confine our attention to equations of degree four or less
so that we will be able to find the roots without resorting to approximation
or iteration. It may help to remember at this point that complex roots, if
any, occur in conjugate pairs if we allow only algebraic equations with *real*
coefficients.

We will have to be careful about special cases that arise when some
of the coefficients are 0. Naturally, conditionals will be useful in sorting
out these exceptions. We start with the innocent-looking linear equation
in one unknown, $ax + b = 0$. For this, we could just write the following:

```
(defun linear (a b) (list (/ (- b) a)))          ;Inadequate version.
```

But this solution does not deal properly with the special cases. If both a and
b are 0, we do not have much of an equation. It is said to be homogeneous,
and any value of x is a solution. The user should be warned and an empty
list returned. If a is 0 but b is not, the equation is inconsistent. There are
no solutions, and again a warning is called for. Finally, if neither a nor b
is 0, we have the obvious result,

$$x = -\frac{b}{a}.$$

Remembering that the value returned should be a list of roots, we arrive
at the following procedure:

```
(defun linear (a b)
  (if (zerop a)
      (if (zerop b)
          (error "Eq. homogeneous ~a*x+~a=0" a b)    ;a = 0 & b = 0
          (error "Eq. inconsistent ~a*x+~a=0" a b))  ;a = 0 & b ≠ 0
      (if (zerop b)
          (list 0)                                   ;a ≠ 0 & b = 0.
          (list (/ (- b) a)))))                      ;a ≠ 0 & b ≠ 0.
```

Note that the second IF could be omitted at the cost of two unnecessary arithmetic operations when b is 0. Also, an error is generated when the equation does not have roots or has an infinite number of roots. The user could in this case be permitted the more elaborate interaction available using BREAK, introduced in chapter 10.

We are now ready to tackle quadratic equations like $ax^2 + bx + c = 0$. If a is 0, this is not really a quadratic equation and the solutions are those of the remaining linear equation $bx + c = 0$. If c is 0, one of the roots is 0 and the other can be found by solving the linear equation $ax + b = 0$. In these two cases we can call on the procedure already defined. If neither a nor c is 0, we can remove the linear term using the transformation $y = 2ax + b$, obtaining the following equation:

$$y^2 + (4ac - b^2) = 0.$$

Using the fact that $x = (y - b)/(2a)$, we could just write the following procedure:

```
(defun quadratic (a b c)                       ;Inadequate version.
  (let ((root (sqrt (- (* b b) (* 4 a c)))))
    (list (/ (+ (- b) root) (* 2 a))
          (/ (- (- b) root) (* 2 a)))))
```

Here ROOT may be complex, but that is in order, because the arithmetic operators can handle complex numbers. This version of QUADRATIC, although easy to understand, once again does not deal separately with the special cases that may arise. It is also wasteful in computation and does not produce the most accurate result possible. We proceed more carefully now. The part of the program that deals with the special cases and computes the discriminant is as follows:

```
(defun quadratic (a b c)
  (cond ((minusp a) (quadratic (- a) (- b) (- c)))
        ((zerop a) (linear b c))                  ;a = 0.
        ((zerop c) (cons 0 (linear a b)))         ;c = 0.
        (t (quadratic-aux a b c (- (* b b) (* 4 a c))))))
```

The first clause in the conditional above ensures that a is not negative. This makes it easier afterward to pick the best method for numerical accuracy and also to order real roots, if any, so that the most positive appears first in the list.

Of course it would be foolhardy to write such procedures without testing each of the major branches. CHECK-QUADRATIC is a test procedure that complements QUADRATIC:

```
(defun check-quadratic (a b c)
  (dolist (x (quadratic a b c))
    (format t "~%For x = ~a, the quadratic yields ~a."
            x
            (+ (* (+ (* a x) b) x) c)))
  (values))
```

Note that this test procedure is not meant to return a value, as indicated by the use of (VALUES). And here are some test cases that check out the first three branches in QUADRATIC:

```
* (check-quadratic -1 2 0)                  ;Tests branches 1 and 3.
For x = 0, the quadratic yields 0.
For x = 2, the quadratic yields 0.
* (check-quadratic 0 2 4)                   ;Tests branch 2.
For x = -2, the quadratic yields 0.
```

Now $x = (y - b)/(2a)$, so if the discriminant is negative, the original equation has the complex conjugate pair of solutions:

$$-\frac{b}{2a} \pm i\,\frac{\sqrt{4ac - b^2}}{2a}.$$

If the discriminant happens to be 0, the two roots coincide at $-b/(2a)$. Finally, when it is positive, there are two real roots, usually given as

$$\frac{-b \pm \sqrt{b^2 - 4ac}}{2a}.$$

Curiously, by viewing the original equation as an equation in the variable $1/x$, we find an alternate form,

$$\frac{2c}{-b \mp \sqrt{b^2 - 4ac}}.$$

This is quickly verified by noting that the sum of the roots must equal $-(b/a)$, and their product must equal (c/a). Why bother with the second form if both are correct? It is a question of numerical accuracy: if b^2 is much larger than the magnitude of $4ac$, the square root of the discriminant will be only a little different from the magnitude of b. The floating-point methods used to represent real numbers in a computer have only limited accuracy, and that accuracy is compromised when two quantities that are nearly equal are subtracted. Thus one of the two roots will be known with considerably less accuracy than the other if we recklessly apply either one of the two formulas alone. Instead, we carefully pick the appropriate formula for each case.

We test the discriminant to see what is to be done next:

```
(defun quadratic-aux (a b c discriminant)
  (cond ((minusp discriminant)                    ;Conjugate pair.
         (quadratic-conjugate (/ (- b) (* 2 a))
                              (/ (sqrt (- discriminant)) (* 2 a))))
        ((zerop discriminant)                     ;Double root.
         (quadratic-equal (/ (- b) (* 2 a))))
        ((minusp b)                               ;Real roots b < 0.
         (quadratic-real-p a
                           (- (sqrt discriminant) b)
                           c))
        (t (quadratic-real-m a                    ;Real roots b ≥ 0.
                             (- (+ (sqrt discriminant) b))
                             c))))
```

Note that the special treatment of the case when the discriminant is 0 can be omitted if the cost of taking the square root of 0 is of no concern and exact equality of the two roots is not imperative. Similarly, special treatment of the case when c is 0 can be removed with only minor loss in accuracy of the result.

We are now ready to write the rest. To make it easier to see what is going on, the work has been divided among four procedures.

```
(defun quadratic-equal (x) (list x x))

(defun quadratic-conjugate (real imaginary)
  (list (complex real imaginary)
        (complex real (- imaginary))))

(defun quadratic-real-p (a rat c)              ;Two real roots & b < 0.
  (list (/ rat (* 2 a))                        ;If a > 0, most positive first.
        (/ (* 2 c) rat)))

(defun quadratic-real-m (a rat c)              ;Two real roots & b > 0.
  (list (/ (* 2 c) rat)                        ;If a > 0, most positive first.
        (/ rat (* 2 a))))
```

Now we test again, this time focusing on the branches of QUADRATIC-AUX:

```
* (check-quadratic 1 2 2)                          ;Tests first branch.
For x = #C(-1 1), the quadratic yields 0.
For x = #C(-1 -1), the quadratic yields 0.
* (check-quadratic 1 4 4)                          ;Tests second branch.
For x = -2, the quadratic yields 0.
For x = -2, the quadratic yields 0.
* (check-quadratic 1 5 6)                          ;Tests third branch.
For x = -2, the quadratic yields 0.
For x = -3, the quadratic yields 0.
* (check-quadratic 1 -5 6)                         ;Tests fourth branch.
For x = 3, the quadratic yields 0.
For x = 2, the quadratic yields 0.
```

The overall program required for this simple exercise may seem surprisingly large. This results from the careful attention to the special cases, the use of the best methods for numerical accuracy, and a desire to avoid repeating calculations.

Someone familiar with certain other programming languages would no doubt have written this procedure quite differently, perhaps as a single large procedure. Several local variables would have been declared and set using the equivalent of SETF. The way illustrated here uses many procedure definitions instead. It is quite common to find LISP programs predominantly employing this multiple-definition, problem-reduction method. This leads to a division of programs into a large number of procedures, each short enough to be easy to understand.

While on the subject of style, note that new variable bindings can be arranged for in a number of different ways. One approach is to break a procedure into parts, with one part calling the other. In this case the parameters of the new subprocedure provide the required bindings. An alternative is the use of LET, which is actually a lot like defining a nameless sub-procedure that happens to be nested inside the main procedure. When many LETs are nested inside one another, however, the pretty-printed version of the LISP procedure begins to look a bit odd, slanting off toward the right, with the space for comments greatly reduced. In order to maintain readability, it is best not to nest LETs too deeply, instead breaking the procedure up into parts that call one another.

Roots of Cubic Equations Can Be Calculated

Next we tackle cubic equations like $ax^3 + bx^2 + cx + d = 0$. These either have one real root and a complex conjugate pair of roots or three real roots. It is helpful to remove the quadratic term using the substitution, $y = 3ax + b$, producing the equation

$$y^3 + 3(3ac - b^2)y + (2b^3 - 9abc + 27a^2d) = 0.$$

In order to find the roots of this simplified cubic, we first find the roots of the quadratic resolvent

$$t^2 + (2b^3 - 9abc + 27a^2d)t - (3ac - b^2)^3 = 0.$$

The roots are found using CUBIC:

```
(defun cubic (a b c d)
  (cond ((minusp a) (cubic (- a) (- b) (- c) (- d)))
        ((zerop a) (quadratic b c d))              ;a = 0.
        ((zerop d) (cons 0 (quadratic a b c)))     ;d = 0.
        (t (cubic-aux a
                      b
                      (quadratic 1                 ;Resolvent.
                                 (+ (* 2 b b b)
                                    (* 9 a (- (* 3 a d) (* b c))))
                                 (expt (- (* b b) (* 3 a c))
                                       3))))))
```

We also need a test procedure and some test cases:

```
(defun check-cubic (a b c d)
  (dolist (x (cubic a b c d))
    (format t "~%For x = ~a, the cubic yields ~a."
            x
            (+ (* (+ (* (+ (* a x) b) x) c) x) d)))
  (values))
* (check-cubic -1 2 3 0)                           ;Tests first and third clauses.
For x = 0, the cubic yields 0.
For x = 3, the cubic yields 0.
For x = -1, the cubic yields 0.
* (check-cubic 0 1 5 6)                            ;Tests second clause.
For x = -2, the cubic yields 0.
For x = -3, the cubic yields 0.
```

If the roots of the resolvent are complex, the cubic has three real roots. If, on the other hand, the roots of the resolvent are real, the cubic has one real root and a complex conjugate pair of roots.

```
(defun cubic-aux (a b roots)
  (if (complexp (first roots))                     ;Check resolvent roots.
      (cubic-real a                                ;Roots complex.
                  b
                  (abs (first roots))              ;Modulus, and
                  (phase (first roots)))           ; argument.
      (cubic-conjugate a                           ;Resolvent roots real.
                       b
                       (cube-root (first roots))   ;Pick out the
                       (cube-root (second roots))))) ; two roots.
```

Here we have used CUBE-ROOT, a procedure that calculates the real cube root of a number. Because this is not a primitive of LISP, you must define it in terms of primitives like EXPT, as you are led to do in a problem. Also note that ABS returns the modulus of a complex number, while PHASE computes the argument, using ATAN applied to the imaginary and the real parts.

Meanwhile, we must be careful to avoid disasters like dividing by 0 or taking the square root of a negative number.[2] A problem might arise, for example, if the primitive PHASE was called with a zero argument (the primitive arbitrarily returns zero in this case). This cannot happen, however, because if a root of the quadratic resolvent was zero if would not be represented as a complex number, and so would not trigger the first clause of the conditional in the procedure above.

Now we can use Cardano's formula. If the roots of the quadratic resolvent are α and β, then the roots of the simplified cubic are given by the following formula, where ω is a complex cube root of one:

$$y = \omega^k \alpha^{1/3} + \omega^{2k} \beta^{1/3}.$$

The powers of this cube root of one, in turn, are given by

$$\omega^k = \cos \frac{2\pi k}{3} + i \sin \frac{2\pi k}{3} \quad \text{for} \quad k = 0, 1, \text{ and } 2.$$

Expanding this result and using the substitution $x = (y - b)/(3a)$, we can write the following:

```
(defun cubic-conjugate (a b r s)                    ;r & s are cube roots.
  (let ((sroot (/ (- (+ r s) b) (* a 3)))
        (real (/ (- (- (/ (+ r s) 2)) b) (* a 3))))
    (if (= r s)
        (cubic-conjugate-equal sroot real)          ;Roots equal.
        (let ((imag (/ (* (- r s) (/ (sqrt 3) 2)) (* a 3))))
          (cubic-conjugate-aux sroot real imag)))))  ;Roots not equal.

(defun cubic-conjugate-equal (sroot droot)          ;Two of roots equal.
  (cons sroot (list droot droot)))

(defun cubic-conjugate-aux (real-root real imag)
  (list real-root                                   ;Real root first,
        (complex real imag)                         ; then comes the
        (complex real (- imag)))))                  ; conjugate pair.
```

We treated separately the special case when the two roots of the quadratic resolvent are equal. In this case two of the roots of the cubic are equal also.

If the roots of the quadratic resolvent are complex, the cubic has three real roots. This is the celebrated *casus irreducibilis* which *cannot* be solved using only rational operations and real roots. We proceed trigonometrically

---

[2]We have, however, not worried about floating point overflow and underflow, issues that would be a concern to someone attempting to write a robust package to be used by others.

and find the roots given by the following, where ρ is the modulus (absolute value) of one of the complex roots of the resolvent and θ is the argument (phase) of this complex root:

$$y = 2\rho^{1/3} \cos\left(\frac{\theta + 2\pi k}{3}\right) \quad \text{for} \quad k = 0, 1, \text{ and } 2.$$

Expanding this result and using the substitution $x = (y - b)/(3a)$, we can write

```
(defun cubic-real (a b rho theta)        ;Rho & theta of complex root.
  (cubic-real-aux a
                  b
                  (* 2 (cube-root rho))
                  (/ (cos (/ theta 3)) -2)
                  (/ (* (sin (/ theta 3)) (sqrt 3)) 2)))
```

Recall that the primitives SIN and COS calculate the sine and cosine of their single argument.

```
(defun cubic-real-aux (a b rd cd sd)        ;Most positive root first.
  (list (/ (- (* -2 rd cd) b) (* 3 a))
        (/ (- (* rd (+ cd sd)) b) (* 3 a))
        (/ (- (* rd (- cd sd)) b) (* 3 a))))
```

We are now ready to test the branches of CUBIC-AUX:

```
* (check-cubic 1 10 31 30)                   ;Tests cubic-real.
For x = -2.0, the cubic yields 0.0.
For x = -3.0, the cubic yields 0.0.
For x = -5.0, the cubic yields 0.0.

* (check-cubic 1 5 8 6)                       ;Tests cubic-conjugate.
For x = -3.0, the cubic yields 0.0.
For x = #C(-1.0 1.0), the cubic yields #C(0.0 0.0).
For x = #C(-1.0 -1.0), the cubic yields #C(0.0 0.0).
```

Roots of Quartic Equations Are Harder To Calculate

We now, with our last breath of air, proceed to quartic equations like $ax^4 + bx^3 + cx^2 + dx + e = 0$. Textbooks advertise several solutions to this type of equation. Unfortunately most, like the Descartes-Euler formula, suffer from poor numerical stability. That is, although formally correct, numerical procedures based on them generate results that are of low accuracy. This, once again, has to do with the inexact nature of the computer's representation for real numbers. Ferrari's method does not suffer from this problem. It is based on a reduction of the quartic into a product of two quadratics with real coefficients. In order to find these quadratics, it is first necessary to solve the cubic resolvent:

$$t^3 - ct^2 + (bd - 4ae)t - (ad^2 + b^2e - 4ace) = 0.$$

If s is the most positive real root of this resolvent, then the quadratics are as follows:

$$2ax^2 + \left(b \pm \sqrt{b^2 - 4a(c-s)}\right)x + \left(s \pm \sqrt{s^2 - 4ae}\right) = 0.$$

The signs of the two square roots have to be picked carefully so that their product equals $(bs - 2ad)$. Note that the product of the two quadratics is actually a nonzero constant times the original quartic, but that does not change the roots.

Fortunately, we arranged for CUBIC to return the real root first in the list, if there is only one, and to return the most positive root first, if there are three real roots. Finally, we can write

```
(defun quartic (a b c d e)
  (cond ((minusp a) (quartic (- a) (- b) (- c) (- d) (- e)))
        ((zerop a) (cubic b c d e))             ;a = 0.
        ((zerop e) (cons 0 (cubic a b c d)))    ;e = 0.
        (t (quartic-aux a
                        b
                        c
                        d
                        e
                        (first (cubic 1          ;Resolvent cubic.
                                      (- c)
                                      (- (* b d) (* 4 a e))
                                      (- (* 4 a c e)
                                         (+ (* a d d)
                                            (* b b e)))))))))
(defun quartic-aux (a b c d e s)                 ;s is root of resolvent.
  (quartic-split a
                 b
                 (sqrt (- (* b b) (* 4 a (- c s))))
                 s
                 (sqrt (- (* s s) (* 4 a e)))
                 (- (* b s) (* 2 a d))))
(defun quartic-split (a b r1 s r2 bs-2ad)
  (if (minusp (* r1 r2 bs-2ad))                  ; sign of r1 r2 same as bs-2ad?
      (append (quadratic (* 2 a) (- b r1) (+ s r2))    ;No.
              (quadratic (* 2 a) (+ b r1) (- s r2)))
      (append (quadratic (* 2 a) (- b r1) (- s r2))    ;Yes.
              (quadratic (* 2 a) (+ b r1) (+ s r2)))))
```

Once again, we would have to be very confident (or foolish) to ignore the need to test this code, so we now write CHECK-QUARTIC:

```
(defun check-quartic (a b c d e)
  (dolist (x (quartic a b c d e))
    (format t "~%For x = ~a, the quartic yields ~a."
            x
            (+ (* (+ (* (+ (* (+ (* a x) b) x) c) x) d) x) e)))
  (values))
```

As an example of the use of this test function, consider

```
* (check-quartic 1 1 -5 1 -6)
For x = #C(0.0 1.0), the quartic yields #C(0.0 0.0).
For x = #C(0.0 -1.0), the quartic yields #C(0.0 0.0).
For x = 2.0, the quartic yields 0.0.
For x = -3.0, the quartic yields 0.0.
```

Actually, because of limitations of floating point arithmetic, it is unlikely that the results returned by a given implementation would be exactly zero as shown here.

Problems

Problem 32-16: Write CUBE-ROOT using the primitive EXPT. Note that (EXPT X Y) returns the principal value of x^y, which is a complex number when the first argument is negative. This is not what we want, so the case of a negative argument has to be treated separately. Also, the result of the computation might not be as accurate as we might hope for. Add one step of the Newton-Raphson iteration

$$x_{n+1} = \frac{1}{3}\left(2\,x_n + \frac{y}{x_n^2}\right)$$

to try to improve upon it. Also write a test function, CHECK-CUBE-ROOT to verify that your procedure works correctly. Here is an example:

```
* (check-cube-root -27)
Cubic root of -27 is -3.0 and -3.0**3 is -27.0
```

Problem 32-17: To check the roots of algebraic equations, it is helpful to have a procedure that finds the coefficients of a polynomial given its roots. Write MAKE-POLY, a procedure that produces a list of coefficients of a polynomial given a list of its roots. Arrange for the higher order coefficients to appear first in the list. Here is an example of MAKE-POLY at work:

```
* (make-poly '(1 2 3 4))
(1 -10 35 -50 24)
* (quartic 1 -10 35 -50 24)
(4.0 3.0 2.0 1.0)
```

Problem 32-18: Another way to check a root is to plug it into the original polynomial to see if the polynomial evaluates to 0. This is what we did in the procedures above for checking QUADRATIC, CUBIC, and QUARTIC. Write POLY-VALUE, a procedure that will evaluate an arbitrary polynomial at a value given as a second argument. Assume the polynomial is given as a list of coefficients, with the high order coefficients appearing first. Here is an example of how POLY-VALUE might be used:

```
* (quartic 1 -10 35 -50 24)
(4.0 3.0 2.0 1.0)
* (poly-value '(1 -10 35 -50 24) 4)
0
```

Problem 32-19: You may have wondered about the initial clauses in the conditionals of QUADRATIC, CUBIC, and QUARTIC. These assure that the first coefficient, a, is positive. That makes it much easier to keep track of what sign intermediate terms and roots of resolvents will have. It is also part of an attempt to always return the most positive real root first in the list of roots. This is important because the solution of the quartic depends on having the most positive real root of the cubic resolvent.

There is a bug, however. The problem is that when the last coefficient of a polynomial happens to be 0, the root 0 is CONSed onto the list of roots computed by a call to a lower-order root finder. Thus the most positive root may be hidden behind a 0. Try, for example,

```
* (quartic 1 4 6 4 2)
```

to see what happens.

There are two approaches to fixing this problem. One is to extract the most positive real root from a list of roots of the resolvent in CUBIC explicitly. Write the procedure MOST-POSITIVE-REAL, and use it in CUBIC in place of FIRST.

Problem 32-20: The other way to solve the previous problem is to make sure that the roots are always ordered correctly in the first place. Write INSERT-ROOT, a procedure that inserts a new root in a list of roots so that the ordering is maintained. That is, the most positive real root comes first in the list. Now all you have to do is replace the appropriate CONSes in QUADRATIC, CUBIC, and QUARTIC with INSERT-ROOT. Although, when used this way, the procedure will not be asked to insert a complex value, make it general enough to deal with this case too, so that it can be used in the next problem.

Problem 32-21: If we use INSERT-ROOT as above, then all procedures except QUARTIC return their roots in order. Replace the two APPENDs in QUARTIC-SPLIT with APPEND-ROOTS, a procedure defined using INSERT-ROOT, so that QUARTIC returns its list of roots ordered as well.

Project 32-4: In the solutions above we sometimes needed only one root of a resolvent equation in order to proceed, yet all roots were calculated and the unused ones discarded. The function QUARTIC, for example, really only needs the most positive real root of the cubic resolvent. Write CUBIC-S, which returns only the most positive real root.

Summary

- It is easy to translate infix notation to prefix.
- Sparse matrices can be represented as lists of lists.
- Complex numbers constitute another numeric data type.
- Roots of quadratic equations are easy to calculate.
- Roots of cubic equations can be calculated.
- Roots of quartic equations are harder to calculate.

References

Methods for numerical computations in general are discussed by Conte and de Boor [1972], Forsythe, Malcomb, and Moler [1977], Hamming [1962], and Hildebrand [1974]. Matrix operations are analyzed in Aho, Hopcroft, and Ullman [1974].

Methods for solving algebraic equations can be found in Burington [1973], Abramowitz and Stegan [1964], and Iyanga and Kawada [1977]. Polynomial arithmetic is discussed by Aho, Hopcroft, and Ullman [1974].

Cody and Waite [1980] provide a cookbook for implementers of mathematical function subroutines. Seminumerical algorithms are treated in detail in Knuth [1981]. Hu [1982] and Sedgewick [1983] discuss many algorithms, including ones for dealing with some of the problems presented here.

Appendix
The Computation of the
Class Precedence List

In this appendix, we explain the CLOS algorithm that computes the class precedence list. Normally the depth-first, left-to-right, up-to-join rules introduced in chapter 14 produce the correct result. But in extreme situations, the CLOS algorithm and the approximating rules produce different results.

The CLOS algorithm is complicated, however, and even wizard-level CLOS programmers try to get by without thinking about it, just as physicists try to get by with Newtonian mechanics rather than dealing with quantum mechanics.

Our explanation consists of English description fortified by examples and by LISP procedures.

Make Initial Lists

We need an empty precedence list, a superclass list, and a direct superclass list. The direct superclass list is a list in which each element consists of a class and its direct superclasses.

To illustrate, we borrow an example from chapter 14. Imagine that we are working with a generic function argument that is an instance of the BOTTOM class and that the following table captures the class hierarchy:

Class	Direct Superclasses
Bottom	S
S	L1 M1 R1
L1	L2
M1	M2
R1	R2
L2	J
M2	J
R2	J
J	Top

From the table, we have the following:

```
()                                      ;Initial precedence list.
(bottom s l1 m1 r1 l2 m2 r2 j top)      ;Superclass list.
((bottom s)                             ;Direct superclass list.
 (s l1 m1 r1)
 (l1 l2) (l2 j)
 (m1 m2) (m2 j)
 (r1 r2) (r2 j)
 (j top))
```

**Make a List of
Precedence Pairs**

The precedence pairs are constructed by replacing each element in the direct superclass list by a sequence of pairs:

```
* (construct-pairs '((bottom s)
                     (s l1 m1 r1)
                     (l1 l2) (l2 j)
                     (m1 m2) (m2 j)
                     (r1 r2) (r2 j)
                     (j top)))
((BOTTOM S)                  ;From bottom and its direct superclasses.
 (S L1) (L1 M1) (M1 R1)      ;From s.
 (L1 L2) (M1 M2) (R1 R2)     ;From l1, m1, and r1.
 (L2 J) (M2 J) (R2 J)        ;From l2, m2, and r2.
 (J TOP))                    ;From j.
```

To define CONSTRUCT-PAIRS, we first define CONSTRUCT-PAIRS-AUX, a procedure that works on individual elements from the direct superclass list:

```
* (construct-pairs-aux '(bottom s))
((BOTTOM S))
* (construct-pairs-aux '(s l1 m1 r1))
((S L1) (L1 M1) (M1 R1))
```

CONSTRUCT-PAIRS-AUX is defined as follows:

```
(defun construct-pairs-aux (l)
  (if (endp (rest (rest l)))
      (list l)
      (cons (list (first l) (second l))
            (construct-pairs-aux (rest l)))))
```

Given CONSTRUCT-PAIRS-AUX, CONSTRUCT-PAIRS is easy to define:

```
(defun construct-pairs (direct-supers)
  (apply #'append (mapcar #'construct-pairs-aux direct-supers)))
```

Make a List of Precedence List Candidates

The list of precedence list candidates is constructed by isolating the classes on the superclass list that do not appear as the second element of any pair on the list of precedence pairs. Initially, this is easy; the only element of the superclass list that survives is BOTTOM:

```
* (filter-classes
    '(bottom s l1 m1 r1 l2 m2 r2 j top)
    '((bottom s) (s l1) (l1 m1) (m1 r1) (l1 l2)
      (m1 m2) (r1 r2) (l2 j) (m2 j) (r2 j) (j top)))
(BOTTOM)
```

Later on, there are situations in which more than one class on the current list of superclasses does not appear as the second element of any pair on the current list of precedence pairs:

```
* (filter-classes
    '(m1 r1 l2 m2 r2 j top)
    '((m1 r1) (m1 m2) (r1 r2)
      (l2 j) (m2 j) (r2 j) (j top)))
(L2 M1)
```

FILTER-CLASSES is defined using a MEMBER form with an elaborate test that compares each class with all second elements on the list of precedence pairs. All classes that fail become candidates:

```
(defun filter-classes (classes precedence-pairs &aux result)
  (dolist (class classes result)
    (unless (member class precedence-pairs
                    :test
                    #'(lambda (x y) (eq x (second y))))
      (push class result))))
```

Select a Candidate

The selected candidate is to move from the candidate list to the precedence list. In general, the selection process requires access to the current precedence list and to the list of direct superclasses. But if there is only one candidate, it is selected straightaway:

```
* (filter-candidates
    '(bottom)
    '()
    '((bottom s) (s l1 m1 r1) (l1 l2) (l2 j)
      (m1 m2) (m2 j) (r1 r2) (r2 j) (j top)))
BOTTOM
```

If there are more than one candidate, the one selected is the one that is a direct superclass of the highest precedence class in the current precedence list. In the following example, the highest precedence class is L1, the one just pushed on. L2 is a direct superclass of L1 but M1 is not:

```
* (filter-candidates
    '(l2 m1)
    '(l1 s bottom)
    '((bottom s) (s l1 m1 r1) (l1 l2) (l2 j)
      (m1 m2) (m2 j) (r1 r2) (r2 j) (j top))))
L2
```

To implement FILTER-CANDIDATES, we must check each candidate against each element of the current precedence list until a direct superclass relation appears. We can step through the candidates and the current precedence list using nested DOLISTs, but then there is a question of what to do when we find the winning candidate. One approach is to use LISP's CATCH and THROW primitives. Both CATCH and THOW forms have identifying symbols as their first arguments. Whenever a THROW form is evaluated, the value of its second argument immediately becomes the value of the surrounding CATCH with a matching identifier:

```
(catch <identifying symbol>
 ...
 (throw <identifying symbol> <result form>)
 ...
 )
```

Using `CATCH` and `THROW` makes it easy to return from the nested `DO` forms in which the candidate classes are tested:

```
(defun filter-candidates (candidates precedence-list direct-supers)
  (cond ((= 1 (length candidates)) (first candidates))
        (t (catch 'found-it
             (dolist (possible-subclass precedence-list)
               (dolist (candidate candidates)
                 (when (member candidate
                               (assoc possible-subclass
                                      direct-supers))
                   (throw 'found-it candidate)))))))))
```

Shrink the List of Precedence Pairs

Not it is time to remove pairs from the list of precedence pairs that have the newly selected element of the precedence list as their first element. To begin, we remove `BOTTOM` from the initial list of precedence pairs:

```
* (filter-pairs
    '((bottom s) (s l1) (l1 m1) (m1 r1) (l1 l2)
      (m1 m2) (r1 r2) (l2 j) (m2 j) (r2 j) (j top))
    'bottom)
((S L1) (L1 M1) (M1 R1) (L1 L2)
 (M1 M2) (R1 R2) (L2 J) (M2 J) (R2 J) (J TOP))
```

Later on, we remove L2 from the list of current precedence pairs making a new, shorter list the current one:

```
* (filter-pairs
    '((m1 r1) (m1 m2) (r1 r2) (l2 j) (m2 j) (r2 j) (j top))
    'l2)
((M1 R1) (M1 M2) (R1 R2) (M2 J) (R2 J) (J TOP))
```

`FILTER-PAIRS` is implemented using a straightforward `REMOVE-IF`:

```
(defun filter-pairs (precedence-pairs winner)
  (remove-if #'(lambda (pair) (eq winner (first pair)))
             precedence-pairs))
```

Repeat

We repeat until all classes are moved from the superclass list to the class precedence list. To do this, we package what we have implemented so far into the definition of ESTABLISH-ORDER. When ESTABLISH-ORDER is ready to return a value, it reverses the precedence list so that it reads from highest precedence to lowest:

```
(defun establish-order (classes direct-supers)
  (let ((precedence-list nil)
        (pairs (construct-pairs direct-supers)))
    (loop
      (when (endp classes) (return (reverse precedence-list)))
      (let* ((candidates (filter-classes classes pairs))
             (winner (filter-candidates candidates
                                        precedence-list
                                        direct-supers)))
        ;;Shrink the list of precedence pairs:
        (setf pairs (filter-pairs pairs winner))
        ;;Move the winning class to the precedence list:
        (setf classes (remove winner classes))
        (push winner precedence-list)))))
```

Now we can test ESTABLISH-ORDER on our example:

```
* (establish-order '(bottom s l1 m1 r1 l2 m2 r2 j top)
                   '((bottom s)
                     (s l1 m1 r1)
                     (l1 l2) (l2 j)
                     (m1 m2) (m2 j)
                     (r1 r2) (r2 j)
                     (j top)))
(BOTTOM S L1 L2 M1 M2 R1 R2 J TOP)
```

And here we test ESTABLISH-ORDER on an example that leads to different results from the depth-first, left-to-right, up-to-join rules:

```
* (establish-order '(bottom a b c d)
                   '((bottom a b c) (a c d) (b c d)))
(BOTTOM A B C D)
```

The approximating rules would produce (BOTTOM A B D C). Here is another example:

```
* (establish-order '(bottom a b c d e)
                   '((bottom a b c) (a c e) (b c d)))
(BOTTOM A B C D E)
```

The approximating rules would produce (BOTTOM A E B D C).

Solutions

Solution 2-1:

ATOM	; Atom.
(THIS IS AN ATOM)	; List.
(THIS IS AN EXPRESSION)	; List.
((A B) (C D)) 3 (3)	; Neither.
(LIST 3)	; List.
(/ (+ 3 1) (- 3 1))	; List
)(	; Neither.
((()))	; List.
(() ())	; List.
((())	; Neither.
())(	; Neither
((ABC	; Neither

Solution 2-2:

```
* (first '(p h w))
P

* (rest '(b k p h))
(K P H)

* (first '((a b) (c d)))
(A B)

* (rest '((a b) (c d)))
((C D))

* (first (rest '((a b) (c d))))
(C D)

* (rest (first '((a b) (c d))))
(B)

* (rest (first (rest '((a b) (c d)))))
(D)

* (first (rest (first '((a b) (c d)))))
B
```

Solution 2-3:

```
* (first (rest (first (rest '((a b) (c d) (e f))))))
D

* (first (first (rest (rest '((a b) (c d) (e f))))))
E

* (first (first (rest '(rest ((a b) (c d) (e f))))))
(A B)

* (first (first '(rest (rest ((a b) (c d) (e f))))))
ERROR

* (first '(first (rest (rest ((a b) (c d) (e f))))))
FIRST

* '(first (first (rest (rest ((a b) (c d) (e f))))))
(FIRST (FIRST (REST (REST ((A B) (C D) (E F))))))
```

Solution 2-4:

```
(first (rest (rest '(apple orange pear grapefruit))))
(first (first (rest '((apple orange) (pear grapefruit)))))
(first
  (first
    (rest
      (rest
        (first
          '(((apple) (orange) (pear) (grapefruit)))))))))
(first
  (first
    (first
      (rest
        (rest
          '(apple (orange) ((pear)) (((grapefruit)))))))))
(first
  (first
    (rest
      (rest
        '((((apple))) ((orange)) (pear) grapefruit)))))
(first (rest (first '((((apple) orange) pear) grapefruit))))
```

Solution 2-5:

```
* (append '(a b c) '( ))
(A B C)
* (list '(a b c) '( ))
((A B C) NIL)
* (cons '(a b c) '( ))
((A B C))
```

Solution 2-6:

```
* (setf tools (list 'hammer 'screwdriver))
(HAMMER SCREWDRIVER)

* (cons 'pliers tools)
(PLIERS HAMMER SCREWDRIVER)

* tools
(HAMMER SCREWDRIVER)

* (setf tools (cons 'pliers tools))
(PLIERS HAMMER SCREWDRIVER)

* tools
(PLIERS HAMMER SCREWDRIVER)

* (append '(saw wrench) tools)
(SAW WRENCH PLIERS HAMMER SCREWDRIVER)
```

```
* tools
(PLIERS HAMMER SCREWDRIVER)
* (setf tools (append '(saw wrench) tools))
(SAW WRENCH PLIERS HAMMER SCREWDRIVER)
* tools
(SAW WRENCH PLIERS HAMMER SCREWDRIVER)
```

Solution 2-7:

```
* (cons (first nil) (rest nil))
(NIL)
```

Solution 2-8:

```
* (length '(plato socrates aristotle))
3
* (length '((plato) (socrates) (aristotle)))
3
* (length '((plato socrates aristotle)))
1
* (reverse '(plato socrates aristotle))
(ARISTOTLE SOCRATES PLATO)
* (reverse '((plato) (socrates) (aristotle)))
((ARISTOTLE) (SOCRATES) (PLATO))
* (reverse '((plato socrates aristotle)))
((PLATO SOCRATES ARISTOTLE))
```

Solution 2-9:

```
* (length '((car chevrolet) (drink coke) (cereal wheaties)))
3
* (reverse '((car chevrolet) (drink coke) (cereal wheaties)))
((CEREAL WHEATIES) (DRINK COKE) (CAR CHEVROLET))
* (append '((car chevrolet) (drink coke))
          (reverse '((car chevrolet) (drink coke))))
((CAR CHEVROLET) (DRINK COKE) (DRINK COKE) (CAR CHEVROLET))
```

Solution 2-10:

```
* (/ (+ 3 1) (- 3 1))
2
* (* (MAX 3 4 5) (MIN 3 4 5))
15
* (MIN (MAX 3 1 4) (MAX 2 7 1))
4
```

**Solutions for
Chapter 3**

Solution 3-1:

```
(defun exchange (pair)
  (list (second pair) (first pair)))      ;Reverse first two elements.
```

To see how EXCHANGE works, suppose the value of SINNERS is (ADAM EVE). Then to evaluate (EXCHANGE SINNERS), the first thing LISP does is evaluate the argument, SINNERS. The value of SINNERS is bound to PAIR while EX-CHANGE is doing its job. Consequently, (SECOND PAIR) is EVE, (FIRST PAIR) is ADAM, and (LIST (SECOND PAIR) (FIRST PAIR)) is (EVE ADAM).

Solution 3-2:

```
(defun construct (front back) (cons front back))
```

Solution 3-3:

```
(defun rotate-left (l) (append (rest l) (list (first l))))
```

Solution 3-4:

```
(defun rotate-right (l) (append (last l) (butlast l)))
```

Solution 3-5: Both of the following work:

```
(defun palindrome (l)
  (append l (reverse l)))
(defun palindrome (l)
  (append (reverse l) l))
```

Solution 3-6:

```
(defun f-to-c (f)
  (- (/ (* (+ f 40) 5) 9) 40))
(defun c-to-f (c)
  (- (/ (* (+ c 40) 9) 5) 40))
```

**Solutions for
Chapter 4**

Solution 4-1:

```
(defun divisible-by-three (n)
  (zerop (rem n 3)))
```

Solution 4-2:

```
(defun palindromep (l)
  (equal l (reverse l)))
```

Solution 4-3:

```
(defun rightp (hypotenuse side1 side2)
  (< (abs (- (expt hypotenuse 2)
             (expt side1 2)
             (expt side2 2)))
     (* .02 (expt hypotenuse 2)))))
```

Solution 4-4:

```
* (and (listp pi)
       (setf result 'set-in-first-and))
NIL                          ;Because PI is not a list.

* result
ERROR                        ;Because RESULT has no value—
                             ;The second AND form was not evaluated.

* (and (numberp pi)
       (setf result 'set-in-second-and))
SET-IN-SECOND-AND            ;Because PI is a number.
* result
SET-IN-SECOND-AND            ;Because RESULT now has a value—
                             ;The second AND form was evaluated.
```

Solution 4-5:

```
(abs x)  ≡  (if (minusp x) (- x) x)

(min a b)  ≡  (if (< a b) a b)

(max a b)  ≡  (if (> a b) a b)
```

Solution 4-6:

```
(not u) ≡ (cond (u nil) (t t))

(or x y z)  ≡  (cond (x) (y) (t z))

(and a b c)  ≡  (cond ((not a) nil) ((not b) nil) (t c))
```

Solution 4-7:

```
(defun check-temperature (x)
  (cond ((> x 100) 'ridiculously-hot)
        ((< x 0) 'ridiculously-cold)
        (t 'ok)))
```

**Solutions for
Chapter 5**

Solution 5-1:

```
(defun skip-first-n (n l)
  (if (zerop n)
      l
      (skip-first-n (- n 1) (rest l))))
```

Solution 5-2:

```
(defun keep-first-n (n l)
  (if (zerop n)
      nil
      (cons (first l) (keep-first-n (- n 1) (rest l)))))
```

Solution 5-3:

```
(defun keep-first-n-cleverly (l n)
  (keep-first-n-cleverly-aux l n nil))
```

```
(defun keep-first-n-cleverly-aux (l n result)
  (if (zerop n)
      (reverse result)
      (keep-first-n-cleverly-aux (rest l)
                                 (- n 1)
                                 (cons (first l) result))))
```

Solution 5-4:

```
(defun add (x y)
  (if (zerop y)
      x
      (add (1+ x) (1- y))))
```

Note that ADD would not be tail recursive if the last line were written as
(1+ (ADD X (1- Y))). Also note that the following solution is more efficient
whenever the value of the second argument is larger than the value of the
first:

```
(defun add (x y)
  (if (> y x)
      (add y x)
      (if (zerop y)
          x
          (add (1+ x) (1- y)))))
```

Solution 5-5:

```
(defun tower-of-hanoi (disks)
  (if (endp disks)
      0                                      ;No disks to move.
      (+ (tower-of-hanoi (rest disks))       ;Store all but the bottom disk.
         1                                   ;Move the bottom disk.
         (tower-of-hanoi (rest disks)))))    ;Move the stored disks again.
```

If there are no disks to move, TOWER-OF-HANOI returns 0 immediately. Otherwise, TOWER-OF-HANOI adds three numbers together: the number of moves to move all but one disk from the source pin to the spare pin; plus one for the move of the bottom disk from the source pin to the destination pin; plus the number of moves to move the temporarily stored disks from the spare pin to the destination pin. Of course the following singly-recursive version is much more efficient:

```
(defun tower-of-hanoi (disks)
  (if (endp disks)
      0
      (+ 1 (* 2 (tower-of-hanoi (rest disks))))))
```

Solution 5-6: MYSTERY computes the depth to which a given expression is nested. Here is an example:

```
* (mystery '(((shallow part)) ((((deep part)))))
5
```

Solution 5-7: STRANGE returns a copy of the expression it is given.

Solution 5-8:

```
(defun presentp (item s)
  (cond ((eql s item) t)
        ((null s) nil)
        ((atom s) nil)
        (t (or (presentp item (first s))
               (presentp item (rest s))))))
```

Note that the line ((NULL S) NIL) is not really necessary because the following line, ((ATOM S) NIL) would catch all empty lists anyway. However, ((NULL S) NIL) is included to make the procedure more transparent.

Solution 5-9:

```
(defun squash (s)
  (cond ((null s) nil)
        ((atom s) (list s))
        (t (append (squash (first s))
                   (squash (rest s))))))
```

Solution 5-10:

```
(defun fibonacci (n)
  (round (/ (- (expt (/ (+ 1 (sqrt 5)) 2) (+ n 1))
              (expt (/ (- 1 (sqrt 5)) 2) (+ n 1)))
           (sqrt 5))))
```

The result of the inner computation is a floating-point number. We used ROUND to turn the result into an integer. Actually, one of the two terms in the difference is always much smaller than the other and so can be omitted safely if we are going to perform a rounding operation in the end anyway. Also, some efficiency could be gained here by computing the square root of 5 just once using LET to hold on to its value.

Solution 5-11:

```
(defun punctuate (l &optional (mark 'period))
  (append l (list mark)))
```

Solution 5-12:

```
(defun fibonacci (n &optional
                    (i 1)
                    (previous-month 1)
                    (this-month 1))
  (if (= n i)                              ;Terminating condition.
      this-month
      (fibonacci n
                 (+ 1 i)                   ;Count up until i = n.
                 this-month
                 (+ this-month previous-month))))
```

Solution 5-13:

```
(defun tail-recursive-expt (m n &optional (product 1))
  (if (zerop n)
      product
      (tail-recursive-expt m
                           (- n 1)
                           (* m product))))
```

Solution 5-14:

```
(defun tail-recursive-reverse (l &optional result)
  (if (endp l)
      result
      (tail-recursive-reverse (rest l)
                              (cons (first l) result))))
```

Solution 5-15:

```
(defun clever-count-atoms (l &optional (count 0))
  (cond ((null l) count)                    ;Return accumulated count.
        ((atom l) (+ count 1))              ;Return count plus one.
        (t (clever-count-atoms
             (rest l)
             (clever-count-atoms (first l) count)))))) ;Count so far.
```

Note that this procedure is *not* tail recursive because CLEVER-COUNT-ATOMS is invoked a second time, after the inner call to CLEVER-COUNT-ATOMS returns. So (REST L), among other things, has to be remembered while the inner recursive form is evaluated. No call to CLEVER-COUNT-ATOMS can just call itself and die—each needs to call itself a second time using the result obtained from the first call to itself.

Solution 5-16:

```
(defun user-defined-list (&rest l) l)
```

Solution 5-17:

```
(defun user-defined-nthcdr (n l)
  (if (zerop n)
      l
      (user-defined-nthcdr (- n 1) (rest l))))
```

Solution 5-18:

```
(defun user-defined-last (l)
  (if (endp (rest l))
      l
      (user-defined-last (rest l))))
```

**Solutions for
Chapter 6**

Solution 6-1:

```
(defun find-book-by-title-words (title-words books)
  (cond ((endp books) nil)
        ((subsetp title-words (book-title (first books)))
         (first books))
        (t (find-book-by-title-words title-words (rest books)))))
```

**Solutions for
Chapter 7**

Solution 7-1:

```
(defun dotimes-factorial (n)
  (let ((result 1))
    (dotimes (count n result)
      (setf result (* (+ 1 count) result)))))
```

Note that this version of DOTIMES-FACTORIAL is somewhat inefficient because
we have to add one to COUNT each time the body of the DOTIMES form is
evaluated. If we did not do this, N would range from 0 to $n - 1$ rather than
from 1 to n.

Solution 7-2:

```
(defun count-outlyers-with-count-if (list-of-elements)
  (count-if #'(lambda (element) (or (> element boiling)
                                    (< element freezing)))
            list-of-elements))
```

Solution 7-3:

```
(defun list-outlyers (list-of-elements)
  (let ((outlyers nil))                     ;Initialize result.
    (dolist (element list-of-elements       ;Establish DOLIST parameter.
                     outlyers)              ;Return form.
      (when (or (> element boiling)         ;Test element against high.
                (< element freezing))       ;Test element against low.
        (setf outlyers                      ;Add element to the result.
              (cons element outlyers))))))   ;Build result.
```

Solution 7-4:

```
(defun list-outlyer-counts (list-of-elements)
  (let ((count-above 0)                          ;Initialize count parameter.
        (count-below 0))                         ;Initialize count parameter.
    (dolist (element list-of-elements            ;Establish DOLIST parameter.
                     (list count-below count-above))   ;Return form.
      (cond ((> element boiling)                 ;Test element against high.
             (setf count-above                   ;Increment COUNT-ABOVE.
                   (+ count-above 1)))
            ((< element freezing)                ;Test element against low.
             (setf count-below                   ;Increment COUNT-BELOW.
                   (+ count-below 1)))))))
```

Solution 7-5:

```
(defun dolist-member (item initial-list)
  (dolist (l initial-list)                 ;Step through all elements.
    (when (eql item l)
      (return t))))
```

Solution 7-6:

```
(defun dolist-reverse (initial-list)
  (let ((result nil))
    (dolist (l initial-list result)        ;Step through all elements.
      (setf result (cons l result)))))      ;Build result using CONS.
```

Solution 7-7:

```
(defun do-factorial (n)
  (do ((result 1 (* n result))             ;Initialize and reset.
       (n n (- n 1)))                       ;Initialize and reset.
      ((zerop n) result)))                  ;Test and return.
```

Solution 7-8:

```
(defun do-member (item initial-list)
  (do ((l initial-list (rest l)))   ;Step through all elements.
      ((or (endp l)                  ;List exhausted?
           (eql item (first l)))     ;First element EQL to ITEM?
       l)))                          ;Return L, which may be NIL.
```

Solution 7-9:

```
(defun do-reverse (initial-list)
  (do ((l initial-list (rest l))                    ;Step through elements.
       (result nil (cons (first l) result)))        ;Build result.
      ((endp l) result)))                            ;Terminate.
```

Solutions for Chapter 9

Solution 9-1:

```
(defun tower-of-hanoi (disks from to spare)
  (unless (endp disks)
    (tower-of-hanoi (rest disks) from spare to)
    (format t "~%Move ~a from ~a to ~a." (first disks) from to)
    (tower-of-hanoi (rest disks) spare to from)))
```

Note that the placement of the FORMAT form between the two recursive calls to TOWER-OF-HANOI is important because the instruction to move the bottom disk must be given after the instructions for moving all but the bottom disk to the spare pin. Similarly, the instruction to move the bottom disk must be given before the instructions for moving the disks back from the spare pin to the destination pin.

Solution 9-2:

```
* (with-open-file (patient-stream "/phw/lisp3/patients.lsp"
                                  :direction :input)
    (do ((patient (read patient-stream nil 'eof)
                  (read patient-stream nil 'eof)))
        ((eq patient 'eof))
      (print patient)))
```

Solution 9-3: Data base files are often large to huge. Under such conditions, it is better to read individual descriptions from a file, rather than forming a long list of descriptions that would consume too much random-access memory.

Solution 9-4:

```
(with-open-file (patient-stream "/phw/lisp3/patients.lsp"
                                :direction :input)
  (with-open-file (nausea-stream "/phw/lisp3/nausea.lsp"
                                 :direction :output)
    (do ((patient-description (read patient-stream nil)
                              (read patient-stream nil))
         (n 1 (+ 1 n)))
        ((not patient-description))
      (format nausea-stream
              "~%Patient ~a is ~a."
              n
              (if (nauseated-p patient-description)
                  "nauseous"
                  "not nauseous")))))
NIL
```

Solution 9-5:

```
(defun echo1 ()
  (loop (print (read))))

(defun echo2 ()
  (loop (print (eval (read)))))
```

Solutions for Chapter 11

Solution 11-1:

```
(defun grandfather (x)
  (when (get x 'father)
    (get (get x 'father) 'father)))
```

The following, more efficient solution binds a LET parameter to the value returned by GET:

```
(defun grandfather (x)
  (let ((father (get x 'father)))
    (when father
      (get father 'father))))
```

Solution 11-2:

```
(defun adam (x)
  (if (get x 'father)
      (adam (get x 'father))
      x))
```

Solution 11-3:

```
(defun ancestors (x)
  (when x
    (cons x (append (ancestors (get x 'father))
                    (ancestors (get x 'mother))))))
```

Solution 11-4:

```
(defun connect (a b)
  (let ((a-neighbors (get a 'neighbors))
        (b-neighbors (get b 'neighbors))
        (result nil))
    (unless (member b a-neighbors)
      (setf (get a 'neighbors) (cons b a-neighbors))
      (setf result t))
    (unless (member a b-neighbors)
      (setf (get b 'neighbors) (cons a b-neighbors))
      (setf result t))
    result))
```

Solution 11-5:

```
(defun distance (city-1 city-2)
  (let ((p1 (get city-1 'position))
        (p2 (get city-2 'position)))
    (sqrt (+ (expt (- (first p1) (first p2)) 2)
             (expt (- (second p1) (second p2)) 2)))))
```

Solution 11-6: The following solution works, but inefficiently, inasmuch as it looks at the white squares, which cannot hold pieces:

```
(defun static-value (board)
  (let ((result 0))
    (dotimes (m 8 result)
      (dotimes (n 8)
        (cond ((eq 'white (aref board m n))
               (setf result (+ 1 result)))
              ((eq 'black (aref board m n))
               (setf result (- result 1)))
              ((eq 'white-king (aref board m n))
               (setf result (+ result 2)))
              ((eq 'black-king (aref board m n))
               (setf result (- result 2)))))))))
```

How could you improve the efficiency of the procedure?

Solutions for Chapter 12

Solution 12-1:

```
(defmacro put (symbol value property)
  `(setf (get ,symbol ,value) ,property))
```

Solution 12-2:

```
(defmacro getq (symbol property)
  `(get ',symbol ,property))
```

```
(defmacro putq (symbol property value)
  `(setf (get ',symbol ,property) ,value))
```

Solution 12-3:

```
(defmacro when-nil (trigger result)
  `(when (not ,trigger) ,result))
```

Solution 12-4:

```
(defmacro letq (argument-list &rest body)
  `(let ,(mapcar #'(lambda (variable-description)
                     (list (first variable-description)
                           (cons 'quote
                                 (rest variable-description))))
                 argument-list)
     ,@body))
```

Solution 12-5:

```
(defmacro define (name-and-parameters &rest body)
  `(defun ,(first name-and-parameters) ,(rest name-and-parameters)
    ,@body))
```

Solution 12-6:

```
(defun punctuate (l &rest marks)
  (append l marks))
```

Solution 12-7:

```
(defmacro punctuate-macro (l &rest marks)
  `(append ,l ',marks))
```

Solutions for Chapter 13

Solution 13-1:

```
(defstruct rock
  (color 'gray)
  (size 'pebble)
  (worth 'nothing))
```

Solution 13-2:

```
(setf high-hopes (make-rock :color 'gold :worth 'high))
```

Solution 13-3:

```
(setf (rock-worth high-hopes) 'nothing)
```

Field	Value	How it Got There
Color	Gold	Supplied in MAKE-ROCK form.
Size	Pebble	Supplied in DEFSTRUCT form.
Worth	Nothing	Supplied in SETF form.

Solution 13-4:

```
(defstruct stud
  (size '2x4)
  (length 8)
  (strength 'medium))
(defstruct (oak-stud (:include stud (strength 'high))))
```

Solutions for Chapter 14

Solution 14-1:

```
(defmethod process ((friend philosopher-friend)
                    (article computer-article)))
```

Solution 14-2:

```
(defclass music-article (article) ())

(defmethod process ((friend friend) (article music-article))
  (print-notification article friend))
```

Solution 14-3: The class precedence list is as follows:

```
political-computer-article          ;Split
political-article                   ;Leftmost superclass.
computer-article                    ;Rightmost superclass.
article                             ;Join
standard-object                     ;Implicit superclass.
t                                   ;Implicit superclass.
```

No reminder is printed:

```
* (process
    (make-instance 'hacker-friend :name 'test-friend)
    (make-instance 'political-computer-article
                   :title "Political Computer Article Test"))
NIL
```

Solution 14-4: The reason notifications are still sent is that the first argument determines method precedence when there is more than one applicable method. When the PROCESS generic function is applied to an entrepreneur friend and to the special-case article, one of the applicable methods is the one specialized to entrepreneur friends and business articles. This method takes precedence over the new one because its first parameter is more specialized.

Solutions for Chapter 15

Solution 15-1:

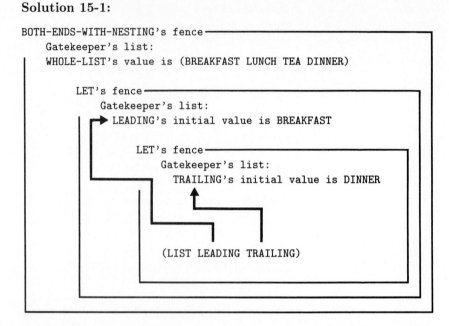

```
BOTH-ENDS-WITH-NESTING's fence
    Gatekeeper's list:
    WHOLE-LIST's value is (BREAKFAST LUNCH TEA DINNER)

        LET's fence
            Gatekeeper's list:
            LEADING's initial value is BREAKFAST

                LET's fence
                    Gatekeeper's list:
                    TRAILING's initial value is DINNER

                (LIST LEADING TRAILING)
```

Solution 15-2: LISP will complain about WHOLE-LIST, saying that WHOLE-LIST is an unbound variable in FRONT-END. The desired value is isolated from FRONT-END by the fence surrounding BOTH-ENDS:

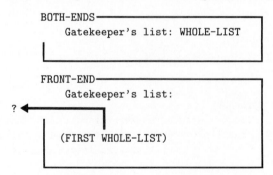

```
BOTH-ENDS
    Gatekeeper's list: WHOLE-LIST


FRONT-END
    Gatekeeper's list:

?

    (FIRST WHOLE-LIST)
```

Solutions for Chapter 17

Solution 17-1:

```
(defmacro enqueue (item queue)
  `(progn (if ,queue
              (setf (rest (last ,queue)) (list ,item))
              (setf ,queue (list ,item)))
          ,queue))
```

```
(defmacro dequeue (queue)
  `(let ((result (first ,queue)))
     (setf ,queue (rest ,queue))
     result))
```

Solution 17-2: Although NCONC replaces only one pointer in the final box representing its first argument, it must first get to that final box by following pointers. As the list grows long, chasing pointers in each recursive call becomes a severe burden.

Solution 17-3:

```
(defun user-defined-nreverse (l &optional reversed-list)
  (if (endp l)
      reversed-list
      (let ((remaining-elements (rest l)))
        (setf (rest l) reversed-list)
        (user-defined-nreverse remaining-elements
                               l)))))
```

Solutions for Chapter 18

Solution 18-1:

```
(defun micro-read-eval-print ()
  (loop
    (format t "~&Micro > ")
    (print (micro-eval (read)))))
```

Solution 18-2:

```
(defun micro-eval (form &optional environment)
  (if (atom form)
      ...
      (case (first form)
        ...
        (m-defun (setf (get (second form) 'm-procedure)
                       `(m-lambda ,(third form) ,(fourth form)))
                 (second form))
        (t ...))))
```

Solution 18-3:

```
(defun micro-eval (form &optional environment)
  (if (atom form)
      ...
      (case (first form)
        ...
        (m-setq (setf (second (assoc (second form) environment))
                      (micro-eval (third form) environment)))
        ...)))
```

Solution 18-4:

```
(setf (get 'm-toggle 'm-procedure)
      (micro-eval
        '((m-lambda (x)
            (m-function
              (m-lambda () (m-setq x (m-not x)))))
          t)))
```

Solutions for Chapter 19

Solution 19-1:

```
(defun depth-first (start finish)
  (do ((queue (list (list start))          ;Initial queue.
              (append (extend (first queue)) ;New paths in front.
                      (rest queue))))        ;Skip extended path.
      ((endp queue) nil)                     ;Queue empty?
    (when (eq finish (first (first queue)))  ;Finish found?
      (return (reverse (first queue))))))    ;Return path, if any.
```

Solution 19-2: Recursive calling schemes lend themselves to perspicuous implementations of depth-first search procedures:

```
(defun depth-first (start finish &optional path)
  (if (eq finish (first path))              ;Finish found?
      (reverse path)                        ;Return path, if any.
      (let ((neighbors (get (first path) 'neighbors)))
        (dolist (neighbor neighbors)        ;Try each neighbor.
          (unless (member neighbor path)    ;Avoid circularity.
            (let ((result (depth-first start ;Recursive call.
                                       finish
                                       (cons neighbor path))))
              (when result (return result)))))))) ;Stop.
```

(This solution may appear to be more complex than the solution of the previous problem. Remember though that there much of the work is done

by EXTEND.) Note how the bindings of PATH on successive recursive calls of
DEPTH-FIRST correspond to the partial paths that are stored in the queue
in our other implementation. Returning from a recursive call restores the
previous binding of PATH, which is shorter by one node than the current
binding. A new node is chosen then, if one is available, to extend the
partial path.

Solution 19-3:

```
(defun best-first (start finish &optional
                                  (queue (list (list start))))
  (cond ((endp queue) nil)                          ;Queue empty?
        ((eq finish (first (first queue)))          ;Finish found?
         (reverse (first queue)))                   ;Return path.
        (t (best-first                              ;Try again.
            start
            finish
            (merge 'list
                   (sort (extend (first queue))
                         #'(lambda (p1 p2) (closerp p1 p2 finish)))
                   (rest queue)
                   #'(lambda (p1 p2) (closerp p1 p2 finish)))
            )))))
```

Solution 19-4:

```
(defun hill-climb (start finish &optional
                                  (queue (list (list start))))
  (cond ((endp queue) nil)                          ;Queue empty?
        ((eq finish (first (first queue)))          ;Finish found?
         (reverse (first queue)))                   ;Return path.
        (t (hill-climb                              ;Try again.
            start
            finish
            (append (sort (extend (first queue))
                          #'(lambda (p1 p2)
                              (closerp p1 p2 finish)))
                    (rest queue))))))
```

Solution 19-5:

```
(defun path-length (path)
  (if (endp (rest path))
      0
      (+ (straight-line-distance (first path) (second path))
         (path-length (rest path)))))
```

```
(defun shorterp (path-1 path-2)
  (< (path-length path-1) (path-length path-2)))

(defun branch-and-bound (start finish &optional
                                      (queue (list (list start))))
  (cond ((endp queue) nil)                           ;Queue empty?
        ((eq finish (first (first queue)))           ;Finish found?
         (reverse (first queue)))                    ;Return path.
        (t (branch-and-bound                         ;Try again.
             start
             finish
             (sort (append (extend (first queue))
                           (rest queue))
                   #'shorterp)))))
```

Solution 19-6:

```
(defun beam (start finish width &optional
                              (queue (list (list start))))
  ;;Trim queue to the required width:
  (setf queue (butlast queue (max (- (length queue) width) 0)))
  (cond ((endp queue) nil)                           ;Queue empty?
        ((eq finish (first (first queue)))           ;Finish found?
         (reverse (first queue)))                    ;Return path.
        (t (beam start                               ;Try again.
                 finish
                 width
                 (sort
                   ;;Extend all partial paths:
                   (apply #'append (mapcar #'extend queue))
                   ;;Sort by distance to final position:
                   #'(lambda (p1 p2) (closerp p1 p2 finish)))))))
```

Solution 19-7:

```
(defun all-paths (start &optional (queue (list (list start))))
  (cond ((endp (extend (first queue)))
         (mapcar #'reverse queue))
        (t (all-paths
             start
             ;;Move incomplete paths to the front:
             (sort (append (extend (first queue)) (rest queue))
                   #'first-path-incomplete-p)))))
```

```
(defun extend (path)
  (mapcar #'(lambda (new-node) (cons new-node path))
          (remove-if #'(lambda (successor) (member successor path))
                     (get (first path) 'successors))))
```

Solution 19-8:

```
(defun time-consumed (path)
  (if (endp path)
      0
      (+ (get (first path) 'time-consumed)
         (time-consumed (rest path)))))

(defun longerp (path-1 path-2)
  (> (time-consumed path-1)
     (time-consumed path-2)))

(defun critical-path (start &optional (queue (list (list start))))
  (cond ((endp (extend (first queue)))
         (reverse (first (sort queue #'longerp))))
        (t (critical-path
             start
             (sort (append (extend (first queue)) (rest queue))
                   #'first-path-incomplete-p)))))
```

Solution 19-9:

```
(defun move-best-to-front (queue predicate)
  (if (endp queue)
      nil
      (let ((result (first queue)))
        (dolist (next (rest queue)
                      (cons result                  ;Return form.
                            (remove result
                                    queue
                                    :test #'equal)))
          (when (funcall predicate next result)
            (setf result next))))))
```

Solution 19-10:

```
(defun transfer (x y a b c)          ;Current contents are X & Y.
  (cond ((= x c)          ;Right amount in crock A.
         (format t "~%I can produce ~a units in A." c)
         nil)
        ((= y c)          ;Right amount in crock B.
         (format t "~%I can produce ~a units in B." c)
         nil)
        ;;If crock A is full, empty it:
        ((= x a) (cons '(empty a) (transfer 0 y a b c)))
        ;;If crock B is empty, fill it:
        ((= y 0) (cons '(fill b) (transfer x b a b c)))
        ;;Will what is in B fit into A?
        ;;If yes, empty B into A:
        ((> (- a x) y) (cons '(empty b into a)
                             (transfer (+ x y) 0 a b c)))
        ;;Otherwise, fill A from B:
        (t (cons '(fill a from b)
                 (transfer a (- y (- a x)) a b c)))))
```

Solution 19-11:

```
(defun water-crock (a b c)
  (cond ((and (> c a) (> c b))
         (format t "~%~a is too large." c))
        ((not (zerop (rem c (gcd a b))))
         (format t "~%Sorry, I cannot produce ~a units." c))
        (t (transfer 0 0 a b c))))
```

Solution 19-12:

```
(defun print-board (board)
  (format t "~%*")                        ;Upper left *.
  (print-horizontal-border board)         ;Upper border.
  (format t "*")                          ;Upper right *.
  (dolist (queen-coordinates board)
    (format t "~%|")                      ;Left border.
    (dotimes (column (length board))
      (if (= column (second queen-coordinates))
          (format t " Q")                 ;Occupied.
          (format t " .")))               ;Not occupied.
    (format t " |"))                      ;Right border.
  (format t "~%*")                        ;Lower left *.
  (print-horizontal-border board)         ;Lower border.
  (format t "*"))                         ;Lower right *.
```

```
(defun print-horizontal-border (board)
  (dotimes (n (+ 1 (* 2 (length board))))
    (format t "-")))
```

Solution 19-13: Starting at row 0, QUEEN attempts to place a queen in column 0. After placing the first queen, it does not make sense to place another queen in the same row, so QUEEN shifts its attention to the next row looking for a safe square. This continues until all queens are placed on the board:

```
(defun queen (size &optional (board nil) (n 0) (m 0))
  (unless (= m size)
    ;;Check for conflict in current row and column:
    (unless (conflict n m board)
      (if (= (+ 1 n) size)
          ;;If all queens placed, print solution:
          (print-board (reverse (cons (list n m) board)))
          ;;Otherwise, proceed to next row:
          (queen size (cons (list n m) board) (+ 1 n) 0)))
    ;;In any case, try with another column:
    (queen size board n (+ 1 m))))
```

The number of solutions increases rapidly with the size of the board, so prepare to be patient if you try QUEEN with large board sizes. There are 92 solutions for the full 8 × 8 chess board; here is the first one produced:

```
* (queen 8)
*-----------------*
| Q . . . . . . . |
| . . . . Q . . . |
| . . . . . . . Q |
| . . . . . Q . . |
| . . Q . . . . . |
| . . . . . . Q . |
| . Q . . . . . . |
| . . . Q . . . . |
*-----------------*

.
.
.
```

Solution 20-1: Like simulation, our forgetting solution propagates from
events to tasks and from tasks to events:

```
(defun forget-event (event)
  (setf (event-time event) 'unknown)
  (dolist (output-task (event-output-tasks event))
    (forget-task output-task)))

(defun forget-task (task)
  (forget-event (task-output-event task)))

(defun simulate (starting-event time)
  (forget-event starting-event)                    ;New line.
  (setf *event-sequence* nil)
  (simulate-event time starting-event)
  (loop
    (if (endp *event-sequence*)
        (return 'done)
        (eval (pop *event-sequence*)))))
```

Solution 20-2:

```
(defun revise-task-duration (task new-duration)
  (setf (task-duration task) new-duration)
  (forget-event (task-output-event task))
  (setf *event-sequence* nil)
  (simulate-task task)
  (loop
    (if (endp *event-sequence*)
        (return 'done)
      (eval (pop *event-sequence*)))))
```

Solution 20-3: ADD-TO-EVENT-SEQUENCE embeds its form argument in a
lexical closure to preserve access to bindings for that form's variables. Note
that other information is included, along with the lexical closure, so that
the proper order can be maintained in *EVENT-SEQUENCE*:

```
(defmacro add-to-event-sequence (form)
  `(setf *event-sequence*
         (sort (cons (list ',(first form)
                           ,(second form)
                           #'(lambda () ,form))
                     *event-sequence*)
               #'earlier-first-p)))
```

The new arrangement of the elements of the *EVENT-SEQUENCE* list requires a slight change to SIMULATE as well:

```
(defun simulate (starting-event time)
  (setf *event-sequence* nil)
  (simulate-event time starting-event)
  (loop
    (if (endp *event-sequence*)
        (return 'done)
        (funcall                            ;EVAL replaced.
          (third                            ;THIRD added.
            (pop *event-sequence*))))))
```

Solutions for Chapter 21

Solution 21-1:

```
(defun make-block (class name width height x y)
  (make-instance class :name name
                       :width width
                       :height height
                       :position (list x y)))
```

Solution 21-2: First, the block class definitions are altered so that there is a default position. You might like to imagine that this is the position at which each block is placed by a part feeder:

```
(defclass basic-block ()
  ((name :accessor block-name :initarg :name)
   (width :accessor block-width :initarg :width)
   (height :accessor block-height :initarg :height)
   (position :accessor block-position :initform '(0 10))
   (supported-by :accessor block-supported-by :initform nil)))
```

Next, blocks are created, without positions except for the table:

```
(defvar *blocks*
  (list
   (make-instance 'table :name 'table :width 20 :height 0 :position '(0 0))
   (make-instance 'brick :name 'b1 :width 2 :height 2)
   (make-instance 'brick :name 'b2 :width 2 :height 2)
   (make-instance 'brick :name 'b3 :width 4 :height 4)
   (make-instance 'brick :name 'b4 :width 2 :height 2)
   (make-instance 'wedge :name 'w5 :width 2 :height 4)
   (make-instance 'brick :name 'b6 :width 4 :height 2)
   (make-instance 'wedge :name 'w7 :width 2 :height 2)
   (make-instance 'ball  :name 'l8 :width 2 :height 2)
  ))
```

Solution 21-7: (SETF BLOCK-POSITION) can be viewed as the two-symbol name of the generic function whose primary method adds values to slots. To add a graphic display procedure to the blocks manipulation program, define a new (SETF BLOCK-POSITION) :AFTER method that activates a display procedure instead of dealing with slots:

```
(defmethod (setf block-position)
           :after
           (new-position (object movable-block))
  <activate display procedure>)
```

Solution 21-8:

```
(defmethod get-space ((object movable-block) (support table))
  (format t "~&For space for ~a, I'll use the home position."
          (block-name object))
  (block-home-position object))
```

Solutions for Chapter 22

Solution 22-1:

```
(defun remove-specializers (parameter-list)
  (let ((accumulate nil))
    (dolist (element parameter-list (reverse accumulate))
      (if (member element lambda-list-keywords)
          (return (reverse accumulate))
          (push (if (listp element)
                    (first element)
                    element)
                accumulate)))))
```

Solution 22-2:

```
(defmacro tell-how (name &rest parameters)
  `(tell-how-aux (list ',name ,@parameters)))
(defun tell-how-aux (given-action)
  (let ((node (find-action given-action)))
    (if (not (null node))
        (cond ((node-children node)
               (format t "~&I did ~a by the following operations:"
                       given-action)
               (dolist (child (node-children node))
                 (format t "~&  ~a" (node-action child))))
              (t (format t "~&I did ~a by just doing it."
                         given-action)))
        (format t "~&I did not ~a." given-action))
    'done))
```

Solution 22-3:

```
(defmacro tell-when (name &rest parameters)
  `(tell-when-aux (list ',name ,@parameters)))
(defun tell-when-aux (given-action)
  (let ((node (find-action given-action)))
    (if (not (null node))
        (format t "~&I did it while I ~a."
                (node-action (find-top-node node)))
        (format t "~&I did not ~a." given-action))
    'done))
(defun find-top-node (node)
  (if (node-action (node-parent node))
      (find-top-node (node-parent node))
      node))
```

Solution 22-4:

```
(defun show-tree (node &optional (leader "")
                                 (addition "")
                                 (arrow ""))
  (format t "~&~a~a~a"
          leader arrow (or (node-action node) 'top-of-tree))
  (when (node-children node)
    (dolist (node (butlast (node-children node) 1))
      (show-tree node
                 (concatenate 'string leader addition)
                 "   |   "
                 "   |--> "))
    (show-tree (first (last (node-children node)))
               (concatenate 'string leader addition)
               "        "
               "   *--> ")))
```

**Solutions for
Chapter 23**

Solution 23-1:

```
(defmethod propagate-via-box ((constraint not-box))
  (let* ((i (constraint-input constraint))
         (o (constraint-output constraint))
         (li (assertion-lower-bound i))
         (ui (assertion-upper-bound i))
         (lo (assertion-lower-bound o))
         (uo (assertion-upper-bound o)))
    (propagate-via-assertion o constraint (- 1 ui) (- 1 li))
    (propagate-via-assertion i constraint (- 1 uo) (- 1 lo))))
```

Solution 23-2:

```
(defclass independent-or-box (ternary-constraint) ())
(defmethod propagate-via-box ((constraint independent-or-box))
  (let* ((a (constraint-input-a constraint))
         (b (constraint-input-b constraint))
         (o (constraint-output constraint))
         (la (assertion-lower-bound a))
         (ua (assertion-upper-bound a))
         (lb (assertion-lower-bound b))
         (ub (assertion-upper-bound b))
         (lo (assertion-lower-bound o))
         (uo (assertion-upper-bound o)))
    (propagate-via-assertion o constraint
              (+ la lb (- (* la lb)))
              (+ ua ub (- (* ua ub))))
    (propagate-via-assertion a constraint
              (if (= 1 ub) 0 (/ (- lo ub) (- 1 ub)))
              (/ (- uo lb) (- 1 lb)))
    (propagate-via-assertion b constraint
              (if (= 1 ua) 0 (/ (- lo ua) (- 1 ua)))
              (/ (- uo la) (- 1 la)))))
```

Solutions for Chapter 24

Solution 24-1:

```
(defun predicates-satisfied-p (predicates argument)
  (cond ((endp predicates) t)
        ((funcall (first predicates) argument)
         (predicates-satisfied-p (rest predicates) argument))
        (t nil)))

(defun match-variable (p d bindings)
  (if (predicates-satisfied-p (extract-predicates p) d)
      (let ((binding (find-binding p bindings)))
        (if binding
            (match (extract-value binding) d bindings)
            (add-binding p d bindings)))
      'fail))

(defun extract-predicates (p)
  (rest (rest p)))
```

Solutions for Chapter 25

Solution 25-1:

```
MAKE-SQUARE-STREAM──────────────────────────────────────
        Gatekeeper's list: N's value is 2

        Nameless procedure's fence────────────────────
            Gatekeeper's list:
```

```
MAKE-SQUARE-STREAM──────────────────────────────────────
        Gatekeeper's list: N's value is 1

        Nameless procedure's fence────────────────────
            Gatekeeper's list:
```

Solution 25-2:

```
(defmacro encapsulate (form)
  `(let ((switch nil) (result nil))
     #'(lambda ()
         (if switch
             result
             (setf switch t result ,form)))))
```

Solution 25-3:

```
(defun stream-rest (stream)
  (let ((tail (second stream)))
    (if (functionp tail)
        (setf (second stream) (expose tail))
        (second stream))))
```

Solutions for Chapter 27

Solution 27-1: First, we initialize *ASSERTIONS* and *RULES*:

```
(setf *assertions* 'empty-stream *rules* 'empty-stream)
```

Next we add assertions:

```
(remember-assertion '(parent laura robert))
(remember-assertion '(parent robert patrick))
```

```
(remember-assertion '(parent patrick sarah))
```

Finally we create the required rules:

```
(remember-rule '(family1
                  (parent (? x) (? y))
                  (ancestor (? x) (? y))))
```

```
(remember-rule '(family2
                  (parent (? x) (? y))
                  (ancestor (? y) (? z))
                  (ancestor (? x) (? z))))
```

Solution 27-2:

- Rule FAMILY1 indicates that Patrick is an ancestor of Sarah because Patrick is a parent of Sarah.

- Rule FAMILY2 indicates that Robert is an ancestor of Sarah because Robert is a parent of Patrick and Patrick is an ancestor of Sarah.

- Rule FAMILY2 indicates that Laura is an ancestor of Sarah because Laura is a parent of Robert and Robert is an ancestor of Sarah.

Evidently, rule FAMILY2 is used more than once.

Solution 27-3:

```
(defun list-variables (pattern &optional names)
  (cond ((atom pattern) names)
        ((eq '? (first pattern))
         ;;Ignore anonymous variable:
         (if (or (eq '_ (second pattern))
                 (member (second pattern) names))
             names
             (append names (rest pattern))))
        (t (list-variables (rest pattern)
                           (list-variables (first pattern)
                                           names)))))
```

Solution 27-4:

```
(defun backward-chain (&rest patterns)
  (let (...)
    (if (endp variables)
        ...
        (do (...)
            (...)
          (let (...)
            (unless (member answer displayed-answers
                            :test #'equal)
              (display-answer answer)
              (setf displayed-answers
                    (cons answer displayed-answers)))
            ;;Only change needed:
            (unless (char= #\, (read-char))
              (return 'no-more)))))))
```

Solutions for Chapter 28

Solution 28-1:

```
(defmacro define-tree (name-of-tree tree-description)
  `(defun ,name-of-tree (word-list)
     (when (and (boundp '*debug*) *debug*)
       (format t "~&~a entered with ~a."
               ',name-of-tree word-list))
     (let ((input word-list))
       (multiple-value-bind
           (result binding word-list)
           (interpret-tree ',tree-description word-list)
         (when (and (boundp '*debug*) *debug*)
           (if result
               (format t "~&~a succeeded consuming ~a."
                       ',name-of-tree
                       (butlast input (length word-list)))
               (format t "~&~a failed leaving ~a."
                       ',name-of-tree word-list)))
         (values result binding word-list)))))
```

Solution 28-2:

```
(defun interpret-branches (branches word-list a-list)
  (if (endp branches)
      (values nil nil word-list)
      (progn
        (when (and (boundp '*debug*) *debug*)
          (format t "~&Starting on  ~a." (first branches)))
        (multiple-value-bind (result binding words-left-over)
            (interpret-tree (first branches) word-list a-list)
          (when (and (boundp '*debug*) *debug*)
            (if result
                (format t "~&Succeeded on ~a." (first branches))
                (format t "~&Failed on    ~a." (first branches))))
          (if result
              (values result binding words-left-over)
              (interpret-branches (rest branches)
                                  word-list
                                  a-list))))))
```

Solution 28-3:

```
(defun interpret-tree (tree word-list &optional a-list)
  (cond ...
        ((eq '* (first tree))
         (do ((word-list word-list (rest word-list))
              (binding-list nil (cons (first word-list)
                                      binding-list)))
             ()
           (multiple-value-bind (result binding word-list)
               (interpret-tree (rest (rest tree))
                               word-list
                               (cons (list (second tree)
                                           (reverse binding-list))
                                     a-list))
             (when result (return (values result
                                          binding
                                          word-list))))
           (when (endp word-list) (return nil))))
        ...))
```

Solution 28-4:

```
(define-tree doctor-tree
  (brnchs (i am worried about * words if-end-rtn
             `(how long have you been worried about ,@words))
          (* words mother * more-words if-end-rtn
            (setf mother t)
            '(tell me more about your family))
          (* words computers * more-words if-end-rtn
            '(do machines frighten you))
          (* words > bad-word * more-words if-end-rtn
            '(please do not use language like that))
          (yes if-end-rtn '(please do not be so short with me))
          (no if-end-rtn '(please do not be so short with me))
          (* words if-end-rtn
            (when (and (boundp 'mother) mother)
              (setf mother nil)
              '(earlier you spoke of your mother)))))

(define-tree bad-word
        (brnchs (darn rtn 'darn)
                (shucks rtn 'shucks)))
```

Solution 28-5:

```
(define-tree student-tree
  (brnchs (* words is * more-words if-end-rtn
             `(= ,(student words) ,(student more-words)))
          (the sum of * words and * more-words if-end-rtn
            `(+ ,(student words) ,(student more-words)))
          (the difference between * words and * more-words
              if-end-rtn `(- ,(student words)
                             ,(student more-words)))
          (* words times * more-words if-end-rtn
            `(* ,(student words) ,(student more-words)))
          (twice * words if-end-rtn
           `(* 2 ,(student words)))
          (the square of * words if-end-rtn
           `(expt ,(student words) 2))
          (* words squared if-end-rtn
           `(expt ,(student words) 2))
          (* words if-end-rtn
           (if (numberp (first words))
               (first words)
               words))))
```

**Solutions for
Chapter 29**

Solution 29-1:

```
(defun compile-elements (tree)
  (cond ...
        ((eq '* (first tree))
         `(do ((word-list word-list (rest word-list))
               (,(second tree)
                 nil
                 (append ,(second tree)
                         (list (first word-list)))))
              ()
           (multiple-value-bind (result binding word-list)
               ,(compile-elements (rest (rest tree)))
             (when result
               (return (values result binding word-list))))
           (when (endp word-list) (return nil))))
        ...))
```

**Solutions for
Chapter 30**

Solution 30-1:

```
(compile-tree multiple-objects
  (brnchs (> objects > multiple-objects
             rtn `(db-union ,objects ,multiple-objects))
          (and > objects rtn objects)
          (> objects     rtn objects)))
```

Solution 30-2:

```
(defmacro make-relation (relation &rest fields-and-records)
  `(setf ,relation
         ',fields-and-records))
```

Solution 30-3:

```
(defun db-show (relation)
  (let ((widths (db-find-field-widths relation)))
    (db-show-record widths (first relation))
    (db-show-record
        widths
        (mapcar #'(lambda (width)
                    (make-string width :initial-element #))
                widths))
    (dolist (record (rest relation) (values))
      (db-show-record widths record))))
```

```
(defun db-show-record (widths fields)
  (format t "~&|")
      (do ((widths widths (rest widths))
           (fields fields (rest fields)))
          ((endp widths))
        (format t " ~va |" (first widths) (first fields)))))

(defun db-find-field-widths (relation &aux result)
  (setf result
        (mapcar #'(lambda (field)
                    (length (format nil "~a" field)))
                (first relation)))
  (dolist (record (rest relation) result)
    (setf result
          (mapcar #'(lambda (number symbol)
                      (max number
                           (length (format nil "~a" symbol))))
                  result
                  record))))
```

Solution 30-4:

```
(defmacro db-extract-value (relation &optional over
                                              &rest projections)
  `(db-extract-value-aux ,relation ',projections))

(defun db-extract-value-aux (relation projections)
  (let ((result (db-project-aux (first relation)
                                (rest relation)
                                projections)))
    (when (rest result)
      (format t "~&I'm taking the first of more than one record."))
    (when (rest (first result))
      (format t "~&I'm taking the first of more than one field."))
    (first (first result))))
```

Solution 30-5:

```
(defmacro db-join (db1 db2 where &rest triples)
  `(cons (append (first ,db1) (first ,db2))
         (db-join-aux (first ,db1)
                      (first ,db2)
                      (rest ,db1)
                      (rest ,db2)
                      ',triples)))
```

```
(defun db-join-aux (fields1 fields2 db1 db2 triples &aux result)
  (dolist (line1 db1 (reverse result))
    (dolist (line2 db2)
      (do* ((triples triples (nthcdr 3 triples)))
           ((endp triples)
            (setf result (cons (append line1 line2) result)))
        (unless (funcall (second triples)
                         (nth (position (first triples) fields1)
                              line1)
                         (nth (position (third triples) fields2)
                              line2))
          (return))))))
```

Solution 30-6: "What suppliers sell tools that the customers need?"

Solution 30-7: "What suppliers sell hammers or wrenches?"

Solutions for Chapter 31

Solution 31-1:

```
(defun similar-magnitude (star spot)          ;Similar magnitude?
  (let ((star-m (star-magnitude star))        ;Get star's magnitude.
        (spot-m (spot-brightness spot)))      ;Get spot's brightness.
    (if (atom star-m)                         ;Check whether variable.
        (< (abs (- star-m spot-m)) 1.0)       ;No, within tolerance?
        (let ((low (first star-m))
              (high (second star-m)))
          (and (> spot-m (- low 1.0))         ;Above lowest magnitude?
               (< spot-m (+ high 1.0)))))))   ;Below highest magnitude?
```

Solution 31-2:

```
(defun map-xy-to-uv (x y trans)               ;From model to image.
  (let* ((c (transform-c trans)) (s (transform-s trans))
         (xo (transform-xo trans)) (yo (transform-yo trans))
         (xd (- x xo)) (yd (- y yo)))
    (values (+ (* c xd) (* s yd))
            (- (* c yd) (* s xd)))))
```

Here is a test case:

```
* (map-uv-to-xy 2.0 3.0
                (make-transform :c (cos 1) :s (sin 1) :xo 1 :yo 2))
-0.4438084
5.303849
* (map-xy-to-uv -0.4438084 5.303849
                (make-transform :c (cos 1) :s (sin 1) :xo 1 :yo 2))
2.0
3.0
```

Solution 31-3:

```
(defun point-match (x y xs ys)
  (let ((dx (- xs x)) (dy (- ys y)))
    (< (sqrt (+ (* dx dx) (* dy dy))) 0.1)))
```

Alternatively, we could use the function DISTANCE defined earlier:

```
(defun point-match (x y xs ys)
  (< (distance x y xs ys) 0.1))
```

Solution 31-4:

```
(defun most-distant-pairs (pairs)
  (let ((p-a) (p-b) (dmax 0))
    (do* ((pairs-a pairs (rest pairs-a))
          (pair-a (first pairs-a)))
         ((endp pairs-a))
      (do* ((pairs-b pairs-a (rest pairs-b))
            (pair-b (first pairs-b)))
           ((endp pairs-b))
        (let* ((star-a (first pair-a))
               (star-b (first pair-b))
               (d (distance-stars star-a star-b)))
          (when (> d dmax) (setf p-a pair-a p-b pair-b dmax d)))))
    (values p-a p-b)))

(defun find-transform (pairs)                 ;Get transformation.
  (if (< (length pairs) 2)                     ;Need two pairs.
      (error "Too few pairs for transformation")
      (multiple-value-bind (p-a p-b) (most-distant-pairs pairs)
        (find-transform-sub p-a p-b))))
```

Solution 31-5: We start with procedures for extracting the centroids of both the set of stars and the set of spots in PAIRS:

```
(defun centroid-stars (pairs)                 ;Work from list of pairs.
  (let ((sumx 0) (sumy 0) (sum 0))             ;Accumulators for totals.
    (dolist (pair pairs)                       ;Step through pairs.
      (let* ((star (first pair))               ;Get star in pair.
             (x (star-x star)) (y (star-y star)))
        (setf sumx (+ sumx x) sumy (+ sumy y) sum (+ sum 1))))
    (values (/ sumx sum) (/ sumy sum))))
```

```
(defun centroid-spots (pairs)              ;Work from list of pairs
  (let ((sumu 0) (sumv 0) (sum 0))         ;Accumulators for totals.
    (dolist (pair pairs)                   ;Step through pairs.
      (let* ((spot (second pair))          ;Get spot in pair.
             (u (spot-u spot)) (v (spot-v spot)))
        (setf sumu (+ sumu u) sumv (+ sumv v) sum (+ sum 1))))
    (values (/ sumu sum) (/ sumv sum))))
```

Then we write a procedure that determines the best-fit rotation given the centroids:

```
(defun find-rotation-sub (pairs xc yc uc vc)
  (let ((sums 0) (sumc 0))
    (dolist (pair pairs)
      (let* ((star (first pair)) (spot (second pair))
             (xd (- (star-x star) xc)) (yd (- (star-y star) yc))
             (ud (- (spot-u spot) uc)) (vd (- (spot-v spot) vc)))
        (setf sumc (+ sumc (+ (* xd ud) (* yd vd))))       ;Dot.
        (setf sums (+ sums (- (* yd ud) (* xd vd))))))     ;Cross.
    (normalize-c-s sumc sums)))
```

Here (x_c, y_c) is the centroid of the stars, while (u_c, v_c) is the centroid of the bright spots. Also, note that we have used the procedure NORMALIZE-C-S, defined earlier, to compute the cosine and sine of the angle of rotation from two quantities that are proportional to the cosine and the sine of this angle.

Now we are ready to recover the transformation as a whole:

```
(defun find-transform (pairs)              ;Find best-fit tranformation.
  (if (< (length pairs) 2)                 ;Need at least two pairs.
      (error "Too few pairs for transformation")
      (multiple-value-bind (xc yc)
          (centroid-stars pairs)                     ;Star centroid.
        (multiple-value-bind (uc vc)
            (centroid-spots pairs)                   ;Spot centroid.
          (multiple-value-bind (c s)
              (find-rotation-sub pairs xc yc uc vc)      ;Rotation.
            (let ((xo (- xc (- (* uc c) (* vc s))))       ;Translation.
                  (yo (- yc (+ (* uc s) (* vc c)))))
              (make-transform :c c :s s :xo xo :yo yo)))))))
```

Solution 31-6: The following computes the rotation and the error, assuming that we have at least two pairs:

```
(defun find-rotation-sub (pairs xc yc uc vc)        ;This version also
  (let ((suma 0) (sums 0) (sumc 0) (sumb 0) (sum 0)) ; computes error.
    (dolist (pair pairs)
      (let* ((star (first pair)) (spot (second pair))
             (xd (- (star-x star) xc)) (yd (- (star-y star) yc))
             (ud (- (spot-u spot) uc)) (vd (- (spot-v spot) vc)))
        (setf suma (+ suma (+ (* xd xd) (* yd yd))))   ;x² + y²
        (setf sumc (+ sumc (+ (* xd ud) (* yd vd))))   ;Dot.
        (setf sums (+ sums (- (* yd ud) (* xd vd))))   ;Cross.
        (setf sumb (+ sumb (+ (* ud ud) (* vd vd))))   ;u² + v²
        (setf sum (+ sum 1))))
    (multiple-value-bind (c s) (normalize-c-s sumc sums)
      (let ((e (sqrt (/ (- (+ suma sumb)
                           (* 2 (+ (* c sumc) (* s sums))))
                        sum))))
        (values c s e)))))
```

The procedure that finds the overall transform looks like this:

```
(defun find-transform (pairs)                        ;Best-fit tranformation,
  (if (< (length pairs) 2)                            ; and error.
      (error "Too few pairs for transformation")
      (multiple-value-bind (xc yc)
          (centroid-stars pairs)                      ;Star centroid.
        (multiple-value-bind (uc vc)
            (centroid-spots pairs)                    ;Spot centroid.
          (multiple-value-bind (c s e)
              (find-rotation-sub pairs xc yc uc vc)   ;Rotation.
            (let ((xo (- xc (- (* uc c) (* vc s))))   ;Translation.
                  (yo (- yc (+ (* uc s) (* vc c)))))
              (list (make-transform :c c :s s :xo xo :yo yo)
                    e)))))))
```

Finally, we also need to change the way we check a transformation:

```
(defun find-match-check (pairs)        ;New version uses error
  (unless (< (length pairs) 2)          ; returned by FIND-TRANSFORM.
    (let* ((tande (find-transform pairs))
           (trans (first tande)) (e (second tande)))
      (when (< e 0.1) (list pairs trans)))))
```

Solution 31-7:

```
(defun find-match-sub (pairs stars spots)     ;Modified fourth version.
  (if (endp stars)                             ;More stars to match?
      (list (find-match-check (reverse pairs)))    ;No check it.
      (let ((star (first stars))               ;First star in list.
            (matches nil))                     ;Place for matches found.
        (dolist (spot spots (reverse matches))   ;Try each spot in turn.
          (when (similar-magnitude star spot)    ;Similar brightness?
            (let ((new (list star spot)))        ;New pair to check.
              (when (distances-check new pairs)     ;Compatible?
                (let ((ans (find-match-sub (cons new pairs)
                                           (rest stars)
                                           (remove spot spots))))
                  (setf matches (append matches ans)))))))))
```

Solution 31-8: The problem with this version of FIND-MATCH-SUB is that typically numerous matches with many wild cards unmatched are generated and passed to FIND-MATCH-CHECK, before the correct, full match is generated. If the set of pairs happens to pass the test, the search is terminated. This means that typically a match containing only a small sub-set of the full set of matched pairs is returned.

In an extreme case, it can happen that a match consisting of only two stars matched to two spots is accepted. If the two stars involved have similar magnitudes, the match may be reversed, so that the computed transformation is wrong.

This is why the fifth version of FIND-MATCH-SUB developed in this chapter looks at all possible matches and then picks the one containing the largest number of matched pairs.

Solution 31-9:

```
(defun recognize-constellation (spots constellations)
  (let ((matches nil))                         ;Place for matches found.
    (dolist (constellation constellations (reverse matches))
      (let* ((stars (constellation-stars constellation))
             (ans (find-match stars spots)))
        (when ans
          (let ((trans (second ans)))
            (setf matches (cons (list constellation trans)
                                matches))))))))
```

Solution 31-10:

```
(defun recognize-constellation (spots constellations)
  (let ((matches nil))                           ;Place for matches found.
    (dolist (constellation constellations (reverse matches))
        (let* ((stars (constellation-stars constellation))
               (ans (find-match stars spots)))
          (when ans
            (let ((pairs (first ans)) (trans (second ans)))
              (setf matches (cons (list constellation trans)
                                  matches))
              (setf spots (remove-spots spots pairs)))))))))

(defun remove-spots (spots pairs)
  (remove-if #'(lambda (spot) (present-in-pair spot pairs))  spots))

(defun present-in-pair (spot pairs)
  (dolist (pair pairs)
    (when (equal spot (second pair)) (return t))))
```

Solution 31-11:

```
(defun similar-triangles (pair-a pair-b pair-c)      ;Triangles similar?
  (let* ((star-a (first pair-a)) (spot-a (second pair-a))
         (star-b (first pair-b)) (spot-b (second pair-b))
         (star-c (first pair-c)) (spot-c (second pair-c))
         (star-ab (distance-stars star-a star-b))
         (star-bc (distance-stars star-b star-c))
         (star-ca (distance-stars star-c star-a))
         (spot-ab (distance-spots spot-a spot-b))
         (spot-bc (distance-spots spot-b spot-c))
         (spot-ca (distance-spots spot-c spot-a)))
    (and (similar-ratio star-ab star-bc spot-ab spot-ab)
         (similar-ratio star-bc star-ca spot-bc spot-bc)
         (similar-ratio star-ca star-ab spot-ca spot-ca))))

(defun similar-ratio (star-d1 star-d2 spot-d1 spot-d2)
  (let ((diff (- (* star-d1 spot-d2) (* star-d2 spot-d1)))
        (norm (sqrt (* star-d1 star-d2 spot-d1 spot-d2))))
    (< (abs (/ diff norm)) 0.1)))
```

Note that we have normalized the cross-ratio by dividing by the geometric mean of the lengths, so that the tolerance in the test is independent of the length of the lines. We arbitrarily allow for a relative error in length of up to a 10%.

Solution 31-12:

```
(defun find-scale (pairs)                    ;Find best-fit scale.
  (if (< (length pairs) 2)                    ;Need at least two pairs.
      (error "Too few pairs to determine the scale")
      (multiple-value-bind (xc yc)
          (centroid-stars pairs)                   ;Star centroid.
        (multiple-value-bind (uc vc)
            (centroid-spots pairs)                   ;Spot centroid.
          (find-scale-sub pairs xc yc uc vc)))))

(defun find-scale-sub (pairs xc yc uc vc)
  (let ((sumxy 0) (sumuv 0))                   ;Sums x² + y² and u² + v².
    (dolist (pair pairs)
      (let* ((star (first pair)) (spot (second pair))
             (xd (- (star-x star) xc)) (yd (- (star-y star) yc))
             (ud (- (spot-u spot) uc)) (vd (- (spot-v spot) vc)))
        (setf sumxy (+ sumxy (+ (* xd xd) (* yd yd))))
        (setf sumuv (+ sumuv (+ (* ud ud) (* vd vd))))))
    (sqrt (/ sumxy sumuv))))
```

Solution 31-13: No change is required, because the magnitude of the sine of the angle is not affected, and the indicated procedures deal only with the magnitude of the sine of the angle, not the angle itself.

Solution 31-14: We can simply use the centers of the lines and the centers of the edges instead of the end points because the centers can be found without knowning which end is which:

```
(defun find-edge-transform (pairs)           ;Get edge transformation.
  (if (< (length pairs) 2)                    ;Need two pairs.
      (error "Too few pairs for transformation")
      (find-edge-transform-sub (first pairs) (second pairs))))

(defun find-edge-transform-sub (pair-a pair-b)       ;Minimal version.
  (let* ((line-a (first pair-a)) (edge-a (second pair-a))
         (line-b (first pair-b)) (edge-b (second pair-b))
         (xa (/ (+ (line-xs line-a) (line-xf line-a)) 2))
         (ya (/ (+ (line-ys line-a) (line-yf line-a)) 2))
         (xb (/ (+ (line-xs line-b) (line-xf line-b)) 2))
         (yb (/ (+ (line-ys line-b) (line-yf line-b)) 2))
         (ua (/ (+ (edge-us edge-a) (edge-uf edge-a)) 2))
         (va (/ (+ (edge-vs edge-a) (edge-vf edge-a)) 2))
         (ub (/ (+ (edge-us edge-b) (edge-uf edge-b)) 2))
         (vb (/ (+ (edge-vs edge-b) (edge-vf edge-b)) 2)))
    (find-transform-aux xa ya xb yb ua va ub vb)))
```

Solution 31-15:

```
(defun check-edge-pairs (pairs trans)           ;Do pairs really match?
  (dolist (pair pairs t)
    (let* ((line (first pair)) (edge (second pair))
           (xs (line-xs line)) (ys (line-ys line))
           (xf (line-xf line)) (yf (line-yf line))
           (us (edge-us edge)) (vs (edge-vs edge))
           (uf (edge-uf edge)) (vf (edge-vf edge)))
      (multiple-value-bind (xsd ysd) (map-uv-to-xy us vs trans)
        (multiple-value-bind (xfd yfd) (map-uv-to-xy uf vf trans)
          (unless (or (and (point-match xs ys xsd ysd)
                           (point-match xf yf xfd yfd))
                      (and (point-match xf yf xsd ysd)
                           (point-match xs ys xfd yfd)))
            (return nil)))))))
```

Solution 31-16: We can start by obtaining the parameters for each line in a convenient form, perhaps something like

$$a\,x + b\,y + c = 0.$$

Then we intersect the two lines using their sets of parameters, by solving two simultaneous linear equations like:

$$a_1\,x + b_1\,y + c_1 = 0,$$
$$a_2\,x + b_2\,y + c_2 = 0.$$

We use the same sub-procedures to perform this computation for edges and for lines.

```
(defun line-parameters (xs ys xf yf)           ;Form ax + by + c = 0.
  (values (- yf ys) (- xs xf) (- (* ys xf) (* xs yf))))

(defun intersect-sub (a-1 b-1 c-1 a-2 b-2 c-2)
  (let ((det (- (* a-1 b-2) (* a-2 b-1))))
    (if (zerop det) (error "Lines do not intersect")
        (let ((det-x (- (* c-1 b-2) (* c-2 b-1)))
              (det-y (- (* c-2 a-1) (* c-1 a-2))))
          (values (/ det-x det) (/ det-y det))))))

(defun intersect (xs-1 ys-1 xf-1 yf-1 xs-2 ys-2 xf-2 yf-2)
  (multiple-value-bind (a-1 b-1 c-1)
      (line-parameters xs-1 ys-1 xf-1 yf-1)
    (multiple-value-bind (a-2 b-2 c-2)
        (line-parameters xs-2 ys-2 xf-2 yf-2)
      (intersect-sub a-1 b-1 c-1 a-2 b-2 c-2))))
```

```
(defun signature (xs-1 ys-1 xf-1 yf-1 xs-2 ys-2 xf-2 yf-2)
  (multiple-value-bind (xo yo)
                       (intersect xs-1 ys-1 xf-1 yf-1
                                  xs-2 ys-2 xf-2 yf-2)
                       (values (distance xo yo xs-1 ys-1)
                               (distance xo yo xf-1 yf-1)
                               (distance xo yo xs-2 ys-2)
                               (distance xo yo xf-2 yf-2))))
(defun line-signature (line-1 line-2)
  (let ((xs-1 (line-xs line-1)) (ys-1 (line-ys line-1))
        (xf-1 (line-xf line-1)) (yf-1 (line-yf line-1))
        (xs-2 (line-xs line-2)) (ys-2 (line-ys line-2))
        (xf-2 (line-xf line-2)) (yf-2 (line-yf line-2)))
    (signature xs-1 ys-1 xf-1 yf-1 xs-2 ys-2 xf-2 yf-2)))
(defun edge-signature (edge-1 edge-2)
  (let ((us-1 (edge-us edge-1)) (vs-1 (edge-vs edge-1))
        (uf-1 (edge-uf edge-1)) (vf-1 (edge-vf edge-1))
        (us-2 (edge-us edge-2)) (vs-2 (edge-vs edge-2))
        (uf-2 (edge-uf edge-2)) (vf-2 (edge-vf edge-2)))
    (signature us-1 vs-1 uf-1 vf-1 us-2 vs-2 uf-2 vf-2)))
```

The two signatures can now be compared in FIND-EDGE-MATCH to ensure that only acceptable partial matches are pursued further.

The above method is not very satisfactory, by the way, when the two lines are almost parallel, because the location of the point of intersection will then be sensitive to small measurement errors in the positions of the end points of the lines. It is better to multiply the four distances obtained above by the magnitude of the sine of the angle between the two lines. The sine of the angle between the lines is proportional to the cross-product of the two lines, and we have already computed this in the process of finding the intersection.

Solution 31-17:

```
(defun similar-length (line edge)              ;Similar length or shorter?
  (let ((dl (line-length line)) (el (edge-length edge)))
    (< el (+ dl 0.1))))
```

The new version of SIMILAR-LENGTH accepts many more matches, and so greatly increases the number of partial matches that have to be explored. It is likely that we will have to find some way of measuring the quality of a match now, so that we can compare matches involving edge-fragments of various lengths. This is somewhat analogous to the situation we encountered when we first permitted wild-card matches. There too we had to develop a measure of the quality of the matches based on the number of pairs that were actually matched.

Note also that an edge may be broken into two (or more) pieces by obscuration. How would you modify the matching procedure to allow more than one edge fragement in the image to match a particular line in the model? How would this additional change affect the computational effort involved in finding a match?

Solutions for Chapter 32

Solution 32-1:

```
(defun pre-to-inf (l)
  (cond ((null l) nil)                              ; Easy case.
        ((atom l) l)                                ; Easy case.
        (t (list (pre-to-inf (second l))            ; Translate part.
                 (opsymbol (first l))               ; Look up symbol.
                 (pre-to-inf (third l)))))))         ; Translate rest.

(defun opsymbol (x)                                 ; Get symbol
  (case x                                           ;  given LISP primitive.
    (setf '=)
    (+ '+)
    (- '-)
    (* '*)
    (/ '/)
    (rem '\\)
    (expt '^)
    (t x)))                                         ; Unrecognized symbol
```

Solution 32-2:

```
(defun pre-to-inf (l)
  (pre-to-inf-aux l -1))                            ; Start with lowest weight.

(defun pre-to-inf-aux (l win)        ; Second arg is precedence weight.
  (cond ((null l) l)                                ; Easy case.
        ((atom l) (list l))                         ; Easy case.
        (t (let ((wout (precedence (first l))))     ; Get weight of new.
             (if (< wout win)                       ; Compare weights.
                 (list (pre-to-inf-sub l wout))     ; Parentheses.
                 (pre-to-inf-sub l wout))))))       ; No parentheses.

(defun pre-to-inf-sub (l wout)                      ; Construct infix.
  (append (pre-to-inf-aux (second l) wout)
          (list (opsymbol (first l)))
          (pre-to-inf-aux (third l) wout)))
```

```
(defun precedence (x)                           ;Find weight
  (case x                                       ; given procedure.
    (setf 0)
    (+ 1)
    (- 1)
    (* 2)
    (/ 3)
    (rem 3)
    (expt 4)
    (t 9)))                                     ;Unrecognized symbol
```

Solution 32-3: Add the following to INF-AUX,

```
(when *trace-flag* (format t "~%AE: ~a OPERATORS: ~a" ae operators))
```

and add the following to INF-ITER,

```
(when *trace-flag* (format t "~%AE: ~a  OPERANDS:  ~a" ae operands))
```

Solution 32-4: Simply replace (> ...) by (not (< ...)).

Solution 32-5: Simply insert the following after the first clause of the conditional in INF-ITER:

```
((and (not (endp ae))
      (or (not (atom (first ae)))
          (= (weight (first ae)) 9)))
 (inf-iter (cons '* ae) operators operands))
```

This procedure makes use of the fact that we chose to assign a weight of 9 to unrecognized "operators."

Solution 32-6:

```
(setf (get '= 'weight) 0)
(setf (get '+ 'weight) 1)
(setf (get '- 'weight) 1)
(setf (get '* 'weight) 2)
(setf (get '/ 'weight) 2)
(setf (get '\\ 'weight) 2)
(setf (get '^ 'weight) 3)

(setf (get '= 'opcode) 'setf)
(setf (get '+ 'opcode) '+)
(setf (get '- 'opcode) '-)
(setf (get '* 'opcode) '*)
(setf (get '/ 'opcode) '/)
(setf (get '\\ 'opcode) 'rem)
(setf (get '^ 'opcode) 'expt)
```

```
(defun weight (operator)
  (let ((weight (get operator 'weight)))
    (if (null weight) 9 weight)))          ;Unrecognized operator.

(defun opcode (operator)
  (let ((opcode (get operator 'opcode)))
    (if (null opcode) operator opcode)))   ;Unrecognized operator.
```

Solution 32-7: Note that | is used to surround atom names containing break or separator characters, so that you have to use \| as shown below:

```
(setf (get '= 'weight) 0)
(setf (get '\| 'weight) 1)
(setf (get '& 'weight) 2)
(setf (get '< 'weight) 3)
(setf (get '> 'weight) 3)
(setf (get '+ 'weight) 4)
(setf (get '- 'weight) 4)
(setf (get '* 'weight) 5)
(setf (get '/ 'weight) 5)
(setf (get '\\ 'weight) 5)
(setf (get '^ 'weight) 6)

(setf (get '= 'opcode) 'setf)
(setf (get '\| 'opcode) 'or)
(setf (get '& 'opcode) 'and)
(setf (get '< 'opcode) '<)
(setf (get '> 'opcode) '>)
(setf (get '+ 'opcode) '+)
(setf (get '- 'opcode) '-)
(setf (get '* 'opcode) '*)
(setf (get '/ 'opcode) '/)
(setf (get '\\ 'opcode) 'rem)
(setf (get '^ 'opcode) 'expt)
```

Solution 32-8:

```
(defun sparse-v-component (v n)
  (if (endp v)
      0                                          ;Easy case.
      (let ((fv (first v)))                      ;First component.
        (cond ((> (first fv) n) 0)               ;Not there.
              ((< (first fv) n)
               (sparse-v-component (rest v) n))   ;Recurse.
              (t (second fv)))))))                ;Found it.
```

Solution 32-9:

```
(defun sparse-v-plus (a b)
  (cond ((endp a) b)                                    ;Termination?
        ((endp b) a)                                    ;Termination?
        (t (let ((fa (first a)) (fb (first b)))         ;Grab components.
             (cond ((< (first fa) (first fb))
                    ;;Copy component of a.
                    (cons fa (sparse-v-plus (rest a) b)))
                   ((< (first fb) (first fa))
                    ;;Copy component of b.
                    (cons fb (sparse-v-plus a (rest b))))
                   (t (let ((sum (+ (second fa) (second fb))))
                        (if (zerop sum)
                            (sparse-v-plus (rest a) (rest b))
                            (cons (list (first fa) sum)
                                  (sparse-v-plus (rest a)
                                                 (rest b)))))))))))
```

Solution 32-10: No. They could be negative too. In fact the indices could be floating-point numbers! The only thing that matters is that they are ordered, so that the procedure can tell in which list to proceed when indices at the head of the two lists are not equal.

Solution 32-11:

```
(defun sparse-v-print (v)
  (format t "~%")
  (sparse-v-print-aux v 1))                             ;Start index 1.

(defun sparse-v-print-aux (v i)
  (unless (endp v)                                      ;Termination.
    (let ((fv (first v)))                               ;First component.
      (if (= i (first fv))                              ;Check index.
          (sparse-v-print-out (second fv) (rest v) (+ i 1))
          (sparse-v-print-out 0 v (+ i 1))))))

(defun sparse-v-print-out (out v i)
  (format t "~a " out)
  (sparse-v-print-aux v i))
```

Solution 32-12: Because of what may appear to be a superfluous extra layer of parentheses around the vectors representing the rows, it is easy to modify the procedure SPARSE-V-PLUS to add matrices instead of vectors. Simply change all calls to SPARSE-V-PLUS to SPARSE-M-PLUS, and all calls to + to SPARSE-V-PLUS! The result is as follows:

```
(defun sparse-m-plus (a b)
  (cond ((endp a) b)                          ;Termination?
        ((endp b) a)                          ;Termination?
        (t (let ((fa (first a)) (fb (first b))) ;Grab components.
             (cond ((< (first fa) (first· fb))
                    ;;Copy component from a.
                    (cons fa (sparse-m-plus (rest a) b)))
                   ((< (first fb) (first fa))
                    ;;Copy component from b.
                    (cons fb (sparse-m-plus a (rest b))))
                   (t (cons (list (first fa)   ;Copy index.
                                  (sparse-v-plus (second fa)
                                                 (second fb))) ;Add.
                            (sparse-m-plus (rest a)
                                           (rest b)))))))))  ;Recurse.
```

Solution 32-13:

```
(defun sparse-v-times-m (v m)
  (if (endp m) nil                            ;Termination?
      (let ((fm (first m)))                   ;Grab first component.
        (cons (list (first fm)                ;Copy index.
                    (sparse-dot-product v (second fm))) ;Dot-product.
              (sparse-v-times-m v (rest m)))))) ;Recurse.
```

So, for example,

```
* (sparse-v-times-m '((1 3.0) (3 -1.0) (4 2.0))
                    '((1 ((1 2.0) (4 5.0)))
                      (2 ((2 1.0) (3 3.0)))
                      (3 ((1 4.0) (2 4.0)))
                      (4 ((2 -5.0) (4 9.0)))
                      (5 ((2 7.0)))))
((1 16.0) (2 -3.0) (3 12.0) (4 18.0) (5 0))
```

Note, however, how this straightforward solution may lead to the inclusion of zero elements when the dot-product is zero. This can be remedied as follows:

```
(defun sparse-v-times-m (v m)
  (if (endp m) nil                                    ;Termination?
      (let* ((fm (first m))                            ;Grab first component.
             (dot (sparse-dot-product v (second fm)))) ;Dot-product.
        (if (zerop dot)
            (sparse-v-times-m v (rest m))             ;Recurse.
          (cons (list (first fm) dot)                 ;Include product.
                (sparse-v-times-m v (rest m)))))))     ;Recurse.
```

Solution 32-14: One way to find the transpose of a matrix is to begin by expanding the list representing the matrix into one that is more symmetrical in the row and column indices:

```
(m-expand '((1 ((2 1.2) (4 1.4)))
            (3 ((1 3.1) (5 3.5) (6 3.6)))
            (4 ((2 4.2)))))
((1 2 1.2) (1 4 1.4) (3 1 3.1) (3 5 3.5) (3 6 3.6) (4 2 4.2)))
```

This can be accomplished using:

```
(defun m-expand (l)                      ;Expand matrix.
  (if (endp l) nil                       ;Termination
      (let ((fl (first l)))              ;Extract column.
        (append (m-expand-aux (first fl) (second fl))
                (m-expand (rest l))))))    ;Recurse.

(defun m-expand-aux (i l)                ;Expand one column.
  (if (endp l) nil                       ;Termination?
      (let ((fl (first l)))              ;Extract element.
        (cons (list i (first fl) (second fl))
              (m-expand-aux i (rest l)))))) ;Recurse.
```

The procedure M-COMPRESS performs the inverse operation:

```
(defun m-compress (mat)  (m-assemble (first (first mat)) nil mat))

(defun m-assemble (n new old)
  (cond ((endp old) (list (cons n                    ;Assemble last.
                                (list (reverse new)))))
        ((= n (first (first old)))                    ;Same row?
         (m-assemble n (cons (rest (first old)) new)
                     (rest old)))                      ;Collect more.
        (t (cons (cons n (list (reverse new)))        ;Assemble row,
                 (m-assemble (first (first old))
                             nil old)))))              ; and do the rest.
```

The row and column indices can be switched around using M-ALTER-FLIP:

```
(defun m-alter-flip (l)
  (if (endp l) nil
      (let ((fl (first l)))
        (cons (list (second fl) (first fl) (third fl))
              (m-alter-flip (rest l))))))
```

Next, it is necessary to sort on the new row indices:

```
(defun m-alter-sort (mat) (m-alter-aux mat nil))
(defun m-alter-aux (old new)
  (if (endp old) new                          ;Termination?
      (m-alter-aux (rest old)                 ;Recurse after
                   (m-insert (first old) new))))   ; inserting first.
(defun m-less (x y)
  (or (< (first x) (first y))                 ;Column number less?
      (and (= (first x) (first y))
           (< (second x) (second y)))))        ;Row number less?
(defun m-insert (x lst)                       ;Insert in right place.
  (if (endp lst) (list x)
      (let ((flst (first lst)))
        (if (m-less x flst) (cons x lst)       ;Fits in here.
            (cons flst (m-insert x (rest lst)))))))   ;Recurse.
```

(Note that we could have used the built-in primitive SORT in the above.)
Finally, all of this can be put together:

```
(defun sparse-m-transpose (l)
  (m-compress (m-alter-sort (m-alter-flip (m-expand l)))))
```

Solution 32-15:

```
(defun sparse-m-times (ma mb)
  (sparse-m-transpose (sparse-m-times-aux (sparse-m-transpose ma)
                                          mb)))
(defun sparse-m-times-aux (tma mb)
  (if (endp tma) nil
      (let ((fa (first tma)))
        (cons (list (first fa)
                    (sparse-v-times-m (second fa) mb))
              (sparse-m-times-aux (rest tma) mb)))))
```

Note the similarity between SPARSE-M-TIMES-AUX and SPARSE-M-TIMES. The only real difference is that we use SPARSE-V-TIMES-M here instead of SPARSE-M-TIMES-V. Unfortunately, we cannot use SPARSE-M-TIMES directly, however, because (SPARSE-V-TIMES-M V M) is not equal to (SPARSE-M-TIMES-V M V).

Solution 32-16:

```
(defun cube-root (y)
  (if (zerop y) 0
      (if (minusp y) (- (cube-root (- y)))
          (cube-root-iter y (expt y 1/3)))))
(defun cube-root-iter (y x)  (/ (+ x x (/ y (* x x))) 3))
(defun check-cube-root (x)
  (let ((answer (cube-root x)))
    (format t "~%Cubic root of ~a is ~a and ~a**3 is ~a."
            x answer answer (expt answer 3)))
  (values))
```

Solution 32-17:

```
(defun make-poly (roots)            ;List of roots is given.
  (poly-aux (list 1                 ;Linear seed polynomial
                  (- (first roots)))) ; using first root.
            (rest roots)))          ;Rest of the roots.
```

The next procedure multiplies a polynomial represented by its coefficients by the linear term $(x - r)$, where the list of coefficients is represented by COEFF and r is the first root in the list ROOTS. The result is a new, larger list of coefficients.

```
(defun poly-aux (coeff roots)       ;Multiply a polynomial by
  (if (endp roots) coeff            ; many linear polynomials.
      (poly-aux (cons (first coeff)
                      (poly-it coeff
                               (first roots)))
                (rest roots)))))
```

In the above, a polynomial is multiplied by a single linear term. Finally, we get to the procedure that does all the work:

```
(defun poly-it (coeff root)         ;Multiply through by one
  (if (endp (rest coeff))           ; linear polynomial.
      (list (* (first coeff) (- root)))
      (cons (- (second coeff)
               (* (first coeff) root))
            (poly-it (rest coeff) root)))))
```

If we use MAKE-POLY to check the roots, we expect to get back the coefficients of the polynomial. In practice, because of limited precision of floating-point representation, we may get slightly different values. These may even have small imaginary components if any of the given roots are complex.

Solution 32-18:

```
(defun poly-value (coeff x)
  (poly-value-aux (rest coeff) x (first coeff)))

(defun poly-value-aux (coeff x val)
  (if (endp coeff) val
      (poly-value-aux (rest coeff)
                      x
                      (+ (* val x) (first coeff)))))
```

Note the use of tail recursion here in implementing Horner's method for computing the value of a polynomial.

   If we use POLY-VALUE to check a root of a polynomial, we expect zero as the answer. In practice, of course, because of limited precision of floating-point representation, we may get some small nonzero value, possibly even with a nonzero imaginary part, if the given root is complex.

Solution 32-19:

```
(defun most-positive-real (l)               ;Get most positive real root.
  (let ((ans (some-real-root l)))
    (if (null ans) (error "No real root in ~a" l)
        (most-positive-real-aux l ans))))

(defun some-real-root (l)                   ;Find any real root.
  (if (endp l) nil
      (if (complexp (first l))
          (some-real-root (rest l))
          (first l))))

(defun most-positive-real-aux (l x)         ;Find most positive real root.
  (if (endp l) x
      (if (complexp (first l))
          (most-positive-real-aux (rest l) x)
          (if (< (first l) x)
              (most-positive-real-aux (rest l) x)
              (most-positive-real-aux (rest l) (first l))))))
```

Solution 32-20:

```
(defun insert-root (new roots)                ;Keep roots ordered.
  (cond ((endp roots) (list new))             ;Easy case, last one.
        ((complexp (first roots))
         (cons new roots))                    ;Real before complex.
        ((complexp new)                       ;New is complex.
         (cons (first roots) (insert-root new (rest roots))))
        ((> (first roots) new)                ;New not highest.
         (cons (first roots) (insert-root new (rest roots))))
        (t (cons new roots))))                ;New most positive.
```

Strictly speaking, the (second) recursive call to INSERT-ROOT is not needed if all we want to do is ensure that the most positive root is first in the list. But why not keep all the real roots sorted while we are at it? It costs little extra.

Solution 32-21: Simply replace the two APPENDs with APPEND-ROOTS, where

```
(defun append-roots (ra rb)
  (if (endp ra) rb
      (append-roots (rest ra)
                    (insert-root (first ra) rb)))))
```

Glossary

A-list	A list of composite elements each containing a symbol, used as a recovery key, along with some data associated with that symbol. Also known as association list.
Abstraction barrier	A virtual wall, produced by procedure abstraction or data abstraction, behind which lower level details are hidden.
Access procedure	A constructor, reader, or writer procedure.
Accessor procedure	In the context of CLOS, a procedure that is used directly to read data from a class object, and indirectly to write data into a class object.
Address	An integer giving the position of a particular chunk of memory, often a byte.
Algorithm	A specification for how to do something. Usually, the specification is an abstract one, not one couched in a particular programming language. However, to be an algorithm, a specification must be concrete enough to be recast as a procedure written in such a language. Some theoreticians insist that a recipe for action must always terminate in a finite number of steps in order to deserve to be called an algorithm.
Antecedent assertion	One of a list of assertions from which a rule's conclusion follows. See *consequent assertion*.

Antecedent consequent rule	A chunk of knowledge expressed in the form of one or more antecedent assertions and one or more consequent assertions. Also known as If-then rule and production rule.
Applicable method	A method whose name appears in the procedure position in a form, and whose parameter specializers are all either the same as the classes of the corresponding arguments in a form, or superclasses of those classes.
Apply	To call a procedure, by applying it to a set of arguments, producing a value and, possibly, side effects. Also known as call.
Arc	A bidirectional connection between two nodes in a net. See *branch*.
Array	The data type for which expressions are stored in places identified by integer indexes.
Artificial intelligence	The field that studies and exploits the computations that connect perception to action.
Assignment	The process of establishing (or changing) a value for a symbol. See *bind*.
Association list	A list of composite elements each containing a symbol, used as a recovery key, along with some data associated with that symbol. Also known as a-list.
Atom	Narrowly, a number or a symbol. Broadly, anything other than a cons cell.
Backquote mechanism	A programming device that simplifies tasks that can be viewed as filling in a template.
Backward chaining	What a rule-based system does when it tries to verify a hypothesis by verifying antecedents that imply that hypothesis. Verification of these antecedent hypothesis in turn requires verification of their antecedents, and so on. See *forward chaining*.
Beam search	A search procedure that differs from breadth-first search in that only some fixed number of the paths that appear to be best, based on heuristic evidence, are retained at every level.
Best-first search	The search procedure that explores a net or a tree by examining the branches that lie beyond the node that seems closest to the goal based on heuristic evidence.
Binary file	A file containing LISP objects represented as bit sequences.
Bind	To reserve a place in memory for a value to be associated with a particular symbol. See *assignment and binding*.
Binding	A place in memory reserved for a value associated with a symbol. Informally, a synonym for value. See *bind*.

Bits	The two-valued switches that anchor the bottom of all computer representations.
Blocks-world program	A classic program that illustrates problem reduction. The problem of putting one block on another is reduced to other problems such as clearing the top, grasping, moving, and ungrasping.
Body	The forms that are evaluated sequentially when a procedure is applied.
Box	The two-pointer entity out of which lists are made in box-and-arrow notation. See *cons cell.*
Box-and-pointer diagram	A representation for lists that stands above the level of detail of the actual bits in a computer, but suggests how the bits are used.
Branch	A unidirectional connection between two places, called nodes, in a net or tree. See *arc.*
Breadth-first search	The search procedure that explores a net or tree level-by-level, exploring all paths of a certain length before looking at any longer paths.
Byte	A chunk of memory, usually consisting of eight bits.
Call	To apply a procedure, by calling it with a set of arguments, producing a value and, possibly, side effects. Also known as apply.
Call by reference	The sort of procedure call for which a change to a parameter variable changes the value of the corresponding argument variable. *Not* used by LISP.
Call by value	The sort of procedure call for which a change to a parameter variable does *not* change the value of the corresponding argument variable.
Cartesian coordinate system	A systematic way of identifying the position of a point by reference to a set of straight line coordinate axes, typically at right angles to one another.
Centroid	The average position of a number of points. The coordinate components of the centroid are averages of corresponding coordinate components of the points. Physically, the center of mass of a set of particles.
Circular list	A list that has one or more pointers back into itself.
Class	The data type that supports inheritance for slots, slot defaults, and the methods of generic functions.
Class precedence list	An ordering of classes, prescribed by CLOS, that helps to determine which applicable primary method is used and the order in which applicable :BEFORE and :AFTER methods are used.

Clause	Part of a COND form. Consists of a test form and consequent forms.
CLOS	An acronym for COMMON LISP Object System.
Combinatorial explosion	The rapid growth in the number of possible ways of choosing alternative combinations of elements as the number of elements grows. In the context of search, the tendency of search trees to develop an almost unthinkably large total number of branches after just a few levels. The severity of the combinatorial explosion depends on the average number of branches emerging from each node.
Comment	Annotation of a procedure as an aid for human programmers, ignored by interpreters and compilers.
Comment translation	A technique for defining procedures by thinking through what they should do in English, or other human language, then writing the result as a series of comments, and finally translating the comments into LISP forms.
Compiler	A program that translates procedure definitions expressed in text form into sequences of computer instructions in preparation for execution.
Complex conjugate	A number obtained by changing the sign of the imaginary part of a given complex number.
Complex contagion	Noncomplex numbers that are about to be combined arithmetically with complex numbers are first converted to equivalent complex numbers by supplying an imaginary part of zero.
Conditional primitive	A primitive that evaluates some of its arguments and returns a value in a manner determined by one or more test forms found among its arguments.
Cons cell	The two-address entity out of which lists are built in computer memory. See *box*.
Consequent	In the context of a conditional primitive, a form that is evaluated or not, depending on the value returned by an associated test form.
Consequent assertion	The assertion that follows from a list of given assertions. See *antecedent assertion*.
Constraint propagation	A process by which values are calculated for arcs in a net. Constraints attached to a node, together with existing values at a subset of the arcs connected to the node, are used to calculate values for other connected arcs. Because the new values, in turn, may enable other constraints to be exploited, a single new value may have far-reaching consequences.
Constructor procedure	A procedure that creates a new data object.
Critical path	The path through a PERT chart that takes the most time.

Cross-product	The cross-product of two vectors is a vector at right-angles to both, with magnitude equal to the product of the magnitudes of the vectors and the sine of the angle between them. The direction of the resulting vector is determined by the right-hand rule. Also known as vector product or outer product. See *dot-product*.
Cursor	The graphic symbol that marks the place in text displayed on a screen where future additions and deletions will appear when using an editor.
Data abstraction	The process of detail hiding through the use of access procedures.
Data driven programming	The programming paradigm identified with the idea that the version of a procedure to use should be determined by the types of the arguments involved. See *object-oriented programming*.
Data type	A class of data objects, typically associated with a family of procedures.
Data-type bits	Bits used to identify the type associated with a particular chunk of memory.
Datum	An expression used to represent knowledge about some real or imagined world.
Debugging primitive	A LISP primitive, such as TRACE, STEP, and BREAK, used as an aid in locating bugs.
Declaration	An expression that tells LISP to handle something in a special way. Declarations are used, for example, to tell LISP that a certain variable is a special variable.
Default value	The value assumed by a variable, field, or slot when no value is explicitly supplied.
Depth-first search	The search procedure that explores a net or tree by picking one branch at each node and pursuing that choice as far as possible before backing up to pursue other choices.
Direct subclass	A class reached by walking downward along one inheritance link.
Direct superclass	A class reached by walking upward along one inheritance link.
Directive	Any part of a FORMAT string that provides instructions on such details as when to go to a new line and how many spaces to allocate to the printed representation of a value. Always introduced by the tilde character.
Divide and conquer	A problem-solving paradigm where a problem is divided into two (or more) smaller, but similar problems. Typically implemented using recursive procedures. See *doubly recursive procedure*.
Dot-product	The dot-product of two vectors is equal to the product of their magnitudes and the cosine of the angle between them. Equivalently, the dot-product is the sum of products of corresponding components of the two vectors. Also known as scalar product or inner product. See *cross-product*.

Doubly recursive procedure	A recursive procedure that may call itself directly twice when invoked.
Dynamic extent	A parameter has dynamic extent if its binding is associated with the time interval bounded by the the time a procedure is applied and the time when that procedure returns a value. Equivalently, if a stack is used to implement special variables, the time between the appearance of a procedure or binding primitive on the stack and by its disappearance.
Dynamic programming	The search technique in which alternate paths to a given place are pruned away as soon as they are developed, leaving only the shortest, thereby greatly reducing the effort that is required to find a solution path.
Dynamic variable	A variable whose value is determined by a record of calls or by a global value in the event that no value is supplied by anything on the record of calls. Also known as special variable.
Element	Part of a list, string, or array.
EMACS	A powerful, popular editor, conceived and implemented initially by Richard M. Stallman. Various versions of EMACS were used in preparing the programs and text for this book.
Encapsulate	To associate a particular binding environment with a procedure by creating a lexical closure.
Environment	A context that determines the bindings of variables.
Evaluation	The process of computing the value of a form.
Event	The instant when a task is started or finished. See *PERT chart*.
Expert system	A system that behaves, in some respects, like a trained person. Often a misnomer for *novice system*.
Expert system shell	A software system that enables users to develop applications by adding domain knowledge only, without further programming. See *inference engine*.
Explanation system	A system that answers questions about behavior.
Expression	Narrowly, an atom or a list. Broadly, anything typically containing symbols. Also known as symbolic expression.
Field	A named place for storing one of the values in an instance of a structure type. See *slot*.
Filter	In the context of mapping over lists, to extract those elements from a list that satisfy a given predicate.

First-rest recursion	A recursive method that examines an entire list, possibly containing sublists, by calling itself on the pieces of the list produced by FIRST and REST.
Floating-point contagion	Integers and ratios that are about to be combined arithmetically with, or compared to, floating-point numbers are first converted to equivalent floating-point numbers.
Floating-point number	The computer's approximation of a real number like 3.141592653....
Form	An expression when viewed as something to be evaluated.
Forward chaining	What a rule-based system does when it starts with a collection of assertions and tries all available rules over and over, adding new assertions as it goes, until the sought after conclusion is reached or no rule can produce a new assertion. See *backward chaining*.
Free variable	A variable lacking a binding when viewed from the perspective of a particular reference form.
Fringe of tree	The leaves of a tree, arranged in linear order, as visited sequentially by a depth-first search procedure. See *depth-first search*.
Funarg	An acronym for <u>fun</u>ction <u>arg</u>ument. An argument that is a procedure object. Also known as procedure argument.
Function	Narrowly, a procedure that has no side effects. Broadly, any procedure.
Garbage collection	The process of reclaiming memory for further use once that memory is no longer accessible through any procedure or variable.
Generator	A procedure that produces a sequence of values. Generators are often implemented as lexical closures in order to isolate their state from other procedures.
Generic function	A group of procedurelike objects, called methods. The argument types appearing in a call to a generic function and the parameter specializers appearing in a method definition determine whether a particular method is an applicable method in the call.
Global value	A value established for use when no procedure or binding primitive supplies a value.
Globally free variable	A special variable for which there is no procedure or binding primitive on the record of calls to supply a value.
Goal tree	A tree recording how goals are achieved by achieving subgoals. See *problem reduction*.
Grammar	A set of patterns that describe legal sentences.

Heuristic

A technique or measurement that works with useful regularity, but not necessarily all the time. Also, a technique or measurement for which our understanding is incomplete.

Hill-climbing search

A search procedure somewhat like depth-first search, except that the next branch pursued at any particular node is the best, based on heuristic evidence, of the branches leaving that node.

If-then rule

A chunk of knowledge expressed in an if-then format, with *if* marking one or more antecedent assertions and *then* marking one or more consequent assertions. Also known as antecedent-consequent rule or production rule.

Implementation language

A language used to implement an algorithm. Often a language used to implement another language. COMMON LISP is generally implemented using a small subset of itself.

Inference engine

Expert systems usually consist of an inference engine and a knowledge base. The inference engine is a general-purpose computer program that uses the knowledge base to infer conclusions. Typically, the knowledge base is in the form of rules and the inference engine does forward or backward chaining. See *expert system shell*.

Inference net

A net consisting of arcs representing assertions and nodes representing logical operators.

Infix notation

Notation for arithmetic expressions where the operator appears between the operands, as in ordinary arithmetic notation. See *prefix notation and precedence weight*.

Inheritance link

A connection between classes that enables information about slots and methods to flow from descriptions of classes to descriptions of individuals.

Input stream

A LISP object that supplies data. Often connected to a file or keyboard.

Instantiation

The process of replacing variables with variable values.

Integer

A whole number, like 105.

Interpreter

A program that carries out the actions specified by definitions expressed in text form, performing the actions called for in the body of those definitions, form by form.

Iterate

To repeat over and over until a stopping criterion is satisfied.

Join

A place where two or more paths come together.

Keychord

A combination of keyboard keys, pressed in concert. Popular in adult text editors like EMACS.

Keyword

Any symbol beginning with a colon character. Often used to match keyword arguments to keyword parameters.

Knowledge engineer	A specialist in extracting knowledge from domain experts and expressing that knowledge in rules or some other artificial-intelligence oriented representation.
Lambda expression	A nameless procedure.
Lexical closure	A procedure packaged with an environment that establishes variable bindings.
Lexical scope	A parameter has lexical scope if its binding is associated with the text interval bounded by the parentheses that delineate a parameter-binding form. See *textual scope*.
Lexical variable	A variable whose binding is determined, ultimately, by the nesting exhibited when procedures are viewed as text. Mediated through virtual fences.
LISP	An acronym for <u>lis</u>t <u>p</u>rocessing.
List	A sequence of elements, each of which may also be a list. A sequence of cons cells, each with a pointer to the next.
Logical constraint	A constraint that limits the truth values taken on by assertions.
Machine Vision	The field of study that concerns itself with methods for generating descriptions of objects based on images obtained by electronic cameras. Typically the descriptions are intended to be used in planning interactions with the imaged environment.
Macro	For LISP interpreters, a procedure that first builds an intermediate form and then evaluates that intermediate form. For LISP compilers, a procedure that produces an expression that is compiled as if the expression were substituted in place of the macro form.
Magnitude	The absolute value of a real number. In the case of a complex number, the square root of the product of the number and its complex conjugate. In the case of a vector, the magnitude of the vector, that is, the square root of the dot-product of the vector with itself. Also known as modulus or norm. See *dot-product and phase*.
Mapping primitive	A primitive that applies a given procedure to the elements in a list. Used to transform, filter, count, or find an item. More generally, a function or procedure that connects entities in the range with entities in the domain of the primitive.
Matrix	A rectangular arrangement of elements, often representing a coordinate transformation from one Cartesian coordinate system to another. Usually represented in LISP by a two-dimensional array.

Message passing   The programming paradigm associated with the idea of sending procedure names to objects. Because what to do is determined by procedures attached to the object's type, message passing can be thought of as an extension of object-oriented programming. See *object-oriented programming.*

Method   A procedurelike object. Groups of methods, that are named identically, but intended for different combinations of argument types, form generic functions.

Module   A collection of procedures that can be isolated by an abstraction barrier from other procedures in a program.

Natural language interface   A program that provides access to a computer data base using English, or other human language.

Nested list   A list that contains one or more lists as elements.

Net   A collection of places, called nodes, and connections between them, called arcs. Unlike trees, nets can have circular paths.

Node   A place in a net connected by arcs.

Number   An atom that makes arithmetic primitives happy. The data type including as subtypes integer, ratio, floating point and complex.

Numerically indexed   Entities identified by integers, as in arrays.

Object   An instance of a data type.

Object-oriented programming   The programming paradigm associated with the idea that a data type should be thought of as a bundle of procedures in addition to a bundle of data-type instances. See *procedure-oriented programming.*

Optional parameter   A parameter that becomes bound to an argument if there are more arguments than are needed to supply values to all preceding required and optional parameters. Otherwise assumes a default value.

Ordinary expression   An expression containing neither variables nor wild-card symbols. Matched to pattern expressions by matching and unification programs. See *pattern expression.*

Output stream   A LISP object that consumes data. Often connected to a file or screen.

Parameter   A variable that is bound to an argument value when a procedure is applied.

Parameter specializer   A class attached to a method parameter that limits the method to applications in which the class is the same as the class of the corresponding argument or a superclass of that class.

Parser　In the context of natural language, a program that analyzes sentences, determining how they are put together. More generally, a program that analyzes sequences.

Path　In the context of files, a series of directory-to-subdirectory connections through a file system's directory tree, usually down to a particular file.

Pattern classification　The process of assigning an unknown entity to a particular class based on a number of observed features. Feature measurements are usually considered to be components of a feature vector, and the space in which this vector lies is divided into regions corresponding to different classes.

Pattern expression　An expression containing variables or wild-card symbols. Matched to ordinary expressions or other pattern expressions by matching and unification programs. See *ordinary expression*.

Pattern matching　The process of matching a general pattern to a specific instance or to another pattern.

PERT chart　An acronym for p̲rogram e̲valuation and r̲eview t̲echnique. Nodes represent tasks of a project. Arcs connect tasks to prerequisite tasks. Work cannot start on any task until its prerequisite tasks are completed.

Phase　The angle whose cosine and sine are proportional to the real and imaginary parts of a given complex number with the same proportionality factor. Also known as argument. See *magnitude*.

Pointer　A link between boxes in box-and-arrow notation. More concretely, an address linking cons cells.

Precedence list　See *class precedence list*.

Precedence weight　In infix notation, possible ambiguity is resolved by assigning precedence weights to operators. Operands between operators of different weight are attached to the adjacent operator of greater weight. (So $a+b*c \equiv a+(b*c)$, since $*$ has greater precedence weight than $+$). See *infix notation*.

Predicate　A procedure that returns either nonNIL or NIL, meaning true or false.

Prefix notation　Notation for arithmetic expressions where the operator precedes (is prefixed to) the operands. LISP can be thought of as using prefix notation, since the procedure name always precedes the arguments. See *infix notation*.

Primitive　A built-in procedure.

Principal value　Many functions, such as nth-roots and inverse trigonometric functions, have multiple values (for example, both -1 and $+1$ are square roots of 1). By convention, a particular one of these multiple values is called the principal value (for example, the value between $-\pi/2$ and $+\pi/2$ is chosen in the case of the arc-tangent function).

Probability system In the context of expert systems, a system that computes the reliability of a conclusion.

Problem reduction In the context of problem solving, the technique by which a problem is broken up into more easily solved subproblems. In the context of programming, the technique by which a procedure is defined in terms of subprocedures.

Problem-solving paradigm Any technique for solving problems, such as problem reduction, divide and conquer, search, forward chaining, or backward chaining.

Procedurally indexed Identified by access procedures, as in structure types and classes.

Procedure A step by step specification, expressed in a programming language, such as LISP, of how to do something.

Procedure abstraction The process of detail hiding through layering of procedures and subprocedures.

Procedure argument An argument that is a procedure object. Primitives like MAPCAR use a procedure argument. Also known as a funarg.

Procedure object A procedure represented so as to be ready for application. To be distinguished from the same procedure expressed as text.

Procedure-oriented programming The programming paradigm identified with the idea that procedures are the primary things to think about, rather than the objects that the procedures work on. See *object-oriented programming*.

Production rule A chunk of knowledge expressed in the form of one or more antecedent assertions and one or more consequent assertions. Also known as if-then rule and antecedent-consequent rule.

Program A collection of procedures that work together.

Programming cliché A broadly useful template for building procedures or procedure fragments.

Progressive envelopment A technique for defining procedures by working out which LISP primitives are needed through a sequence of increasingly more complex experiments.

PROLOG An acronym for programming with logic. A language focused on pattern matching and backward chaining.

Prompt The symbol displayed on the screen by LISP when resting, waiting for you to type something.

Property list A collection of property names and corresponding values, associated with a symbol.

Pruning   Cutting off parts of a search tree based on evidence that the sought after solution is not to be found in the part discarded. See *tree*.

Push-down stack   A linear arrangement of elements from which elements can be removed only from the end at which they are added. Also known as first-in last-out queue. See *stack and queue*.

Queue   A linear arrangement of elements from which elements can be removed only from the end opposite to the one to which they can be added. Also known as first-in first-out queue. See *push-down stack*.

Ratio   A rational number, like 22/7.

Rational canonicalization   When the result of an arithmetic computation with complex numbers, whose components are integers or ratios, happens to produce an imaginary part that is zero, then the result is converted into an equivalent integer or ratio (This does not happen when the components of the complex number are floating-point numbers).

Reader procedure   A procedure that retrieves data.

Record   A set of values, one for each field associated with a particular relation.

Recursive call   A procedure call in which a procedure calls itself, possibly indirectly.

Recursive procedure   A procedure defined such that it may use a value returned by a call to itself, either directly or indirectly through intervening procedure calls.

Reduction   In the context of tail recursion, a single derived problem whose solution provides the answer to a given problem directly, without further computation. The derived problem is typically simpler than the original problem.

Relational database   A database consisting of sets of relations.

Relation   A set of records, each of which supplies a set of field-value pairs.

Representation   A vocabulary of symbols, together with some conventions for arranging them so as to form descriptions.

Rest parameter   A parameter that becomes bound to a list of excess argument values if there are more arguments than there are required and optional parameters.

Restriction feature   A feature found in matching languages that enables you to restrict the values that a pattern variable can be bound to.

Root of Polynomial   An argument for which the value of a given polynomial is zero.

Rule   See *if-then rule*.

Rule-based expert system	An expert system built out of if-then rules. Generally involves forward chaining or backward chaining. See *expert system*.
Rule of good programming practice	Any rule that leads to programs that are easier to write, understand, debug, and maintain.
Search	The process of finding a path through a net or tree. More generally, the process of finding an item that satisfies a particular criterion in a given search space.
Semantic grammar	A grammar whose patterns involve semantic categories, like *tool*, not just syntactic categories, like *noun*.
Sequence	A list, or a simple vector, such as a string.
Shell	A software system that enables users to develop applications by adding domain knowledge only, without further programming. Also known as expert system shell.
Side effect	Anything a procedure does that persists after it returns its value.
Simple vector	A one-dimensional array that is simple (that is, one that uses only the features we introduced in this book.
Simulator	A program that imitates something step by step, typically the evolution of a project or a physical process.
Singly recursive procedure	A recursive procedure defined in such a way that it may call itself directly at most once.
Slot	A named place to store values in a class instance. See *field*.
Solution by radicals	Method for finding roots of a polynomial that involves only ordinary arithmetic operations and extraction of roots.
Source file	A file consisting of LISP objects represented as character sequences. Also known as a text file.
Source language	The language in which a programmer prepares procedure definitions.
Special binding	The binding of a special variable.
Special form	Any one of a small group of primitives whose members are all treated as special cases by LISP interpreters and compilers. Many primitives that look like they should be special forms are actually macros that are written in terms of special forms.
Special variable	A variable whose value is determined by walking up the record of calls or by a global value in the event that no value is supplied by anything on the record of calls. Also known as dynamic variable.

Spherical trigonometry	The study of the properties of curvilinear triangles drawn on a sphere with portions of great circles as sides.
Split	A place where two or more paths separate.
Stack	A dynamic record of those procedures and binding primitives that have been called, but that have not yet returned a value.
State variable	One of the variables whose collective values fully determine the future course of a computation or physical process, given that all current and future inputs are known.
Stream	Any producer or consumer of a sequence of data objects.
String	A sequence of characters bounded by double quote characters at the beginning and end. A simple vector of characters. See *sequence and simple vector*.
Subclass	A class reached by walking downward along a series of one or more inheritance links.
Superclass	A class reached by walking upward along a series of one or more inheritance links.
Symbol	A fundamental LISP data type. A symbol can have a value, name a procedure, and provide access to a property list. Represented in text, roughly, as a sequence of alphanumeric characters, not all of which are numeric characters.
Symbolic expression	Narrowly, an atom or a list. Broadly, anything typically containing symbols. Also known as expression.
Symbolically indexed	Identified by symbol names, as in property lists.
Tail recursive procedure	A recursive procedure defined in such a way that all recursive calls to itself are reductions. See *reduction*.
Target language	The language into which a compiler translates source-language programs.
Task	Something that needs to be done to complete a project. See *PERT chart*.
Template	A pattern showing how the parts of a form are put together.
Text	LISP objects represented as character sequences.
Text file	A file consisting of LISP objects represented as character sequences. Also known as a source file.
Textual scope	What lexical scope should have been called. See *lexical scope*.
Top-level element	A list element that is directly contained by that list. To be distinguished from the elements buried in sublists.

Transformation   In the context of mapping over lists, the construction of the elements of a new list from the elements of a given list.

Transition tree   A diagram that expresses the word-order constraints in sentences. Used extensively in natural-language interfaces.

Transition-tree grammar   A grammar, represented as a net, in which each node has at most one entering arc.

Tree   A collection of places, called nodes, and directed connections between nodes, called branches. A tree has a designated root node from which all other nodes can be reached by moving along branches. Unlike nets, trees cannot have circular paths.

Trigger   In the context of a COND form, to pass the test associated with one of the COND's clauses. In the contex of if-then rules, to satisfy all the antecedent assertions.

Unification   The process of comparing two pattern expressions to see if they can be made identical by a consistent set of substitutions.

Unit vector   Vector of unit magnitude. See *vector and magnitude*.

Variable   A symbol when viewed as something to which a value can be assigned.

Vector   In a mathematical context, an element of a vector space, often represented by its components with respect to a particular Cartesian coordinate system. In LISP, a one-dimensional array, the elements of which may represent the components of a vector in the mathematical sense.

Virtual fence   A boundary thrown up when procedures or binding primitives are called. Analysis of nested virtual fences is used to determine which values lexical variables have.

Writer procedure   A procedure that changes data.

Bibliography

Abelson, Harold and Gerald Jay Sussman (1984), *Structure and Interpretation of Computer Programs*, MIT Press, Cambridge, Massachusetts.

Abramowitz, M. and I. A. Stegan (editors) (1964), *Handbook of Mathematical Functions with Formulas, Graphs, and Mathematical Tables*, National Bureau of Standards, United States Department of Commerce.

Aho, Alfred V., John E. Hopcroft, and Jeffrey D. Ullman (1974), *The Design and Analysis of Computer Algorithms*, Addison-Wesley, Reading, Massachusetts. Reprinted 1976.

Allen, John (1978), *Anatomy of LISP*, McGraw-Hill, New York.

Bratko, Ivan (1986), *PROLOG Programming for Artificial Intelligence*, Addison-Wesley, Reading, Massachusetts.

Brooks, Rodney A. (1985), *Programming in COMMON LISP*, Wiley, New York.

Burington, R. S. (1973), *Handbook of Mathematical Tables and Formulas*, Fifth Edition, McGraw-Hill, New York.

Charniak, Eugene, C. Riesbeck and D. McDermott (1980), *Artificial Intelligence Programming*, Lawrence Erlbaum Associates, Hillsdale, New Jersey.

Church, Alonzo (1941), "The Calculi of Lambda-Conversion," *Annals of Mathematical Studies*, Vol. 6, Princeton University Press, Princeton, New Jersey. Reprinted by Klaus Reprints, New York, 1965.

Cody, William J. Jr. and William Waite (1980), *Software Manual for Elementary Functions*, Prentice-Hall, Englewood Cliffs, New Jersey.

Conte, S. D. and C. de Boor (1972), *Elementary Numerical Analysis—An Algorithmic Approach*, Second Edition, McGraw-Hill, New York.

Cornish, Merrill (1987), "Rapture, Ecstacy and LISP," *Computerworld*, October.

Feigenbaum, Edward A., Pamela McCorduck, and H. Penny Nii (1989) *The Rise of the Expert Company*, Times Books, New York.

Forsythe, G. E., M. A. Malcomb, and C. B. Moler (1977), *Computer Methods for Mathematical Computations*, Second Edition, Addison-Wesley, Reading, Massachusetts.

Grimson, W. Eric L. and Ramesh S. Patil (1987), *AI in the 1980's and Beyond: An MIT Survey*, MIT Press, Cambridge, Massachusetts.

Grimson, W. Eric L. and Tomás Lozano-Pérez (1984), "Model-Based Recognition and Localization from Sparse Range and Tactile Data," *The International Journal of Robotics Research*, Vol. 3, No. 3, Fall.

Grimson, W. Eric L. and Tomás Lozano-Pérez (1987), "Localizing Overlapping Parts by Searching the Interpretation Tree," *IEEE Transactions on Pattern Analysis and Machine Intelligence*, Vol. 9, No. 4, July.

Hamming, R. W. (1962), *Numerical Methods for Scientists and Engineers*, McGraw-Hill, New York.

Harris, Larry R. (1977), "A High Performance Natural Language Processor for Data Base Query," *ACM SIGART Newsletter* 61.

Hildebrand, F. B. (1974), *Introduction to Numerical Analysis*, Second Edition, McGraw-Hill, New York.

Horn, Berthold K. P. (1986), *Robot Vision*, M.I.T. Press, Cambridge, Massachusetts and McGraw-Hill, New York.

Horn, Berthold K. P. (1984), "Extended Gaussian Images," *Proceedings of the I.E.E.E.*, Vol. 72, No. 12, pp. 1671–1686, December.

Horn, Berthold K. P. (1987), "Closed Form Solution of Absolute Orientation using Unit Quaternions," *Journal of the Optical Society A*, Vol. 4, No. 4, pp. 629–642, April.

Horn, Berthold K. P. (1987), "Relative Orientation," Memo No. 986, Artificial Intelligence Laboratory, MIT, Cambridge, Massachusetts.

Horn, Berthold K.P. and Katsushi Ikeuchi (1984), "The Mechanical Manipulation of Randomly Oriented Parts," *Scientific American*, Vol. 251, No. 2, pp. 100–111, August.

Hu, T. C. (1982), *Combinatorial Algorithms*, Addison-Wesley, Reading, Massachusetts.

Iyanga, S. and Y. Kawada (editors) (1977), *Encyclopedic Dictionary of Mathematics* (English tranlation), MIT Press, Cambridge, Massachusetts.

Keene, Sonya E. (1989), *Object-Oriented Programming in COMMON LISP*, Addison-Wesley, Reading, Massachusetts, and Symbolics Press, Cambridge, Massachusetts.

Knuth, Donald E. (1968), *The Art of Computer Programming, Volume 1, Fundamental Algorithms*, Addison-Wesley, Reading, Massachusetts.

Knuth, Donald E. (1973), *The Art of Computer Programming, Volume 3, Sorting and Searching*, Addison-Wesley, Reading, Massachusetts.

Knuth, Donald E. (1981), *The Art of Computer Programming, Volume 2, Seminumerical Algorithms*, Second Edition, Addison-Wesley, Reading, Massachusetts.

McCarthy, John (1960), "Recursive Functions of Symbolic Expressions and their Computation by Machine, Part I," *Communications of the ACM*, Vol. 3, No. 4.

McCarthy, John (1978), "History of LISP," *ACM SIGPLAN Notices*, Vol. 13, No. 8. Also in *History of Programming Languages*, Richard L. Wexelblat (Ed.), Academic Press, New York.

McCarthy, John, P. W. Abrahams, D. J. Edwards, T. P. Hart, and M. I. Levin (1962), *LISP 1.5 Programmer's Manual*, MIT Press, Cambridge, Massachusetts.

Quinlan, J. Ross (1983), "Inferno: A Cautious Approach to Uncertain Inference," *The Computer Journal*, Vol. 26, No. 3.

Rich, Charles and Howard E. Schrobe (1976), "Initial Report on a LISP Programmer's Apprentice," Technical Report 354, Artificial Intelligence Laboratory, MIT, Cambridge, Massachusetts.

Sedgewick, Robert (1983), *Algorithms*, Addison-Wesley, Reading, Massachusetts.

Siklóssy, Laurent (1976), *Let's Talk LISP*, Prentice-Hall, Englewood Cliffs, New Jersey.

Stallman, Richard M. (1987), *GNU EMACS Manual, Sixth Edition*, Free Software Foundation, Cambridge, Massachusetts.

Steele, Guy L. Jr., with contributions by Scott E. Fahlman, Richard P. Gabriel, David A. Moon, and Daniel L. Weinreb (1984), *COMMON LISP Reference Manual*, Digital Press, Bedford, Massachusetts.

Touretzky, David S. (1984), *LISP—A Gentle Introduction to Symbolic Computation*, Harper and Row, New York.

Waters, Richard C. (1985), "The Programmer's Apprentice: A Session with KBEmacs," *IEEE Transactions on Software Engineering*, Vol. SE-11, No. 11.

Waters, Richard C. (1988), "Using Obviously Synchronizable Series Expressions Instead of Loops," *International Conference on Computer Languages*, IEEE Press.

Wilensky, Robert (1986), *COMMON LISPcraft*, W. W. Norton, New York.

Winograd, Terry (1972), *Understanding Natural Language*, Academic Press, New York.

Winston, Patrick Henry (1984), *Artificial Intelligence*, Second Edition, Addison-Wesley, Reading, Massachusetts.

Winston, Patrick H. and Karen A. Prendergast (editors) (1984), *The AI Business: Commercial Applications of Artificial Intelligence*, MIT Press, Cambridge, Massachusetts.

Index of LISP Primitives Used in this Book

Index of
LISP Definitions

General Index

Software

Software in support of this book is available via the INTERNET. To learn how to obtain this software, send a message to lisp3@ai.mit.edu with the word "help" on the subject line. Your message will be answered by an automatic reply program that will tell you what to do next.